Philippines
a travel survival kit

Jens Peters

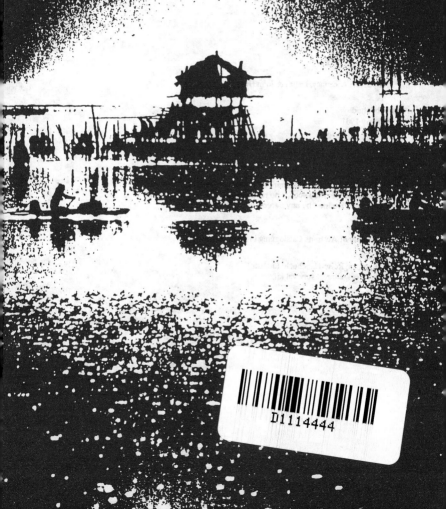

Philippines – a travel survival kit

4th edition

Published by
Lonely Planet Publications Pty Ltd (ACN 005 607 983)
PO Box 617, Hawthorn, Vic 3122, Australia
Lonely Planet Publications, Inc
PO Box 2001A, Berkeley, CA 94702, USA

Printed by
Singapore National Printers Ltd, Singapore

Photographs by
Krzysztof Dydynski (KD)
John Pennock (JPk)
Jens Peters (JP)
Paul Steel (PS)
Tony Wheeler (TW)

Front cover: A jeepney, Dallas & John Heaton, Scoopix Photo Library

First Published
February 1981

This Edition
May 1991

National Library of Australia Cataloguing in Publication Data

Peters, Jens.
[Philippinen, Reise-Handbuch. English.]
Philippines – a travel survival kit.

4th ed.
Includes index.
ISBN 0 86442 096 X.

1. Philippines – Description and travel – 1975 – Guide-books. I. Title.

915.990447

Jens Peters

Jens, born in 1949 in West Germany, studied advertising, communications and arts education in Berlin. Since 1970 he has travelled for several months each year in countries outside Europe. So far he has visited the Philippines (his favourite country in South-East Asia) 30 times and spent over six years there. In 1977 he became involved in travel writing and has since worked as a freelance journalist for various travel magazines and published several guidebooks about tropical countries on his own.

From the Publisher

This fourth edition of Philippines was once again comprehensively updated by Jens Peters. The book was edited at the Lonely Planet office in Australia by Adrienne Costanzo and Tom Smallman, and Krzysztof Dydynski was responsible for design, cover design, title page and maps.

Thanks must also go to Lyn McGaurr for copy-editing; Eleanor Finlay, Geoffrey Hull and Sydney Translations, Chris Taylor, Tom Smallman, Diana Saad and Rob van Driesum for their combined efforts at translating the German edition; Susan Mitra and Tom Smallman for all their editorial guidance; Alan Tiller and Diana Saad for proofreading; Chris Lee Ack for map drawing; Vicki Beale for design assistance; Ann Jeffree for additional design assistance; and Sharon Wertheim for the index.

This Book

In addition to the many German-speaking travellers who contributed to the new German edition of Jens Peters' guide, we would also like to thank our readers (apologies if we've misspelt your name) who took the time to write in with their contributions to this guide and to *South-East Asia on a Shoestring*. These include:

Charles (USA), Maria Ahlqvist (Sw), Nowa Allaf (Aus), Stacie R Allard (J), Joseph Allen (USA), Martin Armstrong (UK), Martin Aust (UK), Helvits Ayelet (Isr), Claire Aylmer (UK), Sr Carol Base (Phil), Ray Bates (USA), M & G Belloni (It), Scott Bergstein (USA), Henri R Bernier (USA), Carole Billingham (UK), Bruce Bonnell (USA), Todd Boulanger (USA), Roger Bound, Richard Boyance (F), Ardy Briede (Nl), Gerhard Bro (Dk), Rumagangrang Cabalagnan (Phil), Dekin Patina Campol (Phil), Lior Carmel (Isr), Allan Chatenay (C), Russ Christensen (USA), Jennifer Clarke (UK), Stephen Clay (UK), Antonio Coassin (Aus), Jennifer Cooper (Ber), Mark Covert (USA), Janet Cowan (USA), Ken Cuddy (Aus), Perry Dawes (Aus), Andrew Dawson (Aus), Rikki Deere (USA), Larry Deming (HK), Mike Dickens, Dave Dixon (USA), C Donaghy (HK), Michael Doolan (Aus), Jane Drover (UK), Pete Drylie (UK), Claire Duiker (USA), Gregory Dunn (UK), Graham Eames (Aus), Edward (Nl), Lawton D Ellery (Aus), Steven Elliott (USA), Cliff Ewing (Aus), Tim Farson, S Fazsy (CH), Dinah Ferrance (USA), Philippe Fossier (USA), Jonathan Frank (USA), Stephen Frazer (Aus), Friesen (J), Randall Fujikawa (USA), Marco Garcia (USA), E Geutskens (Nl), Belinda Goldsmith (UK), Richard Gregory-Smith (Aus), A H Griesdoorn

(Phil), Klaus & Mila Haberl (D), G Hadfield (UK), Bertil Hagnell (Sw), Henrix K Hansen (Dk), Peter Hanske (D), Richard Harding (Aus), Bill Harvey (Aus), A M Healy (Aus), Rene Heremans (B), Judith Hicks (USA), J M Hodges (UK), Fredrik Hoglund (Sw), A G Holmberg (Aus), Lindy Hope, Soren Horn (Dk), Willem Hubben (C), Phillip A Humphrey (Aus), J P Hundersmark (Nl), Richard Jacobi (USA), Steffan Jonsson (Sw), Kryss Katsiavriades (UK), Lars Lagberg(Sw), Dr H Lai Song Tat (S), A Laufer (Phil), Milton Lever (Aus), Regina Mapua Lim, Ron Lindblom (USA), Steven Livett (Aus), Suzanne Llamado, Tim Lockhardt (UK), Alvin Low (USA), Gary Loyd (USA), Claudia Kolatek (J), Richard Lydon (USA), Joe McGinley (Aus), Stuart McIntosh (Aus), J Denis Macrae (Phil), Althea Maddrell (HK), Paul Mascitti (In), Sue Mathieson (Aus), Takeshi Matsuzawa (J), T Mazur (Aus), Richard Meixsel (USA), Chris Meskens (Bel), Ruth Meyer (UK), Boris Minnarert (Nl), Peter Morgan (HK), Pat Morris (Aus), Charles Mulholland (Aus), Patrick Mundas (USA), D & P Murray (Aus), Ouit Nakar (Phil), Leif Ohlson (Sw), Henry Oscar (Phil), Neal Oshima, Jurgen Ott (D), Ian Owen (Aus), Stephen Owen (UK), James Paolelli (USA), Rod Parkes (HK), Clem Parry (Aus), Colin Paterson, Peter Peoska (C), A L Perrier (NZ), Pete, John Pike (Aus), Don Pirot (C), J A Plampin (UK), Steve Powey (UK), Pete J Raia (USA), David Reeve (Aus), Jeff Rigsby (USA), Peter Ritson (Phil), John Rothschild (USA), Sylvia Rushbrooke (Phil), Tim Ryan (Aus), Ayni R Salvante (Phil), Tom Sawyer (Aus), Martin Schmid, David Scott (Aus), Ian Shuck (UK), Tania Sironic (Aus), Tina Sironic (Aus), Roger Smith (USA), Terry Smith (Aus), Ray Spears (USA), Lonnie Spencer (USA), John Spouge (UK), Liz Street (Aus), Charlie Gapuz Te (Phil), T R Thomas (UK), Peter Thomas (USA), David Thornton, Kees van der Ree (CH), Stephen Villagracia (Phil), Michael Vincent (Aus), Rolf Vogler (CH), Sandro Waldmeyer (CH), Kevin & Sally Walsh (Phil), Michelle Ward (Aus), Simon Watson-Taylor (UK), Jack West (Phil), Walter Willey (USA), Maurice J Wood (Aus), Gino Yongco (Phil), David Yu (Tai), Jason Zakay (Isr), H Zurcher (C), Harold Kearns (USA).

A – Austria, Aus – Australia, B – Belgium, Bel – Belize, Ber – Bermuda, C – Canada, CH – Switzerland, D – Germany, Dk – Denmark, F – France, G – Greece, HK – Hong Kong, I – India, In – Indonesia, Isr – Israel, It – Italy, J – Japan, N – Norway, Nl – Netherlands, NZ – New Zealand, Phil – Philippines, S – Singapore, Sw – Sweden, Tai – Taiwan, UK – United Kingdom, USA – United States of America

Warning & Request

Things change, prices go up, schedules change, good places go bad and bad ones go bankrupt – nothing stays the same. So if you find things better or worse, recently opened or long since closed, please write and tell us and help make the next edition better!

Your letters will be used to help update future editions and, where possible, important changes will also be included as a Stop Press section in reprints.

All information is greatly appreciated, and the best letters will receive a free copy of the next edition, or any other Lonely Planet book of your choice.

Price Increases

As we went to press, prices in the Philippines increased by 20% to 50%. The price of petrol, for instance, jumped from 8P to 16P a litre. However, the exchange rate has also increased: at the start of 1990 the US dollar was worth 22P, but by the end of 1990 it was worth 30P. So, although you have to pay more for everything, you also get more pesos for your money.

Contents

MAP LEGEND

BOUNDARIES

- International Boundaries
- Internal Boundaries
- National Parks, Reserves
- The Equator
- The Tropics

SYMBOLS

- NEW DELHI ... National Capital
- BOMBAY ... Provincial or State Capital
- Pune ... Major Town
- Barsi ... Minor Town
- Post Office
- Airport
- Tourist Information
- Bus Station, Terminal
- 66 ... Highway Route Number
- Mosque, Church, Cathedral
- Temple, Ruin or Archaeological Site
- Hostel
- Hospital
- Lookout
- Camping Areas
- Picnic Areas
- Hut or Chalet
- Mountain
- Railway Station
- Road Bridge
- Road Rail Bridge
- Road Tunnel
- Railway Tunnel
- Escarpment or Cliff
- Pass
- Ancient or Historic Wall

ROUTES

- Major Roads and Highways
- Unsealed Major Roads
- Sealed Roads
- Unsealed Roads, Tracks
- City Streets
- Railways
- Subways
- Walking Tracks
- Ferry Routes
- Cable Car or Chair Lift

HYDROGRAPHIC FEATURES

- Rivers, Creeks
- Intermittent Streams
- Lakes, Intermittent Lake
- Coast Line
- Spring
- Waterfall
- Swamps
- Reefs
- Glacier

OTHER FEATURES

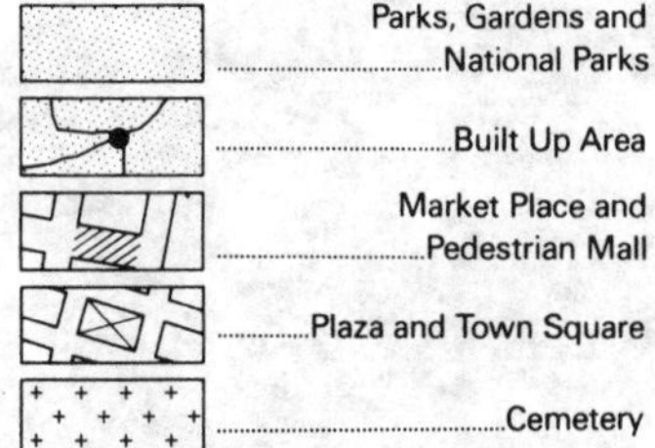

Note: Not all the symbols displayed above will necessarily appear in this book

Introduction

Despite a massive increase in tourism in Asia, the Philippines is still a paradise for globetrotters. Mass tourism in recent years has certainly changed the land and people of the Philippines but so far the changes have not gone too far and have been relatively limited in their scope. To get out and explore the 7000-plus islands of the Philippines still requires a little effort and energy.

It is the variety this country offers that is so interesting for the traveller. The bustling capital of Manila contrasts with lonely islands fringed with superb beaches and gardens of coral. There are towns where you will find mainly bars and discos, but you can also visit mountain tribes who still live according to their own laws and traditions. There are huge rice terraces built eons ago with the most primitive tools; wide sugar-cane fields with subterranean rivers and lakes; or shadowy palm forest groves and dense jungle.

Nor should the extraordinarily friendly people be forgotten – this, the Filipinos like to remind you, is 'where Asia wears a smile'. For the traveller, the Philippines offers the further advantages of reasonable accommodation and food at pleasantly low prices. The myriad islands of this island nation are connected by such frequent boat services that island hopping is a real pleasure.

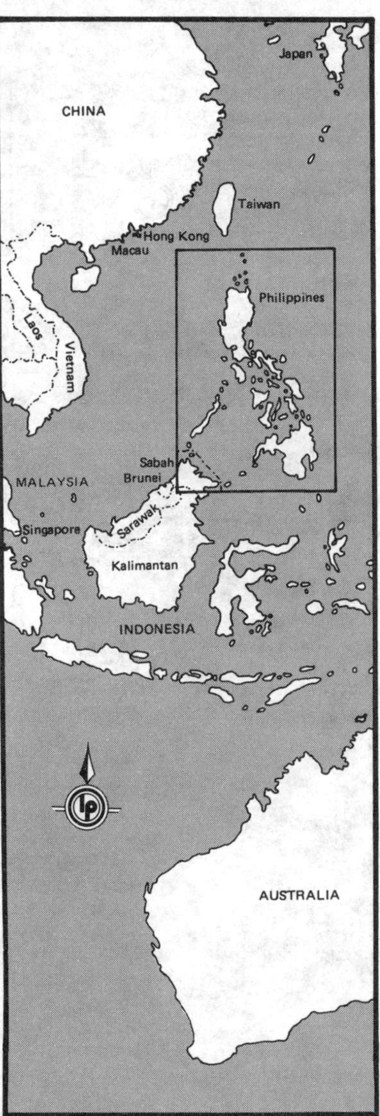

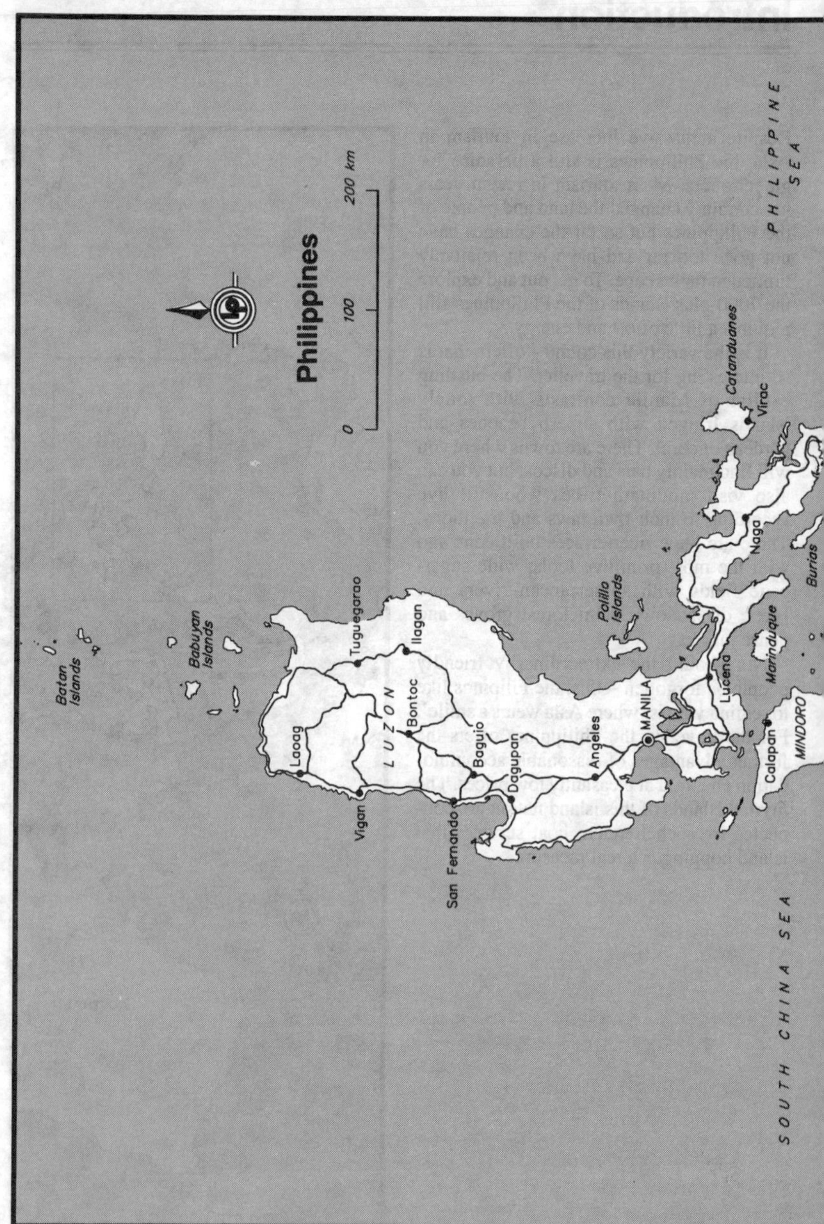
Philippines
0
100
200 km
Batan Islands
Babuyan Islands
Laoag
Vigan
Tuguegarao
Ilagan
LUZON
Bontoc
Baguio
San Fernando
Dagupan
Angeles
MANILA
Polillo Islands
Lucena
Catanduanes
Virac
Naga
Burias
Marinduque
Calapan
MINDORO
PHILIPPINE SEA
SOUTH CHINA SEA

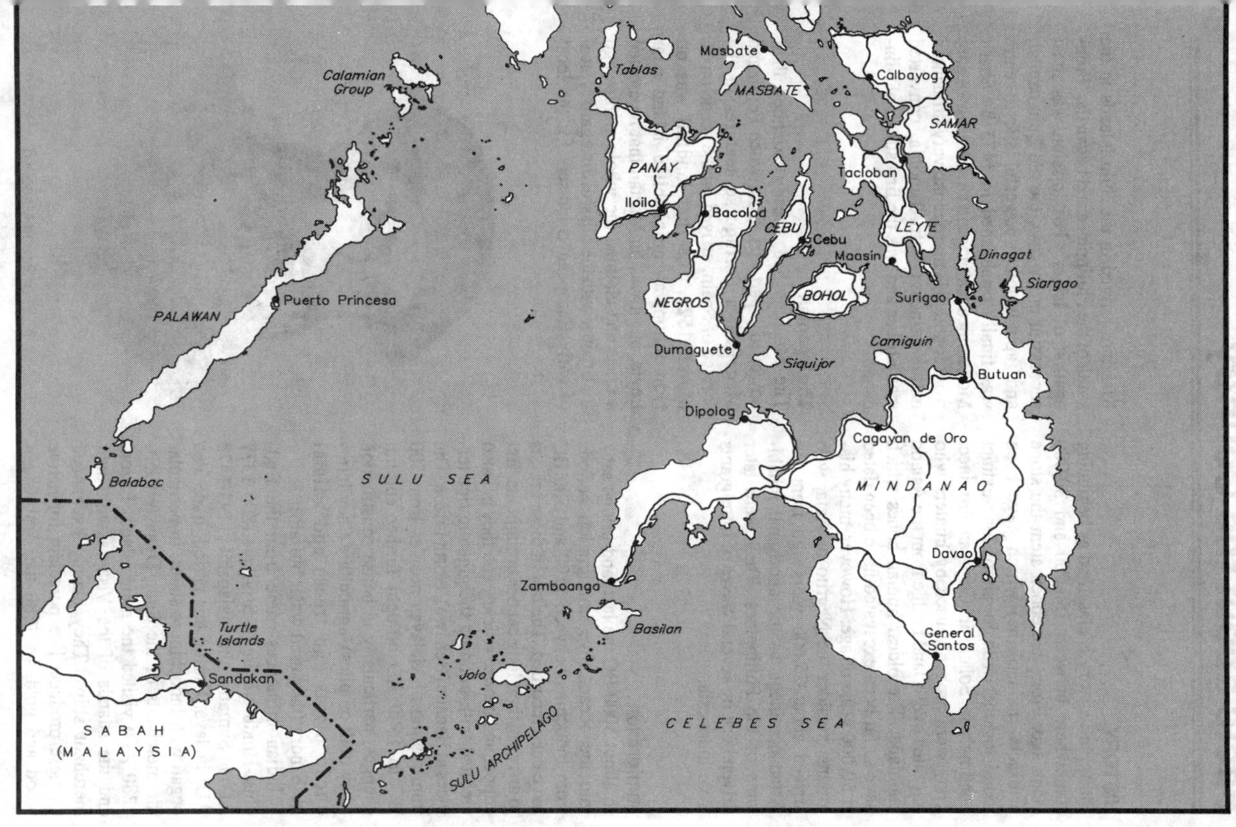
Calamian Group
Tablas
Masbate
MASBATE
Calbayog
SAMAR
PANAY
Tacloban
Iloilo
Bacolod
CEBU
Cebu
LEYTE
Maasin
Dinagat
Siargao
Puerto Princesa
PALAWAN
NEGROS
BOHOL
Surigao
Camiguin
Dumaguete
Siquijor
Butuan
Dipolog
Cagayan de Oro
Balabac
SULU SEA
MINDANAO
Davao
Zamboanga
Turtle Islands
Basilan
General Santos
Sandakan
Jolo
SABAH
(MALAYSIA)
CELEBES SEA
SULU ARCHIPELAGO

Facts about the Country

HISTORY

Philippine history is classified as beginning somewhere between 150,000 and 30,000 years ago. From this epoch stem the stone artefacts (palaeoliths) which have been found together with fossils of long-extinct mammals in Solano in Cagayan Province. They were probably used by hunters who migrated over a land bridge from the Asiatic mainland. The oldest human bones which have so far been excavated have been dated at 50,000 years of age. However, many historians consider the Negrito or Aeta, who arrived about 25,000 years ago from the Asian continent, as the aboriginal inhabitants of the Philippines. They were later driven back by several waves of immigrants from Indonesia.

Immigration

In about 5000 BC the last land bridge sank into the ocean. Five immigration periods from Indochina between 1500 and 500 BC have been recorded. The last of these groups to arrive in their long canoes brought the first copper and bronze articles, and they are also credited with building the gigantic rice terraces at Banaue (Banawe), North Luzon. The immigration of Malayan peoples from 500 BC to 1500 AD brought further cultural changes, particularly in house construction (they built on piles), agriculture (they introduced plants and trees) and animal husbandry (they used water buffalo).

Indian influences came from the Buddhist-Hindu empire of Srivijaya (800-1377 AD) in Sumatra, and Majapahit (1293-1478 AD) in Java. During this period, trade also began with Indochinese states. In particular the merchants of the Sung Dynasty (960-1280 AD) visited the main island, Luzon, and the islands of the Visayas with their merchant ships. They mainly exchanged Chinese products like porcelain for native wood and gold. In 1380 the Arab-taught Makdum arrived in the Sulu Islands in the south of the Philippines and began the 'Propagation of Islam'. His mission was most successful in Bwansa, the old Sulu capital, and Tapul Island. A powerful Islamic centre was finally established in 1475 by Sharif Mohammed Kabungsuwan, a Muslim leader from Johore. He married the very influential native princess Putri Tunoma, converted many tribes and was the first sultan of Mindanao.

The Spanish

The Muslims had already extended their power to a part of Luzon, when Ferdinand Magellan, a Portuguese seafarer in the service of Spain, arrived on the scene on 16 March 1521. His first landfall was on Homonhon, an uninhabited island near Leyte, but it was on Mactan that he erected a cross and claimed the whole archipelago for Spain – with the blissful disregard typical of early European colonisers for the local

Ferdinand Magellan

inhabitants' claim to their country. Lapu-Lapu, a proud Filipino chief, opposed the Spanish authority and this led to a battle in which Magellan was killed.

Ruy Lopez de Villalobos was the next to try and claim the islands for Spain. He reached the island realm with an expedition in 1543 and named it 'Filipinas' after King Philip II of Spain. The permanent Spanish colonial occupation of the Philippines began in 1565. In November of that year Miguel Lopez de Legaspi landed with his fleet at Bohol. In Tagbilaran he sealed a blood-friendship with the island ruler Rajah Sikatuna, conquered Cebu a short time later and erected the first Spanish fort in the Philippines. He was obviously very energetic.

In 1571 Legaspi conquered Manila and a year later the whole country, with the exception of the strictly Islamic Sulu Islands and Mindanao, was under Spain's domination. With the zeal typical of the Spanish at the time, churches were built and the propagation of Catholicism began.

The Push for Independence

Until 1821 the Philippines was administered from Mexico. Attempts by the Dutch, Portuguese and Chinese to set foot in the Philippines were successfully repelled by the Spanish, though the British managed to occupy Manila for a short time in 1762 during the Seven Years' War. They reluctantly handed it back to Spain under the conditions of the Treaty of Paris signed in 1763.

After the opening of the Suez Canal in 1869, many young Filipinos left their country to study in Spain and other European countries. They brought back with them new ideas and thoughts of freedom. In 1872 there was a revolt in Cavite by about 200 Filipino soldiers against their Spanish masters. It was quickly put down, but it signalled the start of a determined struggle for freedom and independence.

The spiritual founders of the independence movement were the Filipino thinkers and patriots Marcelo H del Pilar, Graciano Lopez Jaena, Juan Luna and Dr Jose Rizal. The critical writings and poems of Rizal inspired many Filipinos in their fight for freedom. When Jose Rizal founded the 'Liga Filipina' in 1892, he was exiled as a revolutionary agitator to Dapitan, Mindanao. Andres Bonifacio then founded the secret organisation Katipunan. In August 1896 the armed struggle for independence broke out, first in Manila and later throughout the country. On 30 December 1896, after an absurd mockery of a trial, Rizal was executed by the Spanish authorities. He spent the last weeks before his death in the dungeon of Fort Santiago in Manila. General Emilio Aguinaldo replaced Bonifacio as leader of the revolution in March 1897.

The USA

In 1898, as a result of a dispute over Cuba, a war between Spain and the USA broke out. Under Admiral Dewey the Spanish fleet was decisively beaten in Manila Bay. The Filipinos, seizing their chance to strike against the Spanish, fought on the side of the USA, and on 12 June 1898 General Aguinaldo declared the Philippines independent. The Americans, however, ignored the role the Filipinos had played in the war and paid the Spanish US$20 million for the latter's ex-possession: this was ratified by the Paris Peace Treaty of 10 December 1898. General Aguinaldo was not recognised as president of the revolutionary government. The Filipinos had to begin the struggle against foreign domination again – this time against the formidable USA.

After President Roosevelt recognised the newly drawn-up Philippine constitution, Manuel L Quezon was sworn in as President of the Philippine Commonwealth.

WW II

After the attack on Pearl Harbour, Japanese troops landed on Luzon and conquered Manila on 2 January 1942. The Filipino and US troops suffered defeats with high casualty rates in battles at Corregidor Island and on the Bataan Peninsula. This brought about the brutal Japanese military rule which contined until 1944, when General Douglas

MacArthur fulfilled his promise to return and liberate the Philippines from the Japanese. US troops landed at Leyte and, under their lead, the islands were recaptured from the Japanese forces.

On 4 July 1946 the Philippines received full independence. The first president of the republic was Manuel Roxas. His successors were Elpidio Quirino, Ramon Magsaysay, Carlos Garcia and Diosdado Macapagal.

The Marcos Years

Ferdinand E Marcos was elected to power in 1965 and, unusually for the Philippines, was re-elected in 1969. The Marcos government found the country to be in a chaotic state. Corruption and crime had become the order of the day. People talked of the 'Wild East'.

In 1972 Marcos declared martial law and began to implement his concept of the 'New Society'. Within a short time some changes were apparent – guns disappeared from the streets, crime decreased and improvements in public health were made, but the land reform law of October 1972 only partly abolished land rents.

In foreign policy, the joining of international organisations like ESCAP (Economic & Social Commission for Asia & the Pacific), ASPAC (Asian & Pacific Council), ASEAN (Association of South-East Asian Nations) and the Colombo Plan was successful. The Philippines was also a provisional member of GATT (the General Agreement on Tariffs & Trade).

Political peace, tax abatement and low wages were reasons for foreign companies to invest money again in the Philippines from the mid-1970s on. Not all Filipinos agreed with this political peace, and communist guerrillas of the NPA (New People's Army) and members of the MNLF (Moro National Liberation Front) tried to force change through violence. The opposition parties, the Democratic Socialist Party and the Philippine Democratic Party, had no influence on internal politics. The Communist Party of the Philippines was prohibited. Although martial law was abolished in January 1981, Marcos could continue his dictatorial form of government with so-called presidential decrees.

In the presidential election of June 1981, Marcos was confirmed as head of state for another six years, but the result was contested and allegations of vote-rigging were loud and many. Parliamentary elections were held in 1984 and the opposition UNIDO (United Nationalist Democratic Organisation, an amalgamation of 12 parties) won 63 of the 200 seats. The independent candidates won eight seats, and the government party, KBL (Kulisang Bagong Lipunan – New Society Movement), won 125, including the mandate for 17 which were directly decided by Marcos.

Cory Aquino

A deciding factor in the surprise success of the opposition was not only the dissatisfaction of a large proportion of the population over the state of the economy, but also the response of many voters to the murder of the liberal opposition politician and popular former senator Benigno Aquino upon his return from exile on 21 August 1983. This, more than anything, sharpened the political awareness of all levels of society and moved hundreds of thousands of people to protest. The snap election planned for 7 February 1986 saw the opposition unite for the first time under Aquino's widow, Corazon 'Cory' Aquino of the Philippine Democratic Party (PDP-Laban), and her vice-presidential running mate Salvador Laurel, leader of UNIDO. They were pitted against the team of Marcos and Tolentino.

In the past Marcos had been in a position to decide more or less the outcome of the election, but this time events were being closely monitored by both internal and external sources. Cory Aquino rallied the people in a campaign of civil unrest and national protest of the nonviolent Gandhian kind. Banks, newspapers and companies favoured by Marcos were boycotted and 'People Power' began to make itself felt. The last straw for Marcos came when Defence Minister Juan Ponce Enrile and Armed Forces

Vice-Chief of Staff Fidel Ramos joined the Aquino camp together with military units.

Following the election, both candidates claimed victory and on 25 February both Ferdinand Marcos and Cory Aquino were sworn in as president in separate ceremonies. Later that same day Marcos fled into exile in Hawaii and Cory Aquino stood unopposed. She annulled the constitution and abrogated parliament.

This historic change of leadership was not really a revolution and it hardly touched the country's elite and the structures of power.

Through her ousting of the dictator, Cory Aquino became a national hero and an international celebrity. She restored democracy to the Philippines by re-establishing the political institutions of a democratic parliament and a supreme court.

Although she commanded considerable political power at the beginning of her presidency, she did not manage to bring either the military or the feudal families under control. The president could only partly fulfil the Filipinos' hopes for wellbeing and democracy.

Today the Philippines is perhaps the freest country in South-East Asia, displaying an amazing economic growth which in 1987 and 1988 reached a figure of no less than 6%. Nevertheless, the great majority of the population, living at a bare subsistence level in miserable conditions, has hardly benefited from this new prosperity. The fall of the inflation rate, which according to official statistics sank from the record high of 50.34% in 1984 to 8.6% in February 1989, must undoubtedly be interpreted as a sign of economic recovery. But at the same time the foreign debt still amounts to a crippling US$30 billion, an astronomically high figure for the country. Land reform, a much-discussed subject and long awaited by landless Filipinos, has so far not even passed the preliminary stage.

As president and commander-in-chief of the military, Cory Aquino has survived seven attempted coups, the latest staged in Mindanao in October 1990. Her fall would certainly plunge the country into chaos again. If there was a honeymoon period for this woman of integrity, it has probably now run out: the critical tone in national politics is growing sharper and the winds of discontent seem to be blowing stronger than before. Even if she has not proved to be the long-hoped-for strong political leader and something of her old charisma has dimmed, the most powerful widow in the country has retained her credibility and can count on the trust of the people. However, Cory Aquino herself has stated that when her term of office is over she will not stand for re-election.

GEOGRAPHY

The Philippines officially consists of 7107 islands of which only 2000 are inhabited. Only about 500 of the islands are larger than one sq km and 2500 aren't even named. In descending order of size the biggest islands are:

Luzon	104,683 sq km
Mindanao	94,596 sq km
Palawan	14,896 sq km
Panay	12,327 sq km
Mindoro	10,245 sq km
Samar	9,949 sq km
Negros	9,225 sq km
Leyte	6,268 sq km
Cebu	5,088 sq km
Bohol	4,117 sq km
Masbate	4,047 sq km

The total area of the Philippines is 299,404 sq km. From north to south the Philippines stretches for 1850 km and from east to west for 1100 km. The highest mountain is Mt Apo, near Davao in Mindanao, at 2954 metres. Mt Pulog, east of Baguio in North Luzon, is the second at 2930 metres. There are over 37 volcanoes in the Philippines, 17 of which are classed as being active, including the Mayon Volcano near Legaspi in South Luzon. The longest rivers are the Cagayan River, the Rio Grande de Pampanga and the Agno River in Luzon, and the Rio Grande de Mindanao and the Agusan River in Mindanao.

The islands of the Philippines can be

divided conveniently into four groups. First there's Luzon, the largest and northernmost island and the site of the capital, Manila. The nearby islands of Marinduque (which is sandwiched between Mindoro and Luzon) and Mindoro are generally included with Luzon. At the other end of the archipelago is the second largest island, Mindanao. From Mindanao's south-western tip, the islands of the Sulu archipelago form stepping stones south to Borneo. Third is the tightly packed island group known as the Visayas, which fills the space between Luzon and Mindanao. Seven major islands make up this group: Panay, Negros, Cebu, Bohol, Leyte, Samar and Masbate. Cebu is the central island of the group and Cebu City is the shipping centre for the entire Philippines – from there ships run to places throughout the country. Finally, off to the west, there's the province of Palawan with more than 1700 islands. The main island is Palawan, which is long and narrow and forms another bridge from the Philippines to Borneo.

Forces of Nature

The earth's crust, the lithosphere, is only about 70 km thick and is composed of several small and large plates. Earthquakes occur depending on the amount of friction between these horizontal plates. Among the six large plates, also called continental or tectonic plates, are the Eurasian and the Pacific plates and in between is squeezed the small Philippine plate. Strong earthquakes are fairly rare, but there are light tremors from time to time.

One of the worst earthquakes to strike the Philippines this century hit large parts of the country on 16 July 1990. Measuring 7.7 on the Richter scale, the temblor killed over 1600 people and destroyed over 20,000 buildings, leaving more than 100,000 people homeless. Several strong aftershocks caused further damage to roads and houses. The worst affected cities were Baguio, Cabanatuan and Dagupan, all in northern Luzon.

The breaking points in the earth's crust are marked by deep trenches, high mountain ranges and volcanoes. The most prominent volcanic chain leads from Alaska and the Aleutian Islands, past the Siberian Kamchatka Peninsula, the Kuril Islands and Japan to the Philippines, where there are 37 volcanoes, at least 17 of which are active. The Mayon Volcano in South Luzon erupted slightly in May 1985, but the last serious eruption was in October 1984, when a dangerous series of eruptions necessitated the temporary evacuation of 70,000 inhabitants.

Luzon and the northern Visayas also lie in the typhoon belt. Some of the whirlwinds wandering from the Pacific to the Chinese mainland also affect the Philippines. Violent storms can occur from June to January, although August to November are the peak months for typhoons. Typhoons nearly always cause power failures, and fires (often caused by candles being blown over) frequently follow. Overloaded electrical points, open fires and arson are other causes of the many fires in the Philippines.

CLIMATE

The climate in the Philippines is typically tropical – hot and humid year round. Although the weather pattern is fairly complex, it can be roughly divided into the dry season – January to June – and the wet season – July to December. January is usually the coolest month and May the hottest, but the average temperature is usually around 25°C throughout the year. However, like everywhere in the world, the Philippines weather is not 100% predictable.

December to February is the 'cool dry' period while March to May is the 'hot dry' period. You can expect rain every day in July, August and September. In May, Manila usually has daytime temperatures of 35°C to 40°C and at night it doesn't drop much below 27°C. This is the time of year when the rich citizens of Manila head for the perpetual spring of Baguio and the mountain provinces.

The best time to travel is from December

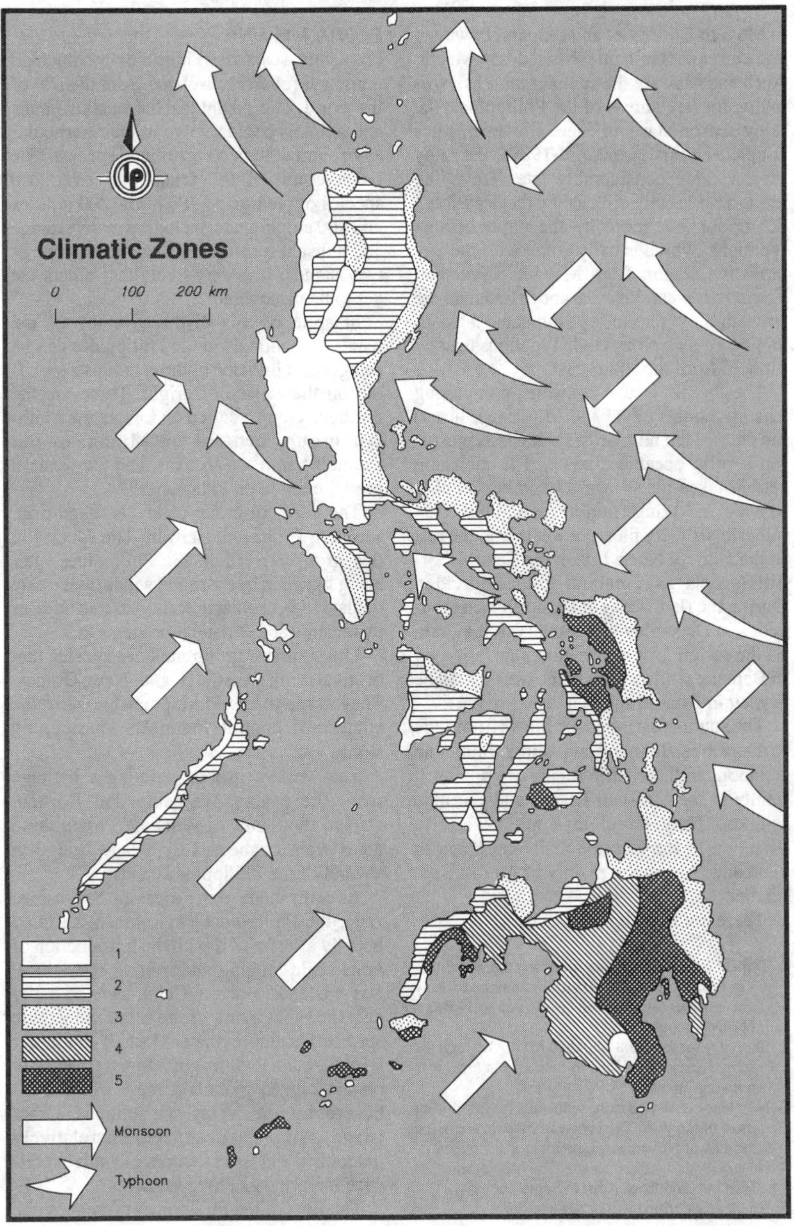
Climatic Zones
0
100
200 km
1
2
3
4
5
Monsoon
Typhoon

to May. In December and January, however, you can expect rain on the east coast. March, April and May are the summer months. Normally, for large areas of the Philippines, the rainy season starts in June. However, for a couple of years in the mid-1980s, the rainy season came considerably late. Travelling around isn't really affected by the occasional downpour, but more by the unpredictable typhoons, which usually come with the wet monsoon season from May to November. The south-west Visayas and Mindanao lie beneath the typhoon belt, but can occasionally be hit by a crosswind. Typhoons usually blow in from the south-east.

The Pacific Ocean coastline, comprising Luzon, Samar, Leyte and Mindanao, lies in the path of the north-east tradewinds, ensuring a mild oceanic climate. The monsoon season takes place from December/January to May and brings rain to the Pacific coast but primarily dry pleasant weather to the rest of the land. In North Luzon the Central Cordillera acts as a natural climate divider. During the first weeks of the north-east monsoons in December and January, it may rain on the eastern side of this mountain range, eg in Banaue; while a little to the west it may be dry, eg in Bontoc and Sagada.

The south-west monsoon blows from June to December/January and brings rain. The typhoons in the Pacific region are predominantly in the Marshall Islands and Caroline Islands. They travel in a north-westerly direction to the Chinese mainland between June and November, mainly in August/September.

There are five climatic zones:

1 Typical South-East Asian monsoon climate. Long dry season from November/December to May and intense rainy period from June to November/December.
2 Short dry season from March to May. Although the rainy season from June to February is long, it is not very intense.
3 No clear-cut dry season, with rain falling during most of the year. The heaviest showers are in the months of November, December and January.
4 No clearly defined dry season. The heaviest rainfall is in the months of April to September.
5 No clearly defined wet or dry season.

FLORA & FAUNA

For many years the Philippine archipelago remained relatively isolated from the rest of the world. This meant that the existing plants and animals could evolve in their particular environment to become unique species. The latest count of the fauna lists over 200 species of mammals, 580 birds, 200 reptiles and 100 amphibians, including many strange and unusual specimens found on only one or two islands. It is very likely that others are yet to be discovered.

In spite of this diversity, many of the plants and animals in the Philippines can be categorised into one of three groups depending on their place of origin. These are the northern group, centred on Luzon; the southern group, centred on Mindanao but extending into the Visayas; and the western group, centred on Palawan.

The northern group claims heritage from southern China and Taiwan. The species in this group arrived in the Philippines after being blown in by monsoon winds (in the case of plant life), drifting in with the ocean tides, or by means of other natural phenomena.

The southern group includes species that originated in Australia and New Guinea. They came to the Philippines by using the islands of central Indonesia as stepping stones.

The western group, claiming a heritage from the Malay peninsula and Borneo, arrived thousands of years ago, when these areas were connected by a land bridge to several of the Philippine islands.

As with many other areas of South-East Asia, the Philippines environment suffered heavily after WW II with the introduction of large-scale logging and mining operations. Some islands, notably Cebu, were so badly damaged that many of the more vulnerable species became extinct. Most of the larger islands retain their original forest cover only on the rugged mountain tops, which form havens for the plants and animals. Other islands, like Palawan, remain relatively untouched and there visitors can still experience the original Philippines.

The flora of the Philippines presents some

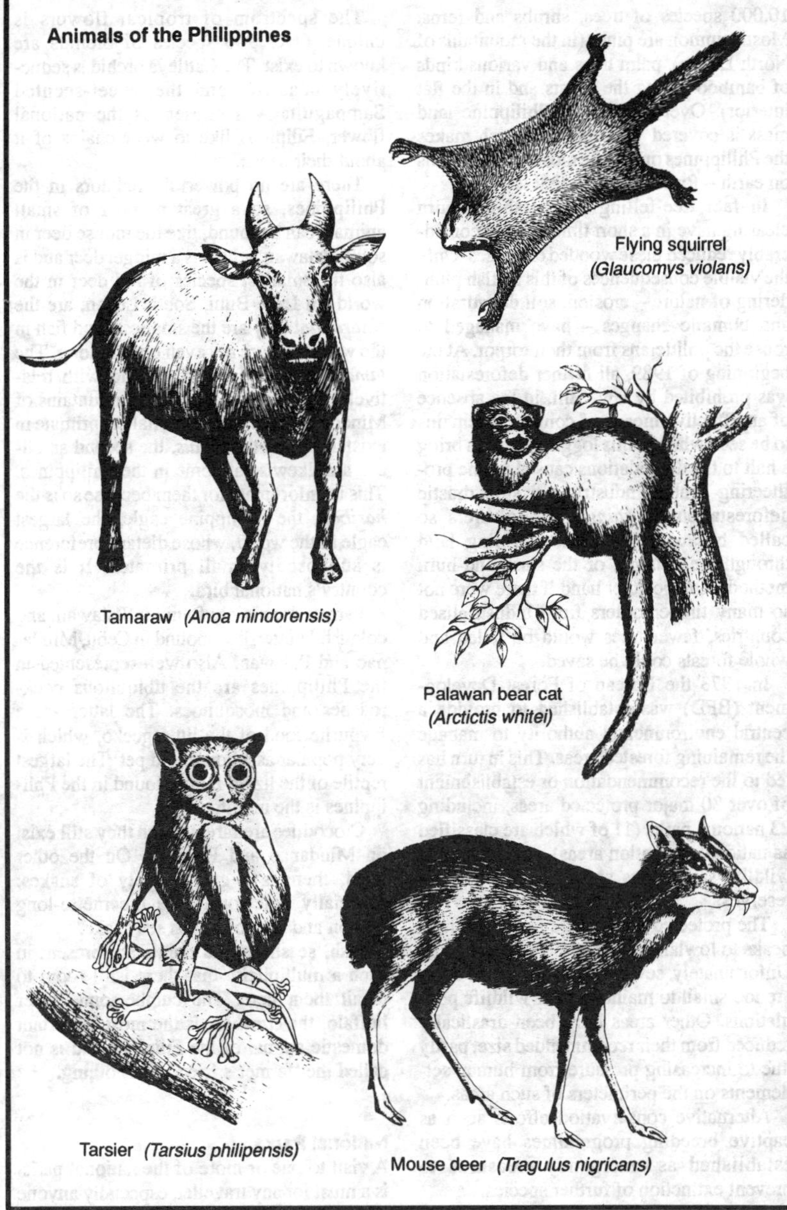
Animals of the Philippines
Flying squirrel
(Glaucomys violans)
Tamaraw (Anoa mindorensis)
Palawan bear cat
(Arctictis whitei)
Tarsier (Tarsius philipensis)
Mouse deer (Tragulus nigricans)

10,000 species of trees, shrubs and ferns. Most common are pines (in the mountains of North Luzon), palm trees and various kinds of bamboo (along the coasts and in the flat interior). Over half of the Philippine land mass is covered with forests, which makes the Philippines one of the most wooded lands on earth – for the present, that is.

In fact tree-felling and slash-and-burn clearing have in a short time already considerably reduced these wooded expanses. Only the visible consequences of this selfish plundering of nature – erosion, soil dehydration and climatic changes – have managed to rouse the politicians from their torpor. At the beginning of 1989, all further deforestation was prohibited by law. Still, in the absence of an effective means of control, it remains to be seen whether this logging ban can bring a halt to the depredations caused by the profiteering timber industry and stop drastic deforestation by *kaingineros* (clearers so called because they create farming land through the *kaingin*, or the slash-and-burn method). On the other hand if there were not so many timber orders from industrialised countries, fewer trees would be felled and whole forests could be saved.

In 1973 the Bureau of Forest Development (BFD) was established to provide a central environmental authority to manage the remaining forested areas. This in turn has led to the recommendation or establishment of over 30 major protected areas, including 23 national parks (11 of which are classified as national recreation areas), seven national wildlife sanctuaries and three strict nature reserves.

The protected areas range from mountain peaks to lowland rainforests and coral reefs. Unfortunately, several of the protected areas are too small to maintain their wildlife populations. Other areas have been drastically reduced from their recommended size, partly due to increasing pressure from human settlements on the perimeters of such areas.

Alternative conservation efforts such as captive breeding programmes have been established as emergency measures to prevent extinction of further species.

The spectrum of tropical flowers is unique. Over 900 species of orchids are known to exist. The Cattleya orchid is seductively beautiful and the sweet-scented Sampaguita was chosen as the national flower; Filipinos like to wear chains of it about their necks.

There are no powerful predators in the Philippines, so a great number of small animals can be found, like the mouse deer in south Palawan, which is a midget deer and is also the smallest species of red deer in the world. In Lake Buhi, South Luzon, are the *sinarapan*: they are the smallest food fish in the world and are not even one cm long. The *tamaraw*, a wild dwarf buffalo with relatively short horns, lives in the mountains of Mindoro. The *tarsier*, the smallest primate in existence, and the *tabius*, the second smallest, are likewise at home in the Philippines. This is unfortunate for them because so is the *haribon*, the Philippine eagle, the largest eagle in the world, whose dietary preference is supposedly small primates. It is the country's national bird.

Parrots are mainly found in Palawan, and colourful butterflies abound in Cebu, Mindanao and Palawan. Also well represented in the Philippines are the ubiquitous cockroaches and mosquitoes. The latter are a favourite food of the little gecko, which is very popular as a household pet. The largest reptile of the lizard family found in the Philippines is the monitor.

Crocodiles are rare, though they still exist on Mindanao and Palawan. On the other hand, there is a great variety of snakes: especially noteworthy are the metre-long python and the poisonous sea snake.

Fish, seashells and corals are present in such a multiplicity that there isn't room to detail them here. The cumbersome water buffalo, the *carabao*, is the most important domestic animal of the Filipinos and is not called the 'farmer's friend' for nothing.

National Parks

A visit to one or more of the national parks is a must for any traveller, especially anyone

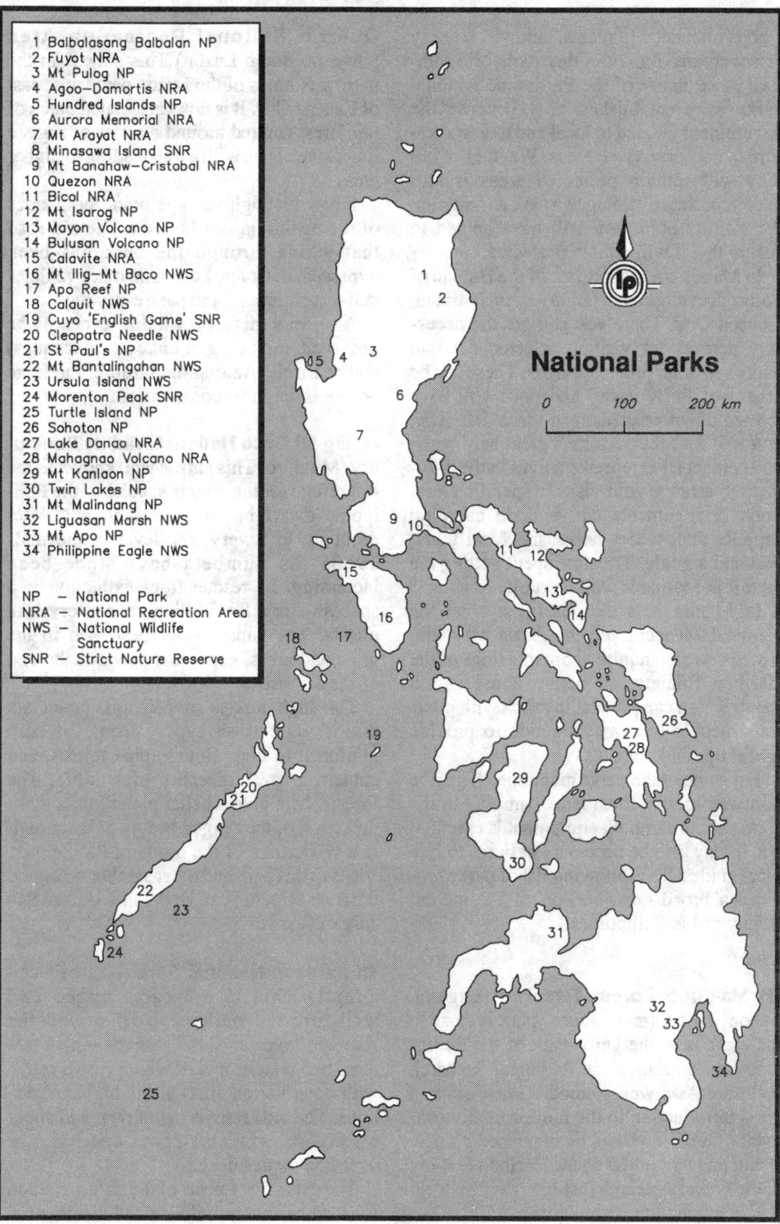
1 Balbalasang Balbalan NP
2 Fuyot NRA
3 Mt Pulog NP
4 Agoo-Damortis NRA
5 Hundred Islands NP
6 Aurora Memorial NRA
7 Mt Arayat NRA
8 Minasawa Island SNR
9 Mt Banahaw-Cristobal NRA
10 Quezon NRA
11 Bicol NRA
12 Mt Isarog NP
13 Mayon Volcano NP
14 Bulusan Volcano NP
15 Calavite NRA
16 Mt Ilig-Mt Baco NWS
17 Apo Reef NP
18 Calauit NWS
19 Cuyo 'English Game' SNR
20 Cleopatra Needle NWS
21 St Paul's NP
22 Mt Bantalingahan NWS
23 Ursula Island NWS
24 Morenton Peak SNR
25 Turtle Island NP
26 Sohoton NP
27 Lake Danao NRA
28 Mahagnao Volcano NRA
29 Mt Kanlaon NP
30 Twin Lakes NP
31 Mt Malindang NP
32 Liguasan Marsh NWS
33 Mt Apo NP
34 Philippine Eagle NWS
NP – National Park
NRA – National Recreation Area
NWS – National Wildlife Sanctuary
SNR – Strict Nature Reserve
National Parks
0 100 200 km

who is interested in plants, animals, scenery or adventure. As with other parts of South-East Asia, many of the Philippine national parks were established only because the government yielded to local and tourist pressure to conserve these areas. Whether or not they will remain protected areas is still uncertain. Just by going to a park and signing the visitors book you will have helped to ensure that it will remain protected.

In Manila the main office of the Bureau of Forest Development (BFD) is in Diliman, Quezon City. There you can get the necessary permits for visiting selected national parks and other protected areas. These can be organised fairly easily and once you have written down your planned visits officially, you will find the permits a great help when you contact BFD representatives in the provinces to arrange your visits to specific areas. Such arrangements can include camping supplies and, where necessary, local transport and a guide. The time spent getting the permit in Manila is well worth it.

In Manila it is also useful to visit the National Museum and the Ayala Museum, where you can inquire about meetings of the Haribon Society, an active conservation group which can put you in touch with interested people who may be able to provide useful tips and contacts.

For some of the parks mentioned here, the best way to visit them is by camping in the areas. Some camping equipment is essential and it may also be necessary at times to hire local guides. The following list of parks provides a broad cross-section of the natural beauty of the Philippines.

Mt Makiling Forest Reserve (Laguna, Luzon) This former national park is close to the campus of the University of the Philippines at Los Banos and its Forest Research Institute. As a well-studied area, it offers a good introduction to the rainforest environment. It is often visited by organised groups. If you make inquiries to the Haribon Society or the Forest Research Institute, they may put you in touch with such a group.

Quezon National Recreation Area (Quezon, South Luzon) This park is in the narrow isthmus of the Luzon peninsula, east of Lucena City. It is now an isolated patch of rainforest centred around a series of rugged limestone crags, with a trail leading to higher areas.

From this high vantage point, both sides of the peninsula can be seen. The old road that winds through the park has been bypassed, but a few buses and other vehicles still travel through the park every day.

A wide variety of wildlife can still be observed including monkeys (macaques) and squirrels. Among the birdlife, the large hornbills are most conspicuous.

Mt Ilig-Mt Baco National Wildlife Sanctuary (Mindoro) This park is well known as the last refuge for the unique species of the Philippine dwarf buffalo, the tamaraw. After dropping to a very low level in the mid-1960s, its numbers have since been increasing. Its rescue from extinction is a success story for Philippine conservation efforts. The tamaraw are best seen in the grassland areas, especially towards the end of the dry season.

The high forests of Mindoro cover six major vegetation types, from lowland rainforest to high altitude pine forests, and contain a great diversity of wildlife. The forests there give a better picture than those on Luzon of the rugged beauty of the mountain wilderness of the northern Philippines. Visits to this park and other smaller protected areas on Mindoro can be organised from San Jose or Roxas.

Mt Kanlaon National Park (Negros Occidental) This is a large, rugged and well-forested park centred around the Kanlaon Volcano (2465 metres), which features two craters, one of which is still active with open barren areas at the higher elevations. The old crater is cylindrical and about a km wide, while the newer crater is now over 250 metres deep.

The extensive forests of the park are noted for their abundant wildlife and also feature many waterfalls and small crater lakes hidden by the trees. It is a major refuge for wildlife in the central Philippines and offers an exciting way for the more adventurous traveller to visit a rainforest.

The park's main attraction is climbing the volcano but facilities for visitors are limited. Access to the park can be organised from Bacolod City and through several of the smaller towns closer to the park.

Mahagnao Volcano National Recreation Area (Leyte) This is a small park in central Leyte featuring a crater lake and diverse forest and scenic areas. It is part of the central mountain region of Leyte, extending north to the Lake Danao area, also proposed as a national park.

In 1982 the whole region was surveyed for a planned merger into one large park with trails and visitor facilities. In contrast to Negros, this region offers a relatively easy opportunity to visit a Philippine wilderness area. The main point of access is from Tacloban City. Mahagnao itself is close to the Burauen area.

St Paul's National Park (Palawan) The focal point of this park, on the west coast of Palawan about 70 km from Puerto Princesa, is the Underground River, which is over seven km in length and navigable by rubber dinghy or canoe for most of its length.

The forested limestone peaks around the river area and St Paul Bay add to the park's remarkable beauty. The best access to the river area is by boat from Baheli or Sabang. The river cave plays host to millions of bats and swiftlets, offering spectacular viewing at dawn and dusk. It is possible to camp on the beach not far from the main entrance of the river and it is well worth spending a few days in this beautiful area.

Mt Apo National Park (Mindanao) This park was established in 1936 to protect the highest peak in the Philippines. Mt Apo (2954 metres) is an active volcano near Davao and its snow-capped appearance is actually caused by a thick white sulphur crust.

The most famous inhabitant of the park is the haribon, or the Philippine eagle. The numbers of this spectacular bird were once reduced to a few individuals, but in the last 25 years have grown considerably, due in part to the experimental breeding programme at nearby Baracatan. Observing this splendid bird in the wild can be an unforgettable experience. As well as scanning the sky and tree tops to see an eagle, you should listen for its piercing cry, or for the racket of smaller birds mobbing one, usually when it is resting in the tops of the larger trees near the edge of the forest.

There are several walking trails in the park, including one to the summit of Mt Apo. This park is characteristic of Mindanao's forested volcanic regions and offers spectacular scenery and wildlife. Visits can be organised from nearby Davao City.

GOVERNMENT

The administration of the Republic of the Philippines is subdivided into 12 regions (plus Metro Manila as the National Capital Region) consisting of 72 provinces. Every province consists of a provincial capital and several municipalities, which in turn consist of village communities, or *barangays*. A barangay with an elected head/administrator, the 'barangay captain', is the smallest socio-political administration unit in the Philippines. The term 'barangay' originates from the time the archipelago was settled between 500 BC and 1500 AD. During that time, a barangay (or balanghai) was a large seaworthy outrigger boat which could carry up to 90 passengers and was used by Malayan peoples to migrate to the Philippines. The crews of these boats were probably social groups like village communities or extended families.

National Flag & National Anthem

The national flag of the Philippines has a white triangle on the left. On either side tapering off to the left are two stripes, the top one blue, the bottom one red. The white

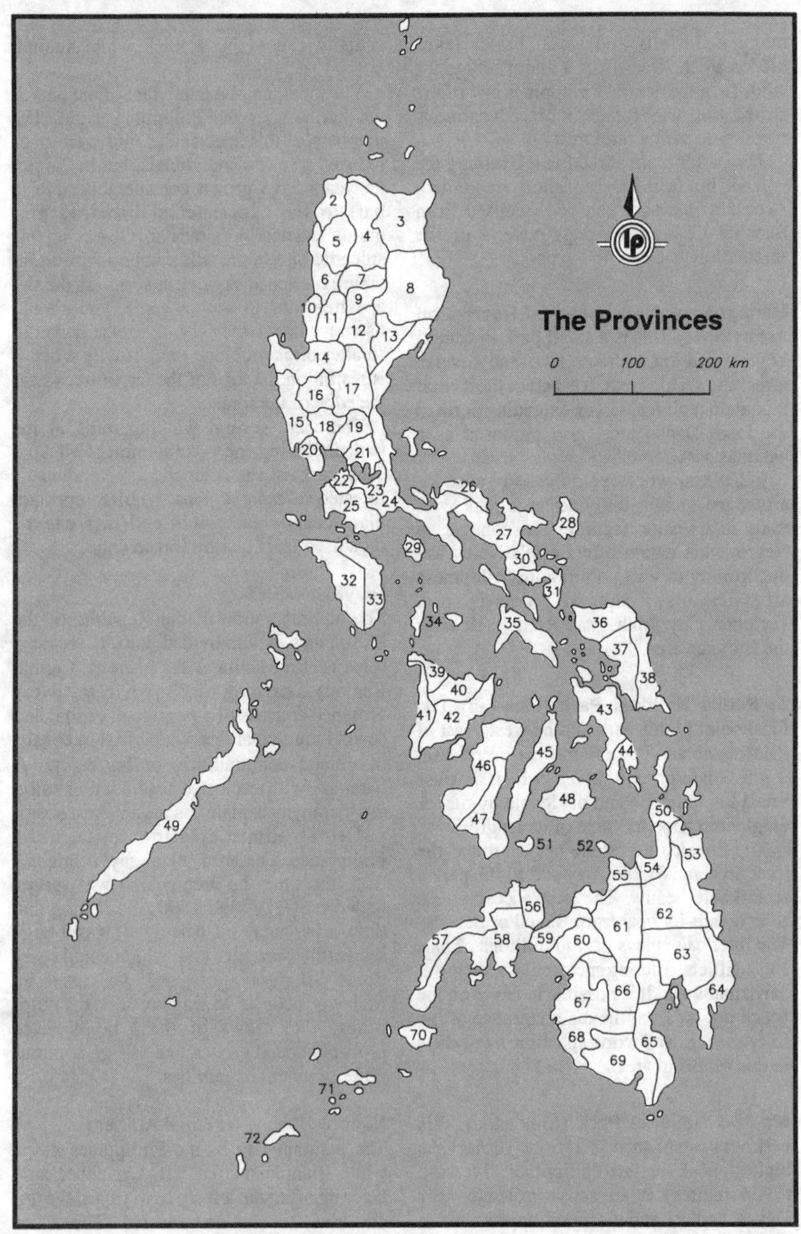
The Provinces
0
100
200 km
1
2
3
4
5
6
7
8
9
10
11
12
13
14
15
16
17
18
19
20
21
22
23
24
25
26
27
28
29
30
31
32
33
34
35
36
37
38
39
40
41
42
43
44
45
46
47
48
49
50
51
52
53
54
55
56
57
58
59
60
61
62
63
64
65
66
67
68
69
70
71
72

1	Batanes	37	Western Samar
2	Ilocos Norte	38	Eastern Samar
3	Cagayan	39	Aklan
4	Kalinga-Apayao	40	Capiz
5	Abra	41	Antique
6	Ilocos Sur	42	Iloilo
7	Mountain	43	Leyte
8	Isabela	44	Southern Leyte
9	Ifugao	45	Cebu
10	La Union	46	Negros Occidental
11	Benguet	47	Negros Oriental
12	Nueva Vizcaya	48	Bohol
13	Quirino	49	Palawan
14	Pangasinan	50	Surigao Norte
15	Zambales	51	Siquijor
16	Tarlac	52	Camiguin
17	Nueva Ecija	53	Surigao del Sur
18	Pampanga	54	Agusan del Norte
19	Bulacan	55	Misamis Oriental
20	Bataan	56	Misamis Occidental
21	Rizal	57	Zamboanga del Norte
22	Cavite	58	Zamboanga del Sur
23	Laguna	59	Lanao del Norte
24	Quezon	60	Lanao del Sur
25	Batangas	61	Bukidnon
26	Camarines Norte	62	Agusan del Sur
27	Camarines Sur	63	Davao del Norte
28	Catanduanes	64	Davao Oriental
29	Marinduque	65	Davao del Sur
30	Albay	66	North Cotabato
31	Sorsogon	67	Maguindanao
32	Mindoro Occidental	68	Sultan Kudarat
33	Mindoro Oriental	69	South Cotabato
34	Romblon	70	Basilan
35	Masbate	71	Sulu
36	Northern Samar	72	Tawi-Tawi

triangle contains three five-point stars and a sun with eight rays. The sun symbolises freedom and its eight rays represent the first eight provinces that revolted against Spanish colonial rule. The stars symbolise the three geographical divisions of the Philippines: Luzon, the Visayas and Mindanao. The blue stripe stands for the equality and unity of the people. The red stripe (placed on top in wartime) symbolises the readiness of the Filipinos to fight to the death for their country.

On 12 June 1898, General Emilio Aguinaldo declared the independence of the Philippines from the balcony of his house in Cavite. On this day the Philippine national flag was raised and the Philippine national anthem played for the first time. In the form of a march, the Marcha Nacional Filipina anthem was composed by Julian Felipe and the words were written by Jose Palma.

ECONOMY

About two-thirds of Filipinos live by fishing, agriculture and forestry. A significant contribution to their diet comes from ocean, coast and freshwater fishing. Rice is the most important agricultural product. The development of new varieties of rice at the International Rice Research Institute in Los Banos, improvements in methods of cultivation and enlargement of the area of cultivation have brought the Philippines closer to self-sufficiency in food production.

The main products for export are coconuts (copra), abaca (Manila hemp), tobacco, sugar cane, bananas, pineapples and, until the declaration of a logging ban by the government in 1989, timber. Cattle farming is still relatively undeveloped. Poultry, pigs, sheep and goats are reared for meat, while buffaloes serve mainly as work animals. The most important minerals are chrome, iron, copper, coal, nickel, gypsum, sulphur, mercury, asbestos, marble and salt. Test drillings for oil have been only partially successful.

The Philippines, like many other Asian countries, is dependent on oil for its energy needs. Every year about US$2 billion has to be spent on crude oil imports. It is hoped that hydroelectric and geothermal power projects will go some way towards improving the energy situation. In 1986 21.6% of the total energy required was produced geothermally, which is equivalent to 8.4 million barrels of oil. The Philippines is second only to the USA in harnessing geothermal energy sources.

Manufacturing occurs principally in and around Manila, and consists mainly of the luxury goods, food, textile and leatherware industries, although the Philippines also manufactures automobile components.

Economic analysts are worried that the Filipino passion for grand and impressive projects, often highly capital intensive, may limit the nation's ability to come to terms with its employment problems. There is a minimum wage set by the state but this often exists only on paper. (See the following Income & Cost of Living section.) The Philippines has a large pool of skilled but underutilised labour.

Tourism is a further source of income and from 1970 to 1980 the tourist flow increased from just 14,000 visitors to over a million. In the years of political unrest from 1983 to 1986 the tourist figures declined, only to shoot up again in 1987, and in 1988 over a million tourists visited the country. Of these approximately 40% were Japanese and 25% from the USA.

Manila had a massive increase in hotel rooms in the 1970s, but this was not followed by a similar development in provincial areas. This lack of development outside Manila may eventually limit the growth of tourism, but it does make the Philippines more enjoyable for the shoestring traveller!

Income & Cost of Living

The basic level of income is fixed by the state. According to law, the lowest possible wage of a working person is 90 pesos per day, equivalent to about US$3. Tariff rates are numerous but exist only on paper, considerably few of these being in fact observed. There are also clear discrepancies in income between city and country. Here are some examples of average wages in the Philippines: labourers or restaurant staff (without tips) receive US$75 per month; office workers or teachers, US$140 per month; engineers, US$390 per month. To cover the basic necessities of life, a family of five members needs at least 6000 pesos per month.

Similarly, prices are considerably higher in the cities than in rural areas. In the country a Filipino meal costs no more than US$2. A bottle of beer (O.33 litres) can be had for the equivalent of US$0.25, and about US$0.17 is charged for soft drinks like Coca-Cola. Naturally everything is a good deal dearer in exclusive restaurants and bars. For instance, you'll pay about US$1 for a Coke at the swimming pool of the Manila Pavilion Hotel, while a beer in one of the Ermita nightclubs will cost around US$1.50.

PUBLIC HEALTH

Much progress has been made in public health since 1975, when the Ministry of Health started an intensive programme to combat sickness and disease. Preventative measures, production of preserved food and dietary education are key points in this health campaign. Town health centres, mobile centres, mobile sickness treatment stations, free treatment and issue of necessary medicines have sustained the programme.

There has been a general decrease in the mortality rate, particularly in that of mothers and babies. The most significant diseases are still pneumonia, tuberculosis, heart and intestinal diseases and bronchitis.

Out of a total of 845 hospitals, 570 are privately run. There are 252 hospitals in Metro Manila alone, 34 of which are run by the government. Undoubtedly the best and most well known are the Medical Center and the Philippine Heart Center for Asia. Both have above-average quality staff and are equipped with modern technology, but the treatment of the population in general is certainly not up to this standard. There are simply too few hospitals, doctors and nurses. An intensive collaboration between the Community Development Planning Council, which has been set up for village sanitation, and the government health service can only be welcomed.

POPULATION

In 1988 the population stood at 60 million. The trend is for the number of inhabitants of the Philippines to grow at a rate of 2.4% a year. The Philippines' family planning programmes are hampered not only by the strong Catholicism of the Filipinos but also by the usual Asian wish for the 'insurance' of a large family in old age. Filipinos are inclined to be very fond of children and have on average six children to a family. Consequently, you will hear of 'family planting' rather than 'family planning', although the government is putting a great deal of effort into popularising the concept of birth control.

Nearly 40% of the population of the Philippines lives in the city, while the other 60% lives in the country. Fifty-three per cent of Filipinos are under 20 years of age, while those who are 65 or over account for only 7% of the population. The ratio of males to females is almost even, averaging out at 100 females to 99.7 males.

Manila is the largest city with 1.6 million people, but including the suburbs such as Quezon, Caloocan and Pasay, the population of Metro Manila is over eight million. Other major cities are Davao, Cebu, Iloilo, Zamboanga, Bacolod, Angeles, Butuan and Cagayan de Oro.

CULTURAL MINORITIES

Some six million Filipinos make up the so-called cultural minority groups or tribal Filipinos, which collectively comprise 12% of the total population. This figure includes the four million Muslims.

There are 60 ethnological groups altogether distributed mainly around North Luzon (Ifugao, Bontoc, Kalinga, Ilokano), central Luzon (Negrito), Mindoro (Mangyan), and western Mindanao and the Sulu Islands (Muslim). Many of these groups are looked after by the ONCC (Office for Northern Cultural Communities), OSCC (Office for Southern Cultural Communities) or OMA (Office of Muslim Affairs). These agencies are responsible for protecting the cultural minorities' way of life and for assisting the government in bringing material and technical aid to these people to assist their integration into mainstream Philippine society. The minorities themselves decide whether to use this service, and if so what type of aid they require.

It would be beyond the scope of this book to describe all the ethnological groups in the Philippines, but a selection of those which represent an important part of the population structure and which are accessible to foreign travellers follows.

Apayao

The Apayao prefer to live close to the rivers, particularly along the shores of the Apayao and Matalang rivers in the highlands of the Ilocos and Abra provinces in north-west Luzon. They call themselves *isneg* and are the descendants of the feared head-hunters in the Central Cordillera. Their leaders, named *mengal*, are celebrated, wealthy warriors with appropriately large followings. Positions of leadership are not inherited but are accorded the warrior with the greatest ability and charisma. The Apayao believe in ghosts

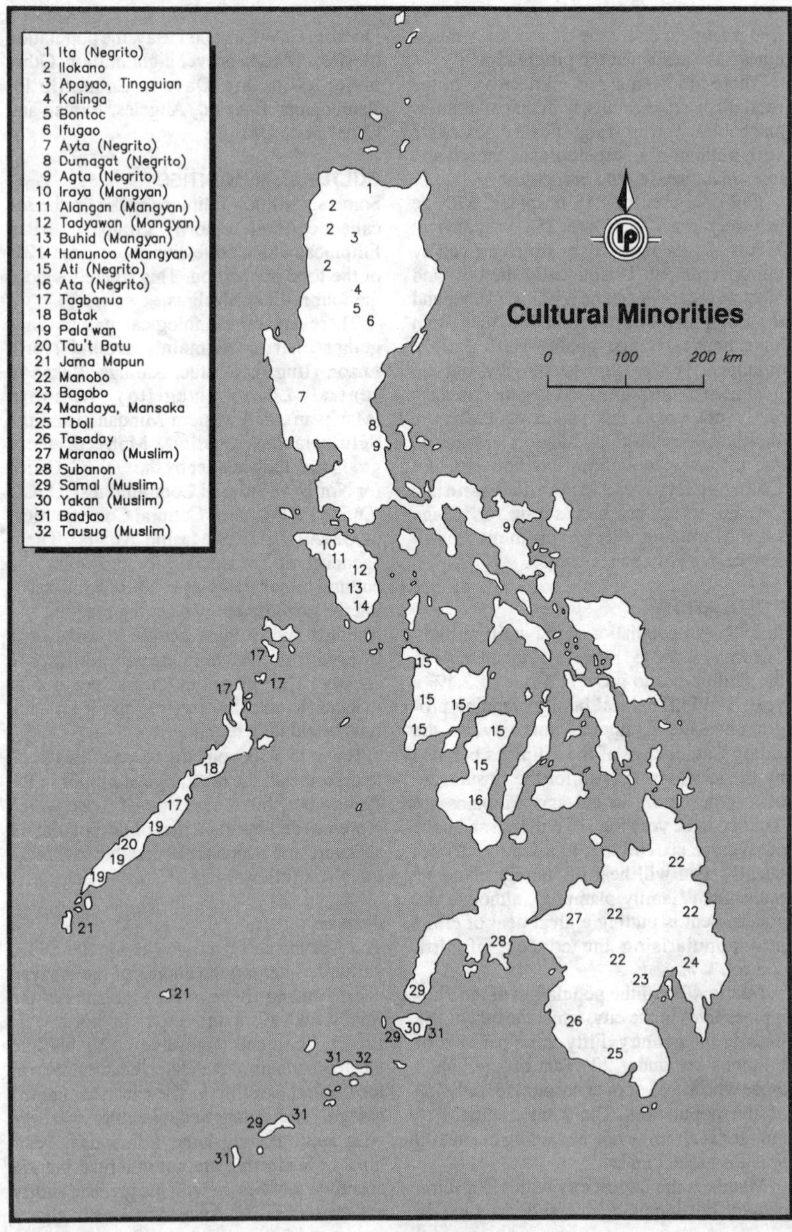
Cultural Minorities
0 100 200 km
1 Ita (Negrito)
2 Ilokano
3 Apayao, Tingguian
4 Kalinga
5 Bontoc
6 Ifugao
7 Ayta (Negrito)
8 Dumagat (Negrito)
9 Agta (Negrito)
10 Iraya (Mangyan)
11 Alangan (Mangyan)
12 Tadyawan (Mangyan)
13 Buhid (Mangyan)
14 Hanunoo (Mangyan)
15 Ati (Negrito)
16 Ata (Negrito)
17 Tagbanua
18 Batak
19 Pala'wan
20 Tau't Batu
21 Jama Mapun
22 Manobo
23 Bagobo
24 Mandaya, Mansaka
25 T'boli
26 Tasaday
27 Maranao (Muslim)
28 Subanon
29 Samal (Muslim)
30 Yakan (Muslim)
31 Badjao
32 Tausug (Muslim)

Apayao house

which may take the form of people, animals, giants and monsters. They are protected by Anglabbang, the best and highest god of the head-hunters.

Badjao

The Sulu archipelago in the south of the Philippines, as well as the coast and waters of north-east Borneo and east Indonesia, are the domain of the Badjao (or Bajau, Badjaw). They are sea gypsies, many of whom still live in small boats as extended families. Today, however, most of them have given up a nomadic way of life and have settled in houses built on stilts on coral reefs far out in the ocean or on sandbanks near the coast. No-one knows exactly how many Badjao there are, but the figure is estimated at about 30,000, two-thirds of them living in Philippine waters. They are said in legend to have originated in Johore in Malaysia.

A Badjao boat, or *lipa* (pronounced 'leepa'), is made of wood, is seven to 12 metres long, and has a removable roof over its central section. The long, thin hull is fitted with individual slats, serving as a flat base on which to stand when punting or spearing fish. The catch is then hung out to dry in the stern. There is a little oven over the stern where fish can be cooked. Apart from seafood, the mainstay of the Badjao diet is cassava: a nourishing stew that is prepared using the cassava tuber, which is rich in starch.

Sea cucumbers are gathered to be sold for use in Chinese restaurants but before they are sold they are cooked, cleaned and dried. In recent years seaweed has developed into a marketable crop. The Badjao, having adopted a settled lifestyle, have planted regular fields of seaweed grown on long stalks under the water around their homes. After the harvest it is stretched out on the platform of the villages to dry, and is later sold to chemical and pharmaceutical companies.

The Badjao try to fit in with their neighbours who, in the Sulu Islands, are the Samal and the Tausug. On the sea the Badjao consider themselves part of a mystical animist world ruled by the great god Tuhan, but many of them closer to land have adopted Islam. Despite Mecca, they are still afraid of *saitan*, the spirits of the winds, the fish, the trees, the hills and so on, because these will cause sickness if they are angry. Only the *jin*, a sort of magician or medicine man, can make contact with these spirits and try to appease them or drive them out and thereby eventually heal the sick.

A marriage celebration lasts for two days and only takes place when there is a full moon. The whole village joins in. After much clanging of *kulintangan* (xylophones), *tambol* (drums) and *agung* (gongs) men and women dance the *igal*, a traditional dance. Polygamy is allowed but is seldom practised. Couples rarely have more than five children.

The dead are buried on special islands which serve as graveyards and these are only visited for burials. Because contact with the spirits of the dead is maintained, the sea people are tied to the land. Before burial the corpse is washed and wrapped in a white sheet. As well as personal treasures, provisions are placed in the grave for the journey to the beyond.

Batak

The Batak are seminomadic hunter-gatherers. They live together in many small groups in the hills and coastal regions of north-east Palawan. During the rainy season, groups join together to form larger communities.

The leaders, or *kapitan*, of the small groups nominate one person, also known as a kapitan, to lead the larger community during this time. The kapitan makes all the important decisions, such as choice of settlement, sharing of work and organisation of gathering activities. During this settled period the Batak also plant crops.

Encroaching civilisation and disease have tragically decimated these shy indigenous people. One can only hope that international attempts being made to stop these people disappearing entirely are successful.

Ibaloy house

Bontoc

The ethnic minorities of the Central Cordillera (Apayao, Bontoc, Ibaloy, Ifugao, Kalinga, Kankanai, Tingguian) in North Luzon are often classified together as *Igorot.* Trinidad Pardo de Tavera, a Philippines scholar, interprets this designation as 'People of the Mountains', but, since the 200,000 mountain inhabitants differ quite considerably culturally, it is not correct to regard or discuss the different ethnic minorities collectively as Igorot. It is remarkable that in the literature on the main ethnological groups of this area it is frequently only the Bontoc who are dealt with in connection with the Igorot.

The Bontoc live in thoroughly organised village communities. Their houses are built close to the ground, and every village, *(iti)*, has two further important accommodation arrangements – *ato* and *olog*. The village elders live in the ato, where social and political decisions are made and religious ceremonies prepared. An ato also serves as a guesthouse and as sleeping quarters for young bachelors. Women are strictly prohibited from entering.

About 10 girls of marriageable age live in the olog, a flat house with an extraordinarily small entrance. This building is taboo to married men: only bachelors are allowed to enter an olog and spend the night with their intended wives. Before they get that far, both partners must fulfil certain rules of the game – the man must promise to marry his partner in the event of pregnancy; if he doesn't keep

Bontoc houses

his promise, he will be socially isolated and not permitted to enter the ologs again. The invitation and permission to spend the night together must be issued by the girl, and as a sign of her consent, she 'steals' a small item of his property. Every Bontoc understands this hint, and when many tobacco pouches or pipes are purloined during the day in the village, you can bet the ologs will be crowded that night.

The Bontoc were feared head-hunters, and justice in the mountains is strictly 'an eye for an eye, a tooth for a tooth', or more appropriately, 'a head for a head'. *Tuf-ay* (spear), *kalasag* (shield), *kaman* (head-axe) and *sangi* (satchel) comprise the equipment of a warrior. The sangi serves as a carrier for the enemy's head. When a successful warrior returns from his expedition, there is a great celebration for two days in the village. As a sign of his heroic deed the hero is tattooed on the chest: this is known as *chak-lag* and is much coveted, as it symbolises strength and bravery. The tattooing on the arms of male and female Bontoc is called *pango*. *Fatek* simply means tattoo.

The Bontoc believe in a better life after death; their funerals are not sorrowful occasions and only the heads of the family are in mourning. The most important requisite of the ceremony, which lasts for several days, is a death seat, the *sungachil*. A short time after a person's death, the body is placed in an upright position in the death seat, bound fast and placed so as to be visible to all who pass in front of the house. The shroud is selected according to the status of the family. Old women sing the *anako*, the death song, and a pig is sacrificed and eaten. After nightfall, a sort of recitation begins, called *achog*, in which the life history of the dead person is reflected upon. This ritual can be quite merry as it is very difficult to get a coherent, objective account of the deeds accomplished by the deceased during their lifetime. Daybreak or exhaustion of the participants ends this part of the funeral ceremony.

The body of one of their warriors killed and decapitated by an enemy is left without ceremony in the vicinity of a track leading to the enemy village. This stands as a reminder to the enemy village that the warrior's death will be avenged.

Ifugao

No other people of the Philippines apart from the Tasaday have attracted more attention than the Ifugao. They are the builders of the gigantic rice terraces of Banaue and the surrounding area. Over the last 2000 years they have shaped a technical and architectural masterpiece with bare hands and primitive tools. The imposing terraced landscape was constructed step by step from the bottoms of the valleys up to heights of 1000 metres or more. These are productive rice fields with a perfectly functioning irrigation system on the steep mountain slopes. The boundary walls have a total length of about 20,000 km. From this measurement the rice terraces of the Ifugao exceed by far those of the Bontoc and Kalinga. They are often justifiably referred to as the eighth wonder of the world.

The life of the Ifugao is full of ceremonies and celebrations at which *tapuy*, a rice wine, plays an important part, whether it's at a funeral or at the carving up of a wild pig brought in by the hunters. They originally learned the rice wine manufacturing process from Chinese traders. Rice harvested under the full moon is preferred, and, in order to accelerate the process of fermentation, the rice is partly boiled in fresh, clean water.

Ifugao house

After adding a minimal quantity of sugar, the promising pot contents are emptied into an earthenware vessel, sealed and left for six months to ripen. After this period, the Ifugao can enjoy themselves over a pleasant-tasting tapuy (see the Food & Drink section in the Facts for the Visitor chapter). It is also possible that an undrinkable, sour liquid will result from mistakes made in the manufacturing process.

The Ifugao build their houses on piles; the windowless space under the pyramid-shaped roof is used as a bedroom, kitchen and storeroom. In order to please the gods, the skull of a sacrificed pig is fixed on the outside of the house. The greatest occasion for the sacrifice of a pig is the return of a successful head-hunter.

For the Ifugao, too, head-hunting is a legitimate way of executing tribal judgements. For example, in October 1977, when an Ifugao youth was run over by a bus and fatally injured, the village council decreed that either the driver or a member of his family must die, and the execution was carried out. Ten years later the driver of a bus belonging to the Pantranco line caused a serious traffic accident with fatal consequences for several Ifugao near Banaue. When the bus company refused to admit responsibility for the deaths and injuries, axes were sharpened in the villages in question. After that no bus driver would drive into the Ifugao district for fear of getting an axe in his neck, and, until the last damages payment was made Pantranco had to hand over the Manila to Banaue route to local jeepneys.

The war dance, *bangibang*, is a component of this traditional vengeance. Equipped with spears, shields and axes, the warriors dance on the walls of the rice fields, their heads adorned with *katlagang*, a form of headdress made of leaves. The person who will carry out the act of vengeance is determined by using a chicken. The warriors form a circle, kill a chicken and leave it to die in the circle. The one chosen is the one closest to the chicken when it finally comes to rest after its final death throes.

Ilokano

The Ilokano are of Malay ancestry. About 200 to 300 BC they came through Borneo, Palawan and Mindoro to Luzon where they settled. The most significant part of the group settled the coastal strips and the adjoining mountain regions in northern and north-western Luzon.

Already settled ethnic groups like the Isnega and Tingguian could not resist the new wave of immigration and were pushed into the hinterlands. Before the Ilokano were confronted with Christian beliefs, they had a multitiered and complicated system of gods and spirits. Only fragments of their superstitions have persisted, however, and these are mainly ornamental – such as amulets and lucky charms which are generally only worn by the inhabitants of outlying Ilokano villages.

Kalinga

The Kalinga live north of the Bontoc. They are also head-hunters. Wars and head-hunting expeditions have been largely restricted through the peace pact, *budong*, which they have worked out. This treaty declares above all that a Kalinga whose honour has been impugned does not lose the respect of the tribe if, instead of beheading the enemy, he accepts a water buffalo (for example) as payment. A significant effect of this ruling is the initiation of social and family ties between different groups.

Like the Bontoc, the Kalinga also have a house for the men and village elders. They call it *dapay*. However, there is not a typical house for marriageable girls and women. It can be any house and is indistinguishable from the others from the outside; the Kalinga name for it is the *ebgan*. Here the evening courtship takes place, the initiation songs are sung, stories told or flutes played. Successful suitors spend the night with their women in the ebgan and both partners have the opportunity to consider a common future together. If they decide to separate, the event of a pregnancy is no hindrance as there are no disadvantages for the parents or the child, who is later declared legitimate by the tribal community.

A marriage is prepared for over a long period by different ritual acts. Earthquakes, landslides and other bad omens can draw out the required ceremonies for months. When all the formalities have at last been accomplished, a house is built for the engaged couple. According to Kalinga tradition, marriages can only be celebrated in the *Dadawak* (the season for marriages) months of March, September or October.

Mandaya & Mansaka

The Mandaya live in the north-eastern and south-eastern part of Davao del Norte on Mindanao. *Mandaya* means 'inhabitant of the highlands'. The Mansaka are classified ethnologically with the Mandaya. They were originally highland people who settled in clearings deep in the mountains, though today many Mansaka live in the eastern coastal regions of Davao Bay.

Animism is strongly practised by both groups, as demonstrated by the many idols carved out of wood which stand in their houses and fields. Also noteworthy are the numerous examples of silver work. Hardly any other ethnic group would use more silver to produce ornaments than the Mandaya. Even more striking than the ear adornments and finger rings are the large round chain pendants which are worn by men and women and are frequently made from coins.

Mangyan

Over 50,000 Mangyan live on Mindoro. The majority of them live in the dense jungles of the mountainous interior. The Mangyan are subdivided into the Iraya, Hanunoo, Alangan, Tadyawan, Batangan, Buhid and Ratagnon.

In earlier times the majority of the Mangyan lived and fished along the coast, but later they retreated to the hills, changed their lifestyle and took up agriculture. They did not go there of their own free will but were driven back by new settlers. In their culture land belongs to everyone. If someone approaches them with deeds of title, these peace-loving people simply withdraw.

Despite the inevitable influences of civilisation, the traditions and culture of the Mangyan have survived. Distances are measured in *yells* (screams), which is the distance over which one scream is audible.

In the south of Mindoro there are settled Hanunoo who are often referred to as 'true Mangyan'. They have their own form of writing in an elaborate syllabic script. *Hanunoo* means 'real' and 'true'. They also have their own postal system. If they want to send messages across great distances, they carve the text into a piece of bamboo and place it into a particular bamboo post. These 'post boxes' are spread over the entire area in specially designated or well-known positions. If the Mangyan come across one of them they read all the letters and deliver

Kalinga houses

those with destinations which are on their route, either personally or by placing them in a more advantageous 'post box'.

The *ambahan*, the stories told by the Mangyan, are also recorded by being carved in bamboo. A typical ambahan has each line is made up of seven syllables. These poems are of a social nature. Thus they may be read to children to discipline them, or they may be given to an adult to read in cases where speaking directly with the person may be embarrassing or painful.

Maranao

The province of Lanao del Sur in the north of Mindanao is the homeland of the Maranao (or Maranaw). They are the 'people of the lake' – Lake Lanao. Of all the Philippine Muslim groups, the Maranao were the last to be converted to Islam. They successfully defended themselves against all colonisation attempts by the Spaniards and Americans, for which their natural environment provided a not inconsiderable protection. Their culture and religion have both developed without interference.

Baong brass vessel

Langguay brass vessel

Examples of Maranao art

Today the Maranao are concerned with preserving and maintaining their cultural identity. Marawi City, lying on the northern tip of Lake Lanao, is an important spiritual centre for Muslims. Several Islamic-oriented schools and the Mindanao State University (MSU), a southern branch of the University of the Philippines, are here.

Maranao are skilled artisans and capable merchants. Cloth, wood and metal work collectively is the second most important sector of their economy; only agriculture is more important. They have a leading position in the country in the production of brass work.

Negrito

There are approximately 25,000 Negrito in the Philippines. The various Negrito groups call themselves names like Agta, Alta, Ita, Ati, Ata and Aeta, which all mean 'man' or 'person'. They live dispersed over many islands but are principally found in eastern Luzon. They can be readily distinguished from all other Filipinos by their physical characteristics: they are darker and rarely taller than 1½ metres. Their hair is short and woolly-crinkly, often decorated with a bamboo ornament. Sometimes they still wear scanty clothing made out of tree bark.

The Negrito are nomads and only a few of them have settled in one place. Instead of living in solid houses, they live in huts built from twigs, branches, foliage and grass. Sometimes they lay out small fields in which they plant sweet potatoes, rice and vegetables; they also hunt and gather fruit. Bows and poison-tipped arrows are their weapons.

Seafaring Negrito are called Dumagat. You meet them occasionally on secluded beaches on the Pacific coast of North Luzon, where they settle temporarily in hastily built huts.

The Negrito do not have laws, nor do they feel themselves bound to any authority. When decisions have to be made, the decision of the head of the family is accepted and followed.

Pala'wan

The Pala'wan live in the highlands of south Palawan. Their villages consist of three to 12 houses. They are led by a number of *panlima*, who are administrators and are also meant to help maintain the peace. The Pala'wan's religion has been influenced by Hindu and Islamic elements. The highest deity is *Ampo*, who is believed to pass on responsibility for the regulation of the affairs of humanity to his subordinate gods, the *diwats*. The practice of the religion also includes social activities such as communal dancing, singing and drinking of rice wine. A marriage is only agreed upon after lengthy negotiations between the two families concerned and is often arranged when the couple are still children.

Tasaday

The Tasaday live in the mountains deep within the tropical rainforest of South Cotabato Province on Mindanao. The discovery of the Tasaday by the outside world has caused considerable controversy.

They were first discovered in the early 1960s by a hunter named Dafal, but the first 'official' meeting didn't take place until June 1971. Their good health was remarkable; from the earliest time until their discovery, these seminaked cave and forest dwellers lived only on the fruit they gathered and the fish, frogs, tadpoles and crabs they caught. They had not yet discovered hunting or agriculture and used only primitive stone tools.

Because of their isolation, at least 50,000 years of evolution had completely passed by them. According to some reports, the 25 clan members had no contact at all with the outside world until they met Dafal. They did not even know of the existence of other groups of people outside their forest. It's worth reading John Nance's book *The Gentle Tasaday* (Harcourt Brace Jovanovich, New York, 1975; Victor Gallancz, London, 1975), which offers a fascinating eyewitness account with many photos.

However, in early 1986, Dr Oswald Item of Switzerland, *Stern* reporter Walter Unger and Jay Ullal published some disconcerting revelations suggesting that the sensational discovery of the Tasaday had been nothing but a publicity stunt cleverly staged by Manuel Elizalde, who at the time was chief of PANAMIN (Presidential Assistance on National Minorities; the bureau has since been disbanded).

It was quite a pickle for everyone involved. Scholars and journalists from all over the world who had been convinced that the Tasaday were genuine demanded further proof and explanations. The Department of Anthropology convened an ultimately inconclusive symposium, and even the 12th International Congress of Anthropological & Ethnological Sciences held in Zagreb, Yugoslavia, in 1988, was unable to bring the controversy to a satisfactory resolution. Only a testimonial issued by the Filipino Congress, which had arranged for some Tasaday to be flown to Manila in order to clarify the question, could bring about a provisional settling of the heated debate. The authenticity of the Tasaday as an ethnic group was then officially confirmed by the highest government authorities.

Tausug

The majority of Tausug live on the island of Jolo in the Sulu archipelago. They describe themselves as 'people in the current' and were the first in the Philippines to accept Islam. Nevertheless, traditional customs are still maintained. Thus a Tausug wedding, *pagtiaun*, is among the richest, most colourful festivals celebrated anywhere on the Sulu Islands. The ceremonies and celebrations last a week. An important part of the activity is the *pangalag*, a wedding dance to the sound of gongs and drums.

The Tausug love freedom and are proud of their bravery. They are renowned as skilled seafarers, diligent traders and excellent business people. Prosperity and pride have helped make the Tausug the dominant tribe from Zamboanga to Sitangkai. Their cultural wealth is exhibited through their dress, the architecture of their houses and in the style of their brass artefacts, jewellery and weapons.

Tau't Batu

The Tau't Batu are referred to as 'people of the rock'. They live in caves in the Signapan Basin, north-west of Mt Mantalingajan, the highest peak in Palawan. They only leave their caves to hunt, gather fruit or harvest cassava and rice in unobtrusive fields. Other sources of nutrition, such as bats and birds, are found inside the caves. Their belief demands that nature be compensated for the death of any of the animals. Animals which have been killed will therefore be replaced by a representation in stone or wood.

A particular social custom is ***bulun-bulun***, the communal living of several families brought about through the necessity to share nourishment. The Tau't Batu were officially discovered only in 1978. In order to protect the lifestyle and habitat of this peaceful little group, the Signapan Basin has been declared off limits to outsiders and this is strictly enforced.

T'boli

An estimated 60,000 T'boli live in about 2000 sq km in the south-western corner of Mindanao. The area is known as the Tiruray Highlands and their culture is centred in the triangle formed by the villages of Surallah, Polomolok and Kiamba, near Lake Sebu.

The T'boli do not have a village community structure. They live in houses set well apart from each other along the ridges of the highlands. In some cases, when there are close family ties, three or four houses are clustered together. Called long houses, or more colloquially, *gunu bong*, they stand on two-metre-high posts and are about 15 metres long and 10 metres wide. The T'boli are monogamous people, but polygamy is allowed and is sometimes practised by the more prosperous as a status symbol.

T'boli long house

T'boli women have a passion for decoration and adorn themselves with ornamental combs, earrings, necklaces and chains, arm and foot bracelets, finger and toe rings and heavy, bell belts. You seldom see one without a head covering, either a *kayab*, originally a turban of abaca, more often today a simple towel; or a colourful *s'laong kinibang*, a large, round hat with a diameter of about half a metre. The traditional clothing of both men and women consists of *t'nalak* – a material woven from abaca with a dark brown background lightened by red and beige designs. It takes several months to weave, but the weaving of the *kumo*, the wedding dress, takes even longer. This typical metre-long T'boli covering has great significance in the wedding ceremony.

Yakan

The Yakan mainly live on Basilan Island in the south of the Philippines, although some have settled near Zamboanga on Mindanao. They are peace-loving Muslims who live by agriculture and cattle breeding. The most important house in a village is the *langgal*, or prayer house, which is run by an imam. All larger annual ceremonies take place here, too. Absolutely essential elements to any festival are music and games, with water buffalo fights being particularly thrilling.

The Yakan are famous as exceptional weavers. A part of their unusual traditional clothing is the *kandit*, a red belt several metres long which is wrapped around the hips to hold up skintight trousers. Adornments men wear include a colourful turban known as a *pis*, or a helmet-shaped hat called a *saruk*. Old women can still be found with overlong artificial fingernails known as *suploh*.

Warning

Before you go into areas set aside for the indigenous people, please examine your motives carefully. If you just want to 'check out the natives' and take pictures for your slide night, you are very misguided. You won't be welcome, and will recognise this fact fairly promptly.

Most cultural minorities are quite friendly to strangers and foreigners. Should you be invited to eat with them, don't refuse without good (for example, religious) reasons, as it could be taken as an insult to the host. On the other hand don't eat too much as the first invitation is usually followed by a second, then a third and so on. If they sing a song for you in the evening, you should have a song on hand to sing in return. Saying that you can't sing or don't know any songs will not get you off the hook as they won't believe you. A song book may be useful if you intend visiting many minorities.

Don't refer to Muslims as Moro. The tag 'Moro' was first used by Spaniards who viewed the Muslims with contempt, probably because the Spaniards resented not being able to bring them under their yoke, as they did with the other population groups. Although many Muslims today proudly name themselves Moro, there are still some who feel discriminated against when a foreigner calls them by this name.

ART & CULTURE

The Philippines has developed a mixed culture from the historical blending of foreign influences with native elements. Today the Muslims and some of the isolated tribes are the only people whose culture remains unadulterated by Spanish and American influences. The ability of the Filipinos to improvise and copy is very apparent: you need only see how the army jeeps left by the Americans were converted into colourful, shining-chrome taxis through painstaking, detailed work before the Filipinos began the serial production of these vehicles themselves.

What would a Philippine townscape be like without these unusual jeepneys? In Metro Manila about 40,000 'discos on wheels' are registered. But since 1980 most of the loudspeakers have been silenced because the 'stereo disco sound' was banned by the state. It's also rumoured that jeepneys will be replaced by the gradual introduction of buses. Something will then be missing – just as the loud, pounding rhythm of the disco music is already missing.

Pop and folk music from the West is perfectly imitated by the local bands, which is one reason why Filipino musicians are in great demand in South-East Asia from Jakarta all the way to Tokyo.

The small gallery shops in the tourist belt of Ermita reflect the high level of Filipino painting: from impressionism to realism virtually all styles are represented. Handicrafts of natural fibres, shells, brass and wood show the technical and formal crafts and the abilities of these talented people.

The ideas of the New Society propagated by Marcos really caught the national consciousness of the Filipinos in the 1970s, just as People Power did in the 1980s. People recollected their cultural heritage and began to care about their traditional arts and crafts. Consequently, the national language is strongly used today in theatre and literature and *kundimans* – romantic and sentimental love songs – are popular again. The good old folk dances, foremost among them the national dance *tinikling*, have even become a new tourist attraction. Well-known dance troupes like Barangay, Bayanihan, Filipinescas or Karilagan have even found a spot on popular TV shows. The most successful interpreters of Philippine folk songs are the Mabuhay singers.

National Clothing

For men, there is no obligation to wear either a tie or a suit, even at highly official political receptions. The *barong tagalog* is the rational alternative: it is a long-sleeved shirt which lets the air through and is worn over the trousers. Underneath, it is customary to wear a T-shirt. The short-sleeved style is known as a *polo barong*. These cool, semi-transparent shirts with their fine embroidery date from the Spanish era when Filipinos were required to wear their shirts untucked, and the barong became a symbol of national consciousness. Fine barongs are made from *pina*, a fibre made from the pineapple plant. The *terno* is the typical Philippine dress worn by women, recognisable by its stiff butterfly sleeves. It is only worn on formal occasions. The general fashion for women follows Western trends.

Cinema

Filipino films are produced in great number, dealing mainly with variations on the themes of violence and clichéd love stories. Productions like *Mababangong Bangungot* by Kidlat Tahimik are rare. This socially critical film was screened overseas under the title *The Perfumed Nightmare*.

In January 1981 the first film festival in Manila took place at the Philippines International Convention Center. After the success of this trial run and both first official festivals of 1982 and 1983 in the specially built film theatre, the organisers hoped that the Manila International Film Festival (MIFF) would be recognised internationally as are the festivals in Cannes, Berlin and Venice and that these cities would send their representatives. But further MIFFs, for economic and probably political reasons, have not taken place.

Sports & Games

The Filipinos are sports enthusiasts. Basketball is their favourite sport and there has been a professional league since 1975. On the popularity scale, chess and boxing are near the top. Consequently, a lot of money was wagered on the outcome of the world heavyweight boxing championship in 1975 (when Mohammed Ali fought Joe Frazier in the 'thriller in Manila'), the World Basketball Championships in 1978 and the chess championship in 1978 (between Korshnoi and Karpov).

Tennis, golf, horse racing, bicycle races and motor racing do have some followers, but are not in the category of a national sport. As a team sport in schools, volleyball is second in popularity to basketball.

It's only rarely that you'll see a game of the once popular *sipa* being played. It's a game played with a plaited ball which is kicked over a net using feet, knees, elbows or the head (a similar idea to volleyball). It is now only played in a few areas in Mindanao and occasionally in Rizal Park in Manila.

The real passion is reserved for games that involve betting. Many pesos are risked at jai alai and cockfights. Jai alai (pronounced 'high aligh') is a frantically fast ball game played in a court rather like a squash court. The players have a shovel-like holder (cesta) with which they hurl a small, hard ball (pelota) against the wall. Their opponent must try to catch the rebounding ball and then hurl it back. The final winner is decided by a knockout competition and bets are placed on the outcome.

Manila and Cebu have jai alai courts, which are known as frontons. Because of game fixing, betting on Sunday and public holidays was forbidden by the the Presidential Committee on Good Government (PCGG) and the courts were closed. However, a reopening of the frontons may soon be possible.

In the meantime those who wish to bet on Sundays and public holidays can go to a *sabong* or cockfight. The fights take place in a wooden arena known as a cockpit and there is great activity as early as 8 am. Before each fight several bookkeepers *(kristos)* come into the ring to encourage the spectators to part with their money and to take the bets. They use a sign language for betting and, amazingly, nothing is noted down – it's all committed to memory. Four fingers raised means P40, horizontal fingers signify hundreds and fingers pointed downwards means thousands – but check this first if you intend to participate!

While bets are being taken, the very expensive cocks are brought out and stirred up for the fight. Like boxers they fight in different weight classes. Each cock is equipped with a razor-sharp spur fastened behind the leg. This deadly spur usually brings a fight to an end after a few seconds.

A 'non-pro', injured or sickly cock must be pecked twice by the winner. Only then is the fight officially over. Should the champion cock choose not to perform this concluding rite, the fight may be declared a draw. Wounded cocks are 'patched up' by experts behind the cockpit; the dead ones end up in the pot.

Filipinos & Foreigners

You can't blame the Filipinos if they are sceptical and distant towards foreigners. As history shows, foreigners have generally not come to the Philippines with friendly intentions. In spite of this, every visitor is heartily welcomed: the Filipinos are very sociable and tolerant and their natural openness surprises many visitors.

There is much to be learned by citizens of industrialised nations who like to be alone. Leisure hours which you may want to spend alone in a restaurant or pub will have to be given up. Chatty people ready to ask questions are always close at hand, especially if there is a possibility of alcohol.

It is very difficult for most foreigners to understand the psyche of the Filipino, especially, for example, when the Filipino may risk a possible 'loss of face' – a painful and embarrassing situation which the Filipino will try to avoid. As a result, they may give out completely false information quite comfortably rather than admit they don't know. Or they will just grin at you benignly pretending they didn't understand your question.

Even if a particular idiosyncrasy of the Filipinos is unpleasant or uncomfortable, you shouldn't become belligerent. You will achieve a lot more by being polite or sharing a joke. Foreigners who indulge in exaggerated reticence, arrogance or who take the opportunity to lord it over the locals financially or culturally, will never find a friend in the Philippines. They will have to make do with being ignored or mistreated.

Filipinos are strongly oriented towards the outside world. As a rule they don't place much store by anything produced in their own country. Imported wares are always in much greater demand than the best locally made products. They'll only make exceptions in the case of 'export quality' goods manufactured in the Philippines, which, though intended for sale abroad, sometimes appear on the local market. Try telling Filipinos that we foreigners often keep our best quality products for ourselves and export cheaper stuff far and wide and they'll stare at you in disbelief: what next!

One thing Filipinos and foreigners have in common is the discovery of the Philippines as a tourist centre. Most Filipinos know very little about their own country. There are chiefly financial and geographical reasons for this, but there's also the traditional lack of interest in one's neighbouring island. When people have the money, they prefer to fly to Hong Kong or Europe for shopping and sightseeing, or if possible go to the USA. Until recently the slogan 'See the Philippines first' was hardly able to attract a single travel-happy Filipino. But now the situation has changed noticeably. With so many foreigners streaming into the country, travelling around and to all appearances having a fine time, Filipinos are becoming curious about their long-ignored homeland. After all, if outsiders are so attracted to the islands, there must be something worth seeing.

Gifts You can bring a lot of happiness to children and adults in the Philippines through small tokens of appreciation, so take some small things to give such as ballpoint pens, coins, cigarettes, matches, lighters, stickers, photos of yourself or bottles of perfume and other obvious imports (possibly with well-known trademarks clearly displayed).

Filipinos are very inquisitive and interested in where the visitor comes from and what it's like there. To show them, or to offer them a gift in return for hospitality you have received, you can make good use of postcards from your country. People also like to look at pictures of your home, family, animals and plants. These things are good conversation starters.

You will be well liked if you're friendly – it doesn't cost anything. There's a fine local saying: 'A smile gives more light than electricity'.

RELIGION

The Philippines is unique for being the only Christian country in Asia – over 90% of the population claim to be Christian, more than 80% of whom are Roman Catholic. The Spanish did a thorough job!

Largest of the minority religious groups are the Muslims (about 8%) who are found chiefly on the island of Mindanao and along the Sulu archipelago. When the Spanish arrived toting their cross, the Muslims were just getting a toehold in the region. In the northern islands their influence was only small and was easily displaced, but in the south, the people had been firmly converted and Christianity was never able to make a strong impression.

About 4% of Filipinos belong to the Philippine Independent Church, which was founded by Gregorio Aglipay in 1902 as a nationalist Catholic church. The Iglesia ni Kristo is the largest community of Protestant believers, to which 4% of the population belongs. Baptists, Methodists, Mormons, Jehovah's Witnesses and members of other sects make up about 2%. Except for a tiny percentage of Buddhist believers, the remainder of the population are animists.

FIESTAS & FESTIVALS

There are many town fiestas which take place on the numerous national holidays over the whole year. An expensive festival is held for two or three days in honour of the appropriate patron saint. It is hard to understand how some of the families shoulder the financial burden: the enormous expenses incurred bear no relation to the poverty and hardship of everyday life in the Philippines. Food and drink are offered with lavish generosity and at the end of the fiesta some visitors even get the money for their journey home pressed into their hands. One or more bands are hired, and musicians and entertainers add to the atmosphere of a people's festival. There is also usually a beauty contest in which the contestants are heavily sponsored. Foreigners and visitors from distant towns get the same royal treatment as friends and relatives.

January

Appey This is a three-day thanksgiving festival of the Bontoc for a bounteous harvest.

1 January

New Year's Day As in Western countries the new year is colourfully and loudly welcomed. Families come together to celebrate the traditional *media noche*, the midnight meal. The streets are incredibly noisy and can be dangerous: fireworks are shot off for several days before new year, often resulting in the loss of fingers and thumbs. Every year unintended and premature explosions of illegally produced fireworks result in chaotic scenes at the hospitals. Many of those affected do not live to see the next new year.

First Sunday in January

Holy Three Kings' Day This is the official end of the Christmas season. The children receive their last Christmas presents on this day. In Santa Cruz and Gasan on Marinduque, the imitation kings are led on horseback through the town. Spectators throw coins and sweets to the children who run alongside the procession.

9 January

Black Nazarene Procession What is probably the largest procession of the Philippines begins early in the afternoon in Quiapo at the Quiapo church. Thousands of Catholics crowd the streets in this part of Manila when the 'Black Nazarene', a life-size statue of Christ made of blackwood, is carried through the town.

Third Weekend in January

Ati-Atihan This festival in Kalibo on Panay is the Rio de Janeiro or New Orleans Mardi Gras of the Philippines. It's an important and spectacular festival, when the town rages for three days. People dance, sing and play drums. Thousands of people, outrageously costumed and cleverly masked, celebrate around the clock until the last evening, when a long procession of excited participants ends the intoxicating festivities.

The origins of the festival date back to the middle of the 13th century, when 10 Datu families had to flee from Borneo. They sailed northeast and landed on the Philippine island of Panay, where the resident Ati – small, dark Negrito people – gave them a piece of land on which to settle. A festival was celebrated and the newly arrived people blackened their faces so they would look just like the local Ati.

Many years later the Spaniards, who had converted much of the country to Christianity, used this ritual to deceive unfriendly Muslims and counter their attempts to influence Kalibo. They got the inhabitants to dye their skin black, wear warlike clothing and pretend they were Ati. The victory against the Muslims was interpreted as being achieved through the intervention of Santo Nino, the child Jesus, and thus the festival started to take on a religious significance.

Third Sunday in January

Sinulog – Santo Nino de Cebu This is the climax of the week-long festival of Pasundayag sa Sinulog. Groups of people, all dressed in costume, gather around the capital buildings until about noon when they make their way through the streets of Cebu City, sometimes marching, sometimes dancing the peculiar Sinulog steps and shouting 'Pit Senyor'. Sinulog is the traditional dance of the old women followers, who can also be seen dancing by themselves in front of the Basilica Minore del Santo Nino and Magellan's Cross any day of the week. 'Pit Senor' means 'viva el Senor', by which is meant 'long live Santo Nino' (the child Jesus). Hotels are nearly always booked out on the holiday weekend.

Sinulog is also celebrated in Kabankalan on Negros during this weekend. As well as the actual Sinulog on the Sunday there are also horse fights on the Saturday.

Fourth Weekend in January

Ati-Atihan in Ibajay One weekend after the festival in Kalibo, another festival takes place in Ibajay, 30 km to the north-west. According to the statements of the people of Ibajay, their Ati-Atihan is the original and only true one – maybe it's true. At least it's fair to say that though this festival is not supported financially by commercial interests or attended by hordes of tourists, the locals, dressed in their simple but original costumes, celebrate with as much enthusiasm as the people in Kalibo.

Dinagyang This festival in Iloilo City includes parades, but the spectators are quiet and passive, unlike the crowds at the similar Ati-Atihan activities in Kalibo.

January/February

Chinese New Year Depending upon the lunar calendar, Chinese New Year celebrations take place some time between 21 January and 19 February. There are ritual and traditional dragon dances in Manila's Chinatown.

February

Saranggolahan In many villages and towns this is the beginning of the kite-flying season. People of all ages take part in competitions with kites of the most varied forms, colours and sizes.

2 February

Feast of Our Lady of Candelaria This is a town festival with processions and parades in honour of Our Lady of Candelaria, the patron saint of Jaro, a district of the city of Iloilo. It's the biggest religious event in the western Visayas.

11 February

Feast of Our Lady of Lourdes This celebration is held in memory of the appearance of the 'Lady of Lourdes' in Lourdes, France. It takes place in Kanlaon St, Quezon City and includes processions in the evening. The feast is also celebrated in San Juan del Monte, Bulacan Province.

14 February

St Valentine's Day This is a day for lovers – an important date for the romantic Filipinos. Small gifts and valentine's cards are personally delivered or sent, and couples dress up to go to a nice restaurant, dance in a disco or go to the movies. Filipinos are deeply upset if they have to spend St Valentine's Day without a valentine.

22 to 25 February

People Power Days These are thanksgiving days for the end of the Marcos era, peacefully brought about by the people. The Epifanio de los Santos Ave (EDSA) in Quezon City was the main scene of the so-called People Power revolution, and on this wide street the reinstalment of democracy is now celebrated every year.

26 February

Dia de Zamboanga This is a festival held by and for Muslims and Christians with cultural offerings, exhibits, regattas and religious ceremonies, in which the old Spanish and Muslim traditions of the city are given expression.

March/April

Moriones Festival Around Easter there are many passion plays in the Philippines. The most popular and colourful is the Moriones Festival in Marinduque. The Roman soldier Longinus, not Jesus, is the focus of the week-long play. Longinus is blind in one eye and as he pierces the right side of the crucified Jesus with his spear, blood flows out of his blind eye and suddenly he can see again with both eyes. The first thing he sees is Christ's passage to heaven; Longinus announces the incident and must flee. The Roman warriors want to stop this 'rumour' and capture him on Easter Sunday. His execution by beheading is the climax of the play.

Maundy Thursday (official holiday) Apart from Good Friday, Maundy Thursday is the most intensively celebrated day of the holy week. Deep in thought, people attend church, most of the traffic comes to a halt and a perceptible silence reigns throughout the country. On Thursday and Good Friday almost everything is closed or stops – even Philippine Airlines' flights. Things start again on Easter Saturday.

Good Friday (official holiday) The many crucifixions and scourges which take place throughout the country have grown into a real tourist attraction! The best known places for this are San Fernando (Pampanga Province), Antipolo (Rizal Province), Manila and Jordan (Guimaras Island).

Easter Sunday (official holiday) At daybreak throughout the land, church bells are rung to herald the resurrection of Christ. Also at dawn, separate mother and son processions – symbolising the risen Christ's meeting with his mother – begin, concluding under a bamboo and flower arch.

9 April

Bataan Day (official holiday) This is a national remembrance day at the Mt Samet Shrine recalling the disastrous battle against the Japanese in WW II and the degrading 'death march' on the Bataan Peninsula.

27 April

Bahug-Bahugan sa Mactan Magellan's landing and the battle which led to his death are acted out on the beach of Mactan, on Mactan Island, Cebu. There are fights in the water but be early: some years the activities start at 8 am and are all over a couple of hours later.

28 April to 1 May

Binirayan – Handuyan Over 700 years ago 10 Malayan political fugitives from Borneo reached the Panay coast. They were made welcome by the Negrito chief Marikado and were allowed to settle in Malandog near present-day San Jose de Buenavista. The landing and settlement are re-enacted using time-honoured costumes and decorated boats. This festival has been celebrated since 1974, but the date has tended to vary and if it continues will probably only be held on alternate years. The most interesting part – the landing of the boats – usually starts early in the morning.

April, May or June

Turumba Festival Turumba means falling, leaping, jumping, skipping or dancing. This describes the behaviour of the participants in the procession in Pakil, Laguna Province.

1 to 30 May

Flores de Mayo – Santacruzan Throughout the whole country, processions in honour of the Virgin Mary take place in the afternoon and evening. Young girls in white dresses decorate the statues of Mary with flowers. An attractive focus of the processions in the flowering month of May are the most beautiful Filipinas of the local villages.

1 May

Labor Day This is a national holiday but no important activities are held.

3 May

Carabao Carroza Water buffalo races are held in Pavia, a few km north of Iloilo on Panay Island. The fastest water buffaloes from the surrounding 18 *barrios* (neighbourhoods) run against each other in a final deciding race. The beauty queens are carried to the race track on festively decorated sleds. Be there by 8 am. There is a town fiesta on the following day.

6 May

Fall of Corregidor War veterans and other nostalgic people visit the fortified island in Manila Bay in memory of the battle in 1942.

14 & 15 May

Carabao Festival This is a two-day celebration in honour of the patron saint of the settlers in San Isidro. Farmers lead decorated water buffaloes to the church square in a long procession on the afternoon of 14 May. There they kneel and are blessed. The next day the water buffalo races take place. Festivals are held in Pulilan (Bulacan Province), San Isidro (Nueva Ecija Province) and Angono (Rizal Province).

15 May

Pahiyas The patron saint San Isidro is also honoured in Lucban and Sariaya, Quezon Province. On the day of the harvest festival, the house façades are attractively decorated with agricultural products. There is a procession in the afternoon. The huge leaves and blooms, which look like coloured glass and shine in the sun, are particularly decorative on Lucban. They are made out of *kiping*, a rice dough, following a traditional recipe and method and eaten at the end of the festival, or given to the guests. The procession takes place in the afternoon.

17 to 19 May
Fertility Rites This three-day festival in Obando (Bulacan Province) is dedicated to the three patron saints of the city. The Obando Festival became famous for its procession, a series of dances based on earlier fertility rites. On 17 May young unmarried men dance through the streets in the hope of soon finding a bride. The following day, unmarried women try their luck. The last day is given to childless couples who show their desire to have children through their participation in this festival.

12 June
Independence Day This is a national holiday with military parades.

24 June
Feast of San Juan Bautista The deeds of St John the Baptist are re-enacted on this day in San Juan, Manila. Friends, relatives and curious spectators are 'baptised'. Water is thrown from, and at, passing cars – keep your camera in a plastic bag!

Parada ng Lechon In Balayan, Batangas, St John's Day is celebrated with a 'suckling pig parade'.

28 to 30 June
Apung Iro (Apalit River Parade) The inhabitants of Apalit (Pampanga Province) show their reverence for St Peter with a boat parade.

First Sunday in July
Pagoda sa Wawa This is a river procession with the Holy Cross of Wawa in the pagoda boat. It takes place in Bocaue, Bulacan Province, just 30 km north of Manila.

29 July
Pateros River Fiesta Pateros, a suburb of Manila, is the centre of duck breeding. From here Manila is supplied with the Filipino delicacy *balut* (see the Food & Drink section in the Facts for the Visitor chapter). The fiesta recalls the killing of a legendary crocodile which threatened the existence of the balut suppliers.

August
Kadayawan sa Dabaw For two weeks in August, Davao City on Mindanao celebrates the Orchid Festival, the Fruit & Food Festival and the Tribal Festival.

Third Weekend in September
Penafrancia Festival The ceremonious and colourful river festival in Naga City, South Luzon, has become a great tourist attraction. The climax is the spectacular boat parade on the Naga River in honour of the Blessed Virgin of Penafrancia.

7 to 12 October
Zamboanga Hermosa This is a festival with cultural performances, religious ceremonies, exhibitions, regattas and the choosing of Miss Zamboanga. The festival is dedicated to the patron saint of the city, Nuestra Senora del Pilar.

Second Weekend in October
La Naval de Manila This procession goes along the main streets of Quezon City to the Domingo Church. It commemorates the victorious sea battle against the Dutch plunderers in the year 1646. This festival is also celebrated in Angeles City in Pampanga Province.

19 October
MassKara Festival On the weekend closest to 19 October, the largest festival on Negros takes place in Bacolod. There are street dances and groups of people wearing costumes and friendly, smiling masks.

1 November
Undas (All Saints' Day) On this national holiday families meet at the cemetery and stay there the whole night. Numerous lights, candles and flowers on the graves make an impressive sight. There are booths and stalls in front of the cemetery.

23 November
Feast of San Clemente On this feast day a boat parade takes place in Angono, Rizal. It is a thanksgiving by the fishing people in honour of their patron saint, San Clemente.

30 November
Bonifacio Day This is a national holiday in tribute to Filipino heroes, most especially in honour of Andres Bonifacio, who headed the Katipunan, the revolutionary movement formed to fight the Spaniards.

Late November, early December
Grand Canao This is a festival of the hill clans

in Baguio, North Luzon. There are dances and rituals in which, among other things, victorious warriors are honoured and water buffaloes, pigs and chickens are sacrificed. There are also agricultural exhibitions and craft demonstrations.

8 December

Feast of Our Lady of the Immaculate Conception On this feast day a boat procession is held at night on the fishing waters of Malabon in the north-west of Metro Manila.

16 to 25 December

Simbang Gabi You can hear Christmas carols practically all over the Philippines from about the beginning of November. Officially, however, the Christmas season begins on 16 December. Following the old traditions, religious Filipinos go to night masses, *simbang gabi*, which are held before dawn.

24 December

Giant Lantern Festival The most spectacular lantern parade and contest in the Philippines takes place in San Fernando, Pampanga Province. Some of the *parol* (coloured paper lanterns) are so large they must be drawn by a tractor. Be at the big church by about 8 pm and you won't miss anything. After midnight mass the most beautiful lantern will be chosen.

25 December

Christmas This family day, as in practically all Christian countries, is awaited with great excitement by children. However, grown-ups also seem to wait for a Christmas present impatiently, and ask repeatedly for a week beforehand: 'Where is my Christmas?'

28 December

Holy Innocents' Day Just as people in the West play April Fools' Day tricks on 1 April, so do Filipinos try to catch one another out on this day.

30 December

Rizal Day This is a national holiday with street parades in memory of the Filipino national hero, Dr Jose Rizal, who on this day in 1896 was executed by the Spaniards. Statues of him are decorated with flowers, and national flags are lowered to half-mast.

Muslim Festivals

There are also some important dates associated with the Muslim calendar. As the Islamic calendar is lunar, it is 11 days shorter than the Gregorian one, so these dates change each year. The *Hari Raya Poasa*, which marks the end of Ramadan, occurred at the end of May in 1990. In February the *Hariraya Hajji* is the time of pilgrimages to Mecca. Muslims spend most of the 10th day of the 12th month of their calendar in mosques. In March/April, *Maulod-En-Nabi* is the prophet Mohammed's birthday. It is a Muslim holiday with ceremonial readings from the Koran in all mosques.

LANGUAGE

History

Historically, the waves of immigration of alien peoples (Indonesians, Chinese, Malays, etc) and the structure of the country (a series of islands) have brought about a multiplicity of languages and language groups. Today there are about 80 significantly different dialects spoken.

During the period of Spanish occupation, Spanish was taught in schools and, since education is mainly a prerogative of the wealthy, it developed as the language of politicians and the business community. Though small, the influence of Spanish on the local languages is still present today (for instance, in the numerical system and in the Zamboangan language in Chavacano). Spanish was abolished in 1968 as a compulsory subject in higher schools, but is still the mother tongue of a small percentage of the population, mainly the upper class.

Since in an occupied country the language of the colonial overlord often dominates, English became very important with the beginning of the US era. Since the declaration of total independence from the USA in 1946, English has remained the language of commerce and politics in the Philippines. Newspapers, TV, radio announcements and even government statistics are evidence of this.

A National Language The concept of a national language was formed after the Spanish-American War in 1898, but it wasn't until 1936, a year after the formation of the Philippines Commonwealth, that the Institute of National Language was established.

President Manual Quezon declared Tagalog the national language in that year and the appropriate bill was incorporated into the Philippine constitution in 1946.

There were several other contenders for the role of the main language in this multilingual country – among them Cebuano, Hiligaynon and Ilocano. The compromises reached during the 1970s still hold; the constitution of 1973 confirms Filipino as the main language. It is based on Tagalog but contains certain linguistic elements from the other Philippine languages. Since 1978 Filipino has been taught in schools and universities.

At present Filipino is understood by about 50% of the population. In the process of trying to strengthen the national consciousness and to preserve a unique Filipino identity, President Corazon Aquino has given the promotion of a national language priority, and ordered that Filipino be the official language used by all government departments. This applies also to correspondence as well as to the naming of officials and public buildings.

Gestures & Signs

As well as the spoken and written language, the Filipinos use various gestures and signs. The hand movements which mean 'go away' to us signify 'come here' in the Philippines. The brief raising of the eyebrows is generally meant positively. One hisses to gain attention, for example when calling one of the waiters in a restaurant. The thumb is not used to indicate numbers; you indicate two beers, for example, always with the ring finger and the little finger; using your middle finger could get you into trouble. Instead of pointing with your finger, you indicate discreetly by pointing pursed lips in the direction you want. Incidentally, in a *turo-turo* restaurant (turo means 'point') there is no menu: the food is displayed and customers point to what they would like to eat. When you want to pay the bill, look out for one of the waiters and draw a rectangle in the air with your index finger and thumb. Should the waiter or waitress be looking the other way, just hiss briefly. If Filipinos don't understand a question, they open their mouths.

Communicating

It is not vital to know the local language, as English will get you through most situations, but as in any country, locals will be pleased and surprised if you have learned even a few fragments of their language. The following may help.

Some Notes on Pronunciation

In Filipino *p* and *f* are often interchanged (Filipino = Pilipino). This means that a written *p* can be pronounced as an *f*. This interchange is sometimes carried over into English by Filipinos (April = Afril) but it in no way impairs understanding.

A *w* written in Filipino is often pronounced as a *u* (Banawe = Banaue, ikaw = ikau). Double vowels are pronounced separately (paalam = pa-alam). The combination *ng* is pronounced 'nang' and *mga* is pronounced 'manga'.

The syllable *po* underlines courtesy towards elders and persons of respect (eg *Salámat po Ginang Santos*, Thank you Mrs Santos).

Filipino

In the words and phrases below, an accent over the vowel of a syllable means that this syllable is stressed. There is sometimes more than one word given in Filipino.

Some Useful Words & Phrases

and	*at*
who (singular)	*síno*
who (plural)	*sinu-síno*
how	*paáno*
what	*anó*
when	*kailán*
why	*bákit*
How many?	*Ilán?*
How much?	*Gaáno, magkáno?*

People & Pronouns

man	*laláki, laláke*
woman	*babáe*
Mr	*Ginoó*

Mr Santos	*Ginoóng Santos*
Mrs	*Gínang*
Mrs Santos	*Gínang Santos*
Miss	*Binibíni*
Miss Santos	*Binibíning Santos*
child (general)	*batà*
child (own)	*anák*
boy	*bátang laláki*
girl	*bátang babáe*
grandmother/grandfather	*lóla/lólo*
friend	*kaibígan*
unmarried man	*binatà*
unmarried woman	*dalága*
I	*akó*
you	*ka, ikáw*
he/she	*siyá*
they	*silá*
we (I and you)	*táyo*
we (I and others)	*kamí*
you (plural)	*kayó*
old	*matandá*
young	*batà*
tall	*mataás*
short	*pandák*
happy	*maligáya*
sad	*malungkót*
intelligent	*matalíno*
drunken	*lasíng*
handsome, pretty	*pógi, guwápo/a*
ugly	*pángit*

Greetings & Civilities

hello, greetings	*mabúhay*
good morning	*magandáng umága*
good day	*magandáng tanghalí*
good afternoon	*magandáng hápon*
good night	*magandáng gabí*
goodbye	*paálam, adyós*
'bye	*bay*
thank you	*salámat*
thank you very much	*maráming salamat*
please	*pakí*
yes/no	*oó/hindí*
yes/no (polite)	*opó/hindí po*
OK	*síge*
excuse me	*ipagpaumanhín*
only, merely, simply	*lang (lamang)*
again, similarly	*namán*
always, of course	*siyémpre*
good/well	*mabúti*
also good/well	*mabúti rin*
You're welcome.	*Waláng anumán.*
Just a minute.	*Sandalí lang.*
No problem.	*Waláng probléma.*
It's all right.	*Ayós ang lahát.*

How are you?
Kumustá (ka)?
How are you? (plural)
Kumustá (po) kayó?
Well, thank you, and you?
Mabúti salámat, at ikáw?
Where have you been?
Saán ka gáling?
Where are you going?
Saán ka pupuntá?
I'm coming from Talisay.
Gáling akó sa Talisay.
I'm going to Bato.
Pupuntá akó sa Bato.

Small Talk

Do you have...?
Mayroón...?
What did you say?
Anó po?
Who is there?
Síno iyán?
What is your name?
Anóng pangálan mo?
How old are you?
Iláng taón ka na?
Where do you come from?
Tagásaáng bayán ka?
You are beautiful!
Magandá ka!
I like you.
Gustó kitá.
Never mind.
Hindí bále.
I don't know.
Áywan ko (hindí ko alam).
Let's go.
Táyo na (síge na).

I like (that).
Gustó ko (itó).
I don't like...
Ayaw ko...
I'll do it (I'll get it).
Akó na lang.
You do it (You get it).
Ikáw na lang.
Come here.
Halíka díto.
What a pity.
Sáyang.
It's too late.
Hulí na.
I have no time.
Walá akóng panahón.
Are you sure?
Siguradó ka ba?
That's not true (flatterer).
Boléro.
It's none of your business.
Walá kang pakíalam.
Get lost!
Alís diyán!
not yet
walá pa
maybe/perhaps
sigúro
really
talagá
fool
gágo (ka)
crazy, mad
lóko-lóko
rude, insolent
bastós
braggart
mayábang

Getting Around

left/right	*kaliwá/kánan*
straight on	*dirétso*
back	*pauróng (pabalík)*
here/there	*díto/diyán, doón*
near/far	*malápit/malayó*
turn-off	*lumikó*
stop	*pára*
aeroplane	*eropláno*
ship	*barkó*
boat	*bangká*
bus	*bus*
car	*kótse*
taxi	*taksi*
train	*tren*
tricycle	*traysikel*
village	*báryo*
town/city	*bayán/lungsód*
road	*daán, kálye*
street corner	*kanto*
bus station	*estasyón ng bus*
railway station	*estasyón ng tren*
airport	*airport*
petrol station	*estasyón ng gas*
police station	*estasyón ng pulis*
embassy	*embassi*
island	*puló*
ocean, sea	*dágat*
bay	*loók*
coast, shore	*tabíng-dágat*
beach	*baybáy*
river	*ílog*
river mouth	*wawà*
lake	*lawà*
creek	*sapà*
waterfall	*talón*
hill	*buról*
mountain	*bundók*
forest, jungle	*kagubátan*
entrance	*pasukán*
exit	*lábasan*
open	*bukás*
closed	*sarádo*

where
saán
How far is it?
Gaáno malayo?
Where is the post office?
Saán ang koréyo?
Which is the bus for Manila?
Alíng bus ang papuntáng Maynîla?
Where is the bus stop?
Saán ang hintáyan ng bus?
Where do I catch the jeepney?
Saán ang sasakay ng jeepney?

Where does this bus go?
Saán papuntá ang bus na itó?
Where do I get off?
Saán akó dapát babá?
How much is the fare?
Magkáno ang pamasáhe?
What town is this?
Anóng báyan íto?
How many km to...?
Ilán ang kilometro hanggáng...?

Accommodation

hotel *otél*
room *kuwárto*
key *susí*
bathroom *bányo*
bed *káma*
blanket, cover *kubrekáma*
pillow *únan*
mosquito net *kulambó*
toilet *kubíta*

room with bath
kuwárto na may bányo
Do you have air-con?
Mayroón bang air-conditión?
There is no water.
Waláng túbig.
How much is a room?
Magkáno ang isáng kuwárto?
I'll take the room.
Síge kukúnin ko ang kuwártong itó.

Food & Drink

food, meal *pagkaín*
breakfast *almusál*
lunch *panánghalían*
dinner *hapúnan*

plate *pláto*
knife *kutsílyo*
fork *tinidór*
spoon *kutsára*
glass *báso*
cup *tása*
serviette/napkin *serbilyéta*

rice (uncooked) *bigás*
rice (cooked) *kánin*
fish *isdá*

meat *karné*
chicken *manók*
soup *sabáw*
salad *insaláda*
vegetables *gúlay*
potato/sweet potato *patátas/kamóte*
onion *sibúyas*
egg *ítlog*
bread *tinápay*
peanut *maní*

salt *ásin*
pepper (grains) *pamintá*
pepper (powdered) *pamintáng duróg*
vinegar *sukà*
sugar *asúkal*

apple *mansánas*
banana *ságing*
coconut (ripe) *niyog*
coconut (young) *bukó*
guava *bayábas*
jackfruit *langká*
mango *manggá*
orange *kahél*
papaya *papáya*
pineapple *pinyá*

water *túbig*
beer *serbésa*
wine *alak*
coffee *kapé*
black coffee *kapéng matápang*
milk *gátas*
tea *tsa*
ice, ice cubes *yelo*

hot *mainít*
cold *malamíg*
sweet *matamís*
sour *maásim*
spicy *maánghang*
salty *inasnán*
spoiled *sirá*
delicious *masaráp*

I am hungry.
Gutóm akó.
I am thirsty.
Naúuhaw akó.

I am full.
Busóg pa akó.
I have no appetite.
Walá akóng gana.
It is cold.
Malamíg íto.
I want rice & fish.
Gústo ko ng kánin at isdá.
That was a good meal.
Ang saráp ng pagkaín.
How much is one coffee?
Magkáno isáng kapé?
bill
chit or *kuwénta*
The bill please.
Àkina ang kuwénta ko (magkáno).

Shopping

money	*péra*
expensive/cheap	*mahál/múra*
too expensive	*masyádong mahál*
big/small	*malakí/maliít*
old/new (things)	*lumà/bágo*
many/all	*marámi/lahát*
several, few	*kauntí*
broken, destroyed	*sirá*
more	*kauntí pa*
less	*tamá na*

How much is this? (touch)
Magkáno itó?
How much is this? (point)
Magkáno iyán?
What is this/that?
Ano itó?
When will it be ready?
Kailán matatápos?
Do you have/is there...?
Mayroón...?
Do you have any...?
Mayroón ba kayong...?
Do you have anything cheaper?
Mayroón bang mas múra?

Time & Dates

today	*ngayón*
tomorrow	*búkas*
every day	*áraw-áraw*
every night	*gabí-gabí*
tonight	*ngayóng gabí*
last night	*kahapong gabí*
anytime	*maski kailán*
a day	*isáng áraw*
a night	*isáng gabí*
day & night	*áraw-gabí*
every Thursday	*túwing Huwébes*
every afternoon	*túwing hápon*
yesterday	*kahápon*
day before yesterday	*noóng kamakalawá*
day after tomorrow	*sa makalawá*
What time is it?	*Anóng óras na?*

week
linggó
last week
noóng nakaraáng linggó
this week
ngayóng linggóng itó
next week
sa linggóng daratíng
month
buwán
a month
isáng buwán
this month
ngayóng buwáng itó
year
taón
a year
isáng taón
every year
taón-taón
last year
nakaraáng taón (nagdáan na taón)
next year
sa sunód sa taón

Days

Monday	*Lúnes*
Tuesday	*Martés*
Wednesday	*Miyérkoles*
Thursday	*Huwébes*
Friday	*Biyérnes*
Saturday	*Sábado*
Sunday	*Linggó*

Months

January	*Enéro*
February	*Pebréro*

March	*Márso*
April	*Abril*
May	*Máyo*
June	*Húnyo*
July	*Húlyo*
August	*Agósto*
September	*Setyémbre*
October	*Oktúbre*
November	*Nobyémbre*
December	*Disyémbre*

Weather

sun	*áraw*
clear, bright	*malinawág*
clouds, fog, mist	*úlap*
cloudy	*úlap, maúlap*
warm	*mainít*
cold	*malamíg*
lightning	*kídlat, lintík*
rain	*ulán*
rainy	*maulán*
thunder	*kulóg*
storm/typhoon	*bagyó*
wind	*hángin*
windy	*mahángin*

Numbers

0	*walá*
1	*isá*
2	*dalawá*
3	*tatló*
4	*apát*
5	*limá*
6	*ánim*
7	*pitó*
8	*waló*
9	*siyám*
10	*sampú*
11	*labing-isá*
12	*labíndalawá*
13	*labíntatló*
20	*dalawampú*
21	*dalawampút isá*
22	*dalawampút dalawá*
30	*tatlumpú*
31	*tatlumpút isá*
40	*ápatnapú*
50	*limampú*
60	*ánimnapú*
70	*pitumpú*
80	*walampú*
90	*siyámnapú*
100	*isáng daán*
101	*isáng daán at isá*
200	*dalawáng daán*
201	*dalawáng daán at isá*
500	*limáng daán*
1000	*isáng libo*
5000	*limáng libo*

one kg	*isáng kilogram*
two pesos	*dalawáng píso*
three km	*tatlóng kilométro*
five litres	*limáng lítro*
10 cubic metres	*sampúng métro kúbiko*

one-half	*kalahatí*
one-third	*isáng-katló*
one-quarter	*isáng-kapat*

once	*minsan*
twice	*makálawá*
three times	*makatatló*
often	*madalás*
seldom	*bihirà*

For a more complete selection of phrases, basic vocabulary and grammar for travel in the Philippines, see Lonely Planet's *Pilipino Phrasebook*.

An excellent Tagalog language course is available from Audio-Forum, 31 Kensington Church St, London W8 4LL, England, UK. This extensive self-instructional language course, *Beginning Tagalog*, consists of 24 cassettes and two text books totalling 900 pages. It costs roughly UK£230.

Cebuano

Cebuano is the second most widely spoken language in the Philippines. It's spoken in the Visayas and in many parts of Mindanao.

Useful Words & Phrases

who (singular)	*kinsá*
who (plural)	*kinsá-kinsá*
how	*unsaón*
what	*unsa*

when *kánus-a*
where *asá*
why *nganóng, ngáno*
How much? *Tagpila, pila?*
What did you say? *Unsa tó?*

People & Pronouns

man *laláki*
woman *babáye*
Mr *Ginoó*
Mr Santos *Ginoóng Santos*
Mrs *Gínang*
Mrs Santos *Gínang Santos*
Miss *Dalága*
Miss Santos *Dalagáng Santos*
grandmother/grandfather *lolá/loló*
friend *amígo/a*
unmarried man *ulitawó, soltéro*
unmarried woman *dalága, dalagíta*
child *báta*
child (own) *anák*
boy *binatílo*
girl *balagíta*

I *akó*
you *ikáw*
he/she *siyá*
they *silá*
we (I and you) *kitá*
we (I and others) *kamí*
you (plural) *kamó*

old *tigúlang*
young *batán-on*
tall *taás*
short *mabú*
happy *malipáyon*
sad *magu-ol*
intelligent *hawód*
handsome,pretty *gwápo/a*
ugly *ngíl-ad*

Greetings & Civilities

hello, greetings
mabúhay
good morning
maáyong búntag
good day
maáyong udló
good afternoon
maáyong hápon
good night
maáyong gabií
goodbye
babáy, síge
thank you
salámat
thank you very much
dagháng salámat
please
palihóg
yes/no
oó/díli
yes/no (polite)
opó/dilagí
OK
síge, síge taná
only, merely, simply
lang
again, similarly
napúd
always, of course
siyémpre
no problem
walá probléma
It's all right.
Maáyo ang tanán.
good/well
maáyo
also good/well
maáyo sab/maáyo man
and
ug

You're welcome.
Waláy sapayán.
Just a minute.
Kadalí lang.
How are you?
Kumustá (na)?
How are you? (plural)
Kumustá (na) kamó?
Well, thank you, and you?
Maáyo man salámat, ug ikáw?
Where have you been?
Diín ka gíkan/Asá ka gíkan?
Where are you going?
Asá ka muadtó/Asá ka páingon?

I'm coming from Kalibo.
Gíkan ko sa Kalibo/Tayá Kalibo ko.
I'm going to Boracay.
Uadtó ko sa Boracay/Páigon ko sa Boracay.

Small Talk

Who is there?
Kinsá ná?
What is your name?
Unsá may agálan mo?
How old are you?
Píla na may ímong idad?
Where do you come from?
Tagá diíng lúgar ka?
I like you.
Gústo ko nimó.
Never mind.
Síge na lang.
I don't know.
Ámbot lang/Walá ko kahibaló.
Let's go.
Dalí na/Síge na.
I like (that).
Gustó ko (niána).
I don't like...
Díli gustó ko...
I'll do it/I'll get it.
Akó na lang.
You do it/You get it.
Ikáw na lang.
Come here.
Dalí díri.
What a pity.
Anugon.
It's too late.
Awáhi na.
I have no time.
Wa koy panáhon.
Are you sure?
Siguradó ka ba?
not yet
walá pa
maybe/perhaps
tingáli
really
tínuod
That's not true (flatterer).
Boléro.

fool
búgok (ka), bangak
crazy, mad
lúku-lúko
rude, insolent
bastós
braggart
hambugéro, hambugéro
It's none of your business.
Walá kay labot.
Get lost!
Pahápwa dihá!

Getting Around

left/right	*walá/tuó*
straight on	*dirétso*
back	*luyó, mobalík*
here/there	*dínhi/dínha, dídto*
near/far	*dúol/layó*
turn-off	*molikó, nilikó, likó*
stop	*pára*
aeroplane	*eropláne*
car	*kótse, sakyanán*
bus	*track, bus*
boat	*sakayán*
village	*báryo*
town/city	*lungsód/siyudád*
road	*dálan*
island	*puló*
ocean, sea	*dágat*
bay	*loók*
coast, shore	*hunásan*
beach	*baybáyon*
river	*subá*
river mouth	*bába sa subá*
lake	*línaw*
creek	*sápa*
waterfall	*busáy*
hill	*búngtod*
mountain	*búkid*
forest	*lasáng*

How far is it?
Unsa'kaláyo (layo)?
Where is the post office?
Asá man ang post office?
Which bus for Cebu?
Únsang bus ang maodtong Cebu?
Where is the bus stop?
Asa man ang hulatán ug bus?

Where do I catch the jeepney?
Asa ko musakay ug jeepney?
Where does this bus go?
Asa man moadto kíning bus?
Where do I get off?
Asa ko manaóg?
How much is the fare?
Tagpíla ang pléte?

Accommodation

hotel — *otél*
room — *kuwárto*
bath — *bányo*
room with bath — *kuwárto nga anaáy bányo*
bed — *katré*
blanket, cover — *hábol*
key — *yáwi*
pillow — *únlan*
mosquito net — *muskitéro*
toilet — *kasílyas*

Do you have air-con?
Nabáy air-condítion?
There is no water.
Walá túbig.
How much is a room?
Pilá ang usá ka kuwárto?
I'll take the room.
Síge kuhaon ko ang kining kuwárto.

Food & Drink

food, meal — *pagkaón*
breakfast — *pamaháw*
lunch — *paniúdto*
dinner — *panihápon*

plate — *pláto*
knife — *kutsílyo*
fork — *tinidór*
spoon — *kutsára*
teaspoon — *kutsaríta*
glass — *báso*
cup — *tása*
serviette/napkin — *serbilyéta*

rice (uncooked) — *bugas*
rice (cooked) — *kanú*
fish — *isdá*
meat — *karné*
beef — *karnéng báka*
pork — *karnéng báboy*
chicken — *manók*
soup — *sabáw*
salad — *salad*
vegetables — *utan*
potato/sweet potato — *patátas/kamóte*
onion — *sibúyas*
egg — *itlóg*
bread — *tinapáy (pan)*
salt — *ásin*
pepper (grains) — *pamintá (síli)*
pepper (powdered) — *pamintáng ginalíng*
vinegar — *súka*
sugar — *asúkar*

apple — *mansánas*
banana — *ságing*
coconut (ripe) — *lubi*
coconut (young) — *butóng*
guava — *bayábas*
jackfruit — *nangká*
mango — *manggá*
orange — *kahíl*
papaya — *kapáyas*
pineapple — *pinyá*

beer — *serbésa*
water — *túbig*
coffee — *kapé*
black coffee — *maisóg na kapé*
milk — *gátas*
tea — *tsaa*
ice, ice cubes — *ápa*

hot — *inít*
cold — *bugnáw*
sweet — *tamís*
sour — *aslum*
spicy — *hang*
salty — *parát*
delicious — *lamí*
spoiled — *pános*

I am hungry.
Gigútom na akó/Gigútom ko.
I am thirsty.
Guiháw ko/Guiháw na akó.
I am full.
Busóg na akó/Busóg ko.

I have no appetite.
Walá koy gana.
That was a good meal.
Kalami sa pagkaón.
The bill please.
Ang báyronon palíhog.

Shopping

money
kuwárta
expensive/cheap
mahál/baráto
too expensive
kamahál, mahál kaáyo
big/small
dako/gamáy
old/new (things)
dáan/bágo
many/all
dághan/tanán
several, few
gamáy, diyútay
broken, destroyed
gubá
less
hustó na, diyutay
more
gamáy pa

How much is this? (touch)
Tagpíla na?
How much is this? (point)
Tagpíla kaná?
What is this/that?
Unsa ni?
When will it be ready?
Kánus-a matápos?

Time & Dates

today
karón
tomorrow
ugma
every day
káda ádlaw, ádlaw-ádlaw
every night
káda gabií
last night
kagabií
a day
usá kaádlaw, úsang ádlaw
a night
usá kagabií, úsang gabií
day & night
ádlaw-gabií
every Thursday
káda Huwébes
every afternoon
káda hápon
day before yesterday
sa úsang ádlaw
yesterday
gahápon
day after tomorrow
sunód ugma
What time is it?
Usáng orása na?

week
semána, dominggó
last week
niáging semána
this week
károng semanáha, károng dominggó
next week
sa sunód semána, dominggó umáabot
month
bulán
a month
usá kabúlan
this month
károng bulána
year
tuíg
a year
usá kátuig
every year
tuíg-tuíg, káda tuíg
last year
niáging tuíg
next year
sa sunód tuíg

Days

Monday	*Lunés*
Tuesday	*Martés*
Wednesday	*Miyérkoles (Miércules)*
Thursday	*Huwébes (Juéves)*

Friday	*Biyérnes (Viérnes)*
Saturday	*Sábado (Sábao)*
Sunday	*Dominggó*

Months

January	*Enéro*
February	*Pebréro*
March	*Márso*
April	*Abril*
May	*Máyo*
June	*Húnyo*
July	*Húlyo*
August	*Agósto*
September	*Setyémbre*
October	*Oktúbre*
November	*Nobyémbre*
December	*Disyémbre*

Weather

sun	*ádlaw*
clear, bright	*háyag, kláro*
clouds, fog, mist	*pangánod*
cloudy	*pangánod, dághang*
cold	*túgnaw*
warm	*inít*
lightning	*kílat, lintí*
rain	*ulán*
rainy	*ting-ulán*
thunder	*dúgdog, dalúgdog*
typhoon	*bagyó*
wind	*hángin*
windy	*mahángin*

Numbers

0	*walá*
1	*usá*
2	*duhá*
3	*tuló*
4	*upát*
5	*limá*
6	*únom*
7	*pitó*
8	*waló*
9	*siyám*
10	*napuló*
11	*únsi*
12	*dóse*
13	*trése*
20	*báynte*
21	*báynte úno*
22	*báynte dos*
30	*tranta*
31	*tranta'y úno*
40	*kuwarénta*
50	*singkuwénta*
60	*sayesénta, siséenta*
70	*siténta, seténta*
80	*otsénta*
90	*nobénta*
100	*usá kagatós*
101	*usá kagatós ug usá*
200	*duhá kagatós*
201	*duhá kagatós ug usá*
500	*limá kagatós*
1000	*usá kalíbo*
5000	*limá kalíbo*

1 pound (weight)	*usáng librá*
2 pesos	*duhá ka píso*
3 km	*tuló ka kilométro*
5 litres	*limá ka lítro*
10 cubic metres	*napuló ka métro kubíko*

one-half	*tungá*
one-third	*tuló ka tungá*
one-quarter	*upát ka tungá*

once	*usaháy*
twice	*kaduhá, ikaduhá*
three times	*katuló*
often	*pirme, síge síge*
seldom	*tág-sa, tagsa-ón*

Facts for the Visitor

VISAS

The visa you are issued at the airport on arrival in Manila is valid for 21 days. It is possible to get an extension in the Department of Immigration & Deportation, Magallanes Drive, Intramuros, Manila and its offices in Angeles City and Cebu City.

If you arrive in the Philippines with a visa, make sure you let the immigration officer know that you've obtained it. Otherwise you risk having only the customary period of 21 days stamped in your passport.

The cost of extensions is regulated according to the time period proposed. At the conclusion of the period stipulated by the visa, you present your extension application and passport to the various immigration officials, and these documents remain with the Immigration Office (Regular Service) for processing. You can get your extension in about four hours if you pay an 'express service' fee of P250. Keep all receipts, as they are likely to be checked at the airport when you leave the country. (Incidentally, anyone applying for a visa extension dressed in rubber thongs (flip-flops) and shorts can expect to be refused service.) A number of travel agencies and restaurants run by foreigners will offer to take care of your extension application for a reasonable sum, normally between P100 and P200.

If you wish to spend between 21 and 59 days in the Philippines, you should request a 59 day visa from a Philippine embassy or consulate in your country. This will normally be granted free of charge. If you're unable to make your application in person, you should send a letter of request asking for the application forms, and enclose a stamped, self-addressed envelope. Don't send in your passport straight away.

21 to 59 Days

Anyone entering the Philippines without a visa or with only a 21 day visa and wishing to remain in the country for up to 59 days must pay P300 for a 38 day extension (Visa Waiver), plus a P10 'legal research fee'.

59 Days to Six Months

Anyone wishing to stay in the country for more than 59 days, but no longer than six months, has to pay the following fees:

Application and Visa Fee (P350) – not applicable in the case of previously paid visa fees.

Alien Head Tax (P125) – applicable only to persons over 16 years of age.

ACR: Alien Certificate of Registration (P250) – in the case of a second application within the same calendar year; this costs only P150.

Extension Fee (P100) – for each month of the extension period already begun.

ECC: Emigration Clearance Certificate (P250) – the fee can be paid at the airport on departure; you can also make the payment at the Immigration Office, though this must be done no sooner than 30 days before departure.

Legal Research Fee (P10) – additional to every other payable fee with the exception of the Alien Head Tax.

Six Months & Longer

Anyone wishing to remain in the country over six months must, in addition to the extension fees listed earlier, pay a further P400 for a Certificate of Temporary Residence. When departing after a stay of one year or longer, there is a further travel tax to pay to the tune of P1620.

The Immigration Office can order anyone applying for a visa extension of over six months to undergo an AIDS test, and can grant or refuse the application on the basis of the result.

Balikbayan

After repeated alterations to the definitions of eligibility for Travel Tax Exemptions for *Balikbayan* (Filipinos living abroad), the following regulations are now in force: the Filipino Civil Registration Office, or the Philippine embassy or consulate in the new country of residence will provide the applicant with a certificate affirming that no tax has been paid on any income. This can then be forwarded to the Department of Tourism (DOT) for exemption from payment of the travel tax. The department's address is Room 108, Ministry of Tourism Building, Agrifina Circle, Rizal Park, Manila.

Documents

It is necessary to have a valid passport and probably an international health certificate. Some bus and ship companies, as well as Philippine Airlines and Philippine National Railways, have student discounts. It is essential to have a student card. If you want to hire a car, you will need a valid driver's licence from your country of origin – the international driver's permit is not recognised.

Make two copies of your documents and of the receipts of your travellers' cheques and leave one copy at a permanent address so you can send for it if necessary. Either exchange the other copy with your travelling companion for theirs or keep it in your luggage, quite separate from the originals. Identification problems and document replacement in the case of loss or theft will be a lot easier if you take these precautions.

If you take a personal address book containing important addresses and telephone numbers, you should make a copy of them and store them separately from the originals.

Bags kept close to you, money belts and secret pockets are further ways of protecting your money, tickets and documents.

MONEY

A$1	=	P22.1
C$1	=	P24.4
DM 1	=	P17.1
UK£1	=	P50.9
US$1	=	P28.0
NZ$1	=	P16.5

The Philippine currency is the peso (P) – correctly spelt piso but always referred to as the peso. It's divided up into 100 centavos (c). There are coins of 1, 5, 10, 25 and 50 centavos and of 1, 2 and 5 pesos, but the 5 peso coin is rare. Banknotes are available in denominations of 2, 5, 10, 20, 50, 100 and 500 pesos.

It's rather confusing to discover that two distinct peso coins are in circulation (the new coin can easily be mistaken for a 50 centavo coin). Also, there are two different large 25 centavo pieces, three fairly similar 10 centavo pieces and two distinct 5 centavo coins. As for paper money, there are in current use two different sets of bills for the following amounts: P5, P10, P20, P50 and P100.

The US dollar is by far the most recognised foreign currency in the Philippines. Bank of America and American Express travellers' cheques are probably the most widely accepted – you can change them at most banks. Although the safety consideration with travellers' cheques applies as much in the Philippines as anywhere else, cash (US dollars) does, as usual, have its advantages. You will often find it easier to change a small amount of cash rather than a cheque.

In some smaller regional towns there may be no bank at all and the only possibility of changing money may be at a hotel and then at a poor exchange rate. Moneychangers are often faster and more efficient than banks, although it's wise to shop around since their rates do vary. When you do change money try to get a reasonable amount of it in smaller denominations: taxi drivers almost never have change of big notes. In more remote areas it can be difficult to change even P100 notes.

Banks

You'll get the best exchange rate in Manila. The Philippine Commercial International Bank tends to offer a better rate for travellers' cheques than any of the other city banks. In the provinces you may lose as much as 20%. In remote districts only the peso and, possibly, the US dollar will be accepted; in those areas no other currency can be relied upon. Sometimes a bank will give you a better rate for your currency than a moneychanger, at other times the opposite will be the case. You could also be charged for a quick comparison of exchange rates.

Many provincial banks only exchange travellers' cheques to a total value of $US100 or less. Cheques for larger amounts can be cashed only with the consent of the bank manager.

The age of automatic tellers has also reached the Philippines, and several branches of the Bank of the Philippines (in Manila, Baguio, Cebu, Bacolod, Davao and Iloilo) are equipped with these machines. Holders of a plastic keycard are therefore not limited by the opening hours of the bank if they want to withdraw money from their account.

If you are thinking of opening an account with a Philippine bank, you should be aware that only the first P40,000 are insured. By law larger amounts do not have to be reimbursed should the bank suffer bankruptcy. Even two or more accounts at the same bank are not insured beyond a total amount of P40,000 when the holder of each account is the same person.

You are not permitted to take more than P500 out of the country. Unused pesos can be changed only at the banking counter in the departure hall of Ninoy Aquino International Airport; you have to produce an official yellow (or white) exchange slip. These can be obtained from a bank or a licensed money exchange office.

Moneychangers

You'll get a fairly good exchange rate from licensed moneychangers. In Manila these will be found in Mabini St (between Padre Faura and Santa Monica streets) and on the corner of M H del Pilar and Padre Faura streets. Besides your passport (a photocopy of which is taken on your first transaction), you will need to produce the receipts from your purchase of travellers' cheques showing the certified number of each cheque.

The Black Market

Compared with the official exchange rate, the black market pays only a few centavos extra for each US$100 bill. The lower the denomination the lower the exchange. A US$1 bill is worth next to nothing on the black market.

You'll find dealers in front of post offices. In Mabini St, in the Ermita district of Manila, some of them are foreigners. But beware, plenty of tourists have been taken for a ride! The illegal moneychangers ply their trade in the following way. To begin with they'll offer you a perfectly correct rate of exchange. You receive your pesos, the dealer takes the dollars. Then, all of a sudden, the dealer will apologise for having short changed you P50. The dealer takes the pesos back, counts them out again and ostentatiously places the allegedly missing P50 on top of the pile while stealthily removing some other notes from the bottom! Should you realise what's happening and shout 'Police!', the amount will be correct again before you know it.

Another favourite trick is not to pay out in full the agreed sum so as to provoke the irritated customer into cancelling the deal. The customer then gets counterfeit dollars handed back while the dealer keeps the good dollars and pesos! There's no getting away from the fact that most black marketeers are consummate artists when it comes to fraud.

That also goes for the pretty young Filipinas who use their charms to lure male tourists. The tourist wanting to change money is taken in by their tale of poverty and woe, and soon finds himself dealing with their well-fed 'brothers'.

Cash

In the Philippines, unlike many other countries, the rate of exchange is somewhat higher for cash than it is for travellers' cheques. You'll get the best value for large US denominations like US$50 and US$100 bills. When selling currency, bear in mind that only clean banknotes are acceptable. Crumpled, torn or dirty ones will be rejected by moneychangers.

Travellers' Cheques

If you want to keep on the safe side of the

law and are prepared to accept an exchange rate of about 5% lower, you should take travellers' cheques rather than cash with you. Travellers' cheques in US dollars issued by American Express and the Bank of America will be cashed by almost every Philippine bank, and certainly by the Philippine National Bank. Thomas Cook travellers' cheques aren't too popular these days in the Philippines: when you present them you may well be told that only American Express and Bank of America cheques are acceptable.

Hold on to your original purchase receipts, as most moneychangers (and sometimes banks) will not cash cheques unless you can produce this documentation.

Eurocheques

It is becoming increasingly difficult to use Eurocheques in the Philippines. Even in Manila you'll barely find a bank willing to accept this form of payment. Occasionally resident foreigners will be willing to swap their pesos for Eurocheques. You can find out about current possibilities for deals of this sort in foreign-run restaurants and businesses.

Eurocheques certainly have advantages in terms of credit, as each cheque takes about three weeks to be debited from your account.

Credit Cards

Well-known international credit cards such as American Express, Diners Club, MasterCard and Visa are accepted by many hotels, restaurants and businesses in the Philippines. With your MasterCard you can withdraw cash in pesos at any branch of the Equitable Bank: there are plenty of these in Manila, for example on the corner of United Nations Ave and Bocobo St (opposite the Manila Pavilion Hotel), Ermita. You can get US dollars or travellers' cheques in dollars with your Visa card at the Bank of America, Paseo de Roxas, Makati, and you can draw cash on your American Express card at American Express, Philamlife Building, United Nations Ave, Ermita.

It's important to remember that the Equitable Bank has brought out its own national Visa card. Many of the hotels, restaurants and businesses displaying showy posters confirming that they accept 'Visa' are actually referring to this local version of it.

Money Transfer

Having money forwarded can be time consuming. Even transfers by telex often take 10 days or longer. Presumably there's not much in it for the banks.

It's advantageous to have a safe-deposit account, as that way you can arrange for the desired sum of money to be sent by telex. Costs are in the vicinity of $US15 and the waiting time is two days.

In Manila use American Express or the Philippine National Bank – the Bank of America tends to be slow. American Express card holders can get US$1000 in travellers' cheques every 21 days on their card account. Up to 20% of it can be taken in cash. One report suggested that the American Express office in Manila will not advance money just with an American Express card: you have to have a personal cheque as well. So, if you are likely to want to get money this way, carry a couple of your own cheques with you.

Payment will be made in pesos or US dollar travellers' cheques. Most banks are unwilling to pay out dollars in bills. If anything they might offer you the amount in very small bills, which you're better off refusing.

TOURIST INFORMATION

You can often get up-to-date news and travel tips about prices, departure times and so on from other travellers.

For regional information, the representatives of the Department of Tourism (DOT) are available. Don't expect too much of them – they are friendly and helpful but not always terribly knowledgeable. As well as the DOT head office in Manila, there are various overseas offices and regional field offices scattered around the country.

Local Tourist Offices

Around the Philippines the local tourist offices are at:

Angeles
Dau Interchange, Mabalacat, Pampanga (tel 2243, 3016)
Baguio
Ministry of Tourism Complex, Governor Pack Rd (tel 7014, 5415, 5416, 6858)
Cagayan de Oro
Ground Floor, Pelaez Sports Complex (tel 3340)
Cebu City
Fort San Pedro (tel 91503, 82329, 96518)
Davao
Apo View Hotel, J Camus St (tel 74861, 71534)
Iloilo
Sarabia Building, General Luna St (tel 78701, 75411)
La Union
Cresta del Mar Beach Resort, Paringao, Bauang (tel 2411, 2098)
Legaspi
Penaranda Park, Albay District (tel 4492, 4026)
Tacloban
Children's Park, Senator Enage St (tel 2048)
Zamboanga
Lantaka Hotel, Valderroza St (tel 3931, 3247)

In Manila there are tourist offices at Ninoy Aquino International Airport and by Rizal Park. See the Information section in the Manila chapter for more details.

Overseas Reps

Overseas offices of the Philippines Department of Tourism include:

Australia
3rd Floor, Philippine Centre, 27-33 Wentworth Ave, Darlinghurst, NSW 2010 (tel (02) 267 2695/2756)
Hong Kong
21 F Wah Kwong Regent Centre, 88 Queen's Road Central, (tel (5) 8100770)
Japan
Philippine House, 11-24 Nampeidai Machi, Shibuya-ku, Tokyo (tel (03) 464 3630/3635)
Philippine Tourism Center, 2F Dainan Building, 2-19-23 Shinmachi, Nishi-Ku, Osaka 550 (tel (06) 535 5071/2)
Singapore
Philippine Embassy, Office of the Tourism Representative, 20B Nassim Rd, Singapore 1025 (tel 737 3977)
UK
199 Piccadilly, London WIV 9LE (tel (071) 7346358)
USA
Suite 1111, 30 North Michigan Ave, Chicago, IL 60602 (tel 312 782-1707)
Suite 1212, 3460 Wilshire Blvd, Los Angeles, CA 90010 (tel (213) 487 4527)
Philippine Center, 556 Fifth Ave, New York, NY 10036 (tel (212) 575 7915)
447 Sutter St, Suite 523, San Francisco, CA 94018 (tel (415) 433 6666)
Philippine Embassy, 1617 Massachusetts Ave, North West, Suite 304, Washington DC 20036 (tel (202) 483 1414, 842 1664)

GENERAL INFORMATION

Post

Sending Mail If you take your mail straight to the mail distribution centre near the domestic airport, it will be processed and sent out much quicker. You can also send things from the post office in Ninoy Aquino International Airport: it's open on Sundays and public holidays as well. So far all my letters have arrived home safely. If you are sending important items (such as film) out by mail, it is best to send it by registered post. Registered express letters will be delivered – all going well – within five days. Around Christmas especially, you should make sure your letters are stamped immediately so that no-one can remove your postage stamps and use them again. Even at the small post office in Mabini St, Manila, there have been numerous complaints about stamp pilfering.

Unlike the GPO (General Post Office) and the Mabini St Post Office, the Rizal Park Post Office near the Manila Hotel is less frequented, and you may only have to wait there a little while or not at all.

A tip for stamp collectors: at the Manila GPO you can get special release stamps. Go to the special room at the rear on the left-hand side of the building.

Parcels Only parcels weighing less than 10 kg will be dispatched by the Philippine postal service. They must also be packed in plain brown paper and fastened with string. Parcels sent to Europe by surface (sea) mail take from two to four months to reach their destination.

Receiving Mail The Philippine postal system is generally quite efficient. You can get mail sent to you at postes restantes at the

GPO in all the major towns. In Manila you'll find the poste restante to the left, at the back of the GPO. It's open Monday to Friday from 8 am till noon, and from 1 to 5 pm on Saturdays and public holidays.

Make sure your surname is printed clearly and underlined – most missing mail to a poste restante is simply misfiled under given names.

You can also have mail sent to American Express if you're using American Express travellers' cheques or carrying an American Express card. American Express has offices in Manila and Makati and at Angeles City (for the big USAF Clark Air Base there). The Manila address is Clients' Mail, American Express, Philamlife Building, United Nations Ave & Maria Orosa St, Manila. You can get information by calling 8159311 (ask to be connected).

If you wish to send money in a letter to the Philippines, you should only do so by registered letter, otherwise its safe arrival can't be guaranteed. To keep on the safe side, camouflage the valuable item with a piece of carbon paper and then fasten the contents to the envelope with a staple on the outside: there are postal employees with X-ray vision! In fact it's not uncommon for envelopes also stamped on the back to be opened (registered letters are known to carry valuable items!). Post office crooks are capable of removing most of the enclosed money and leaving just a token remainder; or they might switch a US$5 bill for a US$50 one before passing the letter on for 'regular' delivery. Postal money orders present no problem. These take about 10 days.

Opening Hours Opening hours in Philippine post offices are not the same everywhere. Many close at noon, others shut on Saturdays as well. The following opening hours can usually be relied upon: Monday to Friday from 8 am to noon, and from 1 to 5 pm. With few exceptions, post offices are closed on Sundays and public holidays, and at the end of the year there are at least three public holidays: Rizal Day (30 December), New Year's Eve and New Year's Day. During the Christmas period, from mid-December to mid-January, mail is delayed by up to a month (see the Fiestas & Festivals section in the Facts about the Country chapter).

Telephones

You do not find telephones everywhere in the Philippines; in an emergency try the nearest police station, which in many areas will have the only telephone. Telephone numbers are always changing so get hold of a local directory before calling.

In contrast to overseas calls, local calls in the Philippines are full of problems. It can take a ridiculously long time to be connected and the lines over long distances are bad. International calls are a breeze in comparison.

Long-distance overseas calls can be made from most hotels. A three minute station to station call to Europe costs about P300. It's a few pesos cheaper if you call directly from one of the offices of the Philippine Long Distance Telephone Co (PLDT). There are PLDT offices at Escolta St and Taft Ave in Manila as well as at other central locations.

Note that it is far cheaper to make station to station rather than person to person calls from the Philippines: the charges are about 25% less.

Try to call outside business hours (of the country you are ringing) when the waiting time will be considerably less. On Sundays there is a 25% reduction in the charge.

Telegrams

The international telegram service is pretty prompt and reliable, but internal telegrams are likely to be delayed. There are two major domestic telegram companies: RCPI (Radio Communications of the Philippines) and PT & T (Philippine Telegraph & Telephone Corporation).

To Europe, 12-hour telegrams cost about P13.50 a word and to Australia they cost P14.20. Within the Philippines, a telegram to Cebu from Manila, for example, costs about P1.50 a word and takes five hours.

To compare, a telex to Europe costs P60

per minute (four lines) through Eastern Communications.

Electricity

The electric current is generally 220 volts, 60 cycles, although the actual voltage is often less, particularly in some provinces. In some areas the standard current is the US-style 110 volts. An adapter may be needed for Philippine plugs which are usually like the US flat, two-pin type.

Blackouts are common outside the tourist centres, which are usually protected from such inconveniences. A pocket torch (flashlight) is very useful for such occasions.

Time

The Philippines is eight hours ahead of GMT, and two hours behind Australian Eastern Standard Time. Philippine time has a curious nature – it includes lack of punctuality and a need for patience. A rendezvous à-la-Philippine time is basically very loose. Either you are waited for, or you wait. Don't get too upset – tomorrow is another day. In the Philippines the only reliable times are sunrise and sunset. If you have been invited somewhere, do as the locals do and arrive about an hour after the arranged time. This will be considered polite and will save the host the embarrassment of a guest arriving too early.

Business Hours

Businesses open their doors to the public between 8 and 10 am. Offices, banks and public authorities have a five-day week. Some offices are also open on Saturday mornings. Banks open at 9 am and close at 3 or 4 pm, but in southern parts of the Philippines closing time is often 3 or 3.30 pm. Embassies and consulates are open for the public mostly from 9 am till 1 pm. Offices and public authorities close at 5 pm. Large businesses like department stores and supermarkets continue until 7 pm, and smaller shops often until 10 pm.

MEDIA

Newspapers & Magazines

After 20 years of press censorship under Marcos, the change of government brought a flood of new national and local newspapers and magazines indulging in a marvellous journalistic free-for-all. Before, there was a group of four big government-friendly national dailies. Now about 20 publications including the *Manila Bulletin*, the *Philippine Daily Inquirer*, *Malaya*, *The Manila Chronicle*, the *Manila Standard*, *Daily Globe*, *The Philippine Star*, *The Journal* and the *Evening Star* fight for their share in a free market. All are in English. In contrast to the unilateral reporting during Marcos's time the media today represent a fair, critical and objective difference of opinion. *Tempo* and *Peoples* are vigorous tabloid papers, which appear in both English and Tagalog.

A lesser role is played by the Philippine papers *Balita*, *Taliba* and *Ang Pilipino Ngayon*, in keeping with their circulation and layout. In the Sunday editions of various newspapers a magazine is included. Newspapers printed in Manila but sold outside the capital are more expensive because of transport costs.

International events are meagrely reported or analysed in the Philippine mass media. If you want to know more you can get *Newsweek, Time, Asiaweek, Far Eastern Economic Review* and the *International Herald Tribune*. These and other international publications can be found on sale in the larger hotels. The number of comics published and read each week is quite phenomenal.

Radio & TV

Radio and TV operate on a commercial basis and the programmes are continually being interrupted by advertisements. There are altogether 22 TV channels. Five broadcast from Manila, sometimes in English and sometimes in Tagalog. In Manila, with a specially erected antenna you will be able to receive Channel 17 and the Far East Network (FEN). The US Army transmitter broadcasts its programmes from the Clark Air Base in Angeles City.

HEALTH

You probably won't get any of the illnesses described here. However, you might be unlucky or need to help others, in which case the information in this section will be a useful starting point.

Travel health depends on your predeparture preparations, your day-to-day health care while travelling and how you handle any medical problem or emergency that does develop. While the list of potential dangers can seem quite frightening, with a little luck, some basic precautions and adequate information you will experience little more than an upset stomach.

Travel Health Guides

There are a number of books on travel health:

Staying Healthy in Asia, Africa & Latin America (Volunteers in Asia, Stanford, California, 1988). Probably the best all-round guide to carry, as it's compact but very detailed and well organised.

Travellers' Health, Dr Richard Dawood (Oxford University Press, 1986). Comprehensive, easy to read, authoritative and also highly recommended, although it's rather large to lug around.

Where There is No Doctor, David Werner (Hesperian Foundation, Palo Alto, California, 1977). A very detailed guide intended for someone, like a Peace Corps worker, going to work in an undeveloped country, rather than for the average traveller.

Travel with Children, Maureen Wheeler (Lonely Planet Publications, Melbourne, 1990). Includes basic advice on travel health for younger children.

Predeparture Preparations

Health Insurance A travel insurance policy to cover theft, loss and medical problems is a wise idea. There is a wide variety of policies and your travel agent will have recommendations. The international student travel policies handled by STA or other student travel organisations are usually good value. Some policies offer lower and higher medical expense options, but the higher one is chiefly for countries like the USA which have extremely high medical costs. Check the small print:

1 Some policies specifically exclude 'dangerous activities' such as scuba diving, motorcycling, even trekking. If such activities are on your agenda you don't want that sort of policy.
2 You may prefer a policy which pays doctors or hospitals direct rather than you having to pay on the spot and claim later. If you have to claim later, make sure you keep all documentation. Some policies ask you to call back (reverse charges) to a centre in your home country where an immediate assessment of your problem is made.
3 Check if the policy covers ambulances or an emergency flight home. If you have to stretch out you will need two seats and somebody has to pay for them!

Medical Kit A good medical kit is essential, particularly if you are going off the beaten track. Because you can't always get to your main luggage when travelling, for example on a flight, it's recommended that you keep a small medical kit in your hand luggage with medications such as pain-relieving tablets, diarrhoea tablets, eye drops and perhaps Alka Seltzer. Consult your doctor about individual medicines.

A possible kit list includes:

1 Aspirin or Panadol – for pain or fever.
2 Antihistamine (such as Benadryl) – useful as a decongestant for colds, allergies, to ease the itch from insect bites or stings or to help prevent motion sickness.
3 Antibiotics – useful if you're travelling off the beaten track. Choose a good broad-spectrum antibiotic.
4 Kaolin preparation (Pepto-Bismol) or Imodium – for stomach upsets.
5 Rehydration mixture – for treatment of severe diarrhoea, this is particularly important if travelling with children. Lomotil is also useful.
6 Antiseptic, mercurochrome and antibiotic powder or similar 'dry' spray – for cuts and grazes.
7 Calamine lotion – to ease irritation from bites or stings.
8 Bandages and Band-aids – for minor injuries.
9 Scissors, tweezers and a thermometer (note that mercury thermometers are prohibited by airlines).
10 Insect repellent, sunscreen, suntan lotion, chapstick and water purification tablets.
11 Condoms – to avoid sexually transmitted diseases.

Ideally, antibiotics should be administered only under medical supervision and should never be taken indiscriminately. Overuse of antibiotics can weaken your body's ability to deal with infections naturally and can reduce the drug's efficacy on a future occasion. Take only the recommended dose at the prescribed intervals and continue using the antibiotic for the prescribed period, even if the illness seems to be cured earlier. Antibiotics are quite specific to the infections they can treat, stop immediately if there are any serious reactions and don't use them at all if you are not sure that you have the correct ones.

In the Philippines many medicines will generally be available over the counter and the price will be much cheaper than in the West, but they may be marketed under a different name. Some medicines are supposedly available only with a prescription form, but, it seems, it's not compulsory for every pharmacy to see one. Antibiotics are available in Philippine pharmacies without prescription. Manila is the best place to buy antibiotics.

As in other developing countries, be careful of buying drugs, particularly where the expiry date may have passed or correct storage conditions may not have been followed. It's possible that drugs which are no longer recommended, or have even been banned, in the West are still being dispensed. In the bigger cities you have a better chance of getting proper medicine at a clean, well-equipped and busy pharmacy rather than at a small store which sells cigarettes and Coca-Cola as well. In small towns choose a pharmacy connected to a hospital or recommended by a doctor.

Health Preparations Make sure you're healthy before you start travelling. If you are embarking on a long trip make sure your teeth are OK: there are lots of places where a visit to the dentist would be the last thing you'd want to do.

If you wear glasses take a spare pair and your prescription. Losing your glasses can be a real problem, although in many places you can get new spectacles made quickly, cheaply and competently.

If you require a particular medication take an adequate supply, as it may not be available locally. Take the prescription, with the generic rather than the brand name (which may not be locally available), as it will make getting replacements easier. It's a wise idea to have the prescription with you to show you legally use the medication.

Immunisations Vaccinations provide protection against diseases with which you might come into contact. For the Philippines no immunisations are necessary, but the further off the beaten track you go the more necessary it is to take precautions. For the Philippines a yellow fever vaccination is necessary only if you're coming from an infected area. Nevertheless, all vaccinations should be recorded on an International Health Certificate, which is available from your physician or government health department.

When organising your vaccinations make sure you plan well ahead as some of them require an initial shot followed by a booster, while some vaccinations should not be given together. Most travellers from Western countries will have been immunised against various diseases during childhood, but your doctor may still recommend booster shots against measles or polio, diseases still prevalent in many developing countries. The period of protection offered by vaccinations differs widely and some are contraindicated if you are pregnant.

The possible list of vaccinations includes:

Tetanus & Diphtheria Boosters are necessary every 10 years and protection is highly recommended.

Typhoid Protection lasts for three years and is useful if you are travelling for long in rural, tropical areas. You may get some side effects such as pain at the injection site, fever, headache and a general unwell feeling.

Hepatitis A (Infectious Hepatitis) Gamma globulin is not a vaccination but a ready-made antibody which has proven very successful in reducing the chances of hepatitis infection. Because it may interfere with the development of immunity, it should not be given until at least 10 days after administration of the last vaccine; it should also be given as close as possible to departure because of its relatively short-lived protection period of six months.

Hepatitis B As in most tropical countries Hepatitis B occurs in the Philippines. Worldwide this disease kills more people in a single day than AIDS kills in a single year. The vaccine is quite expensive and you need three shots (the second shot four weeks after the first shot; the third shot six months after the second shot); a booster is necessary after every three to five years. For those people intending to spend a lot of time in the tropics, the investment is a worthwhile one.

Yellow Fever Protection lasts 10 years and is recommended if you are coming from places where the disease is endemic, chiefly Africa and South America. You usually have to go to a special yellow fever vaccination centre. Vaccination is contraindicated during pregnancy but if you must travel to a high-risk area it is probably advisable.

Basic Rules

Care in what you eat and drink is the most important health rule; stomach upsets are the most likely travel health problem but the majority of these upsets will be relatively minor. Don't become paranoid, trying the local food is part of the experience of travel after all.

Water Water in the cities should be safe to drink, but if you don't know for certain, always assume the worst. Ice from ice factories should be OK too, but sometimes it comes from tap water frozen in plastic bags, in which case you should be careful. Reputable brands of bottled water or soft drinks are generally fine.

Water Purification The simplest way of purifying water is to boil it thoroughly. Technically this means boiling for 10 minutes, something which happens very rarely!

Simple filtering will not remove all dangerous organisms, so if you cannot boil water it should be treated chemically. Chlorine tablets (Puritabs, Steritabs or other brand names) will kill many but not all pathogens. Iodine is very effective in purifying water and is available in tablet form (such as Potable Aqua), but follow the directions carefully and remember that too much iodine can be harmful.

If you can't find tablets, tincture of iodine (2%) or iodine crystals can be used. Two drops of tincture of iodine per litre or quart of clear water is the recommended dosage; the treated water should be left to stand for 30 minutes before drinking. Iodine crystals can also be used to purify water but this is a more complicated process, as you have to first prepare a saturated iodine solution. Iodine loses its effectiveness if exposed to air or damp so keep it in a tightly sealed container. Flavoured powder will disguise the taste of treated water and is a good idea if you are travelling with children.

Other Drinks Take care with fruit juice, particularly if water may have been added. Milk should be treated with suspicion, as it is often unpasteurised. Boiled milk is fine if it is kept hygienically and yoghurt is always good. Tea or coffee should also be OK, since the water should have been boiled.

Food Salads and fruit should be washed with purified water or peeled where possible. Ice cream is usually OK if the brand name is Magnolia, but beware of street vendors and of ice cream that has melted and been refrozen. Thoroughly cooked food is safest but not if it has been left to cool or been reheated. Take great care with shellfish and fish and avoid undercooked meat. In general, places that are packed with travellers or locals will be fine, while empty restaurants are dubious.

Nutrition If the food you are eating is of low nutritional value, if you're travelling hard and fast and therefore missing meals, or if you simply lose your appetite, you can soon start to lose weight and place your health at risk.

Make sure your diet is well balanced. Eggs, beans and nuts are all safe ways to obtain protein. Fruit you can peel (bananas, oranges or mandarins for example) is always safe and a good source of vitamins. Try to eat plenty of grains (eg rice). Remember that although food is generally safer if it is cooked well, overcooked food loses much of its nutritional value. If your diet isn't well balanced or if your food intake is insufficient, it's a good idea to take vitamin and iron pills.

In hot climates make sure you drink enough – don't rely on feeling thirsty to indicate when you should drink. Not needing to urinate or very dark yellow urine is a danger sign. Always carry a water bottle with you on long trips to avoid dehydration. Excessive sweating can lead to loss of salt and therefore muscle cramping. Salt tablets are not a good idea as a means of preventing dehydration, but adding salt to food can help.

Everyday Health A normal body temperature is 37°C (98.6°F); more than 2°C higher is a 'high' fever. A normal adult pulse rate is 60 to 80 beats per minute (children 80 to 100, babies 100 to 140). You should know how to take a temperature and a pulse rate. As a general rule, when somebody has a fever the pulse increases about 20 beats per minute for each degree Celsius rise in body temperature.

Respiration (breathing) rate can also be an indicator of illness. Count the number of breaths per minute: between 12 and 20 is normal for adults and older children (up to 30 for younger children, 40 for babies). People with a high fever or serious respiratory illness (like pneumonia) breathe more quickly than normal. More than 40 shallow breaths a minute usually means pneumonia.

Many health problems can be avoided by taking care of yourself. Wash your hands frequently as it's quite easy to contaminate your own food. Clean your teeth with purified water rather than water straight from the tap. Avoid climatic extremes: keep out of the sun when it's hot, dress warmly when it's cold. Avoid potential diseases by dressing sensibly. You can get worm infections through walking barefoot or dangerous coral cuts by walking over coral barefoot. You can avoid insect bites by covering bare skin when insects are around, by screening windows or beds or by using insect repellents (an excellent insect repellent is 'Off!').

Seek local advice: if you're told the water is unsafe because of jellyfish, crocodiles or bilharzia, don't go in. In situations where there is no information, play it safe.

Medical Problems & Treatment

Potential medical problems can be broken down into several areas. First there are the climatic and geographical considerations – problems caused by extremes of temperature, altitude or motion. Then there are diseases and illnesses caused by insanitation, insect bites or stings, and animal or human contact. Simple cuts, bites or scratches can also cause problems.

Self-diagnosis and treatment can be risky, so wherever possible seek qualified help. Although treatment dosages are given in this section, they are for emergency use only. Medical advice should be sought before administering any drugs.

An embassy or consulate can usually recommend a good place to go for such advice. So can five star hotels, although they often recommend doctors with five star prices. (This is when that medical insurance really comes in useful!) In some places standards of medical attention are so low that for some ailments the best advice is to get on a plane and go somewhere else.

Climatic & Geographical Considerations

Sunburn In the tropics, the desert or at high altitude you can get sunburnt surprisingly quickly, even through cloud cover. Use a sunscreen and take extra care to cover areas which don't normally see sun, eg, your feet. A hat provides added protection, and you should also use zinc cream or some other barrier cream for your nose and lips. Calamine lotion is good for mild sunburn.

Prickly Heat Prickly heat is an itchy rash caused by excessive perspiration trapped under the skin. It usually strikes people who have just arrived in a hot climate and whose pores have not yet opened sufficiently to cope with greater sweating. Keeping cool but bathing often, using a mild talcum powder or even resorting to air-conditioning may help until you acclimatise.

Heat Exhaustion Dehydration or salt deficiency can cause heat exhaustion. Take time to acclimatise to high temperatures and make sure you get sufficient liquids. Salt deficiency is characterised by fatigue, lethargy, headaches, giddiness and muscle cramps and in this case salt tablets may help. Vomiting or diarrhoea can deplete your liquid and salt levels. Anhydrotic heat exhaustion, caused by an inability to sweat, is quite rare.

Heat Stroke This serious, and sometimes fatal, condition can occur if the body's heat-regulating mechanism breaks down and the body temperature rises to dangerous levels. Long, continuous periods of exposure to high temperatures can leave you vulnerable to heat stroke. You should avoid excessive alcohol or strenuous activity when you first arrive in a hot climate.

The symptoms are feeling unwell, not sweating very much or at all and a high body temperature (39°C to 41°C). Where sweating has ceased, the skin becomes flushed and red. Severe, throbbing headaches and lack of coordination will also occur, and sufferers may become confused or aggressive. Eventually the victims will become delirious or convulse. Hospitalisation is essential, but meanwhile get patients out of the sun, remove their clothing, cover them with a wet sheet or towel and then fan them continually.

Fungal Infections Hot weather fungal infections are most likely to occur on the scalp, between the toes or fingers (athlete's foot), in the groin (jock itch or crotch rot) and on the body (ringworm). You get ringworm (which is a fungal infection, not a worm) from infected animals or by walking on damp areas, like shower floors.

To prevent fungal infections wear loose, comfortable clothes, avoid artificial fibres, wash frequently and dry carefully. If you do get an infection, wash the infected area daily with a disinfectant or medicated soap and water, and rinse and dry well. Apply an anti-fungal powder like the widely available Tinaderm. Try to expose the infected area to air or sunlight as much as possible and wash all towels and underwear in hot water as well as changing them often.

Motion Sickness Eating lightly before and during a trip will reduce the chances of motion sickness. If you are prone to motion sickness try to find a place that minimises disturbance – near the wing on aircraft, close to midships on boats, near the centre on buses. Fresh air usually helps while reading or cigarette smoke doesn't. Commercial antimotion-sickness preparations, which can cause drowsiness, have to be taken before the trip commences: when you're feeling sick it's too late. Ginger is a natural preventative and is available in capsule form.

Diseases of Insanitation

Diarrhoea A change of water, food or climate can all cause the runs; diarrhoea caused by contaminated food or water is more serious. Despite all your precautions you may still have a bout of mild travellers' diarrhoea, but a few rushed toilet trips with no other symptoms is not indicative of a serious problem. Moderate diarrhoea, involving half-a-dozen loose movements in a day, is more of a nuisance. Dehydration is the main danger with diarrhoea, particularly for children, so fluid replenishment is the number one treatment. Weak black tea with a little sugar, soda water, or soft drinks allowed to go flat and diluted 50% with water are all good. With severe diarrhoea a rehydrating solution is necessary to replace minerals and salts. You should stick to a bland diet as you recover.

Lomotil or Imodium can be used to bring relief from the symptoms, although they do not cure the problem. Only use these drugs if absolutely necessary – eg, if you *must* travel. For children Imodium is preferable, but do not use these drugs if the patient has a high fever or is severely dehydrated.

Antibiotics can be very useful in treating severe diarrhoea, especially if it is followed by nausea, vomiting, stomach cramps or mild fever. Ampicillin, a broad spectrum penicillin, is usually recommended. Two capsules of 250 mg each taken four times a day is the recommended dose for an adult. Children aged between eight and 12 years should have half the adult dose; younger children should have half a capsule four times a day. Note that if the patient is allergic to penicillin, ampicillin should not be administered.

Giardia This intestinal parasite is present in contaminated water. The symptoms are stomach cramps, nausea, a bloated stomach, watery, foul-smelling diarrhoea and frequent gas. Giardia can appear several weeks after you have been exposed to the parasite. The symptoms may disappear for a few days and then return; this can go on for several weeks. Metronidazole, known as Flagyl, is the recommended drug, but it should only be taken under medical supervision. Antibiotics are of no use.

Dysentery This serious illness is caused by contaminated food or water and is characterised by severe diarrhoea, often with blood or mucus in the stool. There are two kinds of dysentery. Bacillary dysentery is characterised by a high fever and rapid development; headaches, vomiting and stomach pains are also symptoms. It generally does not last longer than a week, but it is highly contagious.

Amoebic dysentery is more gradual in developing, causes no fever or vomiting but is a more serious illness. It is not a self-limiting disease: it will persist until treated and can recur and cause long-term damage.

A stool test is necessary to diagnose which kind of dysentery you have, so you should seek medical help urgently. In case of an emergency, note that tetracycline is the prescribed treatment for bacillary dysentery, and metronidazole that for amoebic dysentery.

With tetracycline, the recommended adult dosage is one 250 mg capsule four times a day. Children aged between eight and 12 years should have half the adult dose; the dosage for younger children is one-third the adult dose. It's important to remember that tetracycline should be given to young children only if it's absolutely necessary and only for a short period; pregnant women should not take it after the fourth month of pregnancy.

With metronidazole, the recommended adult dosage is one 750 mg to 800 mg capsule three times daily for five days. Children aged between eight and 12 years should have half the adult dose; the dosage for younger children is one-third the adult dose.

Cholera Cholera vaccination is not very effective. However, outbreaks of cholera are often widely reported, so you can avoid such problem areas. The disease is characterised by a sudden onset of acute diarrhoea with 'rice water' stools, vomiting, muscular cramps, and extreme weakness. You need medical help, but treat for dehydration, which can be extreme, and if there is an appreciable delay in getting to hospital, begin taking tetracycline. See the Dysentery section for dosages and warnings.

Viral Gastroenteritis This is caused not by bacteria but, as the name suggests, by a virus. It is characterised by stomach cramps, diarrhoea, and sometimes by vomiting and/or a slight fever. All you can do is rest and drink lots of fluids.

Hepatitis Hepatitis A (Infectious Hepatitis) is the more common form of this disease and is spread by contaminated food or water. The first symptoms are fever, chills, headache, fatigue, feelings of weakness and aches and pains. This is followed by loss of appetite, nausea, vomiting, abdominal pain, dark urine, light-coloured faeces and jaundiced skin; the whites of the eyes may also turn yellow. In some cases there may just be a feeling of being unwell or tired, accompanied by loss of appetite, aches and pains and jaundiced skin. You should seek medical advice, but in general there is not much you can do apart from resting, drinking lots of fluids, eating lightly and avoiding fatty foods. People who have had hepatitis must forgo alcohol for six months after the illness, as hepatitis attacks the liver and it needs that amount of time to recover.

Hepatitis B, which used to be called serum hepatitis, is spread through sexual contact with an infected partner or through skin penetration. It could, for instance, be transmitted via dirty needles or blood transfusions. Avoid having your ears pierced, or tattoos or injections done if you have doubts about the sanitary conditions. The symptoms and treatment of type B are much the same as for type A, but gamma globulin as a prophylactic is effective against type A only. (See the earlier Hepatitis B section under Immunisations.)

Typhoid Typhoid fever is another gut infection that travels the faecal-oral route – ie, contaminated water and food are responsible. Vaccination against typhoid is not totally effective and, as it is one of the most dangerous infections, medical help must be sought.

In its early stages typhoid resembles many other illnesses: sufferers may feel like they have a bad cold or flu on the way, as the early symptoms are headache, sore throat and a fever which rises a little each day until it is around 40°C or more. The victim's pulse is often slow relative to the degree of fever present and gets slower as the fever rises, unlike a normal fever where the pulse increases. There may also be vomiting, diarrhoea or constipation.

In the second week the high fever and slow pulse continue and a few pink spots may appear on the body; trembling, delirium, weakness, weight loss and dehydration are other symptoms. If there are no further complications, the fever and other symptoms will slowly go during the third week. However, you must get medical help before this because pneumonia (acute infection of the lungs) or peritonitis (burst appendix) are common complications, and because typhoid is very infectious.

The fever should be treated by keeping the victim cool; dehydration should also be watched for. Chloramphenicol is the recommended antibiotic but there are fewer side effects with ampicillin. The adult dosage is two 250 mg capsules, four times a day. Children aged between eight and 12 years should have half the adult dose; younger children should have one-third the adult dose.

Patients who are allergic to penicillin should not be given ampicillin.

Worms These parasites are most common in rural, tropical areas and a stool test when you return home is not a bad idea. They can be present on unwashed vegetables or in undercooked meat and you can pick them up through your skin by walking barefoot. Infestations may not show up for some time, and, although they are generally not serious, if left untreated they can cause severe health problems. A stool test is necessary to pinpoint the problem and medication is often available over the counter.

Diseases Spread by People & Animals

Tetanus This potentially fatal disease is found in undeveloped tropical areas. It is difficult to treat but is preventable with immunisation.

Tetanus occurs when a wound becomes infected by bacteria which live in the faeces of animals or people, so clean all cuts, punctures or animal bites. Tetanus is also known as lockjaw, and the first symptom may be discomfort in swallowing, or a stiffening of the jaw and neck; this is followed by painful convulsions of the jaw and whole body.

Rabies Rabies is found in many countries and is caused by a bite or scratch by an infected animal. Dogs are a noted carrier. Any bite, scratch or even lick from an animal should be cleaned immediately and thoroughly. Scrub the area with soap and running water, and then clean with an alcohol solution. If there is any possibility that the animal is infected, medical help should be sought immediately. Even if the animal is not rabid, all bites should be treated seriously as they can become infected or result in tetanus. A rabies vaccination is now available and should be considered if you are in a high-risk situation – eg, if you intend to explore caves (bat bites could be dangerous) or work with animals.

Tuberculosis Although this disease is widespread in many developing countries, it is not a serious risk to travellers. Young children are more susceptible than adults, and vaccination is a sensible precaution for children under 12 travelling in endemic areas. TB is commonly spread by coughing or by unpasteurised dairy products from infected cows. Milk that has been boiled is safe to drink; the souring of milk to make yoghurt or cheese also kills the bacilli.

Diphtheria Diphtheria can be a skin infection or a more dangerous throat infection. It is spread by contaminated dust contacting the skin or by the inhalation of infected cough or sneeze droplets. Frequent washing and keeping the skin dry will help prevent skin infection. A vaccination is available to prevent the throat infection.

Sexually Transmitted Diseases Sexual contact with an infected partner spreads these diseases. While abstinence is the only 100% preventative, using condoms is also effective. Gonorrhoea and syphilis are the most common of these diseases; sores, blisters or rashes around the genitals, discharges or pain when urinating are common symptoms. Symptoms may be less marked or not observed at all in women. Syphilis symptoms eventually disappear completely, but the disease continues and can cause severe problems in later years. The treatment of gonorrhoea and syphilis is by antibiotics.

There are numerous other sexually transmitted diseases, for most of which effective treatment is available. However, there is no cure for herpes and there is also currently no cure for AIDS. The latter is becoming more widespread in the Philippines. Using condoms is the most effective preventative.

AIDS can be spread through infected blood transfusions – note that most developing countries cannot afford to screen blood for transfusions. It can also be spread by dirty needles – vaccinations, acupuncture and tattooing can be as dangerous as intravenous drug use if the equipment is not clean. If you do need an injection, it may be a good idea to buy a new syringe from a pharmacy and ask the doctor to use it.

It is still too difficult to determine with accuracy how widely spread AIDS is in the Philippines and where the main area of its dissemination lies. The only results available are from northern Olongapo and Angeles (where the USAF Clark Air Base operates). Of 10,000 'hospitality' girls examined by US and Philippine doctors there, 55 were positive: 36 from Olongapo and 19 from Angeles. In March 1989 the health authorities registered 13 deaths from AIDS nationwide, one of them in Angeles.

Insect-Borne Diseases

Malaria This serious disease is spread by mosquito bites. Symptoms include headaches, fever, chills and sweating which may subside and recur. Without treatment malaria can develop more serious, potentially fatal effects.

If you are travelling on Palawan and Mindanao where malaria is more widespread than in other parts of the Philippines, it is extremely important to take malarial prophylactics. These are available in various forms of malarial prophylactics, so ask your doctor for advice. They generally have to be taken for a period of time before you depart and after you return.

Antimalarial drugs do not actually prevent the disease but suppress its symptoms. Chloroquine is the usual malarial prophylactic; a tablet is taken once a week for two weeks before you arrive in the infected area and six weeks after you leave it. Chloroquine is quite safe for general use, side effects are minimal and it can be taken by pregnant women. Fansidar, once used as a chloroquine alternative, is no longer recommended as a prophylactic, as it can have dangerous side effects, but it may still be recommended as a treatment for malaria. Chloroquine is also used for malaria treatment but in larger doses than for prophylaxis.

Mosquitoes appear after dusk. Avoiding bites by covering bare skin and using an insect repellent will further reduce the risk of catching malaria. Insect screens on windows and mosquito nets on beds offer protection, as does burning a mosquito coil. Mosquitoes may be attracted by perfume, aftershave or certain colours. The risk of infection is higher in rural areas and during the wet season.

Dengue Fever There is no prophylactic available for this mosquito-spread disease; the main preventative measure is to avoid mosquito bites. A sudden onset of fever, headaches and severe joint and muscle pains are the first signs before a rash starts on the trunk of the body and spreads to the limbs and face. After a few more days, the fever will subside and recovery will begin. Serious complications are not common.

Typhus Typhus is spread by ticks, mites or lice. It begins as a bad cold, followed by a fever, chills, headache, muscular pains and a body rash. There is often a large painful sore at the site of the bite and nearby lymph nodes will be swollen and painful.

While tick typhus is spread by ticks, scrub typhus is spread by mites that feed on infected rodents and exists mainly in Asia and the Pacific Islands. You should take precautions if walking in rural areas in South-East Asia. Seek local advice on areas where ticks pose a danger and always check yourself carefully for ticks after walking in a danger area. A strong insect repellent can help, and serious walkers in tick areas should consider having their boots and trousers impregnated with benzyl benzoate and dibutylphthalate.

Cuts, Bites & Stings

Cuts & Scratches Skin punctures can easily become infected in hot climates and may be difficult to heal. Treat any cut with an antiseptic solution and mercurochrome. Where possible avoid bandages and Band-aids, which can keep wounds wet. Coral cuts are notoriously slow to heal, as the coral injects a weak venom into the wound. Avoid coral cuts by wearing shoes when walking on reefs, and clean any cut thoroughly.

Bites & Stings Bee and wasp stings are usually painful rather than dangerous. Calamine lotion will give relief and ice packs will reduce the pain and swelling. There are some spiders with dangerous bites but antivenins are usually available. Scorpion stings are notoriously painful and can be fatal. Scorpions often shelter in shoes or clothing.

Certain cone shells found in the Pacific have a dangerous or even fatal sting. There are various fish and other sea creatures which have dangerous stings or bites or which are dangerous to eat. Again, local advice is the best suggestion.

Snakes To minimise your chances of being bitten, always wear boots, socks and long trousers when walking through undergrowth where snakes may be present. Don't put your hands into holes and crevices, and be careful when collecting firewood.

Snake bites do not cause instantaneous death and antivenins are usually available. Keep the victim calm and still, wrap the bitten limb tightly, as you would for a sprained ankle, and then attach a splint to immobilise it. Then seek medical help, if possible with the dead snake for identification. Don't attempt to catch the snake if there is even a remote possibility of being bitten again. Tourniquets and sucking out the poison are now comprehensively discredited.

Jellyfish Local advice is the best way of avoiding contact with these sea creatures with their stinging tentacles. The box jellyfish found in inshore waters around northern Australia during the summer months is potentially fatal, but stings from most jellyfish are simply rather painful. Dousing in vinegar will deactivate any stingers which have not 'fired'. Calamine lotion, antihistamines and analgesics may reduce the reaction and relieve the pain.

Bedbugs & Lice Bedbugs live in various places, but particularly in dirty mattresses and bedding. Spots of blood on bedclothes or on the wall around the bed can be read as a suggestion to find another hotel. Bedbugs leave itchy bites in neat rows. Calamine lotion may help.

All lice cause itching and discomfort. They make themselves at home in your hair (head lice), your clothing (body lice) or in your pubic hair (crabs). You catch lice through direct contact with infected people or by sharing combs, clothing and the like. Powder or shampoo treatment will kill the lice and infected clothing should then be washed in very hot water.

Leeches & Ticks Leeches may be present in damp rainforest conditions; they attach themselves to your skin to suck your blood. Trekkers often get them on their legs or in their boots. Salt or a lit cigarette end will make them fall off. Do not pull them off, as the bite is then more likely to become infected. An insect repellent may keep them away. Vaseline, alcohol or oil will persuade a tick to let go. You should always check your body if you have been walking through a tick-infested area, as they can spread typhus.

Women's Health

Gynaecological Problems Poor diet, lowered resistance due to the use of antibiotics and even contraceptive pills can lead to vaginal infections when travelling in hot climates. Maintaining good hygiene and wearing skirts or loose-fitting trousers and cotton underwear will help to prevent infections.

Yeast infections, characterised by a rash, itch and discharge, can be treated with yoghurt, or a vinegar or lemon-juice douche. Nystatin suppositories are the usual medical prescription. Trichomonas is a more serious infection; symptoms are a discharge and a burning sensation when urinating. Male sexual partners must also be treated, and if a vinegar-water douche is not effective, medical attention should be sought. Flagyl is the prescribed drug.

Pregnancy Most miscarriages occur during the first three months of pregnancy, so this is the riskiest time to travel. The last three months should also be spent within reasonable distance of good medical care, as quite serious problems can develop at this time. Pregnant women should avoid all unnecessary medication, but vaccinations and malarial prophylactics should still be taken where necessary. Additional care should be taken to prevent illness and particular attention should be paid to diet and nutrition.

Contraceptive Pills & Tampons Contraceptive pills and tampons are available in the larger towns and in tourist areas, but it's still advisable to take some with you. Tampons are hard to come by, and indeed are hardly known of, so you need to give the pharmacy staff a good description of what it is you are after when you send them off to search the shelves!

DANGERS & ANNOYANCES

Security

If you throw your money on the table in bars and restaurants, or flash large banknotes around, don't be surprised if you get mugged on the corner when you leave. Stupidity is punished and the big and small-time gangsters in Manila are waiting for opportunities, just like their counterparts anywhere else in the world.

Look after your valuables and don't even let on that you have them. You will be taken for a wealthy foreigner regardless, even if you are not well off by Western standards and have saved for ages for your trip. Insolent behaviour will only provoke a challenge. This is particularly the case at Christmas, when the time for love and peace mobilises a whole army of thieves and beggars to pay for their gifts with the help of money from tourists and locals alike.

Here are some hints on how to guard your possessions and look after your own safety:

Money belongs in your front trouser pockets, in a pouch worn around your neck and under your clothes, or in a concealed money belt. Don't make it easy for pickpockets, as they are often very skilful.

Keep shoulder bags or camera bags in body contact; don't let them out of your sight. Develop the habit of keeping your hand underneath them: Filipinos with razors are quiet and quick.

Avoid dark alleys at night, especially if you have been enjoying San Miguel beer or Tanduay rum.

Don't pay your taxi fare until all of your luggage is unloaded.

Deposit valuables in the hotel safe, or rent a safe-deposit box at a large bank: it will cost about P150 a year. This is recommended if you want to deposit tickets, documents, travellers' cheques or souvenirs for any length of time while travelling around the country. An important thing to remember when leaving is that all the banks are closed on public holidays. Unfortunately, it's very difficult to get an empty safe-deposit box: either they are all allocated or the bank will not accept deposits for only a short time.

Don't reveal the name of your hotel and especially not your room number to just anyone who asks for it. In an emergency, give a false address spontaneously and believably.

Look over your hotel room carefully before you check out: anything left behind becomes the property of whoever finds it.

If at any stage you should be held up – by someone on a bike in a dark alley, for instance – don't try to defend yourself. Filipinos shoot quickly.

Wherever there are tourists there are thieves: for example pickpockets and transvestites in Ermita and amateur and professional thieves in the buses to Batangas and the pier for Puerto Galera. Be particularly cautious around Ermita, especially in Mabini St and Rizal Park.

Caution, Trap!

Recently there appears to have been an upsurge of thieves who specialise in robbing travellers, so beware. Usually these situations are provoked by gullibility and misplaced trust. It's only a small percentage of Filipinos who should be avoided and if you keep your wits about you, there should be no problems. It's not necessary to become totally insecure, but the following ruses have all been used:

If someone runs up to you, anxiously advising you that your money has been stolen, stay calm and don't immediately reach for the place where you keep your money. The pickpocket is just waiting for you to give your hiding place away.

A popular spot for deceit is the main Manila office of Philippine Airlines in Roxas Blvd. This is usually a busy place and such activities can go unnoticed. For instance, you may be approached by a very pregnant woman who, working together with a young man, will start chatting and later invite you to a sightseeing tour of the town, or to her home. This offer of friendship will usually end with you losing your money.

I have also had reports of fraud in Baguio and Banaue. Tourists are approached by one or two attractive young Filipinas (or two friendly Filipino men) who are well dressed and speak good English, and are invited for coffee, which tastes a bit strange (not uncommon for native coffee in this area). After five or 10 minutes the visitors are out cold, and wake up 12 hours later in a park or field somewhere with all their valuables gone.

If someone tries to get hold of the name of your bank or your account number under some pretext, be careful. If, as well, either before or after this attempt, you are asked if they can leave some of their stuff with your things, look out. Now they have an excuse to look through your things as well as theirs and possibly find your bank account number, and with this information they can telex your bank to send money to an account they have set up in your name.

If a complete stranger comes up to you, especially in the Ermita district (Mabini St, Pistang Pilipino and Rizal Park) and hands you a line about remembering you (for example 'Hello my friend, do you remember me from the airport...San Fernando...I was your bus driver, etc) and suggests showing you the town or inviting you to dinner, don't accept. Others may claim that they were the customs or immigration officer when you arrived at Ninoy Aquino International Airport recently. They weren't. Another line is: 'We're also strangers here, but we know people who can show us the town together'. Invitations to a party from such a stranger will usually end up with you being drugged, robbed and abandoned.

Another is to claim that a sister will be flying next week to, for example Germany, Australia or the USA and – what a coincidence – will be working as a nurse in the same town as you come from. However, before her departure she would like to be reassured by hearing something more about the country and the town. This is merely a pretext to lure you to a house and rob you. It's a well-practised trick in Baguio.

Beware also of Westerners who either can't or don't want to go home, and talk about 'extremely promising' ideas or having good connections. They will tell you that all they need is an investor and will assure you they're not in the least worried about how small or large the investment might be.

In the Philippines there is a pair of resident foreigners

who bestow bogus hospitality on travellers, take them to their house in the country and present them with a juicy bill afterwards.

Never join a card game with Filipinos – you'll always lose. If the 'cousin' of your host allegedly works at the casino, and offers to coach you in tricks, don't be taken in. I've met people who, after losing three games, still haven't realised the syndicate was working against them.

And then there are the fake police who cruise through the tourist quarters of Manila in twos or threes in a new limousine. They stop tourists from their 'squad' car, showing them a false police badge and, on the pretext of checking for counterfeit currency allegedly in circulation, ask them to step into the vehicle for a few minutes. Then these very experienced and terribly obliging gentlemen will kindly offer to check your money to make sure it's genuine. While doing this they skilfully and swiftly help themselves to some of the cash, and on handing back the rest, will reassure you that the notes are perfectly good. And just to complete the trick, as you alight they'll helpfully draw your attention to the pickpockets and petty criminals (who get bolder every day) allegedly waiting for you on every street corner.

There are a few points you should be aware of so you'll know who you're dealing with. It is extremely rare for Filipino police officers to show a badge as ID: usually their mark of authenticity is the neatly pressed uniform or the revolver hanging loosely from their belt. Plain-clothes police officers are more likely to get about in a T-shirt, jeans and gym shoes, than in smart fashionable suits. Number plates on police cars are, as on all government vehicles, white with red letters and numbers, and the first letter is as a rule 'S'. Number plates of licensed taxis are yellow with black lettering, and those of private vehicles are white with green lettering.

As well as meeting fake police officers, you may come into contact with a related species: false immigration officials, whose favourite haunt is the Intramuros/Rizal Park district. Their game is to demand to inspect tourists' passports, and then to return them only on payment of a handsome sum. In reality genuine immigration officials make only occasional random checks of tourists' passports, and most commonly in the red light district of Ermita. In any case they are normally satisfied with a photocopy: there's no need to have the original on you night and day.

Finally, remember that there will be new ideas and variations each year. Filipino thieves do not lack ingenuity or imagination. Don't let them spoil your trip.

Drugs

Since the early 1980s the laws governing drug abuse have grown increasingly severe in the Philippines. Unauthorised people are absolutely forbidden to handle, own or traffic in drugs.

So-called dangerous drugs are divided into two categories: prohibited drugs (opium, heroin, morphine, cocaine, LSD, marijuana); and regulated drugs (pharmaceutical drugs, sleeping pills, pain killers, etc).

Transgressions are punished very severely. Penalties range from six to 12 years imprisonment plus a fine of P6000 to P12,000 for possession of marijuana and go up to P14,000 to P30,000 plus the death penalty for manufacture, trafficking, or import or export of any of the prohibited drugs. The laws also impose these sorts of penalties for the abuse of regulated drugs, if possession and use is not certified by a doctor's prescription.

If a fine can't be paid in the time allowed, the accused is free to bring in a lawyer, or to obtain the services of the Legal Assistance Office – if its staff can be motivated into action!

FILM & PHOTOGRAPHY

Take sufficient slide film with you as there is not a lot of choice in the Philippines. This is especially true of the provinces, where the use-by date has often expired. Kodak Ektachrome 100 costs about P130, and a 200 costs P180. See the Film & Photography section of the Manila chapter.

There's no problem with normal colour film, which is often preferred by Filipinos. Development is fast and good value. High-gloss prints (nine cm by 13 cm) can be processed in an hour at a cost of P2.50 per print; cheaper processing will take longer.

Officially you are only allowed to bring five cartridges of film in with you, but the customs officials usually turn a blind eye in the case of tourists.

The usual rules for tropical photography apply in the Philippines. Remember to allow for the intensity of the tropical light, try to keep your film as cool and dry as possible and have it developed as soon as possible after exposure.

Although airport X-ray security equipment is said to be safe for films, that doesn't apply to frequent X-rays. If you're going to be passing through airport security checks on a number of occasions, it's wise to remove your film from your bag and have it inspected separately.

Remember that cameras can be one of the most intrusive and unpleasant reminders of the impact of tourism – it's polite to ask people before you photograph them. A smile always helps.

ACCOMMODATION

Have a look at the hotel room before you book in; inspect the showers and toilets and only then pay for the room. There are often cheaper rooms without windows in the inner part of the building. Hotels in the top category charge 25% for service and tax on top of the price of the room.

Throughout the Philippines you will find that prices for single and double rooms are sometimes the same. This is because single rooms sometimes have a double bed and can therefore be used by two people; to the Filipinos this is the same as a double room. Double rooms usually have two beds.

As there are frequently fires in the Philippines, you should check the exits. Having lived through a fire with useless fire equipment, been left hanging between floors in a lift several times due to power blackouts and having had to evacuate from a hotel because of an earthquake in Baguio, I've developed a preference for rooms on the ground floor. That may perhaps seem to be somewhat overcautious.

The lighting in hotel rooms is often rather dim. If in the evenings, instead of going out you want to read or write, you should get a light bulb of at least 60 watts beforehand.

It might be advisable to deposit any valuables in the hotel safe. If a simple drawer is used as a locker, don't entrust your things to the hotel. It is also inadvisable to put a large amount of cash in the care of the hotel reception.

If you do deposit your valuables in the hotel safe, get a receipt with an exact account of the details. Also ask whether you can get them back at any time. The night shift is not always entrusted with a key. When you do get your valuables back, check your cash and travellers' cheques carefully.

If you intend staying anywhere for some time inquire about weekly and monthly rents. For a long stay it is worthwhile taking a furnished apartment. This greatly reduces the expense. Even cheaper accommodation – known as 'bedspacing' – is available on a shared basis.

In the provinces you may often be invited into private homes. It is the custom in the Philippines to offer guests the best food and lodging, but this can be very expensive for the family. Don't take advantage of this custom, but don't offer money directly for your board and keep either – say it's to educate their children, for example.

Should you have accommodation difficulties in smaller towns, go to the mayor or barrio captain. He will quickly arrange some shelter for you and may even find a place for you in the government rest house.

Baths & Toilets

The term 'bath' has generally been used throughout the book to mean a bathroom that is equipped with a toilet and shower. It is only in first class international hotels that you can expect a bathtub. Private Filipino homes normally have a shower and not a bathtub.

The toilets are known as comfort rooms or CRs – *lalake* means 'gentlemen' and *babae* 'ladies' in Filipino. The toilets in restaurants and bars are usually dirty and there is seldom toilet paper, but you will always find clean toilets in the lobbies of the larger hotels. Although Shakey's Pizza Parlours have expensive pizzas they do have clean toilets!

FOOD & DRINK

Many Western travellers regard the Philippine diet as monotonous. Many dairy products are lacking and the daily fare consists of rice and fish, but if you are flexible you can add some variety. There are dairy products like milk, yoghurt, cheese and ice cream in most supermarkets, and meals can be varied by checking out the contents of the cooking pots in restaurants. In a turo-turo restaurant (turo means 'point') there is no menu: the food is displayed and customers point to what they would like to eat.

Of course the choice is more restricted in the country than in the city. In larger towns there are usually a number of Western and Chinese restaurants.

Filipino cuisine – with its Chinese, Malay and Spanish influences – is a mixture of Eastern and Western cuisine. The different dishes in a meal are all served at the same time with the result that certain dishes end up being eaten cold, something which Filipinos normally don't mind. Cold fried eggs for breakfast is a typically less-than-appetising possibility.

Apart from the regular meals, in the mornings and afternoons a more or less extensive snack called *merienda* is taken. Besides this, *pulutan* (small morsels and drinks) appear on the table when alcoholic drinks are served.

Progressive Filipinos usually eat with a spoon and fork; knives are not often used. However, the original *kamayan* mode, namely eating with the fingers off a banana leaf, has come back into fashion, so there is no cutlery laid on the table in a kamayan restaurant. Such restaurants are flourishing throughout the land.

It's worthwhile when travelling around to ask for the speciality of the province, which can be surprisingly good.

Eating & Drinking

As a rule of thumb, it is cheap and worthwhile eating where the locals eat, but even Western food is not that expensive. In some restaurants you can get a complete meal for around P75.

At the eateries in the larger towns, grills are very popular in the evenings. You can get liver, pork, chicken and seafood in the form of barbecue sticks. In the warm summer months of April and May, when selecting your choice of fresh meat for grilling, check it out with your nose first.

Water in the Philippines is always clean and drinkable, at least in the towns. In the country it pays to be a bit more careful. I would advise against ice cream in open containers from a travelling vendor. It would be better to buy the packaged Magnolia Dairy Bars.

The Filipino Menu

Rice is the staple food and will be served with most meals. A particular addition to the make-up of the dish requires skilful preparation.

The following description of Philippine foods and drinks may make it a little easier to choose when confronted with a menu.

Adobo – A national standard dish made from chicken, pork, octopus and/or vegetables and cooked with vinegar, pepper and garlic.

Adobong Pusit – Cleaned cuttlefish is prepared with coconut milk, vinegar and garlic. The ink is used as a special seasoning.

Ampalaya con Carne – Beef with bitter melon, prepared with onions, garlic, soy sauce and some sesame oil. Served with rice.

Arroz Caldo – Fried rice with chicken cooked with onions, garlic and ginger, and black pepper added afterwards.

Asado – Seasonal smoked meat, served with sour papaya strips (atsara).

Aso – Dog! Stray mongrel in a piquant sauce. This is a special dish in central and North Luzon. Because of many protests from dog-loving countries, this practice is now forbidden. The Ifugao have lodged an appeal with the government for exemption, stating that aso is a fundamental part of their culture and tradition.

Atsara – This is a very healthy and vitamin- rich side dish, the Philippine sauerkraut – unripe papayas.

Balut – This is a favourite Filipino snack which will keep you healthy. Baluts can be purchased from street sellers and markets. A balut is a half-boiled, ready-to-hatch duck egg. You can distinguish the beak and feathers! Some baluts still contain some liquid so don't break open the whole egg: make a small hole first.

Bangus (Milkfish) – This is a herring-size fish that is lightly grilled, stuffed and baked.

Batchoy – This consists of beef, pork and liver in noodle soup. A speciality of the western Visayas.

Calamares Fritos – Fried squid.

Calderata – A stew of goat's meat or beef, peas and paprika.

Crispy Pata – Pig skin first cooked then seasoned with garlic, salt, pepper and vinegar, and then baked in oil till crispy. There are many ways of seasoning and preparing it. Crispy pata is often served cut into small pieces. There is usually more crackling than meat – which is how the Filipinos like it!

Gambas al Ajillo – Shelled raw shrimps prepared with olive oil, pepper, salt, some paprika and a lot of garlic. Served with white bread.

Ginataan – Dishes cooked in coconut milk.

Halo-Halo – Dessert made from crushed ice mixed with coloured sweets and fruits (halo-halo means 'all mixed together'), covered with evaporated milk. It tastes noticeably better with a little rum.

Inihaw – Grilled fish or meat.

Kare-Kare – A stew of oxtail, beef shank, vegetables, onions and garlic. The stock can be enriched with peanuts and lightly fried rice, both finely ground.

Kilawin – Small cuts of raw meat lightly roasted, then marinated in vinegar and other spices (ginger, onion, salt).

Kinilaw – Small cuts of raw fish or cuttlefish marinated with spices (ginger, onion, chilli) in vinegar or lemon.

Lapu-Lapu Inihaw – Grilled grouper, seasoned with salt, pepper, garlic and soy sauce. Lapu-Lapu is the most popular fish dish in the country, but is expensive. It was named after the Filipino chief who killed Ferdinand Magellan in battle.

Lechon – Suckling pig served with a thick liver sauce. Lechon (*litson*) is an important dish at fiestas.

Lechon Kawali – Pork leg, crisply baked and seasoned with green papaya, ginger, vinegar and sugar.

Lumpia – Spring rolls filled with vegetables or meat. They are served with soy sauce, vinegar or a slightly sweet sauce.

Lumpia Shangai – These are small fried spring rolls filled with meat, whereas the bigger *lumpia sariwa* are filled with vegetables and served uncooked.

Mami – Noodle soup; when made with chicken it's chicken mami, with beef it's beef mami, etc.

Menudo – Stew made from either small liver pieces or chopped pork, with diced potatoes, tomatoes, paprika and onions.

Misua Soup – Soup made from rice noodles, beef, garlic and onions.

Pancit Canton – This is a spicy noodle dish made with thick noodles which are baked, then mixed with pork, shrimps and vegetables. The pork is cooked in soy sauce beforehand.

Pancit Guisado – This is a noodle dish like pancit canton but is less spicy, and thin Chinese noodles are used.

Pork Adobo – Baked pork is prepared with white coconut milk, garlic, peppercorns and salt. There is usually more fat than meat.

Pork Apritada – Pork is cut into small pieces and baked. The sauce includes pieces of tomato, onions, potatoes, pepperoni and garlic.

Shrimp Rebosado – Shrimps are baked in butter then cooked in a roux.

Sinigang – This is sour vegetable soup with fish (*sinigang na isda*) or pork (*sininang na baboy*). It can be served with rice.

Siopao – A white, steam heated dough ball with a filling such as chicken or pork. A quick snack.

Tahong – Large green mussels are cooked or baked in sauce.

Talaba – Raw oysters are soaked in vinegar and garlic.

Tapa – This is baked dried beef served with raw onion rings. Tapa is also available as a vacuum-packed preserved food but this tastes dreadful – remarkably like plastic.

Tinola – A stew of chicken, vegetables, onions and garlic.

Tropical Fruit

In a tropical country like the Philippines you would expect to find many colourful fruit stalls, but you would be looking in vain. Naturally, fruits like pineapple, bananas, papaya and mangoes are available, but not on every street corner.

Atis (Custard Apple) – Also known as 'sugar apple' or 'cinnamon apple', this fruit has a scaly, grey-green skin and looks rather like a hand grenade. To get at its soft white flesh it's best to cut the custard apple in half and remove its kernel with a knife. The skin is not palatable. The fruit is in season from August to October.

Atis (Custard apple)

Chico (Sapodilla) – This egg-shaped fruit with brown skin contains a soft, sweet, brownish pulp. The skin is normally peeled off but you can also eat it. It's in season from November to February.

Chico (Sapodilla)

Durian (Durian) – This is the name of a thick, prickly fruit, about which opinions are sharply divided: either you're crazy about it or you can't stand it. There's no in-between. This fruit, with its 'hellish stench and heavenly taste', is in season from August to October.

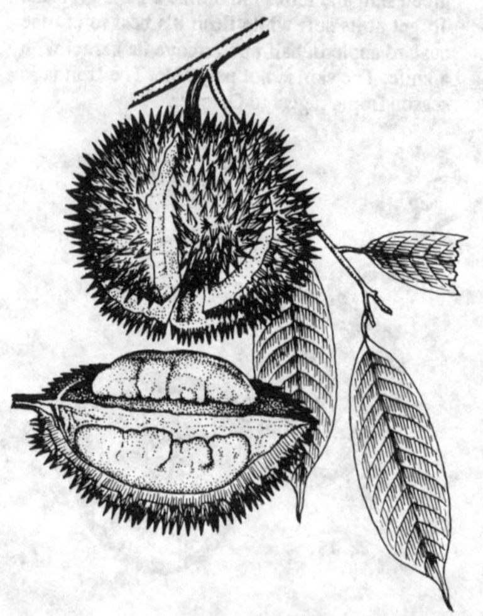

Durian (Durian)

Kaimito (Star Apple) – Slicing a star apple reveals an arrangement of several star shaped segments, hence its name. Soft and very juicy, it is best eaten with a spoon. It's in season from January to March.

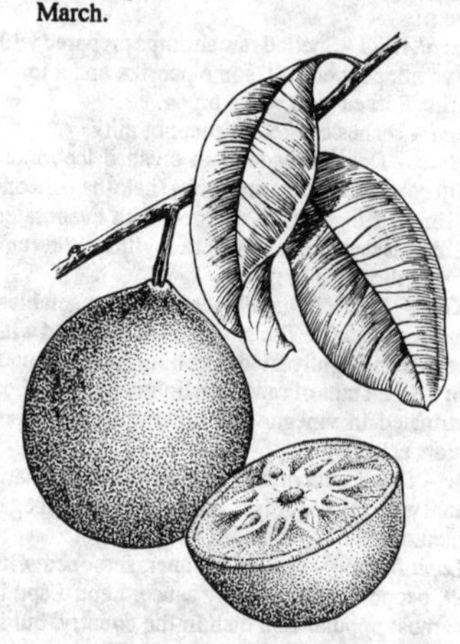

Kaimito (Star apple)

Kalamansi (Kalamansi) – This juicy, green lemon-like fruit is about the size of a pinball. It goes beautifully with black tea and is indispensable in the Filipino kitchen for the preparation of 'happy hour' drinks at sunset or whenever.

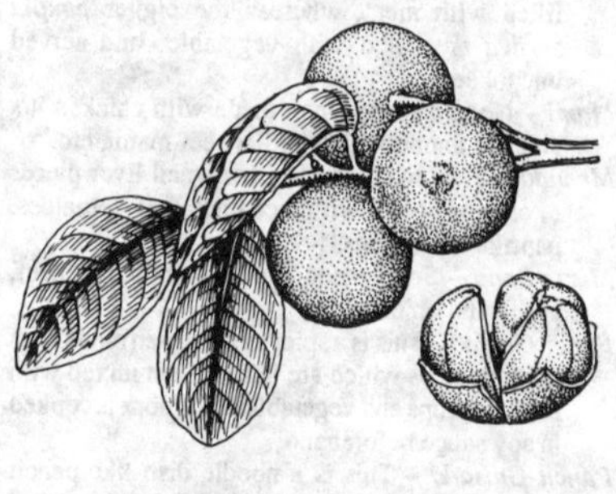

Kalamansi (Kalamansi)

Langka (Jackfruit) – This is a colossus among fruit. Greenish yellow with coarse skin, it can weigh up to 20 kg and may be as big as a blown-up balloon. Filipinos carve its pale yellow flesh into portions and have it in salads or as a vegetable. The jackfruit season is from February to July.

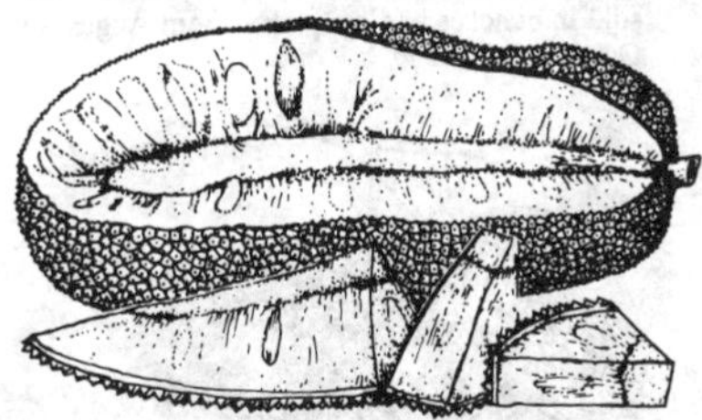

Langka (Jackfruit)

Lanzones (Lanson) – This looks like a little potato. Under its easily peeled, yellow-brown skin is a delicious, translucent flesh. It's in season from August to November.

Lanzones (Lanson)

Mangga (Mango) – This oval shaped fruit can be up to 20 cm long and has a large, flat stone. When the skin is green it is unripe, hard and very sour, but tastes marvellous with salt or a bitter, salty shrimp-paste called bagoong. The flesh of a ripe mango is yellow, juicy and vaguely reminiscent of the peach in taste. It's in season between April and June.

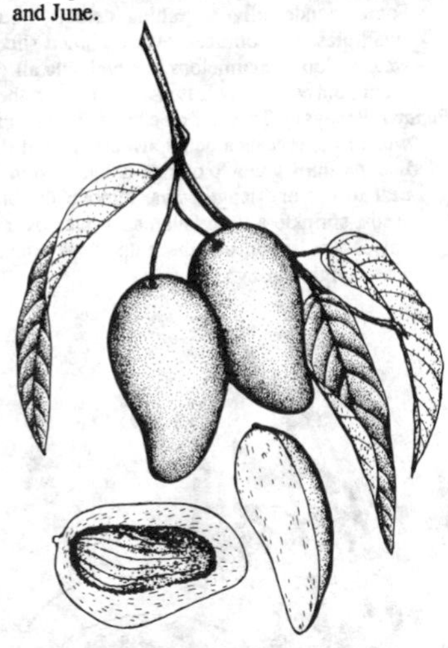

Mangga (Mango)

Mangostan (Mangosteen) – This dark purple fruit is about the size of an apple and has a tough skin. You'll need a knife to get at its sweet, white flesh. It's in season from May to October.

Mangostan (Mangosteen)

Pakwan (Watermelon) – The size of a football, the flesh of this dark-green melon is red and watery. For a wonderfully refreshing dessert, pour a small glass of Cointreau over a chilled slice of watermelon. Watermelons are available all year round, but especially from April to November.

Papaya (Papaya) – This is a species of melon which, when ripe, reveals a delicious, orange-red flesh under a shiny green to orange-coloured skin. It's best to cut one lengthways, remove the black seeds, sprinkle a little kalamansi juice over the halves and spoon out the pulp. Papaya are in season right through the year.

Papaya (Papaya)

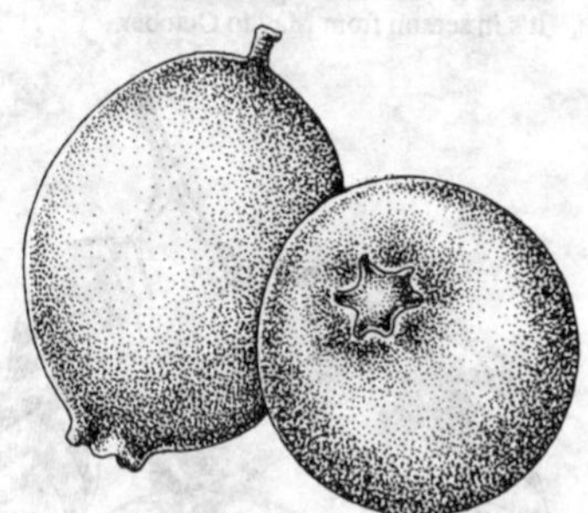

Pasionaryo (Passion fruit)

Pasionaryo (Passion Fruit) – The passion fruit is also known as *maracuja*. Under its skin you'll find a surprisingly sweet, liquid pulp which is best spooned out. The abundant seeds can be eaten too. The passion fruit is mostly available from March to October.

Pina (Pineapple) – Pineapples can be bought the whole year round. They're at their juiciest and sweetest during the main season from March to May.

Rambutan (Rambutan) – This is a funny-looking fruit, shaped rather like an egg with a reddish, hairy skin. Under the cute packaging you'll find a delicious translucent sweet pulp. Rambutans are sold in bunches and are picked from August to October.

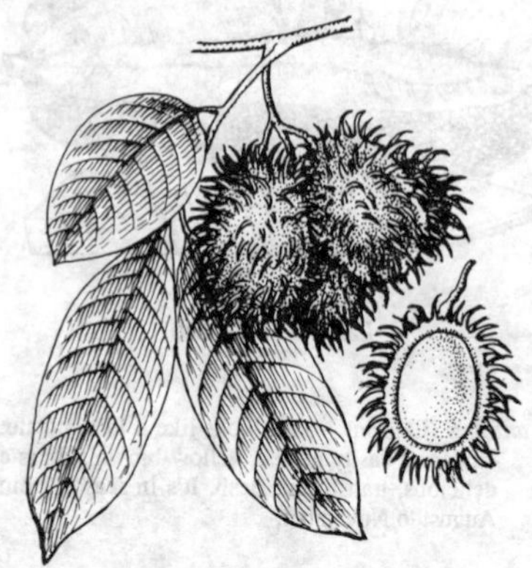

Rambutan (Rambutan)

Saging (Banana) – There are over 20 known varieties. Bananas are available all year round. You can have them not only as freshly picked fruit, but also cooked, grilled, baked or roasted.

Suha (Giant orange)

Suha (Giant Orange) – This fruit also goes by the name of *pomelo* and resembles a huge grapefruit. It tastes rather like a grapefruit too, except that it's somewhat sweeter. You'll have to peel away a very thick skin to get at the flesh, which is usually fairly dry. You can get giant oranges right through the year.

Drinks

Most of the drinks in the Philippines are safe as they are bottled, including milk and chocolate drinks. Fruit juices served with water are also quite safe. However, it's best to avoid unbottled drinks or drinks with ice cubes.

Coconut Juice Only very young coconuts (*buko*) with their soft, nutritious flesh are considered edible in the Philippines. The hard flesh of older coconuts is dried in the sun and processed as copra. If you want to enjoy the delicious, refreshing juice of a young nut, get the fruit seller to open it for you to drink.

Here's a small tip for a taste sensation: pour out some of the coconut milk, insert small pieces of papaya, pineapple and, if possible, mango, top up the contents with rum and let it stand for about 12 hours in the refrigerator.

Alcohol *Tuba* is a palm wine made from the juice of coconut palms. It is tapped from the crown of the tree. Tuba is drunk fresh or after a fermentation process. When distilled it is called *lambanog*.

An alcoholic drink made from fermented sugar cane juice is *basi*, an ice-cooled variant of which has a taste reminiscent of sherry or port. The reddish colour is obtained by adding guava leaves and the bark of the *duhat* tree during fermentation. *Tapuy* (*tapey*) is a rice wine and the end of its six-month fermentation process is eagerly anticipated. Only after this period can you discover whether the aimed-for taste has been achieved or if the wine has become sour and undrinkable.

There are several brands of beer. Apart from the strong Red Horse beer, they are all light and, with a few exceptions, are very good to drink. San Miguel is the most well-known beer and, with over a 90% share of the market, is also the most successful. Relatively new on the market from Denmark is Carlsberg, which is brewed and bottled in the Philippines, but whether it's 'probably the best beer in the world' or not is a matter of taste. A beer from northern Germany is Jever, but whether they continue to import it will depend on sales.

Hard drinks – rum, whisky, gin and brandy – of local manufacture are very good value. The well-aged rums of particularly fine quality are Tanduay, Anejo and Tondena.

Something approximating an egg liqueur can be made by mixing the yolks of six raw eggs, one bottle of gin genebra and half a tin of condensed milk. Preferably served cold. Cheers!

BOOKS & BOOKSHOPS

Manila has a good selection of bookshops – see the Bookshops section in the Manila chapter for details. There is a fairly active local publishing industry, mainly in English. Books on the Philippines tend to fall into either the coffee-table variety or the rather dry facts and history group.

Among the history books is *A Short History of the Philippines* (Mentor Pocketbook, Manila, 1975) by Teodoro Agoncillo; *The Philippines* by Onofre D Corpuz; and *Readings in Philippine History* (Bookmark, Manila, 1965) by Horacio de la Costa, which is good if you're not too fond of formal history. *For Every Tear a Victory* by Hartzell Spence is said to be the best Marcos biography. *Shadows on the Land – An Economic Geography of the Philippines* (Bookmark, Manila, 1963) by Robert E Huke may also be of interest.

Interesting books to look for on specific Philippine topics include *The Truth behind Faith Healing in the Philippines* (National Book Store, Manila, 1981) by Jaime T Licauco. *The Yakans of Basilan Island* (Fotomatic Inc, Cebu City, 1976) by Andrew D Sherfan or *T'boli Art* (Filipinas Foundation Inc, Makati, 1978) by Gabriel S Casal will be of interest to those wanting more information on the people of Mindanao and the south. A handy, easy-to-carry Filipino/English dictionary is *The New Dictionary* (National Book Store, Manila, 1968) by Marie Odulio de Guzman.

MAPS

You can get comprehensive road maps of the Philippines from Petron, Mobil and other petrol companies. Petron's *The Philippine Motorists' Road Guide* is available in bookshops. The trilingual map of the *Philippines* (Nelles Verlag, Munich) is also worth having. Detailed survey maps and sea charts can be obtained from the Bureau of Coast & Geodetic Survey (see the Maps section of the Manila chapter).

For Manila, Metro Manila and environs within a radius of 50 km, Heinrich Engeler's city map of Manila, *Metro Manila*, is recommended. You'll find it at the National Book Store. Bookmark has published the three illustrated city maps *Metro Manila Landmarks*, *Baguio Landmarks* and *Makati*, which offer a bird's-eye view of the modern city's most important streets and noteworthy buildings. The lighthearted *Survival Map of Manila* gives full details on entertainment, restaurants and shopping.

THINGS TO BUY

There are many souvenirs you can buy in the Philippines, particularly in the handicrafts line. Cane work, woodcarving, clothes and articles made of shells are all popular. You can find many items in Manila, particularly around Ermita, in the Ilalim ng Tulay Market at the Quezon Bridge in Quiapo or the Shoemart department store in the Makati Commercial Center, but there is also a wide variety in Cebu, Davao and Zamboanga.

Clothing

The Philippines has become a major manufacturing centre for cheap Western-style clothing, but many men come away from the Philippines with the shirt which is the Filipino national dress – the long-sleeved barong tagalog or its short-sleeved version, the polo barong.

Woodwork

Much of the woodcarving is of the tourist-kitsch variety but you can also find some useful articles such as salad bowls. The Ifugao people in North Luzon's Mountain Province also produce some high-quality woodcarving.

Cane Work & Basketry

In South Luzon abaca products are the main craft. Abaca is a fibre produced from a relative of the banana tree. Its best known end product was the rope known as Manila hemp but today it's made into bags, placemats and other woven products. There's some interesting basket work from Mountain Province and the island of Bohol. Mats and cane furniture are also good buys.

Other Items

Shell jewellery, wind chimes and plain shells are all popular purchases. Zamboanga and Cebu are shell centres. The usual caveat emptor – where the buyer bears the risks of purchase unless the seller provides a warranty – applies to Philippine antiques. Brass ware is a speciality in Mindanao. Hand-woven cottons from Mountain Province are produced in such limited quantities they don't even reach Manila – they're much cheaper in Bontoc or Banaue than in Baguio.

Marble eggs and other marble items come from Romblon. Apart from the pineapple-fibre *(pina)* fabrics, Iloilo is also noted for *santos*, statues of saints. Cebu is the guitar centre of the Philippines, but note that cheap guitars are unlikely to be able to withstand drier, nontropical climates. Lilang's Guitar Factory on Mactan Island is a good place to buy one – you'll find pleasant people, and guitars for P150 to P2500.

ENTERTAINMENT

Cinemas

Cinemas are good value – for a few pesos you frequently get a double feature. There are particular starting times but no fixed entry times, which means there is a constant coming and going during the programmes. Disaster movies, murders and vampires are

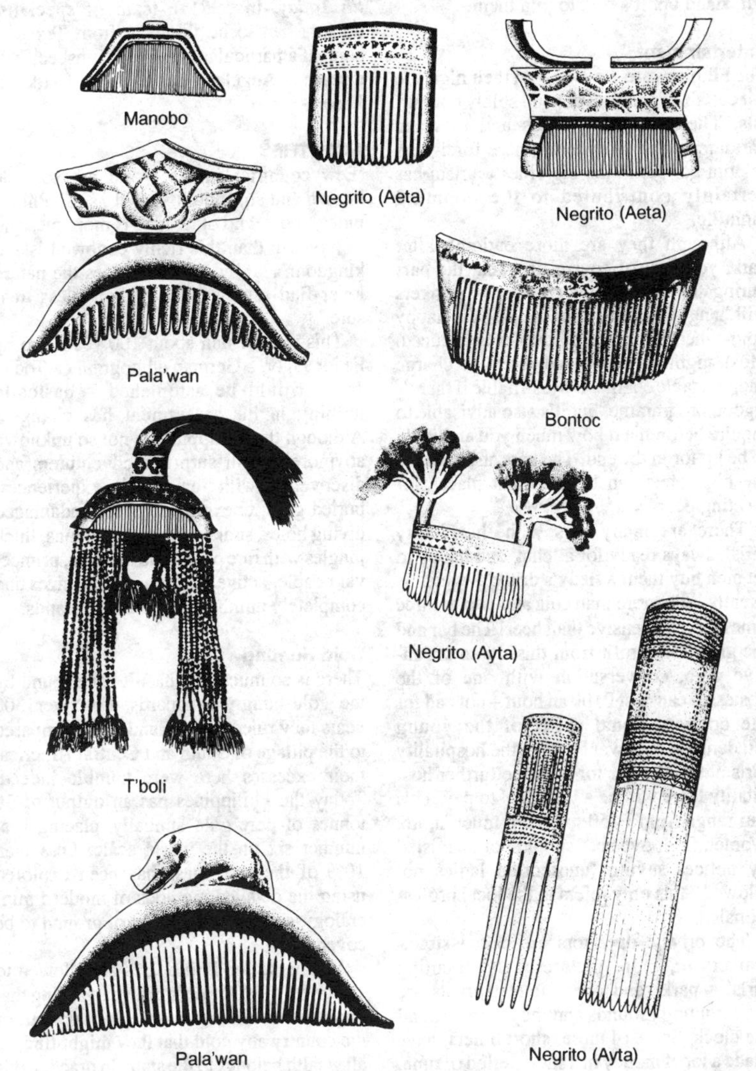

Combs

Decorated combs of wood, horn, bamboo and bone worn as hair ornaments by the various cultural minorities.

the preferred themes. Watch out for the national anthem – sometimes they play it at the end, sometimes at the beginning, usually not at all. If they do play it, all the Filipinos will stand up. It's best to join them.

Entertainment

The Filipinos are very keen on their nightlife – it certainly does not depend solely on tourists. There are bars, clubs and massage parlours in the provinces where foreigners seldom go, but in the big cities tourism has certainly contributed to the booming nightlife.

Although they are more enticing after dark, you can, of course, frequent the bars during the day. However, serious drinkers will hang on to their money until the happy hour when the price of drinks is reduced. Most nightclubs demand a cover charge and/or a table charge. It's justifiable if there's a good programme, but it's also advisable to inquire beforehand how much you are likely to be up for in the end. The bars and clubs of the big hotels can be excellent places for meeting people.

There are many bars with 'hospitality girls' always ready for a 'chat' and happy to let men buy them a 'lady's drink' – which is usually little more than cola and two to three times more expensive than beer! The bar and the girls both profit from this. In an expensive club, conversation with one of the hostesses can cost P100 an hour – not bad for the conversational skills of the young 'student'. If men want to take the hospitality girls out of the bar for possible further hospitality there will be a 'bar fine' to pay. This can range from P150 to much, much more. Women from overseas should not be misled by notices saying 'unescorted ladies not allowed': this only refers to the local professionals.

The private operators are called streetwalkers or, more picturesquely, 'hunting girls' – parks and open-air restaurants are their hunting grounds and they work around the clock. Some of these 'short timers' have made a lot of money in a short period of time. Manila has a somewhat similar reputation to Bangkok and both share a particularly virulent form of VD. Any 'cultural interchange' of an intimate nature should be accompanied by suitable precautions. According to *Bulletin Today*, in 1981 a team of specialist doctors had to be flown in from Texas to combat a particularly resistant 'unspecified' disease at Angeles – at the USAF Clark Air Base.

ACTIVITIES

'Few countries in the world are so little known and so seldom visited as the Philippines, and yet no other land is more pleasant to travel in than this richly endowed island kingdom. Hardly anywhere does the nature lover find a greater fill of boundless treasure.'

This was written about 100 years ago by Fedor Jagor, a German ethnographer. Today Jagor would be astonished – basically nothing in his assessment has changed. Although the Philippines is not so unknown anymore, it still surprises adventurers and discoverers with remarkable experiences: buried gold, unexplored caves, undamaged diving holes, sunken Spanish galleons, thick jungles with rare plants and animals, primaeval people, active volcanoes of all sizes and completely uninhabited paradise islands.

Gold Hunting

There is so much that hasn't been found by the gold-hungry Spaniards. For over 300 years they ruled these islands, yet compared to the pillage of South and Central America, their excesses here were humble indeed. Today the Philippines has an output of 30 tonnes of pure gold annually, placing it at number six on the world scale. Less than 10% of the land mass has been explored using the detailed methods of modern mineralogy, so there is still a lot of ground to be covered.

Visitors to the Philippines are allowed to search for gold, the only drawback being that they are not allowed to keep or take out of the country any gold that they might find, as all wealth belongs to the state. In practice this is not always adhered to very strictly.

Baskets

Baskets of various shapes, patterns and colours of bamboo, rattan, buri and pandanus are made by the cultural minorities of Mountain Province (North Luzon) and the island of Bohol.

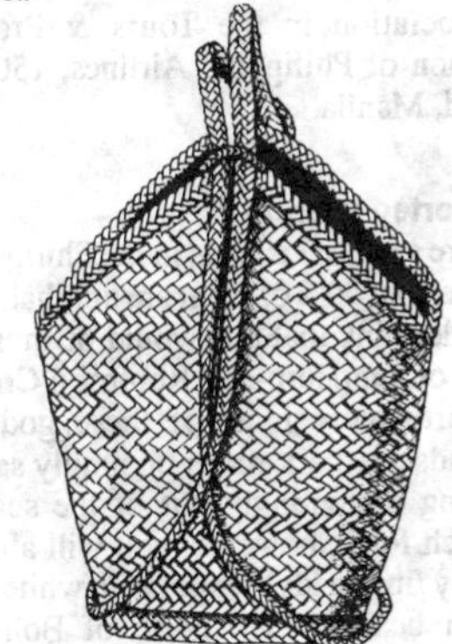

Carry basket

Snake basket

Hand basket

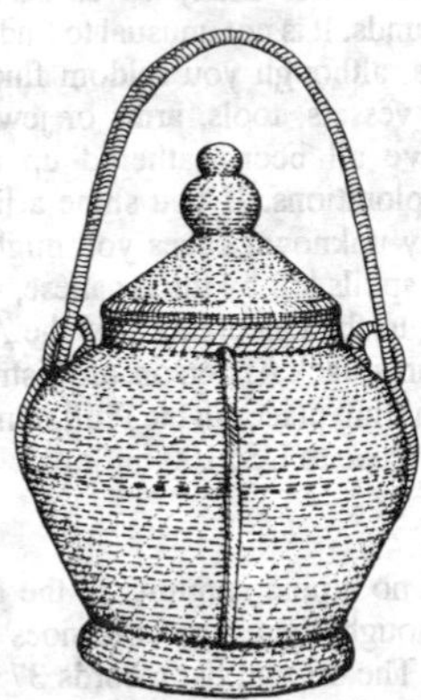

Grain container

Backpack

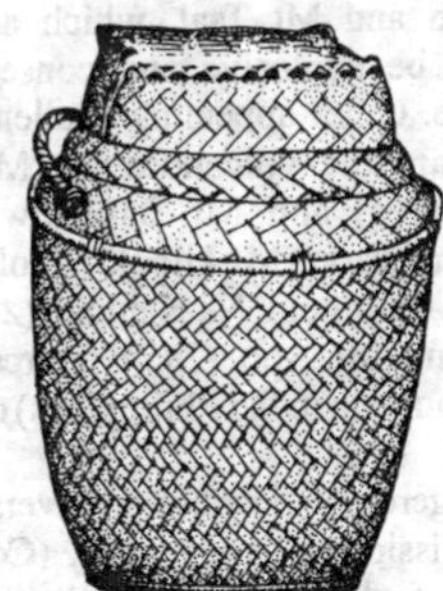

Grain container

The best way to go fossicking is to get in touch with small-claim holders and make yourself known to local gold panners. If you want to follow a hot tip absolutely legally then you must find a Filipino partner for the business and use their name to contract mining rights with the Bureau of Mines & Geo-Sciences.

Caving

Judging from the number of caves in existence, only a handful could have so far been explored. This is because very few Filipinos would willingly go into the unknown depths of the earth! The reasons are fear and superstition or just plain lack of interest.

In earlier times many caves served as burial grounds. It is not unusual to find bones and skulls, although you seldom find artefacts like vessels, tools, arms or jewellery. These have all been gathered up during earlier explorations. If you shine a light in completely unknown caves you might find some war spoils left by the Japanese, which, according to the calculations of the American columnist Jack Anderson, are distributed over 172 hiding places in the Philippines and are worth close to US$100 billion.

Climbing

There are no alpine summits in the Philippines although there are volcanoes worth climbing. The official list records 37 volcanoes, 17 active and 20 dormant, but all unpredictable. The most dangerous include Mt Mayon and Mt Taal, which are both known to be explosive and consequently destructive. Other appealing challenges for climbers are the volcanoes Mt Makiling (1144 metres) and Mt Banahaw (2177 metres) on Luzon; Mt Hibok-Hibok (1322 metres) on Camiguin; Mt Kanloan (2465) on Negros; and Mt Apo (2954 metres – the highest mountain in the Philippines) on Mindanao.

All dangerous volcanoes are overseen by the Commission on Volcanology (Comvol), the centre of which is in the Philippine Institute of Volcanology, Hizon Building, 29 Quezon Ave, Quezon City. This is where you can learn whether or not an eruption is predicted in the foreseeable future. Specific questions about climbs can be answered by the Philippine National Mountaineering Association in the Tours & Promotions section of Philippine Airlines, 1500 Roxas Blvd, Manila.

Deserted Islands

There are 7107 islands in the Philippines and more than 60% of them are uninhabited. One would think that this would be music to the ears of a modern-day Robinson Crusoe, but unfortunately most of these godforsaken islands are stark rocks or simply sandbanks jutting uninvitingly out of the sea. If you search for it, however, you will almost certainly find an idyllic spot with white sand and palm beaches. Try north of Bohol, or in Gutob Bay between Culion and Busuanga. I found 12 isolated islands there in one day!

To really go à la Robinson Crusoe and enjoy it you need something to do, otherwise you'll get bored very quickly in paradise. If you take few supplies, you will soon find your days filled with trying to find more. The sea offers most things: fish, crayfish, sea porcupines, mussels, snails, algae and seaweed.

After just a few days of complete isolation, most budding Crusoes come to the conclusion that it is better to be isolated in pairs or groups. Of what use is the most beautiful place in the world if there is no-one to share it with?

Sailing

Every two years Manila is the destination in the China Sea Race, a classic 1200 km regatta which starts in Hong Kong. This event not only serves to guide the participants through some exotic islands, but also brings with it thousands of spectators from the international yachting scene.

The monsoon which blows steadily from September to May in the north-east guarantees good sailing conditions and many natural harbours invite sailors to rest. It is not uncommon for a crew to decide to spend the winter in one of the beautiful bays of Puerto Galera or Balanacan.

Favourite spots for yachts include the anchorages in the Visayas. For sailing enthusiasts there is also the opportunity to take part in a round trip. You can ask about this at the Manila Yacht Club (MYC) in Roxas Blvd. The MYC is helpful to foreign yachts as well, and will organise guides or an escort from the coastguard when sailing through pirate-infested waters.

Diving

Diving has become a very popular activity in the Philippines and not without reason. This country possesses a large selection of major diving areas, although many underwater sites in recent times have suffered violent ecological damage. To get first class dives you should use proven diving operators who know the remaining good diving sites. One of the most recommended is Asia Divers in Puerto Galera (Anglo-Australian management), represented in Manila by Nena Penar (tel 501075), 1121 M H del Pilar St, near the corner of United Nations Ave, Ermita.

The Department of Tourism quickly recognised the growing popularity of diving and issued the informative *Discover the Philippines through Scuba Diving* guide. It lists 10 dive resorts, 11 dive shops and 16 agencies which offer excursions. For more information you can contact the addresses given in the brochure or the Philippine Commission on Sports, Scuba Diving, in the Tourism Building, Agrifina Circle, Rizal Park, Manila. Good information is also available from Manuel V de la Riva, Dive Adventure Planning, 2169 Agno St Int 4, Malate, Manila. A useful book is *The Diver's Guide to the Philippines* (Unicorn Books Ltd, Hong Kong, 1982) by David Smith and Michael Westlake.

Lots of diving businesses have grown over the last few years and an almost endless variety of programmes is available. During the high season (mid-March to mid-May) mobile dive bases are set up on various islands. You can hire completely equipped diving boats at any time of the year and you can rent anything you need from Manila's diving shops, although it is better to bring some of your own equipment. Philippine Airlines will raise your baggage limit to 30 kg to allow for this, but any oxygen tanks you bring with you must be empty. If you need to buy diving equipment, try Young's Sporting Goods, at 513 Quintin Paredes St, Binondo, Manila. Besides locally made products it also has imported goods from Japan and the USA.

The most beautiful diving sites are far from the settled areas where the underwater scenery is likely to have been destroyed by drainage and dynamite. In the Mindoro Strait, east of the little island of Apo, you will find the Apo Reef. At low tide this reef is partly exposed and is among the most spectacular diving areas in the Philippines.

Probably the best place for diving is in the Sulu Sea on the little-explored Tubbataha Reef. Because of the long distance from the port of departure – it's about 185 km from Puerto Princesa in Palawan – and because of the resultant high costs involved, very few companies offer expeditions to this area. The Quinawanan group is also difficult to get to. It comprises the northern section of the Cuyo Islands and is a protected area for turtles.

Sumilon Island off the south-east coast of Cebu is a year-round favourite. The tourist trade for divers has hardly touched on the fantastic Bacuit archipelago in the north-west of Palawan. Only the Japanese have caught on quickly and built the Ten Knots Resort Hotel on Miniloc Island which caters specifically for divers. In the meantime there is a diving base at El Nido.

Hundreds of years of maritime activity have made sure that the floor of the archipelago is littered with wrecks from typhoons, wars and collisions with reefs. Ideal conditions for exploration are found in the sound between the islands of Busuanga and Culion; in 1944 a fleet of 12 Japanese ships went down here, seven of them in a small protected bay, where the wrecks now lie in 30 to 40 metres of crystal clear water.

For 250 years Spanish galleons travelled

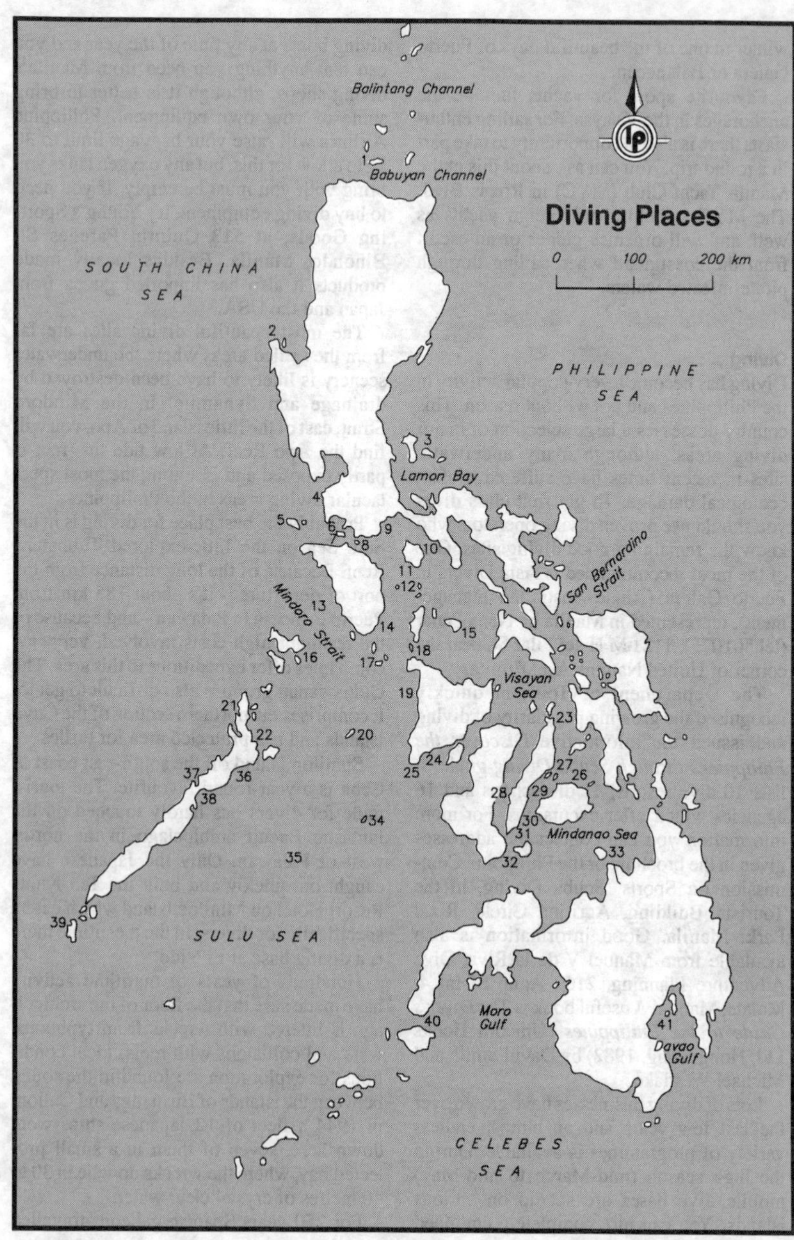
Diving Places
0
100
200 km
Balintang Channel
Babuyan Channel
SOUTH CHINA SEA
PHILIPPINE SEA
Lamon Bay
San Bernardino Strait
Mindoro Strait
Visayan Sea
Mindanao Sea
SULU SEA
Moro Gulf
Davao Gulf
CELEBES SEA
1 2 3 4 5 6 7 8 9 10 11 12 13 14 15 16 17 18 19 20 21 22 23 24 25 26 27 28 29 30 31 32 33 34 35 36 37 38 39 40 41

	DIVING PLACE	DIVING SEASON	ENTRY POINT
1	Fuga Island	April-May	Fuga Island
2	Santiago Island	November-June	Bolinao
3	Polillo Island	April-October	Infanta, Jomalig, Balesin
4	Nasugbu	November-June	Nasugbu Town
5	Lubang Islands	March-June	Catalagan (Batangas Province)
6	Balayan Bay	all year	Anilao
7	Puerto Galera	all year	Batangas City
8	Verde Island	all year	Batangas City
9	Sigayan Bay	all year	San Juan
10	Mopog Island	April-October	Lucena City, Gasan
11	Tres Reyes Islands	April-October	Gasan
12	Dos Hermanas Islands	April-October	Gasan
13	Apo Reef	March-June	San Jose (Mindoro)
14	Buyallao	April-October	Mansalay
15	Cresta de Gallo	March-June	Tablas
16	Calamian Islands	all year	Coron
17	Semirara Island	March-June	San Jose (Mindoro)
18	Boracay Island	all year	Kalibo
19	Batbatan Island	April-June	San Jose (Panay)
20	Cuyo Islands	March-June & October	Cuyo Town
21	Bacuit Bay	November-June	Liminangcong, El Nido
22	Taytay Bay	April-October	Taytay
23	Capitancillo Island	April-October	Sogod
24	Cresta de Gallo	all year	San Joaquin
25	Nagas Island	all year	San Joaquin
26	Danojan Island	all year	Mactan
27	Mactan	all year	Cebu City, Mactan
28	Pescador Island	all year	Moalboal
29	Cabilao Island	all year	Tagbilaran
30	Panglao Island	all year	Tagbilaran
31	Sumilon Island	all year	Dumaguete
32	Apo Island	all year	Dumaguete
33	Mambajao	all year	Balingoan
34	Cagayan Islands	March-June	Cagayancillo
35	Tubbataha Reef	March-June	Puerto Princesa
36	Green Island Bay	April-October	Roxas
37	Ulugan Bay	November-June	Bahile
38	Honda Bay	April-October	Puerto Princesa
39	Balabac Island	all year	Balabac
40	Santa Cruz Island	all year	Zamboanga
41	Talikud Island	all year	Davao

between Manila and Acapulco in Mexico, laden with silver coins, gold, silk, porcelain, pearls, precious stones and other objects of value. Of the more than 30 trading vessels which were lost during this era, 21 sank in the coastal waters near the Philippines, mostly near Catanduanes, Samar and South Luzon. Fairy-tale treasures are said to be spread over the ocean floor and up to now the remains of only 14 of these wrecks have been located.

There is no law in the Philippines against searching for lost galleons. If you find one, however, you must inform the National Museum. If there is a recovery, the discoverer will get a share of the spoils. If you want to explore or photograph a known wreck, you should inform the National Museum of your intentions in writing. It is all too easy as a stranger to be charged with illegal plunder of treasure.

Trekking

There is always movement somewhere in the Philippines. Not just on the freeways and asphalt-covered streets, but along the paths and byways which crisscross the entire archipelago. It's possible to go from the far north to the deep south with minimum contact with motorised transport. On some islands in fact, it is practically impossible to see a car. Batan Island is an example. You can go around the island on a wonderful semisurfaced coast road. Alternatively, there is Lubang where high-wheeled horse carts still dominate the traffic in spite of the introduction of a few jeeps. It is the same in Busuanga. There, once a day, a rattling old bus travels along the dirt road from Coron to Salvacion. The centre and the north of this island are practically free from cars.

There are wonderful opportunities for trekking along the Pacific coast in Bicol Province and Quezon Province in Luzon. If you want to get to know the primaeval landscape of Palawan, then you can try some of the many first-class treks there.

It is also tempting to read the recollections of the treks undertaken by European travellers in the last century, recorded in books which are witness to their love of the Philippines. Two of these are Fedor Jagor's *Travels in the Philippines* (London, 1873); and Paul de la Gironnière's *Adventures of a Frenchman in the Philippines* originally published in 1853 and republished in 1972 by Rarebook Enterprises, Caloocan City.

Useful maps on the scale of 1:250,000 are available in the Philippine Coast & Geodetic Survey, Barraca St, San Nicolas, Manila.

WHAT TO BRING

Bring as little as possible is the golden rule – it's almost always possible to get things you might need and that's far better than carrying too much with you. A backpack is probably the best way of carrying your gear but try to thief-proof it as much as possible and remember that backpacks are prone to damage, especially by airlines, where they easily get caught up on loading equipment. Travel packs are a relatively recent innovation that combine the advantages of a backpack and a soft carry bag. The shoulder straps either detach or can be hidden away under a zip-fastened flap so they do not catch on things.

The Philippines has enough climatic variations to require a fairly wide variety of clothing. At sea level you'll need lightweight gear, suitable for tropical temperatures. In Mountain Province or when scaling the odd volcano, you'll need warmer clothing – jumpers (sweaters) and a light jacket. Bring thongs (flip-flops) for use in hotel bathrooms and showers. A sleeping bag can be particularly useful in the Philippines, especially on overnight boat trips.

If you're a keen snorkeller, bring your mask and snorkel; there are many superb diving areas around the islands. Soap, toothpaste and other general toiletries are readily available, but out in the sticks, toilet paper can be difficult to find. A first-aid kit is useful (see the Health section earlier). A padlock is always worth carrying: you can often use it to add security to your hotel room. When it rains in the Philippines, it really rains so bring a raincoat or umbrella. Other possibilities include a sewing kit, a torch (flashlight), a Swiss army knife, a travel alarm clock, and a mosquito net – the list goes on.

Getting There

AIR

Basically, the only way to get to the Philippines is by plane, and there are only a couple of entry points – Manila and Cebu. There are no regular shipping services into the Philippines.

There are flights to Manila from most of the Philippines' Asian neighbours, including Japan, Hong Kong, Singapore and Malaysia, as well as from Australia, New Zealand, the USA and Europe.

Officially, you must have an onward or return ticket before you're allowed to board a flight to the Philippines. This is even more necessary if you arrive without a visa. It has recently been reported that immigration officials in Manila have been denying entry to travellers who are unable to produce a departure ticket, especially when they don't have a visa stamped in their passport. If this happens, you can only hope to find some friendly person nearby who can quickly arrange the necessary ticket for you. You will find the airline offices upstairs in the airport building.

Other possible but improbable entry points are in Mindanao. From time to time there have been flights between Zamboanga (on Mindanao) and either Kota Kinabalu, Sandakan or Tawau in Sabah (the Malaysian state occupying the north-eastern corner of Borneo). There have also been irregular flights between Davao in the south of Mindanao and north Sulawesi in Indonesia.

At present none of these irregular flights seems to be operating. It's a case of reluctance on all sides. The Filipinos prefer you to enter through Manila and the Indonesians and Malaysians are not very enthusiastic about you arriving in their countries through the places mentioned above either. It's a drag because the idea of making your way through Borneo and then making the short hop across to Mindanao in the Philippines has a lot of appeal. Instead you have to backtrack to Kota Kinabalu and make the much longer and more expensive flight from there to Manila.

Round-the-World Tickets

RTW fares, as Round-the-World tickets are known, have become all the rage of late. Basically, two or more airlines get together and offer a ticket which gets you around the world using only their services. You're allowed stopovers (sometimes unlimited) and you have to complete the circuit within a certain period of time.

Philippine Airlines (PAL) offers a RTW ticket in combination with Sabena and Eastern Air which will take you from Australia to the Philippines, Asia, Europe, the USA and back to Australia for A$2377. The usual Apex booking conditions apply and you have 120 days to complete the circuit. From London, RTW tickets typically cost around UK£1000 to UK£1400, depending on the airlines and routes used.

Circle Pacific Tickets

Circle Pacific fares are a variation on the RTW idea and once again there's an option that includes the Philippines. Continental Airlines and PAL have a ticket that lets you combine the USA, New Zealand, Australia, Asia and the Philippines in a loop around the Pacific. You can make as many stopovers as the two airlines' routes will permit and have up to six months to complete the loop. The ticket must be pruchased at least 30 days before departure, after which the ususal cancellation penalties apply.

Although you must make all reservations before the 30 day cut-off point, you can alter flight dates after departure at no cost so long as you have a revalidation sticker on your ticket. If you want to change your route, requiring your ticket to be rewritten, there's a US$25 charge. Economy class Circle Pacific fares are US$1870 from the USA, A$1799 from Australia or NZ$2711 from New Zealand.

From the USA

From the west coast, Los Angeles or San Francisco, the nonstop economy fare is US$759, and you can tag two stopovers on to this fare at US$25 a time.

Alternatives are the excursion return ticket or the Apex return ticket. Excursion returns have no minimum stay requirements while Apex returns stipulate a seven-day minimum, and a six-month maximum, stay. You're allowed one free stopover on the excursion or Apex fare and extra stops can be added for US$50 each. Payment must be made 21 days in advance, after which the usual cancellation penalties apply. Both tickets have high or low season rates. An excursion return costs US$1024 in the low season, and US$1126 in the high season. Apex returns are marginally cheaper at US$959 and US$1084 respectively.

From Australia

You can fly from Australia to the Philippines with PAL or Qantas. There are two fare seasons – high and low – but the high season level only applies during the school summer break in December and January.

On PAL the one-way economy fares are A$626/743 in the low/high season; return fares are A$743/882 in the low/high season. These fares are valid for a stay of 28 days only. For a stay of 45 days, the return fare in the low season is A$902. With Qantas, one-way economy-class fares to Manila from Sydney, Melbourne or Brisbane are A$690/A$820 in the low/high season. Return fares are A$995/1180 in the low/high season. Qantas also has a special advance-purchase return fare for A$940/1145 in the low/high season.

From New Zealand

There are no direct flights between New Zealand and Manila so there are no real bargains. The cheapest fare available is on Thai International via Bangkok for around NZ$1235.

From Asia

There are lots of flights to the Philippines from its Asian neighbours. Cheap deals tend to vary these days – one day one country is cheaper, the next day another. Currently it appears that Bangkok is no longer the bargain basement and that Hong Kong is the place for good deals.

From Hong Kong the regular economy one-way fare to Manila is HK$908, and you can find discount return fares for around HK$1100. From Japan the one-way fare is Y106,600 but you can get returns for Y53,000. From Korea it costs US$360 one-way or US$730 return.

Out of Malaysia, the regular one-way fare is M$698 and, if you shop around, you can fly return for M$918. Out of Singapore the regular one-way fare is S$699 but, again, discount fares will be available. You can get good fares from these two countries via the Philippines to the USA. In Thailand the regular one-way fare from Bangkok is 8050B and discount one-way tickets cost around 5500B. From Sri Lanka you pay Rs 7616 for the regular one-way fare.

From Europe

PAL and a number of European airlines, including British Airways, connect London and other major European capitals with Manila. The regular economy one-way fare from London to Manila is UK£958 and 90 day excursion return fares cost UK£679. You can get to Manila from London for much less by shopping around London's numerous bucket shops.

Bucket shops are travel agents who specialise in discounting airline tickets – a practice for which London is probably the world headquarters. To find out what fares are available, scan the weekly what's on magazine *Time Out* or the *News & Travel Magazine*, which is free. Two excellent places to look for cheap tickets are Trailfinders, in Earls Court Rd, or STA Travel, in Old Brompton Rd. Typical discount fares between London and Manila are around UK£250 one way or UK£475 return.

Another way to get to the Philippines cheaply from London is to fly to Hong Kong and continue from there. Competition on the

London to Hong Kong route is cutthroat. There are also attractively priced tickets available from London to Australia with the Philippines as a stopover. You can also find good ticket deals to the Philippines in Belgium and the Netherlands.

To reach European destinations, you can fly to London for around US$675.

SEA

Although there are many excellent connections by ship around the Philippine islands, the possibilities of getting to the Philippines from overseas are very limited. You might find a passenger-carrying freight ship out of Hong Kong or Singapore, but, in these containerised days, it is increasingly unlikely. There are regular sea connections between Borneo and Mindanao, but, since smugglers and pirates mainly operate there, you're unlikely to be too popular on arrival.

LEAVING THE PHILIPPINES

Airfares

The Philippines is no place to look for cheap airline tickets. Although Manila has over 300 travel agents, the lack of competition is astounding. Discounts are available but you have to be persistent and shop around. There are lots of agents around the Ermita area, particularly off Roxas Blvd and in T M Kalaw St, by Rizal Park. Check out Mr Ticket Travel in the lobby of the Hotel Swiss Inn, at 1030 Belen St, Paco (tel 5224835; fax 5224840; tlx 65034 HARMONY PN), and Broadway Travel, 1322 Roxas Blvd, Ermita (tel 591924; tlx 63862 MASS PN). You can also try the Youth & Student Travel Association of the Philippines, Ystaphil (tel 8320680; fax 8187948; tlx YSTAPHILPM), at 4227 Tomas Claudio St, Paranaque.

Typical one-way fares from Manila include Bangkok US$190, Hong Kong US$140, Tokyo US$210, Taipei US$146 and Singapore US$215. Pan Am, Northwest, PAL, Korean Airlines and China Airlines have budget fares to the US. To go to the US west coast it costs US$512 in the low season and US$563 in the high. To the east coast it costs US$630 in the low season and US$693 in the high.

Departure

Make absolutely certain you confirm your onward flight with the airline at least 72 hours before departure. It's even better to confirm your outward flight when you arrive. That way you can be fairly certain that your booking has been registered on the computer. Don't check in at the last minute; flights are often overbooked and, in spite of a confirmed ticket, you can find yourself bumped from the flight! If you have excess baggage, it's worth giving the baggage handlers a generous tip and letting them take care of the problem.

Departure Tax When you depart from Ninoy Aquino International Airport, you have to pay a P220 airport tax. You can take up to P500 out with you, and have unused pesos reconverted, but only if you have receipts from official moneychangers or banks. The bank counter is in the exit hall.

One traveller advised keeping enough pesos for taxi fares and departure tax, but not arriving at the airport with too much money. In his case, when a PAL and a Qantas flight both left for Australia on a Sunday night, the bank did not have enough Australian dollars to meet demand. In that situation, it's probably better to change your money into US dollars or another hard currency, rather than trying to change pesos overseas at a bad rate.

WARNING

The information in this chapter is especially vulnerable to change – prices for international air travel are volatile, routes are introduced and cancelled, schedules change, rules are amended and special deals come and go. Airlines and governments seem to take a perverse pleasure in making price structures and regulations as complicated as possible; you should check directly with the airline or a travel agent to make sure you understand how a fare works. In addition, the travel industry is highly competitive and there are many lurks and perks. The upshot of this is that you should get opinions, quotes and advice from as many airlines and travel agents as possible before you part with your hard-earned cash.

The details given in this chapter should be regarded as pointers and not as a substitute for your own careful, up-to-the-minute research.

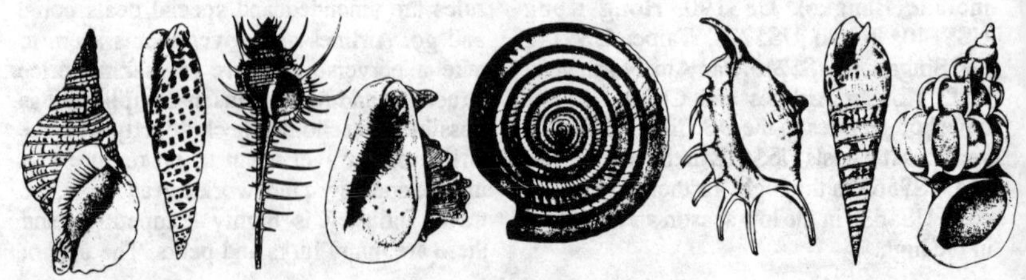

Getting Around

AIR

After practically monopolising the air traffic scene for many years, Philippine Airlines (the state airline) now faces competition from smaller companies like Aerolift and Pacific Airways. Though modest enterprises, these other airlines offer valid alternatives for people travelling in the region. Ever since the catastrophic shipping disasters of the 1980s, there's been a dramatic increase in the use of domestic airlines – the packed-out local commuter planes are proof enough of this. So these days it's very important to book a seat well in advance.

(The Aerolift and Pacific Airways maps show the main routes covered by these airlines; details of their flight schedules are given in the Transport from Luzon section of the Manila chapter.)

Philippine Airlines

PAL flies between nearly all the larger cities. Over the Christmas period, between 15 December and 4 January, all flights are fully booked out.

The flight schedule changes twice a year, but only in minor details, so that you'll have a reasonable idea of what's available in local flights by consulting the information in the Transport from Luzon section in the Manila chapter and allowing for slight variations. When available, a current 'Domestic Flight Schedule' can be obtained at the PAL office in Roxas Blvd. (If there are none printed, you can make your own copy of the table displayed on the first floor). You'll find at least part of the flight schedule reproduced in the tourist magazine *What's on in Manila*, which is available free in the main hotels. The PAL

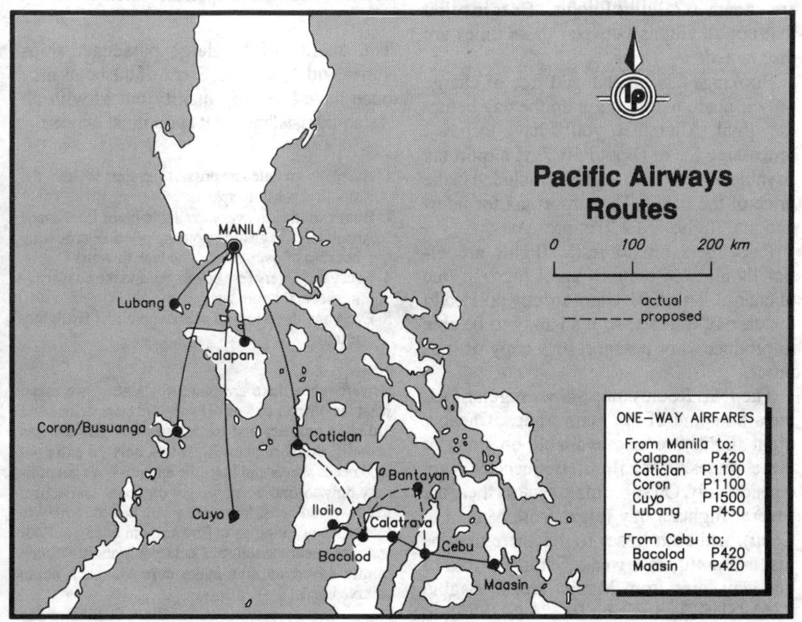

fleet contains jets (A-300, Boeing 737, BAC 1-11) and turboprops (Fokker 50, SD 360, HS 748). Smoking is not permitted on board.

PAL customers are attended to in numerical order in the city offices; even to obtain a small piece of information, you have to take a number and wait your turn. It's always best to ring up if you want quick information. The Manila office has set up a round-the-clock Info-Service on 8323166.

Students under 26 years of age taking round-trip flights (eg, Manila-Cebu-Manila or Manila, Zamboanga, Davao, Cebu, Manila) are entitled to a 15% reduction. As well as your student card, you may be asked to produce your passport (or a copy including the photo) when purchasing the ticket.

PAL also offers a Golden Age Discount of 15% for passengers over 60 years of age. However, the form costs P50 and you have to bring two identification photos and a photocopy of your passport as well.

A general discount of 30% is offered on night flights between 7 pm and 4 am; these are known as 'Bulilit Flights'. Bear in mind that not all flights between these times are discounted.

Bookings can be changed free of charge only if made before noon on the day before the flight. After that, you'll have to pay a processing fee of about P50. Any airport tax payable on domestic flights is included in the price of the ticket. The airport tax for international flights is P220 at present.

Passengers on domestic flights are officially allowed only 18 kg of luggage free of charge. This limit is not strictly policed in the case of tourists, so it's handy to be able to produce your passport or a copy of it as proof.

The PAL Routes map shows regular PAL fares on some of the main routes. Cheaper night flights are also available on some of these routes. PAL flight frequencies vary considerably. On some main sectors there are several flights a day (eight from Manila to Cebu), while on lesser routes there may be just a few flights a week. Sample prices of one-way fares from Manila are: to Baguio P363 ($US13); to Cebu P1376 ($US50); to Puerto Princesa P1180 ($US42); to Davao P1788 ($US64).

BOAT

Wherever you go there's always a boat ready to take you to the next island. For short trips, outrigger boats or pumpboats are used. The motor is at the back – a very noisy arrangement. A 16 hp pumpboat uses five litres of fuel for an hour's speedy motoring, so you can work out the cost of chartering.

The quality of the passenger ships of the inter-island operators varies greatly. The flagships of several companies run on the prestigious Manila, Cebu, Zamboanga, Davao route. They are punctual and fast and the service is relatively good; some boats even have a disco on board.

Third class (deck class or sun deck) is quite acceptable. Bunks or camp beds (depending on the quality of the vessel) are under cover and protected from sun and rain, whereas the cabins and dormitories below decks are often cramped and sticky.

The quality of the large passenger ships varies widely as well. Some of the boats may once have been top quality but as with all Asian inter-island boats you must expect:

1 As many people as possible crammed into the smallest possible space
2 Bunks welded to every available bit of floor space
3 Absolutely disgusting toilets, often overflowing because of overuse and the lack of water
4 Lousy food, very few beverages and the boat arriving several hours late
5 Everyone throwing up everywhere if it is slightly rough

Beware when there are two 3rd classes – we asked what the difference was between 3rd class deluxe and 3rd class ordinary and the answer was, 'Deluxe has bedding, ordinary doesn't'. It was only P5 extra but who needs sheets and blankets anyhow? We got ordinary only to find when we got on board that deluxe had reserved beds. In ordinary you had to fight with thousands of Filipinos to find a sq cm of empty floor space not near the toilets. Luckily a friendly Filipino family saved us, but make sure to check about reserved beds!

Piers & Jill Beagley

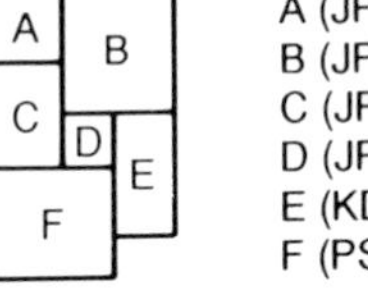

A (JP)
B (JP)
C (JP)
D (JP)
E (KD)
F (PS)

Top: Calesas are found in Manila, Vigan and Cebu City (JP)
Bottom: Tricycles (TW)

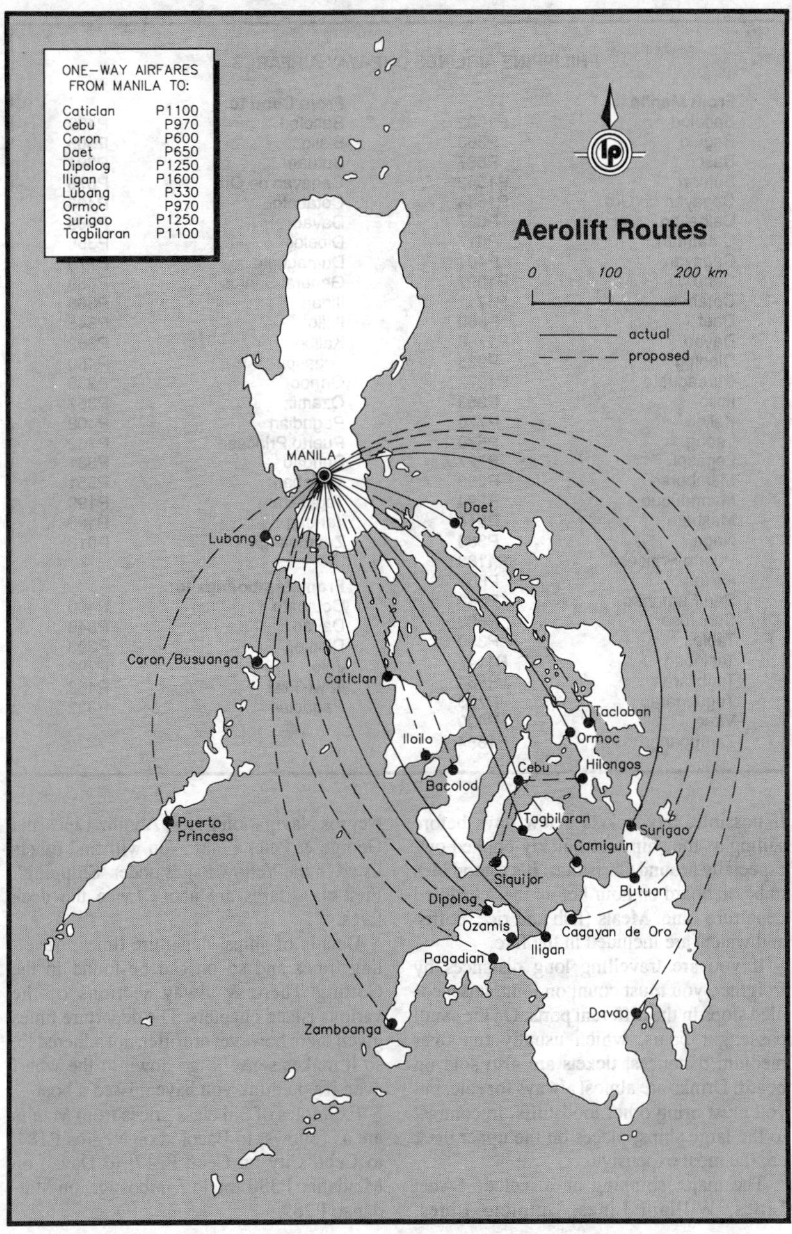
ONE-WAY AIRFARES
FROM MANILA TO:
Caticlan P1100
Cebu P970
Coron P600
Daet P650
Dipolog P1250
Iligan P1600
Lubang P330
Ormoc P970
Surigao P1250
Tagbilaran P1100
Aerolift Routes
0 100 200 km
actual
proposed
MANILA
Lubang
Daet
Coron/Busuanga
Caticlan
Tacloban
Ormoc
Iloilo
Hilongos
Cebu
Bacolod
Tagbilaran
Puerto
Princesa
Surigao
Camiguin
Siquijor
Butuan
Dipolog
Ozamis
Cagayan de Oro
Iligan
Pagadian
Davao
Zamboanga

PHILIPPINE AIRLINES ONE-WAY AIRFARES

From Manila to:	
Bacolod	P1002
Baguio	P363
Basco	P887
Butuan	P1542
Cagayan de Oro	P1534
Calbayog	P637
Catarman	P617
Cauayan	P401
Cebu	P1097
Cotabato	P1711
Daet	P380
Davao	P1788
Dipolog	P935
Dumaguete	P1272
Iloilo	P953
Kalibo	P770
Laoag	P570
Legaspi	P727
Mamburao	P288
Marinduque	P294
Masbate	P514
Naga	P383
Puerto Princesa	P1180
Roxas	P603
San Fernando	P348
San Jose	P693
Tablas	P390
Tacloban	P1147
Tagbilaran	P834
Tuguegarao	P783
Virac	P499
Zamboanga	P1654

From Cebu to:	
Bacolod	P469
Bislig	P505
Butuan	P391
Cagayan de Oro	P675
Cotabato	P495
Davao	P869
Dipolog	P355
Dumaguete	P270
General Santos	P669
Iligan	P363
Iloilo	P545
Kalibo	P382
Legaspi	P450
Ormoc	P236
Ozamiz	P357
Pagadian	P408
Puerto Princesa	P762
Surigao	P331
Tacloban	P551
Tagbilaran	P199
Tandag	P400
Zamboanga	P913

From Zamboanga to:	
Cotabato	P400
Davao	P849
Dipolog	P393
Jolo	P292
Tawi-Tawi	P463
Pagadian	P332

If possible, buy tickets a few days before sailing as the ships are quickly booked out, especially around Christmas. It's a good idea to be on board an hour before the scheduled departure time. Meals (fish and rice, coffee and water) are included in the fare.

If you are travelling long distances by freighter, you must count on long, unscheduled stops in the different ports. On the small passenger boats, which usually run over medium distances, tickets are also sold on board. Drinks are almost always for sale, but you must bring other foodstuffs. In contrast to the large ships, places on the upper deck are the most expensive.

The major shipping lines include Sweet Lines, William Lines, Sulpicio Lines, Negros Navigation Lines, Aboitiz Lines and George & Peter Lines. You will find others listed in the Yellow Pages under 'Shipping'. First-class fares are about twice the deck fares.

Details of ships, departure times, travelling times and so on can be found in the Getting There & Away sections of the various island chapters. The departure times given there however are often not adhered to, so it makes sense to go down to the wharf even if you think you have missed a boat.

Examples of 3rd class prices from Manila are as follows: to Bacolod on Negros P184; to Cebu City on Cebu P217; to Davao on Mindanao P380 and to Zamboanga, on Mindanao P289.

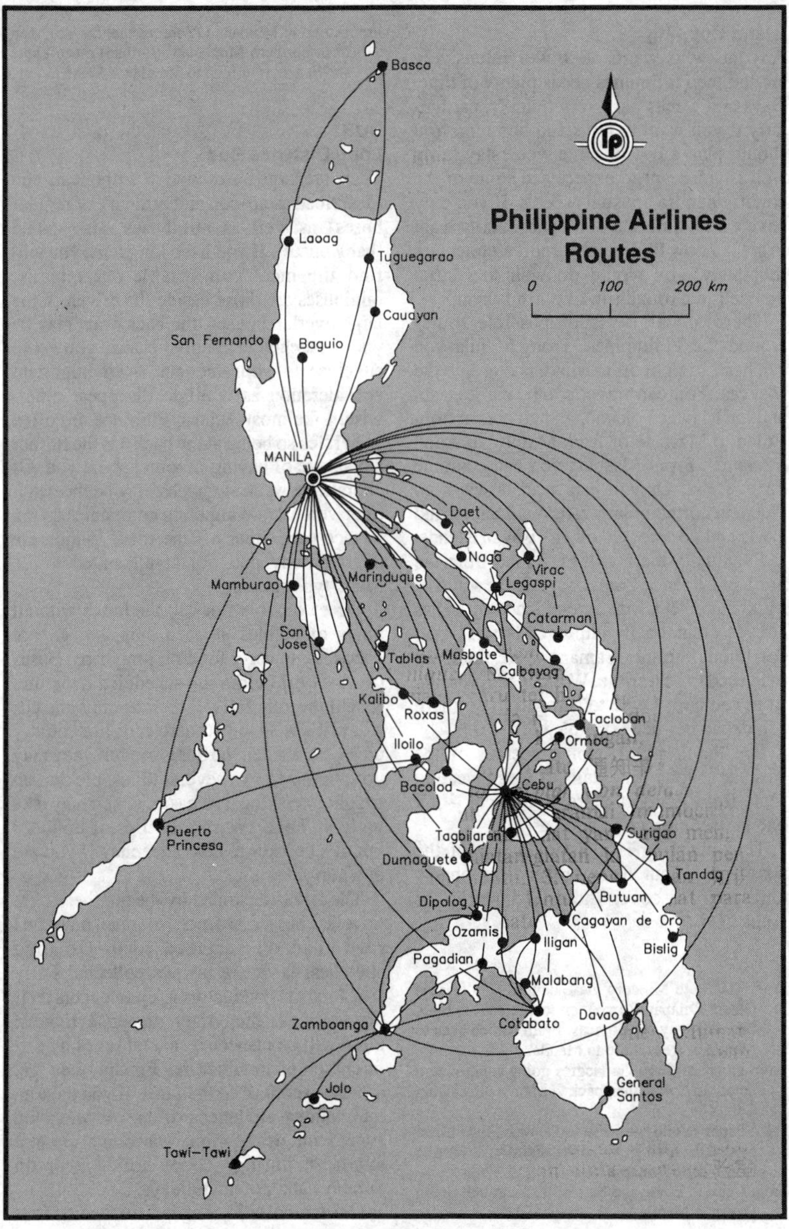
Philippine Airlines
Routes
0
100
200 km
Basco
Laoag
Tuguegarao
Cauayan
San Fernando
Baguio
MANILA
Daet
Naga
Virac
Legaspi
Marinduque
Mamburao
San Jose
Tablas
Masbate
Catarman
Calbayog
Kalibo
Roxas
Tacloban
Ormoc
Iloilo
Bacolod
Cebu
Puerto Princesa
Tagbilaran
Surigao
Dumaguete
Tandag
Butuan
Dipolog
Cagayan de Oro
Ozamis
Iligan
Bislig
Pagadian
Malabang
Zamboanga
Cotabato
Davao
Jolo
General Santos
Tawi-Tawi

Island Hopping

Anyone who wants to travel intensively around the Philippines needs plenty of time. Days and weeks pass very quickly, particularly if you want to go island hopping. You should plan a two or three week stay fairly well if you want to experience some of the country's more unusual aspects. If you only have a little time and don't particularly want to get to know Philippine airport architecture intimately, you would do well to restrict yourself to a round trip of north Luzon.

There are all sorts of possible routes around the Philippines. From Manila you can head straight off to Mindanao or into the Visayas. You can travel south, via Legaspi and the Mayon Volcano, and go across from Bulan to Masbate or from Matnog to Allen on Samar. From Masbate you can continue on to Cebu. Or you can head down from Allen, in northern Samar, through Samar and Leyte and go across to other Visayan islands.

Eventually there will be a road from the north of Luzon to Zamboanga in the south of Mindanao. This Japanese-aided project has already dramatically improved the transport conditions through Samar, where the main road used to be terrible. Work on the crossing from southern Leyte to Surigao in northern Mindanao has been completed.

See the Island Hopping section of the Visayas chapter for details of the interesting route from Puerto Galera to Boracay – it's one fantastic beach to another!

The following is a list of a few of the possibilities, but there are endless opportunities to discover the island world for yourself.

From Manila to Mindoro via Batangas City (Puerto Galera-Calapan-Roxas), on to Tablas/Romblon, then to Panay via Boracay. From Kalibo back to Manila or from Iloilo to Manila.

From Panay to Cebu via Negros going south with a detour to Bohol, then back to Manila direct from Cebu City.

From Panay (Iloilo) or Cebu to Palawan, then travel around the north or the south, returning to Manila from Puerto Princesa.

From Cebu to Leyte and Samar, then through South Luzon to Manila.

From Cebu to Mindanao (Zamboanga, Davao), then from northern Mindanao (Surigao) on to Leyte and Samar, returning to Manila via South Luzon.

BUS

Long Distance Bus

There are large buses with or without air-con (described as air-con and ordinary or regular buses) as well as minibuses, also called 'baby buses'. If you have long legs, you will find the most comfortable seats in the minibuses are those beside the driver. In the large overland buses, the back seats may be your best choice, mainly because you get to sit close to your luggage – an important consideration as it might disappear otherwise. Like most Asians, Filipinos are often travel sick so being at the back has the further advantage of having no-one behind you. Of course, the weak stomachs may be the result of drivers from competing companies trying to race each other off the roads, which are often bumpy and not at all suited to Le Mans-type speeds.

Street vendors flock to the buses with all kinds of edibles at each stop, so it's not necessary to carry food on long trips. Buses often set off before the scheduled departure time if they are full – if there is only one bus a day, it's wise to get there early! In country areas, even when the buses are full, they may go round the town several times, picking up freight or making purchases, which may take up to an hour. For shorter trips of up to 20 km, it's quicker to take a jeepney if you are in a hurry.

The fare is reckoned by the number of km travelled but it costs more to travel on gravel road than on surfaced road. On long stretches, fares are always collected fairly late. First the conductors ask passengers their destinations, then they dispense tickets; these will be inspected several times by different chief conductors. Finally they get around to collecting the fares. If you have an international student card, show it when you state your destination. Discounts are not available during school holidays or on Sundays and public holidays.

One trip costs 75 centavos for the first four

km and 25 centavos for each extra km. So a 100 km trip costs about P25 or about US$1.

Ordinary bus fares from Manila are: to Alaminos (237 km) P66; to Baguio (250 km) P63; to Batangas (110 km) P28; to Olongapo (126 km) P45; to Legaspi (544 km) P183.

See the Getting There & Away section of the Manila chapter for details of where the bus terminals are and for information about local buses.

TRAIN

The railway line from Manila to South Luzon is now the only one operating. Typhoons damage bridges almost every year so that journeys on this stretch can either be frequently interrupted or only partly completed. The line in Panay has been closed for some time. The trains are slow and cost about the same as buses.

CAR RENTAL

Apart from various local firms, the internationally known, reputable companies Avis and Hertz have good, reliable vehicles. You can rent cars by the day, week or month. The cheaper cars are usually booked, so it's worth reserving one if you want a particular model. A Toyota Corolla with air-con and a radio costs US$65 a day, or US$390 a week, including unlimited km. Special rates apply from Monday to Friday (Biz Week) and from Friday to Monday (Weekender). Petrol costs about P7.50 a litre. Avis has several offices in Metro Manila (for example, in Manila Pavilion Hotel and on Roxas Blvd, between Padre Faura and Santa Monica streets), Angeles, Baguio and Cebu City.

MOTORCYCLE

Unlike Thailand or Indonesia, there is no organised setup to hire motorbikes. If you want to rent a motorbike, you have to ask around. For a Honda 125 cc, expect to pay P150 to P300 a day. In Manila you can hire motorbikes from Rent-a-Motorcycle (tel 8322234), 2223 Roxas Blvd, Pasay. You will find motorbikes for sale in the advertisements under 'Classified Ads-For Sale' in the *Manila Bulletin*, especially in the Sunday edition. The most common bike is a 125 cc, but it's better though dearer to buy a 350 cc, as you can overtake faster and more safely. However, outside Manila, parts are hard to come by. A new Honda 125 cc costs about P33,000.

If you buy a bike, make sure you obtain the originals of the following documents:

1 Sale Contract – have it drawn up by a lawyer.
2 Registration Certificate – pink paper, endorsed by the Land Transportation Commission. A numberplate marked 'Ready for Registration' will do.
3 Official Receipt – you need this for the finance office. Get it at the Bureau of Land Transportation.

If you want to sell your motorcycle before leaving the country, you'll be paid in pesos. You can only exchange these (with difficulty) for foreign currency on the black market. It is recommended that you change dollars into pesos before you buy. You can do this officially at the Central Bank, which will give you a receipt for the transaction. With this receipt you can then change the pesos back into dollars without problems.

It's useful to have the owner's manual with you. A tool set, including screwdriver and spark plug key is essential for both types of bike; for the 350 cc it is imperative to take a spare tube, patching kit, spark plugs and chain with you from Manila. The Highway Police insist upon a helmet.

If you are island hopping, you will require a shipment clearance, which you can get from the police before you leave each island. You will also need a photocopy of the Sale Contract or Registration Certificate.

BICYCLE

Although it's dangerous on busy streets, travelling by bicycle can be another interesting way to explore the Philippines.

LOCAL TRANSPORT

Jeepney

These are the most popular form of transport for short journeys. Originally they were reconstructed Jeeps which were left in the

Philippines by the US army after WW II. Few of these old models are left. The new jeepneys, which may be Ford Fieras, are brightly painted in traditional designs and the bonnets are decorated with a multitude of mirrors and figures of horses. They are part of any typical Philippine street scene. Much to the relief of many, the ubiquitous cassette players have now been banned in jeepneys. The jeepneys' route is indicated and the official charge is 75 centavos for the first four km (most charge P1), and 25 centavos for each extra km. When you want to get out, just bang on the roof, hiss or yell 'para' (stop).

In the provinces, it is important to negotiate a price before setting out on a long trip over unfamiliar territory. Before you start, ask other passengers about the price or check in a nearby shop, and then confirm the price with the driver. This may save you an unpleasant situation when you reach your destination. Jeepneys usually only leave when full (or overflowing) with passengers, so you must allow for long waiting periods, especially if you are in a hurry. If you are prepared to pay for the empty 'seats' you can get the driver to leave immediately.

If you climb into an empty jeepney and the driver takes off straight away, it usually means you'll be charged for a Special Ride. If you don't want this, you must make it clear that you are only prepared to pay for a regular ride. You might need to get the driver to stop straight away, especially if no more passengers are getting on. It costs about P600 to rent a jeepney for a day and more if the roads are in bad condition; petrol is extra.

Safety Tip If several men get into the jeepney straight after you and try to sit near you or get you to change seats under some pretext, they may be intent on relieving you of your valuables. Get out immediately.

Taxi

Under no circumstances should taximeters be switched off. Flat fare arrangements always favour the driver. It doesn't hurt to show taxi drivers that you know more than they think, so that they won't take roundabout routes. The initial charge is P2.50, which includes the first 500 metres, then P1 for each further 250 metres. If possible, have small change handy as it is difficult to get change for anything over P20. If a taximeter has obviously been rigged and is running too fast, the only sensible thing is to stop and take another taxi.

In spite of fines of up to P5000, countless taxis still have rigged meters. Pay particular attention to the price display if the driver honks the horn every few seconds. Sometimes horn and meter are linked up and the meter adds a unit every time the horn is sounded! Make sure the meter is turned on when you start. In Manila the most reliable seem to be the Golden Cabs (black with a gold-coloured roof), but unfortunately there are not many of them around. The taxis that wait outside the big hotels, bus stations, wharves and air terminals almost always have meters that run fast. It usually pays to walk to the next street. New taxis are fitted with a digital indicator that cannot (yet!) be interfered with.

PU-Cab

These are small taxis without meters; their minimum price is P10 for a town journey. For longer journeys you pay correspondingly more and need to negotiate the fee beforehand. You will find PU-Cabs in Cebu City, Bacolod, Davao, Zamboanga and some other places, but not Manila.

Trishaw

These are bicycles with sidecars for passengers. As transport becomes increasingly motorised, trishaws are becoming rarer, even in the provinces. Prices start at about P1.25 per person for a short trip.

Tricycle

These are small motorcycles or mopeds with sidecars for passengers and go much better than you might think. The fare must be negotiated, and is usually around P1 for a short ride.

Calesa

These two-wheeled horse-cabs are found in Manila's Chinatown, in Vigan, where they fit the local scene very well, and in Cebu City, where they are called *tartanillas*. In Manila, Filipinos pay about P10 for short trips; tourists are usually charged more. Establish beforehand if the price is per person or per calesa.

Manila

Metro Manila was formed by merging 17 towns and communities. Manila, San Nicolas, Binondo, Santa Cruz, Quiapo and San Miguel form the nucleus of the city, where you will find the markets (Divisoria Market, Quinta Market), the churches (Quiapo Church, Santa Cruz Church), the shopping streets (Rizal Ave, Escolta St), Chinatown (Binondo, Ongpin St), the official home of the president (Malacanang Palace in San Miguel) and many, many people.

The name Manila was originally two words: *may* and *nilad*. *May* means 'there is', and *nilad* is a mangrove plant which used to grow on the banks of the Pasig River. The bark of the mangroves gave a natural soap which the locals used for washing their clothes.

Three years after he founded the colony, King Philip II of Spain called the town *Isigne y Siempre Leal Ciudad*, meaning 'distinguished and ever loyal city'. This charming name could not, however, replace the name Maynilad. If you want to know what Maynilad looked like in the middle of the last century, read Fedor Jagor's classic book *Travels in the Philippines*, published in 1873.

Rizal Park, better known as Luneta Park, is the centre of Manila and is the city's most important meeting place. The two most popular areas for tourists flank Rizal Park. To the north is Intramuros, the Spanish walled city which was badly damaged during fierce fighting in WW II. To the south of Rizal Park is the area where the more peaceful modern invaders are drawn – Ermita and Malate. Here you will find most of Manila's hotels, restaurants and active nightspots. It is known as the 'tourist belt', and its main street is the waterfront Roxas Blvd. Ermita is about 10 km north-west of Ninoy Aquino International Airport (NAIA).

Manila's business centre is Makati, where the banks, insurance companies and other businesses have their head offices. The embassies of many countries are also here. At the edge of Makati, along E de los Santos Ave (almost always called EDSA), lies Forbes Park, a millionaires' ghetto with palatial mansions and its own police force.

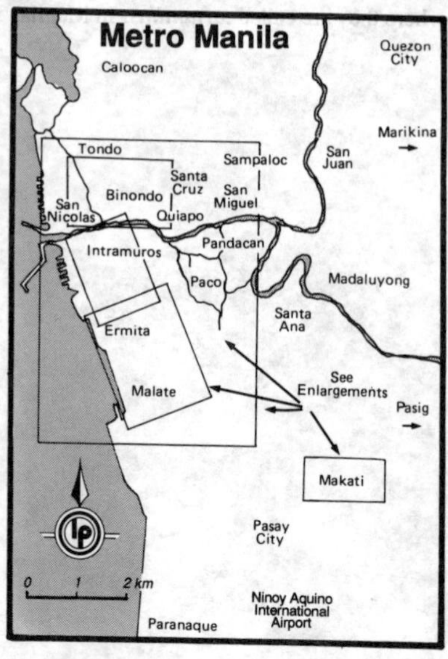

At the other extreme is Tondo, Manila's main slum. It's estimated that 1½ million Filipinos live in slums in Metro Manila, and Tondo has 180,000 living in 17,000 huts in just 1½ sq km. Other areas of Manila which may be of interest to the traveller include Caloocan City, a light-industrial engineering and foodstuff preparation centre, and Quezon City, the government centre, where you'll also find the Philippine Heart Center for Asia, the 25,000 seat Araneta Coliseum and the four-sq-km campus of the University of the Philippines (UP).

ORIENTATION

Although Manila is a fairly sprawling town, it's quite easy to find your way around. Like Bangkok, however, Manila has a number of 'centres'. Makati, for example, is the business centre, while Ermita is the tourist centre. The area of most interest to visitors can be defined by the Pasig River, Manila Bay and Taft Ave. The river forms the northern boundary of this rectangular area, while the bay and Taft Ave form the western and eastern boundaries.

Immediately south of the river is the oldest area of Manila, which includes Intramuros and is where you'll find most of the places of historic interest in Manila. The GPO (General Post Office) and the Immigration Office are also in this area. Further south is the open expanse of Rizal Park (Luneta Park) which extends from Taft Ave to the bayside Roxas Blvd. This is the central meeting and wandering place in Manila. (Beware of pickpockets here and in areas like Santa Cruz.) South of the park is Ermita, the tourist centre, which has cheaper (and some more expensive) accommodation, restaurants, airline offices, nightlife and pretty much everything else you'll need.

Further south again are Malate and Pasay City, where there are many up-market hotels, particularly along the bay, on Roxas Blvd. The modern Cultural Center is built on reclaimed land jutting into the bay. Continue down Taft Ave to the airport or travel southeast from Taft Ave to Makati. North of the river are the sprawling slums of Tondo, the crowded and interesting Chinatown area and the main railway station.

INFORMATION

Tourist Information

There are three Department of Tourism (DOT) information centres in Manila: a reception unit at Ninoy Aquino International Airport, another at the nearby Nayong Pilipino Complex, and the main Tourist Information Center (tel 599031 and 501928) on the ground floor of the Tourism Building, Agrifina Circle, Rizal Park. At the international airport, the DOT counter is just behind customs. The staff there will be pleased to check on the availability of hotel rooms for you.

Post

The quickest way to send mail from the Philippines is to take it to the Air Mail Distribution Center near the Domestic Airport or the office in the arrivals area at Ninoy Aquino International Airport, which is open every day. Particularly at Christmas, make sure you see your mail being stamped so that the stamps can't be removed and resold. There are a lot of complaints about the small post office in Mabini St. By contrast, the Rizal Park Post Office near the Manila Hotel is not as busy as the GPO or the Mabini St office.

Money

Manila is the best place to change money. The rates moneychangers offer are better than those at banks, and they're better in Manila than elsewhere in the country. Carry lots of change or small bills: when you get out into the country, changing P100 notes can be difficult.

Foreign Embassies & Consulates

The addresses of foreign embassies and consulates in Metro Manila are:

Australia
BPI Building, Ayala Ave, Makati (tel 8177911)

Austria
Prince Building, Rada St, Makati (tel 8179191)

Belgium
Don Jacinto Building, Dela Rosa St, Makati (tel 876570-74)

Canada
Allied Bank Building, Ayala Ave, Makati (tel 8159536)

Denmark
Citibank Building, Paseo de Roxas, Makati (tel 856756, 8191906)

France
Filipinas Life Building, Ayala Ave, Makati (tel 876561-65)

Germany
Solid Bank Building, Paseo de Roxas, Makati (tel 864906)

India
2190 Paraisa St, Makati (tel 872445)

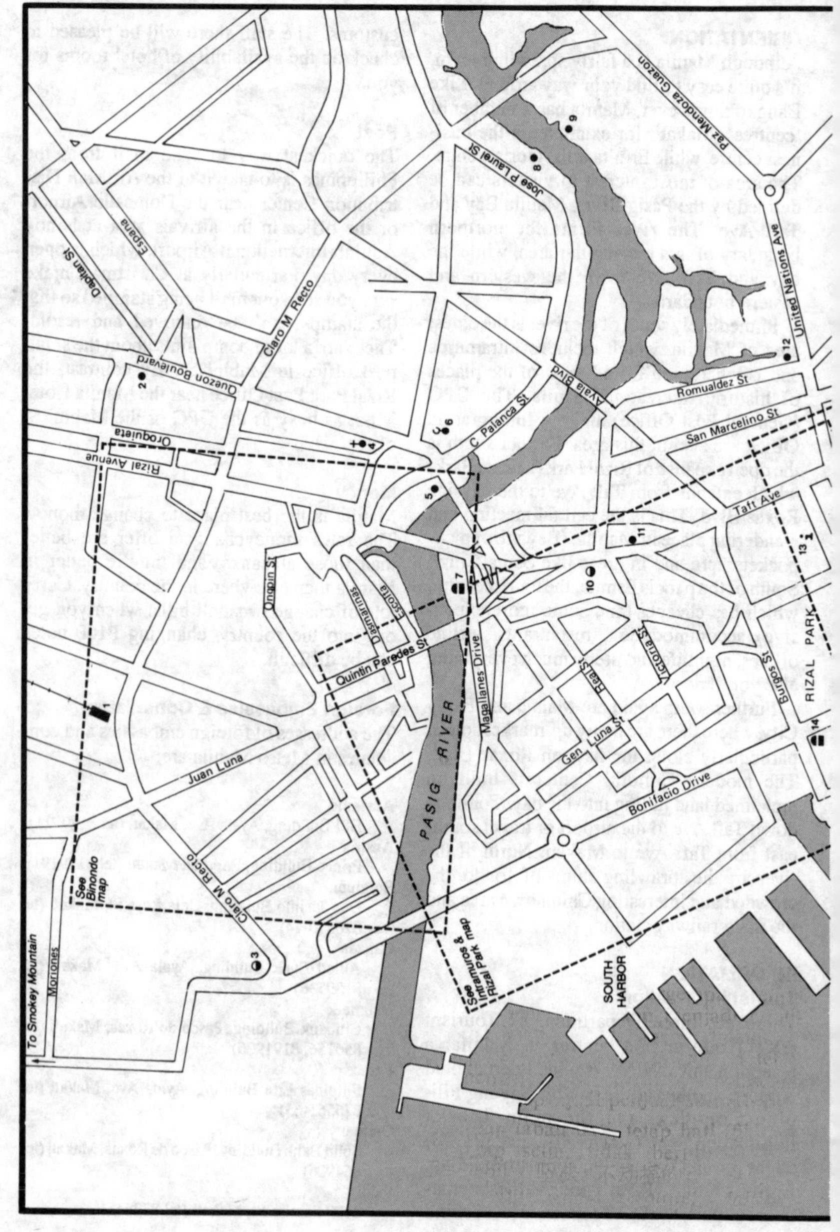
Paz Mendoza Guazon
Jose P Laurel St
United Nations Ave
Romualdez St
San Marcelino St
Taft Ave
RIZAL PARK
Ayala Blvd
C Palanca St
Dapitan St
Espana
Claro M Recto
Quezon Boulevard
Oroquieta
Rizal Avenue
Ongpin St
Escolta
Dasmarinas
Quintin Paredes St
Magallanes Drive
PASIG RIVER
Victoria St
Real St
Gen Luna St
Burgos St
Bonifacio Drive
Juan Luna
Claro M Recto
See Binondo map
See Intramuros & Rizal Park map
SOUTH HARBOR
Morriones
To Smokey Mountain
1
2
3
4
5
6
7
8
9
10
11
12
13
14

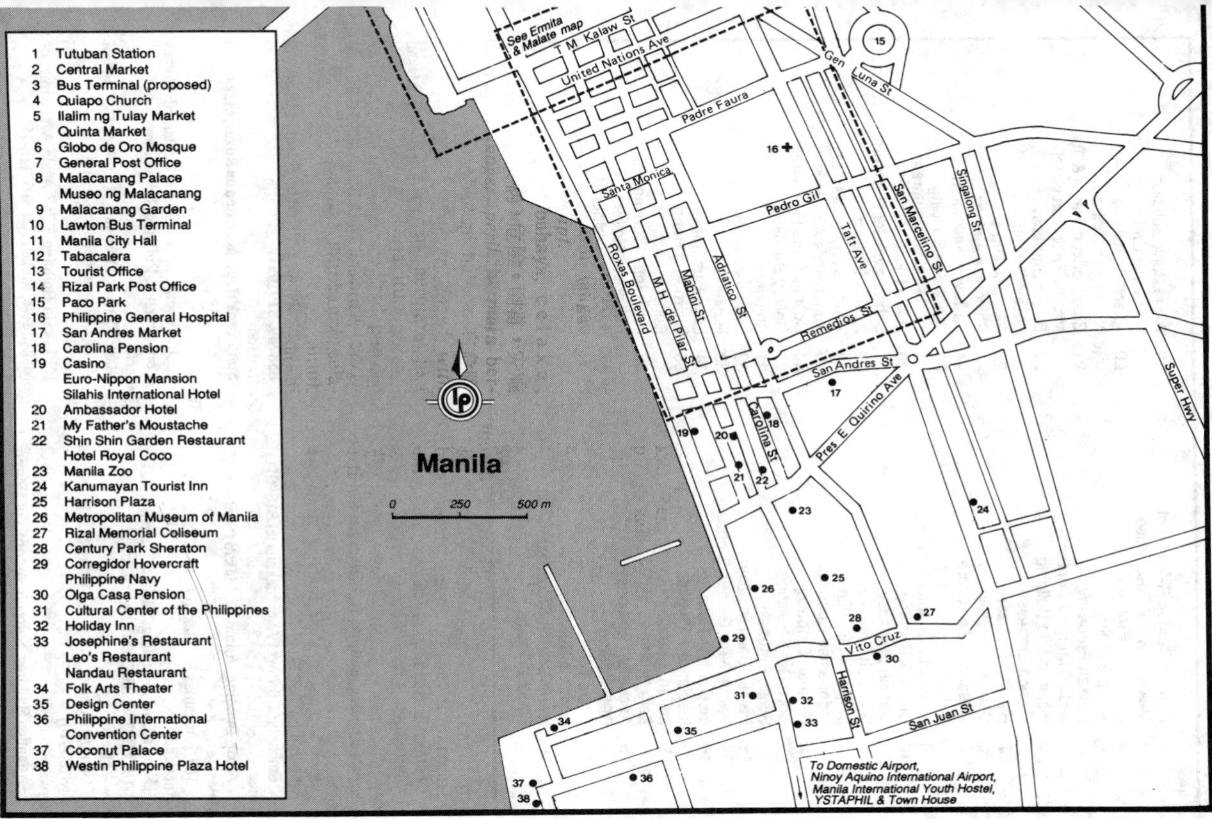
1 Tutuban Station
2 Central Market
3 Bus Terminal (proposed)
4 Quiapo Church
5 Ilalim ng Tulay Market
Quinta Market
6 Globo de Oro Mosque
7 General Post Office
8 Malacanang Palace
Museo ng Malacanang
9 Malacanang Garden
10 Lawton Bus Terminal
11 Manila City Hall
12 Tabacalera
13 Tourist Office
14 Rizal Park Post Office
15 Paco Park
16 Philippine General Hospital
17 San Andres Market
18 Carolina Pension
19 Casino
Euro-Nippon Mansion
Silahis International Hotel
20 Ambassador Hotel
21 My Father's Moustache
22 Shin Shin Garden Restaurant
Hotel Royal Coco
23 Manila Zoo
24 Kanumayan Tourist Inn
25 Harrison Plaza
26 Metropolitan Museum of Manila
27 Rizal Memorial Coliseum
28 Century Park Sheraton
29 Corregidor Hovercraft
Philippine Navy
30 Olga Casa Pension
31 Cultural Center of the Philippines
32 Holiday Inn
33 Josephine's Restaurant
Leo's Restaurant
Nandau Restaurant
34 Folk Arts Theater
35 Design Center
36 Philippine International
Convention Center
37 Coconut Palace
38 Westin Philippine Plaza Hotel
Manila
0
250
500 m
See Ermita & Malate map
T M Kalaw St
United Nations Ave
Gen Luna St
Padre Faura
Santa Monica
Pedro Gil
Taft Ave
San Marcelino St
Singalong St
Roxas Boulevard
M H del Pilar St
Mabini St
Adriatico St
Remedios St
San Andres St
Pres E Quirino Ave
Carolina St
Super Hwy
Vito Cruz
Harrison St
San Juan St
To Domestic Airport,
Ninoy Aquino International Airport,
Manila International Youth Hostel,
YSTAPHIL & Town House

1 Korean Garden Restaurant
2 Makati Central Post Office
3 Japanese Embassy
4 Alpap Building
Korean Embassy
5 Makati Medical Center
6 Filipinas Life Building
French Embassy
7 Belgian Embassy
Don Jacinto Building
8 Casalinda Bookstore
Philbanking Building
9 Mandarin Oriental Hotel
10 Citibank Building
Danish Embassy
Swedish Embassy
11 Indonesia Building
Indonesian Embassy
12 German Embassy
Solid Bank Building
Swiss Embassy
13 Pacific Bank Building
Papua New Guinea Embassy
14 Insular Life Building
Insular Life Theater
15 Italian Embassy
Zeta Building
16 Australian Embassy
BPI Building
17 Bistro RJ
Olympia Building
18 Marie Christine Building
Thai Embassy
19 Allied Bank Building
Canadian Embassy
20 Atlantica Building
Norwegian Embassy
21 Blue Horizon Travel & Tours
Manila Peninsula Hotel
22 British Embassy
Locsin Building
23 PAL Building
Philippine Airlines
24 La Tasca Restaurant
25 Creekside Building
Thai Room Restaurant
26 Metro Disco
Schwarzwälder Restaurant
27 Ayala Museum
28 Aling Asiang Restaurant
29 Aunt Mary's Aunt Restaurant
30 Cosmic Plate Restaurant
Gallery Building
31 Shakey's
32 Landmark Shopping Center
33 Rustan's
34 Love Bus Station
35 Bistro Ang Hang
Sunvar Plaza
36 Hotel Inter-Continental
Philippine Airlines
37 Pensione Virginia
Ville de Saigon Restaurant

Indonesia
Indonesia Building, Salcedo St, Makati (tel 856061-68)
Italy
Zeta Building, Salcedo St, Makati (tel 874531)
Japan
Visa Section: Sikatuna Building, Ayala Ave, Makati (tel 858291)
Embassy: Gil Puyat Ave, Makati (tel 8189011)
Korea
Alpap Building, Alfaro St, Makati (tel 8175705)
Malaysia
107 Tordesillas St, Makati (tel 8174581-85)
Netherlands
King's Court Building, Pasong Tamo St, Makati (tel 886768, 887753)
New Zealand
Gammon Center Building, Alfaro St, Makati (tel 8180910)
Norway
Atlantica Building, Salcedo St, corner of Herrera St, Makati (tel 881111)
Papua New Guinea
Pacific Bank Building, 6766 Ayala Ave, Makati (tel 880386)
Singapore
ODC International Plaza Building, 219 Salcedo St, Makati (tel 8161764)
Sweden
Citibank Building, Paseo de Roxas, Makati (tel 858749, 8191951)
Switzerland
Solid Bank Building, Paseo de Roxas, Makati (tel 8190202-05)
Taiwan
Pacific Economic & Cultural Center, BF Homes Condominium Building, Intramuros
Thailand
Marie Christine Building, 107 Rada St, Legaspi Village, Makati (tel 8155219)
UK
LV Locsin Building, 6752 Ayala Ave, corner of Makati Ave, Makati (tel 8167116-18)

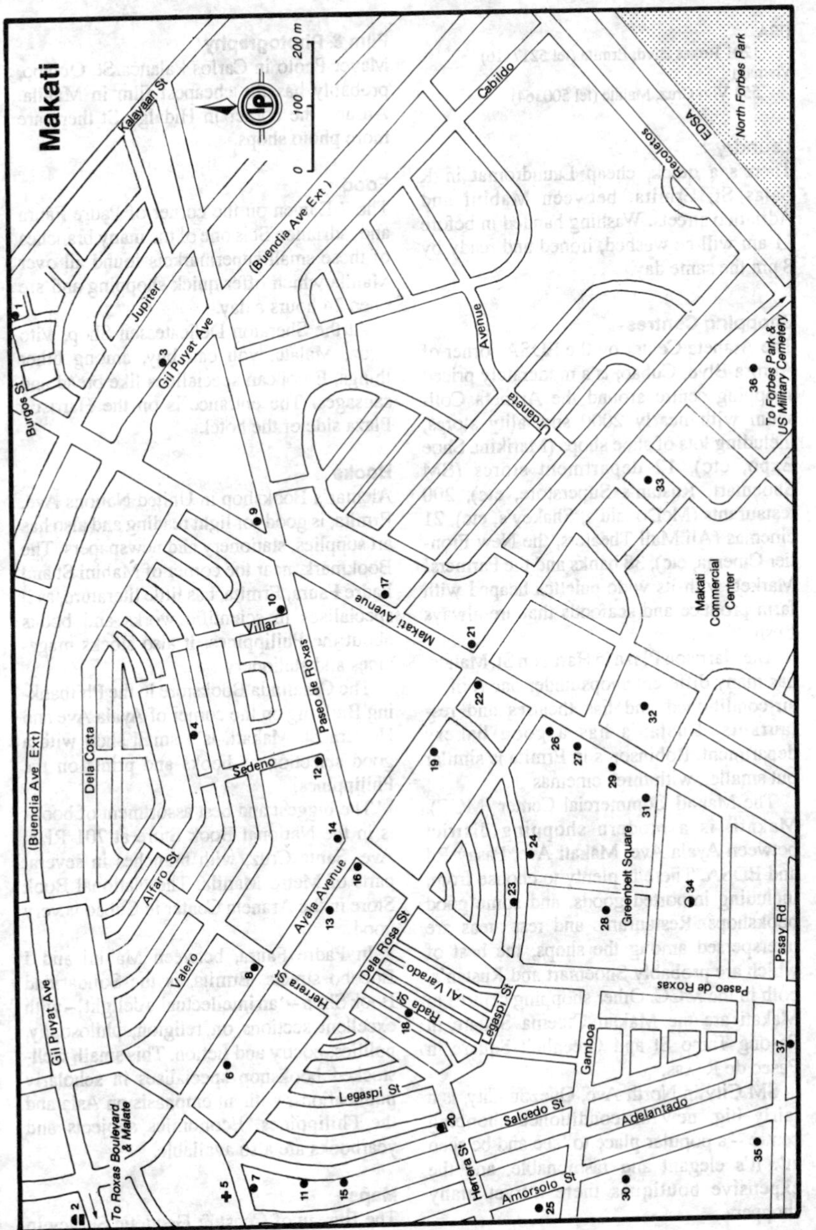
Makati
0
100
200 m
Kalayaan St
Jupiter
Burgos St
Gil Puyat Ave
(Buendia Ave Ext)
Cabildo
Recoletos
EDSA
North Forbes Park
Avenue
Urdaneta
To Forbes Park & US Military Cemetery
Makati Avenue
Paseo de Roxas
Villar
Sedeno
Dela Costa
(Buendia Ave Ext)
Gil Puyat Ave
Alfaro St
Valero
Ayala Avenue
Dela Rosa St
Herrera St
Al Varado
Rada St
Legaspi St
Legaspi St
Gamboa
Salcedo St
Adelantado
Herrera St
Amorsolo St
Paseo de Roxas
Pasay Rd
Makati Commercial Center
Greenbelt Square
To Roxas Boulevard & Malate

USA
1201 Roxas Blvd, Ermita (tel 5217116)
Vietnam
554 Vito Cruz, Malate (tel 500364)

Laundry

There's a quick, cheap Laundromat in R Salas St, Ermita, between Mabini and Adriatico streets. Washing handed in before 11 am will be washed, ironed and ready by 8 pm the same day.

Shopping Centres

The Araneta Center on the EDSA corner of Aurora Blvd, Cubao, is a moderately priced shopping centre around the Araneta Coliseum with nearly 2000 speciality stores, including lots of shoe shops (Marikina Shoe Expo, etc), 12 department stores (SM Shoemart, Rustan's Superstore, etc), 200 restaurants (McDonald's, Shakey's, etc), 21 cinemas (Ali Mall Theaters, the New Frontier Cinema, etc), 38 banks and the Farmers' Market, with its wide palettes heaped with farm produce and seafoods that are always fresh.

The Harrison Plaza in Harrison St, Malate, has many different shops under one roof, is air-conditioned and has theatres and restaurants. Rustan's has a good bakery department. Robinson's in Ermita is similar but smaller, with three cinemas.

The Makati Commercial Center (MCC), Makati, is a modern shopping district between Ayala Ave, Makati Ave, Pasay Rd and EDSA. There is plenty to choose from, including imported goods, and some good bookshops. Restaurants and rest areas are interspersed among the shops, the best of which are probably Shoemart and Rustan's, both in the MCC. Other shopping centres in Makati are the Makati Cinema Square in Pasong Tamo St and Greenbelt Square in Paseo de Roxas.

SM City in North Ave, Quezon City, is a fairly big, new air-conditioned shopping centre – a popular place to 'see and be seen at'. It's elegant and fashionable, and the expensive boutiques there attract many shoppers.

Film & Photography

Mayer Photo in Carlos Palanca St, Quiapo, probably has the cheapest film in Manila. Around the corner in Hidalgo St there are more photo shops.

Food

The 7-Eleven on the corner of Padre Faura and Adriatico St is one of the many branches of these small supermarkets found all over Manila which offer quick shopping and are open 24 hours a day.

At the Sheraton Delicatessen Shop, Vito Cruz, Malate, you can buy, among other things, European specialities like bread and sausages. The entrance is on the Harrison Plaza side of the hotel.

Books

Alemar's Bookshop in United Nations Ave, Ermita, is good for light reading and also has art supplies, stationery and newspapers. The Bookmark, near the corner of Mabini St and Padre Faura, Ermita, has little literature, as it specialises in scientific works and books about the Philippines. It also stocks magazines and stationery.

The Casalinda Bookstore in the Philbanking Building on the corner of Ayala Ave and Herrera St, Makati, is a small shop with a good selection of books and prints on the Philippines.

The biggest and best assortment of books is in the National Book Store at 701 Rizal Ave, Santa Cruz, with branches in several parts of Metro Manila. The National Book Store in the Araneta Center in Cubao is very good.

In Padre Faura, between Mabini and J Bocobo streets, Ermita, is the Solidaridad Book Shop – 'an intellectual's delight' – with excellent sections on religion, philosophy, politics, poetry and fiction. This small, well-stocked bookshop specialises in scholarly publications, with an emphasis on Asia and the Philippines. Economics subjects and yearbooks are also available.

Maps

The Bureau of Coast & Geodetic Survey in

Barraca St, San Nicolas, has detailed maps, including nautical charts. It is open Monday to Friday from 8 am to noon and from 1 to 5 pm.

Diving Equipment

Young's Sporting Goods, 513 Quintin Paredes St, Binondo, is probably the best shop in Manila for diving equipment, with lead, masks from P375, tanks, shoes, harpoons and other spare parts, but they don't refill tanks. They sell mainly US products, but also some Japanese.

RIZAL PARK

This is a real oasis in the centre of the city and is popularly known as Luneta Park. There are flowers, fountains, wide lawns and, of course, plenty of music attracting thousands of strolling Filipinos every day in the late afternoon and evening. If you're there at 5 am, you can see the first eager Chinese doing their t'ai chi. Sunday is a family day, and at about 5 pm there are free concerts. On New Year's Day there are great celebrations here. You can buy food in the cafeteria but the orders have to be written down as the waiters are deaf-mutes.

It is interesting to watch the changing of the guard at the Rizal Memorial, which is close to where the national hero Dr Jose Rizal was executed by the Spaniards on 30 December 1896. His farewell poem, *Mi Ultimo Adios* (My Last Farewell), is inscribed on a brass plaque in many languages.

Tucked away between the monument and the fishpond (towards Kalaw St) is Rizal's Fountain – a well from Wilhelmsfeld, a village near Heidelberg in Germany. They say that Rizal used to drink from this well during his Heidelberg student days.

At the side of the park nearest the water is a children's playground, where you can enjoy the colourful Manila Bay sunsets. On the opposite side, near the Ministry of Tourism, the roller-skating rink with its big globe and the topographical model of the Philippines, there is another playground, with wonderful large stone statues of dinosaurs and monsters.

On either side of the open-air auditorium are the Chinese and Japanese gardens, which are popular meeting places for couples.

INTRAMUROS

Literally the city 'in walls', Intramuros is the Manila of the past. This is where Legaspi erected a fortress in 1571 after his victory over the Muslims. Following attacks by the Chinese fleet and a fire, the Filipinos were forced to build the wall. A wide moat all around made the bulwark complete. Within the walls, the most important buildings were the numerous feudal lords' houses, 12 churches and several hospitals. Only Spaniards and Muslims were allowed to live within the walls; Filipinos were settled on what is now the site of Rizal Park. Likewise, the Chinese were housed in the range of the cannons, about where the City Hall stands today. Neither the Dutch nor the Portuguese managed to storm this fortress and the attacks of the Sulu pirates were also unsuccessful.

Intramuros was almost totally destroyed by bomb attacks in WW II. The San Agustin Church remained relatively undamaged and the Manila Cathedral was rebuilt after the war. During the restoration, Puerta Isabel II and Puerta Real, two of the original seven gates of the city, were also restored.

A few houses are also well worth seeing, like the Casa Manila in the San Luis Complex and the El Amanecer, both in General Luna St.

Fort Santiago

The most important defence location of the Intramuros fortress-city was Fort Santiago. From this strategic location, at the mouth of the Pasig River, all activity in Manila Bay could be observed. During the Japanese occupation in WW II, innumerable Filipino prisoners lost their lives in the infamous dungeon cells which lay below sea level – at high tide there was no escape. Dr Jose Rizal also spent his last days in a narrow cell at this

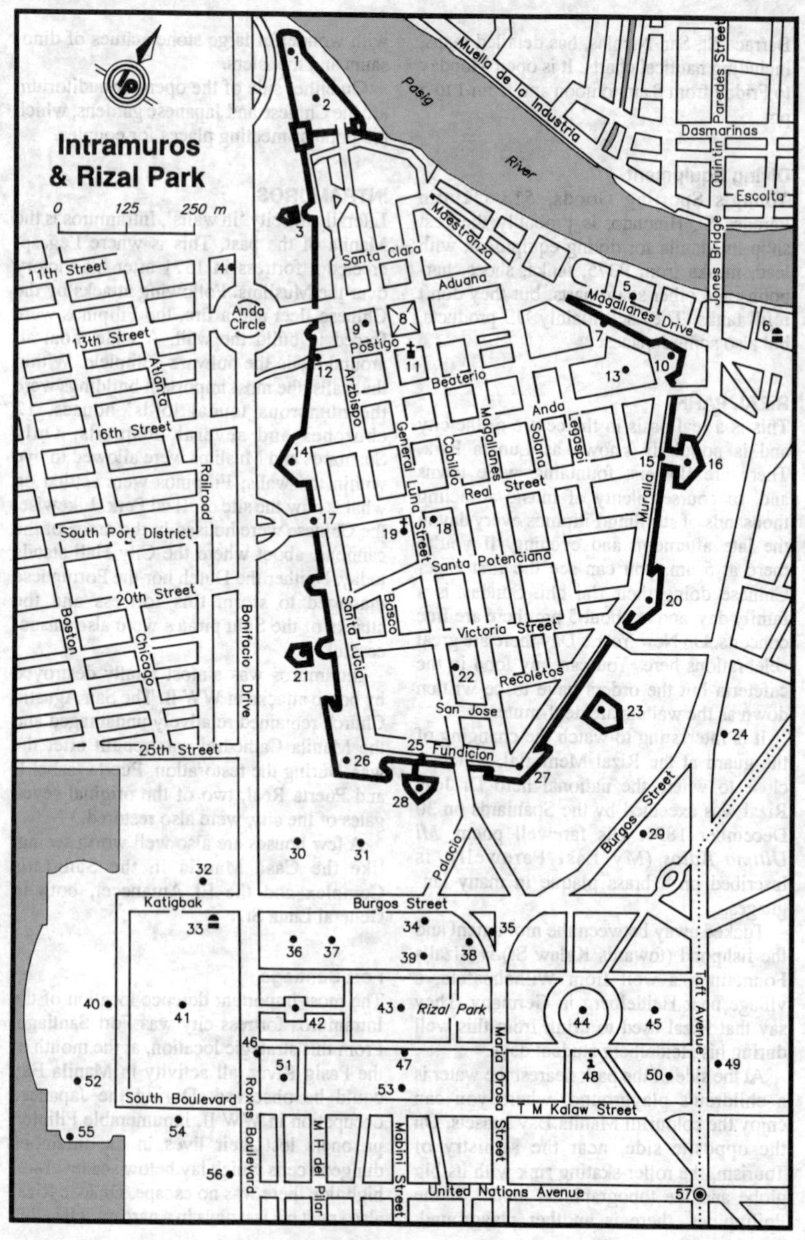
Intramuros
& Rizal Park
0 125 250 m
Pasig
River
Muella de la Industria
Dasmarinas
Quintin Paredes Street
Escolta
Jones Bridge
Maestranza
Santa Clara
Aduana
Magallanes Drive
11th Street
13th Street
16th Street
20th Street
25th Street
Anda Circle
Atlanta
Postigo
Arzbispo
Beaterio
Anda
Solana
Legaspi
Magallanes
Cabildo
General Luna Street
Real Street
Muralla
Railroad
South Port District
Santa Potenciana
Santa Lucia
Basco
Victoria Street
Recoletos
San Jose
Fundicion
Bonifacio Drive
Boston
Chicago
Palacio
Burgos Street
Taft Avenue
Katigbak
Rizal Park
Roxas Boulevard
M H del Pilar
Mabini Street
Maria Orosa Street
T M Kalaw Street
South Boulevard
United Nations Avenue
1
2
3
4
5
6
7
8
9
10
11
12
13
14
15
16
17
18
19
20
21
22
23
24
25
26
27
28
29
30
31
32
33
34
35
36
37
38
39
40
41
42
43
44
45
46
47
48
49
50
51
52
53
54
55
56
57

1 Rizal Shrine
2 Fort Santiago
3 Revellin de San Francisco
4 Seamen's Club
5 Immigration Office
6 General Post Office
7 Puerta Isabel II
8 Plaza Roma
9 Palacio del Gobernador
10 Bastion de San Gabriel
11 Manila Cathedral
12 Puerta del Postigo
13 Letran College
14 Bastion de Santa Lucia
15 Puerta del Parian
16 Revellin del Parian
17 Puerta de Santa Lucia
18 Casa Manila Museum San Luis Complex
19 San Agustin Church
20 Bastion de Dilao
21 Fortin San Pedro
22 El Amanecer
23 Revellin de Recoletos
24 Manila City Hall
25 Puerta Real
26 Bastion de San Diego
27 Bastion de San Andres
28 Aquarium
29 National Museum
30 Legaspi & Urdaneta Monument
31 Golf Course
32 Manila Hotel
33 Rizal Park Post Office
34 Planetarium
35 Artificial Waterfall
36 Rizal's Execution Spot
37 Chinese Garden
38 Japanese Garden
39 Concerts in the Park Open-Air Stage
40 Quirino Grandstand
41 Parade Ground
42 Rizal Memorial
43 Central Lagoon
44 Agrifina Circle
45 Philippines Model
46 Sightseeing Tours in Double-Decker Buses
47 Cafeteria
48 Tourist Office
49 Jai-Alai Stadium
50 Children's Playground
51 Rizal's Fountain
52 Children's Playground
53 National Library
54 Army & Navy Club
55 Harbour Trips Harbor View Restaurant
56 US Embassy
57 United Nations Avenue Metrorail Station

fort before his execution by the Spaniards in 1896.

Today Fort Santiago is a memorial. There is an open-air theatre, the Rizal Shrine and a display of old cars which used to belong to important Filipino personalities.

In early 1988, Fort Santiago was turned inside out, with government permission, by US gold-seekers who, by excavating, hoped to uncover the legendary war treasure of the Japanese general Yamashita, which was rumoured to have been hidden in the Philippines. All excavations were in vain, of course.

The fort is open daily between 8 am and 10 pm.

San Agustin Church

The first constructions of the San Agustin Church were destroyed by fires in 1574 and 1583. In 1599 the foundation stone for the present construction was laid. The massive church was not damaged by the earthquakes of 1645, 1754, 1852, 1863, 1880, 1968 and 1970, nor by the bombardment in the fighting around Manila in February 1945. San Agustin is the oldest existing stone church in the Philippines. From 1879 to 1880, the crystal chandeliers came from Paris, the walls and roofs were masterfully painted by two Italian artists, and the choir stalls were carved by the Augustinian monks themselves. In a small chapel to the left of the high altar lie the mortal remains of Legaspi. There is a museum and a contemplative inner courtyard adjoining the church.

Manila Cathedral

This cathedral, with its great cupola, is the Philippines' most significant Catholic church. It is in the Plaza Roma at Intramuros. With the help of the Vatican, the building, which was destroyed in WW II, was rebuilt from 1954 to 1958; some old walls were restored and integrated into the new construction. The large organ with its 4500 pipes came from the Netherlands and is the largest in Asia.

QUIAPO CHURCH

This church became famous because of its large crucifix of black wood. The Black Nazarene was carved in Mexico and brought to the Philippines by the Spaniards in the 17th century. Each day, especially on Friday, thousands of Catholics come to the church to pay homage to the crucifix. The climax of the adoration is the procession on 9 January and in Passion Week (the week between Passion Sunday and Palm Sunday, before Easter) on Monday and Friday.

CHINESE CEMETERY

It may seem irreverent to recommend a cemetery as a tourist attraction but this one should not be missed. It contains some of the most ostentatious tombs in the world. There are actual houses with mailboxes and toilets – some even have an air-conditioner. Things get lively on All Saints' Day (1 November), when the descendants of the dead come to visit their ancestors, just as Catholic Filipinos do. Most Sundays, in fact, it's a fascinating place to visit. One of the attendants who live there will take you round if you settle on a fee first; they have some amazing stories to tell. It's also just as well to have their company for safety reasons if it is a quiet day and you are going around the outside of the area, which is crossed by several streets and is about as big as Rizal Park.

The Chinese Cemetery is in the north of the suburb of Santa Cruz, just where Rizal Ave becomes Rizal Ave Extension. It has two entrances: the North Gate, which is almost always closed, and the South Gate, which is tucked away and can be reached from Aurora Ave. Apart from taxis, the best way to get there from Ermita is by Metrorail to Abad Santos Station. From there it is about 350 metres to the right. A tricycle from the station costs about P1 per person; taking one saves asking the way. Otherwise you can get a jeepney at Mabini St or Taft Ave going towards Caloocan City; they carry the sign 'Monumento'. Get off at Rizal Ave, on the corner of Aurora Ave. It will cost you P50 to drive through the cemetery.

1 Tutuban Railway Station
2 Seng Guan Buddhist Temple
3 Quan Yin Chay Restaurant
4 D Jose Metrorail Station
5 Philippine Rabbit Bus Terminal
6 Vegetarian Food Garden
7 National Book Store
8 Divisoria Market
9 Home Garden Vegetarian Restaurant
10 Mandarin Villa Restaurant
11 Spring Garden Food Palace
12 Food Stalls
13 Stampmakers
14 Third Welcome Gate
15 Binondo Church
Plaza Calderon de la Barca
16 Second Welcome Gate
17 Fairmart Department Store
18 Shoe World
19 Santa Cruz Church
Santa Cruz Plaza
20 Carriedo Metrorail Station
21 Young's Sporting Goods
22 Bureau of Coast & Geodetic Survey
23 First Welcome Gate
24 General Post Office

CHINATOWN

Chinatown is not a clearly defined suburb but a cultural and business district that takes in parts of Santa Cruz and Binondo, roughly the area between the three Chinese-Philippine friendship stores called the Welcome Gates. (See the Binondo map.) From Ermita you cross the Pasig River over the Jones Bridge, between the Immigration Office and the GPO, to the First Welcome Gate, also known as the 'Arch of Goodwill'. The southern part of Chinatown begins here. From Quintin Paredes St, which runs through the

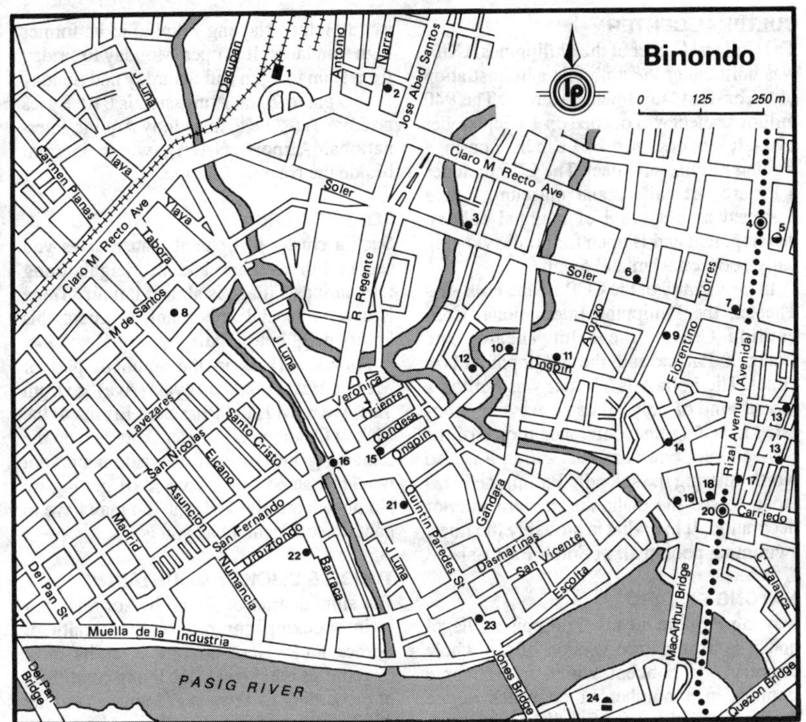

gate, several little streets seem to wind crazily towards the big east-west curve of Ongpin St that stretches between the other two Welcome Gates.

Ongpin St is the main business street of Chinatown, but in the next streets you can also find exotic shops like herb-scented drug stalls, well-stocked Chinese groceries, small teahouses and spacious restaurants. In contrast with the Chinatowns of other Asian cities, this one is very busy on Sunday.

MALACANANG PALACE

The Malacanang Palace is the single most noteworthy attraction in the suburb of San Miguel. It is in Jose P Laurel St, on the banks of the Pasig River. Malacanang is a derivation of the old Filipino description *May Lakan Diyan* meaning 'here lives a nobleman' and referring to the Spanish aristocrat Luis Rocha, who built the palace. In 1802 he sold it to an important Spanish soldier. From 1863 the nobleman's house was used as the domicile of the Spanish heads of government. Later, the Americans also used the palace as their residence.

The first Philippine head of state, Manuel Quezon, occupied the palace. It was used as the seat of office by President Marcos until his reign ended in February 1986, when the palace was opened to the public. It has since been renovated, redecorated and reopened as a museum of 'historical, art and heritage values'. (For more information about the museum, see the Museums section in this chapter.) President Aquino continues to govern from the adjoining Palace Guest House.

CULTURAL CENTER

The Cultural Center of the Philippines (CCP) was built under the umbrella administration of the ex-first lady Imelda Marcos. The P40 million project was opened on 19 September 1969. It was designed by Leandro Locsin, a leading Filipino architect. The CCP includes a theatre, art gallery and museum. It was designed as a symbol of national cultural development and is open for public viewing daily between 9 am and 5 pm.

In the vicinity of the CCP are the Folk Arts Theater, the Philippine International Convention Center, the Film Theater, the Coconut Palace and the Philippine Plaza Hotel. The Folk Arts Theater was built in a record time of only 70 days. Anyone interested in seeing the conference rooms of the Convention Center can take a tour. It is also worth entering the splendid Philippine Plaza Hotel to see the elaborate modern interior decoration. It has what is probably the finest swimming pool in all of South-East Asia.

NAYONG PILIPINO

Nayong Pilipino means 'Philippine village' and it is a miniature version of the whole country – a concept which has become popular in a number of countries in the region. Typical houses and distinctive landscapes have been built on the 35 hectare site, which represents the archipelago's various regions and its diverse cultural minorities. Jeepneys take you through the sites for free, or you can rent a bicycle or tricycle with a sidecar. There is boating on the lake, fishing, a covered walk-in aviary, a big aquarium (somewhat sparsely stocked), cool herbal gardens and more.

The shops are a good way for newly arrived visitors to the Philippines to get acquainted with what's available in the various islands. It may be worth visiting the Philippine Museum of Ethnology (see the Museums section in this chapter). When I last visited, there was Muslim dancing in the Mindanao section on Saturday afternoons between 3 and 4 pm.

Service and entertainment declined after 1988, although the Tourist Office has promised to return Nayong Pilipino to its former high standards. It is open Monday to Friday from 9 am to 6 pm and Saturday and Sunday from 9 am to 7 pm. Admission is P10. Buses go from Taft Ave to the Ninoy Aquino International Airport (NAIA), which is right beside the Nayong Pilipino.

FORBES PARK

Such a cluster of opulent mansions as you see in Forbes Park and its neighbouring Dasmarinas Village is almost unique. There is even a special police unit to guard this luxury neighbourhood.

Forbes Park is in the southern part of Makati. Buses marked 'Ayala (Ave)' go from Taft Ave or M H del Pilar St in Ermita to the Makati Commercial Center. You then do the remaining km by taxi as visitors on foot wouldn't stand much chance of getting in. No photos are allowed and you may have to hand in your camera as you go in.

TONDO & SMOKEY MOUNTAIN

The slum quarter of Tondo in North Harbor is in shocking contrast to the wealth of Forbes Park. Here poverty is at its most extreme, as is evident in the living conditions of (according to Terre des Hommes) around 3000 families of five to eight members each, who live in huts on the municipal tip – the Smokey Mountain – combing the stinking, smouldering refuse for anything usable, like bottles or tin, which can be sold to the dealers living nearby on Honorio Lopez Blvd.

If you are interested in the burning social problems of the Philippines in general and Tondo in particular, you will find wonderful conversationalists in two sisters of the order of Mother Teresa: Sister Mary Andrea and Sister Ursula (a German and a Filipina). Helping hands are welcome and medication is gratefully received. Look for the Missions of Charity at 683 del Pan St, San Nicolas, Metro Manila (a children's house) or at 287 Tayuman St (houses for the dying and a children's tuberculosis ward).

The Canossa Health Center was established in Tondo in the beginning of 1984, and there are always two or three German doctors on duty from the Committee of Doctors for the Third World. They are delighted to get visitors and will gladly discuss Tondo's problems with anyone who is interested.

US MILITARY CEMETERY

The US Military Cemetery is directly east of Forbes Park. Here, in rank and file, are the bodies of 17,000 US soldiers who died in the Philippines during WW II. In the circular memorial built on a rise are numerous good pictures of the battles of the Pacific. It's worth seeing.

It is about two km from where Ayala Ave meets EDSA. The extension of Ayala Ave is called McKinley Rd and leads through Forbes Park, past San Antonio Church, the Manila Golf Club and the Manila Polo Club directly to the cemetery.

FAITH HEALERS

The unorthodox methods of the infamous Filipino faith healers are now world famous. Clearly some of these 'doctors' are no more than money-grubbing charlatans, but others are so skilful that even sceptics gape in awe.

Many patients travel to Baguio, some to Pangasinan Province, but there are also healers in Metro Manila. Anyone can watch after obtaining the consent of the patient.

For further information, get in touch with the Philippine Spiritual Health Foundation Inc (tel 5210771), Manila Midtown Hotel, on the corner of Adriatico St and Pedro Gil, Ermita. The founder of this organisation is the famous and businesslike faith healer Alex Orbito, who also owns the travel bureau Orbit Tours. The private address of Alex Orbito, where he also conducts consultations, is 9 Maryland St, Cubao, Quezon City.

MUSEUMS

You will find many interesting museums in Manila; they are listed here in alphabetical order.

The **Ayala Museum** in Makati Ave, Makati, specialises in high points of Philippine history, chronologically presented in over 60 showcase dioramas. There is also an ethnographic section which features artefacts, weapons and ships. Behind the museum is an aviary and tropical garden under a gigantic net. The museum is open from 9 am to 6 pm Thursday to Sunday, and the charge is P20 (P10 for students). The museum is just 200 metres from the Manila Peninsula Hotel. Admission to the aviary costs P22 (no student discount).

The **Carfel Seashell Museum** at 1786 Mabini St, Malate, was originally a small private collection of the shells found in Philippine waters. The display room is on the 1st floor, and below is a shop selling shells, coral and shell ornaments. It is open from 9 am to 6 pm Monday to Saturday and admission is P10 (P5 for students).

The **Casa Manila Museum** in General Luna St, Intramuros, is one of the first examples of the restoration which Intramuros is undergoing. With its beautiful inner courtyards and antique furnishings, it is a faithful reproduction of a typical Spanish residence. Downstairs is a model of Fort Santiago and the bulwarks of Intramuros as well as a photographic display. Attached to the museum is the Restaurant Muralla. The museum is open from 9 am to noon and from 1 to 6 pm daily except Monday, and admission is P10.

The **Central Bank Money Museum** is in the Central Bank Compound in Roxas Blvd, Malate. It is part of the Metropolitan Museum and is on the level of the Cultural Center. It not only has coins and bank notes, but shell and ornament currency also. It is open from 10 am to 5 pm daily except on Monday and admission is free. The **Metropolitan Museum of Manila** has changing displays of various art forms, including some 'old masters'. It is open daily except Monday from 9 am to 6 pm. Admission is free.

The **Coconut Palace** is in the Cultural Center Complex, which is in Roxas Blvd, Malate. This former guesthouse of the Marcos regime, made of the best tropical timbers, was erected in 1981 especially for the visit of the Pope. It is open daily except Monday from 9 am to 4 pm and admission is P100.

The **Cultural Center Museum** on Roxas Blvd, Malate, has Oriental and Islamic art on permanent display on the 4th floor. The art displays in the main gallery are changed from time to time. It is open Monday to Friday from 9 am to 6 pm and admission is P2.

The **Lopez Memorial Museum** is in the Chronicle Building (ground floor), Neralco Ave, Pasig. This is a private museum with a valuable collection of more than 13,000 Filipino books. The collection of historical travel literature is remarkable and includes one of three existing copies of *De Moluccis Insulis* (The Moluccan Islands) by Maximillianus Transylvanus. The work dates back to 1524 and is the first printed account of Magellan's voyage to the Philippines. Also on display are some important oil paintings, some of them award-winning works by the well-known classical Filipino artists Felix Resurreccion Hidalgo and Juan Luna. It is open Monday to Friday from 8.30 am to noon and from 1 to 4 pm. Admission is P15.

The **Museo ng Malacanang** is in Jose P Laurel St, San Miguel. When you visit the Malacanang Palace, it seems as if the family of former president Marcos has just left its 'modest residence'. Here you can see Imelda's famous shoes, Ferdinand's bedroom, their grandson's mini-Mercedes and many more of the extravagant luxuries which their successor Cory Aquino firmly renounced. It is open Monday and Tuesday from 9 to 11 am and 1 to 3 pm and Thursday and Friday from 9 to 11 am for guided groups. Admission is P200. There is public viewing on Thursday and Friday from 1 to 3 pm , at a cost of P10; on Saturday from 9 am to noon and from 2 to 5 pm the public viewing is free. Tickets can be bought at the palace gates, where you also have to go through a security check. The crush on Saturday and on the cheap afternoons is tremendous. On certain official occasions the palace and museum are closed to the public. For information about these ring 407775 and 5212301. There are jeepneys from Quiapo Market at Quezon Bridge to the palace.

The University of Santo Tomas, in Espano St, Sampaloc, the oldest university in the Philippines, houses the **Museum of Arts & Sciences**. It has an extensive collection of historic documents and a noteworthy library with more than 180,000 volumes. It is open Monday to Friday from 9 am to noon and from 3 to 6 pm. Admission is free.

The **National Museum** in Burgos St, Rizal Park, has many prehistoric finds, including a piece of the skull of 'Tabon Man' found in Tabon Cave, Palawan. There are also displays of pottery, weapons, costumes and ornaments. The museum is open Monday to Saturday from 9 am to noon and from 2 to 5 pm. Admission is free.

The **Philippine Museum of Ethnology**, Nayong Pilipino, Pasay City, offers comprehensive information on the lifestyles of the so-called cultural minority groups. Tools, weapons, musical instruments and everyday utensils are on display. Written explanations and photos illustrate the differences between the various Filipino tribes. It is open Monday to Friday from 9 am to 6 pm and Saturday and Sunday from 9 am to 7 pm. Admission is free.

Puerta Isabel II in Magallanes Drive, Intramuros, displays liturgical objects, *carrosas* (processional carriages) and some old bells. It is open daily except Monday from 9 am to noon and from 1 to 6 pm. Admission is free.

The **Rizal Shrine** at Fort Santiago, Intramuros, is a memorial to the national hero, Dr Jose Rizal. You can see some personal effects and his death cell. The shrine is open daily from 9 am to noon and from 1 to 5 pm but closed on public holidays. Entrance is P2.50.

The **San Agustin Museum**, San Agustin Church in General Luna St, Intramuros, has been established since 1973 in the Augustinian monastery. You can see frescoes, oil paintings, antique choir stalls, precious robes and other liturgical items. It is open daily from 8 am to noon and from 1 to 5 pm. Admission is P15.

MARKETS

The **Baclaran Flea Market**, one of the biggest markets in Manila, is in Roxas Blvd,

Baclaran, near the Baclaran Church. Every day, from Roxas Blvd up as far as Harrison St (the Metrorail South Terminal), good-value clothing, food, flowers and household goods are on sale. The busiest time is on Wednesday, when the many churchgoers come looking for bargains after mass.

Central Market in Quezon Blvd, Santa Cruz, is a big market hall full of clothing and accessories such as T-shirts, bags and shoes.

Divisoria Market, San Nicolas, is in Santo Cristo St and the side streets nearby. It is a bright, lively market where examples of almost everything produced in the Philippines are sold at reasonable prices. There is a good vegetables and fruit section. Look out for pickpockets here!

Pistang Pilipino is near Pedro Gil, between M H del Pilar and Mabini streets, Malate. It is a fairly lifeless market, mainly for tourists. 'Fixed price...but I give you good discount'! Still, it's a good place to find out about the country's handicrafts, and if you're a clever shopper you could do extremely well.

Quinta Market in Carlos Palanca St, Quiapo, is also called the Santa Cruz or Quiapo Market. It is by Quezon Bridge, near Quiapo Church, and sells textiles, household goods and many other things. Handicrafts are sold in the **Ilalim ng Tulay Market** under the bridge, and not far away is the **Rajah Sulimon Market**, a Muslim market near the Globo de Oro Mosque.

San Andres Market, San Andres St, Malate, has a wide range of top-quality tropical fruit. Perhaps the best and certainly the dearest fruit market in Manila, it is also open at night.

PLACES TO STAY

Manila has a very wide range of accommodation and it shouldn't be too hard to find something to suit you. The tourist centre is Ermita, where you will find most of the government offices, while the business centre is in Makati. Most of the cheaper places to stay at are in, or very close to, Ermita. There are a few top-end hotels in Ermita, but quite a few more are strung out along the bay, fairly close to Ermita, in Malate and Pasay City. Some of the top-end places can also be found in Makati.

PLACES TO STAY – BOTTOM END

There are a lot of hostel-style places around Manila, many offering dormitory accommodation. A number are close to Ermita, generally in or just off Taft Ave, away from the bay.

Youth Hostel Philippines (tel 592507) at 1572 Leon Guinto St has dorm beds in fan-cooled rooms for P42; there's a P2 discount for YHA members. There are also singles/doubles for P75/95. It's basic and relatively good, but, although the doors are shut at 12.30 am, it's very noisy.

The *Manila International Youth Hostel* (tel 8320680; fax 8187948; tlx 41316 YSTAPHILPM) at 4227 Tomas Claudio St, Paranaque, has dorm beds for P75 (YHA members P50). It is a good, clean house with a garden. This is the office of YSTAPHIL, the Youth & Student Travel Association of the Philippines. It is next to the Excelsior Hotel, on the corner of Roxas Blvd.

The *Manda Pension House* is at 1307 F Agoncillo St, on the corner of Padre Faura, Ermita. Simple rooms with fans are P80 and you can get a discount for a week's stay.

The *Carolina Pension* (tel 5223961) at 2116 Carolina St, Malate, has simple accommodation. Single rooms with fan cost from P75 to P175, and doubles with fan and bath cost P150 and with air-con and bath P225.

Lucen's Pension House (tel 5222389) at 2158 Carolina St, Malate, has basic, clean rooms with fan for P160, with fan and bath for P195 and with air-con and bath for P275. It's next to the big Victoria Court Motel and has a small restaurant.

The *Town House* (tel 8331939) at the Villa Carolina Townhouse, 201 Roxas Blvd, Unit 31, Paranaque, has dorm beds with fan for P50, singles with fan for P80, doubles with fan from P140 to P180 and with fan and bath for P220. It is pleasant, with a friendly atmosphere created by Bill and Laura, who like travelling themselves. It's in a small side

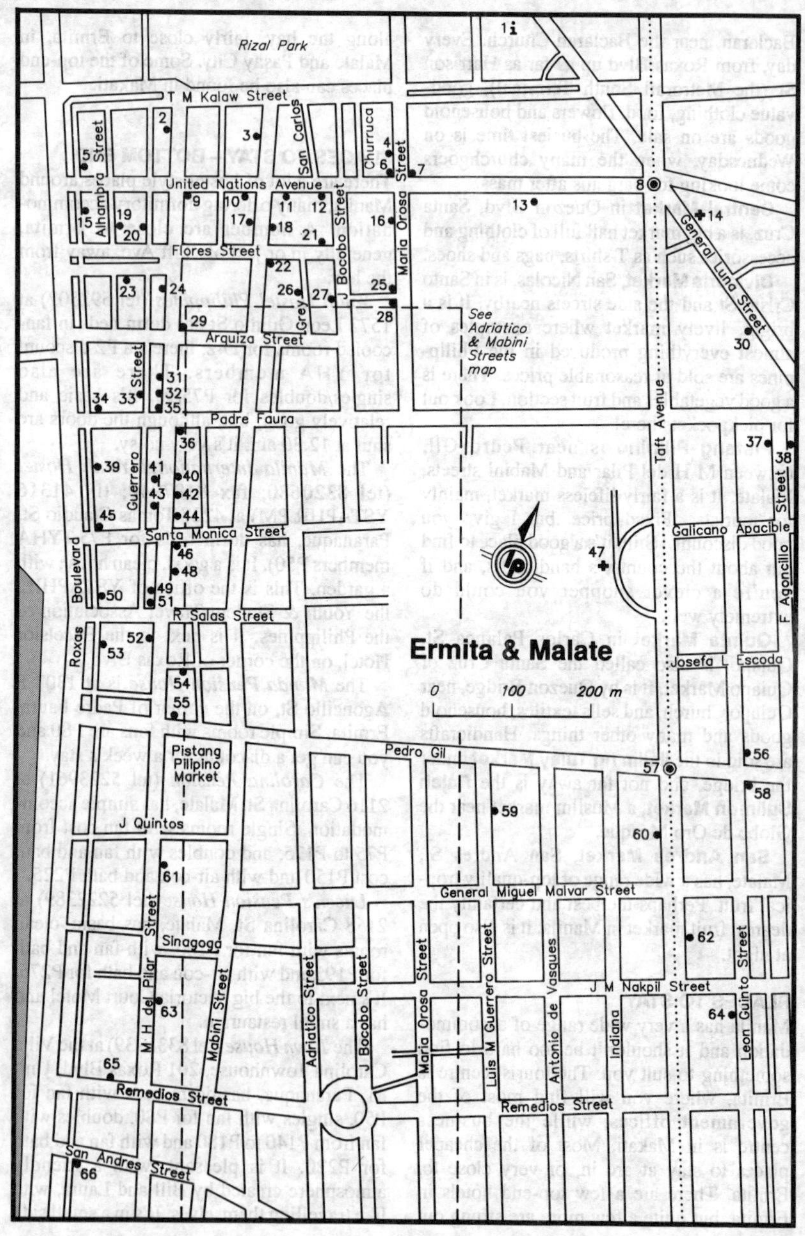
Rizal Park
T M Kalaw Street
Alhambra Street
San Carlos
Churruca
Maria Orosa Street
United Nations Avenue
J Bocobo Street
Flores Street
Grey
Arquiza Street
See Adriatico & Mabini Streets map
Padre Faura
Guerrero
Street
Santa Monica Street
Boulevard
Roxas
R Salas Street
Ermita & Malate
0
100
200 m
Pistang Pilipino Market
Pedro Gil
J Quintos
Sinagoga
M H del Pilar Street
Mabini Street
Adriatico Street
J Bocobo Street
Remedios Street
San Andres Street
Maria Orosa Street
Luis M Guerrero Street
Antonio de Vasques
Indiana
General Miguel Malvar Street
J M Nakpil Street
Leon Guinto Street
Remedios Street
Taft Avenue
General Luna Street
Galicano Apacible
F Agoncillo
Street
Josefa L Escoda
1
2
3
4
5
6
7
8
9
10
11
12
13
14
15
16
17
18
19
20
21
22
23
24
25
26
27
28
29
30
31
32
33
34
35
36
37
38
39
40
41
42
43
44
45
46
47
48
49
50
51
52
53
54
55
56
57
58
59
60
61
62
63
64
65
66

1 Tourist Office
2 Hong Kong Restaurant
3 Mabini Mansion
4 Kentucky Fried Chicken
5 Dutch Inn
Majestic Apartments
6 McDonald's
7 Manila Pavilion Hotel
8 United Nations Avenue Metrorail Station
9 Nino di Roma
10 Southern Cross Bar & Club
Southern Cross Inn
11 Moulin Rouge Theater Club
12 Alemar's Bookshop
13 Western Police Station
14 Manila Medical Center
15 Bayview Prince Hotel
16 Max's
17 Club 21
18 Jodi's Place
19 Swagman Hotel
20 Au Bon Vivant
21 Hotel Soriente
22 Birdwatcher's Bar
Swagman Birdwatcher
23 Mayumi Inn
New Park Lodge
24 Myrna's
25 Bulwagang Pilipino
26 Richmond Pension
27 Barrio Fiesta
28 Pension Filipinas
29 Hotel La Corona
30 Jetset Executive Mansion
31 Diamond Inn
32 Sandico Apartment Hotel
33 Pool Bar
34 Aurelio Hotel
35 Iseya Hotel & Restaurant
Rooftop Restaurant
36 Mrs Wong
37 Manda Pension House
38 Casa Dalco
39 Broadway Travel
Avis Rent-a-Car
40 Exotic Garden Restaurant
New Bangkok Club
Superstar
Swiss Hut
41 Lili Marleen
42 Guernica's
Lafayette
43 Edelweiss
44 Aida's
45 Shinmen Restaurant
46 Firehouse
Romanza Lodge
47 Philippine General Hospital
48 Rol's Ihaw Ihaw Restaurant & Beer Garden
49 Australian Club
50 Boulevard Mansion
51 Hula Hut
Rosie's Diner
52 Fischfang
Sleepy Cheaper Guesthouse
53 Philippine Airlines
54 Old Heidelberg
Swiss Bistro
55 White House Tourist Inn
56 Youth Hostel Philippines
57 Pedro Gil Metrorail Station
58 New Casa Olga Pension
59 Tropicana Apartment Hotel
60 Philippine Long Distance Telephone Company (PLDT)
61 Pension Natividad
62 Philippine Airlines
63 Weinstube
64 Casa Solanie Apartelle
65 Shakey's Malate
66 Aristocrat Restaurant

street called Sunset Drive and is only about five minutes away by taxi (which costs P15) from the Domestic Airport and Ninoy Aquino International Airport.

Richmond Pension (tel 585277) is at 1165 Grey St, Ermita, in a quiet little side street. It has singles/doubles with fan for P120/200. The rooms are small but clean.

Remedios Pensionne House (tel 5220163) at 609 Remedios St, Ermita, is simple and homely. It has singles with fan for P150, doubles with fan and bath for P250, and singles/doubles with air-con and bath for P350/400.

The *Circle Pension* (tel 5222920) at 602 Remedios St, Malate, is basic but comfortable with singles/doubles with fan for P250/330. Air-con is P100 extra.

Casa Dalco (tel 598522, 508825) at 1318 F Agoncillo St, on the corner of Padre Faura, is a beautiful house and has friendly owners. Singles/doubles with fan cost P130/150, with air-con P200 and with air-con and bath P300.

Casa Dalco (tel 507558) at 1910 Mabini St, Malate, has singles with air-con for P300 and singles/doubles with air-con and bath for P320/360. It's a good place with a restaurant.

The *Pension Natividad* (tel 5210524) at 1601 M H del Pilar St, Malate, has dorm beds with fan for P70 and with air-con for P100, and rooms with fan and bath for P250, and with air-con and bath for P400/450. It has a pleasant atmosphere.

The *Sleepy Cheaper* (tel 5219019) at 1511 M H del Pilar St, Ermita, has simple but clean singles/doubles with fan for P125/150 and with fan and bath for P250.

The *Olga Casa Pension* (tel 587647) at 1674 Mabini St, Malate, has singles/doubles with fan for P145/170 and doubles with fan and bath for P195. It has wide beds and a restaurant.

Another *Olga Casa Pension* (tel 596265) is at 640 Vito Cruz, Malate, near the Sheraton Hotel (properly known as the Century Park Sheraton). It has singles/doubles with fan for P160/180 and with fan and bath for P200, and doubles with air-con and bath for P300.

The *New Casa Olga Pension* is in Leon Guinto St, on the corner of Pedro Gil, Malate. Singles/doubles with fan are P120/140 and doubles with fan and bath are P200. The beds are wide and you can leave luggage at the hotel.

The *Lucky Pensionne* (tel 5214845) is at 1726 Adriatico St, Malate. It has a restaurant and the rooms are clean but very small. Singles/doubles with fan cost P120/160. Visitors are not allowed.

The *Malate Pensionne* (tel 593489, 585489) at 1771 Adriatico St, Malate, has dorm beds with fan for P65 and with air-con for P75, and rooms with fan for P180, with fan and bath for P250 and with air-con and bath for P300. It is relatively pleasant, although the rooms on the street side are somewhat noisy. A good, reasonably priced restaurant opens on to the garden. Lockers can be rented and luggage left without charge for up to two weeks. An airport service is planned. Prostitutes from the Strip, which is not far away, are not encouraged.

The *White House Tourist Inn* (tel 5221535) at 465 Pedro Gil, Ermita, has rooms with fan for P180, with fan and bath for P270 and with air-con and bath for P370. It is quite a reasonable house and has a restaurant.

New Park Lodge, at 418 N S de Guia St, Plaza Ferguson, Ermita, is an unadorned place that is reasonably quiet. It has rooms with fan for P125 and with air-con for P200/220.

The *Luisa Pension House* (tel 5218929) at 1320 Mabini St, Ermita, opposite the Tower Hotel, has singles/doubles with fan for P150/170 and with fan and bath for P180. It is fairly basic and the rooms are small. A better *Luisa Pension House* (tel 598956) is in J Bocobo St, Ermita, where rooms with fan are P170 and with fan and bath P200. It used to be called the Ryokan Pension House.

The *Diamond Inn* at 1217 M H del Pilar St, Ermita, has rooms with air-con and bath for P250 and is relatively good, with wide beds. The street side is noisy.

La Soledad Pension House (tel 500706) at 1529 Mabini St, Ermita, has singles/doubles with fan for P100/150 and doubles with air-con for P250. It's a good place, with a common room and kitchen facilities you can use. It is directly over the Grand Café disco.

The *Santos Pension House* (tel 595628) is at 1540 Mabini St, Ermita. It has dorm beds with fan for P60, rooms with fan for P165, with fan and bath for P195 and with air-con and bath for P295. The rooms vary in quality but are all clean, and there is a restaurant.

Romansa Lodge (tel 5212930) at 470 Santa Monica St, Ermita, has rooms with fan for P150 and with air-con and bath for P230/270. It is unpretentious and good. Rooms are also available by the hour. The rooms over the Firehouse Bar are noisy.

The *Mabini Pension* (tel 594853) is at 1337 Mabini St, Ermita. It has dorm beds for P80, rooms with fan for P180/220, with fan and bath for P280 and with air-con and bath for P400. The rooms are good but vary in standard. The owner, Urs, is Swiss and the people there are friendly and helpful.

The *ECA Pension House* (tel 5218769, 595257) is at 1248 J Bocobo St, Ermita, near the Luisa Pension House. It has singles with fan from P140 to P180, singles/doubles with fan and bath for P200/240 and doubles with fan for P200 and with air-con and bath for P350.

The *Pension Filipinas* (tel 5211488) at 542 Arkansas St, on the corner of Maria Orosa St, Ermita, is reasonable and has singles/doubles with fan for P150/240 and with air-con for P200/290.

The *Swagman Birdwatcher* is a good, comfortable place with a pub and restaurant on the corner of Flores and Mabini streets, Ermita. Rooms with fan are P200.

The *Yasmin Pension* (tel 505134) in Arquiza St, Ermita, is a quiet place with rooms with air-con and bath for P400.

PLACES TO STAY – MIDDLE

The *Sandico Apartment Hotel* (tel 592036) in M H del Pilar St, Ermita, has rooms with air-con and bath for P330/350. The rooms are pleasant, with fridges and TVs.

The *Majestic Apartments* (tel 507606-07) is at 1038 Roxas Blvd, on the corner of United Nations Ave, Ermita. Rooms with air-con and bath cost from P350 to P400. The dearer rooms have fridges and cooking facilities.

The *Dutch Inn* (tel 599881-85) at 1034-1036 Roxas Blvd, Ermita, is a good place with big rooms. Rooms with air-con and bath cost from P264 to P336, while apartments cost from P480 to P600.

The *Ermita Tourist Inn* (tel 5218770-73) is at 1549 Mabini St, on the corner of Soldado St. Rooms with air-con and bath cost from P425 to P495. You can also get weekly and monthly rates. It is a pleasant place and the daily menus in the ETI Restaurant are good value.

Another quiet, clean place but with rather small rooms is the *Mayumi Inn* (tel 594551, 586465) at 430 Plaza Ferguson, Ermita, where singles/doubles with air-con and bath cost P380/430.

The *Manila Tourist Inn* (tel 597721) at 487 Santa Monica St, Ermita, has rooms with air-con and bath for P550.

The *Iseya Hotel* (tel 592016-18; fax 5224451; tlx 40328 NEDSCOT PM) at 1241 M H del Pilar St, Ermita, has a restaurant, and singles/doubles with air-con and bath for P480/500. The rooms have TVs, and the dearer ones also have fridges.

The *Southern Cross Inn* (tel 586883, 586951; tlx 40406 SCROSS PM) at 476 United Nations Ave, Ermita, has small rooms but is well kept. The entrance is in Mabini St. Singles/doubles with air-con and bath cost P500/520.

The *Swagman Hotel* (tel 505816, 505828; tlx 49960 ATTN SWAGGY) at 411 A Flores St, Ermita, is pleasant. Rooms with fan and bath are P430 and with air-con and bath are from P540. The air-con rooms have a fridge and TV. There is a 24 hour restaurant and airport service.

The *Royal Palm Hotel* (tel 582736-40; fax 5220768; tlx 62310 ROPALM PN) is attractive, good quality and also has a restaurant. It is at 1227 Mabini St, Ermita, and has rooms with air-con and bath for P590/650. The dearer rooms are more spacious.

Las Palmas Hotel (tel 506661-69; fax 5217089; tlx 65030 LASPAL PN) is at 1616 Mabini St, Malate. It has very good singles/doubles with air-con and bath from P630/720. There is a restaurant, and you can get weekly rates.

The *Kanumayan Tourist Inn* (tel 573660-69) at 2284 Taft Ave, Malate, is a good, quiet place with a 24 hour restaurant and a beautiful swimming pool in the garden. It has rooms with air-con and bath for P448/560 and doubles with air-con, bath and kitchen for P672. There is another entrance at 2317 Leon Guinto St.

The *Hotel Swiss* (tel 5224841; fax 5224840; tlx 65034 HARMONY PN), at 1030 Belen St, Paco, has very comfortable rooms with TV, air-con and bath from P700 and suites from P1120.

The *Casa Solanie Apartelle* (tel 508641-45; tlx 65058 MANF PN) at 1811 Leon Guinto St, Malate, has rooms with air-con and bath for P492/537. It is quiet with a friendly atmosphere and a coffee shop.

The *Rothman Inn Hotel* (tel 5219251-60) at 1633-35 Adriatico St, Malate, has rooms with TVs. Singles/doubles with air-con and bath cost from P610 to P720; the more expensive rooms have fridges. There is also a restaurant.

Directly above the International Supermarket, on the corner of Flores and J Bocobo streets, Ermita, is the *Hotel Soriente* (tel 599133), where well-kept rooms with air-con and bath are P542.

The *Pensione Virginia* (tel 878690) is a quiet, relatively inexpensive place in Makati with a well-cared-for appearance. It is at 816 Pasay Rd, San Lorenzo Village, and singles/doubles with air-con and bath are P600/700.

The *Cherry Lodge Apartelle* (tel 507631-34) at 550 J Bocobo St, Ermita, has rooms with air-con and bath from P600/650, suites for P1400 and also weekly and monthly rates. There are round beds, TVs, and the dearer rooms have fridges. It is also a short-time hotel.

The *Aurelio Hotel* (tel 509061; fax 3619419; tlx 23315 HOA PH) is on the corner of Padre Faura and Roxas Blvd, Ermita. It has singles with air-con and bath from P840 to P980, and doubles with air-con and bath for P1200. The rooms have TVs, and there is also a restaurant and a swimming pool.

Robelle House (tel 881931-35) is good value for Makati. It is at 4402 Valdez St, opposite the International School. Singles with air-con and bath cost from P700, doubles with air-con and bath cost P760, and suites cost P850. There is a restaurant and a swimming pool in a pleasant local atmosphere.

The *Hotel La Corona* (tel 502631-34; fax 505513; tlx 62383 ETDCOR PN) at 1166 M H del Pilar St, Ermita, has rooms with air-con, TV and bath from P1500. Suites costing from P2300 have a fridge and jacuzzi. Monthly rates apply.

The *Sundowner Hotel* (tel 5212751; fax 5215331; tlx 63746 SUNDER PN) at 1430 Mabini St, Malate, has an attractive lobby and a newspaper stand with international papers. Singles/doubles with air-con and bath cost P930/1062. The dearer rooms have fridges.

The *Ambassador Hotel* (tel 506011; fax 5215557; tlx PN 63413) at 2021 Mabini St, Malate, has rooms with air-con and bath for P1333/1528. It has a restaurant and swimming pool.

The *Hotel Royal Coco* (tel 5213911; tlx 65065 ATRUM PN) at 2120 Mabini St, Malate, is an attractive and comfortable place that offers rooms with TV, air-con and bath from P1275/1525 and suites cost from P2400.

PLACES TO STAY – TOP END

Manila has plenty of 1st class hotels. Many of them, like the Philippine Plaza and the Sheraton, offer reductions of 40% in the off season from June to September. Others, like the Manila Midtown Hotel, cut their price by 50% for a stay of four weeks. The elegant Manila Hotel can be ranked with the Raffles in Singapore, the Oriental in Bangkok and the Peninsula in Hong Kong as among the oldest and most reputable hotels in South-East Asia. The new Philippine Plaza, with its 700 rooms, seems by contrast modern and elaborate. For a real extravagance, the Imperial Suite there is available – a penthouse with 10 rooms and your own butler for US$2000 a night. Those who will settle for a mere five super rooms but who still need their own butler, swimming pool and garden, can book the Mandarin Suite at the Mandarin Oriental Hotel in Makati. It only costs US$1800.

Hotels

The following hotels are probably the twelve best in this category. All contain numerous bars, restaurants and nightclubs. The guests have the use of swimming pools, saunas and tennis courts. To the price given in US dollars, you have to add a 10% service charge and a 13.7% government tax.

Century Park Sheraton (tel 5221011; fax 5213413; tlx 40489 SHERMLA PM) is in

Vito Cruz in Malate. Rooms with air-con and bath cost from US$99 to US$109 and suites cost from US$190.

The *Holiday Inn* (tel 597961-80; fax 5223985; tlx 63487 HOLIDA PN) has rooms with air-con and bath from US$85/90 and suites from US$150. It is at 3001 Roxas Blvd, Pasay City.

The *Hotel Inter-Continental* (tel 8159711; fax 8171330; tlx 23314 ICH PH) is in Ayala Ave, Makati. Singles/doubles with air-con and bath cost from US$155/170.

The *Hyatt Regency* (tel 8312611; fax 8335913; tlx 45327 HATTMLA TM) at 2702 Roxas Blvd, Pasay City, has rooms with air-con and bath from US$135.

The *Mandarin Oriental Hotel* (tel 8163601; fax 8172472; tlx 63756 MANDA PN) in Makati Ave, Makati, has rooms with air-con and bath from US$130/150 and suites from US$240.

The *Hotel Nikko Manila Garden* (tel 8104101; fax 8171862; tlx ITT 45883 GARDEN PM) is on Fourth Quadrant, Makati Commercial Center, Makati. It has rooms with air-con and bath from US$94/106 and suites from US$140.

The *Manila Hotel* (tel 470011; fax 471124; tlx 63496 MHOTEL PN) at Rizal Park, Ermita, has rooms with air-con and bath from US$110/125, suites from US$180 and a penthouse for US$1900.

The *Manila Midtown Hotel* (tel 573911-40; fax 5222629; tlx 27797 MNLMID DH) in Pedro Gil, Ermita, has rooms with air-con and bath from US$87/98.

The *Manila Pavilion Hotel* (tel 57311; fax 5223531; tlx 40773 PVL HTL MNL) in United Nations Ave, Ermita, has rooms with air-con and bath from US$100/110 and suites from US$200.

The *Manila Peninsula* (tel 8193456; fax 8154825; tlx 22507 PEN PH) is on the corner of Makati and Ayala avenues, Makati. Rooms with air-con and bath cost from US$140/155 and suites from US$300.

The *Silahis International Hotel* (tel 573811; fax 2573811; tlx 66627 SIHSSM PN) has rooms with air-con and bath from US$75/80.

The *Westin Philippine Plaza Hotel* (tel 8320701; fax 8323485; tlx 40443 FILPLAZA PM) has rooms with air-con and bath from US$100/120 and suites from US$270.

Apartments

If you're going to stay long in Manila it may be worth considering apartments instead of hotel rooms. It is possible to find apartments with cooking facilities, air-con, a fridge, TV and so on for a monthly rent of from P5000 to P10,000, depending on what is provided. A month's rent must be paid in advance, and a deposit is required for the electricity. Rentals are monthly, weekly, and sometimes even daily. The daily rates include electricity and are around P300 to P500. Apartments in Makati are often very dear, while those in Ermita and Malate are seldom available, especially the cheaper ones, so it's a good idea to book early. You will find places to rent listed in the weekend editions of the large daily papers.

The *Broadway Court* (tel 782931-35; tlx 22099 UNI PH) is at 16 Dona Juana Rodriguez St, New Manila (Quezon City). It has one-room apartments costing P500 daily and P6000 monthly, and has a coffee shop and tennis court.

The *Jetset Executive Mansion* (tel 5214029-30; fax 344430) is at 1205 General Luna St, Ermita. It has rooms with air-con and bath for P450 and one-room apartments for P650 daily (monthly by arrangement). There is also a restaurant.

The *Victoria Mansions* (tel 505056, 575851; tlx 45693 STARS PM), 600 J M Nakpil St, Malate, has one-room apartments for P250 to P300 daily and P7500 monthly.

Pearl Garden Apartel (tel 575911) at 1700 Adriatico St, Malate, has one-room apartments for P575 daily and P12,000 monthly. Two-room apartments cost P1200 daily and P19,200 monthly. There is also a restaurant.

The *Dakota Mansion* (tel 5210701-22; tlx 40442 MANHOTEL PM), on the corner of Adriatico and General Miguel Malvar streets, has one-room apartments for P770 daily and P12,300 monthly. Two-room apartments cost P1200 daily and P20,000 monthly. It has a restaurant and swimming pool.

The *Casa Blanca I* (tel 596011-18; tlx 66755 PHC PN) at 1447 Adriatico St, Ermita, has one-room apartments for P600 daily and P7700 monthly. Two-room apartments cost P600 daily and P13,000 monthly.

The *Boulevard Mansion* (tel 5218888; tlx 41127), 1440 Roxas Blvd, has studios for P770 daily and P12,000 monthly; standard one-room apartments for P816 daily and P13,000 monthly; suites for P933 daily and P16,000 monthly; and a penthouse for P2,680 daily and P50,000 monthly. It also has a coffee shop.

At the *Dona Petronila Mall* (tel 595355, 587550) at 1184 Mabini St, Ermita, you can get a one-room apartment for P380 to P400 daily, P2000 to P2200 weekly and P4500 to P5000 monthly.

The *San Carlos Mansion* (tel 590981), at 777 San Carlos St, Ermita, has one-room apartments for P450 to P550 daily, P2750 to P3500 weekly and P9000 to P12,000 monthly. Two-room apartments cost P600 to P700 daily, P3900 to P4600 weekly and P14,000 to P15,000 monthly.

The *Mabini Mansion* (tel 5214776) is at 1011 Mabini St, Ermita. A one-room apartment costs P770 daily and P12,360 monthly. A two-room apartment is P1282 daily and P18,540 monthly There is a coffee shop here.

The *Tropicana Apartment Hotel* (tel 590061-76; tlx 27645 TAH PH, 40171 TROPTEL PM) at 1630 Luis M Guerrero St, Malate, has standard one-room apartments for P750 daily, P4750 weekly and P15,500 monthly. Deluxe one-room apartments are P860 daily, P5400 weekly and P23,700 monthly. Standard two-room apartments are P1300 daily, P8200 weekly and P23,700 monthly. Deluxe two-room apartments are P1500 daily, P9700 weekly and P29,000 monthly. It has a restaurant and a swimming pool.

The *Euro-Nippon Mansion* (tel 5213921) at 2090 Roxas Blvd has one-room apartments for P675 daily and P14,000 monthly.

The *Traveller's Inn* (tel 857061) at 7880 Makati Ave, Makati, has one-room apartments for P900 daily and P10,000 monthly.

PLACES TO EAT

Manila's restaurants have an impressive diversity of cuisines and prices. Connoisseurs have the opportunity to try the local fare as well as the pleasures of other Asian cooking and European and American dishes. Fast food is available, or you can enjoy the generous fixed-price buffets provided by the top-class hotel restaurants at your leisure.

In most restaurants in Ermita you can get a decent meal for roughly P50 to P100. In Adriatico St, where there is a wide range of Asian places, prices are a bit higher. For a meal of several courses you can expect to pay from P100 to P200.

The top restaurants in Makati and in the luxury hotels are expensive, but a real gourmet would probably be prepared to pay the P200 to P300 or more charged for the excellent food, service and atmosphere. Sometimes these meals are accompanied by cultural entertainment or a fashion show. A lunch buffet costs about P120 to P180.

Good wine in a good restaurant will cost at least P300 a bottle. Wine is imported and transport costs and import duties make it very expensive. Maybe San Miguel beer is a better choice.

Only a few top restaurants insist on formal dress such as ties, jackets or barongs. Otherwise casual clothes are quite all right. However, even in a middle-range restaurant, thongs (flip-flops), shorts or singlets would be pushing tolerance a bit far.

The prices given for the following restaurants are the approximate current costs of dinner for one person. Drinks are not included, nor are extra helpings or expensive items like lobster tails by the dozen or caviar by the kg. With buffets in top hotels, 25% is added for government tax and the service charge.

Filipino Food

Ermita is a good place to explore for Filipino food, especially along M H del Pilar St.

There are also some good places in Makati. *Mother Sachi* in Gil Puyat Ave (Buendia Ave), between Pasong Tamo St and Ayala Ave, Makati, is self-service, with good, reasonably priced vegetarian dishes. Its specialities are shepherd's pie, Bhagavad fruit pie and soya fish. It is open Monday to Saturday from 11 am to 9 pm with meals for about P75. *Cosmic Plate* in the Gallery Building, Amorsolo St, Makati, is another good vegetarian restaurant with different dishes each day. A health-food shop is attached. It is open daily from 11 am to 9 pm; a meal costs about P75.

Aida's in M H del Pilar St, Ermita, is a reasonably priced 'turo-turo' restaurant, partly open air, which sometimes has good munggo (bean) soup. It is open daily around the clock; a meal costs about P50.

Myrna's, also in M H del Pilar St, Ermita, is a typical simple Filipino restaurant. It serves good bangus (milkfish) and is crowded at meal times. It is open Monday to Saturday from 7 am to 11.30 pm and a meal costs about P50.

The Coffee Tree, on the corner of Mabini and R Salas streets, has good Filipino food and a cheap American breakfast. It is open Monday to Saturday from 7 am to 10.30 pm; a meal costs about P75.

Mabini House in Mabini St, Ermita, serves Filipino and Chinese food, with good rice and noodle dishes. It is open daily from 7 am to 10 pm with meals for about P50.

Calle 5 in Mabini St, Ermita, is a big open-air restaurant which has good squid. There is live music in the evenings. It is open daily from 8 am to 3 am; a meal costs about P100.

The *Harbor View* in South Blvd, at the end of Rizal Park, right where the harbour trip starts, is a pleasant place by the waterfront to watch the sunset and catch a fresh breeze while having a beer and enjoying good Filipino food like sinigang (vegetable soup) or bangus. It's open Monday to Saturday from 10 to 2 am and Sunday from 10 am to midnight. Meals cost about P75.

The *Seaside Market* in Roxas Blvd, Baclaran (near Baclaran Church), is a real market where you can buy freshly caught fish and have it prepared cheaply at the little adjoining restaurants. It is open all hours and a meal costs from P50 to P75.

At *Leo's*, on the corner of Roxas Blvd and Dapitan St, you can eat à la carte or choose your fish and have it prepared as you wish. It is open daily all hours and a meal costs from P75 to P100.

The *Seafood Market* in J Bocobo St, Ermita, is relatively dear, but is a good seafood restaurant. It's almost like a real market: guests do their own selecting and then take their filled baskets to the cooks to be prepared as they wish. It is especially busy at night but the waiting time is usually short. You can round off the menu with coffee and cakes at the *Café Alps* next door. There is another *Seafood Market* in Makati Ave, Makati. It is open daily from 10 am to midnight; a meal costs about P200.

Rol's Ihaw Ihaw in M H del Pilar St, Ermita, is an open-air seafood restaurant with a popular beer garden right alongside. It is open daily from 8 am to 1 am with meals for about P100.

Barrio Fiesta in J Bocobo St, Ermita, is a good, medium-priced restaurant with branches all over the country. It has an extensive menu with specialities like crispy pata and kare-kare (stew). It is open daily from 8 am to 1 am and a meal costs about P75. There is another *Barrio Fiesta* in Makati Ave, Makati.

The *Bulwagang Pilipino* on the corner of Arkansas St and Maria Orosa St, Ermita, is another good Filipino restaurant, open daily from 9 am to 11 pm; it charges about P100 for a meal.

At the *Palais daan* in Adriatico St, Malate, you can get good Filipino dishes and seafood. It is open daily from 10 am to 1 am and charges about P150 for a meal.

The *Aristocrat*, on the corner of Roxas Blvd and San Andres St, Malate, is a big, medium-priced restaurant. It is very popular with local people and the most popular of the six Aristocrat restaurants in Metro Manila. It is open 24 hours a day all week and charges about P75.

Josephine's in Roxas Blvd, Pasay City, is a well-known and popular seafood restaurant with a lot of choice and live combo music in the evenings. It is open daily from 9 am to midnight; a meal costs about P125.

Nandau on the corner of Roxas Blvd and Lourdes St, Pasay City, is an excellent seafood restaurant which specialises in food from the province of Zamboanga del Norte in Mindanao – blue marlin, for example. It is open daily from 11 am to 11 pm and a meal costs about P175.

The *Patio Mequeni* in Remedios St, Malate, is a pleasant, simply furnished restaurant that specialises in dishes from Pampanga Province. It is open Monday to Saturday from 11 am to 3 pm and from 6 pm to midnight. A meal costs about P100.

At the *Kamayan Restaurant* in Padre Faura, Ermita, you can eat with your fingers in true Filipino style. There is a wide range of dishes from all over the Philippines. It is open daily from 11 am to 2 pm and from 5 to 10 pm. A meal costs about P200.

Aling Asiang in the Plaza Building, Legaspi St, Greenbelt Square, Makati, is a well-run speciality restaurant with authentic dishes from various provinces. It is open from 11 am to 11 pm daily with meals for about P150.

Ang Bistro sa Remedios, on the corner of Adriatico and Remedios streets, Malate, is an elegant restaurant serving special dishes from Pampanga Province. It is open from 11 am to 2 pm and from 6 pm to midnight daily; a meal costs about P200.

Asian Food

Chinese *Mrs Wong* on the corner of Padre Faura and M H del Pilar St is well patronised. It is open daily from 10 am to 7 am and a meal costs about P50.

The *Hong Kong Restaurant* in M H del Pilar St, Ermita, is a long-established typical Chinese restaurant with good noodle soup. It is open daily from 10 am to 4 am and a meal costs about P75.

Kowloon House is in Mabini St, Malate. A basic but pleasant restaurant, it is open daily from 8 am to 10 pm; a meal costs about P50.

The *Sea Palace* in Mabini St is a good and relatively cheap Chinese restaurant which also has Filipino food. It is open from 11 am to 2.30 pm and from 6 to 11.30 pm daily with meals for about P100.

The *Shin Shin Garden* in Mabini St, Malate, is good but somewhat dear. It is open from 11 am to 2 pm and from 6 to 10 pm daily and a meal costs about P200.

The *Taipekey Restaurant* in Adriatico St, Malate, is also good but dear. It is open from 11 am to 2 pm and from 5 to 9 pm; a meal costs about P150.

Eva's Garden in Adriatico St, Ermita, is pleasant and reasonably priced. It is open Monday to Saturday from 11.30 am to 2 pm and from 5 to 10 pm and Sunday from 5 to 10 pm. A meal costs about P100.

Quan Yin Chay in Soler St, Chinatown, is a small restaurant which has good-value vegetarian foods and fruit juices. It is open daily from 8 am to 9 pm and a meal costs about P25.

Mandarin Villa in Ongpin St, Chinatown, is one of the biggest Chinese restaurants in the area. It is open daily from 11 am to 10 pm with meals for about P100.

Indian & Arabian *Al-Sham's* in Mabini St, Malate, has Arabian, Indian and Pakistani food, with mutton, lamb and goat meat dishes, and curries and vegetarian food. It is open daily from 11.30 am to 10.30 pm; a meal costs about P150. There is another *Al-Sham's Restaurant* in Makati Ave, Makati.

A good Indian restaurant in Padre Faura, Ermita, is the *Kashmir*, which serves mainly north Indian and Pakistani dishes, hot or mild as required, and vegetarian foods. It is open from 10 am to 11 pm daily and meals cost about P200. There is another *Kashmir Restaurant* on the corner of Makati Ave and Guerrero St, Makati.

Indonesian The *Café Lerop* in Adriatico St, Malate, has Indonesian and Malaysian dishes with an especially good rijsttafel. It is

Top: Entrance to Fort Santiago, Manila (TW)
Bottom: Black Nazarene procession in Quiapo, Manila (JP)

Top: Bullock-led cane cart, Manila (TW)
Bottom: The ubiquitous jeepney (JP)

open Monday to Saturday from 11 am to 2 am and meals cost about P150.

Japanese The *Iseya Restaurant* in Padre Faura, Ermita, serves a business lunch that, at P50, is very good value. It is open daily from 11 am to 2 pm and from 5 to 11 pm and its usual meals are about P75.

The *Yamato* in Adriatico St, Ermita, is good for sushi and tempura. It is open daily from 11 am to 2 pm and from 5.30 to 10.30 pm and meals cost about P75.

The *Tempura-Misono* is a very popular Japanese restaurant in the Hyatt Regency Hotel, Roxas Blvd, Pasay City. Meals cost about P400.

Korean The *Korean Village* in Adriatico St, Malate, is supposed to be the biggest Korean restaurant in Manila. Its specialities are spare ribs and beef stew. It is open Monday to Saturday from 11 am to 2 pm and from 5 to 10 pm and meals cost about P150.

The *Korean Palace* is also in Adriatico St, Malate, and competes with the Korean Village. It is open from 11 am to 2 pm and from 5 to 10 pm daily and meals cost about P150. Another Korean restaurant is the *Korean Garden* in Burgos St, Makati, which charges about P200 and is open daily from 11.30 am to 2.30 pm and from 5.30 to 10.30 pm.

Thai The *Sukhothai* in Makati Ave, Makati, is an unpretentious place with good, reasonably priced food. It is open Monday to Saturday from 11 am to 2 pm and from 5 to 10 pm with meals for about P75.

Flavours & Spices in New Garden Square, on the corner of Legaspi St and Greenbelt Drive, Makati, is a good restaurant where you can also buy Thai spices. It is open from 11 am to 10 pm and meals cost about P150.

Another good restaurant is *Taste of Thailand* in the Mile Long Building, Amorsolo St, Makati, which is open daily from 11.30 am to 2 pm and 6.30 to 10 pm. Meals cost about P150.

The *Thai Room* in the Creekside Building, Amorsolo St, Makati, has standard dishes like tom yan and Thai curries and its menus are varied daily. It is open Monday to Saturday from 11 am to 3 pm and from 6 to 10 pm. Meals cost about P150.

Vietnamese The *Vietnam Food House* in Harrison St, Pasay City, is small but popular, with different specialities each day. A meal costs about P75 and it is open from 9 am to 7.30 pm daily.

The *Ville de Saigon* in Pasay Rd, Makati, has Vietnamese cuisine with a French touch and also vegetarian dishes. It is open daily from 11.30 am to 2.30 pm and from 5.30 to 11.30 pm. A meal costs P200.

Western Food

US Mainland *Steak Town* in Adriatico St, Malate, has good steaks and seafood, soup, salad, bread, dessert and coffee. It is open from 8 am to 2 am daily and meals cost about P200. There is another Steak Town Restaurant in Makati Ave, Makati.

The *New Orleans* in La Tasca Building, Greenbelt Square, Legaspi St, Makati, specialises in US and Creole dishes, especially steaks and barbecued ribs, along with pretty good New Orleans jazz. It is open from 11 am to 2.00 pm and from 6 pm to midnight daily. Meals cost about P250.

At the *Café Adriatico*, on the corner of Adriatico St and Remedios Circle, Malate, the usual menu features steaks, salads, seafood and fondue, topped off with various kinds of coffee and a good choice of cocktails. It's a trendy place to meet at night after the theatre. It is open Monday to Friday from 10 am to 6 am and Sunday from 2.30 pm to 6 am. Meals cost about P250.

Mario's in Makati Ave, Makati, has good steaks and salads, seafood, French and Spanish soups and Californian wines. It is open Monday to Saturday from 11 am to 2.30 pm and from 5.30 to 11 pm, and Sunday from 5.30 to 11 pm. Meals cost about P200.

Max's in Maria Orosa St, Ermita, is one of the 10 branches of Max's in Manila. It serves chicken roasted in various ways as well as standard Filipino dishes. It is open daily from 8 am to 11 pm and meals cost about P100.

Australian & UK From the *Rooftop Restaurant*, on the corner of Padre Faura and M H del Pilar St, Ermita, you can enjoy a good view over Manila Bay. It is an Australian restaurant and beer garden on top of the Iseya Hotel and is open daily all hours; on Sunday there's an Aussie barbecue for P100. Normally, meals cost from P100 to P150.

The *Southern Cross* in United Nations Ave, Ermita, is a combined Australian bar and club open 24 hours a day with meals from P100 to P150.

German, Austrian & Swiss *Lili Marleen* in M H del Pilar St, Ermita, has homely German dishes at reasonable prices. Menus vary daily. It is open from 10 am to 3 am and meals cost about P75.

Edelweiss in M H del Pilar St, Ermita, cooks German, Austrian and Swiss food and specialises in fondue. It is open from 10 am to 2 pm and meals cost about P100.

The *München Grill Pub* in Mabini St, Ermita, has Bavarian dishes and is open daily from 10 to 2 am. Meals cost about P100.

Jodi's Place in Mabini St, Ermita, has German food. It is open from 10 am to 2 am daily and meals cost about P100.

Fischfang in M H del Pilar St, Ermita, is also German. It is open daily all hours and meals cost about P75.

Old Heidelberg in Soldado St, Ermita, is a German restaurant with a small beer garden. It is open daily from 9 am to 3 am and meals cost about P100.

The *Schwarzwälder* in Makati Ave, Makati, has German dishes like bratwurst and eisbein (knuckle of pork) with sauerkraut plus a salad bar and different sorts of coffees. It is open daily from 11.30 am to 2.30 pm and from 5.30 pm to 3 am. Meals cost about P200.

The *Swiss Hut* in M H del Pilar St, Ermita, has good, reasonable Swiss specialities. It is open from 11 am to 3 am and meals cost about P100.

The *Swiss Bistro* in Soldado St, Ermita, has good Swiss food and is a popular meeting place. It's open daily from 10 am to 3 am and meals cost about P100.

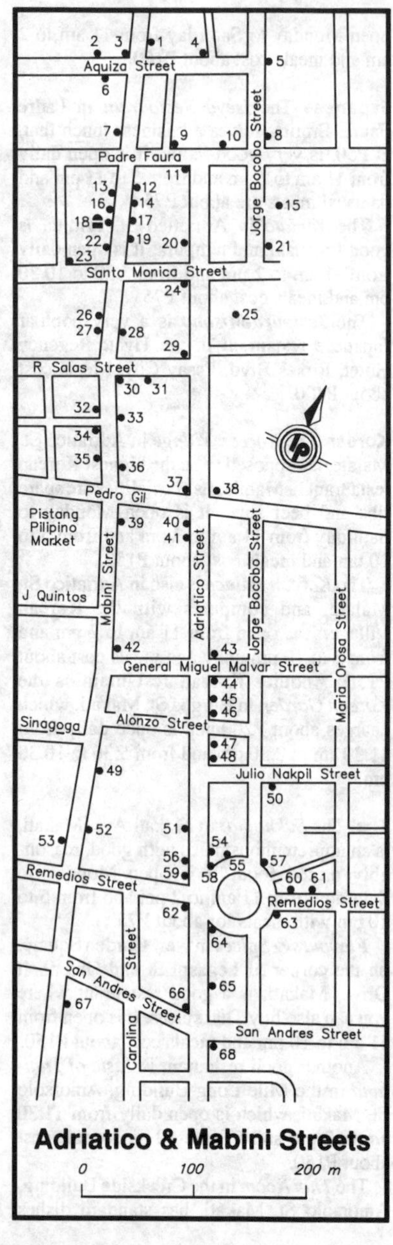

Adriatico & Mabini Streets

1	Dona Petronila Mall
2	Yasmin Pension
3	Shakey's Mabini
4	Socialite Club
5	Café Alps
	Seafood Market
6	Holandia Restaurant
7	Bookmark
	Royal Palm Hotel
8	ECA Pension House
	Luisa Pension House
9	Jollibee
	Kamayan Restaurant
	Kashmir Restaurant
10	Solidaridad Book Shop
11	7-Eleven
12	Mister Donut
13	PTT Telegram
14	Luisa Pension House
	München Grill Pub
15	Food Stalls
16	Tower Hotel
17	Calle 5
18	Mabini Pension
	Post Office
19	T'Boli Arts & Crafts
20	Eva's Garden Restaurant
21	Cherry Lodge Apartelle
22	Moneychanger
23	Manila Tourist Inn
24	Yamato Japanese Restaurant
25	Robinson's
26	Al-Sham's
27	Kowloon House
28	Sundowner Hotel
29	Casa Blanca I
30	Coffee Tree
31	Laundromat
32	La Solidad Pension House
33	Santos Pension House
34	Ermita Tourist Inn
	Galactica Travels Inc
35	Mabini House
36	Boomerang Club
37	El Comedor Restaurant
38	Manila Midtown Hotel
39	Las Palmas Hotel
40	Zamboanga Restaurant
41	Rothman Inn Hotel
42	Olga Casa Pension
43	Dakota Mansion
44	Pearl Garden Apartel
45	Taipekey Restaurant
46	Palais daan Restaurant
47	Lucky Pensionne
48	Steak Town Restaurant
49	Sea Palace Restaurant
50	Victoria Mansion
51	Malate Pensionne
52	Carfel Seashell Museum
53	Hobbit House
54	Hard Rock Café
55	Moviola
56	Korean Village Restaurant
57	Patio Guernica
58	Café Adriatico
59	Korean Palace Restaurant
60	Remedios Pension House
61	Empress Garden Restaurant
62	Ang Bistro sa Remedios
63	Circle Pension
64	Prego Restaurant
	Limelight Theater
65	D'Partner's Disco
66	Café La Jazz
67	Casa Dalco
68	Café Lerop

French *Lafayette* in M H del Pilar St, Ermita, is a café-restaurant open daily from 11 am to midnight. Meals cost from P150 to P200.

L'Orangerie in Zodiac St, Makati, is a very up-market French restaurant with some original dishes. It is open Monday to Friday from 11 am to 3 pm and from 6 to 11 pm. Meals cost about P400.

Dutch & Swedish *Holandia* in Arquiza St is a Dutch restaurant open Monday to Saturday from 10 am to 1 am and Sunday from 4 pm to 1 am. Meals cost about P100.

Italian *Nino di Roma*, on the corner of United Nations Ave and M H del Pilar St, Ermita, is an Italian restaurant with a wide range of pizzas and pasta dishes. It is open from 8 am to midnight daily and meals cost about P100. Another place with good pasta and pizzas is the *Italian Village* in Makati Ave, Makati, which opens from 11 am to 11 pm daily and costs about P200.

Mexican *Aunt Mary's Aunt* in Greenbelt Square, Makati Ave, Makati, is a good, reasonably priced place where you can get a pitcher (six glasses) of margarita for P110. It is open daily from 11 to 2 am and meals cost about P75.

Tia Maria in General Luna St (a side street off Makati Ave), Makati, has cocktails and good Mexican food. It is open Monday to Saturday from 11 am to midnight and Sunday from 5 pm to midnight. Meals cost about P100.

Spanish *Guernica's* in M H del Pilar St, Ermita, has typical dishes like paella, but also steaks. Guitar music provides atmosphere. It is open Monday to Saturday from 11 am to 2 pm and from 6 pm to midnight, and Sunday from 6 pm to midnight. Meals cost about P200. There is another *Guernica's* in Pasay Rd, near EDSA, Makati.

Patio Guernica in J Bocobo St, near Remedios Circle, Malate, has common Spanish dishes, steaks and vegetarian food. It is busy but not as lively as the older Guernica's in M H del Pilar St. It is open Monday to Saturday from 11 am to 2 pm and from 6 pm to midnight, and Sunday from 6 pm to midnight.

El Comedor, on the corner of Adriatico St and Pedro Gil, Ermita, has traditional Spanish food plus some specialities and a relatively cheap lunch special. It is open daily from 11 am to 3 pm and from 6.30 to 10.30 pm. Meals cost about P250.

The *Muralla* in the San Luis Complex, General Luna St, Intramuros, has Spanish and Filipino food. It is open daily from 11 am to 2 pm and from 6 to 11 pm. Meals cost about P250.

Fast Food

There are lots of reasonably priced small food stalls in J Bocobo St that sell Filipino snacks and meals from around P20. They open daily from 8 am to 10 pm.

Rosie's Diner in M H del Pilar St, Ermita, is comfortable and always fairly full, in the style of a US snack-bar of the 1950s – all that's missing is the Wurlitzer. It is open all day every day and a meal costs from P50 to P75.

Shakey's Mabini in Mabini St, Ermita, sells pizzas with thick or thin dough, but their spaghetti is a bit dear. There is loud live music in the evenings. It is open daily from 11 am to 5 am and a meal costs from P75 to P100. There is also *Shakey's Malate* in Remedios St, open from 11 to 5 am, *Shakey's Makati* in Makati Ave, open from 9 am to midnight, and *Shakey's Greenhills* in Padilla Ave, open from 10 to 2 am.

The *Pizza Hut* in Harrison Plaza, Malate, is one of eight in Metro Manila. It specialises in pan pizzas and is a popular place in a busy shopping centre. It is open daily from 10 am to midnight; a meal costs from P75 to P100.

If you're really hanging out for a hamburger, *McDonald's* in United Nations Ave, Ermita, sells the 'real thing'. It is open daily from 7 am to midnight and a hamburger usually costs about P50.

Jollibee in Padre Faura, Ermita, is one of a Filipino burger chain with lots of outlets. Its specialities are chickenjoy and champ with cheese; a full breakfast may also be offered. It is open Monday to Saturday from 7 am to 10 pm and Sunday from 7.30 am to 9.30 pm. A meal costs about P50.

Kentucky Fried Chicken in Harrison Plaza, Malate, has the traditional crispy chicken. It is open daily from 10 am to midnight and costs about P75. There are Kentucky Frieds all over Manila. Another is in Maria Orosa St, opposite the Manila Pavilion Hotel.

Mister Donut in Mabini St, Ermita, has a good choice of excellent doughnuts and good coffee – not a bad breakfast alternative. It is open all hours every day and costs about P25.

Buffets

You can get breakfast buffets daily from 6 to 10 am at the *Sundowner Hotel* in Mabini St, Ermita, for about P90; *The Brasserie* in the Mandarin Oriental Hotel, Makati Ave, Makati, for about P130; the *Café Coquilla* in the Manila Pavilion Hotel, United Nations Ave, Ermita, for about P125; and the *Café*

Ilang-Ilang and *Lobby Lounge*, Manila Hotel, Rizal Park, Ermita, for about P145.

The *Café Vienna* in the Holiday Inn, Roxas Blvd, Pasay City, has buffets for breakfast Monday to Friday from 6 to 10 am for P100; lunch Monday to Friday from noon to 2 pm for P110; and dinner Tuesday to Saturday from 7 to 10 pm for P150. It has Continental and international cuisines.

The *Concourse* in the Hotel Nikko Manila Garden, Fourth Quadrant, Makati Commercial Center, Makati, has an international cuisine with breakfast buffet daily from 6 to 10 am for P100 and a lunch buffet daily from 11.30 am to 2 pm for P130.

The *1930's Banquet Hall*, Admiral Hotel, Roxas Blvd, Malate, has a Filipino lunch buffet Monday to Saturday from 11.30 am to 2 pm for about P120. The *Champagne Room* in the Manila Hotel, Rizal Park, Ermita, has a lunch buffet with international cuisine Monday to Friday from noon to 3 pm for about P230, and on Sunday at the same times for about P250. For Italian food, the *Roma* in the same hotel has a lunch buffet Monday to Friday from noon to 3 pm for P210.

The *Lobby Bar* in the Manila Pavilion Hotel, United Nations Ave, Ermita, has a daily lunch buffet from 11 am to 2 pm for P135, and *Pier 7* in the Philippine Plaza Hotel, Cultural Center Complex, Malate, has one from 11.30 am to 2.30 pm daily at P180 for steaks and seafood (a speciality).

ENTERTAINMENT

Jai Alai

The corruption-ridden Jai Alai and casino operations have been shut down by the new Presidential Commission on Good Government. It is not yet decided if they will be allowed to reopen – check when you get there.

The Jai Alai Fronton (stadium) is on Taft Ave across from Rizal Park. (Jai alai is a version of pelota played by two or four players.) Games used to be played daily in the late afternoon except on Sundays and public holidays.

Casinos

Soon after the Marcos era, the big casino in the renamed Ninoy Aquino Ave at the Ninoy Aquino International Airport was closed, as were all other casinos in the area, by the Commission on Good Government set up by the Aquino government. In the meantime, the Casino Filipina, which has branches all over the country, is doing big business. In Manila you can play in the *Silahis Hotel*, Roxas Blvd, Malate, and in the *Manila Pavilion Hotel*, United Nations Ave, Ermita. Entry is free and players in casual clothes or even beachwear are admitted.

Cockfights

There are several cockpits in Manila – the Philippine Cockers Club in Santa Ana; the Olympic Stadium at Grace Park, Caloocan; Libertad in Dolores St, Pasay City; Elorde in Santos Ave, Paranaque; and La Loma in Calavite St, Quezon City. Fights are staged on Sundays and feast days. Admission is from P20 to P200.

Cinemas

Films are advertised in the daily papers. Some cinema districts are Rizal Ave, Santa Cruz, and in *Robinson's* in Adriatico St, Ermita. Beware of pickpockets and bag snatchers in the cinemas.

Concerts

In Paco Park, Ermita, Paco Park Presents puts on free chamber music at 6 pm on Friday.

The Puerta Real Evenings which take place every Saturday night at 6 pm in Intramuros are free musical entertainment in the greenery near the aquarium by the old fortress wall.

A Free Concert in the Park takes place every Sunday at 5 pm in Rizal Park.

Horse Racing

Races are held on Saturday and Sunday afternoons and Wednesday evenings. Check the daily papers for more information, or contact the Philippine Racing Club (tel 879951, 863442) or the Manila Jockey Club (tel 7111251). The courses are at the Santa Ana Race Track, A P Reyes Ave, Santa Ana, and in the San Lazaro Hippodrome, Felix Huertas St, Santa Cruz.

Planetarium

The Planetarium is in the grounds of Rizal Park; you go in from Burgos St. There are audiovisual demonstrations daily at 10.30 am and 1.30 and 3.30 pm. Admission is P2.

Folk Dances

There is Muslim dancing on Saturday at 3 pm in the Mindanao section of Nayong Pilipino (the Philippine Village) at Ninoy Aquino International Airport in Airport Ave, Pasay City. These displays were put on here for many years and then almost ceased, but the Tourist Office has promised to restore them as a tourist attraction, so it's worth inquiring about them.

Pistahan in the *Philippine Plaza Hotel*, Cultural Center Complex, Malate, has a dinner and cultural show every evening from 7 pm featuring Filipino food, songs and dancing. At 6 pm a torch ceremony is held. Without drinks it costs about P350 per person.

Pistang Pilipino, on the corner of M H del Pilar St, Pedro Gil and Mabini St, Malate, has a cultural performance each afternoon and evening. Admission is free. For the special variety show at 11 pm, you pay a P50 cover charge or P150 for the the show and a buffet. Then at midnight there is a disco.

The Zamboanga Restaurant in Adriatico St, Malate, has Filipino and Polynesian dancing with dinner from 7 to 8.30 pm. Seafood dishes like fisherman's delight are a speciality. It is open daily from 9 am to 11 pm and costs about P100.

Theatre

Performances are irregular, so check the arts section of the daily papers or inquire at the Tourist Office (tel 599031, 501703) or at the theatre itself.

The Cultural Center of the Philippines (CCP) is on Roxas Blvd, Malate (tel 8321125).

The Folk Arts Theater is in the Cultural Center Complex, Roxas Blvd, Malate (tel 8321120).

The Insular Life Theater (Repertory Philippines) is in the Insular Life Building, Ayala Ave, Makati (tel 8173051).

The Meralco Theater is in the Meralco Building, Ortigas Ave, Pasig (tel 7219777).

The Metropolitan Theater is in Lawisang Bonifacio, Lawton Plaza, Ermita (tel 484721).

The Rajah Sulayman Theater is an open-air theatre in Fort Santiago, Intramuros.

Zoo

You will find the Manila Zoological & Botanical Gardens at the southern end of Mabini St, at the beginning of Harrison St, in Malate. The Philippine eagle which you can see there and the tamaraw, a dwarf buffalo from Mindoro, are of great interest but otherwise the miserable accommodation (small enclosures, no shade, no plants) and the obvious neglect suffered by most of the creatures on display illustrate the usual Asian, and especially Filipino, attitude to animals. Animal lovers are advised to give it a miss. If you do want to visit the zoo, it is open daily from 8 am to 6 pm.

Bars & Nightclubs

All the big hotels have bars and nightclubs. The most exclusive nightspots with excellent live music are found on Roxas Blvd. A few steps from the bayfront in the Ermita area you are in the heart of it. M H del Pilar St between United Nations Ave and Pedro Gil is a nonstop line of go-go bars and cocktail lounges.

In contrast to the sometimes rather tasteless décor of the Filipino bars are the big, more elaborate places like *Superstar* mostly run by expatriates. Some of these, such as *Firehouse*, have excellent video-rock setups. In places like the *Australian Club*, the happy hour starts in the afternoon and low beer prices make sure it lives up to its name. Outside the happy hour, however, the prices are much the same as in the Makati nightclubs (such as *Cathouse*) that you find in the Makati Ave and Burgos St area.

Filipinos like clubs which have stimulating entertainment – say, a model show. These so-called disco-theatres are mainly in Quezon City – *Bigwig* in Quezon Ave, for example – but there are also a few in touristy Ermita, such as *Moulin Rouge* in United Nations Ave.

Bistros & Music Lounges

Bistros are enjoying a growing popularity in Manila. All the trendy people go there to be with the 'in' crowd. New names are always being added to the accepted meeting places, and of course others quietly disappear. The ones given here are well established and should survive for some time. Most places don't allow thongs (flip-flops) or shorts.

Bistro Ang Hang in the Sunvar Plaza on the corner of Pasay Rd and Amorsolo St, Makati, has highly spiced dishes. It is open Monday to Saturday from 11 am to 2 am and Sunday from 11 am to 3 pm and from 6 pm to midnight.

The *Bistro RJ* in the Olympia Building, Makati Ave, Makati, has live '50s and '60s music, including Beatles and Beach Boys titles. It is open daily from 6 pm to 3 am. Admission costs P50 on Sunday and Monday, P75 on Tuesday and Thursday and P100 on Wednesday, Friday and Saturday.

The *Café Adriatico* in Adriatico St near Remedios Circle, Malate, started Manila's craze for bistros and is still a favourite. It is open Monday to Saturday from 10 am to 6 am and Sunday from 2 pm to 6 am.

The *Calesa Bar* in the Hyatt Hotel, Roxas Blvd, Pasay City, has good show bands. It is open Monday to Saturday from 7.30 pm to 2 am.

The *Hard Rock Café* in Adriatico St, Malate, has half a small plane protruding outside as if crashed; inside you can watch rock videos. It is open Monday to Saturday from 5 pm to 3 or 4 in the morning.

Moviola in Remedios Circle, Malate, is a piano bar and restaurant open Monday to Saturday from 11 am to 4 am and Sunday from 6 pm to 4 am.

The *Kuh Lesesma Music Museum* in Virra Mall (near the Unimart Supermarket), Greenhills Shopping Center, San Juan, is a comparatively new place that had the unusual concept of combining memorabilia of various stars with live appearances by well-known artists and show bands. The museum is open daily from 5.30 pm to 1 am, and the music lounge from 8 pm to 1 am. Admission is P50 Sunday to Thursday and from P150 to P350 Friday and Saturday, depending on the show.

The *Penguin Café* in Remedios St near Remedios Circle, Malate, can be quite a lively place. It's open Tuesday to Sunday from noon to 2 pm and from 6 pm to 2 am.

The *Siete Pecados* in the Philippine Plaza Hotel in the Cultural Center Complex, Malate, has show bands from 7.30 or 8 pm and is open daily from 5 pm to 1.30 or 2 am.

Discos

'Let's go disco' is as much a part of the Philippine lifestyle as reading comics or smoking menthol cigarettes, so naturally these modern dance-palaces abound. Among the best is *Billboard* in Makati Ave, Makati, a modern disco and video bar that's very popular with the young Filipino trendies. It is open daily from 5 pm to 4 am, and has happy hours Monday to Friday from 5 to 7 pm. Admission is P50 on Friday and Saturday; otherwise it's free.

La Cage in Roxas Blvd, Pasay City, has become the late-night haunt of the colourful mix of people who used to frequent the Coco Banana, once so beloved by gays and transvestites, but now closed.

Lost Horizon in the Philippine Plaza Hotel, Cultural Center Complex, Malate, has good sound with live music and a DJ. It is open daily from 7 pm to 2 or 3 am and admission is free.

Metro in Makati Ave, Makati, seems to be the one preferred by the local film and show stars. It is open daily from 9 pm to 4 am and admission is P50 or P75.

Rumours in South Drive, Makati Commercial Center, Makati, is about the biggest disco in Manila, fitted out with the newest technical equipment. It is open daily from 9 pm to 4 am and admission is P50

At the *Stargazer* in Silahis Hotel, Roxas Blvd, Malate, you use an outside lift to go up to the laser disco, which has a panoramic view over all Manila. It is open daily from 9 pm to 4 am and admission is P75 or P100.

The *Club Valentino* is in the Manila Midtown Hotel, on the corner of Pedro Gil and Adriatico St, Ermita. It is open daily from 10 pm to 4 am. There's a floorshow on Saturday. Admission is free.

Folk Clubs

The *Hobbit House* at 1801 Mabini St, Malate, has a good international atmosphere and the dubious attraction of waiters who are all dwarfs. The minimum order after 8.30 pm is P60. Mexican dishes are a speciality. It is open daily from 7 pm to 2 am. Admission is P50, except when Freddie Aquilar is performing, when it is P120. This most popular interpreter of the Philippines performs his songs of social criticism here about twice a week, usually Tuesday and Saturday. A group called Asin is also popular for its attractive lyrics.

My Father's Moustache in M H del Pilar St, Malate, is a small rustic folk pub that is very relaxed. It has a special Mongolian barbecue. It is open daily from 5 pm to 2 am.

You can hear country & western music daily from 6 pm to 2 am in the *Club 21* in Mabini St, Ermita.

Jazz

Jazz is also enjoying an increase in popularity. Therefore it is safe to assume that there will soon be more places than those listed here.

At present you can hear jazz daily from 6 to 11 pm in the *Lobby Court* of the Philippine Plaza Hotel, Cultural Center Complex, Malate. There are also regular Sunday evening performances in the *Clipper Lounge* of the Mandarin Oriental Hotel, Makati Ave, Makati, and in the *Concourse Lounge* of the Manila Garden Hotel, Makati Commercial Center, Makati.

The main rendezvous for jazz enthusiasts however is *Birdland*, on the corner of Tomas Morato St and Timog Ave, Quezon City, where showbands appear Monday to Saturday from 6 pm to 2 am. There is a cover charge of from P75 to P120.

Pubs

Among the pubs in Ermita and Malate that are not pick-up joints are *Lili Marleen*, *Edelweiss*, *Guernica's*, *Silver Bar*, *Swiss Hut* and the *Weinstube*, all in M H del Pilar St; *Southern Cross* in United Nations Ave; *Holandia* in Arquiza St; *Birdwatcher's Bar* on the corner of Flores St and Mabini St; and the *Boomerang Club* in Mabini St.

You can also spend some pleasant afternoons and evenings in the restaurant bars with swimming pools, thus making a stay in noisy Manila's polluted air a little more bearable. Among these open-air oases are the *Pool Bar*, tucked away in Guerrero St, a small side street off Padre Faura, by the Aurelio Hotel, and *Treasure Island*, a nice little place among the lagoon-like swimming pools of the Philippine Plaza Hotel, where you can have a tropical cocktail while enjoying the magnificent display of the sunset over Manila Bay.

THINGS TO BUY

The full name of Philtrade Exhibits is the Philippine Center for International Trade and Exhibition. It is in Roxas Blvd, Pasay City, and here you can see goods that are manufactured in the Philippines for export. Prices are relatively high, but it's all right to bargain.

Silahis in General Luna St, Intramuros, has a wide range of handicrafts from the whole country. It's in the basement of the restored El Amanecer, and above are the Chang Rong Antique Gallery and the Galeria de las Islas.

In Paterno and Puyat streets (side streets off Rizal Ave), Santa Cruz, stampmakers with the skill of surgeons will cut cheap rubber stamps like signatures, for P30 in 15 minutes.

At the La Flor de la Isabela cigar factory, Tabacalera, on the corner of Romualdez St and United Nations Ave, Ermita, single visitors or groups can be shown how the world-famous Coronas are made. You can also buy cigars and, if you like, have the boxes engraved with initials. They prefer you to book (tel 508026).

T'boli Arts & Crafts in Mabini St, Ermita, sells the handicrafts of the T'boli, who are one of the ethnic minorities on Mindanao. This small shop is up some steps, opposite the post office, between Santa Monica St and Padre Faura.

GETTING THERE & AWAY

Air

Manila has two airports. For flights within the Philippines you use the Domestic Airport. Small airlines like Aerolift and Pacific Airways have a small terminal building each, while Philippine Airlines uses the main building; flights to Cebu go from the Cebu Terminal, which is slightly to the side. You have to tell the taxi driver well in advance which terminal you want as well as the name of the airline and the destination. It is rumoured that Manila's present Domestic Airport will soon be relocated in the old international airport, just beside the new Ninoy Aquino International Airport (NAIA) – supposedly in 1991. It remains to be seen what will happen.

When you depart from NAIA, you will have to pay a departure tax of P220. (For further information see the Getting There chapter.)

The Philippine Airlines offices are, with very few exceptions, open Monday to Saturday from 8.30 am to 5 pm and closed on Sundays and holidays. Philippine Airlines has a 24 hour telephone information service (tel 8323166). Destinations, flight times, arrival and departure times of Aerolift, Pacific Airways and Philippine Airlines are given in the Getting Around chapter.

(See the Getting There and Getting Around chapters for details of international and domestic flights to and from Manila, and the Getting Around section of this chapter for information about transport from NAIA to the city and to the Domestic Airport.)

Following is a list of the airline offices in Manila:

Philippine Airlines

PAL Building, Legaspi St, Makati (tel 888174, 8171479) (open Monday to Saturday from 8.30 am to 5 pm)

Hotel Intercontinental, Ayala Ave, Makati (tel 8160238, 884178) (open Monday to Saturday from 8.30 am to 5 pm)

Ninoy Aquino International Airport, Pasay City (tel 8310622, 8310716) (open daily from 6 am to the time of the last PAL flight)

Domestic Airport, Pasay City (tel 8320990-91, 8316541) (open daily from 4 am to 8 pm)

Botica Boie Building, Escolta St, Binondo (tel 475014, 492003) (open Monday to Saturday from 8.30 am to 5 pm)

S & L Building, 1500 Roxas Blvd, Ermita (tel 504461, 586662) (open Monday to Friday from 8.30 am to 5 pm, and Saturday and holidays from 8.30 am to noon)

Manila Hotel, Rizal Park, Ermita (tel 494010, 495377) (open Monday to Saturday from 8.30 am to 5 pm)

PWU Building, Taft Ave, Malate (tel 503844, 591857) (open Monday to Saturday from 8.30 am to 5 pm)

Central Bank Building, Mabini St, Malate (tel 507878, 507051) (open Monday to Saturday from 8.30 am to 5 pm)

Belson Finance Building, EDSA, Mandaluyong (tel 705969, 708050) (open Monday to Saturday from 8.30 am to 5 pm)

BPI Arcade, Aurora Blvd, Cubao, Quezon City (tel 999891, 977216) (open Monday to Saturday from 8.30 am to 5 pm)

De los Santos Building, Quezon Blvd Extension, Quezon City (tel 7122743, 7122756) (open Monday to Saturday from 8.30 am to 5 pm)

Aerolift

Chemphil Building, 851 Pasay Rd, Makati (tel 8172361, 8172369)

West Maintenance Area, Domestic Airport, Pasay City (tel 8331694)

Tickets also available from:

Broadway Travel, Chateau Marie Building, Roxas Blvd, Ermita (tel 591924, 5212903)

Blue Horizon Travel & Tours, Manila Peninsula Hotel, Ayala Ave, Makati (tel 876071-76)

Mabini Pension, 1337 Mabini St, Ermita (tel 594853)

Sunshine Run, 451 Pedro Gil, corner of M H del Pilar St, Ermita (tel 506601, 506606)

Pacific Airways

Domestic Airport Rd, Pasay City (tel 8322731-32, 8332390-91)

Bus

All bus companies use a combination of

ordinary buses and air-con buses, but there aren't too many of the latter. You can ring and inquire about exact departure times and possibly reserve a seat. Both Sarkies' Tours (tel 597658, 508959) and Sunshine Run (tel 584787, 584102) specialise in tours in North and South Luzon using air-con buses. You can also get tickets and make reservations at Galactica Travels Inc (tel 5218770), in the Ermita Tourist Inn, on the corner of Mabini and Soldado streets, Ermita.

There is no central bus terminal in Manila. The terminals of the individual companies are scattered all over the city. Most of them are easy to reach by Metrorail. The Ministry of Transportation is planning to move several terminals from the city centre to the outskirts. This would affect the Lawton Terminal, which is presently opposite the City Hall and from which buses leave for the provinces of Batangas, Laguna, Quezon and Cavite. Check if a final decision has been made.

Following is a list of the addresses and major routes of the principal bus companies in Manila:

Baliwag Transit (tel 350860) in Rizal Ave Extension and 2nd Ave, Grace Park, Caloocan City, has buses going north to Bulacan Province, Baliwag and San Jose. Get to its terminal by Monumento jeepney from Mabini St. The nearest Metrorail station is R Papa Station.

BLTB (tel 8335501) is in EDSA, Pasay City. It has buses going south to Batangas, Calamba, Lucena, Nasugbu and Santa Cruz. Get to its terminal by Baclaran jeepney or bus from Taft Ave or M H del Pilar St and change in or before Baclaran. The nearest Metrorail station is EDSA Station.

Dagupan Bus (tel 976123) in New York St, Quezon City, has buses going north to Alaminos, Baguio, Dagupan and Lingayen. Get to its terminal by taking a Cubao jeepney from Taft Ave or a Makati Love Bus from M H del Pilar St to the Ayala Commercial Center; then catch another Love Bus to Cubao.

Dangwa Tranco (tel 7312859) in 1600 Dimasalang St, Sampaloc, has buses going north to Baguio and Banaue. Get to its terminal by Blumentritt jeepney from Taft Ave. The nearest Metrorail station is Tayuman Station.

Farinas Trans (tel 7314507) in M dela Fuente St, on the corner of Laong Laan, Sampaloc, has buses going north to Vigan and Laoag. Get to its terminal by Blumentritt jeepney from Taft Ave. The nearest Metrorail station is Tayuman Station.

Lawton Terminal, opposite City Hall, has recently been named Liwasang Bonifacio, but people aren't really used to this yet. JAM Transit, Laguna Transport and BLTB buses going south leave from here for Batangas, Lucena and Santa Cruz. Get to its terminal by Monumento jeepney from Mabini St or Taft Ave. The nearest Metrorail station is Central Terminal.

Maria de Leon (tel 7314907) in Gelinos St, on the corner of Dapitan St, Sampaloc, has buses going north to Vigan and Laoag. Get to its terminal by Blumentritt jeepney from Taft Ave. The nearest Metrorail station is Bambang Station.

Pantranco North (tel 997091, 951081) at 325 Quezon Blvd, Quezon City, has buses going north to Alaminos, Aparri, Baguio, Baler, Bolinao, Lingayen and Tuguegarao. Get to its terminal by Pelcoa or Project 8 jeepney from Taft Ave or Mabini St, though these are not frequent.

Philippine Rabbit (tel 7115819) is in Santa Cruz at 819 Oroquieta St, with another entrance in Rizal Ave. It has buses going north to Angeles City, Baguio, Balanga, Mariveles, San Fernando (Pampanga) and Tarlac. Get to its terminal by Monumento jeepney from Mabini St. The nearest Metrorail station is D Jose Station. Philippine Rabbit has another terminal (tel 343488, 3614490) on the corner of 2nd Ave and Rizal Ave Extension, Grace Park, in Caloocan City. Buses leave for Laoag, San Fernando (La Union) and Vigan in the north. There may possibly also be buses leaving from Santa Cruz or from the company's new terminal at 256 North Diversion Rd, Balintawak, Quezon City (tel 359574, 346264). Get to this terminal by Monumento jeepney from Mabini St. The nearest Metrorail station is R Papa Station.

Philtranco (tel 8335061) in EDSA, Pasay City, has buses going south to Cagayan de Oro, Calbayog, Catbalogan, Daet, Davao, Legaspi, Lucena, Naga, Tacloban and Sorsogon. Get to its terminal by Baclaran jeepney or bus from Taft Ave or M H del Pilar St and change in or before Baclaran. The nearest Metrorail station is EDSA Station.

Superlines (tel 984910) at 670 EDSA in Quezon City has buses going south to Daet and Lucena. Get to its terminal by Cubao jeepney from Taft Ave.

Times Transit (tel 7314180) at 1716 Laong Laan, Sampaloc, has buses going north to Bangued, Laoag, San Fernando (La Union) and Vigan. Get to its terminal by Blumentritt jeepney from Taft Ave. The nearest Metrorail station is Tayuman Station.

Victory Liner (tel 3611506, 3611514) at 713 Rizal Ave Extension, Caloocan City, has buses going north to Alaminos, Iba, Olongapo and Mariveles.

Get to its terminal by Monumento jeepney from Mabini St. The nearest Metrorail station is North Terminal (Monumento). Victory Liner has another terminal (tel 8335019) at 651 EDSA, Pasay City, with buses going north to Baguio, Iba and Olongapo. Get to this terminal by Baclaran jeepney or bus from Taft Ave or M H del Pilar St and change in or before Baclaran. The nearest Metrorail station is EDSA Station.

Train

See the Getting Around chapter for details.

Boat

Nearly all inter-island boats leave Manila from North Harbor. If you have trouble finding it ask a coastguard opposite Pier 8.

Next to the North Harbor piers are the docking facilities of the Del Pan Bridge (coming from the sea it is the first bridge over the Pasig River). Various small vessels to neighbouring islands depart from here but they don't have any schedule.

To get to North Harbor from Ermita by taxi costs about P30. There is a rather roundabout way of getting there by jeepney, although it goes through inner suburbs with heavy traffic and can take up to an hour. From Mabini St or Taft Ave you get a jeepney to Divisoria; there you change into a jeepney for North Harbor.

To go from North Harbor to Ermita or other suburbs after a ship has docked, it is extremely difficult to get a taxi with a properly adjusted meter. The 'fixed price' is between P50 and P100.

The small travel bureau Galactica Travels Inc (tel 5218770) sells tickets for the shipping companies Aboitiz Lines, Palawan Shipping Corporation and Sweet Lines, so you don't always have to go to the offices on the wharves.

The following companies have offices in Manila:

Aboitiz Lines
  King's Court Building, Pasong Tamo St, Makati (tel 887451, 8164875)
  Pier 4, North Harbor, Tondo (tel 217581, 2173339, 218175)
  Destinations: Panay, Romblon

Asuncion Shipping Lines, 3038 Jose Abad Santos St, Tondo (tel 7110590)

Carlos Gothong Lines
  Pier 10, North Harbor, Tondo (tel 213611, 214121)
  Destinations: Cebu, Mindanao, Panay

Negros Navigation Lines
  Negros Navigation Building, 849 Pasay Rd, Makati (tel 864921-25)
  Pier 2, North Harbor, Tondo (tel 217526, 219071, 217477)
  Destinations: Negros, Panay, Romblon

Palawan Shipping Corporation
  551 Victoria St, Intramuros (tel 405294, 491372, 483611)
  Pier 10, North Harbor, Tondo
  Destinations: Panay, Cuyo, Palawan

Sulpicio Lines
  415 San Fernando St, San Nicolas (tel 479621, 475346)
  Pier 12, North Harbor, Tondo (tel 201781)
  Destinations: Cebu, Leyte, Masbate, Mindanao, Negros, Palawan, Panay, Samar

Sweet Lines
  Pier 6, North Harbor, Tondo (tel 201791, 263527)
  Destinations: Cebu, Mindanao

William Lines
  1508 Rizal Ave Extension, Caloocan City (tel 3610764)
  Pier 14, North Harbor, Tondo (tel 219821, 405458)
  Destinations: Cebu, Leyte, Mindanao, Palawan, Panay, Romblon, Samar

GETTING AROUND

Ninoy Aquino International Airport (NAIA)

Near the luggage collection point, you will find telephones provided for you to make free local (Manila) calls. These give you the opportunity of booking a hotel room while you wait for your luggage to appear. It costs P20 or US$1 to use a luggage trolley; the charge includes the service of a porter, but, unlike the trolleys, porters can be hard to locate.

If you want to confirm a connecting flight or your return flight before leaving the airport, you'll find the counters of all the major airlines two floors up; take the staircase in front of the arrival hall exit.

Airport Transport

International Airport to the City Unfortunately, they don't seem to have heard of the saying 'The first impression is the most important' in Manila. Since 1975 I've been arriving at the international airport at least twice a year, and almost each time my arrival has been marred by some inconvenience. Comparing Manila with other Asian cities, like Bangkok or Hong Kong, you can't help wondering why this place seems unable to provide a smooth arrival for visitors. And why on earth can't airport staff manage to arrange efficient transport to a hotel for visitors who are tired and worn out after many hours in a plane? For years the airport managers have been experimenting with various changes, none of which ever seem to benefit incoming travellers.

For instance, the reliable and inexpensive airport buses that once serviced a large number of hotels in different suburbs disappeared from the scene overnight. Then the Golden Cabs (black with a gold-coloured roof), which were equipped with meters that actually worked properly, were ousted from the arrival platform. With these gone, there were only the highly suspect yellow taxis to ferry tourists to the city – some of the fares charged would make your hair stand on end. For a trip from the airport to Ermita/Rizal Park, which normally should cost no more than P40 (US$2), up to US$50 has been demanded! If you get off with paying P100, you should consider yourself lucky. The latest plan is to allow only Aircon Taxis to service the airport. Their set charges would be something like P220 to Pasay, P300 to Ermita and Makati, and P380 to Quezon City. It can only be hoped that the elimination of all competition will be prevented by a massive protest on the part of the numerous Filipino air passengers.

Bus There are still regular buses from the international airport, many of them bound for Ermita and downtown Manila, and the taxis are in fierce competition with them. You will find the buses standing about 150 metres to the right of the exit. The grey California buses now follow the highway – not a particularly pleasant route. It's better to travel to Ermita on the yellow DMTC buses, which have their terminus in Quiapo. These go along Taft Ave and you can alight at the corner of Pedro Gil or wherever. But be warned: there are plenty of 'pocket slashers' riding these buses and they are constantly on the lookout for big spoils! You might be better off investing a few pesos in a taxi ride, or, for a mere P15, get a taxi to the Metrorail terminus in Baclaran; from there it's P3.50 to Pedro Gil Station or United Nations Ave.

Taxi You can get a Golden Cab from the departure level; these taxis take passengers from the city to the airport and are normally supposed to return empty. (To go to the departure level, take the staircase a few metres from the main exit in the arrival hall.)

If there are still ordinary taxis to be found at the departure level these days, they'll probably be standing some 50 metres to the left of the exit. The taximeter is supposed to be switched on just before the taxi starts off. If the driver tells you that the counter is out of order, you're quite entitled to get out again. However, ordering the driver to stop and let you out after you've gone 500 metres can be awkward, especially at night.

The starting fee in taxis is P2.50; when you reach the tourist quarter of Ermita, a correctly functioning taximeter will show about P40 (prices are as at September 1990). Certain taxi drivers, however, while switching off the meter at the end of the trip, nimbly turn it forward P20 or so! Other taxi drivers will proudly hand you typed 'official' fare lists, often impressively set in a leather binder with gold lettering. Be aware that these have no legal validity whatsoever and are simply another crude attempt to defraud unsuspecting tourists.

Keep your cool and don't allow yourself to be provoked if you encounter problems with a driver on the way to the hotel. You're in a much better position to win a fight when you and your luggage are already out of the taxi and you can call on the hotel staff for support.

Hotel Transport If instead of a fairly expensive taxi fare you'd rather spend your money on a decent hotel room, you can book a room for the first night at one of the accommodation counters near the main exit in the arrival hall. Most of the hotels represented offer a free limousine service for patrons arriving at the airport.

If you can't book ahead, and the hotel of your choice is booked out, you can (during the daytime) wait in the hotel lobby until a room becomes vacant. But remember that few guests tend to check out after midday. A polite request at the reception counter will usually find a member of staff willing to ring other hotels for a vacant room for you.

International Airport to the Domestic Airport Travellers landing in Manila and proceeding to another destination within the Philippines have to transfer to the nearby domestic airport. PAL provides passengers with a free bus service. As this shuttle bus is mostly underbooked, a friendly smile will normally get passengers of other airlines on it too. The bus only departs, however, when it has at least one PAL passenger on board. The shuttle bus counter is at the arrival platform exit.

A taxi ride from the international airport to the domestic airport generally costs no more than P15, but you can be charged up to P150.

Bus

Around Manila, city buses only display their final destination on the sign on the front. That can be a large complex like the NAIA, a street name like Ayala (for Ayala Ave in Makati) or a whole suburb like Quiapo (north of Pasig River). The fare is 75 centavos for the first four km and 25 centavos for every km after that. At the end of Rizal Ave Extension there is a statue of Andres Bonifacio, known as the 'Monumento', a very popular destination and stop for jeepneys and buses.

The air-con Love Buses are very popular in Manila. They are blue (with red hearts) operate on several main routes and charge a flat rate of P8.50. Have small change to hand, as bus drivers usually cannot change large notes. The Escolta-Ayala/Medical Center bus is a useful one for tourists – the Love Bus goes from the Calle Escolta (Binondo/Santa Cruz) through Ermita (M H del Pilar St) to Makati (the embassies) and the Makati Commercial Center. It returns through Mabini St in Ermita. There are no fixed stops on the way. Don't throw your ticket away, as there are frequent inspections.

Train

The Metrorail LRT (Light Rail Transit) is an overhead railway which runs on concrete pylons several metres high, linking the suburbs of Caloocan City and Pasay City. The line runs from North Terminal (Monumento) in Caloocan City, over Rizal Ave to Central Terminal near the Manila City Hall and on over Taft Ave to South Terminal in Baclaran, Pasay City. The fare is a flat rate of P3.50, irrespective of the number of stations you travel to. Instead of tickets, you have to buy tokens that open the barriers to the platforms. Smoking, eating and drinking are all forbidden both on the platforms and in the trains. Bulky objects which may cause obstruction will not be carried.

Following are the stations from north to south, and some of the prominent city features nearby:

North Terminal (Monumento)
  Andres Bonifacio Monument, EDSA, Victory Liner Bus Terminal
5th Ave Station
  Caloocan City
R Papa Station
  Philippine Rabbit Bus Terminal (2nd Ave), Baliwag Transit Bus Terminal
Abad Santos Station
  Chinese Cemetery
Blumentritt Station
  Chinese Hospital, San Lazaro Hippodrome
Tayuman Station
  Dangwa Tranco Bus Terminal, Farinas Trans Bus Terminal, San Lazaro Hippodrome
Bambang Station
  Maria de Leon Bus Terminal, Times Transit Bus Terminal, University of Santo Tomas
D Jose Station
  Claro M Recto St (cinemas), Philippine Rabbit Bus Terminal (Santa Cruz)

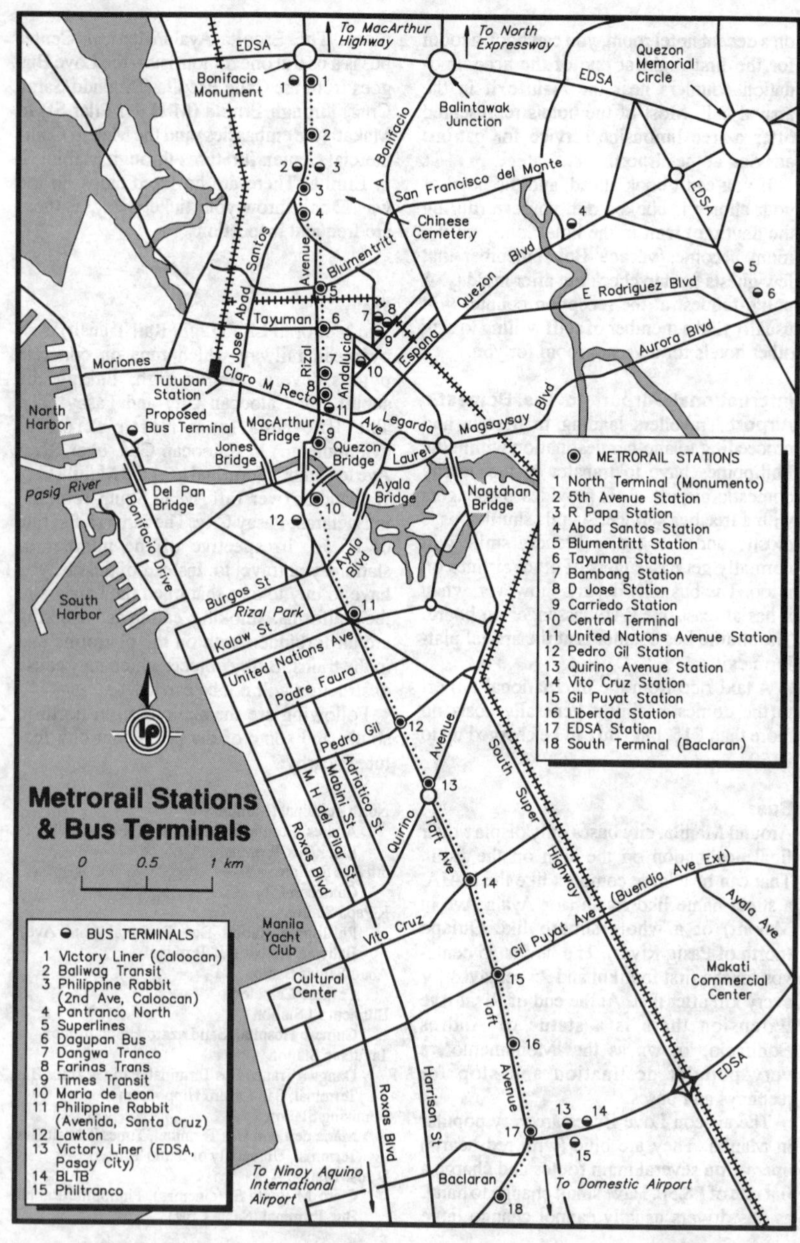

Metrorail Stations & Bus Terminals
To MacArthur Highway
To North Expressway
EDSA
Bonifacio Monument
Balintawak Junction
Quezon Memorial Circle
A Bonifacio
San Francisco del Monte
Chinese Cemetery
Jose Abad Santos
Rizal Avenue
Blumentritt
Quezon Blvd
E Rodriguez Blvd
Tayuman
Andalucia
Espana
Aurora Blvd
Moriones
Tutuban Station
Claro M Recto Ave
Legarda
Magsaysay Blvd
North Harbor
Proposed Bus Terminal
MacArthur Bridge
Jones Bridge
Quezon Bridge
Laurel
Pasig River
Del Pan Bridge
Ayala Bridge
Nagtahan Bridge
Bonifacio Drive
Ayala Blvd
South Harbor
Burgos St
Rizal Park
Kalaw St
United Nations Ave
Padre Faura
Pedro Gil
Quirino Avenue
South Super Highway
M H del Pilar St
Mabini St
Adriatico St
Roxas Blvd
Taft Ave
Gil Puyat Ave (Buendia Ave Ext)
Ayala Ave
Vito Cruz
Manila Yacht Club
Cultural Center
Makati Commercial Center
Harrison St
Taft Avenue
To Ninoy Aquino International Airport
Baclaran
To Domestic Airport
0 0.5 1 km
METRORAIL STATIONS
1 North Terminal (Monumento)
2 5th Avenue Station
3 R Papa Station
4 Abad Santos Station
5 Blumentritt Station
6 Tayuman Station
7 Bambang Station
8 D Jose Station
9 Carriedo Station
10 Central Terminal
11 United Nations Avenue Station
12 Pedro Gil Station
13 Quirino Avenue Station
14 Vito Cruz Station
15 Gil Puyat Station
16 Libertad Station
17 EDSA Station
18 South Terminal (Baclaran)
BUS TERMINALS
1 Victory Liner (Caloocan)
2 Baliwag Transit
3 Philippine Rabbit (2nd Ave, Caloocan)
4 Pantranco North
5 Superlines
6 Dagupan Bus
7 Dangwa Tranco
8 Farinas Trans
9 Times Transit
10 Maria de Leon
11 Philippine Rabbit (Avenida, Santa Cruz)
12 Lawton
13 Victory Liner (EDSA, Pasay City)
14 BLTB
15 Philtranco

Carriedo Station
  Chinatown, Escolta, Ilalim ng Tulay Market, Quinta Market, Quiapo Church, Santa Cruz Church
Central Terminal
  GPO, Immigration Office, Intramuros, Lawton Bus Terminal, Manila City Hall, Metropolitan Theater
United Nations Ave Station
  Manila Doctor's Hospital, Manila Medical Center, Manila Pavilion Hotel, Paco Park, Rizal Park, Tourist Office, Western Police District
Pedro Gil Station
  Manila Midtown Hotel, PLDT (Philippine Long Distance Telephone Company)
Quirino Ave Station
  Malate Church, San Andres Market
Vito Cruz Station
  Central Bank, Cultural Center, De la Salle University, Harrison Plaza, Sheraton Hotel
Gil Puyat Station
  Cartimar Market, Philtrade Exhibits
Libertad Station
  Libertad Cockpit, Pasay Market
EDSA Station
  BLTB Bus Terminal, Philtranco Bus Terminal, Victory Liner Bus Terminal
South Terminal (Baclaran)
  Baclaran Church, Baclaran Flea Market, Seaside Market

Taxi

Always have some change ready when you board a taxi in Manila, as there's no guarantee the driver will have any. The flag-down charge is P2.50, after which it is P1 for the first 500 metres and P1 for each subsequent 250 metres. If the price hasn't already gone up, TOMMI (Taxicab Operators of Metro Manila) would certainly like to see it raised. The BOT (Bureau of Transportation) will agree to an increase only when all taxis have been fitted with a modern meter which cannot be fiddled with.

Jeepney

You need to get to know Manila a bit before you can travel through the city by jeepney without problems. Crowding and the limited view make it hard to see where you are going, so a seat by the driver is desirable. Jeepney routes are fixed. Their main streets and stops are shown on the side of the vehicle and mostly on the windscreen as well. For example, jeepneys with the sign 'Baclaran, Harrison, Santa Cruz, Rizal, Monumento' will go from Baclaran in Pasay City, through Harrison St to Harrison Plaza, then down Mabini St, back down M H del Pilar St – both one-way streets – past the City Hall (Lawton), to the suburb of Santa Cruz, then down Rizal Ave and Rizal Ave Extension to Monumento in Caloocan City.

Jeepneys on the north-south route are almost always marked 'Baclaran' or 'Libertad' to show the southern end of their route, both in Pasay City. The northern end could be Monumento (Caloocan City, at the end of the Rizal Ave Extension); Blumentritt (a street in northern Santa Cruz, by the Chinese Hospital and near the Chinese Cemetery); or Divisoria (the Divisoria Market in the suburb of San Nicolas). Jeepneys in Ermita run along M H del Pilar St and Mabini St (those marked 'Harrison') or Taft Ave (those marked 'Taft'). Jeepneys whose north-eastern destination is shown as 'Project 2', 'Project 3' or 'Project 4' are going to Cubao, while those marked 'Project 6' and 'Project 8' are heading for Quezon City. The fare is 75 centavos for the first four km; most charge P1.

See also the Jeepneys section of the Getting Around chapter.

Driving

Traffic in Manila is chaotic and noisy, especially to someone who is used to fairly strict traffic controls. There are few bus stops and these are not always used. Buses and jeepneys stop wherever they see a fare to pick up and then taxis of various companies try to get in ahead of them. Horns and hand signals are used most often, brake lights and blinkers rarely, and traffic-lane markings seem to be thought a waste of paint. However, the Filipinos are used to these conditions and there are few accidents – the battered vehicles usually last longer than their appearance would lead you to believe. If you want a cheap and pleasant form of inner-city public transport, try the Metrorail.

Tours

For a quick and relatively cheap overview of Manila you should organise something for yourself, but preferably not during the rush hour in late afternoon, when traffic is heavily congested.

Try using the air-con Love Buses for transport. Get on a Love Bus in M H del Pilar St in Ermita which is going in the direction of Ayala/Medical Center and travel to the terminus at Makati Commercial Center, where you can sightsee, shop or visit the Ayala Museum. Then get another Love Bus from the Commercial Center to Cubao in Quezon City. In the Araneta Center in Cubao are numerous restaurants and cinemas as well as excellent opportunities for shopping and window shopping. From there, catch another Love Bus to Quiapo/Escolta, which will take you past numerous ministries and other official establishments, and the central part of the city. From Escolta, head in the direction of Ayala/Medical Center and get off at Ermita.

Students of the German School in Manila have suggested another tour which uses a variety of public transport and goes through Tondo, Binondo and Chinatown. Get on a Love Bus at M H del Pilar St in Ermita travelling towards Ayala/Medical Center and go as far as the intersection of the Southern Expressway (South Super Highway) and Gil Puyat Ave (Buendia Ave). Continue by train from Buendia Station to the terminus at Tutuban. Departure times are about once an hour in either direction (4.30, 5.30, 6.30, 8.20, 9.30 and 10.30 am). The last part of the train trip is through the slums of Tondo.

From the terminus at Tutuban, walk to nearby Narra St, where you will find the Temple of 10,000 Buddhas (Seng Guan Buddhist Temple). Then go back to Claro M Recto Ave, past the station and a little further on turn left into Tabora St. Continue on to Divisoria Market and then along the river and through the Second Welcome Gate to Binondo Church. This is where Chinatown starts – the busy Ongpin St runs from here to the Santa Cruz Church. Halfway along, right at the Ongpin North Bridge, there are lots of little stalls offering a variety of delicious foods, particularly vegetable and seafood dishes. From Carriedo Station you can get the Metrorail to Pedro Gil Station, Taft Ave, and from there walk back to your starting point.

An extension of the walk from Carriedo Station is to go along Carriedo St to Quiapo Church, or along Carlos Palanca St (Echague St) past Quinta Market to Quezon Bridge, with its cheap craft shops in the Ilalim ng Tulay Market. From there, you can go to Quiapo Church or to the Globo de Oro Mosque with its shining gold dome and the nearby Rajah Sulimon (Muslim) Market.

TRANSPORT FROM LUZON

To the Batan Islands

Air From Manila to Basco via Laoag there is a PAL flight on Thursday and Sunday. On Monday, Wednesday and Saturday flights go via Tuguegarao.

To Bohol

Air Aerolift flies daily from Manila to Tagbilaran; PAL flies from Manila to Tagbilaran on Monday, Wednesday and Friday.

Boat The William Lines' MV *Misamis Occidental* leaves Manila on Friday at 9 am for Tagbilaran via Dumaguete on Negros, taking 36 hours.

To Catanduanes

Air PAL flies daily from Manila to Virac and from Legaspi to Virac.

Boat The MV *Virac* or the MV *Antipolo* leaves Tabaco daily for Virac at 11 am, taking three hours or more.

To Cebu

Air PAL and Aerolift both have daily flights from Manila to Cebu City; PAL also has a daily flight from Legaspi to Cebu City.

Boat Several vessels run between Manila and Cebu City. The Sweet Lines' MV *Sweet Baby* departs on Sunday at noon and on

Thursday at 9 am, taking 22 hours. The William Lines' MV *Dona Virginia* leaves on Sunday at 10 am and Wednesday at 8 pm, taking 20 hours. The Sulpicio Lines' MV *Davao Princess* leaves on Sunday at 10 am, taking 23 hours, while their MV *Filipina Princess* leaves on Tuesday at 10 am and Friday at 8 pm, taking 21 hours.

To Leyte

Air Aerolift has flights on Monday, Tuesday, Thursday, Friday and Saturday from Manila to Ormoc. PAL has daily flights from Manila to Tacloban.

Bus Air-con Philtranco buses leave Manila daily at 7 am and 5 pm for Tacloban. The travelling time including the ferry trip from Matnog to San Isidro is 25 hours. It is possible to pick up these buses on the way – in Legaspi, for instance, at 3 am or 5 pm – if seats are available, but they seldom are.

Boat The Sulpicio Lines' MV *Cebu Princess* leaves Manila on Friday at 10 am for Ormoc, via Masbate and Calbayog, taking 45 hours. The William Lines' MV *Tacloban City* leaves on Monday at 1 pm for Tacloban via Catbalogan and on Friday for Tacloban direct. The time taken (direct) is 24 hours.

To Lubang

Air Pacific Airways has flights from Manila to Lubang daily and Aerolift has flights on Tuesday, Thursday, Saturday and Sunday.

Boat The William Lines' MV *Edward* leaves Manila for Tilik on Friday at noon, taking seven hours. The Asuncion Shipping Lines' MV *Asuncion X* leaves Manila for Tilik on Saturday at 10 pm, taking eight hours, and their MV *Catalyn A* leaves Manila for Tilik on Tuesday at 10 pm, taking eight hours.

To Marinduque

Air PAL has daily flights from Manila to Marinduque.

Boat There is one ship a day from Lucena to Balanacan. Departure time varies as it is dependent upon the tides, but is usually around 10 am. Passengers are taken by outrigger boats out to the ship, which is anchored off the coast. The trip takes four hours. There is a BLTB bus from Manila to Lucena which goes directly to the wharf. BLTB (tel 833550) can give you the departure time of the bus and probably the sailing time of the ship as well.

There is also one ship a day from Lucena to Buyabod, the port for Santa Cruz, which takes five hours. The situation about sailing times is the same as for the ship going to Balanacan.

To Masbate

Air PAL has daily flights from Manila to Masbate and from Legaspi to Masbate on Monday, Wednesday, Friday, Saturday and Sunday.

Boat The Sulpicio Lines' MV *Cebu Princess* leaves Manila for Masbate at 10 am on Friday. It takes 17 hours. The William Lines' MV *Cebu City* leaves Manila for Masbate on Saturday at midnight, taking 16 hours.

From Bulan there is one boat daily leaving at noon and taking four hours. There may possibly be a second boat.

To Mindanao

Air From Manila, PAL has daily flights to Cagayan de Oro, Cotabato, Davao and Zamboanga, and flights on Monday, Wednesday, Thursday and Saturday to Butuan.

Aerolift has daily flights from Manila to Dipolog, flights on Monday, Wednesday, Friday and Sunday to Surigao and flights on Tuesday, Thursday and Saturday to Iligan.

Bus Air-con Philtranco buses run daily from Manila to Davao, leaving at 7 am and 5 pm. Travelling time including the ferry from Matnog to San Isidro and from Liloan to Surigao is 45 hours. It is possible to pick up the bus on the way – at Legaspi, for example, at 3 am or 5 pm – if seats are available (but they seldom are).

Boat The Carlos Gothong Lines' MV *Our Lady of Lourdes* leaves Manila at 6 pm on Tuesday for Butuan. It takes 35 hours.

The Negros Navigation Lines' MV *Santa Ana* leaves Manila for Cagayan de Oro on Friday at 2 pm. It takes 42 hours and goes via Iloilo on Panay.

The Sulpicio Lines' MV *Davao Princess* leaves Manila for Davao on Sunday at 10 am. It takes 50 hours, going via Cebu City.

The Sulpicio Lines' MV *Dipolog Princess* leaves Manila for Dipolog on Wednesday at midnight. It takes 38 hours and goes via Dumaguete on Negros. It continues on to Cagayan de Oro and Ozamiz.

The Sweet Lines' MV *Sweet Glory* leaves Manila on Tuesday at 7 pm for Zamboanga. It takes 36 hours and continues on to Davao.

The William Lines' MV *Manila City* leaves Manila on Thursday at 7 pm for Zamboanga. It takes 36 hours and continues on to Davao.

The Sulpicio Lines' MV *Cotabato Princess* leaves Manila on Saturday at 3 pm for Zamboanga, taking 45 hours and going via Estancia and Iloilo on Panay. It continues on to Cotabato.

To Mindoro

Air Pacific Airways has daily flights from Manila to Calapan. PAL has daily flights from Manila to Mamburao and San Jose.

Bus A through trip from Manila to Puerto Galera starts from the Sundowner Hotel in Mabini St, Ermita, daily at 9 am. The air-con bus goes to Batangas to the MB *Sikat II*, which leaves at noon and arrives in Puerto Galera at 2.30 pm. Bookings and tickets (P180) are arranged at the Sundowner Hotel. Buses from Manila to Batangas leave the Lawton and BLTB bus terminals regularly; see the Batangas section of the Around Manila chapter.

Boat Two boats go daily from Batangas to Calapan, at 5 pm and 6 pm, taking three hours. You can catch a jeepney from Calapan to Puerto Galera the next morning, taking two hours.

There are three boats daily from Batangas to Puerto Galera. The MS *Princess* (Express) costs P50, leaves at 11 am and takes two hours. The MB *Sikat II* costs P80, leaves at noon and takes 2½ hours. The ferry MS *Queen* costs from P25 to P40, leaves at 12.30 pm and takes two hours or more. A Special Ride by outrigger boat should not cost more than P400.

The William Lines' MV *Edward* leaves Manila on Friday at noon for Sablayan. It takes 18 hours, going via Tilik on Lubang. The same boat goes from Manila on Monday at 7 pm to San Jose, taking 16 hours.

To Negros

Air PAL has daily flights from Manila to Bacolod and Dumaguete.

Boat There are three Negros Navigation Lines ships each week from Manila to Bacolod. The MV *Don Claudio* sails on Sunday at 9 am, taking 24 hours. The MV *Don Julio* leaves on Tuesday at 10 am, taking 21 hours. The MV *Santa Maria* leaves on Friday at 2 pm and takes 28 hours, going via Roxas on Panay.

From Manila to Dumaguete, the Sulpicio Lines' MV *Dipolog Princess* sails on Wednesday at midnight and takes 30 hours; the William Lines' MV *Misamis Occidental* goes on Friday at 9 am, also taking 30 hours.

To Palawan

Air From Manila to Coron, Aerolift has flights on Monday, Wednesday, Thursday and Saturday and Pacific Airways has daily flights.

Pacific Airways flights go from Manila to Cuyo on Monday, Wednesday and Friday.

PAL has daily flights from Manila to Puerto Princesa.

Boat The Palawan Shipping Lines' MV *Princess of Antique* leaves Manila for Cuyo on the 5th and 19th of each month at 1 pm. It takes 42 hours, going via San Jose de Buenavista on Panay. From Cuyo it goes on to Puerto Princesa.

The William Lines' MV *Masbate I* leaves

Manila for Puerto Princesa on Tuesday at 7 am, going via Odiongan on Romblon, and on Friday at 7 pm, going via Malay on Panay. It takes 30 hours.

The Sulpicio Lines' MV *Palawan Princess* leaves Manila for Puerto Princesa on Thursday at midnight, taking 24 hours.

The Asuncion Shipping Lines has several ships going from Manila to various towns on Palawan. The MV *Asuncion X* leaves Manila for Coron on Saturday at 10 pm, via Tilik on Lubang. It takes 26 hours and continues on to Culion. The MV *Catalyn A* leaves Manila for Coron on Tuesday at 10 pm, via Tilik on Lubang. It takes 26 hours and continues on to Culion. The MV *Asuncion IV* leaves Manila for El Nido on Wednesday at 11 pm. It takes 30 hours and continues on to Liminangcong. The MV *Asuncion VI* leaves Manila for Dumaran on Monday at 10 pm. It takes 38 hours and goes on to Roxas, Caramay and Puerto Princesa. This ship sometimes goes via Tilik on Lubang before sailing to Dumaran.

To Panay

Air Aerolift and Pacific Airways have daily flights from Manila to Caticlan. PAL has daily flights from Manila to Iloilo, Kalibo and Roxas.

Boat The MV *Super Ferry 1*, Aboitiz Lines, leaves Manila on Sunday at 2 pm for Boracay, taking 22 hours. This ship goes via Dumaguit (near Kalibo on Panay) where it stops for two hours. From Boracay it continues to Iloilo.

The Aboitiz Lines' MV *El Cano* leaves Manila for Dumaguit on Monday at noon, taking 20 hours.

The Sulpicio Lines' MV *Cotabato Princess* leaves Manila on Saturday at 3 pm for Estancia, taking 17 hours.

There are three ships from Manila to Iloilo. The Negros Navigation Lines' MV *Santa Florentina* leaves on Sunday at 12.30 pm and their MV *Santa Ana* leaves on Friday at 2 pm. Both take 24 hours. The Sulpicio Lines MV *Philippine Princess* leaves on Tuesday at 10 am and takes 22 hours.

The William Lines' MV *Masbate I* leaves Manila on Friday at 6 pm for Malay (near Boracay on Panay), taking 14 hours.

The Carlos Gothong Lines' MV *Our Lady of Guadalupe* leaves Manila on Wednesday at noon for New Washington, taking 20 hours.

For Roxas from Manila, the Aboitiz Lines' MV *El Cano* leaves on Thursday at noon. It goes via Romblon town on Romblon and takes 29 hours. The Negros Navigation Lines' MV *Santa Maria* leaves on Friday at 2 pm and takes 17 hours. The Carlos Gothong Lines' MV *Our Lady of Fatima* leaves on Saturday at 6 pm and takes 19 hours.

To Romblon

Air PAL has daily flights except Sunday from Manila to Tugdan on Tablas.

Boat The William Lines' MV *Masbate I* leaves Manila for Odiongan on Tablas on Tuesday at 7 am. It takes 12 hours.

The Negros Navigation Lines' MV *Santa Maria* leaves Manila for Romblon town on Friday at 2 pm, taking 13 hours, and the Aboitiz Lines' MV *El Cano* leaves Manila for the same destination on Thursday at noon, taking 16 hours.

There are also several boats weekly from Lucena which go to Romblon town or to Magdiwang on Sibuyan.

To Samar

Air PAL has daily flights from Manila to Calbayog and Catarman.

Bus Air-con Philtranco buses leave Manila daily at 7 am and 5 pm for Calbayog and Catbalogan, taking 23 and 25 hours respectively, including the ferry from Matnog to San Isidro. It is possible to get on these buses in Legaspi at 3 am and 5 pm if there is room, but seats are not often available.

Boat The Sulpicio Lines' MV *Cebu Princess* leaves Manila for Calbayog on Friday at 10 am, taking 19 hours.

The William Lines' MV *Tacloban City*

leaves Manila for Catbalogan on Monday at 1 pm, taking 22 hours.

There are two to four ferries daily, depending on the season, from Matnog to Allen and San Isidro. They usually leave between 6 am and 8 am when the Philtranco bus from Manila arrives, but there may also be one between 10 am and noon and during the afternoon. The crossing takes one hour or more.

Around Manila

All the trips described in this chapter can be done as day trips from Manila. The map shows towns that can be reached by bus within three hours. Olongapo, Pagsanjan and Matabungkay, however, deserve an overnight stay.

Some destinations can be combined – the volcano at Tagaytay and the beach at Matabungkay, for example. Some towns can be visited on the way to other destinations: Olongapo is on the way to the Hundred Islands and Pagsanjan is on the way to South Luzon.

There is an expressway from Metro Manila north to Dau and Mabalacat, a little beyond Angeles, and another south to about Calamba. Buses using expressways rather than the ordinary roads carry the sign 'Expressway'.

BATAAN PENINSULA

It's not possible to do a round trip of the Bataan Peninsula. The stretch from Bagac to Olongapo is blocked for military reasons by the Philippines Navy. At Morong, about a thousand Vietnamese boat people live in a place known as the 'Procession Center'.

On Mt Samat, a little to the south of Balanga, the provincial capital, is Dambana ng Kagitingan, a national monument to the victims of the Battle of Bataan. There is a cross over 90 metres high from which you get a good view over the former battlefield and Manila Bay.

At present a great debate rages in the Philippines as to whether the USA should retain its bases in Olongapo, Subic Bay and Angeles after 1991 and how much it should pay. (The Military Bases Agreement signed shortly after WW II expires in 1991.) An undercurrent of anti-USA sentiment directed towards the bases is making itself felt, especially in the south of Bataan.

A large part of the south of the peninsula is industrialised. Most of the almost 650 manufacturing plants in the province, including the biggest, are in the Export Processing Zone in Mariveles, where textiles, clocks, electrical appliances and automobile parts are made.

Getting There & Away

Lots of Philippine Rabbit Company buses leave Manila daily for Balanga, Mariveles and Morong. Most go to Balanga. The travelling time to Mariveles is three hours.

Several Victory Liner buses run daily from Olongapo to Balanga, taking an hour or more.

SAN FERNANDO (Pampanga)

Don't confuse San Fernando (Pampanga), the capital of Pampanga Province, between Manila and Angeles, with the San Fernando that is the capital of La Union Province on the coast, north-west of Baguio. This town is notorious at Easter because on Good Friday at noon you can see at least one believer being nailed to a cross in a rice field outside the gates of the city. And on 24 December a spectacular parade of oversized lanterns mounted on trucks is driven through the town. (See also the Fiestas & Festivals section in the Facts about the Country chapter.)

Places to Stay

The simple *Pampanga Lodge*, opposite the big church, is pleasant, with singles/doubles with fan for P60/90 and doubles with fan and bath for P100. You can also get 12 hour rates. It has a restaurant.

Getting There & Away

Only a few buses go direct from Manila to San Fernando along the old MacArthur Highway. Most use the quicker expressway. There are several Philippine Rabbit and Victory Liner buses every day. Buses from Manila to Olongapo almost always go into San Fernando; if necessary, you can get a jeepney from the nearest crossroads into the town. The buses take about an hour.

Numerous Victory Liner buses go from Olongapo through San Fernando daily, almost all on the way to Manila or Baguio. Travelling time is an hour or more.

You can get reasonably priced jeepneys from Angeles to San Fernando daily. Most come from Mabalacat or Dau, north of Angeles. Victory Liner buses from Baguio to Olongapo go through Angeles and San Fernando and it is possible to get on them. This trip takes 30 minutes.

OLONGAPO

The US Navy is stationed here and while this is not a good reason for a visit, what has sprung up around the base makes the town interesting. There are countless bars, nightclubs, massage parlours, pubs and cinemas. Some of the best rock, country & western and disco music can be heard in the clubs. Olongapo is the place for relatively inexpensive entertainment. Attempts to promote Olongapo as the 'fun city of the Philippines' centre around the twice-yearly Mardi Gras. On long weekends in February and during April and May there is beer, music and dancing on Magsaysay Drive, where most nightclubs are.

From Olongapo you can easily do a day trip to Mt Samat on the Bataan Peninsula. Take a Victory Liner bus from Olongapo to Balanga and from there go on by jeepney or minibus to the Mt Samat turn-off. The last seven km you have to hike uphill. A hat is recommended.

Places to Stay

Bayside Hotel (tel 5440) at 1697 Rizal Ave has single rooms with fan for P75, and singles/doubles with fan and bath for P100/120. Those are '24 hour' prices, so you can guess what the rooms are usually used for. You pay daily in advance, but it's good value and the beds are wide so a single is good for two. The price drops by P20 if you check in after 6 pm. Check out time is 11 am. It's near the Victory Liner bus station.

The *MGM Hotel* at 87 Magsaysay Drive is in the middle of the lively red-light district but is reasonable. It has rooms with fan and bath for P180 and with air-con and bath for P300. The air-con rooms have TV. Check out time is 11 am.

The *Moonstone Apartments* (tel 5301) at 2132-2148 Rizal Ave is probably the best hotel in the town. It has doubles with air-con and bath from P530 to P600. TV costs P40 extra. Apartments cost from P650. Monthly rates are available. All rates are payable daily in advance. It has a restaurant, coffee shop and swimming pool. It is near the big market, a few minutes on foot from the Victory Liner Terminal in the direction of Manila.

Getting There & Away

From Manila, several Victory Liner buses leave the bus terminal in Pasay (EDSA) for Olongapo daily, and also from Caloocan (the Rizal Ave Extension). The trip takes two to three hours. There are also several Victory Liner buses from Alaminos to Olongapo daily, taking about six hours. You may have to change at Santa Cruz.

Victory Liner buses run roughly hourly from 5.30 am to 5.30 pm daily between Baguio and Olongapo and it is possible to board them at Angeles. In Angeles you can also catch a San Fernando jeepney, get out at the turn-off to Olongapo and wait for the next bus. Travelling time from Baguio is six hours; from Angeles, it takes two hours. Victory Liner buses also run several times a day from San Fernando to Olongapo, taking an hour or more.

BARRIO BARRETTO & SUBIC

By comparison with Olongapo, the bars in Barrio Barretto and Subic are basic, with entertainment at about the jukebox level. When the fleet's in, however, things are pretty wild and the uninhibited goings-on – especially in Subic – can tempt hard-bitten marines in a mood for a fling after long weeks at sea to jump ship.

There are several resorts along the 12 km of coast between Olongapo and Subic but the beaches themselves are not particularly good. They are better north of Subic Bay,

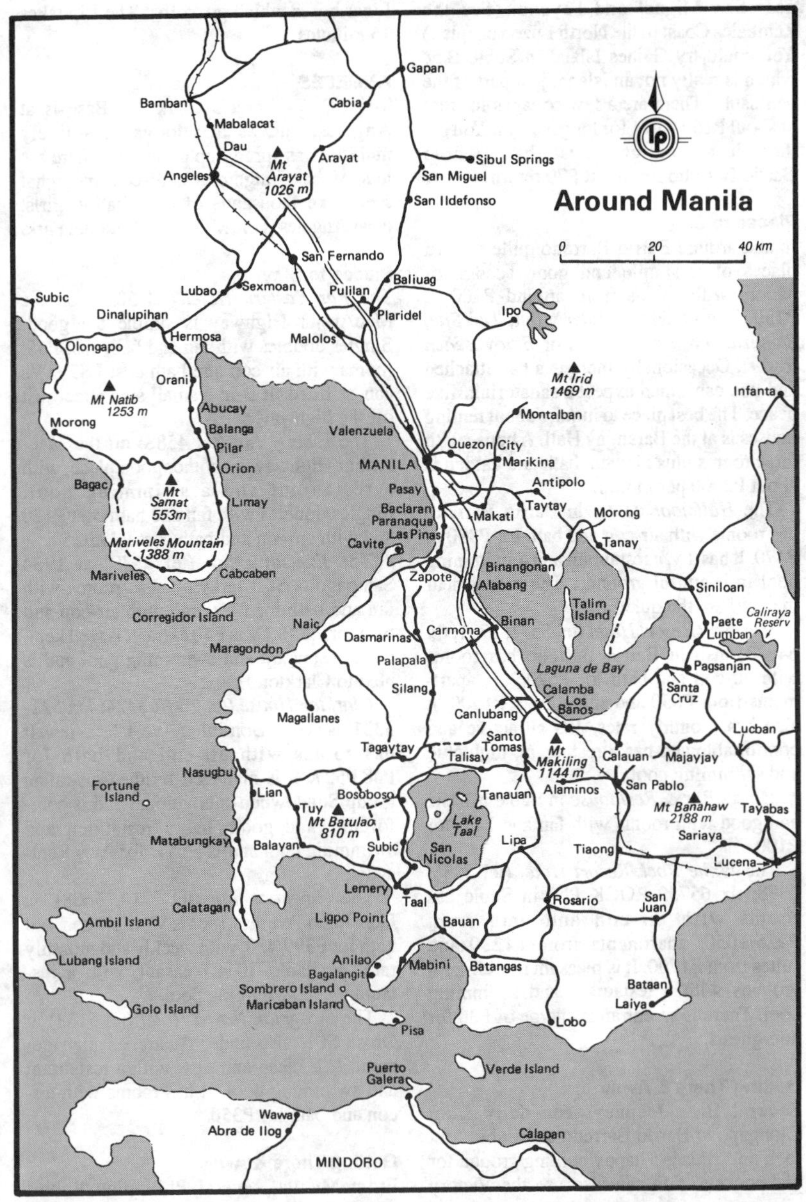
Around Manila
0 20 40 km
Gapan
Bamban
Cabia
Mabalacat
Dau
Mt Arayat 1026 m
Arayat
Sibul Springs
Angeles
San Miguel
San Ildefonso
San Fernando
Baliuag
Lubao
Sexmoan
Pulilan
Subic
Dinalupihan
Plaridel
Ipo
Hermosa
Olongapo
Malolos
Mt Irid 1469 m
Orani
Infanta
Mt Natib 1253 m
Abucay
Morong
Balanga
Valenzuela
Montalban
Pilar
Quezon City
Orion
MANILA
Marikina
Bagac
Mt Samat 553m
Antipolo
Limay
Pasay
Taytay
Baclaran
Makati
Morong
Paranaque
Las Pinas
Mariveles Mountain 1388 m
Cavite
Tanay
Mariveles
Cabcaben
Binangonan
Zapote
Alabang
Siniloan
Talim Island
Corregidor Island
Naic
Binan
Paete
Caliraya Reserv
Carmona
Dasmarinas
Lumban
Maragondon
Palapala
Laguna de Bay
Pagsanjan
Silang
Calamba
Santa Cruz
Los Banos
Magallanes
Canlubang
Lucban
Tagaytay
Santo Tomas
Mt Makiling 1144 m
Talisay
Calauan
Majayjay
Nasugbu
Fortune Island
Lian
Bosoboso
Tanauan
Alaminos
San Pablo
Tuy
Mt Batulao 810 m
Lake Taal
Mt Banahaw 2188 m
Tayabas
Matabungkay
Sariaya
Balayan
Subic
Lipa
Tiaong
San Nicolas
Lucena
Lemery
Taal
Rosario
San Juan
Calatagan
Ambil Island
Ligpo Point
Bauan
Lubang Island
Anilao
Mabini
Batangas
Bagalangit
Sombrero Island
Bataan
Maricaban Island
Laiya
Golo Island
Pisa
Lobo
Puerto Galera
Verde Island
Wawa
Abra de Ilog
Calapan
MINDORO

near San Miguel and beyond. (See the Zambales Coast in the North Luzon chapter.) You could try Gaines Island in Subic Bay, which is really not an island, just part of the peninsula. There are a few cottages for rent at about P100 – less for longer stays. You get there in an outrigger boat (banca) from Barrio Barretto for about P70 return.

Places to Stay

In and around Barrio Barretto quite a lot of places offer simple and good accommodation, with rooms from around P100 to P150. You could try *Rider's Inn*, *The Site*, *Samurai Inn*, *Bamboo Inn* or *Baloy Beach Resort*. Occasionally there is a bar attached and you can't then expect a sanatorium-like peace. The best place to inquire about renting houses is at the Barangay Hall. A house with three rooms plus kitchen, bath and garden is about P2000 per month.

The *Halfmoon Hotel* in Barrio Barretto has rooms with air-con and bath for P390 to P470. It has TV, a restaurant and a swimming pool in beautiful grounds. The rooms near the pool are the quietest.

Marmont Resort Hotel (tel 5571, 3791; tlx 64873) also in Barrio Barretto has rooms with air-con and bath for P620/700, apartments from P850 and suites from P1500. It also has monthly rates. It's attractive and comfortable and has a restaurant, nightclub and swimming pool.

Mina's Bar & Resthouse in Subic is basic and good with rooms with fan and bath for P100.

The *White Rock Resort Hotel* (tel 5555, 2398; tlx 65759 ROCK PN) in Subic has rooms with air-con and bath from P925/1050, apartments from P1230 and suites from P1700. It is pleasant in well-kept grounds with a restaurant and swimming pool. There is an entrance charge of P30 for non-guests.

Getting There & Away

Several Blue Jeepneys run daily from Olongapo to Barrio Barretto and Subic. But look out – this is a happy hunting ground for pickpockets. You can also use the Victory Liner buses which go to Iba. The trip takes 15 minutes.

ANGELES

The US Air Force's Clark Air Base is at Angeles, and as at Olongapo, a lively nightlife has sprung up around it. There are lots of bars, nightclubs, discos and what seem like thousands of 'hospitality' girls. Near Angeles is the Mt Arayat National Park.

Places to Stay

The *Far Eastern Hotel* (tel 5014) on the MacArthur Highway is simple but good. Singles/doubles with fan and bath cost P65; rooms with air-con and bath cost P85. TVs can be hired. It is in a small side street just off the highway.

The *Liberty Inn* (tel 4588) on the MacArthur Highway is another good place, with a restaurant and a swimming pool. Singles/doubles with fan and bath cost P120 and with air-con and bath cost P235/250.

The *Executive Inn* (tel 3939) at 1934 Sampaguita St, Clarkview, has rooms with fan and bath for P120 and with air-con and bath for P200. TV is P40 extra. It is well kept, has a restaurant and swimming pool and is next to Clarkton House.

Clarkton House (tel 2667, 3424; fax 521-5331) is at 620 Don Juico Ave, Clarkview. It has rooms with air-con and bath for P483/527. It is managed by the Australian group Sundowner International and is comfortable and good, has a restaurant and swimming pool and is a base for Avis Rent-a-Car.

The *Hawaiian Inn* (tel 2714, 5608) on Don Juico Ave has rooms with air-con and bath for P399/450, with weekly and monthly rates available. It is pleasant, with a restaurant and swimming pool.

The *Swagman Narra Hotel* (tel 5133) in Orosa St is also under Australian management. It is clean and tidy, with a restaurant and swimming pool. It has rooms with air-con and bath for P350.

Getting There & Away

From Manila, several Philippine Rabbit

buses run daily to Angeles, taking an hour or more. Be careful about buses which are not marked 'Expressway/Dau', as these follow side streets and make lots of stops. You can also take a bus from any of the companies – Philippine Rabbit, Victory Liner, Pantranco, Farinas or Maria de Leon Trans – to Baguio, Laoag, Vigan, San Fernando (La Union), Dagupan or Alaminos, get out at Dau and go the short way back to Angeles by jeepney or tricycle. To go from Angeles to Manila you can get a Philippine Rabbit bus at its terminal in Angeles or catch a bus in Dau coming from North Luzon. In addition, an air-con bus leaves Manila daily at around 8.30 am from the Sundowner Hotel, Mabini St, for Clarkton House, returning at 10 am.

Another air-con bus leaves Manila daily at 1 pm from the Birdwatcher's Bar, Mabini St, for the Swagman Narra Hotel, returning at 3 pm. And the so-called Clark Bus or Embassy Bus leaves daily at about 10 am and 5 pm from the Manila Pavilion Hotel, Maria Orosa St entrance, for Clark Air Base. This bus comes from Ninoy Aquino International Airport and also stops at the Holiday Inn, Philippine Plaza, Admiral Hotel, Silahis Hotel and the US Embassy. It leaves Angeles for Manila at 7 am and 2 pm.

Hourly Victory Liner buses run from Olongapo to Angeles daily. They take two hours. In Olongapo you can also get a Manila bus, get out in or before San Fernando (Pampanga) and wait for a bus or jeepney to Angeles.

Victory Liner buses run from Baguio to Angeles hourly every day from 5.30 am to 5 pm. They are the ones marked 'Olongapo'. The trip takes four hours. Buses from other companies such as Philippine Rabbit and Pantranco travel from Baguio to Manila via Dau; it is just a short way from Dau to Angeles by jeepney or tricycle. Similarly, to go from Angeles to Baguio it's best to go to Dau and get on one of the buses from Manila.

Numerous buses of various companies travel daily from Laoag, Vigan and San Fernando La Union to Dau on the way to Manila. If you get out in Dau, it's only a short way by jeepney or tricycle to Angeles. To go from Angeles to San Fernando La Union, Vigan or Laoag, it's best to go to Dau and get on the buses coming through from Manila.

CORREGIDOR ISLAND

The fortified island of Corregidor was important in WW II. Even earlier, in 1898, Corregidor was used by the USA in its war against Spain because of its strategic position at the entrance to Manila Bay. Construction of the Malinta Tunnel began 25 years later and it served as General Douglas MacArthur's headquarters from December 1941 to March 1942, as Filipinos and Americans struggled in vain against the Japanese invaders. Quezon left by submarine and eventually MacArthur was smuggled out on a PT boat. After the island fell, the infamous Bataan Death March commenced there. Today ruins of the military installations and ordnance can be inspected, and there are elaborate plans for restoration. On the highest point of the island stands the Pacific War Memorial.

Getting There & Away

Organised daily excursions from Manila to Corregidor at a cost of P950 per person include transport from hotel to wharf, the boat trip and a guided round tour by bus on the island, as well as a generous buffet lunch on the return trip. The MV *Island Cruiser* leaves daily at 7.30 am and 1.30 pm from the clipper landing near the Manila Hotel and Rizal Park. For further information call 588809 or 5210791. The MV *Tristar* belonging to the Tristar Sea Ventures Corporation leaves from the hover-ferry terminal by the Cultural Center, Roxas Blvd. Sailing dates and times are Tuesday, Thursday, Saturday and Sunday (possibly only Saturday and Sunday) between 7 and 7.30 am. The trip takes two hours and you are back in Manila by about 4 pm.

An economical alternative to the organised tour is to go under your own steam via Mariveles on the Bataan Peninsula. Take one of the many daily Philippine Rabbit buses to Mariveles; the first leaves at 4.30 am. It is a three-hour trip. Get out just before

Mariveles at the covered bus stop shortly after Cabcaban. From there, for P3 to P5, you can get a trishaw or tricycle to take you down the old National Highway to the former Villa Carmen Beach Resort, where the owner of the Villa Carmen arranges round trips by boat to Corregidor for P350.

You could also get a bus to Balanga and then do the last bit in a minibus or jeepney going to Mariveles down the old National Highway, as this goes past the gate of the Villa Carmen. Returning to Manila, the last Philippine Rabbit bus leaves Balanga at about 6 pm.

There is a landing fee of P10 per person at Corregidor. At weekends it is sometimes possible to make arrangements for shared transport with the Americans from the US Navy base in Subic who like making day trips from Mariveles to the island fortress.

LAS PINAS

This small town is famous for its unique bamboo organ in the San Jose Church. Started in 1816 by the Spanish Father Diego Cerra, it was made from bamboo to save money and was finally completed in 1824. Standing over five metres high, it has 832 pipes of bamboo and 122 of metal. From 1973 to 1975 it was overhauled in Germany and now sounds as good as new. Asmall shop in the church porch sells records and cassettes of bamboo-organ music. The real thing can be heard on Sunday or during the Bamboo Organ Festival which lasts for a week every February. It's a social occasion, with internationally famous organists, choirs and ensembles. On normal weekdays the organ can only be seen from 2 to 4 pm.

Las Pinas also makes jeepneys and the people in the workshops are quite happy to have you looking around, although they are closed on Sunday. As you leave the church, the Sarao Jeepney Factory is about three km further south on the main street.

Getting There & Away

In Manila there are plenty of buses to Las Pinas that you can stop in Taft Ave. Destinations shown will be either Zapote or Cavite. It takes half an hour. Another possibility is to get a jeepney to Baclaran (you can get one from M H del Pilar St in Ermita), then go on with a Zapote jeepney to Las Pinas.

If you want to go on from Las Pinas to Tagaytay or Matabungkay, you can go into the main street and get into any of the many buses coming through from Manila on the way to Nasugbu.

CAVITE

This town on the southern side of Manila Bay has no real tourist attractions to offer and its beaches, like Lido Beach, are not particularly good. It does, however, make a pleasant day trip from the city, and the fair and leisure park known as Covelandia is nearby. The Philippines Navy is stationed at Cavite. The Aquinaldo House Museum in Kawit, Cavite, is worth seeing.

Places to Stay

The spacious *Puerta Azul Beach Resort* (tel 574731-40; tlx 64546 AZUTEL PN) in Ternate, 40 km south-west of Cavite, has rooms with fan and bath for P900. It is well kept, with a restaurant and coffee shop. There are facilities which belong to a local country club but for a small charge may be used by hotel guests. These include a swimming pool for P25, a tennis court from P65, squash courts for P75 an hour, a golf course for P350, Hobie Cats for P170 and windsurfers for P120.

Marbella Marina Beach Resort (tel 8185021), also in Ternate, has rooms with air-con and bath from P1100. It is attractive and comfortable, with a restaurant, tennis court, golf course and swimming pool. It also has Hobie Cats and windsurfers.

Getting There & Away

Numerous buses leave the Lawton Terminal in Manila daily and can be stopped in Taft Ave. Travelling time is half an hour.

TAGAYTAY (Taal Volcano)

Due to its high altitude (600 metres) and cool climate, Tagaytay was once proposed as an alternative summer resort to Baguio. The sprawling town offers visitors superb views of the volcanic island with its crater lake, but only if the weather is clear. The volcano is one of the smallest in the world. If you want to climb it, you can make arrangements before you leave Manila through the Volcanology Commission (tel 608303) in Quezon City. However a permit to cross the lake and stop at the island is not essential. A good route is from Talisay, 17 km to the east. An attractive alternative route is to go on to Batangas and then to San Nicolas.

About 10 km east of Tagaytay, on Mt Sungay (710 metres), are the ruins of the Palace in the Sky, the villa built by Ferdinand Marcos for the state visit of Ronald Reagan. From here you have a marvellous view of Lake Taal to the south, Laguna de Bay to the east and almost as far as Manila to the north. You come from Tagaytay in a jeepney bound for Villa Adelaida, get out at the last stop and do the last few metres to the top on foot.

Places to Stay

Emma's Place, Silang Crossing, is homely and run by very nice people. They have rooms for P50/100.

The *Taal Vista Lodge* is clean and good. It has rooms with air-con and bath for P850 but it also has two-person tents for P75, with mattresses and linen costing P15 extra. At the lookout in front of the lodge, folk dances with native music often take place at noon; the entrance fee is P15 and is added on to the bill if you consume something in the restaurant (it's really only worth a bottle of beer).

Villa Adelaida (tel 267), Foggy Heights, has rooms with fan and bath for P600. At weekends it can be 20% dearer. It is pleasant, with a restaurant and swimming pool. Coming from Manila, you turn to the left instead of the right at the crossroads before Tagaytay. The Villa is by the road that runs down to the lake. You can make reservations in Manila (tel 876031-39).

Getting There & Away

Several BLTB buses run daily from Manila to Tagaytay, marked 'Nasugbu'. There are also others that pass through. The trip takes an hour or more.

From Talisay to Tagaytay there are three to eight jeepneys a day on the 17 km of dusty, narrow road. It costs P10 per person and a Special Ride costs P200.

To get to Tagaytay from Pagsanjan you go by jeepney to Santa Cruz. There you get a Manila bus and get out at the junction at Calamba. From Calamba you go by jeepney through Binan to Palapala and from there you get a bus to Tagaytay. It takes about three hours. Or, instead of getting out at Calamba, you can continue on to Alabang and there change to a jeepney to Zapote, where you can catch a bus from Manila heading for Tagaytay.

TALISAY

Talisay is on the edge of the lake and is a good starting point for trips to the volcanic island. The return boat trip costs P275 with a guide, P200 from, for example, Rosalina's Place. You might have to cope with heavy swells and may occasionally get sopping wet, so a plastic bag for the camera is a good precaution.

About five km west of Talisay in Buco, on the edge of Lake Taal, is an old seismological station of the Philippine Institute of Volcanology & Seismology (PHIVOLC). Its scope has been extended to that of a 'Science House', with staff always on duty and information available on the work of vulcanologists, the instruments and the geological history of Lake Taal.

Places to Stay

Rosalina's Place, Banga, has rooms for P50/90 and with fan and bath for P60/100. It is simple and good and has a restaurant. It lies a little outside Talisay, opposite the International Resort.

Getting There & Away

From Manila the trip to Talisay is in two stages. First you get one of the numerous daily BLTB buses marked 'Lemery' or 'Batangas' and go as far as Tanauan. From there you can get a jeepney in the public market going to Talisay. Total travelling time is two hours.

From Tagaytay, the 17 km road to Talisay drops down to the lake and is dusty, narrow and little used, except by the three to eight jeepneys that run daily. The fare is P10 per person; a Special Ride is about P200. The last one leaves from the Aquino Monument, about two km from the Taal Vista Lodge, at 5 pm.

To reach Talisay from Pagsanjan you begin by catching a jeepney to Santa Cruz. Then catch a Manila bus and get out at the junction at Calamba. From there, catch a jeepney to Tanauan, where you can pick up a jeepney to Talisay. Total travelling time is about two hours. Instead of going through Calamba, you can use jeepneys from Pagsanjan and Santa Cruz via San Pablo to Tanauan and Talisay.

From Batangas, it's best to use the many daily Manila buses to get to Tanauan. This route is also served by jeepneys, but buses are more comfortable. In the public market in Tanauan you can get a jeepney to Talisay. Total travelling time is two hours.

NASUGBU & MATABUNGKAY

Matabungkay has the most popular beach in the neighbourhood of Manila, so on weekends there are lots of day-trippers. Although the sand is not dazzlingly white, it's not bad and the water is clean. Among the main attractions are thatched-roof rafts with tables and chairs which can be hired for around P100 per day and anchored over the reef to act as platforms from which to swim and snorkel. The hirer also brings out food and ice-cold drinks to order. Day trips to nearby Fortune Island can be arranged for P300 to P400.

The beaches at Nasugbu are worth noting. The one at White Sands is three to four km to the north and can be reached by tricycle or outrigger boat. Out of Nasugbu, in the direction of the beach, is a good seafood restaurant, the Dalam Pasigan and, about 20 km west of Nasugbu, at the foot of Mt Batulao, is the exclusive Batulao Resort Hotel, with swimming pool and facilities for sports like riding, golf, tennis, squash, bowling, billiards and table tennis.

Places to Stay

The *Swiss House Hotel*, Matabungkay, has rooms with fan for P200/350. It is well kept and has a restaurant.

The *Twins*, Ligtasin/Matabungkay, has rooms with fan and bath for P350/400. It is good quality and has a restaurant.

The *Matabungkay Beach Resort*, in Matabungkay, has rooms with air-con and bath for P350/400. It is attractive and comfortable, with a restaurant, swimming pool and tennis court.

The *Coral Beach Club*, Matabungkay, has rooms with fan and bath for P400. It has been well maintained and has a restaurant.

White Sands Beach Resort, in Muntingbuhangin Cove, Natipuan, Nasugbu, has cottages with fan and bath for P625/795. There is no electricity but it is pleasant and has a restaurant. Reservations can be made in Manila (tel 8335608).

The *Maya-Maya Reef Club* (tel 233), Nasugbu, has cottages with fan and bath for P940 and cottages with air-con and bath for P1400. It is popular, with a restaurant, swimming pool and tennis court in attractive grounds. There is also a diving shop. Reservations can be made in Manila (tel 8106858, 8159289; fax 8159288; tlx 4233 BATO PU).

Punta Baluarte Inter-Continental Resort, Calatagan, has rooms with air-con and bath for P1200/1500. It has a restaurant, swimming pool, golf course and tennis courts and is about 20 km south of Matabungkay. You can make reservations in Manila (tel 894011, 8159711; tlx RCA 23314 ICH PH).

Getting There & Away

BLTB buses leave Manila almost hourly every day for Nasugbu. An air-con bus goes at 11.30 am. It takes about two hours. To get to Matabungkay, it's best to get out at Lian and do the last few km by jeepney. These leave about 100 metres from the bus stop in the direction of the centre of the town. Special Rides in a tricycle cost about P50.

There are also jeepneys that run from Nasugbu to Matabungkay via Lian.

At 12.30 pm, a BLTB bus goes from Manila to Matabungkay and on to Calatagan, which saves changing at Lian.

From Batangas to Matabungkay and Nasugbu is a three or four-stage trip by jeepney: jeepney from Batangas to Lemery, jeepney from Lemery to Balayan, jeepney from Balayan to Nasugbu or from Balayan to Balibago and jeepney from Balibago.

BATANGAS

There is talk of developing an industrial zone in and around Batangas, the provincial capital, which would provide a convenient location for foreign investors. The South Super Highway is to be extended to Batangas and the possible reopening of the old Manila-to-Batangas railway is being considered. The depth of Batangas Bay and the ease with which harbour facilities could be constructed are also being put forward as advantages Batangas has over other regions.

Tourists mainly use Batangas as a transit point on the way to Puerto Galera on Mindoro. However, it is also a good point from which to make day trips to Lake Taal, to the hot springs at Calamba and Los Banos, to Banuan Beach and to Grethel Beach near Lobo. Tabangao, on the further part of the rocky coast, is just seven km from Batangas and offers good diving and snorkelling.

Places to Stay

J.C.'s Pension House in M H del Pilar St has rooms with fan for P60/120 and with air-con and bath for P250. It is attractive and comfortable.

The *Guesthaus* (tel 1609), 224 Diego Silan St, on the corner of M H del Pilar St, has rooms with fan for P70 and with fan and bath for P100. It is clean and comfortable.

The *Mascor Hotel* (tel 3063) on Rizal Ave Extension has rooms with fan and bath for P150/250 and with air-con and bath for P200/300. It is pleasant and has a restaurant and disco. It is on the outskirts, towards the harbour.

The *Alpa Hotel* (tel 2213), Kumintang Ibana, has rooms with fan for P50/100, with fan and bath for P127, with air-con for P187/209 and with air-con and bath for P330/385. It is well kept and has a restaurant and swimming pool. It is on the outskirts in the direction of Manila.

Getting There & Away

Always ask for Batangas City when inquiring about transport, otherwise there will be confusion as to where in the Batangas Province you wish to visit. Several buses leave the Lawton Terminal in Manila daily for Batangas. You can also stop them in Taft Ave, but by then the best seats are often taken. If you want the harbour in Batangas, look for the buses for Batangas Pier. Air-con buses go from the BLTB Terminal but not all go through to the pier, in which case you have to get a jeepney down to the dock. The trip takes two hours or more. Beware of pick-pockets on these buses – they often operate in teams of three.

If you arrive in Batangas from Mindoro, you can take one of the Manila buses waiting at the pier and go directly to Manila, or go into town by jeepney and get a bus there – either the regular bus or a BLTB air-con bus to Pasay/Manila.

If you are going from Manila to Batangas and on towards Puerto Galera, there is a daily combined bus and ship service from the Sundowner Hotel in Mabini St, Ermita, leaving at 9 am.

There is an interesting back-roads route from Batangas to Manila via Lemery which allows for a detour to Lake Taal. Go by jeepney from Batangas to Lemery; the road is dusty and not very good, so the best seat is that next to the driver. Then take a jeepney to San Nicolas on the south-western edge of the lake. The last jeepney back to Lemery leaves at 5 pm, which gives you ample time to catch the last BLTB bus in Lemery for Pasay/Manila. If instead of Manila you are heading for Santa Cruz or Pagsanjan, then you change at Calamba.

To go to Batangas from Pagsanjan quickly, take a jeepney to Santa Cruz; from there, catch a Manila-bound bus as far as

Calamba. From Calamba, either take a jeepney directly to Batangas or take a jeepney to Tanauan and then can catch a Batangas-bound bus travelling from Manila.

LOBO

Lobo is about 30 km south-east of Batangas. From there it's three km by tricycle to the beautiful Grethel Beach, a favourite Filipino retreat for school holidays and weekends. The Submarine Garden, a few km away, is said to be worth seeing. There is also a daily boat to Calapan on Mindoro.

Places to Stay

On Grethel Beach there are several cottages for P200 per day, but with some determined bargaining you may be able to halve the price. As there is no restaurant, you will usually have to provide your own food, although the owner may be willing to supply basic meals.

The *Blue Lodge*, Masaguisit, has dormitories with fan for P60, rooms for P75/100, with fan for P100/125 and with fan and bath for P175/200.

Getting There & Away

Several jeepneys run daily to and from Batangas. It takes an hour or more.

ANILAO

In Anilao there are various diving centres where you can arrange trips to diving spots in Balayan Bay near Cape Bagalangit and near Sombrero and Maricaban islands. Boat hire for a day trip to Sombrero Island is around P500.

The beach at Anilao is not recommended. You can, however, hire thatched bamboo rafts with tables and chairs for P250 at places like the Anilao Beach Resort. These are anchored some distance out from the beach and are good platforms for swimming and snorkelling.

Places to Stay

Because Anilao is a tourist haunt, accommodation is expensive. It is worth getting away from the centre. The *San Jose Lodge* on the edge of town has rooms for P75/100. The *Anilao Beach Resort* (tel 8341641), also out of town on the beach, has rooms with bath for P275/300. It is pleasant and good and has a restaurant.

The *Aqua Tropical Resort* has a Manila address: c/o Aqua Tropical Sports, Manila Midtown Hotel, Pedro Gil, Ermita (tel 587908, 5216407; fax 8189720; tlx 27706 ATTRA PH). It has rooms with fan for P540, with fan and bath for P860 and with air-con and bath for P1200 and P1800. It is attractive and comfortable and has a restaurant and swimming pool. It also has diving equipment and organises diving trips. It is near Bagalangit, a few km south-west of Anilao. You can also reach it from Anilao by boat.

Getting There & Away

From Batangas, there are several buses and jeepneys daily, although it may be necessary to change at Mabini. The trip takes an hour or more.

LEMERY

From Lemery you can get to Ligpo Point, eight km to the south, with the small Ligpo Island just offshore. It is a favourite place for divers, even though the underwater setting is fairly ordinary. The beach here is better than the one at Anilao.

Places to Stay

The only possible accommodation seems to be at the *Vila Lobos Lodge*, which is a simple, rather noisy place with small rooms and a disco. Rooms with fan and bath are P50 and with air-con and bath are P80.

Getting There & Away

Several BLTB buses do the three-hour trip to and from Manila daily. From Batangas several jeepneys run daily. The road is poor and dusty and the trip takes an hour or more.

SAN NICOLAS

You can cross fairly cheaply from San Nicolas to the volcanic island in Lake Taal. The round trip costs about P200. If you set out very early, you may see a magnificent sunrise. For a few pesos extra the boatman may guide his passengers up to the old crater with the lake inside it. It is easy to get lost on the way down to the lake, so it is advisable to have a guide. On the edge of the old crater live a few shepherds who know the island well and can act as guides.

There are four craters on the island. If you are climbing to the new crater, which last erupted in 1965, you don't need a guide. It doesn't take long and there is no need to stay overnight in San Nicolas.

Boats also go to the island from Subic, a little north of San Nicolas. The road along the lake's edge between Subic and San Nicolas is practically impassable for ordinary vehicles.

Places to Stay

You can ask for a room at the store, where you can sit outside on the corner of the plaza. It is also where you arrange for boats.

The *Playa del Sol* is relatively pleasant. Rooms with fan and bath cost P200, but except in the summer months of March, April and May they may be bargained down to much less.

The *Lake View Resort* has basic cottages with rooms for P75.

Getting There & Away

Several jeepneys run daily from Lemery to San Nicolas. The trip takes half an hour. The last jeepney from San Nicolas to Lemery leaves at 5 pm. See also details for getting to and from Batangas.

CALAMBA

The national hero Jose Rizal was born in Calamba. Rizal House, with its garden, is now a memorial and museum. In Tadlac, a small village between Calamba and Los Banos, you can stay with fishermen's families and go night fishing on Laguna de Bay. Near the village is the lovely Alligator Lake, a deep volcanic lake without alligators! About a km towards Los Banos you see the sign Rainbow Falls'. From here it is a half-hour walk to the refreshing 25 metre high waterfall in a gorge full of lush tropical vegetation.

Places to Stay

The *Villa Pansol* (tel 2095) has rooms with air-con and bath for P500. It is well kept, with a restaurant and swimming pool in pleasant grounds.

Getting There & Away

The numerous buses leaving Lawton Terminal in Manila daily marked 'Los Banos' and 'Santa Cruz' go through Calamba. The trip takes an hour.

In Batangas, the buses marked 'Manila' leaving the pier and market frequently every day go through Calamba. The trip takes about an hour.

Similarly, in Santa Cruz and Pagsanjan, numerous Manila-bound buses go through Calamba every day, taking an hour.

LOS BANOS

The University of the Philippines (UP) has a forestry institute with a botanical garden in Los Banos. The garden is not so botanical but it has a big swimming pool. Not far from the UP is the IRRI (International Rice Research Institute). Look for the sign 'UP Los Banos' on the main road.

Los Banos is noted for its hot springs in which you can have a bath as a health treatment. Most resorts are outside the town, along the highways as far as Calamba. The Crystal Resort is reported to be very beautiful and is recommended. It is five km away towards Manila but entry is P40.

Not far from Los Banos is the Philippine Art Center, from where you get a good view over Laguna de Bay and Alligator Lake. A Special Ride there in a jeepney costs P20. At nearby Mt Makiling there is a nice park with zoo and pool and good views. Jeepneys to the Scout Jamboree Park go there.

Anyone interested in orchids should visit Prof 'Totoy' Mendoza and his wife, Poly, at 'Kaligay', 89 Lopez Ave – 200 metres in the direction of the college from the main bus stop in the middle of town. Totoy Mendoza also has a big experimental and hybridisation station 800 metres up Mt Banahaw. Anyone who wishes can join his regular excursions to the orchid farm and spend one or more days (and some cold nights) in these beautiful surroundings. The accommodation is simple but well cared for. Guests are not taken on a commercial basis but P100 should be contributed for one night and two meals.

Places to Stay

Makiling Lodge has rooms for P100 and with air-con and bath for P200. Take a jeepney in Los Banos towards City Springs; Makiling Lodge is about 100 metres from the City of Springs Resort.

Lakeview Health Resort Hotel is in Lopez St. It has rooms with fan and bath from P150 and with air-con and bath from P350. It is comfortable and good, with a restaurant and swimming pool.

Getting There & Away

Numerous buses leave Manila daily from the Lawton Terminal for Los Banos. Buses marked 'Santa Cruz' also travel through Los Banos. Travelling time is an hour or more.

From Santa Cruz and Pagsanjan, the numerous buses marked 'Manila' go through Los Banos. The trip takes an hour.

ALAMINOS

Alaminos is known for Hidden Valley, a fascinating private property and resort with lush tropical vegetation and several springs. This wonderful natural area is a paradise for botanists and a popular subject for filming and photography. It is part of Alaminos but is five km from the centre. Tricycles firmly demand P50 for the short stretch from Alaminos to the gates. Here visitors are again hit hard. Admission has gone up to P500 on normal weekdays and P600 on Sundays and holidays. This includes a drink on arrival, buffet lunch, snacks in the afternoon and use of the facilities such as the swimming pool, showers, changing rooms, etc. Take your swimming gear.

Places to Stay

Hidden Valley Springs has rooms with air-con and bath from P700 and P800. It also has cottages. Breakfast is included. It is pleasant and has a restaurant. The overnight tariff includes entry to the resort. Reservations are made in Manila (tel 509903).

Getting There & Away

Several BLTB, Philtranco and Superlines buses leave Manila daily and go through Alaminos, such as those marked 'San Pablo', 'Lucena', 'Daet', 'Naga' and 'Legaspi'. The trip takes an hour or more.

Mt Makiling lies between Los Banos and Alaminos, so the way from Los Banos is a bit roundabout. Go by jeepney from Los Banos to San Pablo, then take either a Manila-bound bus or a Tanauan-bound jeepney to Alaminos. The trip takes an hour.

SAN PABLO

San Pablo is known as the City of the Seven Lakes. It's a good centre for walks. There's one to Sampaloc Lake, which has restaurants standing on piles along the lakeside, and others to Pandin Lake and Yambo Lake. The remaining four lakes are Calibato, Mohicap, Palakpakin and Bunot.

Climbers may like to tackle the nearby Mt Makiling, a volcanic mass of 1144 metres with three peaks. This is best reached from Alaminos or Los Banos. If you are starting from San Pablo, the best climb is the 2188 metre Mt Banahaw. This dormant volcano, with its springs and waterfalls, is credited with mystical powers, and especially at Easter, many Filipinos come to meditate and pray in the ravines and to drink or bathe in the 'holy water' of the splashing streams. The climb usually begins at Kinabuhayan, which is reached by jeepney from San Pablo. Three days are needed for the climb.

About 10 km south of San Pablo, just before Tiaong, is the Villa Escudero, a coconut plantation and resort combined. Admission is P80. In this complex, reminiscent of the Spanish colonial era, it is worth seeing the museum, which has many valuable historical and cultural artefacts.

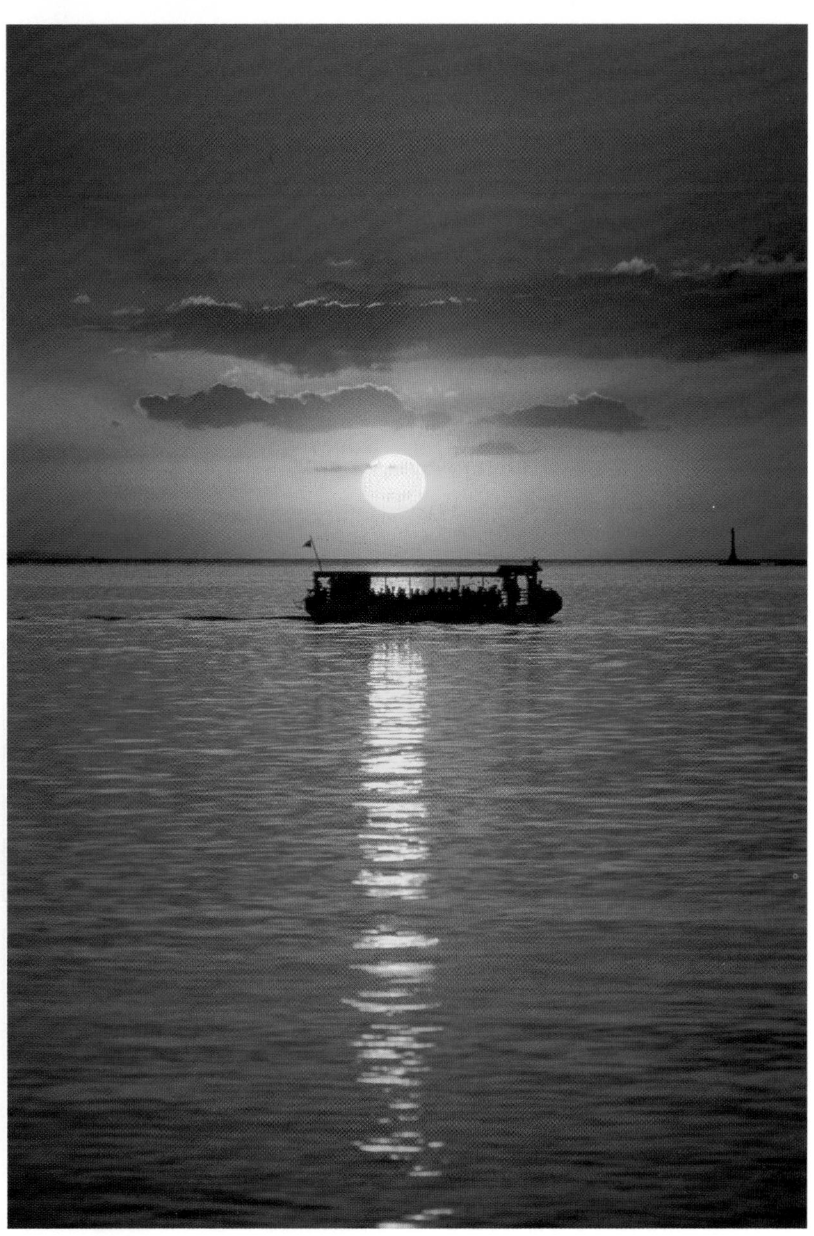

A harbour tour boat at sunset, Manila Bay (JPk)

Top: Dawn at Lake Taal, Batangas (JPk)
Bottom: Batad village and rice terraces near Banaue, North Luzon (JPk)

Places to Stay

City Inn Agahan, 126 Colago Ave, is very simple, with rooms for P30/60.

Sampaloc Lake Youth Hostel (tel 4448) is in Efarca Village, Schetelig Ave. Here dorm beds cost P70. Get there by tricycle from the church or plaza in San Pablo for P2.

San Rafael Swimming Pool Resort has rooms for P250/400. Cottages are also available. It has two swimming pools.

The *Villa Escudero* (tel 2379), Tiaong, has rooms with bath from P360/450. It also has cottages. It is good and has a restaurant. Reservations can be made in Manila (tel 593698, 5210830).

Getting There & Away

Several BLTB, Philtranco and Superlines buses leave Manila daily marked 'Lucena', 'Daet', 'Naga' and 'Legaspi'. All of these go through San Pablo. The trip takes two hours.

From Pagsanjan you get to San Pablo in two stages. First take a jeepney from Pagsanjan to Santa Cruz, then catch another jeepney to San Pablo. It takes an hour or more.

Numerous jeepneys run daily from Los Banos to San Pablo. It takes half an hour.

PAGSANJAN

A trip to Pagsanjan (pronounced pag-sanhan) is a must on every Philippine tour itinerary. The last section of Francis Ford Coppola's Vietnam War film *Apocalypse Now* was filmed here. The Magdapio Waterfalls are only part of Pagsanjan's attractions; it's the river trip through the picturesque tropical gorge which is the real draw card. Two 'banqueros' will paddle you upstream against the strong current in a banca or canoe. It's a feat of strength which taxes even two men paddling together. At the last major waterfall you can ride on a bamboo raft for an extra P10. You come downstream at a thrilling speed. Shooting the rapids is most exciting in August and September, when the river is high. Don't hold too tightly to the sides of the boat and keep your hands inside or your fingers may be crushed. Use a plastic bag to keep the camera dry.

All things included, the officially fixed price of this harmless bit of fun is P150. (Up to three people can ride in a banca, so if you go alone, it costs P300.) However, tips may be requested, even demanded vehemently. Readers' letters have told of boat operators making most aggressive demands at times – sums of from P500 to P1000 were mentioned. Anyone who, halfway to the waterfall, is not prepared to promise an extra payment is not, according to most reports, going to enjoy the rest of the trip. So pay up or suffer. You can, of course, skip the trip, save your money and let others be annoyed. The banqueros organised by the Youth Hostel, Pagsanjan Falls Lodge and Willy Flores Lodge are not supposed to demand extra money.

Don't go on weekends, when there are so many tourists that it's like an anthill. If you stay overnight in Pagsanjan and leave for the falls at sunrise, you'll be on the river long before the hordes arrive. As sunlight comes late in the deep valleys, photographers will have difficulty taking pictures with normal equipment in the very early morning.

You get a good view over Pagsanjan and its surroundings from the watertanks on the hill above the school. Steps go up to the school from Mabini St – which runs parallel to Rizal St, the main street – and the path to the hill starts at the school.

The Pagsanjan Town-Fiesta is on 12 December.

Places to Stay

A good rule for most places in Pagsanjan is to find your own way there. The place is not too big and guides are not needed, especially since the host is expected to pay them a commission and so your room will end up costing more!

Pagsanjan Youth Hostel (tel 2124), 237 General Luna St, has dorm beds with fan for P30, singles/doubles for P60/65 and doubles with fan for P80. It is basic and run by friendly, helpful people who will also help arrange boat trips. Go through the city gate to the end of Rizal St, turn right over the river, then right again. The hostel is a fair way down on the left. Look for the sign.

Willy Flores Lodge, 821 Garcia St, has rooms for P40/80 and with fan for P50/100. It is simple, with a homely atmosphere, and staff will help to organise boat trips.

La Tour de Pagsanjan Lodging House (tel 1231), F de San Juan St, has dorm beds for P50, rooms for P80/90 and with fan for P100/120. Two rooms share a bath. There is a motorbike for hire at P250 a day.

Miss Estella y Umale's *Riverside Bungalow* (tel 2465), at 792 Garcia St, has two bungalows with rooms with fan and bath for P150 and with air-con and bath for P300. It's not far from Willy Flores and Miss Estella is a good cook.

Camino Real Hotel (tel 2086), 39 Rizal St, has rooms with fan for P200, with fan and bath for P150/225, with air-con for P300 and with air-con and bath for P350. It is attractive and comfortable, with large rooms and a restaurant.

Pagsanjan Falls Lodge (tel 1251) has rooms with fan and bath for P350 and with air-con and bath for P450/500; it also has a restaurant. It is poorly maintained, however, and is a popular pick-up joint for elderly gays looking for young boys, so male guests need to make it clear they're not interested or they'll be continually pestered. Try to get room No 10, 11 or 12 in the coconut grove as these have verandas looking straight out on to the river. There is also a very beautiful pool.

Pagsanjan Village Hotel (tel 2116), Garcia St, has pleasant singles for P100, singles/doubles with fan for P150/200, doubles with air-con for P250 and doubles with air-con and bath for P350.

Places to Eat

The *Dura-Fe Restaurant* in General Jaina St has very good food – try the sweet & sour fish. It closes at 8.30 pm. Also recommended is the *D & C Luncheonette* in National Rd near Falls Lodge. The small restaurant opposite is good and the staff will cook almost anything for you if you order in advance.

Getting There & Away

Numerous Laguna Co buses leave the Lawton Terminal in Manila daily for Santa Cruz. Some even go right through to Pagsanjan. They can also be hailed in Taft Ave. In addition, BLTB buses run from Manila to Santa Cruz. This takes two hours. The last few km from Santa Cruz are done by jeepney. Special Rides by tricycle are not necessary, even when the driver tries to persuade the innocent foreigner to the contrary.

Organised day tours from Manila can be arranged for about US$30 at the various travel agencies and the Tourist Office. This way all costs are covered and you may avoid hassles with banqueros.

There are two shortcuts in going from Tagaytay to Pagsanjan which save you going right back to Manila. One involves travelling by bus to Zapote, then by jeepney to Alabang, by bus to Santa Cruz and by jeepney to Pagsanjan. Alternatively, take a bus from Tagaytay to Palapala, then a jeepney through Binan to Calamba, then a bus to Santa Cruz and a jeepney to Pagsanjan.

To get to Pagsanjan from Batangas, it's quickest to get a Manila-bound bus as far as Calamba. There, get a bus coming from Manila to Santa Cruz and go on to Pagsanjan by jeepney.

If you are going to South Luzon from Pagsanjan, there are several Supreme Lines buses daily running from Santa Cruz to Lucena, taking about three hours. If you don't want to wait for a bus, you can go by jeepney from Santa Cruz to Lucban and then get another jeepney to Lucena. All buses from Manila marked 'Daet', 'Naga', 'Legaspi', etc, go through Lucena, so you don't have to go right back to Manila.

AROUND PAGSANJAN

Visits to the following destinations make good day trips from Pagsanjan. Paete is the best known Philippine centre for wood carving in ebony. The Japanese Garden is a memorial to the Japanese soldiers who died in WW II in and around Pagsanjan. Caliraya Reservoir is a massive artificial lake with resorts like Sierra Lakes and Lake Caliraya Country Club featuring water skiing and windsurfing. The village of Lucban, halfway along the road to Lucena, is a good example of what villages must have looked like during the era of Spanish rule. Lucban has its harvest festival on 15 May (see the Fiestas & Festivals section in the Facts about the Country chapter).

North Luzon

With over 100,000 sq km, Luzon is the largest island in the Philippines. About half of all Filipinos live there. It plays a leading role in the Philippines' economic and cultural affairs and the number of its tourist attractions is second to none. For central Luzon see the Around Manila chapter.

Most impressive in North Luzon are Mountain and Ifugao provinces, with their rice terraces and numerous ethnic minorities, but many travellers are attracted to the Hundred Islands National Park and the beaches on Lingayen Gulf. The cultivated provinces of Ilocos Norte and Ilocos Sur are less frequently visited. The historic town of Vigan with its old Spanish churches and extensive sand dunes is in Ilocos Sur.

The massive earthquake that struck the Philippines on 16 July 1990 had its epicentre in Nueva Ecija Province, North Luzon. The cities of Cabanatuan, the capital of Nueva Ecija, and Baguio, a popular mountain resort in Benguet Province, 175 km north of Manila, were the worst hit. The earthquake caused the collapse of several hotels in Baguio (see the Places to Stay section under Baguio).

The West Coast

THE ZAMBALES COAST

The mountainous province of Zambales borders on the South China Sea to the west. Along the coast, between San Antonio and Iba there are several beaches, some of which are over several km long, and some of which have places where you can stay the night. You will find beaches that have not been visited much up to now about 80 km north of Iba, on Dasol Bay. One of these is Tambobong White Beach, 15 km outside Dasol. Also remarkable are the extensive salt works north of Santa Cruz.

San Antonio & San Miguel

After about an hour's travel from Olongapo, you get to San Antonio, a pleasant little town with a clean market. Twice a day there is a power jeep over the five-km trip from the plaza south-west to Pundaquit. Tricycles only go as far as the river (two km away). Pundaquit is a small fishing village on a sheltered bay. From there you can arrange to cross to Camera and Capones islands for P150 to P200. Both islands have white beaches and are rocky, but parts of Capones Island are covered with palms and bushes. There is a lighthouse at the western end of the island which juts out from the sea like a cathedral. The lighthouse keeper is the only person who lives on the island, but, occasionally, a few Americans come here to go diving.

From Pundaquit you can walk along the wide beach to San Miguel and beyond, after crossing a fairly shallow river. There is a US Naval Communication Station in San Miguel.

Places to Stay *San Miguel Hotel* in San Miguel has basic rooms with fan and bath for P100 and with air-con and bath for P150.

Hi-Way Resthouse at West Dirita, San Antonio, is a fairly reasonable place with rooms with fan for P90, with fan and bath for P140 and with air-con and bath for P220 (with TV for P260). The rooms here can also be rented for three, eight and 16 hours.

Big Food Resthouse in San Miguel has rooms with fan and bath for P150 and with air-con and bath for P200. It is pleasant and quite a lot better than either of the other two places.

Places to Eat The *Meathouse Carlsberg Garden Restaurant* in San Miguel serves both Filipino and German dishes. The *San Miguel Restaurant* offers good Filipino cuisine with live music.

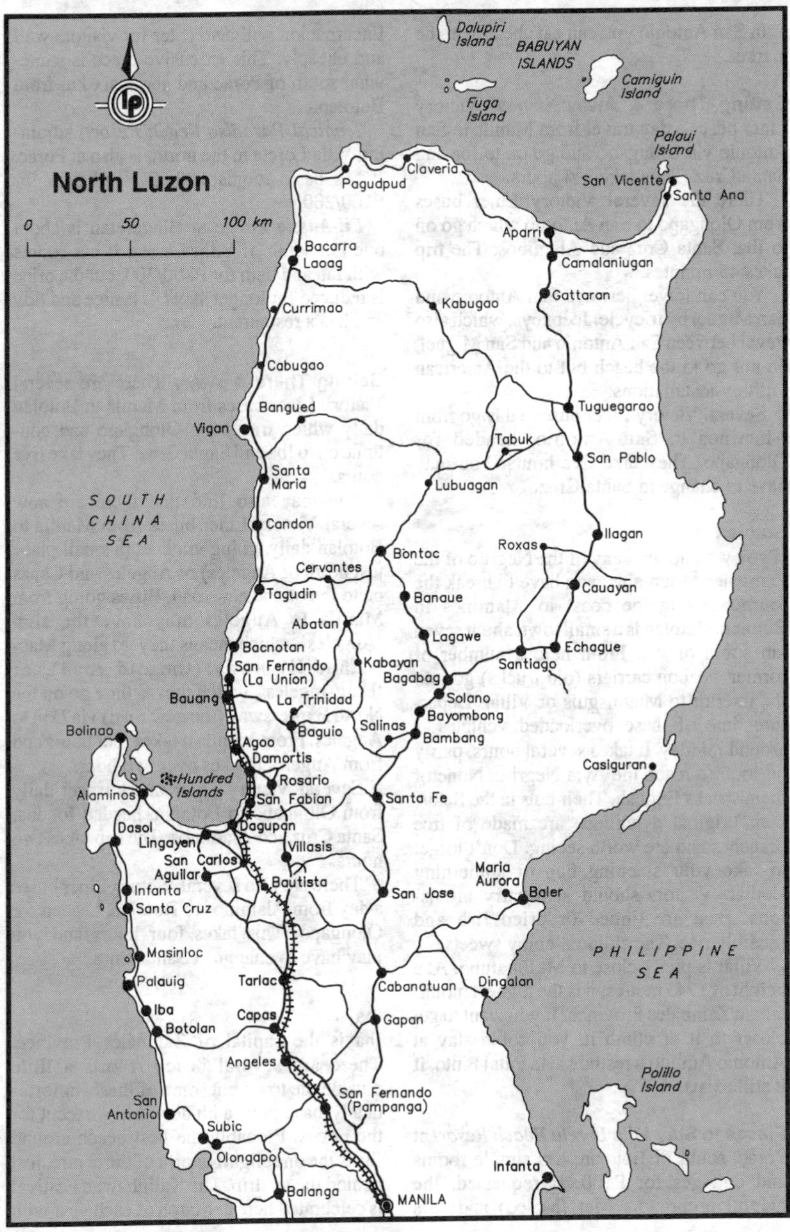
North Luzon
0
50
100 km
Dalupiri Island
BABUYAN ISLANDS
Camiguin Island
Fuga Island
Palaui Island
Claveria
Pagudpud
San Vicente
Santa Ana
Aparri
Camalaniugan
Bacarra
Laoag
Gattaran
Currimao
Kabugao
Cabugao
Tuguegarao
Bangued
Vigan
Tabuk
San Pablo
Santa Maria
Lubuagan
SOUTH CHINA SEA
Candon
Ilagan
Roxas
Bontoc
Cervantes
Tagudin
Banaue
Cauayan
Abatan
Lagawe
Echague
Bacnotan
Santiago
Kabayan
San Fernando (La Union)
Bagabag
Solano
Bauang
La Trinidad
Bayombong
Bolinao
Baguio
Salinas
Bambang
Agoo
Damortis
Casiguran
Hundred Islands
Rosario
Alaminos
San Fabian
Santa Fe
Dasol
Dagupan
Lingayen
Villasis
San Carlos
Aguilar
Bautista
Maria Aurora
Infanta
San Jose
Baler
Santa Cruz
Masinloc
PHILIPPINE SEA
Palauig
Tarlac
Cabanatuan
Dingalan
Iba
Capas
Gapan
Botolan
Angeles
Polillo Island
San Fernando (Pampanga)
San Antonio
Subic
Olongapo
Infanta
Balanga
MANILA

In San Antonio you can eat cheaply in the market.

Getting There & Away Several Victory Liner buses a day travel from Manila to San Antonio via Olongapo and go on to Iba and Santa Cruz. They take 3¾ hours.

There are several Victory Liner buses from Olongapo to San Antonio which go on to Iba, Santa Cruz and Alaminos. The trip takes 45 minutes.

You can travel between San Antonio and San Miguel by tricycle. Jeepneys, which also travel between San Antonio and San Miguel, do not go to the beach but to the American military installations.

Several Victory Liner buses a day go from Alaminos to San Antonio, headed for Olongapo. They take five hours. You may have to change in Santa Cruz.

Botolan

If you want to visit any of the Negrito of the Zambales Mountains, you have to break the journey along the coast to Alaminos in Botolan. Botolan is a small town about seven km south of Iba. From here a number of former weapon carriers (old trucks) go into the interior to Maguisguis or Villar. Departure time of these overloaded vehicles is around midday. It takes several hours, partly on foot, to reach the Ayta Negrito. None of them speaks English. Their huts in the fields, their original dwellings, are made of tree branches and are worth seeing. Don't forget to take your sleeping bag or something similar. Visitors should also carry provisions. Best are tinned or dried fish and possibly rice. The children enjoy sweets.

Villar is pretty close to Mt Pinatubo. At a height of 1745 metres, it is the highest mountain in Zambales Province. If you want to get closer to it or climb it, you could stay at Antonio Aquino's resthouse in Patal Pinto, if it still exists.

Places to Stay *Villa Loreta Beach Resort* at Porac, south of Botolan, has simple rooms and cottages for P100. If requested, the helpful proprietors Mat (Mateo) and Mrs Encarnacion will also cater for visitors well and cheaply. This extensive place is somewhat south of Porac and about six km from Botolan.

Tropical Paradise Beach Resort, adjoining Villa Loreta to the north, is also at Porac. It has basic rooms with fan and bath for P100/200.

Fil-Aussie Lodge at Binoclutan is about one km south of Villa Loreta. It has rooms with fan and bath for P200/300, but the price is reduced for longer stays. It is nice and tidy and has a restaurant.

Getting There & Away There are several Victory Liner buses from Manila to Botolan daily which travel via Olongapo and continue on to Iba and Santa Cruz. They take five hours.

You may also find that there are now several Victory Liner buses from Manila to Botolan daily, going via Dau (a small place just north of Angeles) or Angeles and Capas on to Iba on the new road. Buses going from Manila to Angeles may have the sign 'Angeles', which means they go along MacArthur Highway (the old road), or 'Dau/Angeles', which means they go on the North Expressway (the new road) via Dau to Angeles. From Manila it takes four hours and from Angeles it takes over two hours.

Several Victory Liner buses travel daily from Olongapo to Botolan, headed for Iba, Santa Cruz and Alaminos. The trip takes two hours.

There are also several Victory Liner buses a day from Alaminos to Botolan, headed for Olongapo. This takes four hours and you may have to change at Santa Cruz.

Iba

Iba is the capital of Zambales Province. There are several beach resorts a little outside the town but some of these, unfortunately, have gone a bit downhill – except for the prices. Probably the best beach around Iba is the one slightly north of the centre, just behind the airstrip. The Kalighawan Festival is celebrated here in March of each year with

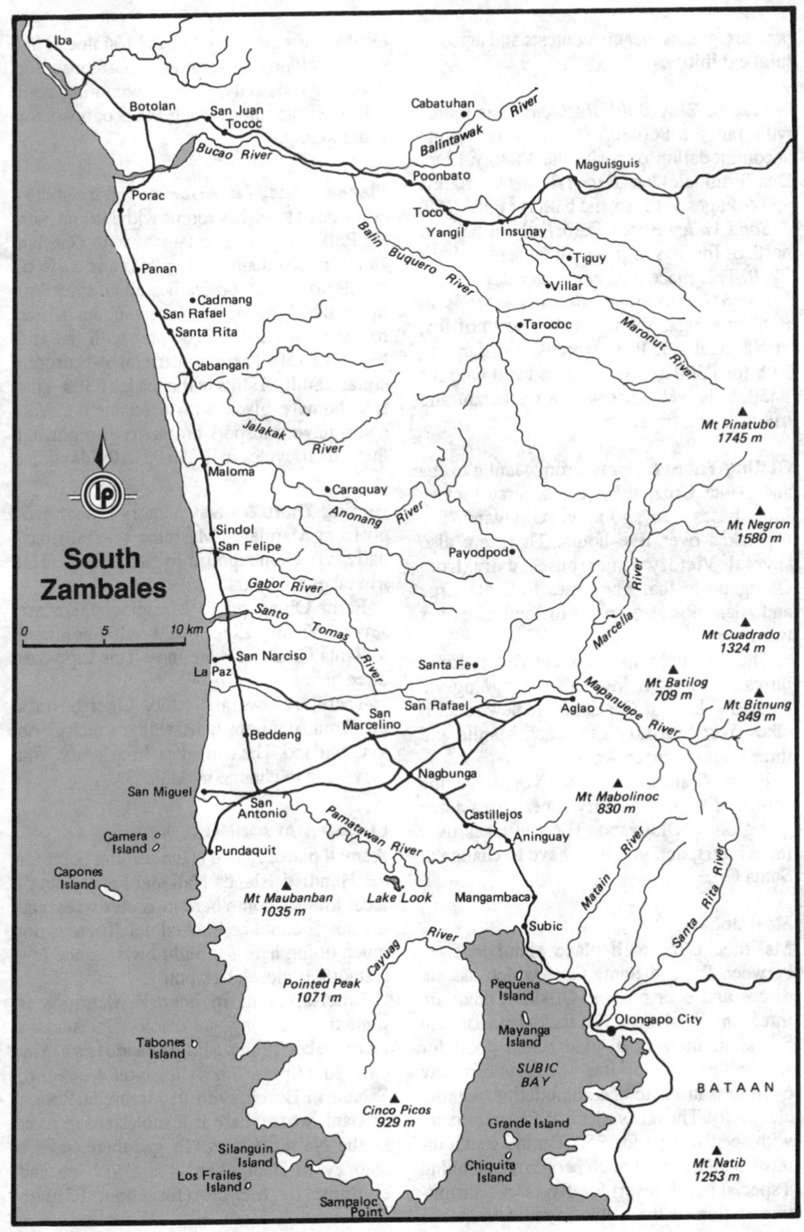
South
Zambales
0
5
10 km
Iba
Botolan
San Juan
Tococ
Bucao River
Cabatuhan
Balintawak River
Poonbato
Maguisguis
Porac
Toco
Yangil
Insunay
Balin Buquero River
Tiguy
Villar
Panan
Cadmang
San Rafael
Santa Rita
Tarococ
Maronut River
Cabangan
Jalakak River
Mt Pinatubo
1745 m
Maloma
Caraquay
Anonang River
Mt Negron
1580 m
Sindol
San Felipe
Payodpod
Gabor River
Santo Tomas River
Marcella River
Mt Cuadrado
1324 m
San Narciso
La Paz
Santa Fe
Mt Batilog
709 m
Mapanuepe River
Mt Bitnung
849 m
San Rafael
Aglao
San Marcelino
Beddeng
Nagbunga
San Miguel
San Antonio
Mt Mabolinoc
830 m
Castillejos
Pamatawan River
Aninguay
Camera Island
Pundaquit
Capones Island
Mt Maubanban
1035 m
Lake Look
Mangambaca
Matain River
Santa Rita River
Subic
Cayuag River
Pointed Peak
1071 m
Pequena Island
Olongapo City
Tabones Island
Mayanga Island
SUBIC BAY
BATAAN
Cinco Picos
929 m
Grande Island
Silanguin Island
Chiquita Island
Mt Natib
1253 m
Los Frailes Island
Sampaloc Point

parades, games, beauty contests and agricultural exhibitions.

Places to Stay *Balili Resthouse* has rooms with fan for P60/80. This is very simple accommodation opposite the Victory Liner Bus Terminal. *Vicar Beach Resort* has rooms and cottages with fan and bath for P300/350.

Sand Valley Beach Resort, about one km north of Iba, has rooms with fan and bath for P280. This place has seen better days.

Rama International Beach Resort is in Bangantalinga, about four km north of Iba, in National Rd. It has rooms with fan and bath for P300 and with air-con and bath for P450. It is well kept with a restaurant and offers diving trips.

Getting There & Away From Manila to Iba and Santa Cruz, there are several Victory Liner buses a day, going via Olongapo. The trip takes over five hours. There are also several Victory Liner buses daily from Olongapo to Iba. The buses to Santa Cruz and Alaminos also go via Iba and take over two hours.

There should also be several Victory Liner buses a day from Manila to Iba going via Dau/Angeles and Capas on the new road. It takes over four hours to reach Manila and three hours to reach Angeles.

From Alaminos to Iba, you have the choice of several Victory Liner buses a day going on to Olongapo. The trip takes over three hours, and you may have to change in Santa Cruz.

Masinloc

Masinloc is a small place about halfway between Iba and Santa Cruz which has six discos and beer houses. Offshore there are three small islands. On the island of San Salvador, there is a wide beach good for snorkelling and diving and you can stay overnight in basic accommodation without electricity. The crossing costs P5 per person, with special trips for P50. On the southernmost island, some Dutch people are planning a special beach resort for divers. A transmitting station of the Catholic radio Veritas is located on a peninsula near Masinloc. This setup includes a beautiful guesthouse for invited guests only, with a swimming pool and other amenities, such as speedboats for water skiing.

Places to Stay *Little Hamburg* at the southern edge of town has rooms with fan and bath for P80. There is a restaurant with German and Filipino cuisine and there is also a disco.

Puerto Asinan Lodge lies about three km north of Masinloc at Kahawangan. It has rooms with fan for P100 and with fan and bath for P150. There is also a three-bedroom cottage built on stilts in the sea for P300. This is a homely place with a restaurant. You could have transport problems at night but there are tricycles for P3 to P5 in the daytime.

Getting There & Away Victory Liner buses go from Manila to Masinloc several times daily, via Olongapo on to Santa Cruz. The trip takes six hours.

From Olongapo to Masinloc, there are several Victory Liner buses a day going on to Santa Cruz and Alaminos. This trip takes three hours.

There are several Victory Liner buses a day from Alaminos to Masinloc which go on to Olongapo. The trip takes three hours. You may have to change in Santa Cruz.

LUCAP & ALAMINOS

A small place, Lucap is the starting point for the Hundred Islands National Park. Lots of local tourists come here in Easter week and the hotels could be booked out. There is not much doing here for night owls, as the few restaurants close at 10 pm.

Entertainment in nearby Alaminos is limited to bowling and discos. On Sundays there are cockfights a little outside town. You can do trips from Alaminos to Agno, Sabangan Beach, with its Umbrella Rocks, or Bani, where there is a subterranean river in the Nalsoc Caves. To get there, take a jeepney to Bani, then go on to Tiep and continue by tricycle (for about P30) to Colaya.

Places to Stay

The following prices are for the off season. For the high season, which is Easter week and the weekends in April and May, some hotels raise their tariffs by about 50% to 100%.

Most of the accommodation is in Lucap. *Kilometre One Tourist Lodge* has rooms with fan for P65/110. It is simple and clean and has a restaurant. It also serves as a youth hostel. *Gloria's Cottages* has rooms with fan and bath for P100.

Lucap Hotel has dorm beds with fan for P60, rooms with fan for P100/180, with fan and bath for P120/200, with air-con for P180/250 and with air-con and bath for P200/300.

Maxime by the Sea has rooms with fan and bath from P80/150 and with air-con and bath for P200/250. It is pleasant and comfortable and has a restaurant and a beautiful terrace.

Last Resort has rooms with fan and bath for P250 and with air-con and bath for P350. It is fairly pleasant and has a restaurant and boating facilities. You can make reservations in Manila (tel 5214073).

Ocean View Lodge has rooms with fan for P110/135, with fan and bath for P120/150 and with air-con and bath for P380/450. It is well kept and has a restaurant. You can make reservations in Manila (tel 7324668).

Alaminos Hotel in Quezon Ave, Alaminos, has rooms for P60/80, with fan and bath for P100/120 and with air-con and bath for P200/220. This place is clean and fairly good and also has a restaurant.

Places to Eat

You can eat cheaply in Lucap at the small *Canteens* by the wharf. Some lodges have restaurants, such as the *Ocean View Restaurant*, which also offer quite inexpensive and good meals. Apart from the *Last Resort Restaurant*, restaurants close quite early on most days, sometimes even by 8 pm.

At Alaminos, the *Plaza Restaurant* is worth a visit; sometimes there are folk singers. You could also try the *Imperial Restaurant*.

Getting There & Away

You can travel by tricycle between Alaminos and Lucap. The regular cost is P6 for up to four passengers, but you will be charged as much as P30.

Dagupan Bus and Pantranco North buses go hourly every day from Manila to Alaminos. They take five hours. You may have to change at Lingayen. These buses go via Dau/Angeles, where you can also board them.

Several Victory Liner buses a day travel between Olongapo and Alaminos, taking six hours. You may have to change at Santa Cruz.

A few Pantranco North buses a day go from Baguio to Alaminos. The last bus leaves at about 11.20 am. The trip takes four hours and you may have to change at Dagupan.

To travel from Banaue to Alaminos you will have to take the early Baguio bus that leaves at about 5 am from Banaue then get off at Rosario and board a Dagupan, Lingayen or Alaminos bus coming from Baguio.

HUNDRED ISLANDS

The Hundred Islands aren't palm-fringed dream islands, but coral formations of varying sizes with scrub and occasionally small, white beaches. They are of limited appeal for snorkelling, as the water isn't always crystal clear. The supposedly colourful underwater world has also been damaged by the long-standing use of dynamite for fishing and often can hardly be seen.

Places to Stay & Eat

Take adequate food supplies with you if you want to spend a night or several days on an island. The cheapest place for food is the market at Alaminos and you should be able to get a can of water from the hotel at Lucap. The fee for putting up your own tent is P10 a day on Quezon, Governor's and Children's islands. You can rent a so-called pavilion on Quezon Island for P200 or a two-roomed cottage for six people on Governor's Island for P600. On Children's Island there are tents of various sizes for between P50 and P150. Water is provided and there are toilets and fireplaces.

Getting There & Away

To get to Hundred Islands National Park, you first have to go to Alaminos. There is a direct connection to Alaminos from Manila. You can also go via Olongapo and along the Zambales coast (see the Around Manila chapter). There is a third possible route from Manila to Zambales, which should be open by now, going along the road from Capas, north of Angeles, through the Zambales Mountains.

The fare from Lucap to the Hundred Islands National Park by outrigger boat, which can take up to six persons, has been fixed officially at P200 plus P5 entry fee per person. You can also go on an island round trip which will cost you between P50 and P80, depending on the duration and extent of the trip. This makes it possible to choose your 'own' island and be dropped off there, but don't forget to fix a time to be picked up on the return trip. Four or five hours of island life will probably be quite enough, especially when there is no shade. Most day-trippers go to Quezon Island, particularly on weekends. You can get drinks at the kiosk there.

BOLINAO

Bolinao is a little town which hasn't yet been overrun by tourists. If you want beautiful beaches, you'll have to go a few km further as there aren't any close by. For a bit of variety, you could arrange to cross to one of the offshore islands. Take your own snorkelling equipment as it is next to impossible to find even a pair of goggles in Bolinao.

The museum on the outskirts of town has a collection of Philippine flora and fauna which is worth a look, but, because of the lack of money, it has only a few historical items. In the town centre is the church, which dates back to 1609. It used to double as a fortress during attacks by pirates and by the English, Japanese and Americans. If you can catch the priest when he is not too busy, he might tell you more about those times. He might also show you round and let you have a look at the antiquated kitchen with its antique utensils.

Places to Stay

The *A & E Garden Inn* in the centre of town, next to the Pantranco Bus Terminal, has rooms with fan for P60/80, with fan and bath for P100/120 and with air-con and bath for P250/300. It is simple but clean and has a good restaurant. You can also rent tree houses there.

The *Celeste Sea Breeze Resort* by the sea has rooms with fan and bath for P100/150. It is basic but comfortable and has a restaurant. You can hire outrigger sailing boats there. *Capitan Cascante* is also by the sea and has rooms for P50 and cottages for P200. There is a restaurant.

Getting There & Away

Several jeepneys and minibuses a day leave the market at Alaminos for Bolinao. You can also catch a Pantranco North bus, which takes one hour.

Both Dagupan Bus and Pantranco North buses run several times a day from Manila to Bolinao. It takes six hours and you may have to change at Lingayen or Alaminos.

LINGAYEN

Lingayen is the capital of Pangasinan Province, which dates back to about 1611. Lingayen Beach is outside the town. As on other well-known beaches at the southern end of the Lingayen Gulf, none of them particularly impressive, you will find many Filipinos from polluted Manila in search of recreation.

Places to Stay

The *Viscount Hotel* (tel 137) in Maramba Blvd has rooms with fan and bath for P100 and with air-con and bath for P200. It is clean and good and has a restaurant.

The Lion's Den on Lingayen Beach has rooms with fan and bath for P180. It has a restaurant, but if you want to buy fresh fish and vegetables in the nearby market, where you can go by tricycle for P1, the hotel

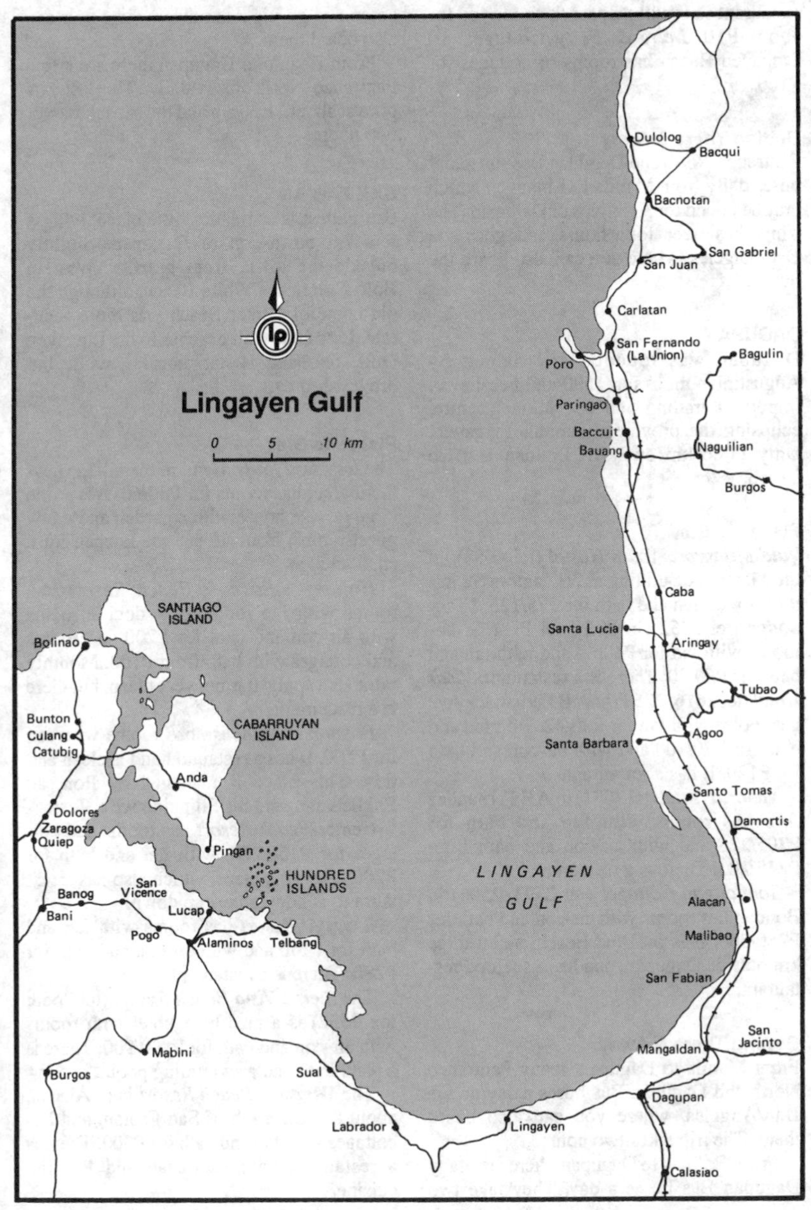

Lingayen Gulf
0 5 10 km
Dulolog
Bacqui
Bacnotan
San Gabriel
San Juan
Carlatan
San Fernando
(La Union)
Poro
Bagulin
Paringao
Baccuit
Bauang
Naguilian
Burgos
Caba
Santa Lucia
Aringay
Tubao
Santa Barbara
Agoo
Santo Tomas
Damortis
SANTIAGO
ISLAND
Bolinao
Bunton
Culang
Catubig
CABARRUYAN
ISLAND
Anda
Dolores
Zaragoza
Quiep
Pingan
HUNDRED
ISLANDS
LINGAYEN
GULF
San
Vicence
Banog
Bani
Lucap
Pogo
Alaminos
Telbang
Alacan
Malibao
San Fabian
San
Jacinto
Mangaldan
Mabini
Burgos
Sual
Dagupan
Labrador
Lingayen
Calasiao

restaurant staff will prepare them for you for about P10. *Letty & Betty Cottages* on Lingayen Beach has rooms or cottages for P100.

Getting There & Away

Pantranco North and Dagupan Bus run many buses daily from Manila to Lingayen which may be bound for Alaminos or Dagupan. The trip takes over four hours and goes via Dau/Angeles, where you can also board the bus.

DAGUPAN

Dagupan was founded and named by Augustinian monks in 1590 and became an important trading and educational centre, eclipsing the provincial capital, Lingayen. Only three km away in Bonuan is Blue Beach.

Places to Stay

Villa Milagrosa Youth Hostel (tel 4658), in the Maramba Building at 26 Zamora St, has rooms with fan and bath for P75/125. *Lucky Lodge* (tel 3452) in M H del Pilar St has rooms with fan for P40/60 and with fan and bath for P60/80. There is a restaurant. *Vicar Hotel* (tel 2616, 3253) in A B Fernandez Ave has rooms with fan for P30/42, with fan and bath for P70/100 and with air-con and bath for P120. It has a restaurant.

Victoria Hotel (tel 2081) in A B Fernandez Ave has rooms with fan and bath for P205/225 and with air-con and bath from P245/280. There is a restaurant.

Tondaligan Cottages (tel 2593, 2595) in Bonuan has rooms with air-con and bath for P280/360. It is on Blue Beach, about three km outside Dagupan, and has a seafood restaurant.

Getting There & Away

From Manila to Dagupan, many Pantranco North and Dagupan Bus buses a day go via Dau/Angeles, where you can also board them. The trip takes two hours.

From Bolinao to Dagupan, there are many Dagupan Bus buses a day. They take two hours and go via Alaminos, where you can also board them.

From Baguio to Dagupan there are a few Pantranco North buses daily. The last bus goes at about 11.20 am and the trip takes over two hours.

SAN FABIAN

San Fabian is a friendly little place, lying a few km north-east of Dagupan. Slightly outside the town, from Nibaliw West to Bolasi, stretches White Beach, although the old name of Center Beach was more accurate. Like almost all beaches in the Lingayen Gulf, the sand is not dazzling white but brownish-grey.

Places to Stay

The *Residenz Patty Mejia* in the village near the market has rooms for P30/60. It is a fine large private house with a garden and a few guest rooms. You can use the kitchen for a small charge.

Holiday Village & Beach Resort has rooms with fan for P60/75, double rooms with air-con and bath for P200 and rooms and cottages with bath from P100. Monthly rates also apply. It is not very clean, but there is a restaurant.

Breman's Resthouse has rooms with fan for P100. It has a restaurant and is clean and tidy. This place is managed by Ron, an Englishman, and his Filippino wife, Tess.

Center Beach Resort has rooms and cottages for P150/200, with fan and bath for P200/250. This place, which also has a restaurant, is now rather run down.

Lazy 'A' Resort has rooms with fan and bath for P150 and with air-con and bath for P280. There is a restaurant.

The *Sierra Vista Beach Resort* (tel 7668; fax 7532) is a nice little hotel with rooms with air-con and bath for P800/900. There is a restaurant and a swimming pool.

The *Windsurf Beach Resort* is in Alacan, about six km north of San Fabian, and has cottages with fan and bath for P300. There is a restaurant with European and Filipino cuisine.

Getting There & Away

A few Pantranco North buses go south from Baguio to San Fabian daily. Take any headed for Dagupan or Alaminos. The last bus leaves at about 11.20 am and takes two hours.

From San Fernando (La Union) to San Fabian, there are many minibuses a day, going on to Dagupan. The trip takes two hours.

From Dagupan to San Fabian, there are many buses a day. Take either a minibus going to San Fernando or one of a few Pantranco North buses going to Baguio. It will take 30 minutes. Some of these buses may be coming from Lingayen or Alaminos.

ARINGAY & AGOO

Agoo and Aringay lie between San Fabian and Bauang. In Aringay, the small Don Lorenzo Museum is opposite the old church.

Worth seeing in Agoo is the basilica, which was rebuilt in 1892 after a severe earthquake. It has a Shrine of Our Lady and is the most important place of pilgrimage of La Union Province during Holy Week. The climax of the *Semana Santa* (Holy Week) activities is the procession on Good Friday.

Next to the Agoo Municipal Hall is the Iloko Museo. This is a small museum with liturgical objects, antique furniture and china. Next door, in Imelda Park, visitors can pass the time in a beautiful tree house. On the northern outskirts of Agoo is a large stone statue of an eagle, marking the start of the Marcos Highway, which leads to Baguio. On the way there, near Pugo, is the former Marcos Park with golf course, swimming pool, hostel and cottages. Towering over it all is a huge bust of Marcos which has been partly carved into the rock.

Places to Stay

The *Agoo Playa Resort* has rooms with aircon and bath from P720/840. It is attractive and comfortable and beautifully laid out. There is a restaurant and a swimming pool.

Getting There & Away

There are numerous Philippine Rabbit, Times Transit, Farinas Trans and Maria de Leon buses from San Fernando (La Union) to Agoo, all going to Manila. The trip takes one hour.

From Manila, take any bus heading for San Fernando, Vigan or Laoag; the trip takes five hours.

BAUANG

Bauang has developed into the most popular beach resort in North Luzon. The places to stay mentioned here are only a small cross section, as there are many others. Nearly all of them are on the long, grey beach between Baccuit and Paringao, a little to the north of Bauang proper and about five km south of San Fernando. You can't see much from the road except a few signposts. If you are arriving by bus or jeepney, it is best to warn the driver or conductor that you want to be dropped off at the hotel of your choice. If it is booked out, the best way to find alternative accommodation is to walk along the beach. There is a tourist office for this region in the Cresta del Mar Hotel.

The small White Beach at Poro Point near the Wallace Air Base, offers snorkelling and is a good alternative to the beach at Bauang.

In Naguilian, 10 km east of Bauang, they manufacture *basi* (an alcoholic drink made from fermented sugar-cane juice), which is reputed to be the best in the country and is especially popular with Ilokanos. Its reddish colour is caused by adding guava leaves and duhat bark to the sugar-cane juice. Basi tastes a bit like sherry or port.

Places to Stay

Jac Corpuz Cottages at Baccuit has rooms from P80. They are basic cottages between the resorts of Lourdes and Leo Mar.

Lourdes Beach Homes at Baccuit have rooms with fan and bath for P100/120. These are large cottages which have, unfortunately, seen better days.

There are rooms with fan and bath for P120/150 at *Leo Mar Beach Resort* at Baccuit. They are unadorned but homely. If the price is significantly higher than this, try to bargain. This place has a restaurant. At this southern end of the beach, you will also find the *Hide Away Beach Resort*, a large house with rooms with fan from P150 to P380. There is also a restaurant.

Mark Teresa Apartel (tel 3022) on the highway at Paringao has apartments with two bedrooms for P300. It has favourable monthly rates but is often booked out. Next to it is the *Château Inn* with clean rooms with fan for P150. This place has a rooftop restaurant.

China Sea Beach Resort (tel 414821) at Paringao has rooms with fan and bath for P450/550. It is pleasant and has cottages in treeless grounds. It also has a restaurant and a swimming pool.

The *Coconut Grove Resort* (tel 414276) at Paringao has rooms with air-con and bath for P525. There is a restaurant and a swimming pool, but the main attraction is the outdoor lawn bowl complex.

The *Bali Hai Resort* (tel 412504) at Paringao has rooms with fan and bath for P425/510 and with air-con and bath for P510. It is attractive and comfortable and has nice cottages. Weekly or monthly rates can be arranged. It has a restaurant, windsurfing and Hobie Cats.

The *Cabana Beach Resort* (tel 412824, fax 414496) at Paringao has rooms with air-con and bath for P540. It has a restaurant and a beautiful swimming pool with a bar, so you can also go windsurfing or take a course in diving.

Cresta del Mar (tel 413363, 413297) at Paringao has rooms with air-con and bath from P675. This attractive place has a restaurant and a swimming pool.

Places to Eat

Try one of the resort restaurants along the beach for a change, though their prices are slightly higher than most places. The cuisine at the *Anchorage* is good, as it is at the *Fisherman's Wharf* and *Bali Hai*. Also worth trying is the Mongolian barbecue at the *Cabana* on Saturday nights.

The *Ihaw-Ihaw Restaurant*, next to the Tobacco Roll Disco on the highway, serves grills. You can also eat well and cheaply at the pleasant little *Jasmin Restaurant* on the same side of the road towards San Fernando. They serve Filipino and European dishes. You will find very reasonably priced food at the *Château Rooftop Restaurant*, which is also on the highway.

Entertainment

Entertainment is limited mainly to billiards and videos in a few of the resort restaurants. There is dancing at the *Tobacco Roll Disco* on the highway, where it is pretty dark. There are more discos and a few bars in Poro Point junction near San Fernando. You can get there by tricycle from Bauang Beach for P15, but to get back to the beach the drivers charge P20.

Getting There & Away

There are plenty of Philippine Rabbit, Times Transit, Farinas Trans and Maria de Leon buses between Manila and Bauang. Take any going to San Fernando, Vigan and Laoag. The trip takes over five hours. These buses go via Dau/Angeles and you can board them there. At Christmas, when many buses are full, you may get a reasonable seat by taking a jeepney to the bus companies' terminals in San Fernando and catching a bus there.

To go from Baguio to Bauang you have a choice of several Philippine Rabbit and Marcitas Liner buses bound for San Fernando. The trip takes over an hour. The trip along the winding Naguilian Rd down to the coast is especially attractive in the late afternoon. For the best view, sit on the same side as the driver. You can also go by jeepney, which is a bit faster than the bus.

There are many jeepneys daily from San Fernando to Bauang. You can get off on the highway near the beach resorts. The jeepneys take 30 minutes.

From Laoag and Vigan there are several Philippine Rabbit, Times Transit, Farinas Trans and Maria de Leon buses a day, all going to Manila. The trip to Bauang takes five hours from Laoag and three hours from Vigan.

The best way to catch a bus on the

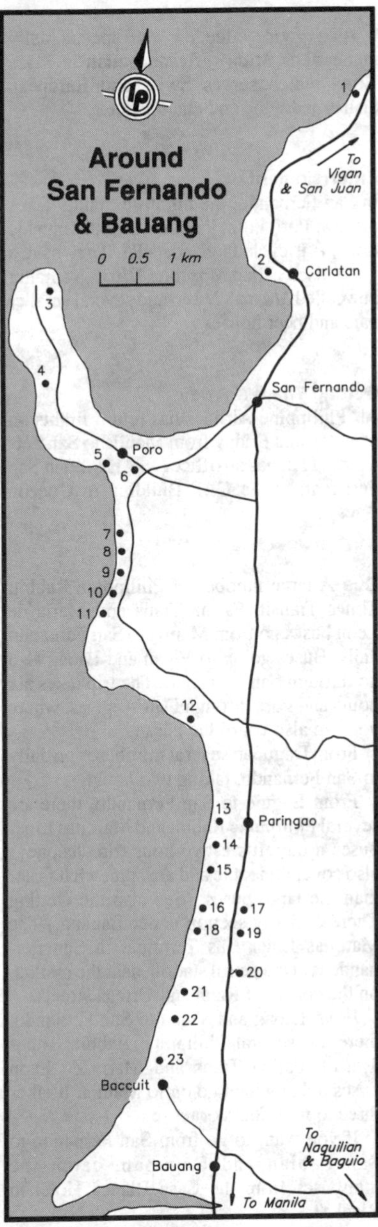

1	Hacienda Beach Resort
	Mona Liza Cottages
2	Oceana Apartments
3	Wallace Air Base
4	Voice of America Radio Station
5	Miramonte Beach Resort
6	Nightclub District
7	Driftwood Resort
8	Acapulco Beach Resort
9	Ocean Deep Resort
10	Blue Lagoon Beach Resort
11	Sunset Bay Swiss Beach Resort
12	California Resort
13	Bali Hai Resort
	Fishermans Wharf Beach Resort
	Sea Breeze Resort
14	Cabana Beach Resort
15	Anchorage Hotel
	China Sea Beach Resort
	Coconut Grove Resort
16	Cresta del Mar Hotel
	Sunset Palms Beach Resort
17	Château Inn
	Mark Teresa Apartel
18	Long Beach Hotel
19	Jasmin Restaurant
20	Ihaw-Ihaw Restaurant
	Tobacco Roll Disco
21	Leo Mar Beach Resort
22	Jac Corpuz Cottages
	Lourdes Beach Homes
23	Family Beach
	Hide Away Beach Resort

highway from Bauang to Manila is to stop every bus until you get one that suits you.

SAN FERNANDO (LA UNION)

Also called the city of the seven hills, San Fernando is the capital city of La Union Province. There is a beautiful view over the South China Sea from Freedom Park, also known as Heroes' Hill. You can also get good views from the Bayview Hotel on the Gapuz Zigzag Rd, near the Provincial Capitol Building. The Museo de La Union, next to the Provincial Capitol, gives a cultural overview of the province. It's closed on weekends. The Chinese Pagoda and the Macho Temple, which are at the northern edge of town, bear witness to the Chinese influence in San Fernando. From 12 to 16 September, the Chinese-Filipino religious community holds an annual celebration of the Virgin of Caysasay at the Macho Temple.

Places to Stay

The *Casa Blanca Hotel* (tel 3132) in Rizal St has rooms with fan for P60/70, with fan and bath for P80/100 and with air-con and bath for P130/160. This fine, large house is simple and reasonably good.

Plaza Hotel (tel 2996) in Quezon Ave has rooms with fan and bath for P175/210 and with air-con and bath from P265/290. It is nice and clean and has a restaurant.

About three km south-west of San Fernando, along the beach at Poro Point, there are several resorts. Two of them are the *Sunset Bay Swiss Beach Resort* (tel 414843) with rooms with air-con and bath for P450, and the *Ocean Deep Resort* (tel 414440; fax 414439) with rooms with fan and bath for P175/250. The latter also offers scuba diving instructor courses.

Oceana Apartments (tel 413611-13) at Carlatan, slightly north of San Fernando, has apartments with one bedroom and air-con for P450 and with two bedrooms for P800. It is pleasant and has a kitchen and TV. This place offers favourable monthly rates.

The *Hacienda Beach Resort* in Urbiztondo, near San Juan, about five km north of San Fernando, has rooms and cottages for P150/200. There is a restaurant serving European meals. Also in Urbiztondo is the *Mona Liza Cottages* (tel 414892), which has rooms for P100/150. The restaurant there serves smoked fish as a speciality.

Places to Eat

The *New Society Restaurant* in Burgos St at the market serves excellent Chinese meals. The soup served with the special meal alone is worth the money. The Filipino and Chinese meals at the *Mandarin Restaurant*, the *Crown Restaurant* and the *Garden Food Center* are good and cheap. All three of these are in Quezon Ave near the town plaza.

Also good value are the special daily menus at the *Midway Restaurant* in the Plaza Hotel which serves Swiss and European dishes and wine and champagne.

Entertainment

In San Fernando, the nightlife mainly takes place at Poro Point junction, slightly outside town. A tricycle there costs P5. They have a good disco called *Mascotte Disco*, a smaller one called *Mama's Disco* and several smaller bars and beer houses.

Getting There & Away

Air Philippine Airlines has return flights on Monday and Friday from Manila to San Fernando. PAL has an office (tel 412909) in San Fernando at the CAP Building in Quezon Ave.

Bus A large number of Philippine Rabbit, Times Transit, Farina Trans and Maria de Leon buses go from Manila to San Fernando daily. Buses going to Vigan and Laoag also go through San Fernando. The trip takes six hours and goes through Dau/Angeles, where you can also board the bus.

From Dagupan several minibuses go daily to San Fernando, taking two hours.

From Baguio to San Fernando, there are several Philippine Rabbit and Marcitas Liner buses a day. It's a two-hour trip. Jeepneys also cover this route and are somewhat faster than the large buses. (See also the Getting There & Away section under Bauang.) The Marcitas Liner Bus Terminal in San Fernando is at the petrol station, near the market, on the corner of Rizal and Ortega streets.

From Laoag and Vigan to San Fernando, there are several Philippine Rabbit, Times Transit, Farina Trans and Maria de Leon buses a day which go on to Manila. It takes three to four hours or more.

If you want to go from San Fernando to San Fabian and Dagupan, catch the minibuses from the Casa Blanca Hotel in Rizal St.

The Mountains

BAGUIO

Baguio (pronounced Barg-ee-o with a hard 'g') is the summer capital of the Philippines. Baguio has a population of about 180,000. This City of Pines, City of Flowers or City of Lovers, as it is also known, is certainly the most popular place for Filipinos to travel. Filipinos who can afford it move to this town, which is at an altitude of 1500 metres, during the hot summer months. Easter is the peak season and some hotels may raise their prices. There are supposed to be 200,000 visitors, but it's a mystery where they all stay. They rave about the zigzag road (Kennon Rd) and the cooler climate, and can't understand why others don't always share their enthusiasm.

Baguio lacks the typical Philippine atmosphere. Except for its wonderful market, the town could just as well be in some European mountain region. Somehow even the people here are different from the lowland Filipinos. Their features are harsher and they lack the carefree jollity characteristic of Filipinos. The people you meet in the streets at night are a cheerless lot in their woolly jackets, in contrast to the usual laughing faces and colourful T-shirts with cheeky slogans.

Keep in mind that Baguio is a favourite hunting ground of various tricksters who will claim acquaintance with you at the airport or immigration office for ulterior motives. Stay clear of them.

City Market

The things on sale here are mostly local products made or grown in Benguet Province, which is the area around Baguio. You will find basket ware, textiles, silver jewellery and woodcarvings as well as vegetables, fruit, honey and so on. Look out for the strawberries and the sweet, heavy strawberry wine. In the meat section, the grinning dog heads are no longer sold. After strong international criticism, this highland delicacy was forbidden by the government, so dog meat is no longer prominently displayed at markets where Westerners go. The traditional arts and crafts of the mountain dwellers are sold in the adjoining Maharlika Livelihood Center, a large complex with numerous shops. You can buy woodcarvings at more reasonable prices there, direct from the makers in the so-called Woodcarver's Village. You will find it in Asin Rd, about four or five km west of Baguio.

Burnham Park

Burnham Park is a green reserve with a small artificial lake in the middle of town. It is named after Daniel H Burnham, the town planner of Baguio. There is boat hire, a children's playground and other attractions. Be careful at night, as people have been attacked here.

Mountain Province Museum

This small museum, next door to the tourist office, gives a vivid picture of the life of the cultural minorities in the Central Cordillera (a mountain chain). The opening hours are from 9 am to noon and from 1.30 to 5 pm. Admission costs P5.

St Louis Filigree

Young silversmiths are trained in the St Louis University trade school. You can watch them make the finest filigree. Their work is sold in the St Louis Filigree Shop at fixed prices, but not all have a hallmark. If you want one, arrange to get it while you are there. The opening hours for both the workshop and the shop are Monday to Saturday from 8 am to noon and from 1 to 5 pm.

Easter School

The Easter School of Weaving is on the north-western outskirts of Baguio. The weavers make tablecloths and clothing and you can watch them at work.

Lourdes Grotto

There is a statue of Our Lady of Lourdes here and if you climb the 225 steps, you will get a beautiful view of the surrounding countryside. There is an even better view from Mines

1 Easter School of Weaving
2 Baguio Village Inn
3 Times Transit Bus Terminal
4 Leisure Lodge
5 Honeymoon Disco
6 Dream World Disco
7 Jeepneys to Bell Church
Philippine Rabbit Bus Terminal
8 Baguio Garden Inn
Country Music World
9 Dangwa Tranco Bus Terminal
Skyland Express Bus Terminal
10 Silver Lodge
11 Travellers Lodge
12 Market
13 Jeepneys to Dominican Hill, Lourdes Grotto & Asin Hot Springs
14 Diamond Inn
Folkden
15 Emerald Inn
Highland Lodge
16 Swagman Attic Hotel
17 Pier 66
18 Brent School
19 St Louis Filigree Shop
20 Maharlika Livelihood Center
21 Town Hall
22 Cypress Inn
23 168 Folkhouse
Orange County
24 Mido Hotel
Sunshine Restaurant
25 Marcitas Liner Bus Terminal
26 Philippine National Bank
27 New Plaza Hotel
28 Fire Place
29 456 Restaurant
Baguio Goodwill Lodge
30 Jeepneys to Mines View Park
31 Cathedral
32 Ganza Steak & Chicken House
33 Bread of Life
34 Sizzling Plate
35 Patria de Baguio
Songs Music Lounge
36 Philippine Airlines
37 Mount Crest Hotel
38 Burnham Hotel
39 Mario's Restaurant
40 Post Office
41 Amapola Café
42 Benguet Pine Pensione
43 Burnham Park
44 The Solibao
45 Pantranco North Bus Terminal
46 Victory Liner Bus Terminal
47 Casa Vallejo
48 Mountain Province Museum
49 Tourist Office
50 Convention Centre

View Park, which is 2½ km out of town, behind the Baguio Botanical Gardens.

Camp John Hay

Camp John Hay is a recreation base of the US Army, which is at the south-eastern edge of Baguio. Everything there, apart from the sleeping quarters and duty-free shops, is open to the public, including tourists. Among other things, there is a library with reasonably recent American papers and magazines. They have a theatre, a bowling alley, tennis courts, a golf course and several bars and restaurants.

At the *Halfway House*, the *19th Tee Patio* and the *Main Club*, you can get American beer, Californian wine and excellent, varied and filling meals. The *Lone Star Steak House* serves outstanding steaks and good wine.

To get to the base, take a jeepney or taxi from the centre of town to the main gate. There are shuttle buses about every hour and military taxis in the camp.

Baguio Botanical Gardens

These gardens, about one km out of town, were for a time named after the then first lady Imelda Marcos but are now known again by their original name. You can see several types of houses typical of the Central Cordillera here. There is also a handicrafts centre with a souvenir shop – a rather touristy affair. You can combine a trip to the botanical gardens with an excursion to Wright Park (1½ km out of town) and Mines View Park, where you can go horse riding and from which you can get a beautiful panoramic view of the valley and the mountains.

To get there take a jeepney from Magsaysay Ave, opposite the city market, or from Mabini Rd, between Session and Harrison roads.

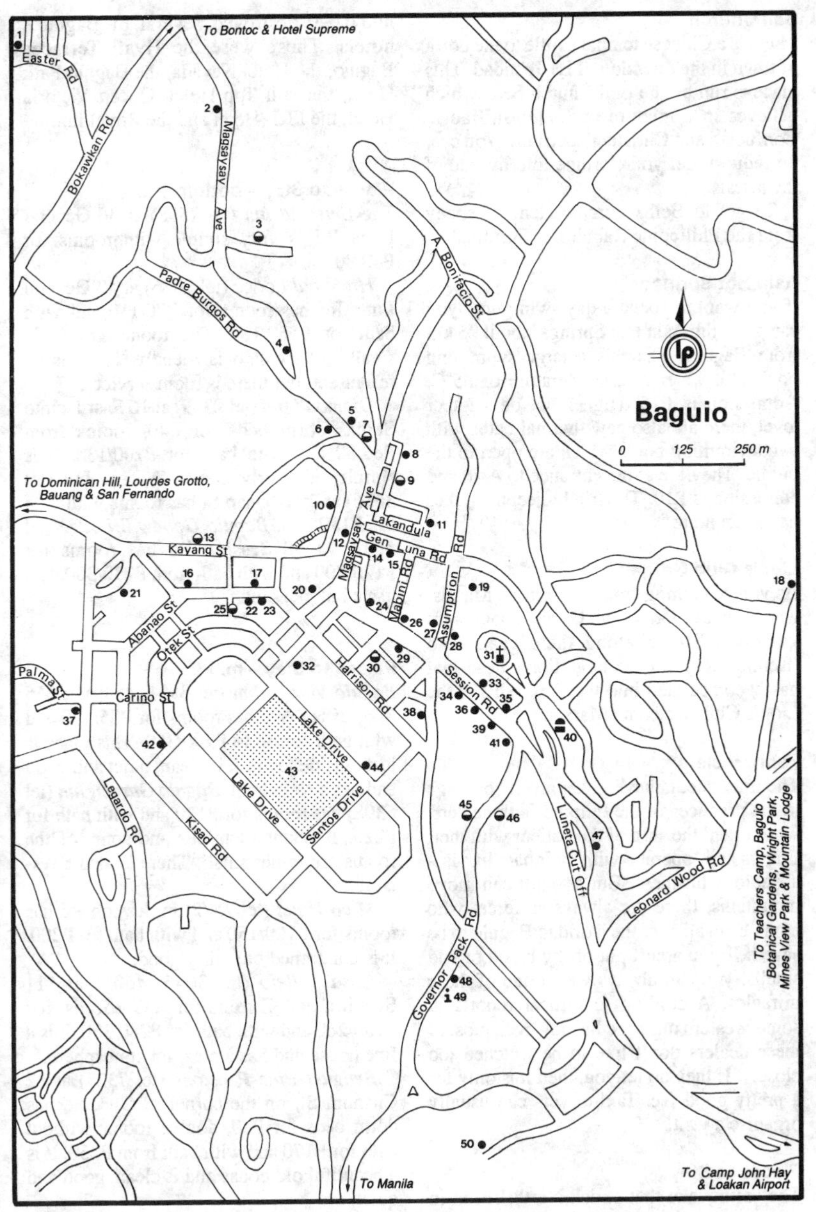
Baguio
0 125 250 m
To Bontoc & Hotel Supreme
To Dominican Hill, Lourdes Grotto, Bauang & San Fernando
To Manila
To Camp John Hay & Loakan Airport
To Teachers Camp, Baguio Botanical Gardens, Wright Park, Mines View Park & Mountain Lodge
Easter Rd
Bokawkan Rd
Magsaysay Ave
Padre Burgos Rd
A Bonifacio St
Lakandula
Gen Luna Rd
Kayang St
Mabini Rd
Assumption Rd
Abanao St
Otek St
Palma St
Carino St
Harrison Rd
Session Rd
Lake Drive
Santos Drive
Legardo Rd
Kisad Rd
Luneta Cut Off
Leonard Wood Rd
Governor Pack Rd

Bell Church

There is a Chinese temple a little to the north of town in the direction of La Trinidad. This place is run by the Bell Church Sect, which believes in a mixture of Buddhist, Taoist, Confucian and Christian doctrines. You can, on request, get your fortune told by one of the priests.

To get to Bell Church, catch a jeepney from the Philippine Rabbit Bus Terminal.

Asin Hot Springs

If you want to spend a day swimming, you can go to the Asin Hot Springs, about 25 km from Baguio. There is a large swimming pool with water at a temperature of 35°C. Admission is P15. Higher up, on another level, there are also new thermal baths with two swimming pools which are open to the public. They are at the entrance to Asin and admission is P10. The trip by jeepney takes barely an hour.

Lion's Club Gorge

As you're coming from or going to Manila, watch out at Lion's Club Gorge, about eight km out of town along the zigzag road (Kennon Rd), for the large lion's head that has been sculpted into the rock. This is the Lion's Club Welcome Marker.

Faith Healers

The mass media have given much coverage to the practices of the Filipino faith healers, who 'open' the skin of the patient with their fingers and 'operate' with their bare hands – a dubious business. But as faith can move mountains, there are always sufferers who come from all over the world to Baguio to be saved. If you aren't put off by blood or bad smells, you can always watch one of these miracles. According to critical reports in some Western mass media, however, most of these healers don't like to be watched too closely. If they do let you, then it is only for a pretty good fee. Taxi drivers can usually organise a visit.

Places to Stay

The earthquake that struck North Luzon in mid-1990 destroyed several of Baguio's hotels. These were the Hyatt Terraces Baguio, the Hotel Nevada, the Baguio Park Hotel, the Hill Top Hotel, Queen Victoria Hotel, the FRB Hotel and the Royal Inn.

Places to Stay – bottom end

The *Emerald Inn* (tel 2578) at 36 General Luna Rd is very simple with rooms for P40/80.

Highland Lodge (tel 7086) at 48 General Luna Rd has rooms for P70/110 and with bath for P150/180. The rooms are fairly small, but the staff is friendly. There is no restaurant, but there is room service.

Diamond Inn (tel 2339) at 16 East Jacinto St has dorm beds for P40, rooms from P60/80 and with bath for P100/130. It is simple but fairly good. *Cypress Inn* (tel 3656) at 29 Abanao St has rooms with bath for P150/200. *Baguio Goodwill Lodge* (tel 6634) at 58 Session Rd has rooms for P120/200 and with bath from P250/300. It is basic but pleasant.

Places to Stay – middle

Baguio Village Inn (tel 3901, 4649) at 355 Magsaysay Ave has rooms for P85/170 and with bath for up to P200/350. This place is just outside town. It is clean, quiet and good and has a restaurant. *Baguio Garden Inn* (tel 6398) has rooms for P120 and with bath for P225. It is unpretentious and some of the rooms are rather small. There is also a restaurant.

Mido Hotel (tel 2575) in Session Rd has rooms for P100/150 and with bath for P200. It is unadorned but fairly good.

Casa Vallejo (tel 3045, 4601) at 111 Session Rd Extension has rooms for P180/260 and with bath for P280/380. It is a fine house and has a pleasant atmosphere.

Benguet Pine Pensione (tel 7325) at 82 Chanum St, on the corner of Otek St, has dorm beds for P80, double rooms without bath for P170 and with bath from P250. It is a beautiful old house and is clean, good and quiet.

Places to Stay – top end

New Plaza Hotel (tel) 4038) at 2 Assumption Rd has rooms with bath for P360/470. It is clean and good and has a restaurant.

Mountain Lodge (tel 4544, 6175) at 27 Leonard Wood Rd has singles/doubles with bath for P350/400 and double rooms with a fireplace for P450. It is attractive and comfortable.

Burnham Hotel (tel 2331, 5117) at 21 Calderon St has rooms with bath for P396/430. This is a fine, tastefully decorated house which also has a restaurant.

Swagman Attic Hotel (tel 5139) at 90 Abanao St has rooms with bath for P387, and with TV for P430. This place is managed by Australians and is pleasant with a restaurant.

Hotel Supreme (tel 2855) at 416 Magsaysay Ave, just outside town, has rooms for P454/567 and with bath from P504/617. It is clean, quiet and good and has a restaurant.

Places to Eat

The restaurant in the Dangwa Tranco Bus Terminal is good and cheap. The Chinese *Kayang Restaurant* in Magsaysay Ave has menus which change daily, but it closes at 9 pm and you can't get beer after 8.30 pm.

Both *The Solibao* and the *Ganza Steak & Chicken House* are in Burnham Park and have tables outside.

If you are looking for Thai cuisine, ask for the *Taste of Thai*, which is small and cheap.

The *Amapola Café*, at the upper end of Session Rd, is a combination of pub, restaurant, sidewalk café and art gallery (on the second floor). It offers good steaks, tasty bread and native coffee.

There are other restaurants of varying quality and price in Session Rd. One of these is the *Sizzling Plate*, where you can have a proper breakfast.

Pier 66 in Abanao St is a popular beer garden with fast food.

The meals at the *456 Restaurant* are rather dear and not particularly good.

At the *Bread of Life* coffee shop, you can enjoy imported cheeses and European sausages as well as coffee and bread.

The *Star Café* serves a hearty Ifugao breakfast.

Entertainment

There are several good folk music centres in Baguio. Among the most popular are the *Fire Place* in Assumption Rd and *Folkden*, in the street by the Diamond Inn. The *168 Folkhouse* in Abanao St stays open around the clock. *Orange County* is just a few doors away and has both country & western and rock & roll music.

At the back of the Baguio Garden Inn is the entrance to the *Country Music World*, where you can sometimes enjoy well-sung Igorot songs. Jazz is played at *Songs*, a music lounge at the Patria de Baguio, in Session Rd.

Opposite and around the Philippine Rabbit Bus Terminal, you will find a few go-go bars and discos, such as *Dream World Disco* and *Honeymoon Disco*. Slightly better clubs like *Chapparal* are on the Marcos Highway.

Getting There & Away

Air Philippine Airlines has one flight between Manila and Baguio daily except Monday and Friday. The trip takes 50 minutes.

If you're catching a flight to Manila, you can get a jeepney from Baguio to Laokan Airport which leaves from Mabini Rd, between Session and Harrison roads.

Bus From Manila to Baguio, there are plenty of Philippine Rabbit, Pantranco North, Victory Liner, Dagupan Bus and Dangwa Tranco buses daily, taking six hours. Buses go via Dau/Angeles, where you can also board the bus.

From Olongapo, you can get to Baguio by Victory Liner bus. These leave hourly and take six hours. They pass through Angeles, where you can also board the bus.

From Dagupan to Baguio, there are several Pantranco North buses a day, taking two hours.

From San Fernando, several Philippine Rabbit and Marcitas Liner buses travel daily

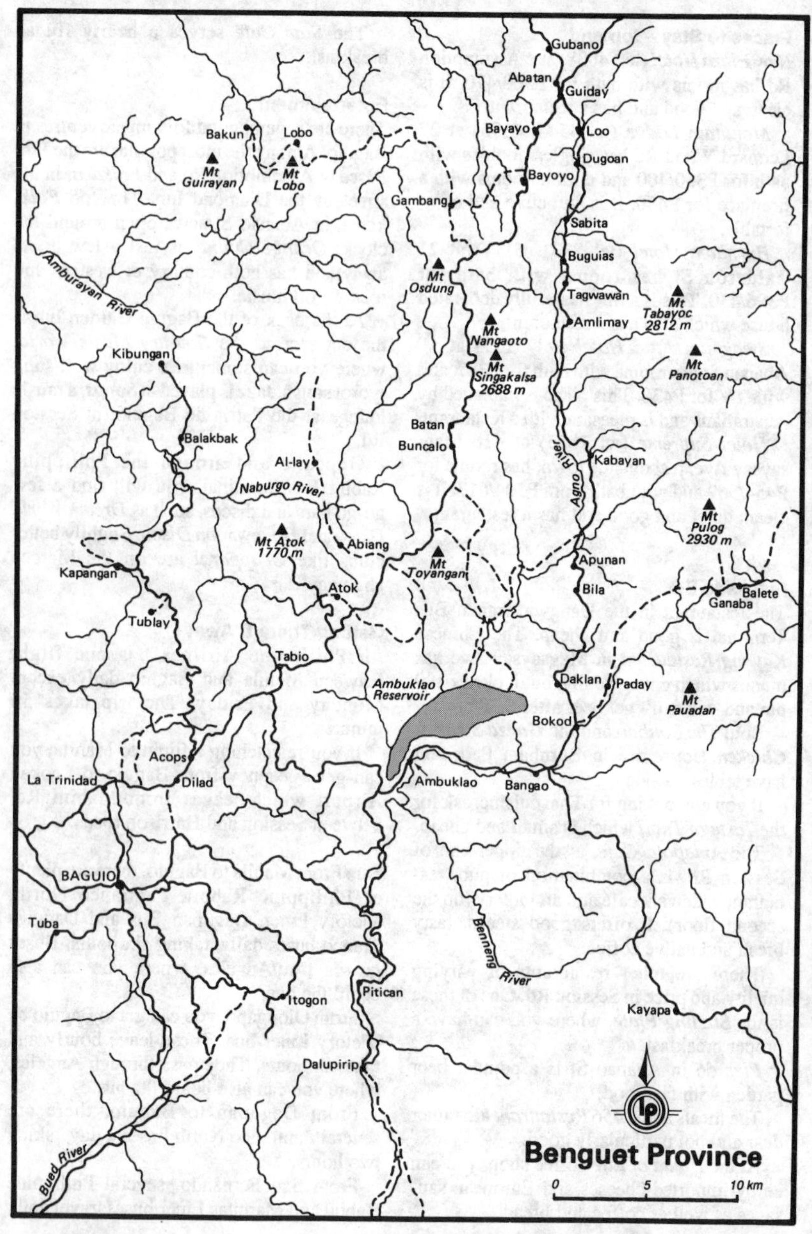
Gubano
Abatan
Guiday
Bakun
Lobo
Bayayo
Loo
Mt Guirayan
Mt Lobo
Dugoan
Bayoyo
Gambang
Sabita
Amburayan River
Mt Osdung
Buguias
Tagwawan
Mt Tabayoc 2812 m
Mt Nangaoto
Amlimay
Kibungan
Mt Singakalsa 2688 m
Mt Panotoan
Batan
Balakbak
Buncalo
Kabayan
Al-lay
Naburgo River
Agno River
Mt Pulog 2930 m
Mt Atok 1770 m
Abiang
Mt Toyangan
Apunan
Kapangan
Bila
Atok
Ganaba
Balete
Tublay
Tabio
Daklan
Paday
Mt Pauadan
Ambuklao Reservoir
Bokod
Acops
Ambuklao
Bangao
La Trinidad
Dilad
BAGUIO
Tuba
Benneng River
Itogon
Pitican
Kayapa
Dalupirip
Bued River
Benguet Province
0
5
10 km

to Baguio. It takes two hours and the last bus leaves at about 5.30 pm. The bus goes via Bauang, where you can also board the bus. You can also go by jeepney.

From Banaue, the Dangwa Tranco buses run a daily service to Baguio, leaving at 6.45 and 7.30 am, and sometimes at 5 am. They follow the southern route via Bayombong, San Jose and Villasis, taking nine hours.

From Bontoc, Dangwa Tranco buses run daily to Baguio, leaving at 6, 7, 8 and 9.15 am. The trip takes eight hours.

From Sagada there is a Dangwa Tranco bus which runs to Baguio at about 6 or 6.30 am in seven or more hours. Sometimes there are two buses a day, and there may also be a bus coming from Besao which you can board. Look out for buses from Sagada and other places in Mountain Province, which have sometimes been stopped by the military searching passenger luggage for marijuana.

The trip from Baguio to Manila takes 30 minutes less than in the reverse direction, as the first part is downhill.

KABAYAN

Kabayan is well known for the many burial caves of the local Ibaloy tribe. There are mummies with their legs hunched up against their bodies lying in hollow tree trunks which serve as coffins. Some are said to be at least 500 years old. Because some of the caves were plundered in the 1970s, the nearest and best known of them have since been sealed. Those that are still open can only be reached with guides after long marches. You can also see some mummies in a small museum in the Town Hall.

Places to Stay & Eat

If the *Youth Hostel* has not yet been finished, you will have to stay in private houses, for instance with the person in charge of the post office. You can get meals at the *Brookside Café*, but this closes at 8 pm.

Getting There & Away

There is a daily Dangwa Tranco bus from Baguio to Kabayan, leaving at about 9.30 am. The trip takes over six hours. There is no connection for Abatan to the north. To get there, you have to walk or take the daily bus back to Baguio.

SAGADA

Sagada is a pleasant little place in the mountains, known for its caves and hanging coffins. If you are a climber and are curious to see them, you would be well advised to get one of the locals to guide you through these caves. A well-known and experienced guide is Jacinto Degay, who lives next to St Theodores Hospital, but staff at the guesthouses can find you a competent guide. The usual cost is P25 per person and P25 per lamp. You need a kerosene lamp, as a torch won't offer enough light. Careful guides will put up ropes for safety at dangerous spots. Good footwear is also important for a visit to the caves.

A guide is not essential for most of the burial caves. They are not very far from the centre of town – at most a 30 minute walk away. Among these are the Matangkib, Sugong, and Lumiang caves. Sumaging Cave (Big Cave) does not contain any coffins. You need a guide to go into this cave, as a thorough exploration can take up to six hours. A guide is also recommended if you want to visit Crystal Cave.

Weavers make beautiful materials at the Sagada Weaving & Souvenir Shop, and you can buy traditional woven goods at fairly reasonable prices.

Places to Stay

The *Sagada Guest House* has rooms for P25/50, P30/60 for one night only. It is clean with warm water and has good and reasonably priced meals.

St Josef's Guest House has rooms for P25/50, is clean and pleasant and serves good communal meals.

Julia's Guest House has rooms for P50 or P60 for one night only. It is comfortable and has big rooms. You can get good vegetarian meals there.

The *Green House* has rooms for P25/50. It is an older private house which is quiet and has four rooms to let, with use of kitchen,

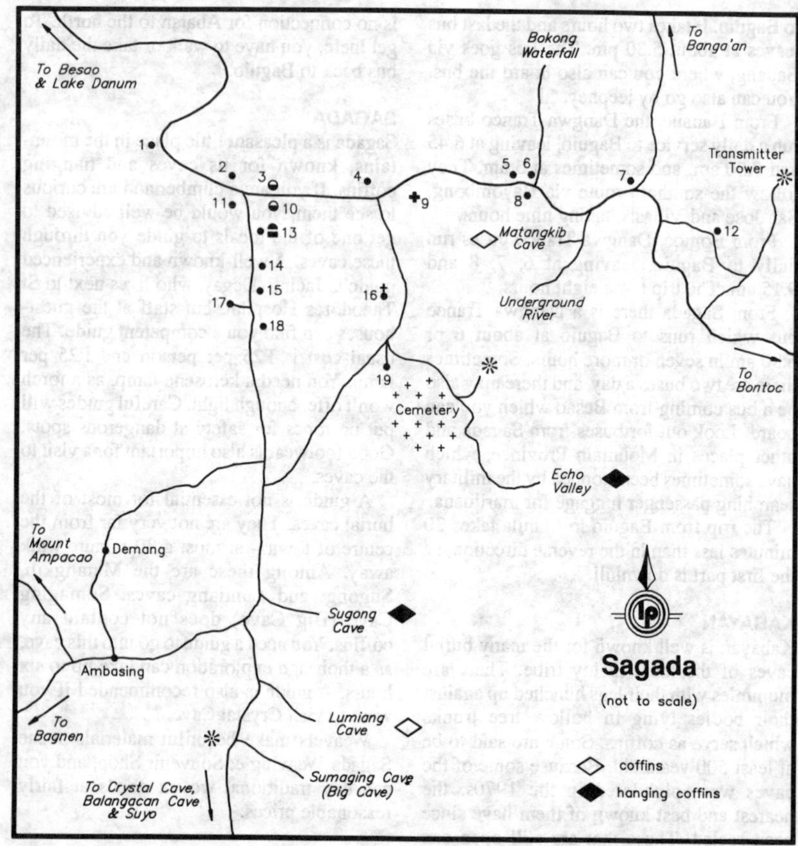

living and dining rooms. There is warm water.

Traveller's Inn has rooms for P25/50 and is in a quiet location. It has a nice atmosphere.

Mapiyaaw Sagada Pension has dorm beds for P20, and singles/doubles with bath for P40/70. It is a little outside the centre and is good quality.

Places to Eat

You can eat well and cheaply at the *Moonhouse Café* and at the *Shamrock Café*; the latter serves several Mountain Province specialities. Several of the guesthouses serve large evening meals and breakfasts, but you should book ahead.

Getting There & Away

Several Dangwa Tranco, Skyland Express and Lizardo Trans buses leave Baguio daily for Sagada. The departure times are 6 am and 7 or 7.30 am and the trip takes eight hours. The Dangwa Tranco buses, which are usually pretty full, come to Baguio from La Trinidad, which is a few km north of Baguio. If you want a good seat, take a jeepney from Baguio to La Trinidad Bus Terminal well

1 Sagada Guest House
2 Town Bakery
3 Buses to Baguio
4 St Josef's Guest House
5 Sagada Weaving & Souvenir Shop
6 Traveller's Inn
7 Studio Eduardo Masferré
8 Cangbay's Store
9 Hospital
10 Jeepneys to Bontoc
11 Market
12 Mapiyaaw Sagada Pension
13 Bank
Municipal Hall
Police Station
Post Office
14 Shamrock Café
15 Julia's Guest House
16 St Mary's Church
17 Green House
18 Moonhouse Café
19 St Mary's High School

before the scheduled departure time. Sit next to the driver or on the right side of the bus for the best view. It gets fairly cool, so take a jacket or jumper out of your luggage before it gets stowed away.

From Bontoc to Sagada, there are at least two jeepneys daily, usually leaving at 8 am, 9.30 am and 1.30 pm. It takes one hour.

An unusual way to go to Sagada is from Vigan via Bangued, right across Abra Province (see the Vigan to Bangued & Sagada section in this chapter).

AROUND SAGADA

A visit to Bokong Waterfall with its natural swimming pool is worthwhile and very refreshing after touring the caves in Sagada. It's a little hard to find, so you may have to ask for directions. It takes about 30 minutes to get there on foot from Sagada. To get there from the market, walk in the direction of Banga'an, then turn left after the Sagada Weaving & Souvenir Shop.

A little further towards Bontoc, near the turn-off to Banga'an, don't miss a visit to Eduardo Masferré's studio. His photographs of life in the villages of Mountain Province in the '30s, '40s and '50s are worth seeing. A selection of his impressive work has been published in an illustrated book. His son sells copies of individual photos. According to some reports, however, they will seldom arrive if sent as postcards.

You can walk from Sagada to Banga'an in about an hour through a beautiful landscape with rice terraces. There is also supposed to be a connection by jeepney now. About one hour outside Banga'an is a beautiful waterfall, which you can reach if you follow the path behind the school, going down through the rice terraces.

BONTOC

At an altitude of about 900 metres, Bontoc is the centre of Mountain Province. In and around Bontoc live the Bontoc tribe. A little to the north are the Kalinga and, to the southeast, the Ifugao tribes. (See the section on Cultural Minorities in the Facts about the Country chapter.) You can get a good overview of the differences and similarities between the mountain tribes in the small but excellent Bontoc Museum. The friendly staff is always happy to give detailed information about the life in Mountain Province. The opening hours are from 8 am to noon and from 1 pm to 3 pm. Admission is P10. The museum has a picture of the Tucucan Bridge, also known as Monkey Bridge. This was made of bamboo and similar materials and was in Tucucan, a small place four km northeast of Bontoc, on the road to Tabuk. Unfortunately, the bridge collapsed in 1986 and was replaced by an uninteresting modern construction.

Woven materials are made on old looms in and around Bontoc, for example, in the All Saints Elementary School and in Barangay Samoki, a village on the other side of the river. As well as woven materials, locals also make simple utensils. It takes about 30 minutes to walk from Bontoc to Samoki.

If you feel like a soothing massage after your strenuous walks up and down mountains, go to the Massage Centre of Bontoc. There are two blind masseurs who, for P40, will give a professional massage lasting almost two hours.

There is a branch of the Philippine National Bank (PNB) in Bontoc if you want to change any money.

Places to Stay

The *Mountain Hotel* (tel 3018) has basic rooms for P25/40-50 and has a restaurant. The *Bontoc Hotel* has rooms for P25 per person. It is simple and homely and has a restaurant. *Chico Terrace* (tel 3099) has rooms with bath for P25 per person. It is basic but well kept and has rooms with three or five beds.

Happy Home Inn (tel 3021) has singles/doubles for P30/50 and double rooms with bath for P150. It is basic but habitable and has hot showers for an extra P5. You can also get a good walking map of Bontoc and its surroundings.

The *Pines Kitchenette & Inn* has rooms for P35/70 and with bath for P140. It is nice and clean and has a restaurant.

Places to Eat

You can get good cheap meals in the restaurants at the Bontoc and Mountain hotels. There is also the Pines Kitchenette & Inn where you can get a good cheap breakfast as well as other meals.

Getting There & Away

There are five Dangwa Tranco buses from Baguio to Bontoc a day. Departure times are at 6, 7, 8, 9 and 10 am. The trip takes eight hours. Some buses start in La Trinidad, a few km north of Baguio, and are generally pretty full when they get to Baguio. If you want a good seat, it is worth going the short distance from Baguio to La Trinidad by jeepney.

From Banaue to Bontoc there is one jeepney which leaves at about 6.30 to 7.30 am and sometimes earlier. There is also a daily bus, except on Sundays, which leaves between 10 and 11 am and takes over two hours. Jeepneys take almost an hour less. A special jeepney ride costs P500.

The bus connection between Tuguegarao and Bontoc via Tabuk and Lubuagan is probably still suspended. It is a bad stretch which takes 10 hours. The bus goes via Roxas, Santiago and Banaue.

There are at least two jeepneys a day from Sagada to Bontoc. They leave at 5.45 to 6.15 am and 11 am to noon. The trip takes one hour.

There is a cross trip from San Fernando to Bontoc and Sagada, leaving from Tagudin (50 km north of San Fernando) and going as far as Cervantes. Two jeepneys leave at 6 to 6.30 am from Bitalag Rd junction, about five

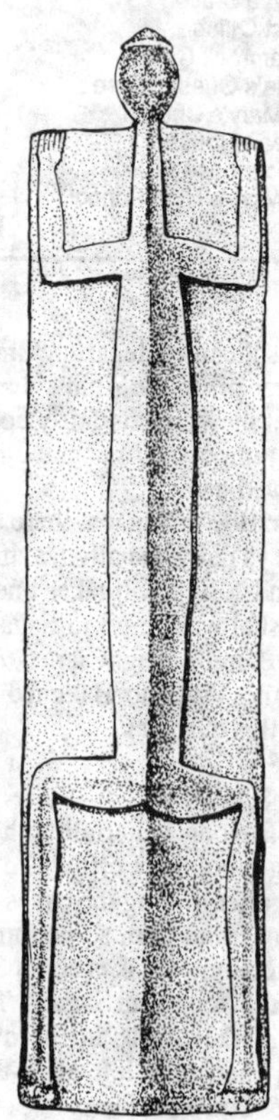

Bontoc shield – Filipinos used shields made of engraved buffalo leather or carved out of wood to protect themselves in battle.

km north of Tagudin. There is nothing after that time on this stretch. The road is bad and it's a very time-consuming trip. If your jeepney gets to Cervantes too late, you won't get an onward connection until 5 am the next morning, when you can catch a bus going to Baguio via Abatan. There are jeepneys during the day on this stretch. At Abatan you can take a bus coming from Baguio which goes to Bontoc or Sagada.

To go from Abatan to Cervantes there is a Dangwa Tranco bus coming from Baguio which leaves between 10 and 11 am. You can also get a jeepney from Abatan to Mankayan and from there go on by minibus to Cervantes. In the afternoon, this connection may not be available. From Cervantes to Tagudin at least there is a daily jeepney at 1 and 3 pm. On Thursdays, which is market day, there is an additional jeepney at 11 am. There is no problem getting connecting buses at Tagudin and at Bitalag Rd junction heading either north or south.

Hints for Drivers The trip from Baguio to Bontoc is very beautiful and interesting, but strenuous too as some sections of the road are very bad. The cementing of this so-called mountain highway is, however, making progress. The only possible overnight stop is at the Mount Data Lodge north of Abatan, which has double rooms with bath for about P300, though you may be able to negotiate a discount.

AROUND BONTOC

Bugnay

Bugnay is a Kalinga village and is a pretty expensive place for travellers. You will be asked P20 or more for a local guide or for the 'new bridge construction'. They also charge an extra few pesos for taking photographs. There are other charges as well as the obligatory gifts. It is advisable to take no more valuables than necessary, as several attacks have been reported in this area.

Fighting is now going on between the CPAL (Cordillera People's Liberation Army) and the NPA (New People's Army), so travelling through this area is dangerous.

Getting There & Away You can get a bus from Bontoc to Tabuk via Banaue, Santiago and Roxas which leaves at 7.30 to 8 am. Buses between Bontoc and Tabuk via Bugnay, Tinglayan and Lubuagan are probably still suspended.

From Bontoc to Tinglayan going via Bugnay there is a daily jeepney, which leaves after the arrival of the bus from Baguio between 1 and 2 pm. There are several checkpoints on this stretch and the soldiers will search your luggage thoroughly. They will also want to see identity documents, but are usually satisfied with a photocopy of your passport.

The jeepney returning from Tinglayan to Bontoc does not leave till 6 am the following morning. A day trip from Bontoc to Bugnay is therefore impossible. To charter a jeepney would cost at least P600, and then only if you can find one. You can add to this the cost of presents and of a guide, whom you should have for safety reasons alone. All in all, it would be an expensive business.

Malegcong

You get the best view of the rice terraces from this village. They are even better here than in Bauang. It may be possible to obtain up-to-date information on life in Malegcong and in the mountains from the English-speaking teacher there.

You should carry some provisions, particularly water, and gifts for the locals. The forest inspectors are not too keen on lots of matches being handed out indiscriminately as there have been numerous forest fires due to carelessness. Whatever you do, don't take alcohol for a general drinking session. A small gift is not just recommended, it's compulsory unless you want to be muttered and sworn at by all the villagers.

Getting There & Away There is not supposed to be any connection by jeepney from Bontoc to Malegcong any more. It takes three hours on foot, which is quite a walk. It can get very hot. Take some kind of headcover as well as provisions, including water.

There may still be a jeepney from Bontoc

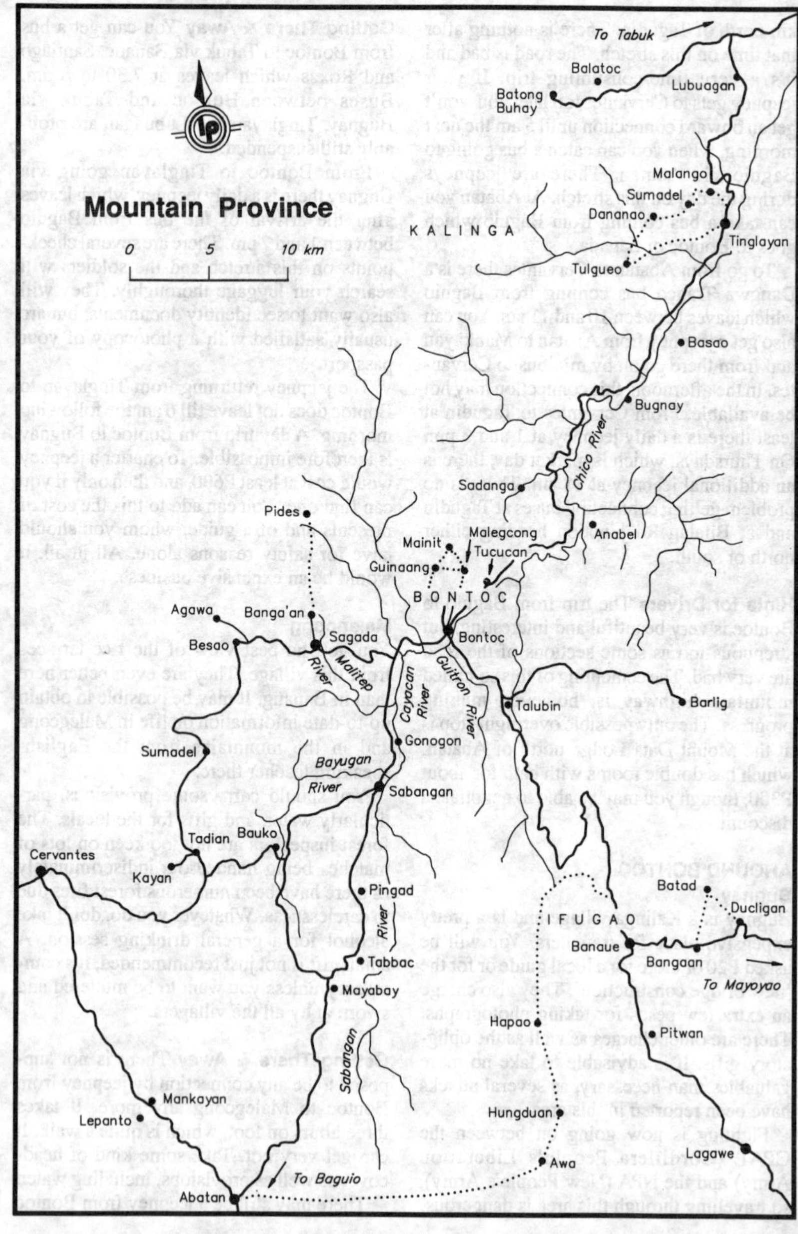
Mountain Province
0
5
10 km
To Tabuk
Balatoc
Lubuagan
Batong Buhay
Malango
Sumadel
Dananao
Tinglayan
Tulgueo
KALINGA
Basao
Bugnay
Chico River
Sadanga
Anabel
Pides
Mainit
Malegcong
Tucucan
Guinaang
BONTOC
Agawa
Banga'an
Sagada
Besao
Bontoc
Malitep River
Cayocan River
Guitron River
Talubin
Barlig
Gonogon
Sumadel
Bayugan River
Sabangan
Tadian
Bauko
Cervantes
Kayan
Pingad
Batad
Ducligan
IFUGAO
Banaue
Bangaan
To Mayoyao
River
Tabbac
Mayabay
Hapao
Pitwan
Sabangan
Mankayan
Lepanto
Hungduan
Lagawe
Awa
To Baguio
Abatan

to Guinaang at 6.30 to 7 am. Just before the village of Guinaang, on the right, there is a track to Malegcong which goes past rice terraces to a mountain summit where you have to turn right to get to Malegcong. The walk from Guinaang to Malegcong takes two hours. From Malegcong you can walk back to Bontoc, which takes two hours. You will first pass rice terraces and the track runs downhill, until you reach a road which vehicles can use. The trip from Malegcong to Bontoc takes two hours.

Mainit

Mainit means hot. Even the springs in this little place where people pan for gold are hot.

There is a jeepney which leaves Bontoc daily for Guinaang at about 6.30 to 7 am. From there it is about 45 minutes on foot down the mountain to Mainit.

There may be a jeepney in the afternoon from Guinaang back to Bontoc. There is also a track from Mainit to Malegcong. It is hard to find, so a guide may be useful. The track starts before you get into Mainit, at a sulphur spring, which you can smell a long way off. If you are coming from Guinaang, you have to turn right at the sulphur spring and follow the track past the rice terraces to Malegcong.

Tinglayan & Kalinga Villages

Tinglayan is a good starting point from which to visit Kalinga villages. From there you can try to get to the villages with Kalinga who have been to see their relatives in hospital. Still, the area must be regarded as dangerous because of several ambushes and numerous fights between the politically distinct units of the NAFP (New Armed Forces of the Philippines), the NPA and the CPLA. You should check the situation before you go there.

The following round trip will take at least three days on foot, including stopovers in the villages. You can count on three hours from Tinglayan to Tulgueo, one hour or more from Tulgueo to Dananao, two hours from Dananao to Sumadel and one hour from Sumadel to Malango. From Malango you get on to the main road and go back to Tinglayan.

Always get a guide to take you from one village to the next to reduce the likelihood of an attack. Women are normally honoured and treated with respect by the Kalinga, as a Kalinga who attacks a woman loses face for good, yet they should also have a guide. Unfortunately, generous travellers have caused expectations of handouts. There have been reports of emphatic demands for hundreds of pesos for the construction of a (non-existent) school.

Lubuagan

In and around Lubuagan, the former government of president Marcos came into direct conflict with the Kalinga because of the Chico Valley dam project, which was to comprise four single dams and produce 1000 megawatts of electricity. The Chico Valley dam would have been the largest in South-East Asia and would have flooded the Kalinga's valleys, forcing them to resettle. The Kalinga were opposed to the move as it would have meant the end of their centuries-old culture, which has developed in isolation of the colonised lowlands. The Kalinga's religion was another reason for their opposition to the move. They live in a world of gods and spirits and show great respect to the dead, so their ancestors' resting places must be left undisturbed.

At first there was only scattered fighting against the surveying for the dam. In 1980, however, following the murder of Bugnay's Chief Macliing Dulag, who had been sabotaging the works of the national energy company, the 20 or so groups of Kalinga, comprising about 100,000 members, formed a united front. Macliing was shot by several volleys of machine-gun fire through the thin walls of his hut and it is said that the murderers were wearing military uniforms. The conflict widened and soldiers and construction workers were beheaded and rebellious Kalinga shot. Members of the communist NPA joined the Kalinga and instructed them in the use of modern M-16 rifles.

Today, relations between the mountain dwellers and the NPA, as well as the government, are anything but harmonious. The

Kalinga now distrust any power which tries to intrude on them. They continue to be vigilant and regard any stranger as a threat – do not venture into the mountains alone.

Ifugao god: Bulul, the protector of rice

Woodcarving

Woodcarving is part of the culture of the Ifugao who live in the Central Cordillera. They like making sacred figures that represent humans in different positions. The most famous wooden figures are the Bulul, male and female gods who, after harvest, are placed at the entrance of the storehouse to protect the rice. The rice gods, attracted by the ceremony, are supposed to inhabit these figures and ensure that the rice not only lasts until the next harvest, but also increases miraculously.

BANAUE

Banaue is at an altitude of about 1200 metres. The rice terraces around Banaue have been called the eighth wonder of the world. It took the Ifugao tribespeople, with their primitive implements, over 2000 years to create this imposing landscape.

There are a number of things to do around Banaue. You can visit several Ifugao villages, take some of the paths through the rice terraces, enjoy the panorama from Banaue View Point or take a refreshing dip in the clear water of Guihon Natural Pool. On the way there you can make a detour to the bronzesmiths of Matanglag, or visit Josef Blas, who makes artistic woodcarvings.

You can buy a useful map of Banaue's surroundings for P2 at the Tourist Information Center, which is next to the market. It shows the way to various interesting sights and describes them in detail on the back.

Peter Gatik is a good guide with excellent information. He lives in Bayongong and conducts trekking tours with small groups from Batad to Bontoc. You will need to pay him a few pesos in advance and allow two days for preparations.

Money

There is an authorised foreign exchange counter at the Banaue Hotel. However, the exchange rate is poor and there is a fee of P50 for each travellers' cheque.

Places to Stay

Jericho Guest House is a reasonable place which has rooms for P25/50. *Happy Homes Inn* (tel 4046) has rooms for P35/60. The basic Ifugao house (a house of the Ifugao tribe that is available for accommodation) is P75. *Travellers Inn* is a simple place with rooms for P35/70.

The *Wonder Lodge* (tel 4017) and *Brookside Inn* both have rooms for P35/70. *Half Way Lodge* (tel 4082) has rooms for P35/60-75 and with bath for P200/250. It is clean, simple and has a restaurant. *Stairway Lodge* has singles/doubles for P35/60-70 and double rooms with bath for P200. It is pleasant and has a restaurant.

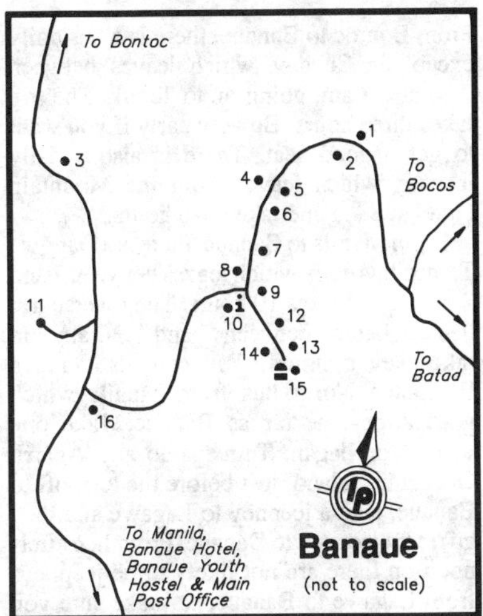

1 Travellers Inn
2 Brookside Inn
3 Terrace Ville Inn
4 Cozy Nook
5 Half Way Lodge
6 Stairway Lodge
7 Green View Lodge
8 Wonder Lodge
9 Valgreg Lodge
10 Market
Tourist Information Center
11 Banaue View Lodge
12 Sanafe Lodge
13 Las Vegas Restaurant
14 Happy Homes Inn
15 Municipal Hall
Post Office
16 Jericho Guest House

J & L Lodge (tel 4035) has rooms for P50/100. It is slightly outside Banaue, on the way to the Banaue Hotel. The Ifugao house costs P150.

Green View Lodge (tel 4022) is a good place with dorm beds for P50 and rooms with bath for P244/315-350. The single rooms are OK for two people.

Terrace Ville Inn has comfortable rooms with bath for P150/300-350.

Fairview Inn has rooms with bath for P250/300-350. It is attractive and comfortable.

Sanafe Lodge (tel 2110) has dorm beds for P55 to P100, singles/doubles with bath for P350/470 and double rooms without bath for P360. There is also a restaurant.

The *Banaue Youth Hostel* has dorm beds for P110. It is administered by the Banaue Hotel, whose swimming pool is available for use.

The exclusive *Banaue Hotel* (tel 4087, 4088) has rooms with bath for P1320/1450 and suites for P3165. It is attractive and comfortable and has a restaurant and a swimming pool.

Places to Eat

Most hotels have a small restaurant or else the staff will cook meals for guests. The following are good and cheap: *Half Way Restaurant*, *Stairway Restaurant*, *Terraces Restaurant* and *Las Vegas Restaurant*. Eating at the Youth Hostel is rather expensive because the portions are small.

The restaurant at the *Banaue Hotel* is excellent and, if there are enough guests, Ifugao dances are held at night. Although these performances are in contrast to the setting and are perhaps out of place, they do seem to be relatively authentic. Admission is P10. On the return to the village at night it is likely to be very dark, so don't forget to take a torch.

There is also live music at the *Patina Bar Folkden*, where you can get beer and snacks quite late.

Getting There & Away

There are two Dangwa Tranco buses from Baguio to Banaue a day, taking the southern route via Villasis, San Jose and Bayombong. They leave at 6.45 and 7.30 am and take nine hours. It is necessary to be at the bus terminal early, as the bus will leave up to an hour early if it is full, especially at Easter.

If you want to go from Baguio to Banaue via Bontoc, you will have to stay the night in Bontoc, as there is no direct connection.

From Bontoc to Banaue, there is a bus daily except on Sunday, which leaves between 7.30 and 8 am, going on to Tabuk. The trip takes three hours. Be very early if you want to get a good seat. There is also a daily jeepney which leaves from the Mountain Hotel at 8 am and takes two hours.

From Manila to Banaue, there is a Dangwa Tranco bus daily which leaves between 7 and 7.30 am and takes 10 hours. The reverse trip leaves Banaue between 7 and 7.30 am and takes seven hours. You can also take a Pantranco North bus from Manila which goes almost as far as Banaue. Take one bound for Ilagan, Tuguegarao and Aparri. Get off in Solano, just before the turn-off to Banaue, take a jeepney to Lagawe and then go on by jeepney to Banaue. From late afternoon on there are not likely to be jeepneys from Lagawe to Banaue, so make sure you don't arrive too late. There is no accommodation in Lagawe.

To go from San Fernando and Bauang to Banaue, take a bus at about 5 or 6 am headed for Manila and get off at the turn-off to Rosario. From there catch the bus from Baguio to Banaue (see above) which gets there about an hour after leaving Baguio. The bus is likely to be full to bursting point, but perhaps some of the passengers will get off there.

From Banaue to Tuguegarao and Aparri take one of the buses mentioned from Banaue to Manila or Baguio and get off at Bagabag, Solano or Bayombong. Then wait for the Manila to Tuguegarao or Aparri bus. The trip takes four or six hours respectively.

From Banaue to Baguio, the Dangwa Tranco buses leave at 6.45 and 7.30 am, and sometimes even at 5 am.

From Banaue to Manila, a Dangwa Tranco bus leaves daily between 7 and 7.30 am, taking seven hours. An air-con Sarkies bus leaves at 10 am and the trip takes seven hours.

Hints for Drivers Because of attacks on private vehicles it is advisable to drive in front of a bus or jeepney.

AROUND BANAUE

Batad & Cambulo

Batad is about 16 km north-west of Banaue. The rice terraces in Batad are in the shape of an amphitheatre. Many Ifugao houses now have corrugated iron roofs, but luckily these have not yet been generally accepted. There is a beautiful waterfall with a natural swimming pool. It's only about an hour's walk away, but it would be better to stay overnight rather than include it in a day's visit to Banaue.

If you want to photograph villagers in Batad, you should ask them first as they either don't want any photos to be taken, or else will demand payment.

About two hours on foot from Batad is Cambulo, a typical little Ifugao village, in the midst of rice terraces. It is advisable to use water purifying tablets in this area. From there you can go along a trail to Kinakin, which is on the main road, in about three hours. It is another eight km back to Banaue.

Places to Stay Accommodation is simple throughout, but the atmosphere is always very friendly. You can stay the night in Batad for P10 or P15 at the *Hillside Inn*, *Mountain View Inn*, *Romeo's Inn*, *Foreigner's Inn* or *Simon's Inn*. This place has good meals, especially Israeli ones.

In Cambulo *Lydia Domanlig* has overnight accommodation for P10. Lydia, the owner, also cooks for her guests.

Getting There & Away For the first 12 km from Banaue to Batad you can go by vehicle, but the rest you have to walk. The Tourist Information Center and several guesthouses, such as the Half Way Lodge, will organise trips by jeepney for P250 to P350. The jeepney will take up to 14 people and the driver will wait at the Batad turn-off until late afternoon or come back for guests at an agreed time. Between Dalican and Bangaan there is a signposted path to Batad. From here it will take you barely two hours. Don't be taken in by 'guides' who just happen to be going the same way to Batad, where they will demand a pretty high price.

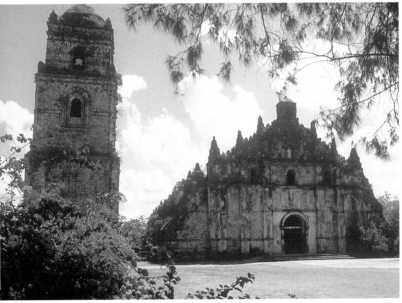

Top: Street scene in Vigan, the Philippines' best preserved Spanish town (KD)
Bottom: A church built in 'earthquake baroque' style in Paoay, North Luzon (JP)

Top left: A typical example of colonial church architecture (JP)
Top right: Pounding rice (JP)
Bottom left: Approaching the Mayon Volcano's symmetrical cone (TW)
Bottom right: Roman centurion at the Moriones Festival, Marinduque (JP)

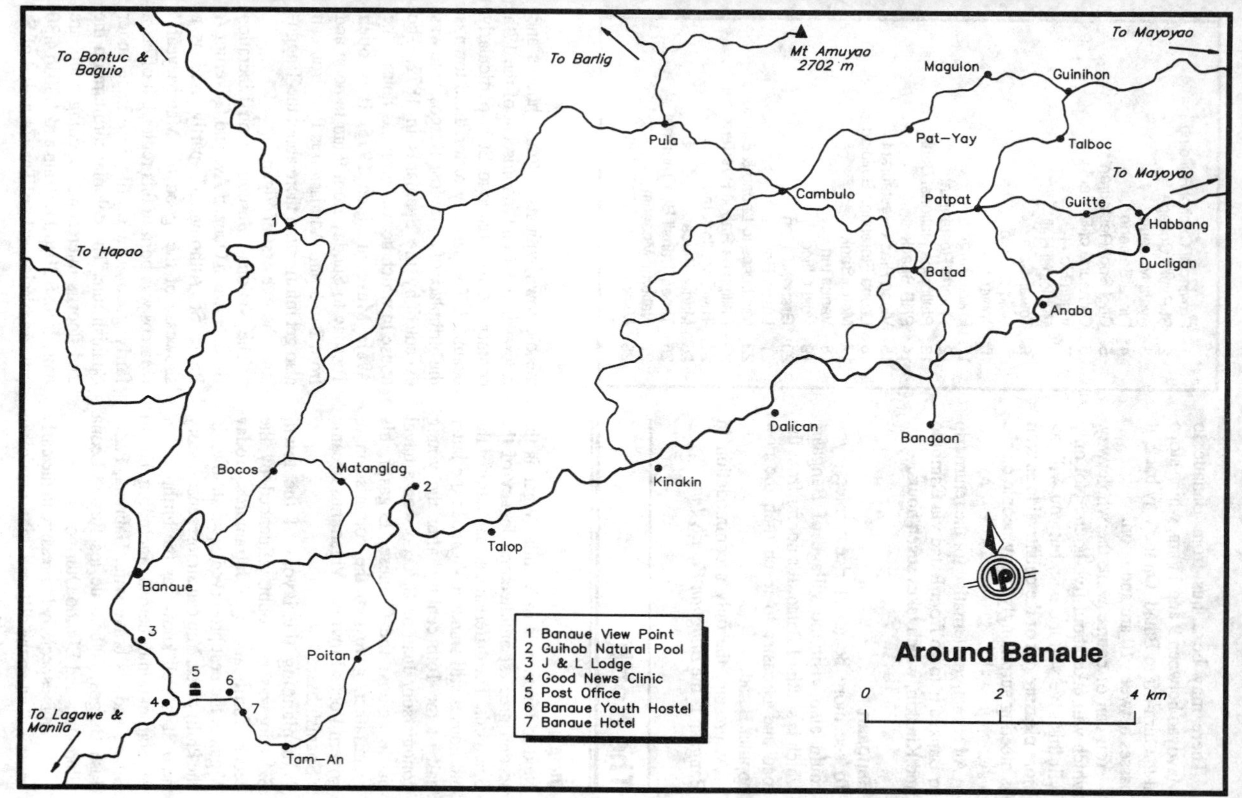

Around Banaue
0
2
4 km
1 Banaue View Point
2 Guihob Natural Pool
3 J & L Lodge
4 Good News Clinic
5 Post Office
6 Banaue Youth Hostel
7 Banaue Hotel
To Bontuc &
Baguio
To Barlig
Mt Amuyao
2702 m
To Mayoyao
Magulon
Guinihon
Pula
Pat-Yay
Talboc
To Mayoyao
Cambulo
Patpat
Guitte
Habbang
To Hapao
Ducligan
Batad
Anaba
Dalican
Bangaan
Bocos
Matanglag
Kinakin
Talop
Banaue
Poitan
To Lagawe &
Manila
Tam-An

There may be a bus from Banaue to Mayoyao between 9 and 11 am, which stops at the turn-off to Batad. On the way back, it passes between 10 am and noon.

You can of course walk the whole way, which will take about five hours. Not only will this save you the fare, but you will get more pleasure out of the countryside as well as meeting surprisingly many people on the way.

An attractive alternative for the return trip to Banaue is to go from Batad via Cambulo and Kinakin, which takes seven hours.

Bangaan

To see more beautiful rice terraces, you could also visit the village of Bangaan, which is south of Batad. It's not far from the road and is easier to reach than the now popular Batad.

At present, the only accommodation in Bangaan is the *Bangaan Family Inn*.

1 Provincial Capitol Building
2 St Paul's College
3 Ayala Museum
4 Plaza Salcedo
5 Cool Spot Restaurant
6 Cathedral of St Paul
7 Vigan Hotel
8 Municipal Hall
9 Tower Café
Unique Café
10 Tower
11 Plaza Burgos
12 Victoria Restaurant
13 Philippine National Bank
14 PNB Snack
15 Vigan Plaza Restaurant
16 Leona Florentina Building
17 Metro Bank
18 Venus Inn
19 Post Office
20 Grandpa's Inn
21 Luzon Hotel
22 Minibuses to Laoag & Bangued
23 Philippine Rabbit Bus Terminal
24 The Cordillera Inn
25 Marius Place
26 Times Transit Bus Terminal
27 National Museum
28 Market

The North

VIGAN

Next to Intramuros in Manila, Vigan is the second greatest architectural legacy of the Spaniards. The difference is that many of the old houses still stand in Vigan. In the latter half of the 16th century, after the young conquistador Juan de Salcedo won a naval battle against the Chinese, Legaspi, his grandfather, gave him the commission to govern Ilocos Province. Vigan thus became a Spanish base.

In planning the layout of the town, Salcedo was no doubt influenced by the secure fortifications of Intramuros. Today Vigan is the best preserved Spanish town in the Philippines. You can almost sense history here. It is well known as the birthplace of several national heroes, including Diego Silang and his brave wife, Gabriela, Padre Jose Burgos, Isabelo de los Reyes, Leona Florentina and Elipido Quirino.

Vigan is especially impressive in the early morning, when the diffused light transforms the old town with its colonial houses and calesas into a scene reminiscent of the 17th century. Mena Crisologo St is particularly beautiful. The partially restored old town is the birthplace of Padre Jose Burgos, who was executed by the Spaniards in 1872. The house in which he was born has housed the Ayala Museum since 1975. It is open Tuesday to Sunday from 9 am to noon and from 2 to 5 pm. Admission is P10. You can also get information there about the Tingguian, who live east of Vigan.

The National Museum is on Liberation Blvd, between Quezon Ave and Governor A Reyes St. Although it's partly used as a showcase of the 'good old Marcos years' (Marcos was born in this region), it offers a fairly good idea of life in Vigan under Spanish rule. The colonial furniture on the 2nd floor is interesting. Opening hours are daily from 8.30 to 11.30 am and 1.30 to 4.30 pm. Admission is free. The Cathedral of St

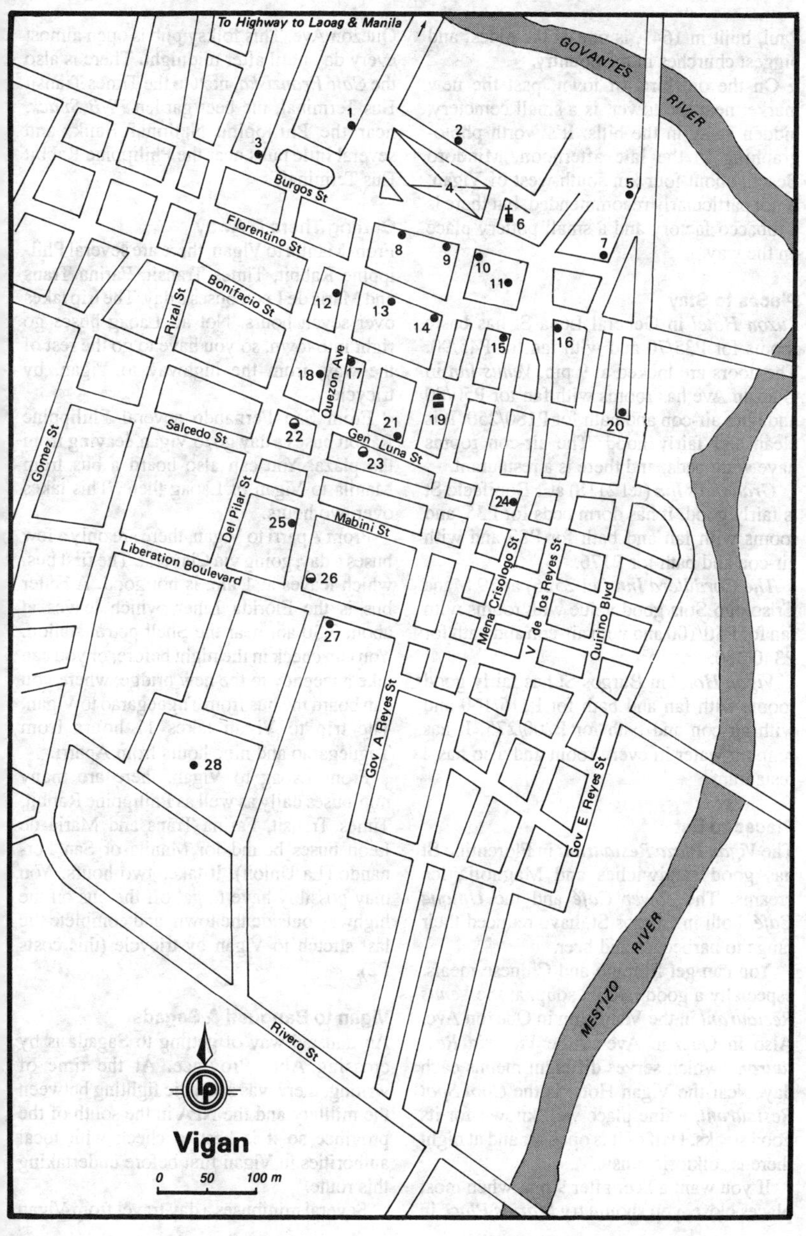
To Highway to Laoag & Manila
Govantes River
Burgos St
Florentino St
Bonifacio St
Rizal St
Quezon Ave
Salcedo St
Gen Luna St
Gomez St
Del Pilar St
Mabini St
Liberation Boulevard
Mena Crisologo St
V de los Reyes St
Quirino Blvd
Gov A Reyes St
Gov E Reyes St
Rivero St
Mestizo River
1
2
3
4
5
6
7
8
9
10
11
12
13
14
15
16
17
18
19
20
21
22
23
24
25
26
27
28
Vigan
0
50
100 m

Paul, built in 1641, is one of the oldest and biggest churches in the country.

On the outskirts of town, past the new market near the tower, is a small cemetery, hidden away in the hills. It's worth photographing in the late afternoon. Mindoro Beach, about four km south-west of Vigan, is not particularly recommended, but there is a tobacco factory and a small pottery place on the way.

Places to Stay

Luzon Hotel in General Luna St has basic rooms for P35/70 and with fan for P45/90. The doors are locked at 9 pm. *Venus Inn* in Quezon Ave has rooms with fan for P50/80 and with air-con and bath for P180/250. It is clean and fairly good. The air-con rooms have wide beds, and there is a restaurant.

Grandpa's Inn (tel 2118) at 1 Bonifacio St is fairly good. It has dorm beds for P35, and rooms with fan and bath for P88 and with air-con and bath for P176.

The Cordillera Inn (tel 2526) at 29 Mena Crisologo St is good value with rooms with fan for P50/100 and with air-con and bath for P340/380.

Vigan Hotel in Burgos St has fairly good rooms with fan and bath for P115/160 and with air-con and bath for P200/275. It has running water in every room and also has a restaurant.

Places to Eat

The *Vigan Plaza Restaurant* in Florentino St has good sandwiches and Magnolia ice creams. The *Tower Café* and the *Unique Café*, both in Burgos St, have reduced their range to barbecues and beer.

You can get Filipino and Chinese meals, especially a good noodle soup, at the *Venus Restaurant* in the Venus Inn in Quezon Ave. Also in Quezon Ave is the *Victoria Restaurant*, which serves different menus each day. Near the Vigan Hotel is the *Cool Spot Restaurant*, a fine place well known for its good steaks. Half of it is open air and at night there is folkloric music.

If you want a beer after 9 pm, when most places close, you should try *Marius Place* in Quezon Ave. This folksy pub is open almost every day until after midnight. There is also the *Café Franziska*, next to the Times Transit Bus Terminal, the beer garden *PNB Snack*, near the Philippine National Bank, and several little pubs near the Philippine Rabbit Bus Terminal.

Getting There & Away

From Manila to Vigan, there are several Philippine Rabbit, Times Transit, Farina Trans and Maria de Leon buses a day. The trip takes over seven hours. Not all Laoag buses go right into town, so you have to go the rest of the way, from the highway to Vigan, by tricycle.

From San Fernando several Philippine Rabbit buses a day go to Vigan, leaving from the plaza. You can also board a bus from Manila to Vigan or Laoag there. This takes over two hours.

From Aparri to Vigan, there are only a few buses a day, going via Claveria. The first bus, which leaves at 1 am, is not good. A better bus is the Florida Liner, which leaves at about 3.30 am near the Shell petrol station. You can check in the night before, or you can take a jeepney to the new bridge, where you can board the bus from Tuguegarao to Vigan. The trip to Vigan takes 11 hours from Tuguegarao and nine hours from Aparri.

From Laoag to Vigan, there are many minibuses daily as well as Philippine Rabbit, Times Transit, Farina Trans and Maria de Leon buses bound for Manila or San Fernando (La Union). It takes two hours. You may possibly have to get off the bus on the highway outside the town, and complete the last stretch to Vigan by tricycle (this costs P2).

Vigan to Bangued & Sagada

An unusual way of getting to Sagada is by crossing Abra Province. At the time of writing, there was sporadic fighting between the military and the NPA in the south of the province so it is best to check with local authorities in Vigan first before undertaking this route.

Several minibuses a day travel from Vigan

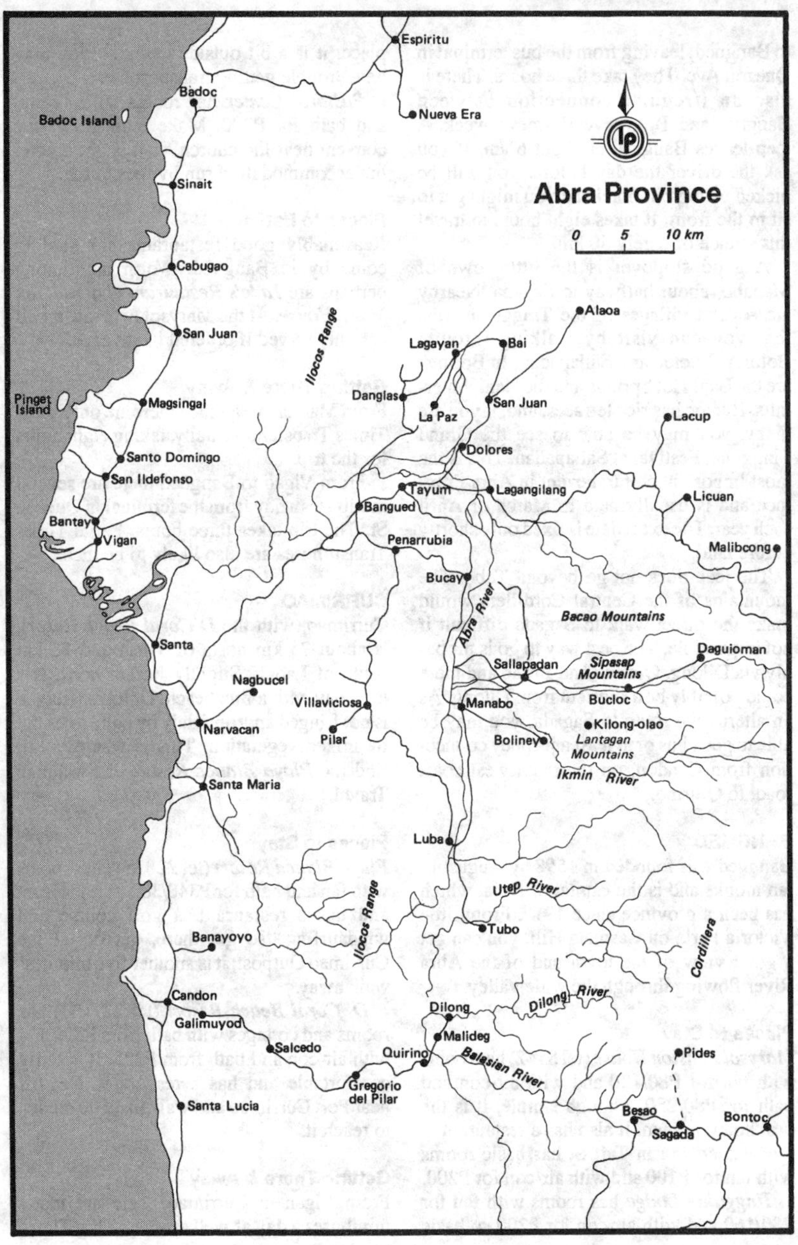
Abra Province
0 5 10 km
Espiritu
Badoc
Badoc Island
Nueva Era
Sinait
Cabugao
San Juan
Ilocos Range
Pinget Island
Magsingal
Santo Domingo
San Ildefonso
Bantay
Vigan
Santa
Nagbucel
Narvacan
Villaviciosa
Pilar
Santa Maria
Banayoyo
Candon
Galimuyod
Salcedo
Santa Lucia
Alaoa
Lagayan
Bai
Danglas
La Paz
San Juan
Lacup
Dolores
Tayum
Lagangilang
Licuan
Bangued
Penarrubia
Malibcong
Bucay
Abra River
Bacao Mountains
Sallapadan
Sipasap Mountains
Daguioman
Bucloc
Manabo
Kilong-olao
Boliney
Lantagan Mountains
Ikmin River
Luba
Utep River
Tubo
Cordillera
Dilong
Dilong River
Malideg
Quirino
Balasian River
Gregorio del Pilar
Pides
Besao
Sagada
Bontoc

to Bangued, leaving from the bus terminal in Quezon Ave. They take three hours. There is also an irregular connection between Bangued and Tubo several times a week. A jeep leaves Bangued at about 6 am. If you ask the driver the day before, you will be picked up at your hotel and you might get to sit in the front. It takes eight hours to travel this stretch of barely 50 km.

A good stopover is the little town of Manabo, about halfway to Sagada. Nearby are several villages of the Tingguian tribe that you can visit by walking through Boliney, Bucloc and Sallapadan. In Boliney are the Bani Hot Springs and the Nani Waterfalls. Bucloc has rice terraces, and, if you are lucky, you may be able to see the Grand Tingguian Festival at Sallapadan. This is the most important cultural event in Abra Province and is usually held in March or April each year. The exact date is fixed only shortly beforehand.

The jeep does not go beyond Tubo. The mountains of the Central Cordillera would make the direct walk to Sagada difficult if not impossible. The best way to go is probably via Dilong, Quirino and Besao and there could possibly be a shortcut from Dilong. As an alternative route to Sagada, you may be able to get a bus or at least a jeepney connection from Candon, on the main west coast road, to Quirino.

BANGUED

Bangued was founded in 1598 by Augustinian monks and is the capital of Abra, which has been a province since 1917. From little Victoria Park, on Casmata Hill, you can get a good view of the town and of the Abra River flowing through the wide valley.

Places to Stay

Marysol Pension House (tel 8542) has rooms with fan for P80/120 and with air-con and bath for P80/250. Though simple, it is the best hotel in town. It also has a restaurant.

Bangued Inn in Taft St has basic rooms with fan for P100 and with air-con for P200.

Tingguian Lodge has rooms with fan for P80/160 and with air-con for P200. A basic place, it is a bit outside town, so you may have trouble getting transport there.

Pastoral Center has rooms with air-con and bath for P200. Make inquiries at the convent near the church, as it is not a hotel but accommodation run by the church.

Places to Eat

Reasonably good restaurants are hard to come by in Bangued. Worth mentioning perhaps are *Jade's Restaurant* and *Yan Yan Mami House*. At the Marysol Pension, meals are only served if ordered in advance.

Getting There & Away

From Manila to Bangued there are only a few Times Transit buses daily, taking eight hours for the trip.

From Vigan to Bangued there are several minibuses a day from the terminal in Quezon St. The trip takes three hours. Large Times Transit buses are also likely to be there.

CURRIMAO

Currimao, with the *D'Coral Beach Resort*, is about 75 km north of Vigan and 25 km south of Laoag. Slightly further north is a long bay with a fine beach. Unfortunately, it is not fringed appropriately by palm trees but by mixed vegetation. This is where you'll find the *Playa Blanca Resort* of Swagman Travel.

Places to Stay

Playa Blanca Resort (tel 220784) has rooms with fan and bath for P340/380. It is pleasant and has a restaurant, a golf course and windsurfing. To get there, get off at the Currimao Outpost; it is another five minutes' walk away.

D' Coral Beach Resort (tel 221133) has rooms and cottages with bath from P250 and with air-con and bath from P325. It is fairly comfortable and has a restaurant. Get off near Port Currimao and walk just 500 metres to reach it.

Getting There & Away

From Vigan to Currimao, there are many minibuses a day as well as several big Times

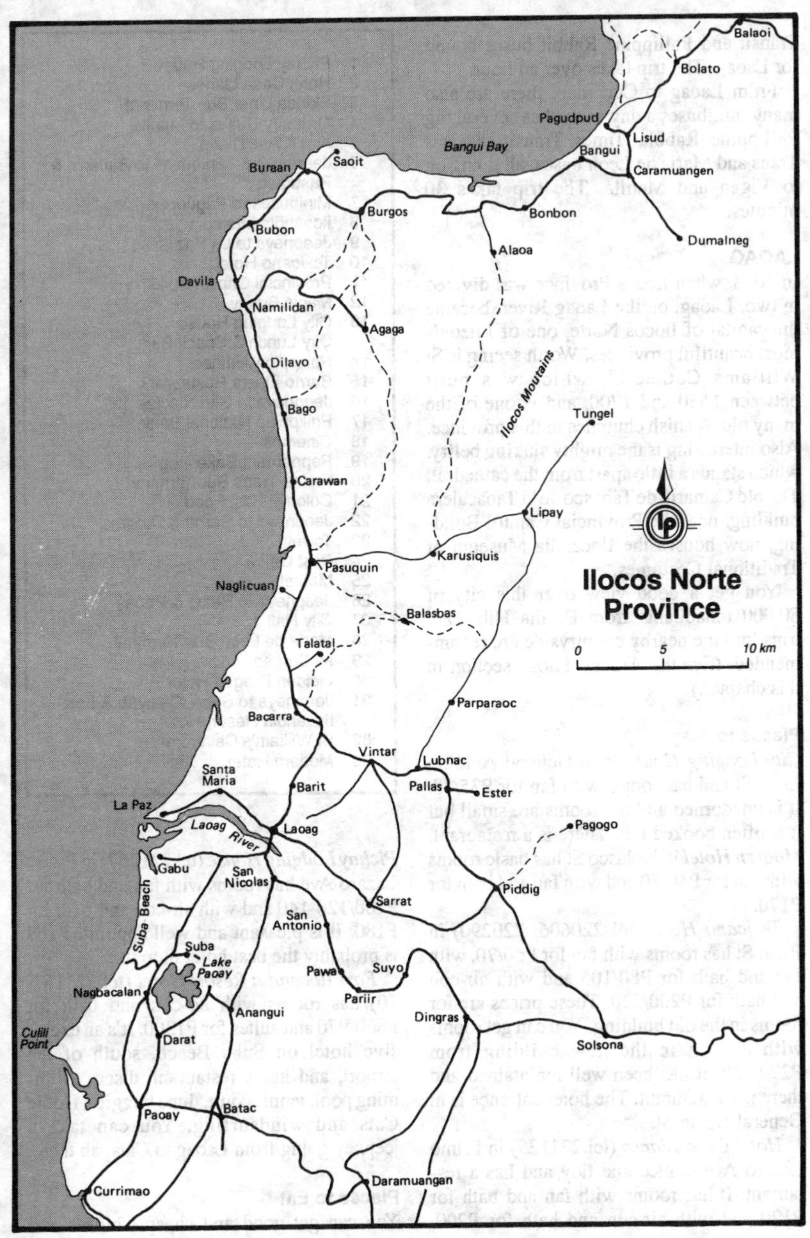
Ilocos Norte Province
0
5
10 km
Balaoi
Bolato
Pagudpud
Lisud
Bangui Bay
Bangui
Caramuangen
Saoit
Buraan
Burgos
Bonbon
Dumalneg
Bubon
Alaoa
Davila
Namilidan
Agaga
Dilavo
Ilocos Moutains
Bago
Tungel
Carawan
Lipay
Karusiquis
Pasuquin
Naglicuan
Balasbas
Talatal
Parparaoc
Bacarra
Vintar
Lubnac
Santa Maria
Barit
Pallas
Ester
La Paz
Laoag River
Laoag
Pagogo
Gabu
San Nicolas
Suba Beach
Sarrat
Piddig
San Antonio
Suba
Lake Paoay
Suyo
Pawa
Pariir
Nagbacalan
Anangui
Dingras
Culili Point
Darat
Solsona
Paoay
Batac
Currimao
Daramuangan

Transit and Philippine Rabbit buses bound for Laoag. The trip takes over an hour.

From Laoag to Currimao, there are also many minibuses a day as well as several big Philippine Rabbit, Times Transit, Farinas Trans and Maria de Leon buses, all going on to Vigan and Manila. The trip takes 30 minutes.

LAOAG

In 1818, when Ilocos Province was divided in two, Laoag, on the Laoag River, became the capital of Ilocos Norte, one of Luzon's most beautiful provinces. Worth seeing is St Williams Cathedral, which was built between 1650 and 1700, and is one of the many old Spanish churches in this province. Also interesting is the mighty sinking belfry, which stands a little apart from the cathedral. The old Camarin de Tabasco de la Tabacalera building, near the Provincial Capitol Building, now houses the Ilocandia Museum of Traditional Costumes.

You get a good view over this city of 80,000 inhabitants from Ermita Hill. Day trips into the nearby countryside are recommended. (See the Around Laoag section in this chapter.)

1 Pichay Lodging House
2 Hotel Casa Llanes
3 Florida Liner Bus Terminal
4 Ordinary Buses to Manila
5 Fire & Ash Disco
6 Jeepneys & Minibuses to Bacarra & Pasuquin
7 Minibuses to Pagudpud
8 Ilocandia Museum
9 Jeepneys to La Paz
10 Texicano Hotel
11 Provincial Capitol Building
12 Magic Bunny
13 City Lodging House
City Lunch & Snack Bar
14 Philippine Airlines
15 Barrio Fiesta Restaurant
16 Jeepneys to San Nicolas
17 Philippine National Bank
18 Cinemas
19 Peppermint Bakeshop
20 Farina Trans Bus Terminal
21 Colonial Fast Food
22 Jeepneys to Sarrat & Dingras
23 Tower
24 Post Office
25 Market
26 Jeepneys to Batac & Paoay
27 City Hall
28 Maria de Leon Bus Terminal
29 McBurgee
30 Golden Dragon Hotel
31 Jeepneys to Suba, Calayab & Fort Ilocandia Resort Hotel
32 St William's Cathedral
33 Modern Hotel

Places to Stay

City Lodging House is in General Antonio Luna St and has rooms with fan for P35/70. It is unadorned and the rooms are small but it is often booked out. There is a restaurant. *Modern Hotel* in Nolasco St has basic rooms with fan for P40/80 and with fan and bath for P170.

Texicano Hotel (tel 220606, 220290) in Rizal St has rooms with fan for P60/70, with fan and bath for P80/105 and with air-con and bath for P200/230. These prices are for rooms in the old building. You can get rooms with air-con in the new building from P270/320. It has been well maintained and there is a restaurant. The hotel entrance is in General Hizon St.

Hotel Casa Llanes (tel 221125) in Primo Lazaro Ave is nice and tidy and has a restaurant. It has rooms with fan and bath for P120 and with air-con and bath for P200.

Pichay Lodging House (tel 221267) in Primo Lazaro Ave has rooms with fan and bath for P100/120-140 and with air-con and bath for P180. It is pleasant and well appointed and is probably the best hotel in town.

Fort Ilocandia Resort Hotel (tel 221167-70) has rooms with air-con and bath for P860/970 and suites for P1300. It's an exclusive hotel on Suba Beach, south of the airport, and has a restaurant, disco, swimming pool, tennis court, dune buggies, Hobie Cats and windsurfing. You can take a jeepney going from Laoag to Calayab there.

Places to Eat

You can get good and cheap Chinese and

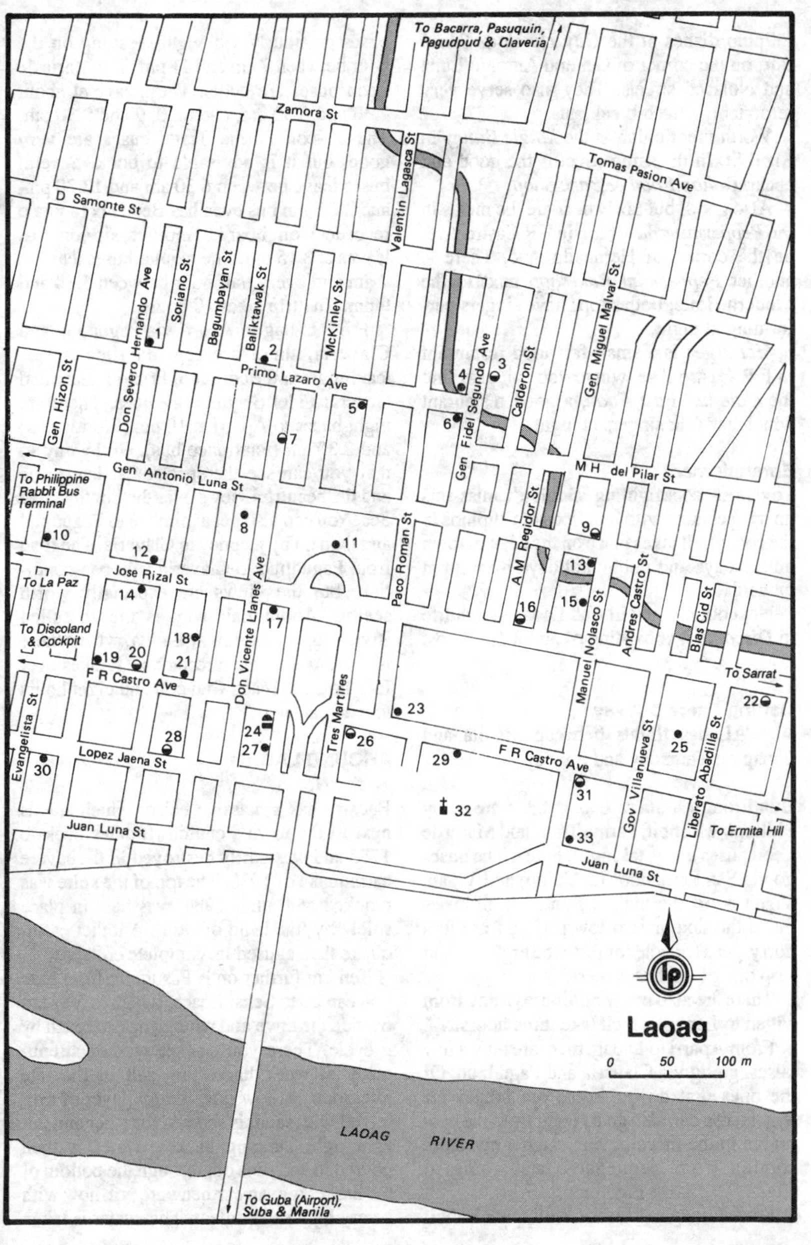

To Bacarra, Pasuquin, Pagudpud & Claveria
Zamora St
Tomas Pasion Ave
D Samonte St
Valentin Lagasca St
Don Severo Hernando Ave
Soriano St
Bagumbayan St
Baliktawak St
McKinley St
Gen Miguel Malvar St
Gen Hizon St
Primo Lazaro Ave
Gen Fidel Segundo Ave
Calderon St
Gen Antonio Luna St
M H del Pilar St
To Philippine Rabbit Bus Terminal
A M Regidor St
Paco Roman St
Jose Rizal St
To La Paz
Don Vicente Llanes Ave
To Discoland & Cockpit
Manuel Nolasco St
Andres Castro St
Blas Cid St
F R Castro Ave
To Sarrat
Tres Martires
Gov Villanueva St
Liberato Abadilla St
Evangelista St
Lopez Jaena St
Juan Luna St
To Ermita Hill
Laoag
0 50 100 m
LAOAG RIVER
To Guba (Airport), Suba & Manila

Filipino dishes at the *City Lunch & Snack Bar*, on the corner of General Antonio Luna and Nolasco streets. They also serve very reasonably priced breakfasts.

Worth mentioning is the *Magic Bunny* in Rizal St. In the same street is the good and cheap *Dohan Food & Bake Shop*.

Also good, but fairly dear are the meals in the *Peppermint Bakeshop* in F R Castro Ave, on the corner of Hernando Ave. There is another *Peppermint Bakeshop* next to the Modern Hotel; both shops have singers performing at night.

McBurgee is a small fast-food restaurant in F R Castro Ave, where you can also find the *Colonial Fast Food*, a good restaurant which has folk singers at night.

Entertainment

Lovers of cockfighting shouldn't miss this noisy spectacle with hundreds of Filipinos in the cockpit. It takes place on the edge of town on Sundays and public holidays from 2 pm onwards.

Next door, you will find Laoag's nightlife in *Discoland*, consisting of about 10 discos.

Getting There & Away

Air PAL has flights between Manila and Laoag on Thursday and Sunday.

Bus From Manila to Laoag, there are many Philippine Rabbit, Farina Trans and Maria de Leon buses a day, taking 10 hours. The buses go via San Fernando (La Union) and Vigan. Vigan is off the highway and not all buses make the detour into town. If you are in a hurry, get a tricycle for P2 to the highway and stop one of the buses there.

There are also many minibuses a day from Vigan to Laoag, which take three hours.

From Aparri to Laoag, there are only a few buses, going via Claveria and Pagudpud. Of the ones that do go, some are bound for Vigan. You can also go by jeepney to the new bridge in the morning and catch a bus there coming from Tuguegarao and going to Vigan. This takes eight hours.

From Laoag to Manila, Philippine Rabbit buses go hourly via Vigan, leaving on the hour between 7 am and 11 pm. The Maria de Leon buses are better. They leave at about 7.30 and 8.30 am, and 8.30, 9 and 9.30 pm. The air-con Farina Trans buses are very good, but it is advisable to book. Several buses leave between 6.30 am and 12.30 pm, and the 7 pm bus even has Betamax (a video recorder) on board. Another air-con bus leaves at 8.15 pm. The regular buses leave at 7 am and every half hour between 5.30 and 9 pm. The trip takes 10 hours.

From Laoag to Aparri via Pagudpud and Claveria, there are few daytime buses, leaving from the corner of Primo Lazaro and General Fidel Segundo avenues. There are night buses to Aparri at 10 pm (Florida bus) and 2.30 am (Pantranco bus). Go by day so that you can see the spectacular landscape and the beautiful views over the South China Sea. You can also get a minibus to Pagudpud and then go by jeepney to Claveria. The road from Pagudpud to Claveria is in bad condition, but the views are especially worth seeing. About half way is the so-called Riviera of the North, at Banua, where there is also a government resthouse. It takes over four hours to reach Claveria and eight hours to reach Aparri.

AROUND LAOAG

To the North

Bacarra has a massive belfry which stands next to the town's church. It dates back to 1783 and was partly destroyed in the severe earthquake of 1930. The top of the spire was crooked and, until 1984, was held in place solely by 'the hand of God'. Another earthquake then caused its complete collapse.

Ten km further on is Pasuquin; from here you can go to Seksi Beach, which is four km outside the town and which you can reach by tricycle. There you can see women strenuously at work harvesting salt in the late afternoon. At low tide, the top layer of salt, mixed with sand, is scraped together and put in a light hanging basket. Water is then poured in and runs out through the bottom of the basket into an earthenware pot, now with a very high salt content. This water is taken to the village and boiled in a large pot until it has almost completely evaporated. The remaining slurry is then ladled out of the pot into a hanging basket, which the remaining water seeps through to form a long, hanging white cone of the finest salt.

To the West

The nearest good beach to Laoag is in La Paz, an unhurried, long drawn-out place at the mouth of the Laoag River. Hardly any vegetation exists on the wide beach, but there are very extensive sand dunes.

To the South-East

A fine country road leads to Sarrat, the birthplace of former president Marcos. The house he was born in, now the Marcos Museum, is full of mementos of his family. It is open Monday to Saturday from 8 am to noon and from 2 to 5 pm, and on Sunday from 8 am to noon and from 1 to 4 pm. Closer to the centre is the restored Sarrat Church and Convent, built in 1779 by Augustinian monks.

Only ruins remain of the church in Dingras, which was destroyed by fire in 1838.

To the South

There is a church in San Nicolas which was built in the latter part of the 17th century and restored in the 19th century. In Batac is the so-called Malacanang del Norte, formerly the vast domain of Marcos and today a public museum.

A few km to the south-west is the fortress-like church of Paoay, which is worth a stop. Its side walls are supported by strong posts. Styled in 'earthquake baroque', this church is probably the most famous in Ilocos Norte. You can also see the scenically attractive Lake Paoay. Going from Paoay through bamboo forests, along the western shore of the lake to Suba, you could make a detour to Suba Beach. The road there is hilly and winding and there are high, extensive sand dunes, more imposing than those at La Paz, where many Philippine films have been shot. It is usually windy on this wide beach and there is good surf.

If you have come up from Paoay by tricycle and want to return to Laoag by jeepney, ask the driver to drop you off at the Fort Ilocandia Resort Hotel or at the Suba Golf Course. The last regular jeepney leaves the hotel at about 4 pm and passes the golf course on the way back to Laoag. The exclusive hotel is about five km south of Gabu, where Laoag Airport is located. Marcos had it built specially for guests on the occasion of the wedding of his daughter Irene to Greggy Araneta in 1983. The tables and seats under cover on the beach belong to the hotel and may be used free of charge. The restaurant is surprisingly cheap.

PAGUDPUD

Pagudpud lies on Bangui Bay, about 60 km north of Laoag, and could become a tourist destination in the near future. The beautiful Sand White Beach at Pagudpud is probably the best and most attractive in North Luzon.

The *Villa del Mar* has simple rooms for P50 to P150 and spacious cottages with two rooms and a kitchen for P300 to P500. Another resort is currently under construction.

Getting There & Away

Buses from Vigan and Laoag to Aparri and Tuguegarao go via Pagudpud. The trip to Pagudpud takes two hours from Laoag and seven hours from Aparri. From Laoag there are several minibuses a day for Pagudpud leaving from Don Vicente Llanes Ave.

CLAVERIA

If you want to sunbathe at Waikiki Beach, you don't have to fly to Hawaii. Claveria too has a Waikiki Beach. It has the same name because of its supposed similarity to the world-famous beach of Honolulu, but that is hardly justified. The NPA is also very active in the surroundings of Claveria.

South of Claveria live the Ita tribespeople. They are Negrito who still go hunting with bow and arrow. If you want to visit them, you have to go about eight km by tricycle and then walk another four km. On the way there you will pass the village of Santa Filomena.

You can make side trips from Claveria to the Babuyan Islands. There is a passenger boat once a week to Calayan Island, north-east of Dalupiri which takes five hours. From Calayan Island, there are boats going to Babuyan Island, further north-east, taking four hours. The people there live in almost total seclusion from modern civilisation. It is suggested that visitors take a few presents or objects for barter even though the value of money is known there. You can sleep and eat at the priest's or the mayor's house.

The 837 metre high Babuyan Claro Volcano, with its two craters, on Babuyan Island is worth seeing. Fuga Island is supposed to be the most beautiful of the Babuyan Islands. As it is the private property of Mr Lim, you need a visitor's permit, which you can get at his timber yard in Claveria. However, the manager or other person authorised to issue a permit is seldom there.

Places to Stay

The cottages on the beach at Claveria were destroyed by a severe typhoon in September 1987, but you can stay in the house of the former owner of Sun Beach Cottages who now runs the Grassroots Restaurants in Claveria.

There is supposed to be accommodation at Taggat, a few km west of Claveria, in the *Company House* and the *Public House* for P30/60. Both houses are adjoining, but they are not designated as hotels. They are about a one-km walk from the bus stop.

Between Claveria and Taggat, next to the Shell petrol station, is the *Traveller's Inn*. This is an old house without electricity, where you can stay for P20.

Getting There & Away

From Aparri to Claveria, there are a few buses daily headed for Laoag or Vigan. The trip takes four hours.

From Tuguegarao to Claveria, there is a daily bus going on to Vigan, which takes five hours.

From Claveria to Aparri, there is a daily AML bus at about 10 am. Additional buses come from Laoag, but the seats are mostly booked out. You can stop the buses in the main street. They take four hours.

There is a daily Pantranco North bus from Claveria to Tuguegarao and Manila at 10 am. This bus also goes close to Aparri. If you want to stop there, get off at the new bridge and continue by jeepney. It takes five hours to get to Tuguegarao and 14 hours to get to Manila.

From Vigan and Laoag to Claveria there are few buses. It takes between four and six hours or more (see the Getting There & Away sections under Vigan and Laoag).

APARRI

It's not worth staying in Aparri, unless you want to do some deep-sea fishing. Big-game fishing is popular in the Babuyan Channel, north of Luzon. The waters around Point Escarpada, near San Vicente, are well known as the best Philippine fishing grounds for marlin. If you want to explore this north-eastern corner of Luzon, you should take the bus from Aparri to Santa Ana. You will have to continue by tricycle to San Vicente if there is no bus or jeepney. From there you can get somebody to take you across to Palaui Island by outrigger boat.

Places to Stay & Eat

Victoria Hotel in De Riviera St has rooms for P30/60. It's basic but fairly clean accommodation. *Pipo Hotel* at 37 Macanaya District has simple rooms with fan for P40/80 and with fan and bath for P60/100, and also has a restaurant.

Dreamland Hotel has rooms with fan for P40/60, with fan and bath for P60/100, and with air-con and bath for P100/150. It's a reasonable place but the rooms in the adjoining bungalow are better than those in the main building. Apart from the *Magnolia Restaurant*, down near the river, this hotel's restaurant is probably the only decent one in town.

Getting There & Away

From Manila to Aparri, there are daily Pantranco North buses more or less hourly.

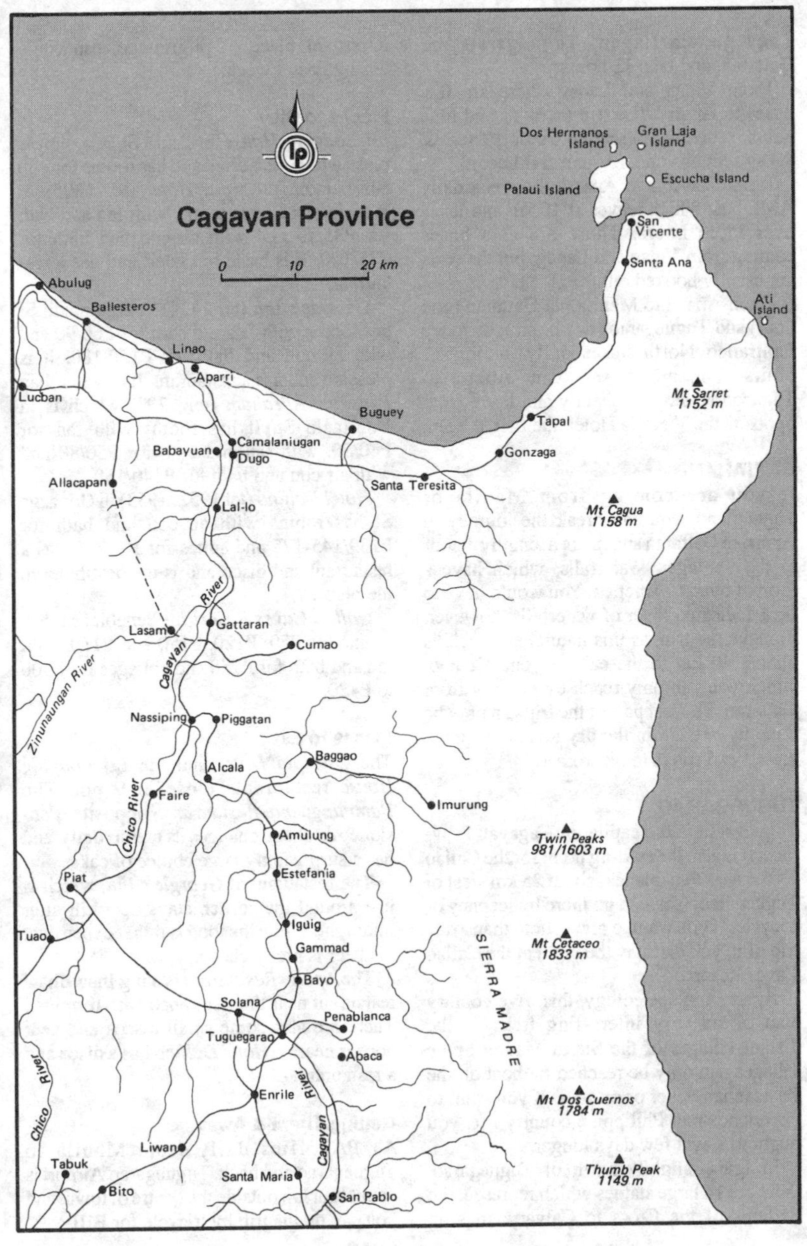
Cagayan Province
0 10 20 km
Dos Hermanos Island
Gran Laja Island
Escucha Island
Palaui Island
San Vicente
Santa Ana
Ati Island
Abulug
Ballesteros
Linao
Aparri
Lucban
Mt Sarret 1152 m
Buguey
Tapal
Camalaniugan
Babayuan
Dugo
Gonzaga
Allacapan
Santa Teresita
Mt Cagua 1158 m
Lal-lo
Cagayan River
Gattaran
Lasam
Cumao
Zinunaungan River
Nassiping
Piggatan
Baggao
Alcala
Chico River
Faire
Imurung
Twin Peaks 981/1603 m
Amulung
Estefania
Piat
Iguig
Tuao
Mt Cetaceo 1833 m
Gammad
SIERRA MADRE
Bayo
Solana
Penablanca
Tuguegarao
Abaca
Enrile
Mt Dos Cuernos 1784 m
Chico River
Liwan
Thumb Peak 1149 m
Tabuk
Bito
Santa Maria
San Pablo

They go via Ilagan, Tuguegarao and Gattaran, and take 11 hours.

From Vigan and Laoag, there are few buses to Aparri. The trip takes 11 and nine hours respectively (see the Getting There & Away sections under Vigan and Laoag).

From Claveria to Aparri, there is a daily AML bus, which leaves at 10 am and takes over three hours. There are also buses coming from Vigan and Laoag, but the seats are usually booked out.

From Aparri to Manila via Gattaran (one hour) and Tuguegarao (two hours), there are Pantranco North buses daily, taking 11 hours. The minibuses from Aparri to Tuguegarao stop frequently and leave from opposite the Victoria Hotel, the first at 7 am.

GATTARAN

If you are coming from Manila or Tuguegarao, you can break the journey to Aparri in Gattaran and make a lengthy detour to the Tanlagan Waterfalls, which have a drop of over 100 metres. You would have to be a dedicated lover of waterfalls, however, to make the trip, as this natural spectacle is almost 40 km to the east, beyond Cumao, which you can only reach by jeepney from Gattaran. The last part of the trip can only be done by vehicle in the dry season, as there are several rivers to be crossed.

TUGUEGARAO

Tuguegarao is the capital of Cagayan Province. It is also the starting point for the Callao Caves near Penablanca, about 25 km west of Tuguegarao. You can go there by jeepney or tricycle. If you want to make more than a day trip of it, you can stay the night at the Callao Caves Resort.

Apart from speleology, this cave country also offers very interesting treks to the distant villages of the Sierra Madre. Some villages can only be reached by boat on the Pinacanuan River or on foot. If you want to experience real Philippine country life, you ought to stay a few days longer.

In Iguig, slightly north of Tuguegarao, there are 14 large statues which represent the Stations of the Cross to Calvary. It is an important place of pilgrimage, especially during Easter week.

Places to Stay

LB Lodging House in Luna St is a simple place with a restaurant and has rooms for P30 per person. *Olympia Hotel* (tel 1805) in Washington St has rooms with fan and bath for P35/79 and with air-con and bath for P75/100. It is basic but good and has a restaurant.

Georgie's Inn (tel 1434) in Aguinaldo St has rooms with fan and bath for P60/90 and with air-con and bath for P150/180. It is pleasant and has a restaurant. It is better than *Pensione Abraham* (tel 1793) which is in Bonifacio St. It has rooms with fan for P40/50, with fan and bath for P50/80 and with air-con and bath for P140/150.

Hotel Delfino (tel 1952, 1953) in Gonzaga St has rooms with air-con and bath for P109/145-175 and suites for P218. It has a restaurant and disco and is the best hotel in the place.

Callao Caves Resort, in Penablanca, has rooms for P50, P120, P150 and P160, with fan and bath for P150 and cottages for P300 to P420.

Places to Eat

The *Olympia Hotel* and the *LB Lodging House* restaurants close at 9 pm. The *Pampanguena Restaurant*, opposite Pensione Abraham, changes its menus daily, and has a surprisingly large choice of cakes.

The restaurant at *Georgie's Inn*, which is just around the corner, stays open till after midnight. While the food is rather expensive, the beer is pretty cheap.

The *Apollo Restaurant* is a big Ihaw-Ihaw restaurant near the Pantranco Bus Terminal. There are also some small discos and beer houses nearby. *Hotel Delfino* has a disco and a restaurant.

Getting There & Away

Air PAL flies daily from Manila to Tuguegarao and back. Tuguegarao Airport is about four km outside the centre of town, and you can do the trip by tricycle for P10.

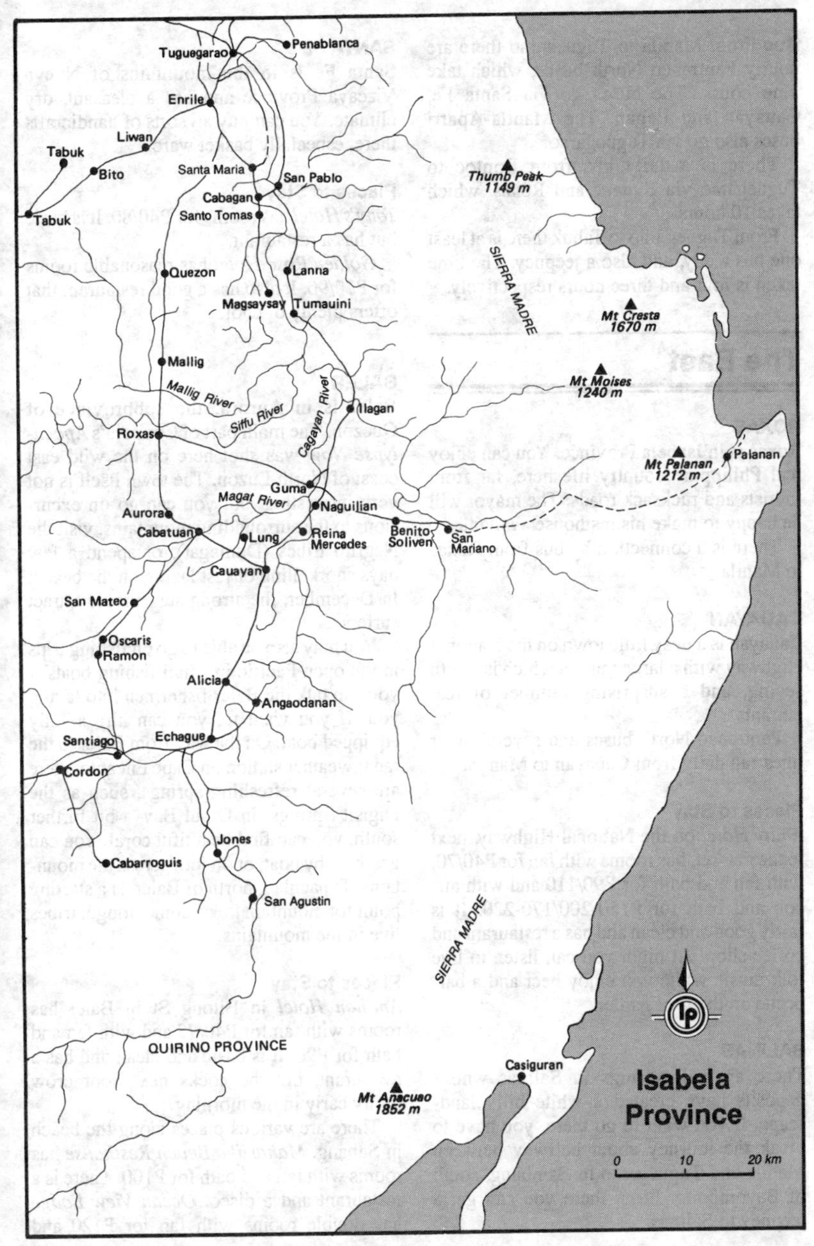
Tuguegarao
Penablanca
Enrile
Liwan
Tabuk
Bito
Tabuk
Santa Maria
San Pablo
Cabagan
Santo Tomas
Quezon
Lanna
Magsaysay
Tumauini
Mallig
Mallig River
Siffu River
Cagayan River
Ilagan
Roxas
Guma
Magat River
Naguilian
Aurora
Cabatuan
Lung
Reina Mercedes
Benito Soliven
San Mariano
Cauayan
San Mateo
Oscaris
Ramon
Alicia
Angaodanan
Santiago
Echague
Cordon
Jones
Cabarroguis
San Agustin
QUIRINO PROVINCE
Thumb Peak 1149 m
SIERRA MADRE
Mt Cresta 1670 m
Mt Moises 1240 m
Mt Palanan 1212 m
Palanan
SIERRA MADRE
Casiguran
Mt Anacuao 1852 m
Isabela Province
0 10 20 km

Bus From Manila to Tuguegarao there are hourly Pantranco North buses, which take nine hours. The buses go via Santa Fe, Cauayan and Ilagan. The Manila-Aparri buses also go via Tuguegarao.

There is a daily bus from Bontoc to Tuguegarao via Banaue and Roxas, which takes 10 hours.

From Tuguegarao to Tabuk there is at least one bus a day, and also a jeepney. The time taken is four and three hours respectively.

The East

ROXAS

Roxas is in Isabela Province. You can enjoy real Philippine country life here, far from tourists and rucksack roads. The mayor will be happy to make his resthouse available.

There is a connection by bus from Roxas to Manila.

CAUAYAN

Cauayan is a busy little town on the National Highway with a large market which is worth seeing, and a surprising number of restaurants.

Pantranco North buses and several other lines run daily from Cauayan to Manila.

Places to Stay

Amity Hotel on the National Highway, next to the market, has rooms with fan for P40/70, with fan and bath for P90/110 and with aircon and bath for P150-200/170-220. It is fairly good and clean and has a restaurant and coffee shop. At night you can listen to live folk music while you enjoy beer and a barbecue on the roof garden.

SALINAS

There are salt springs in Salinas whose deposits have created a white hilly landscape. If you want to go there, you have to break the journey about halfway between Manila and Tuguegarao in Bambang, south of Bayombong. From there you can get a jeepney to Salinas.

SANTA FE

Santa Fe is in the mountains of Nueva Vizcaya Province and has a pleasant, dry climate. You can buy all sorts of handicrafts there, especially basket ware.

Places to Stay

Tony's Hotel has rooms for P40/80. It is basic but has a restaurant.

Golden Rose Hotel has reasonable rooms for P70/90. It also has a good restaurant that offers plenty of choice.

BALER

Baler is in Aurora, the subprovince of Quezon. The main part of Coppola's *Apocalypse Now* was shot here on the wild east coast of North Luzon. The town itself is not very interesting, but you can go on excursions to the surrounding mountains, visit the Negrito tribes (Dumagat), or spend a few days snorkelling or just lazing on the beach. In December, the strong surf should attract surfers.

You may also be able to go on fishing trips in the open Pacific in small fishing boats if you can talk the Baler fishermen into taking you. If you want to, you can hire a fully equipped boat. On the way from Baler to the radar weather station on Cape Encanto, there are several refreshing springs, such as the Digisit Springs. In Dibut Bay, a bit further south, you can find beautiful coral. You can get there by boat, or on foot across the mountains. Dipaculao, north of Baler, is a starting point for mountain treks; some Ilongot tribes live in the mountains.

Places to Stay

Amihan Hotel in Bitong St in Baler has rooms with fan for P40/75 and with fan and bath for P90. It is basic and clean and has a restaurant, but the cocks next door crow pretty early in the morning.

There are various places along the beach in Sabang. *Maharlika Beach Resthouse* has rooms with fan and bath for P100. There is a restaurant and a disco. *Ocean View Lodge* has double rooms with fan for P120 and

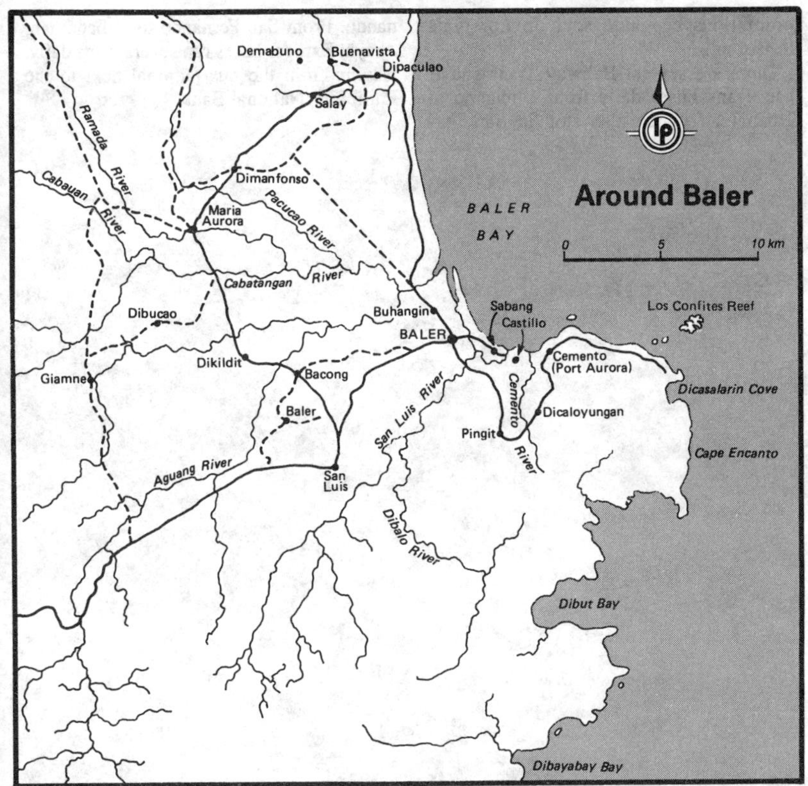

rooms with fan and bath for P100/150 and also has a restaurant. *MIA Surf & Sports Resort* has rooms with fan for P70/100. You can hire surfboards there and take surfing lessons.

If you want bigger surf than that at Sabang Beach, you can get a surf guide to take you to another beach.

Baler Guest House has rooms with fan for P60, with fan and bath for P100 and with air-con for P200.

Getting There & Away

There are several Pantranco North Buses a day from Manila to Cabanatuan, some of which also go through to Baler. You can either take a direct one or one labelled San Jose, Ilagan, Tuguegarao or Aparri. They take 2½ hours. If you are coming from the north, you have to change at Cabanatuan for Baler.

The last bus from Cabanatuan to Baler leaves at 3 pm. The road across the Sierra Madre is bumpy but the views are beautiful. If you are going towards Baler, you get the best view sitting on the left-hand side of the bus. The trip will take you four hours or more.

Roughly halfway, you will come to the entrance to the Aurora Memorial Park, where there are a few restaurants. The bus stops there for half an hour, long enough for a scrumptious eggcaldo soup in Lorelyn's Restaurant.

There are several Baliwag Trans and E Jose Trans buses daily from Olongapo to Cabanatuan which also stop in San Fernando. From San Fernando to Cabanatuan, Arayat Express buses run several trips daily, leaving from the bus terminal next to the Philippine National Bank.

South Luzon

The convoluted peninsula stretching south from Manila has an impressive, volcano-studded landscape which includes the Mayon Volcano. Mayon's symmetrical cone is said to be the most perfect in the world. It's one of the symbols of the Philippines and the most imposing feature of South Luzon. North of Mayon, hot springs dot the active geothermal area around Tiwi, while the slopes of Mt Isarog, near Naga, and Mt Iriga, near Iriga, are home to several Negrito tribes. Between Sorsogon and Matnog, Mt Bulusan, with its long spurs, has earned the area the name of 'the Switzerland of the Orient'.

Between Lucena City and Lamon Bay is the mountainous, heavily wooded Quezon National Park. Forget the little-known beach resorts from Atimonan to Gumaca: those at Daet and San Miguel Bay are better. Good beach weather is rarer here than in other parts of the islands, as the Pacific climate is usually rough. The best time to travel is in April and May. In June and July, thousands of jellyfish may arrive, heralding the typhoon season and making swimming impossible.

Buses go south from Manila through Lucena, Daet, Naga, Iriga and Legaspi. There are several buses daily from the Philtranco Terminal in EDSA, Pasay City. To travel right through to Legaspi takes between nine and 11 hours. There are air-con buses at 8 am and 7 and 8 pm.

The road to Legaspi, the main town in the south, is long and winding – particularly the stretch to Daet. If you want to, you can take one of the large Philtranco buses and follow the Philippine Highway all the way to Matnog at the southern tip.

South Luzon also makes a good departure point for travels to the islands of the Visayas.

LUCENA CITY

Only about three hours from Manila by bus, Lucena is one departure point for boats to Marinduque and Romblon; they leave from the river harbour of Cotta Port, just outside the town. To the north of Lucena, on the road to Pagsanjan, is the little town of Lucban, where you can get a fairly accurate idea of how towns looked in the time of the Spaniards. There is one hotel in Lucban.

It is worth travelling by minibus from Lucena to Quezon National Recreation Area, which is between Lucena and Atimonan. The Maharlika Highway crosses the park and is used by all the large buses, so it is better to take a minibus. These take the old zigzag road and stop at the picnic ground in the middle of the park. There are interesting walks through the jungle-like vegetation, with lovely flowers, monkeys and so on, but it's not so enjoyable if it's raining. If you want to continue south, you can take a minibus to Atimonan and change to a larger bus there.

Forget about Dalahican Beach, six km from Lucena – it's dirty and swampy.

Places to Stay

The *Lucena Fresh Air Hotel & Resort* (tel 712424, 713031) is in the Isabang district, at the edge of the town, on the left as you come from Manila. Singles/doubles with fan cost P55/70, with fan and bath P88-110/103-125 and with air-con and bath P204/219. The rooms have pleasant balconies and you can use the restaurant, swimming pool and other facilities. It's probably become more expensive of late, so perhaps you should ask about the *Tourist Hotel* (tel 714456), which has a restaurant, where singles with fan cost P40, singles/doubles with fan and bath cost P60/80, and with air-con and bath cost P90/110.

Getting There & Away

Plenty of Philtranco, Superlines and BLTB buses go from Manila to Lucena every day. They may be going only as far as Lucena or

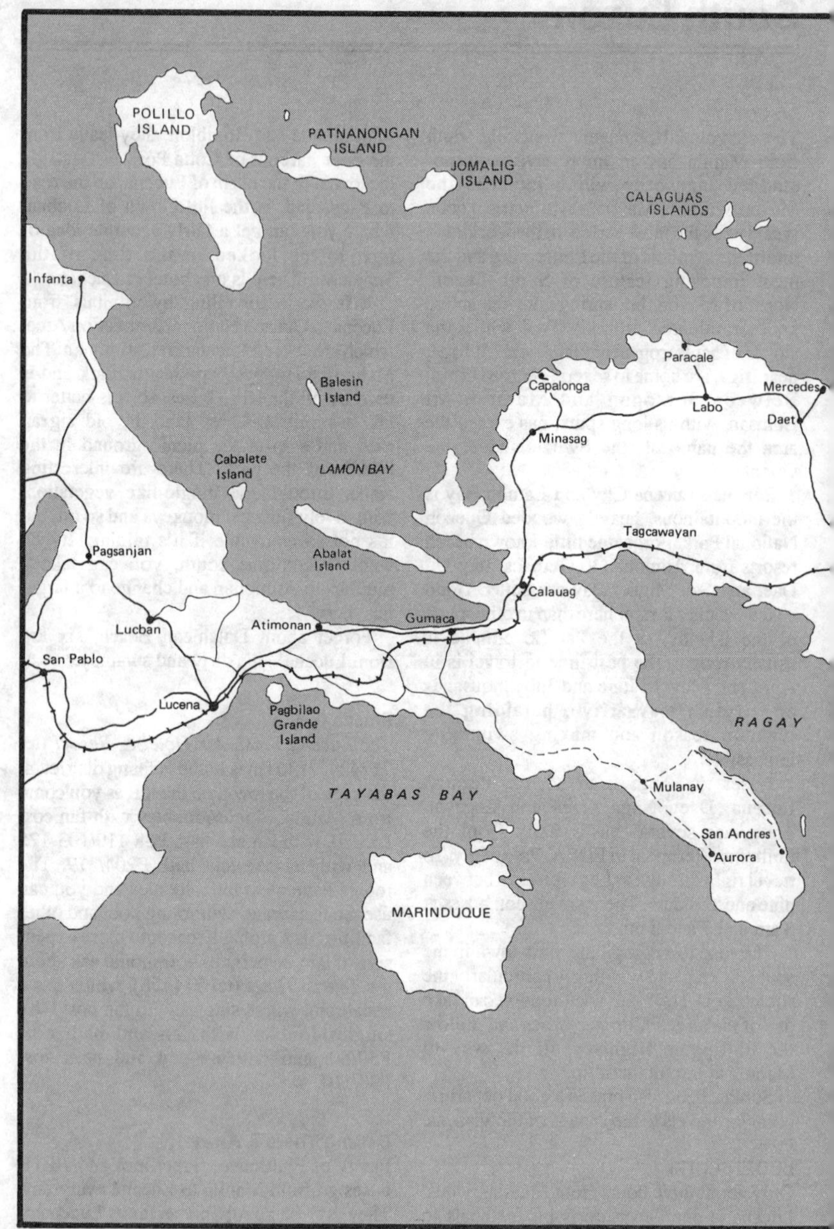
POLILLO ISLAND
PATNANONGAN ISLAND
JOMALIG ISLAND
CALAGUAS ISLANDS
Infanta
Paracale
Capalonga
Mercedes
Balesin Island
Labo
Daet
Minasag
Cabalete Island
LAMON BAY
Tagcawayan
Pagsanjan
Abalat Island
Calauag
Lucban
Atimonan
Gumaca
San Pablo
Lucena
Pagbilao Grande Island
RAGAY
Mulanay
TAYABAS BAY
San Andres
Aurora
MARINDUQUE

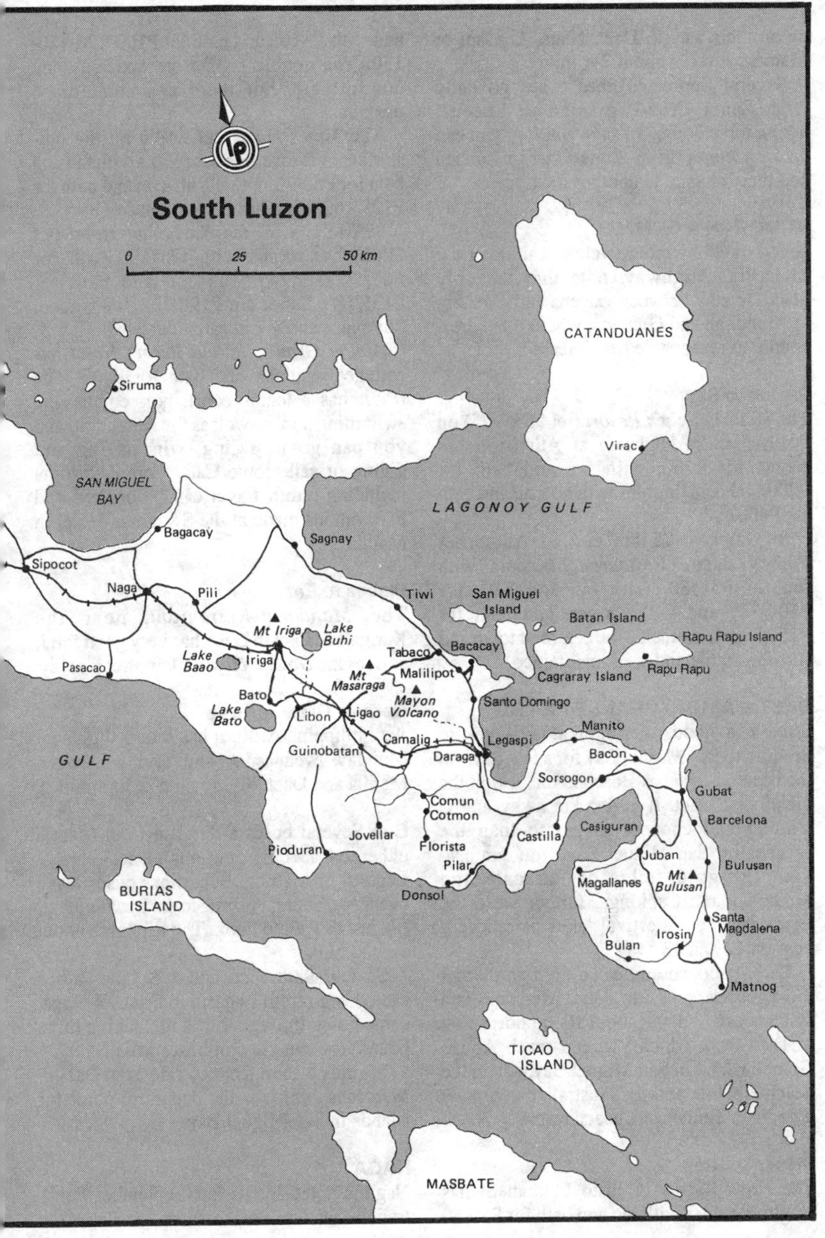
South Luzon
0
25
50 km
CATANDUANES
Siruma
Virac
SAN MIGUEL BAY
LAGONOY GULF
Bagacay
Sagnay
Sipocot
Naga
Pili
Tiwi
San Miguel Island
Batan Island
Mt Iriga
Lake Buhi
Rapu Rapu Island
Lake Baao
Iriga
Tabaco
Bacacay
Pasacao
Mt Masaraga
Malilipot
Rapu Rapu
Cagraray Island
Mayon Volcano
Bato
Santo Domingo
Lake Bato
Libon
Ligao
Manito
GULF
Camalig
Legaspi
Guinobatan
Daraga
Bacon
Sorsogon
Gubat
Comun
Cotmon
Barcelona
Casiguran
Jovellar
Castilla
Florista
Pioduran
Juban
Bulusan
Pilar
Mt Bulusan
Magallanes
BURIAS ISLAND
Donsol
Santa Magdalena
Irosin
Bulan
Matnog
TICAO ISLAND
MASBATE

be on their way to Daet, Naga, Legaspi or Matnog. It takes about 2½ hours.

Several Supreme Lines buses go daily from Santa Cruz/Pagsanjan to Lucena, taking three hours. To save waiting, you can take a jeepney from Santa Cruz to Lucban and there change to another for Lucena.

ATIMONAN & GUMACA

If you travel by motorcycle or car along the Maharlika Highway, note that the only places to stay between Lucena and Daet are at Atimonan and Gumaca, where there are a couple of reasonable beach resorts.

Places to Stay

The *Victoria Beach Resort* (tel 965, 975) on the Maharlika Highway at Atimonan has rooms for P100, with fan and bath for P200/300, and doubles with air-con and bath for P400.

In Gumaca, 25 km east of Atimonan, *Pinky's Lodge & Restaurant* has rooms with fan for P50/80, with fan and bath for P100/120 and with air-con and bath for P150/300. It is outside the centre of town and is comfortable and well maintained.

DAET & APUAO GRANDE ISLAND

Daet is a good overnight stop if you're heading to San Miguel Bay for a few days on the beach. Bagasbas Beach is the best in the vicinity of Daet. It is 4½ km away and is simpler and cheaper to get to than the beaches on San Miguel Bay. You can also visit the gold fields of Paracale and Mambulao. In Caplonga, further west, the Black Nazarene Festival takes place every year on 12 and 13 May.

Early risers should catch the fish market in Mercedes from 6 to 8 am. Mercedes is a small coastal village about 10 km north-east of Daet from which you can reach Apuao Grande Island in San Miguel Bay, where the beach is white and the Australian company Swagman Tours has a beach resort.

Places to Stay

The *Hotel Alegre* in Justo Lukban St has singles/doubles with fan and bath for P50/80 and with air-con and bath for P100-120/120-150. The double rooms are spacious and comfortable, but there is a loud disco upstairs.

The *Mines Hotel* (tel 2483) on the outskirts on Vinzons Ave has rooms with fan and bath for P60/90 and with air-con and bath for P125/160. It's a basic, clean place.

In Moreno St, the *Karigalan Hotel* (tel 2265) has rooms with fan and bath for P67/90, and with air-con and bath for P135/180. Suites are P190/202. It's a good, tidy place and is centrally located.

Apuao Grande Island Resort Hotel has cottages with fan and bath for P400. The resort has a tennis court, golf course and swimming pool as well as the restaurant, and you can go jet-skiing, windsurfing and diving or sail Hobie Cats. Complete tours including return travel can be booked and reservations made at the Swagman Hotel in Manila.

Places to Eat

The *Mandarin Restaurant*, near the Karigalan Hotel in Daet, has very good food, as does the *Golden Horse* a few streets away.

Getting There & Away

Air Philippine Airlines has return flights on Monday, Wednesday and Friday between Manila and Daet. Flying time is 50 minutes.

Bus Several buses a day run from Manila either to Daet only or through Daet to Naga, Legaspi or Matnog. Superlines buses leave every two hours; Philtranco are less frequent. It's just as well to book. The trip takes about seven hours.

Several Philtranco and J B Liner buses each day go from Legaspi to Daet via Naga, some going through to Manila, taking three hours. You can get minibuses from Naga.

It's only a short jeepney ride from Daet to Mercedes, which is the departure point for islands in San Miguel Bay.

NAGA

Naga is noted for its late-September Penafrancia Festival on the river. (See also the

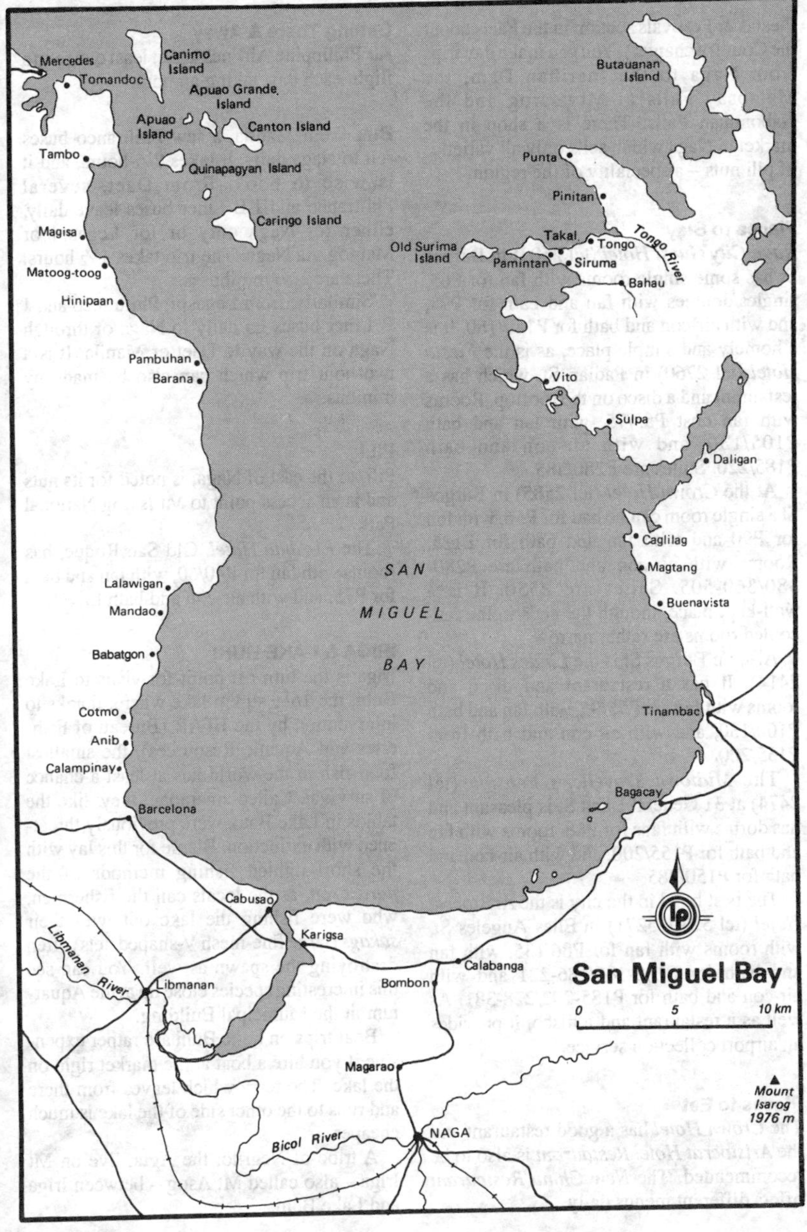
Mercedes
Tomandoc
Canimo Island
Apuao Grande Island
Apuao Island
Canton Island
Tambo
Quinapagyan Island
Caringo Island
Magisa
Matoog-toog
Hinipaan
Pambuhan
Barana
Lalawigan
Mandao
Babatgon
Cotmo
Anib
Calampinay
Barcelona
Cabusao
Karigsa
Libmanan River
Libmanan
Calabanga
Bombon
Magarao
Bicol River
NAGA
Butauanan Island
Punta
Pinitan
Takal
Tongo
Tongo River
Old Surima Island
Pamintan
Siruma
Bahau
Vito
Sulpa
Daligan
Caglilag
Magtang
Buenavista
Tinambac
Bagacay
SAN MIGUEL BAY
San Miguel Bay
0 5 10 km
Mount Isarog 1976 m

Fiestas & Festivals section in the Facts about the Country chapter). You can make day trips from Naga to the Inarihan Dam, the Malabsay Falls at Mt Isarog and the Nabontalan Falls. There is a shop in the market at Naga which sells only all varieties of pili nuts – a speciality of the region.

Places to Stay

Naga City Guest Hotel (tel 2503) in Burgos St has some single rooms with fan for P65, singles/doubles with fan and bath for P95, and with air-con and bath for P150/180. It is a homely and simple place, as is the *Fiesta Hotel* (tel 2760) in Padian St, which has a restaurant and a disco on the rooftop. Rooms with fan cost P55/75, with fan and bath P105/130, and with air-con and bath P185/220. Suites are P280/385.

At the *Crown Hotel* (tel 2585) in Burgos St a single room can be had for P56, with fan for P90 and with fan and bath for P125. Rooms with air-con and bath are P280-380/360-505. Suites are P550. It is a well-kept place, though the beds in the fan-cooled rooms are rather narrow.

Also on Burgos St is the *Lindes Hotel* (tel 2414). It has a restaurant and disco and rooms with fan are P55/95, with fan and bath P100/130, and with air-con and bath from P155/200.

The *Midtown Traveller's Pension* (tel 2474) at 31 General Luna St is pleasant and has dorms with fans for P88, rooms with fan and bath for P155/200, and with air-con and bath for P150/285.

The best hotel in the city is the *Aristocrat Hotel* (tel 5230, 5271) in Elias Angeles St, with rooms with fan for P86/135, with fan and bath for P148-186/186-221 and with air-con and bath for P185-292/228-381. As well as a restaurant and a disco, it provides an airport collection service.

Places to Eat

The *Crown Hotel* has a good restaurant and the *Aristocrat Hotel Restaurant* is also to be recommended. The *New China Restaurant* offers different menus daily.

Getting There & Away

Air Philippine Airlines has at least one return flight each day, taking an hour.

Bus From Manila, a few Philtranco buses run to Naga daily. It takes 8½ hours, and it is wise to book. From Daet, several Philtranco and J B Liner buses leave daily, either for Naga only or for Legaspi or Matnog via Naga. The trip takes 1½ hours. There are also minibuses.

Similarly, from Legaspi, Philtranco and J B Liner buses go daily to Naga or through Naga on the way to Daet or Manila. It is a two-hour trip which can also be made by minibus.

PILI

Pili, to the east of Naga, is noted for its nuts and is an access point to Mt Isarog National Park.

The *El-Alma Hotel*, Old San Roque, has rooms with fan for P40/60, with fan and bath for P75, and with air-con and bath for P150.

IRIGA & LAKE BUHI

Iriga is the turn-off point for visits to Lake Buhi, the 16½ sq km lake where, thanks to intervention by the BFAR (Bureau of Fisheries and Aquatic Resources), the smallest food fish in the world has at least a chance of survival. Called sinarapan, they, like the tabios in Lake Bato, were previously threatened with extinction. Blame for this lay with the short-sighted fishing methods of the *parasarap*, as the locals call the fishermen, who were fishing the lake out with their *sakags* (large fine-mesh V-shaped nets) often destroying the spawn as well. You can see this interesting species close up at the Aquarium in the Municipal Building.

Boat trips on Lake Buhi are rather expensive if you hire a boat at the market right on the lake. The ferry which leaves from there and runs to the other side of the lake is much cheaper.

A tribe of Negrito, the Agta, live on Mt Iriga – also called Mt Asog – between Iriga and Lake Buhi.

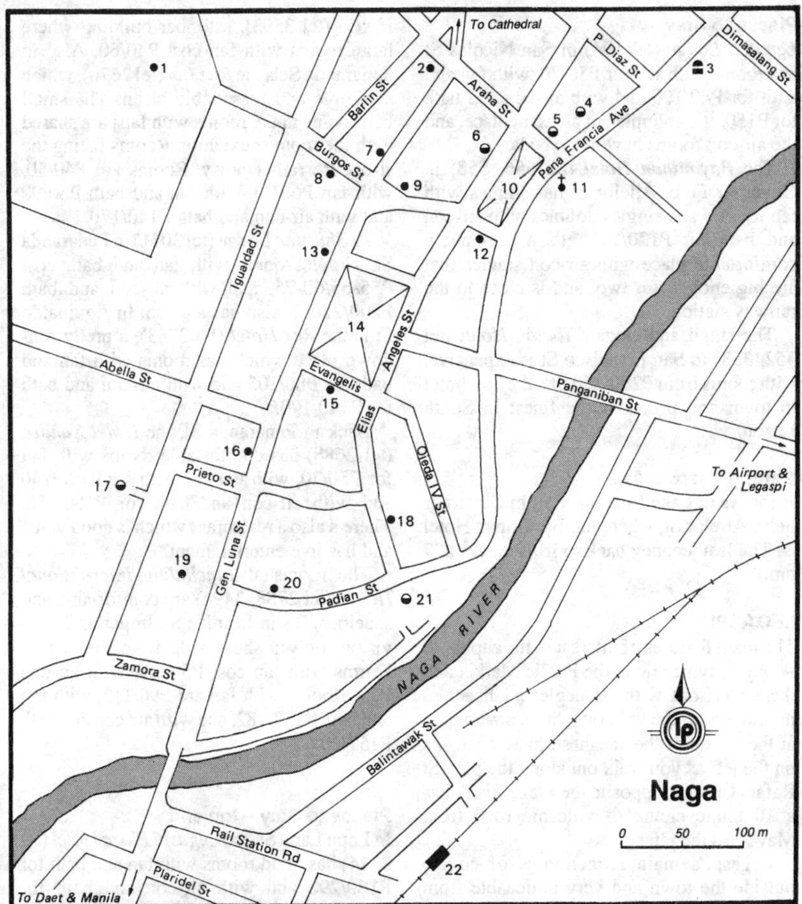

1 University of Nueva Careres
2 Police Station
3 Post Office
4 Philtranco Bus Terminal
5 JB Liner Bus Stop
6 Minibuses to Daet
7 Midtown Traveller's Pension
8 Lindes Hotel
9 Graceland Fast Food
Naga City Guest House
10 Plaza Martinez
11 San Francisco Church
12 Crown Hotel
13 Philippine National Bank
14 Plaza Rizal
15 Naga Garden Restaurant
16 New China Restaurant
17 Jeepneys to Bagacay
18 Aristocrat Hotel
19 Public Market
20 Fiesta Hotel
21 Minibuses to Iriga, Legaspi & Tabaco
22 Railway Station

Places to Stay

Lemar's Lodge (tel 594) in San Nicolas St has rooms with fan for P50/70, with fan and bath for P80/100 and with air-con and bath for P150. It's a simple but pleasant place, and the air-con rooms have wide beds.

The *Bayanihan Hotel* (tel 556, 558) in Governor Felix Alfelor St has singles with fan for P45 and singles/doubles with air-con and bath for P120/165. It's a reasonably comfortable place with air-con singles that are big enough for two, and is close to the railway station.

The small and elegant *Ibalon Hotel* (tel 352, 353) in San Francisco St is expensive, with rooms from P280/360. It's the best hotel in town and probably the finest in South Luzon.

Getting There & Away

Jeepneys to Lake Buhi leave from Governor Felix Alfelor St, where the Bayanihan Hotel is. The last jeepney back to Iriga leaves at 7 pm.

LEGASPI

The main features of interest in the capital of Albay Province lie in the Public Market and the waterfront with its neglected headless monument to the unknown heroes who died at the hands of the Japanese in WW II. It's on the left as you walk out along the pier. St Rafael Church, opposite the Plaza Rizal, has a 10 tonne chunk of volcanic rock from Mayon as the altar.

Legaspi's main attraction is of course outside the town and very noticeable from anywhere in the area: the mighty Mayon Volcano.

The Tourist Office is in Penaranda Park in the suburb of Albay. Jeepneys go there from central Legaspi, and you can get a tricycle from there to the airport for P15.

Places to Stay – bottom end

Peking Lodge (tel 3198) in Magallanes St has rooms with fan for P40/60, with fan and bath for P80/90 and with air-con and bath for P130/150. It's a basic but good hotel.

In Penaranda St is *Catalina's Boarding House* (tel 3593), a timber building where large rooms with fan cost P40/60. Also in Penaranda St is the *Ritz Inn* (tel 2670), which is simple and reasonably clean. The small bathrooms in the rooms with fans are shared with the rooms next door. Rooms facing the street are rather noisy. Rooms are P40/50, with fan P60/70, with fan and bath P80/90 and with air-con and bath P140/170.

At *Shirman Lodge* (tel 3031) in Penaranda St, simple rooms with fan and bath cost P55-65/60-75, and with air-con and bath P200/220. It also has a disco. In Aguinaldo St is the *Rex Hotel* (tel 2743), a pretty run-down place which has rooms with fan and bath for P80/105 and with air-con and bath for P140/190.

Back in Penaranda St, the *Hotel Xandra* (tel 2688) has comfortable rooms with fan for P50/70, with fan and bath for P100/140 and with air-con and bath for P180/250. There's also a restaurant which is good value and has live entertainment.

The rooms at *Tanchuling International House* (tel 2788, 3494) are comfortable and spacious. It's in Jasmine St, Imperial Subdivision, only a short walk from the centre. Dorms with fan cost P50 and with air-con P75. Rooms with fan are P90/112, with fan and bath P137/182, and with air-con and bath P157/202.

Places to Stay – top end

In Lapu Lapu St, the *Legaspi Plaza Hotel* (tel 3344) has good rooms with fan and bath for P180/298 and with air-con and bath for P276/342. It has a restaurant and disco.

The *Hotel Casablanca* (tel 3130, 3131, 3133) in Penaranda St has air-con rooms with bath for P350 and suites for P430. It's an attractive place, with a restaurant and disco.

The *Hotel La Trinidad* (tel 2951-55) is the best hotel in the city area, centrally located in Rizal St, with a swimming pool, coffee shop, restaurant and even a cinema in the complex. Rooms with air-con and bath are P365/430, and suites are P655; there is a free airport service.

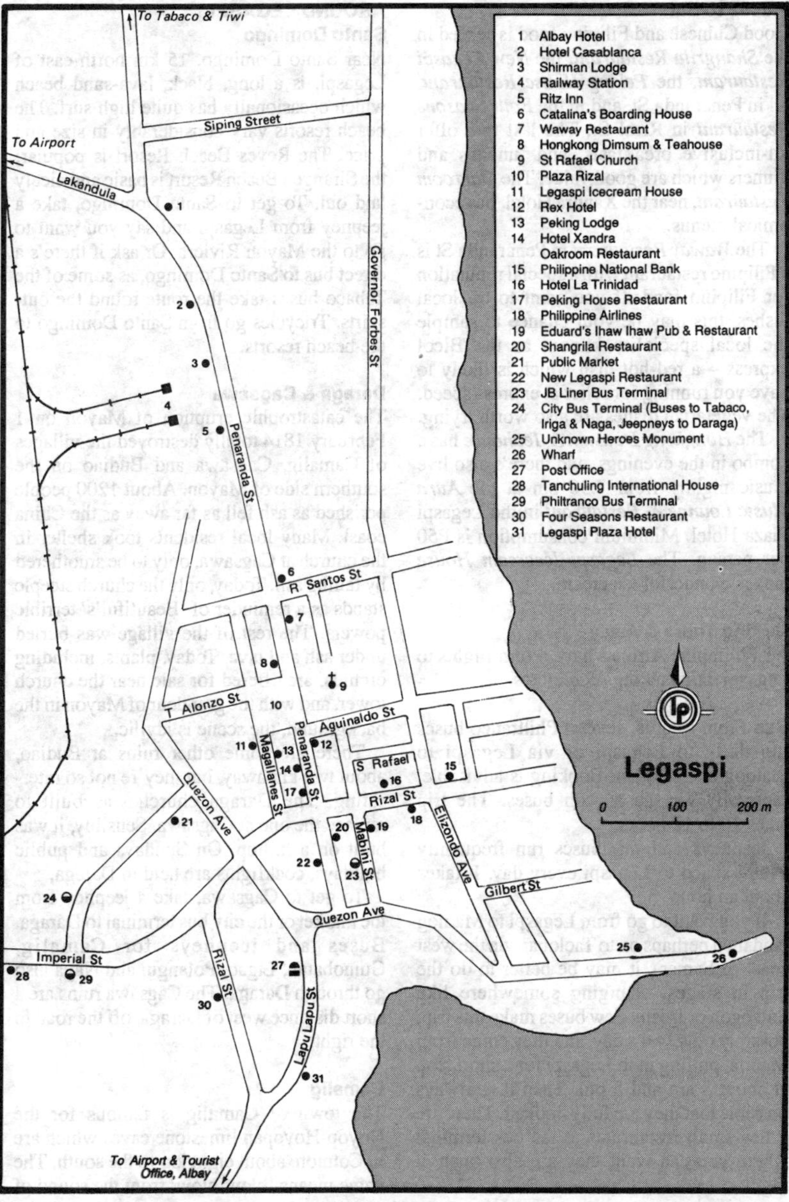
To Tabaco & Tiwi
Siping Street
To Airport
Lakandula
Governor Forbes St
Penaranda St
R Santos St
T Alonzo St
Aguinaldo St
Magallanes St
Penaranda St
S Rafael
Rizal St
Quezon Ave
Mabini St
Elizondo Ave
Gilbert St
Quezon Ave
Imperial St
Rizal St
Lapu Lapu St
To Airport & Tourist Office, Albay
1 Albay Hotel
2 Hotel Casablanca
3 Shirman Lodge
4 Railway Station
5 Ritz Inn
6 Catalina's Boarding House
7 Waway Restaurant
8 Hongkong Dimsum & Teahouse
9 St Rafael Church
10 Plaza Rizal
11 Legaspi Icecream House
12 Rex Hotel
13 Peking Lodge
14 Hotel Xandra
Oakroom Restaurant
15 Philippine National Bank
16 Hotel La Trinidad
17 Peking House Restaurant
18 Philippine Airlines
19 Eduard's Ihaw Ihaw Pub & Restaurant
20 Shangrila Restaurant
21 Public Market
22 New Legaspi Restaurant
23 JB Liner Bus Terminal
24 City Bus Terminal (Buses to Tabaco, Iriga & Naga, Jeepneys to Daraga)
25 Unknown Heroes Monument
26 Wharf
27 Post Office
28 Tanchuling International House
29 Philtranco Bus Terminal
30 Four Seasons Restaurant
31 Legaspi Plaza Hotel
Legaspi
0 100 200 m

Places to Eat

Good Chinese and Filipino food is served in the *Shangrila Restaurant*, the *New Legaspi Restaurant*, the *Peking House Restaurant*, all in Penaranda St, and in the *Four Seasons Restaurant* in Rizal St. The last two offer all-inclusive breakfasts, and lunches and dinners which are good value. The *Oakroom Restaurant*, near the Xandra Hotel, has economical menus.

The *Waway Restaurant* in Penaranda St is a Filipino restaurant with a special reputation for Filipino food. If you want to try local dishes, this may be your chance to sample the local speciality known as the Bicol express – a red-hot dish which is likely to have you running for relief at express speed. The vegetarian dishes are also worth trying.

The *Hongkong Dimsum & Teahouse* has a combo in the evenings, and there's also live music nightly from 7.30 pm at the *Aura Music Lounge & Restaurant* in the Legaspi Plaza Hotel. Minimum consumption is P50 per person. The *Legaspi Icecream House* makes wonderful ice cream.

Getting There & Away

Air Philippine Airlines have return flights to Legaspi daily, taking 45 minutes.

Bus From Manila, several Philtranco buses run daily to Legaspi or via Legaspi to Matnog or Tacloban. Booking is advisable, especially for the air-con buses. The trip takes 10 to 12 hours.

Jeepneys and minibuses run frequently from Tabaco to Legaspi every day. It takes about an hour.

If you want to go from Legaspi to Matnog (and then perhaps on to Tacloban via the west coast of Samar), it may be better to do the trip in stages, changing somewhere like Sorsogon or Irosin. Few buses make this trip, possibly only two a day, and they come from Manila, pulling in to Legaspi for a short stop at about 3 am and 5 pm. Then it is always possible that they are fully booked. There are a few small restaurants at the bus terminal where you can wait; they are also open at night.

AROUND LEGASPI

Santo Domingo

Near Santo Domingo, 15 km north-east of Legaspi, is a long, black, lava-sand beach which occasionally has quite high surf. The beach resorts vary considerably in size and price. The Reyes Beach Resort is popular; the Sirangen Beach Resort is basic and nicely laid out. To get to Santo Domingo, take a jeepney from Legaspi and say you want to go to the Mayon Riviera. Or ask if there's a direct bus to Santo Domingo, as some of the Tabaco buses take the route round the outskirts. Tricycles go from Santo Domingo to the beach resorts.

Daraga & Cagsawa

The catastrophic eruption of Mayon on 1 February 1814 totally destroyed the villages of Camalig, Cagsawa and Budiao on the southern side of Mayon. About 1200 people perished as ash fell as far away as the China coast. Many local residents took shelter in the church at Cagsawa, only to be smothered by falling ash. Today, only the church steeple stands as a reminder of 'Beautiful's' terrible powers. The rest of the village was buried under ash and lava. Today, plants, including orchids, are offered for sale near the church tower, and with the grandeur of Mayon in the background, the scene is idyllic.

There are some other ruins at Budiao, about two km away, but they're not so interesting. The Daraga church was built to replace the one at Cagsawa. Sensibly, it was built on a hilltop. On Sundays and public holidays, cockfights are held in Daraga.

To get to Cagsawa, take a jeepney from the market or the city bus terminal to Daraga. Buses and jeepneys for Camalig, Guinobatan, Ligao, Polangui and Naga also go through Daraga. The Cagsawa ruins are a short distance west of Daraga, off the road to the right.

Camalig

The town of Camalig is famous for the Hoyop-Hoyopan limestone caves which are in Cotmon, about eight km to the south. The name means 'blow-blow' from the sound of

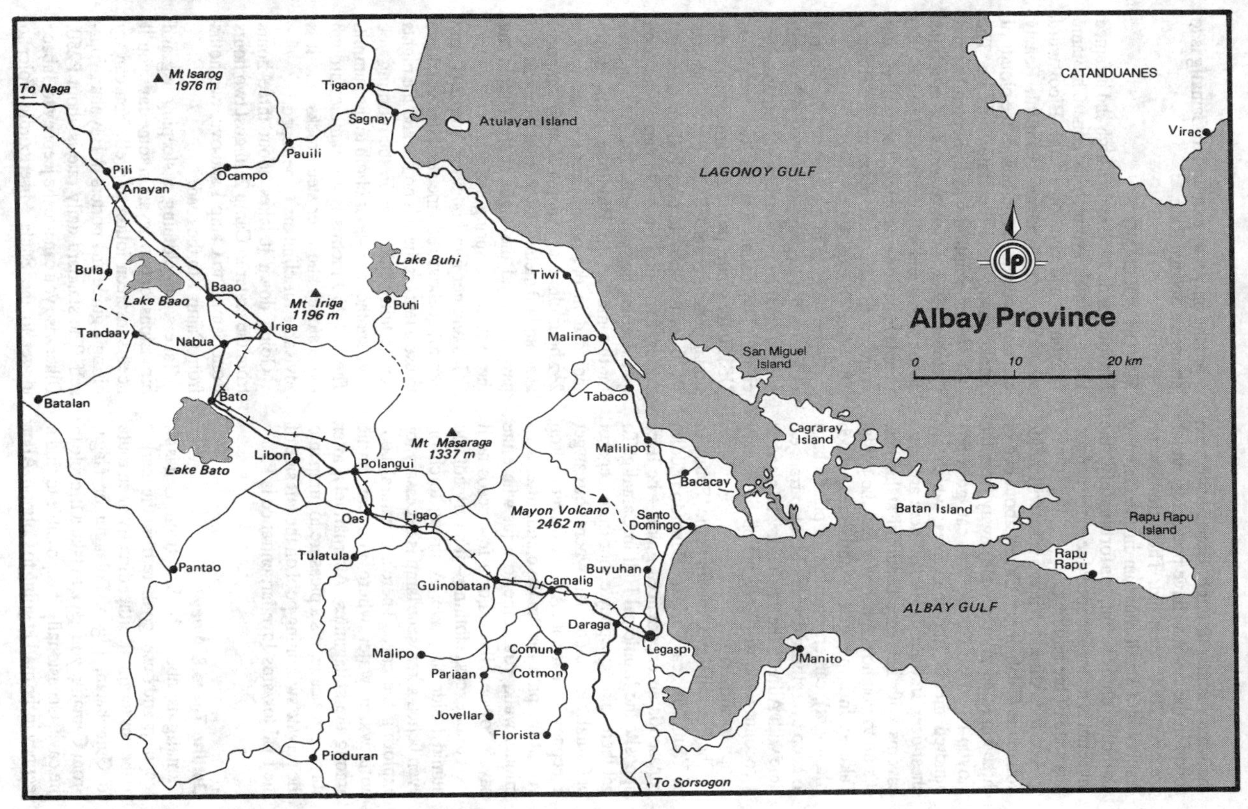
Albay Province
0
10
20 km
CATANDUANES
Virac
LAGONOY GULF
Atulayan Island
To Naga
Mt Isarog 1976 m
Tigaon
Sagnay
Pauili
Pili
Ocampo
Anayan
Lake Buhi
Bula
Lake Baao
Baao
Mt Iriga 1196 m
Buhi
Tiwi
Iriga
Tandaay
Nabua
Malinao
San Miguel Island
Bato
Batalan
Tabaco
Cagraray Island
Mt Masaraga 1337 m
Malilipot
Libon
Polangui
Lake Bato
Bacacay
Batan Island
Mayon Volcano 2462 m
Oas
Ligao
Santo Domingo
Rapu Rapu Island
Rapu Rapu
Tulatula
Pantao
Buyuhan
Guinobatan
Camalig
ALBAY GULF
Daraga
Legaspi
Malipo
Comun
Manito
Pariaan
Cotmon
Jovellar
Florista
Pioduran
To Sorsogon

the wind rushing through. Bones have been found in the caves as have potsherds, which are over 2000 years old. They are now on display in a small museum in the Camalig Catholic church but, unfortunately, the museum is no longer open due to the dangerous state of the building.

Ask for Alfredo Nieva, who will guide you to the Calabidogan Caves, about two or three km (a 45 minute walk) away from the Hoyop-Hoyopan Caves. You can go a few hundred metres into the caves, which are chest-deep in water in parts. There are large caverns with bats and beautiful stalactites. It's up to you how much you pay the guide. Take swimming gear, sandshoes, torch (flashlight), camera and lots of plastic bags to keep everything dry. It's best to arrange a time with Alfredo the day before; he also has a coconut-wine distillery which he is very happy to show off.

The Pariaan Cave, known as the 'Fountain of Youth', is near Pariaan. Eduardo (Eddie) Nalasco is an experienced guide – he lives opposite the Municipal Hall in Camalig. To get there take a jeepney either from Legaspi or Camalig to Guinobatan, where you can get a jeepney for Pariaan. Ask the driver to drop you at the path for the cave and, after a 10 minute walk, you come to a jut where the cave's 'owner' lives. For a few pesos he'll look after excess clothing – it's very hot and humid inside the cave. A strong torch or, even better, a kerosene lamp is necessary for exploring the cave. There's a natural pool with warm water where you can bathe among the stalagmites. Alternatively, after staying in a cave, it's a pleasure to jump into the private swimming pool on the left side of the road towards Jovellar; entrance is P2.

Getting There & Away

Camalig is about 14 km from Legaspi. Jeepneys and buses go there from the market or the bus terminal, either directly or en route to Guinobatan, Ligao, Polangui or Naga. From Camalig, you have to take a tricycle to the cave. Occasionally it is possible to find a jeepney in the market going to Cotmon. After 6 pm the only way to return to Camalig is to arrange a Special Ride.

MAYON VOLCANO

Mayon stands 2462 metres high and is famed for its perfectly symmetrical cone. The name Mayon is a derivation of the Bicol word *magayon*, which means beautiful. Beauty can also become dangerous, as the clouds of smoke rising from the crater indicate. The last violent eruption was in September and October 1984, when a series of eruptions shook towns and villages nearby and 70,000 people had to be evacuated. The most violent eruption to date took place on 1 February 1814 (see Daraga & Cagsawa).

If you want to climb Mayon, the Tourist Office in the Legaspi suburb of Albay will supply detailed information and organise the climb. The usual cost for two people is US$50 for guide, porter and tent; each additional person costs US$20. Provisions cost P120 for two people plus P60 for a second porter if you don't want to carry your food and sleeping bag yourself. You get a jeepney in the market to Buyuhan (this is not included in the price), from where it is a 2½ hour climb to Camp 1 (Camp Amporo) at about 800 metres. If you start late, you will have to spend the night at the simple hut there; there is a spring nearby.

It's another four hours to Camp 2 (Camp Pepito) at about 1800 metres. Here you have to use a tent, as there is no hut and the nights can be fairly cold here. In the morning you have another four-hour climb to the summit. The last 250 metres is a scramble through loose stones and over steep rocks, and it is advisable for climbers to be roped.

Going down it takes about three hours from the crater to Camp 2, almost two hours from Camp 2 to Camp 1 and over two hours from Camp 1 to the road.

Take warm clothing, a sleeping bag and provisions for two days. On some days you'll need sunscreen lotion as well. You can try hiring a guide and porters in Buyuhan yourself. The standard daily rate is about P250. Otherwise you can use the jeepney to Tabaco to get to the Santa Misericordia Volcano

Observatory near Santo Domingo, where the experts working there will arrange for an experienced guide. This costs between P600 and P700 for parties of up to four. At this station you can also find out the present state of volcanic activity and the best route for the existing conditions. To try the ascent without a guide is reckless and irresponsible, as it's easy to get lost at the foot of Mayon. Many of the harmless-looking canyons turn out to be dead ends with sheer drops.

Getting There & Away

To get from Legaspi to the Mayon Resthouse, a forsaken ruin on the northern slope, take a bus or jeepney to Tabaco, then a bus or jeepney to Ligao. Get off at the resthouse turn-off about halfway to Ligao. From there you've got about an eight-km walk up to the resthouse. You can hire a jeepney in Tabaco but it's cheaper to persuade the regular Ligao jeepney drivers to make a small detour to the resthouse and drop you there. You may possibly be able to spend the night on the floor of the Museum of the Mayon Volcano Observatory above the resthouse. Water is available, but you need to have your own supplies. The climb from the observatory

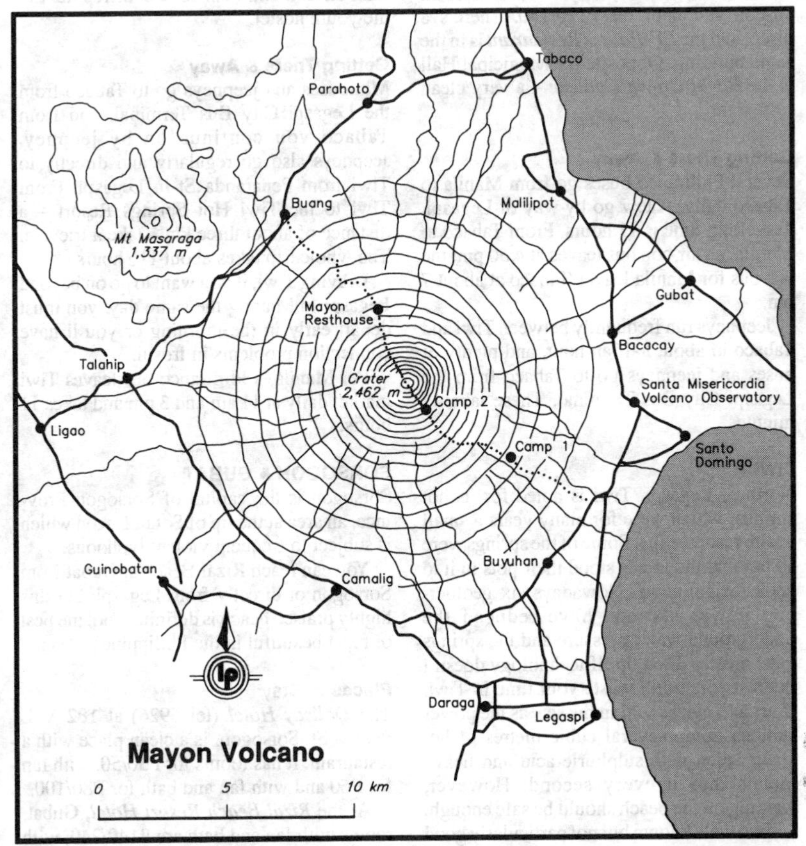

(700 metres) to the top and back can be done in a day.

TABACO

Tabaco is mainly the departure point for the boat to the islands, which leaves daily at 11 am for Virac on Catanduanes, taking 3½ hours. Probably the only thing worth seeing in Tabaco is the two-storey market, where among the wares are some interesting knives.

Places to Stay & Eat

Tony's Hotel in Riosa St near the market has rooms with fan and bath for P50/70 and with air-con and bath for P110/140. There's a disco, and the *EF-Palace Restaurant* is in the same building. Opposite the Municipal Hall is the *Royal Crown Canteen* – a very clean restaurant.

Getting There & Away

Several Philtranco buses go from Manila to Tabaco daily. A few go by way of Legaspi. Travelling time is 11 hours. From Tabaco to Manila, an air-con bus leaves at 4.50 pm; the last bus for Manila leaves Tabaco at about 7 pm.

Jeepneys run frequently between Tiwi and Tabaco in about half an hour, and plenty of buses and jeepneys go to Tabaco from the Legaspi City Bus Terminal. These take 45 minutes.

TIWI

North of Legaspi, Tiwi is noted for its hot springs, which were for many years a small health resort or spa. Some of the springs were so hot that the locals stood their pots in it to cook their dinners. Nowadays six geothermal power stations have reduced the underground water pressure and the springs have mostly dried up. If technology doesn't interest you, don't waste your time in Tiwi. You can't even swim in the sea, as the power stations dump several cubic metres of hot water laden with sulphuric acid and heavy metals into it every second. However, walking on the beach should be safe enough.

Two well-known but not particularly good beaches, with black sand, are Sogod Beach and Putsan Beach. If you walk to Putsan, take a look at the primitive potteries on the way. There are better swimming opportunities on Coral Island – ask how to get there at the hostel.

Places to Stay

Bano Youth Hostel has rooms with fan and bath for P45/95 and with air-con and bath for P170/200. There's an outside swimming pool and thermal baths in the basement.

The *Tiwi Hot Spring Resort* has rooms with fan and bath for P100/150 and doubles with air-con and bath for P200. It's next to the youth hostel.

Getting There & Away

Minibuses and jeepneys go to Tabaco from the Legaspi City Bus Terminal, and from Tabaco you continue on by jeepney. Jeepneys also go regularly and directly to Tiwi from Penaranda St in Legaspi. From Tiwi to the Tiwi Hot Springs Resort – a distance of about three km – take a tricycle. The whole trip takes about 1½ hours.

Leaving Tiwi, if you want to go on beyond Legaspi to Matnog the same day, you must depart early in the morning or you'll have connection problems in Irosin.

For Manila, a Philtranco bus leaves Tiwi market daily at 11 am and 3 pm and takes 11 hours.

SORSOGON & GUBAT

Sorsogon is the capital of Sorsogon Province, an area at the tip of South Luzon which is subject to frequent violent typhoons.

You can reach Rizal Beach at Gubat from Sorsogon or directly from Legaspi, but this highly praised beach is definitely not the best or most beautiful in the Philippines.

Places to Stay

The *Dalisay Hotel* (tel 6926) at 182 V L Peralta St, Sorsogon, is a clean place with a restaurant. It has rooms for P30/50, with fan for P60 and with fan and bath for P80/100.

At the *Rizal Beach Resort Hotel*, Gubat, rooms with fan and bath are P140/240; with

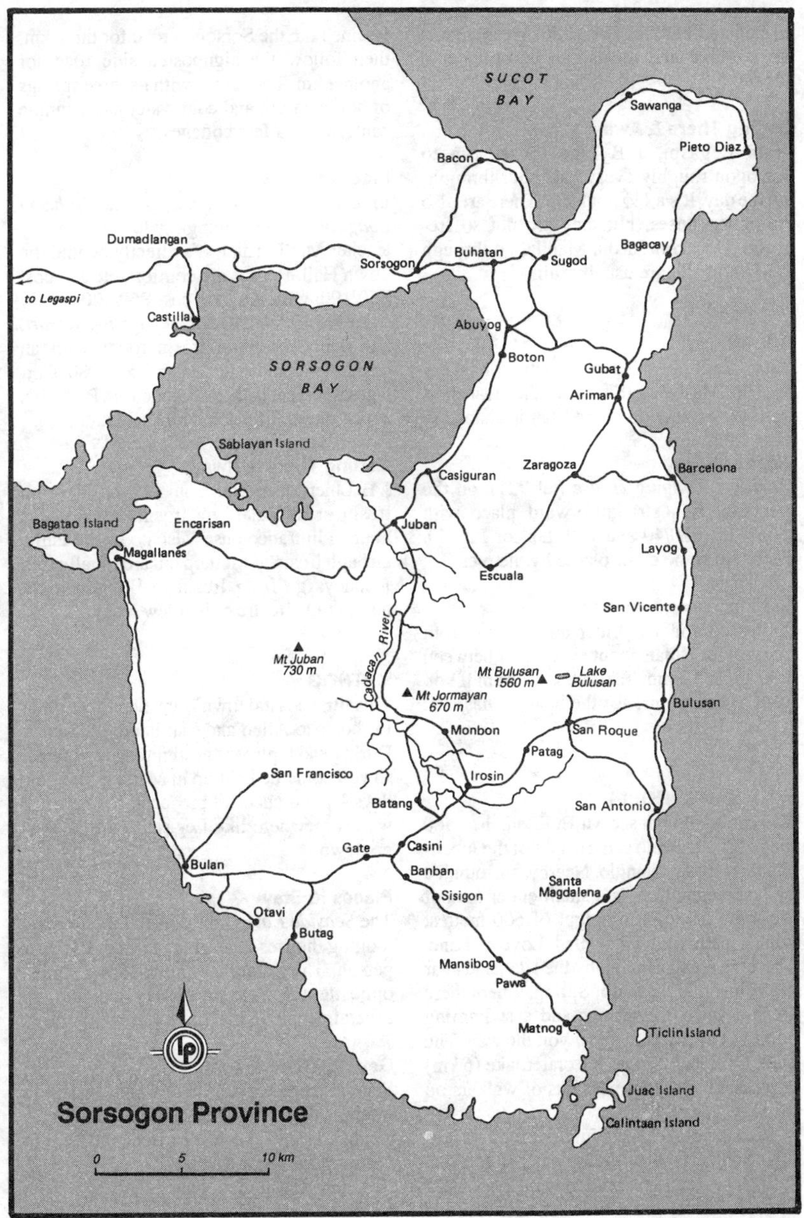
SUCOT BAY
Sawanga
Pieto Diaz
Bacon
Dumadlangan
Bagacay
Buhatan
Sorsogon
Sugod
to Legaspi
Castilla
Abuyog
Boton
SORSOGON BAY
Gubat
Ariman
Sablayan Island
Zaragoza
Casiguran
Barcelona
Bagatao Island
Encarisan
Juban
Magallanes
Layog
Escuala
San Vicente
Cadacan River
Mt Juban 730 m
Mt Bulusan 1560 m
Lake Bulusan
Mt Jormayan 670 m
Bulusan
San Roque
Monbon
Patag
San Francisco
Irosin
Batang
San Antonio
Gate
Casini
Bulan
Banban
Santa Magdalena
Sisigon
Otavi
Butag
Mansibog
Pawa
Matnog
Ticlin Island
Juac Island
Calintaan Island
Sorsogon Province
0
5
10 km

air-con and bath they're P280. Weekly rates are possible and meals can be ordered in advance.

Getting There & Away

From Legaspi, J B Liner buses run to Sorsogon roughly every half hour throughout the day. It's a 1½ hour trip. There are also Philtranco buses, but they are not so frequent. They come from Manila, go through to Matnog and are usually full.

BULAN

Bulan is simply a departure point for a daily boat to Masbate. (See also the Transport from Luzon section in the Manila chapter).

Places to Stay

Mari-El's Lodging House (tel 721), on the pier site, is a straightforward place with rooms for P20/40 and with fan for P25/50. There are some other places by the pier.

Getting There & Away

Philtranco and J B Liner buses leave from Legaspi for Bulan about every hour between 4.30 am and 3 pm. Take a bus by 8 am if you want to be on time for the boat to Masbate. It takes 3½ hours.

BULUSAN & IROSIN

You can't help but see Mt Bulusan, the 1560 metre high volcano at the centre of the Juban-Bulusan-Irosin triangle. Nearby, surrounded by lush vegetation, is a small crater lake of the same name, at a height of 600 metres, with a path round it called Lovers' Lane. There's a small canteen by the lake, and near the volcano is Masacrot Spring, where there are hot and cold springs and a swimming pool, but no signs to show you the way. The walk from Bulusan up the crater lake (6 km) is pleasant and you meet lots of walkers on the way.

Bulusan makes a useful base for a visit to this 'Switzerland of the Orient'. If you like springs you can go to the Mateo Hot & Cold Springs Resort about four km north-east of Irosin. Take the Sorsogon road for three km, then follow the signposted side road for another km. The resort, with its three springs of hot, medium and cold water has a simple canteen and a few cottages.

Places to Stay

In Bulusan you can stay at the *Bulusan Lodging House* belonging to the friendly teacher Mrs Bartilet. It's directly behind the Town Hall. Rooms are comfortable and cost P50/100; with fan they cost P60/120.

At the *Mateo Hot & Cold Springs Resort*, San Benon, Monbon, Irosin, rooms with fan cost P40/80 and with fan and bath P80. Cottages with fan, bath and kitchen are P200. It's a nice, peaceful place with a restaurant.

Getting There & Away

J B Liner buses run from Legaspi daily to Irosin or to Bulan via Irosin. It takes 2½ hours. Philtranco buses also go from Manila through Irosin to Matnog but are usually full. Jeepneys go from Irosin to Bulusan in an hour, but there are only a few a day.

MATNOG

This little coastal town is the departure point for boats to Allen and San Isidro on Samar. During bad typhoons all shipping is stopped, so you could be held up in Matnog for a few days – not a cheerful prospect. It's better to wait somewhere like Legaspi until the seas go down.

Places to Stay

The *Seaside Eatery* and *Villa's Inn* are basic lodging houses charging around P30 per person. The restaurant on the corner almost opposite the Seaside Eatery can put up several people in one big room overnight.

Getting There & Away

Several jeepneys run daily from Legaspi to Irosin, taking one hour. From Matnog, a jeepney usually leaves for Irosin at 7 am to transport the local teachers.

A few Philtranco buses daily go from Legaspi through Matnog en route to

Tacloban. All seats are usually occupied, so it's better to do the trip in stages using other means of transport. It takes three hours. See also Getting There & Away from Legaspi.

TO/FROM SOUTH LUZON

Most transport from Luzon to other islands goes through Manila. See the Transport from Luzon section in the Manila chapter.

Around Luzon

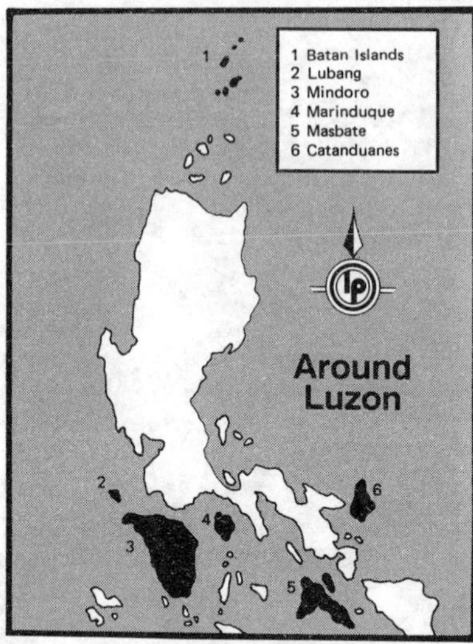

Several islands around the main island of Luzon are also generally grouped with Luzon. They include the Batan Islands, which are scattered off the far northern coast of Luzon; Catanduanes, off the south-eastern coast near Legaspi; and the smaller islands of Lubang, Marinduque and Masbate and the larger island of Mindoro, all off the western coast.

Batan Islands

The Batan Islands are the northernmost islands of the Philippines. Y'ami is only 100 km from Taiwan. The biggest and economically most important islands are Batan, Ibayat and Sabtang. Dinem Island is uninhabited. The climate of the Batan Islands is harsh and changeable. Compared with other parts of the Philippines, all 10 of these islands are hit by typhoons relatively frequently between June and September. From October to February or March it is often wet and stormy. The best months to visit are April and May.

Many Batan Islands houses are built of solid rock and have roofs thickly thatched with cogon grass to resist the weather. They are low, with few windows, and are usually found in small groups in niches protected from the wind. Geographically isolated from the other main islands, the Batanese impress the visitor as being both primitive and strong-willed. You could sometimes imagine yourself to be in a village in Gaul and would probably not be in the least surprised if around the next corner were a venerable druid brewing his potions.

People here protect themselves from sun and rain with a *suot*, a head-covering made from *voyavoy* leaves which reaches right down the back.

Goods which aren't produced on the islands are slightly more expensive here than they are in Luzon, as they have to be flown in or shipped on the occasional freighter. The main crops are garlic, onions, taro yams and camotes. The main occupations are cattle farming and fishing.

BATAN ISLAND

Don't expect very much in the way of sights; in fact, this is part of the island's charm. About the only excitement is the Sunday cockfight. There are a couple of white beaches on the western coast; the southern and eastern coasts are rocky. To the north the landscape of this green and hilly island is dominated by the 1008 metre high Iraya Volcano.

A seldom-travelled and only partly surfaced road runs from Basco to Riacoyde (via Mahatao, Ivana and Uyugan) and then straight across the island back to Mahatao. It's a good track for walking and you come

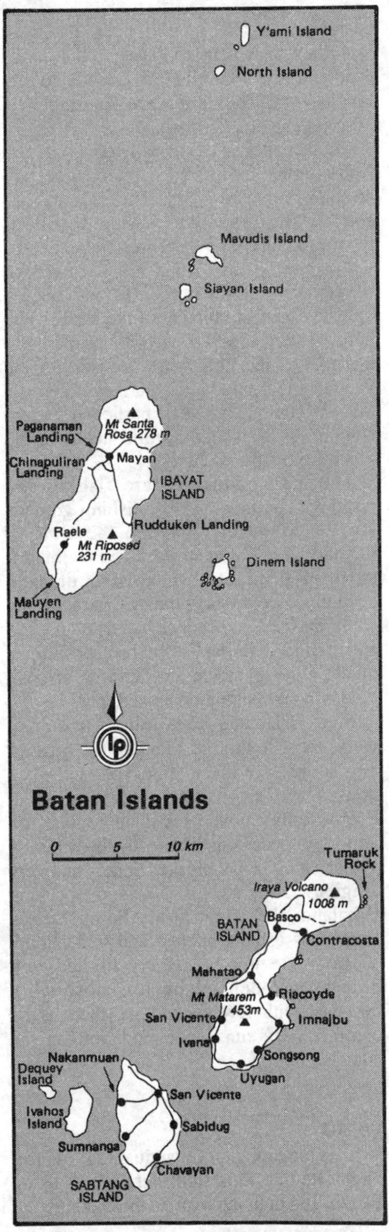

across lovely little villages inhabited by friendly Ivatan, the natives of Batan Island.

Basco

Basco is the capital of this province, which is the smallest in the Philippines – smallest both in area and population. Next to the big church, with its beautiful façade, are numerous governmental buildings which dominate this well-kept town at the foot of Mt Iraya. Just on 5000 people live here. There is a Philippine National Bank (PNB) here which will cash travellers' cheques. In Basco you can hire private jeepneys (P400), motorcycles (P200) and bicycles. Inquire at Mama Lily's Pension House.

Places to Stay *Mama Lily's Pension House* has rooms for P200/350. It is clean and simple and the price includes full board. Guests can use the living room and terrace, and there is a restaurant.

The *School Canteen* has rooms for P50. Food in the School Canteen is inexpensive.

SABTANG ISLAND

In contrast to Batan Island, there are no cars on Sabtang. It is worth going round the island on foot and visiting the four villages. The mayor will place a guide at your disposal who knows the paths and the shortcuts. Through him you will find it easier to get to know the villagers and to see things such as how suots are made. On the eastern coast of the neighbouring island of Ivahos there is an extensive coral reef. You can get there by boat from Nakanmuan or Sumnanga.

There are no hotels on Sabtang, but it is possible to stay with the mayor or the director of the Fishery School. You can also get something to eat there, but since no-one will charge you money or accept it, it is rather nice to 'happen' to have a small gift on hand.

Getting There & Away

A boat goes once a week from Basco to Sabtang Island. If you don't want to wait, you have to go to Ivana, but the jeepney to Ivana usually only goes when a plane lands. In good weather a boat goes daily from Ivana to San Vicente on Sabtang at about 8.30 am and takes about 30 minutes. It should return the next morning.

IBAYAT ISLAND

Ibayat is the largest island of the group. It has few beaches and a rocky coast. A feature of the island is the coconut crab, which is so fond of coconuts that it will climb trees to get them. You can stay and eat with the mayor.

Getting There & Away

The boat service from Basco to Paganaman Landing or Mauyen Landing on Ibayat Island is irregular. Travel time is about four hours. The boats only go in good weather and are fairly unpredictable – not so good if you are on a tight schedule. East of Raele is a landing strip for small aircraft.

TO/FROM THE BATAN ISLANDS

You can get to the Batan Islands from Laoag and Tuguegarao (see the Transport from Luzon section of the Manila chapter). Travel in and out depends first and foremost on the weather. On rainy days, if the partly concreted runway at Basco is wet, planes can neither land nor take off. Delays may also occur, even in the summer months of March, April and May.

To Luzon

Air PAL has flights from Basco to Laoag and Manila on Thursday and Sunday, and flights to Tuguegarao and Manila on Monday, Wednesday and Saturday.

Boat The Avega Exchange Services' MV *LSD* goes from Basco to Manila twice or three times a year.

Catanduanes

Also known as the 'land of the howling winds', this kidney-shaped island lies in the Pacific Ocean, separated from South Luzon by the Magueda Channel and the Gulf of Lagonoy. The province consists of the main island and a few smaller ones, the most important of which are Panay to the north-east and the Palumbanes Islands to the north-west. The latter are Palumbanes, Porongpong and Calabagio.

Catanduanes is mostly hilly. The only flat land is found east of the capital, Virac, and around Bato and Viga. The climate has shaped the landscape. As a result of typhoons, the coastal hills are barely covered with grass, many palms are uprooted or broken off, and steep cliffs and deeply indented bays are typical of the eastern and north-eastern coasts. The typhoons blast into this part of the Philippines straight off the Pacific. In Catanduanes you have to expect rain throughout the year, particularly from November to January, while not quite so much from April to June.

The main industries are fishing and farming. The most prolific fishing grounds are the Magueda Channel, the Gulf of Lagonoy and Cabugao Bay. The main agricultural products are abaca nuts and coconuts, rice, sweet potatoes, cassava and fruits such as avocados, jackfruit, papaya and oranges. Mining has not been developed much, although there are deposits of coal, gold, silver, manganese and copper.

Many islanders have left in search of work, most settling in Manila. The greatest migrations take place after typhoons when houses and crops have been destroyed. People only come back then to visit on important occasions like festivals or family gatherings. The people are friendly and very religious. They are the Bikolano, speaking Bikolano, the language of South Luzon. English is usually spoken and understood. Visitors are nearly always invited into homes, and depend on this hospitality because, with few exceptions, there is no commercially run accommodation on the islands.

VIRAC

Virac is the capital of Catanduanes Province. Favourite day trips from here are to Igang Beach, 10 km to the west; to the Balongbong

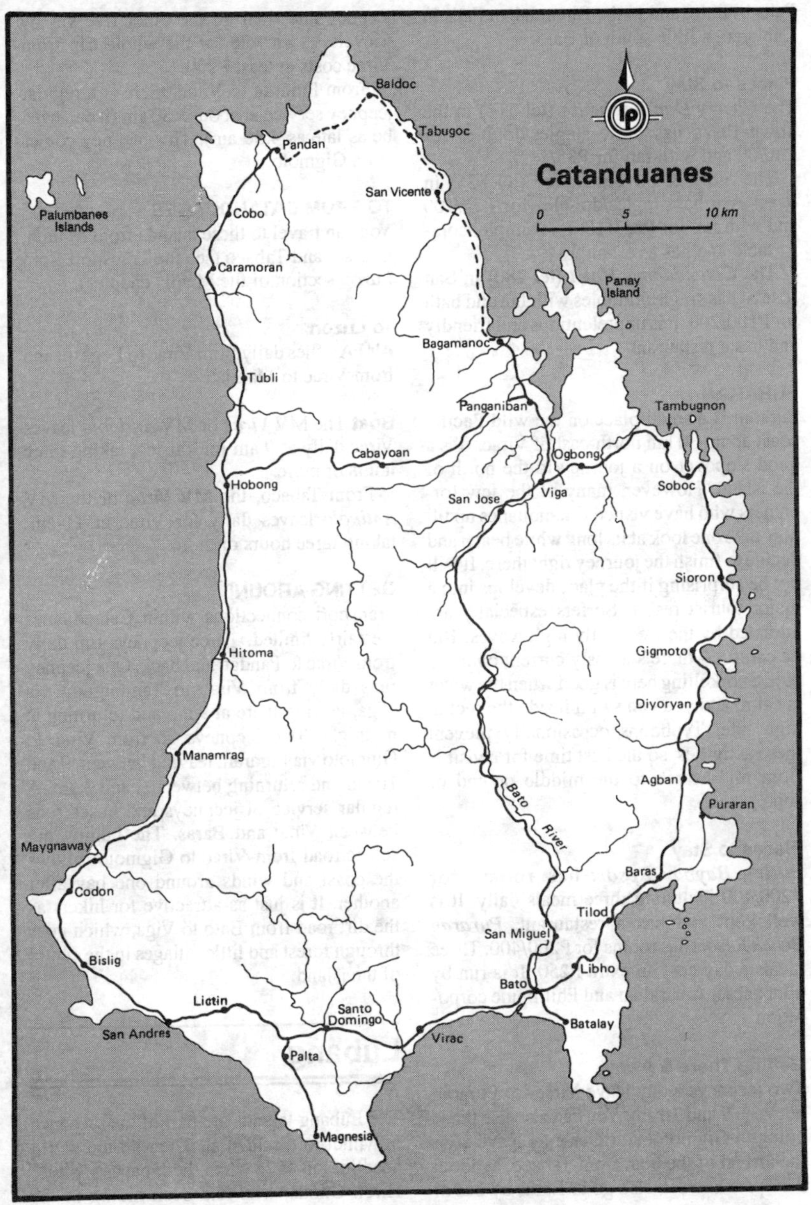
Catanduanes
0
5
10 km
Baidoc
Tabugoc
Pandan
San Vicente
Palumbanes Islands
Cobo
Caramoran
Panay Island
Bagamanoc
Tubli
Panganiban
Tambugnon
Cabayoan
Ogbong
Soboc
Hobong
San Jose
Viga
Sioron
Hitoma
Gigmoto
Diyoryan
Manamrag
Agban
Bato River
Puraran
Maygnaway
Codon
Baras
Tilod
San Miguel
Libho
Bislig
Bato
Lictin
Santo Domingo
Batalay
San Andres
Virac
Palta
Magnesia

Falls in Bato; and to the Binanuahan Falls in Cabugao, a little south of Bato.

Places to Stay

The *Cherry Don Resthouse* (tel 516) in the Town Plaza has basic singles/doubles for P30/60 and with fan for P35/75.

The *Stars & Stripes Lodge* (tel 635) in Rizal Ave has singles/doubles for P75/100 and with fan for P85/110. It is simple, comfortable and has a restaurant.

The *Catanduanes Hotel* (tel 280) in San Jose St has singles/doubles with fan and bath for P100/200. It is unpretentious and friendly and has a restaurant.

PURARAN

Puraran is a small place on the wild Pacific coast about 30 km north-east of Virac. It is a good stopover on a journey to the north of the island. However, many of the few foreigners who have visited Catanduanes up till now take one look at its long white beach and decide to finish the journey right there. It will not be surprising if the place develops into a major tourist resort. Surfers especially are attracted by the frequently high waves. But be careful – there's a nasty current over the reef. Snorkelling here is good when the water is calm, and you can swim inside the reef at high tide. Typhoons occasionally prevent these activities, so the best time for a visit is from mid-March to the middle or end of June.

Places to Stay

Puting Baybay Resort has rooms for P200/400 including three meals daily. It is well kept and has a restaurant. *Puraran Beach Resort* has rooms for P200/400. Three meals a day cost an extra P250. It is run by a Japanese, Australian and Philippine corporation.

Getting There & Away

Two jeepneys a day leave Virac for Puraran between 9 and 10 am. You can also use those going to Gigmoto. Another may leave after the arrival of the boat from Tabaco, at about 2.30 pm. You can also go to Baras by bus or jeepney and then go the other five km by tricycle. A tricycle for the whole trip from Virac costs at least P200.

From Puraran to Virac, there is a regular jeepney service at about 3.30 am (it can even be as late as 4.30 am). This jeepney comes from Gigmoto.

TO/FROM CATANDUANES

You can travel to these islands from Manila, Legaspi and Tabaco (see the Transport from Luzon section of the Manila chapter).

To Luzon

Air PAL flies daily from Virac to Legaspi and from Virac to Manila.

Boat The MV *Virac* or MV *Antipolo* leaves Virac daily at 9 am for Tabaco, taking three hours or more.

From Tabaco, the MV *Virac* or the MV *Antipolo* leaves daily for Virac at 11 am, taking three hours or more.

GETTING AROUND

Transport connections within Catanduanes are fairly limited. Three jeepneys run daily from Virac to Pandan and back. One jeepney runs daily from Virac to Tambugnon via Viga, leaving there at 9 am and returning at midnight. Two jeepneys go from Virac to Gigmoto via Puraran, leaving between 9 and 10 am and returning between 2 and 3 am. A regular service of jeepneys and buses runs between Virac and Baras. The bumpy but scenic road from Virac to Gigmoto follows the coast and winds around one bay after another. It is just as attractive for hikers as the dirt road from Bato to Viga, which goes through forest and little villages in the centre of the island.

Lubang

The Lubang Islands are part of the province of Mindoro Occidental. They hit the world headlines in 1974 when the Japanese soldier Hiroo Onoda, who had been hiding in the mountains of Lubang for 30 years, finally decided it was time to give himself up as a WW II prisoner of war. Fumio Nakahura, a captain in the Japanese Imperial Army, held out for another six years before being discovered in April 1980 on Mt Halcon on Mindoro.

The people of Lubang earn their income mainly from the sale of garlic. They would like to share in the profits from tourism but seem at present most likely to inspire only one wish in visitors: to leave for Manila or Mindoro as soon as possible. I found people in Tilik and further south-east to be distant to the point of being unfriendly. As you go from Tilik towards Lubang, attitudes become noticeably more relaxed.

TILIK

You can't travel around much here because of the lack of transport, but the country around Tilik is good for walks, such as the one to Como Beach near Vigo. It's no tropical paradise, but there's some real surf and it's not crowded. There's a beautiful sandy beach at Tagbac, west of Lubang, but the sea floor is muddy. If you go by paddle boat from Tilik to the other side of the bay, make sure there is at least a 15 cm clearance above the water line. The centre of the bay is exposed and even a light wind can blow water into the boat. It's easy to get thoroughly drenched.

Places to Stay

There is no commercial accommodation available in Lubang, so you will have to find a family who will rent you a room. Just ask at the church or one of the shops.

TO/FROM LUBANG

You can get here from Luzon and Mindoro (see the Transport from Luzon section of the Manila chapter and the To/From section of the Mindoro chapter).

To Luzon

Air Pacific Airways flies daily from Lubang

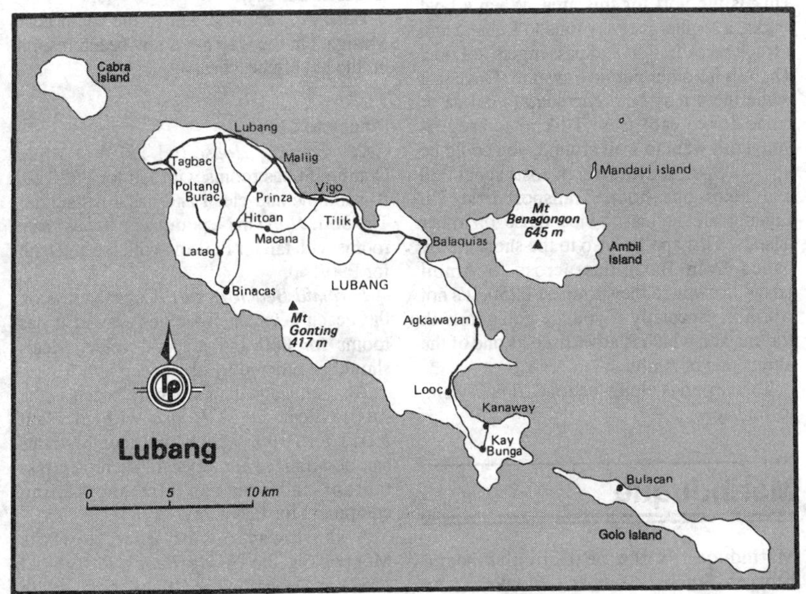

to Manila and Aerolift goes on Tuesday and Thursday.

Boat The William Lines' MV *Edward* leaves Tilik for Manila on Sunday at 9 am, taking seven hours.

The Asuncion Shipping Lines' MV *Asuncion X* leaves Tilik for Manila on Wednesday at 10 am, and their MV *Catalyn A* leaves Tilik for Manila on Saturday at 10 am. Both take eight hours.

To Mindoro

Boat The William Lines' MV *Edward* leaves Tilik for Sablayan on Friday at 10 pm, taking seven hours.

To Palawan

The Asuncion Shipping Lines' MV *Asuncion X* leaves Tilik for Coron on Sunday at 8 am, and their MV *Catalyn A* leaves Tilik for Coron on Wednesday at 8 am. Both take 16 hours and continue on to Culion.

GETTING AROUND

Tilik is the port for this area. When a boat docks, a regular jeepney runs to Lubang and a truck takes freight and passengers to Looc. There is no other public transport. Once in a while there may be a *carretela* (a calesa or horse-drawn cab) from Tilik to Lubang. If you don't want to wait around, you could be up for a Special Ride, which costs about P50 and takes one hour. Transport costs on Lubang are at least twice those on other islands. This applies also to the short trip by banca from Balaquias across to Ambil Island, for which they now ask P250. It's not worth it, especially if you are going to look for the jade which is advertised as one of the attractions of Ambil.

The airport is along the road from Lubang to Tagbac.

Marinduque

Marinduque is the near-circular island between South Luzon and Mindoro. The Marinduquero are Tagalog and most of them come from Batangas and Quezon provinces.

Coconuts and rice are the main agricultural products. Two mining companies extract iron ore and copper; there are large copper deposits at Labo near Santa Cruz. The main tourist attraction is the Moriones Festival at Easter, which is great fun and which everyone joins in with good humour (see the Fiestas & Festivals section of the Facts about the Country chapter). This is when Marinduque gets most of its tourists. At other times there aren't many around, as the tourist industry here is just getting going.

BOAC

Boac, on the Boac River, is the capital of Marinduque Province. It is a pretty little town towered over by a massive church with a richly decorated altar built on a hill. Of the passion plays performed all over the island at Easter, each claiming to be the best, the star production of the Moriones Festival is the one staged in Boac from Easter Thursday to Easter Sunday.

Boac Airport is 12 km to the south near Masiga. On the way are a few beach resorts on the pebbly beaches.

Places to Stay

Cely's Lodging House (tel 1519) at 10 de Octubre St has rooms with fan for P60/120. It is simple and clean and has a restaurant. The *Boac Hotel* in Nepomuceno St has basic rooms with fan for P60 and with fan and bath for P90/140.

Pyramid Beach Resort, Caganhao, is on the beach between Boac and Cawit. It has rooms for P60 and is good value. Meals should be ordered in advance.

Also on Caganhao's pebbly beach is the *Aussie Pom Guest House* with pleasant rooms for P100. Weekly and monthly rates can be arranged on request. There is a restaurant and you can hire snorkelling equipment for P20 a day.

A short way out of Boac, towards Mogpog, is the *Swing Beach Resort* (tel 1252) in Deogratias St. It has rooms (with

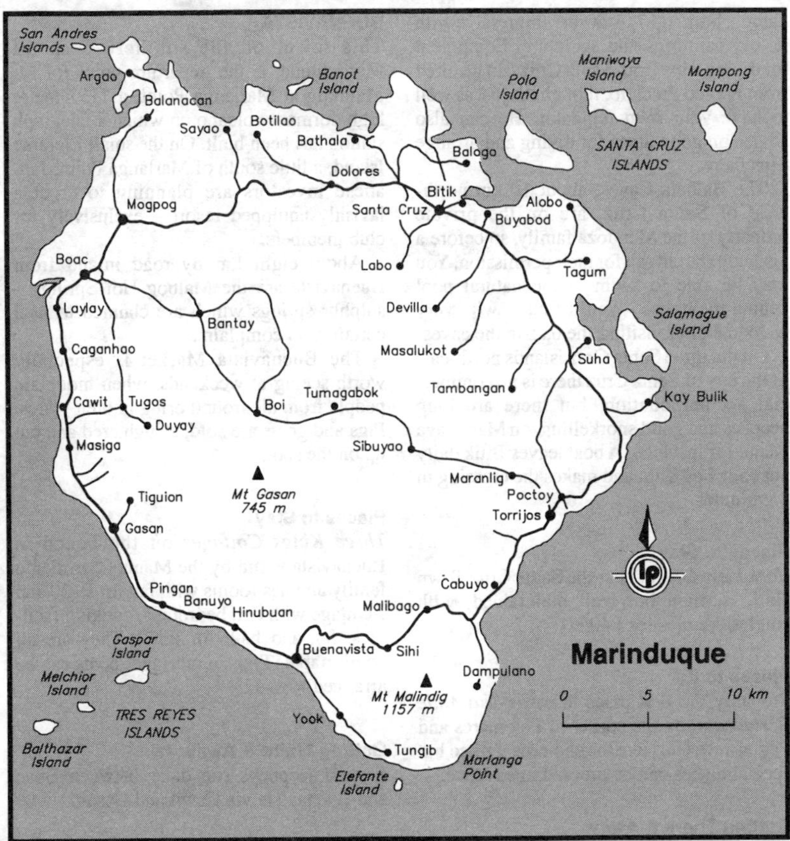

four beds) for P150 per person or P300 per person for full board.

In Cawit, the *Sunraft Beach Hotel* has rooms and cottages with bath for P100. It is basic but relatively good. The *Seaview Hotel* has good, clean rooms with fan and bath for P185/245.

BALANACAN

This small town in north-west Marinduque has a little harbour in a sheltered bay which provides shipping services to and from Lucena on Luzon.

LTB Lodge is a simple place near the wharf, where there are a few small restaurants. Rooms are P30/60 and with fan P50/80.

Getting There & Away

There aren't many jeepneys between Boac and Balanacan daily. It's safer to rely on those that meet the boats.

SANTA CRUZ

Although Boac is the capital of Marinduque, Santa Cruz has the most inhabitants. Its great church, built in 1714, is very impressive with its old paintings and sculpture. Equipment for diving trips from Santa Cruz can be hired from Franco Preclaro, though it's just as well to have your own regulator. He can also advise on good areas for diving and arrange trips there.

The Bathala Caves, about 10 km north-west of Santa Cruz, are on the private property of the Mendoza family, so before a visit you should ask for their permission. You may be able to swim in the natural pool behind the house – you'll find a swim very welcome after visiting the bats in the caves!

On the three Santa Cruz islands north-east of the city of Santa Cruz there is no commercial accommodation, but there are long beaches and good snorkelling, on Maniwaya Island for instance. A boat leaves Bitik daily at about 7 or 8 am and makes the crossing in 45 minutes.

Places to Stay

Park View Lodge, near the Santa Cruz Town Hall, is plain but well maintained, with singles/doubles for P40/80.

Places to Eat

Probably the best place to eat is *Tita Amie Restaurant*, on the corner of Palomares and Pag-asa streets. Here the choice is limited but special dishes can be ordered in advance.

Getting There & Away

Several jeepneys run daily from Boac to Santa Cruz via Mogpog.

GASAN

Like Boac and Mogpog, Gasan is heavily involved in the Easter passion play. Handcrafted basket ware and ornaments are made here; in the UNI Store, for example, you can see how the carved wooden birds are painted.

Places to Stay

UNI Lodge near the Municipal Building is basic but relatively good, with rooms with fan for P50/100. Tricycles, motorcycles and a jeep can be hired here.

BUENAVISTA

This town, on the southern coast of Marinduque, is the departure point for Mt Malindig at Marlanga Point, a 1157 metre high dormant volcano on which a telegraph station has been built. On the small Elefante Island, a little south of Marlanga Point, Japanese investors are planning to erect a lavishly equipped resort – exclusively for club members.

About eight km by road inland from Buenavista are the Malbog Hot Springs – sulphur springs which are claimed to heal certain skin complaints.

The Buenavista Market is especially worth seeing at weekends, when mountain people from all around bring in their wares. Pigs and goats are sold, slaughtered and cut up on the spot.

Places to Stay

Three Kings Cottages on the beach at Buenavista is run by the Manuel Sarmiento family and has rooms with fan for P120 and a cottage with two bedrooms, cooking facilities, fan and bath for P300. They are all comfortable. Trips in outrigger boats can be arranged.

Getting There & Away

Several jeepneys run daily between Boac and Buenavista via Cawit and Gasan.

TRES REYES ISLANDS

It's a 30 minute trip in an outrigger boat from Buenavista to the outlying Tres Reyes (Three Kings) Islands. Although Balthazar and Melchior islands are rocky and uninhabited, the third, Gaspar, has a small village and a lovely coral beach that is good for snorkelling and diving. In 1980 the wreck of a Chinese junk that sank 200 years ago was discovered about 100 metres north of Gaspar Island in 38 metres of water. Although most of its rich cargo of porcelain has already been salvaged, from time to time local divers bring up a few more finds, so the treasure hunt goes on.

TORRIJOS

White Beach at Poctoy near Torrijos is probably the best beach on Marinduque. The outlying coral reef is good for snorkelling and the beach has a magnificent view of Mt Malindig.

Maranlig and Sibuyao, both north-west of Torrijos, make good day trips. Maranlig has cockfights on Sundays; Sibuyao is on a plateau with rice terraces. A jeepney runs daily to Maranlig. There is only one to Sibuyao and that is on Sunday, which is market day.

You can go over to the beach on Salamague Island by boat in an hour, but the Salamague Island Resort, opened a few years ago, is no longer regularly open to guests. It is suffering from a lack of customers and is usually closed.

Places to Stay

A typhoon destroyed the White Beach Cottages but local people only 50 metres or so from the beach rent rooms with cooking facilities for P50. Try Leonard Pilar or Jose Roldan. In Torrijos the mayor, Ben Cordero Lim, has rooms for P50.

Getting There & Away

A few jeepneys run daily from Buenavista to Torrijos via the hill town of Malibago, but be careful, as from late afternoon they don't go beyond Malibago.

There aren't many jeepneys from Santa Cruz to Torrijos. It is safest to rely on those which meet the boat.

TO/FROM MARINDUQUE

You can get to Marinduque from Luzon or Mindoro (see the Transport from Luzon section of the Manila chapter and the To/From section of the Mindoro chapter).

To Luzon

Air PAL flies daily from Boac to Manila.

Boat There is one boat daily from Balanacan to Lucena at 6 am, taking four hours. There is another boat to Lucena, also leaving at 6 am, from Buyabod, the harbour for Santa Cruz. This one takes five hours.

To Mindoro

A boat leaves Gasan for Pinamalayan on Mindoro daily at 10 am, taking three hours or more.

Masbate

The province of Masbate includes Masbate Island and the smaller Ticao and Burias islands. Although the island group is officially part of the Bicol region, the influence of the Visayas is unmistakable, so the Cebuano and Hiligaynon languages are also frequently spoken. Before WW II, Masbate was a leading gold field. Today it is noted for its meat production, having some herds of cattle as large as 4000 head. Fishing is also important economically. Tourism doesn't mean much here, as few foreigners come to these islands, which are off the main traffic routes, so visitors accustomed to rusticity will have a pleasant time here. Even basic commercial overnight accommodation is really only available in the towns of Masbate, Mobo, Aroroy and Mandaon. Lovers of tuba should try the white variety, which is a speciality of Masbate.

MASBATE

The town of Masbate is the capital of the province but hasn't a great deal of note beyond the harbour, the market and numerous stalls which line the streets. It is the base for air and sea travel to places like South Luzon. A few km south-east, in Mobo, is Bitu-on Beach, a popular place to visit, with a beach resort whose cottages are a good alternative to the hotels in the town.

Places to Stay

The *Crown Hotel* in Zurbilo St has basic rooms with fan for P50/100. The *St Anthony Hotel* (tel 263) in Quezon St has simple rooms with fan and bath for P120/180 and with air-con and bath for P250/280.

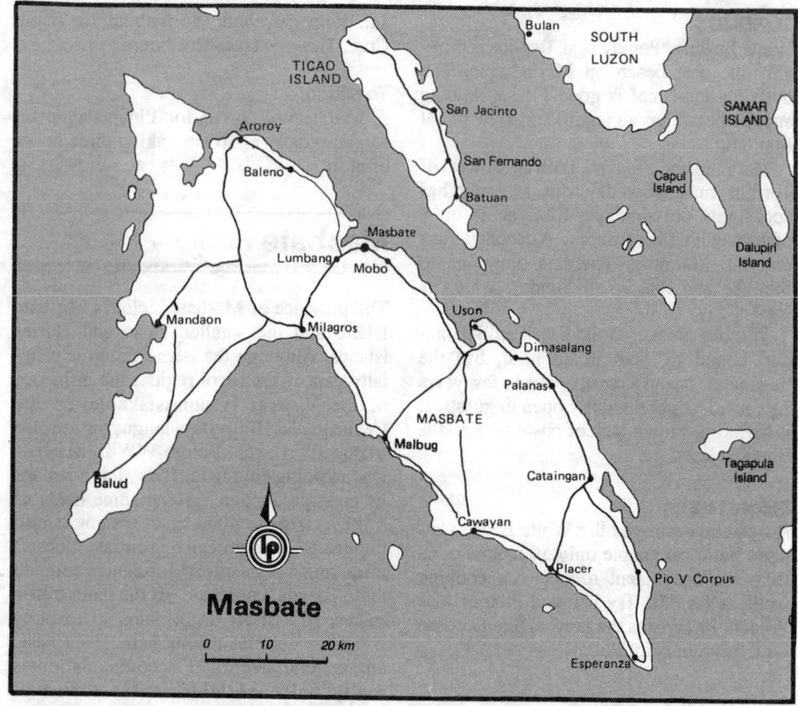

Places to Eat
For a good, reasonably priced meal try *Peking House* in the port area or the *Petit Restaurant* opposite the St Anthony Hotel in Quezon St.

MANDAON

Boats go from Mandaon to Sibuyan Island in Romblon Province. Near the town is Kalanay Cave, where numerous archaeological finds have been made.

Mesa's Lodging right on the beach has rooms for P25/50.

Getting There & Away
Several jeepneys and buses run daily from Masbate to Mandaon, taking two hours. Try to get a seat on the roof if you want a good view of some lovely landscapes.

TO/FROM MASBATE

You can get to Masbate from Cebu, Luzon, Romblon and Samar (see the Transport from Luzon section of the Manila chapter and the To/From sections of the chapters on the other islands).

To Cebu

Boat The Sulpicio Lines' MV *Cebu Princess* leaves Masbate for Cebu City on Saturday at 8 am. It takes 45 hours, going via Calbayog on Samar and Ormoc on Leyte. The boat comes from Manila.

To Luzon

Air PAL has flights from Masbate to Legaspi daily except for Tuesday and Thursday, and daily flights from Masbate to Manila.

Boat A boat leaves Masbate daily for Bulan at 5 am, taking four hours. There may be a second boat some other time during the day.

The Sulpicio Lines has two ships running from Masbate to Manila – the MV *Bohol Princess* on Monday and the MV *Cebu Princess* on Wednesday. Both leave at 2 pm and take 19 hours.

To Romblon

Boat There is one ship a week from Mandaon to Sibuyan Island, leaving on Wednesday or Thursday at 7 pm. After a short trip, it anchors for a time in Maolingon Bay (about 15 to 30 minutes by boat from Mandaon), before going on at about 1 am. The journey takes five hours. You can only find out the exact departure time in Mandaon. Information given in other places varies widely and is not reliable.

To Samar

Boat Two Sulpicio Lines' ships run from Masbate to Calbayog – the MV *Cebu Princess* on Saturday and the MV *Bohol Princess* on Thursday. Both leave at 8 am and take four hours.

Mindoro

Mindoro is the next big island to the south of Manila. It is divided into Mindoro Occidental, which is the western part, and Mindoro Oriental, the eastern part. Only the coastal strip is heavily populated. In the jungles and mountains inland there are various groups of the Mangyan tribes (see the Cultural Minorities section of the Facts about the Country chapter).

Fishing and the cultivation of rice and coconuts are the main economic activities, with some cattle raising around San Jose. Although the name Mindoro is a contraction of the Spanish *Mina de Oro*, meaning 'gold mine', no major gold discovery has yet been made. The difficult terrain has also limited Mindoro's potential for copper and iron-ore mining, and the main mining activity has been the quarrying of marble. There has, however, been some promising oil prospecting in the south-west.

The usual tourist route on Mindoro is from Puerto Galera to Roxas and Mansalay, via Calapan. Puerto Galera is popular for its beaches and extensive coral reefs. Roxas is the starting point for boat trips to Tablas and Boracay islands, and from Mansalay you can get to the villages of the Mangyan. Except in dry seasons, the more isolated coast of Mindoro Occidental is impassable by land; you can only tour it by boat.

PUERTO GALERA

The fine beaches and excellent diving at Puerto Galera have been attracting travellers for some time. For about 50 years, it has been regarded by zoologists, botanists and students of the University of the Philippines as an ideal place to study the eco- structure of animals, plants and microorganisms in almost undisturbed natural conditions. In 1934, the UP Marine Biological Station was set up. Forty years later, the United Nations Man & Biosphere Program International declared Puerto Galera a nature centre. It was at this time that the media also discovered the attractions of Puerto Galera as a tourist resort, and the place took off.

The town's new wealth has attracted foreign interest and investment. It has also split the population into two opposing camps: the developers and the environmentalists. The developers see in tourism the business opportunity of a lifetime and advocate expansion at any price. The environmentalists are concerned about the detrimental effects development is having on the customs and morals of the inhabitants and on the natural features of their environment. Comparisons with the beginning of tourist developments in Kuta Beach in Bali, Hikkaduwa in Sri Lanka and Pattaya in Thailand have some basis. Puerto Galera has something of all three: there are joints and magic mushrooms; occasionally there is nude bathing; and gays and girls from Ermita come here with their boyfriends of various nationalities.

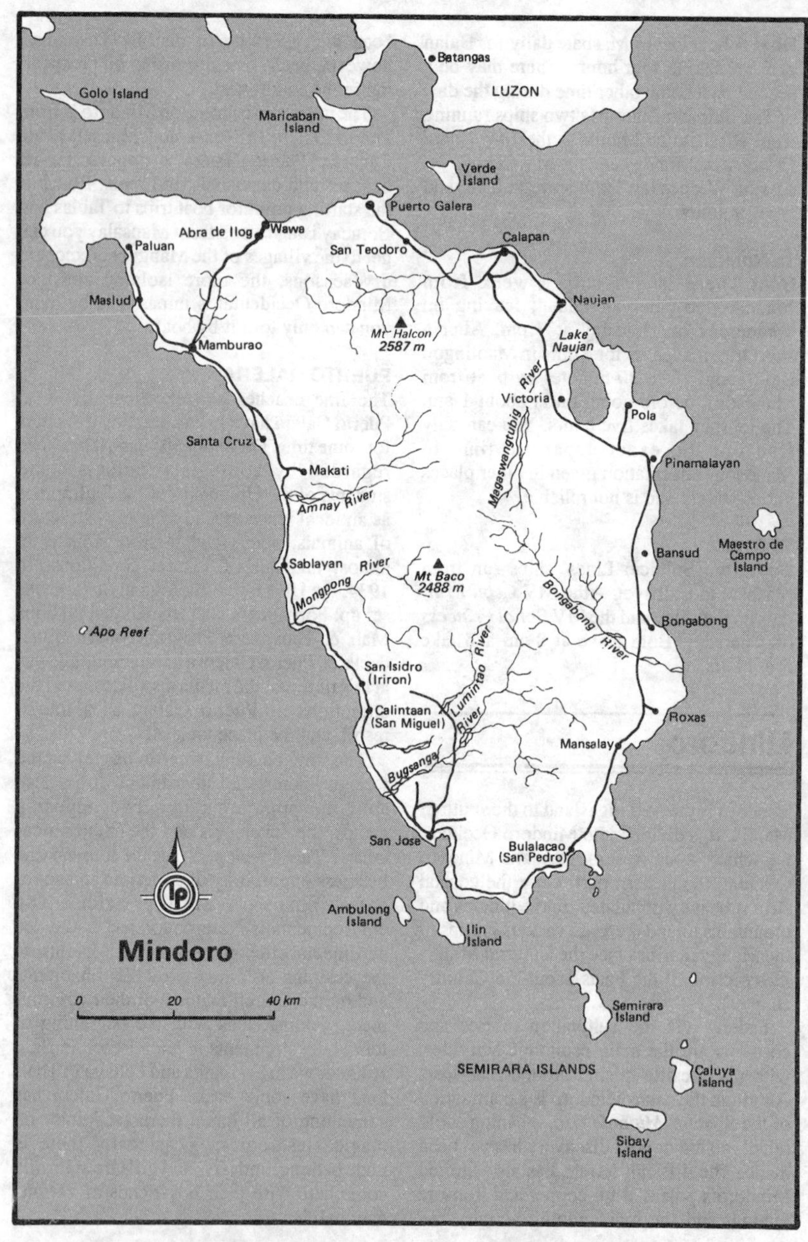
Batangas
LUZON
Golo Island
Maricaban Island
Verde Island
Puerto Galera
Wawa
Abra de Ilog
Paluan
San Teodoro
Calapan
Naujan
Maslud
Mt Halcon 2587 m
Lake Naujan
Mamburao
River
Victoria
Pola
Magaswangtubig
Santa Cruz
Pinamalayan
Makati
Amnay River
Maestro de Campo Island
Bansud
Sablayan
River
Mt Baco 2488 m
Mongpong
Bongabong
Bongabong River
Apo Reef
Lumintao River
San Isidro (Iriron)
Calintaan (San Miguel)
River
Roxas
Mansalay
Bugsanga
San Jose
Bulalacao (San Pedro)
Ambulong Island
Ilin Island
Mindoro
0
20
40 km
Semirara Island
SEMIRARA ISLANDS
Caluya Island
Sibay Island

It's a trendy place which tourism, unless carefully supervised, could easily destroy. The adage that tourism is like fire – it can cook your food but it can also burn down your house – should be heeded in Puerto Galera. Considering the tourism potential of this little beauty spot, the disruption of the environment has so far been kept within bounds. In fact, the locals have made short shift with bolo and bullet of some over-zealous and ignorant foreign investors.

Puerto Galera has a most beautiful natural harbour, and the view from the deck of the ferry as you come through the Batangas Channel is a delight. Spanish galleons once sought shelter here from typhoons, and the name dates from that era, when this was the gateway for Spanish traders on their way to China, India, Sumatra and Java. In the small museum by the church you can see pieces of pottery from various Chinese dynasties as well as a fine collection of shells.

The journey from Manila by bus and boat is comfortable by Philippine standards and only lasts about five hours. Although it can be rainy and somewhat cool, most visitors come to Puerto Galera in December and January. Tourist numbers have usually declined by mid-March, but sunny and exceptionally still weather can still be enjoyed between June and October.

Puerto Galera is on the blacklist of the drug authorities, so be prepared for an occasional clamp-down. Spot checks are common when the ferry arrives.

The Rural Bank in Puerto Galera changes cash and may also change travellers' cheques. The Margarita Shopping Center changes both cash and travellers' cheques.

Places to Stay

Christine's Place on the edge of town on the quiet Balete Beach has basic rooms for P60. So does *Malou's Hilltop Inn*. *Melxa's Greenhill Nipa Hut* has rooms with fan for P60/120. It is also quite simple. *Bahay Pilipino* has basic rooms with fan for P70/100, and has a restaurant. *Jelliz* has rooms with fan for P60/100. It is a straightforward place with a restaurant.

The *Fishermen's Cove Beach House* is on a quiet bay about a km out of town towards White Beach. It has rooms for P50 and with bath for P100. It is good value and has a restaurant.

Cathy's Travellers Inn has rooms for P50, with bath for P100, and a cottage with bath for P150. It is homely and is about two km out of town towards Halige Beach and Boquete Beach.

The *El Canonero Marivelis Hotel* is right near the wharf and has rooms with fan and bath for P100. It is nice and tidy and has a restaurant. *Villa Margarita Bamboo House* has basic rooms with fan and bath for P100. *Villa Margarita White House* has rooms with fan and bath for P100-125/150. It is well maintained and has a restaurant.

The *Outrigger Hotel* is on Hundora Beach on the southern edge of town. It has rooms with fan and bath for P180 and is comfortable. It has a restaurant.

Holiday Garden Apartelle belongs to the Villa Margarita. It has good, clean rooms with fan and bath for P250 and apartments with fan and bath for P400.

Encenada Beach Resort is about 1½ km out of town towards Sabang. It has rooms and cottages with fan and bath for P280. It is pleasant, beautifully laid out, and has a restaurant. You can go windsurfing and water skiing and use Hobie Cats. Reservations can be made in Manila at Puerto Galera Bus & Ferry, Sundowner Hotel (tel 5213344), Mabini St.

Tanawin Lodge consists of small fully furnished two-storey houses with living rooms and bedrooms. It has rooms and cottages with bath for P600 to P1100. The grounds are the nicest in Puerto Galera and it has a restaurant and a swimming pool with a bar. Bookings can be made in Manila at the Executive Run, Sundowner Hotel (tel 5221435), Mabini St.

Places to Eat

Around the docks at Puerto Galera various restaurants serve European and Filipino dishes. Among these are *El Canonero Restaurant*, the *Rendezvous Restaurant* and the

Typhoon Restaurant. The cuisine is international at the *Villa Margarita White House* and the *Jelliz Bar & Restaurant*, while the *Pier Pub* serves pizzas.

Getting There & Away

You can go from Manila to Puerto Galera via Batangas (see the Transport from Luzon section of the Manila chapter). Several jeepneys run from Calapan to Puerto Galera every day between 7 am and 4 pm, leaving from the market. The trip takes two hours. A Special Ride by outrigger boat from Calapan to Puerto Galera costs P350.

From Mamburao to Abra de Ilog one jeepney runs daily at 6 am. It takes two hours or more. It may go the rest of the way to the wharf at Wawa. If not, get another jeepney or a tricycle. The boat for Puerto Galera leaves Wawa between 8 and 9 am, sometimes earlier. If there's no boat, as sometimes happens, you're up for a Special Ride at P400. The regular price is P15 (not the P50 which is sometimes demanded after the boat arrives). The trip takes two hours or more.

The trip from San Jose to Puerto Galera has to be done in several stages. The jeepney from San Jose to Bulalacao leaves between

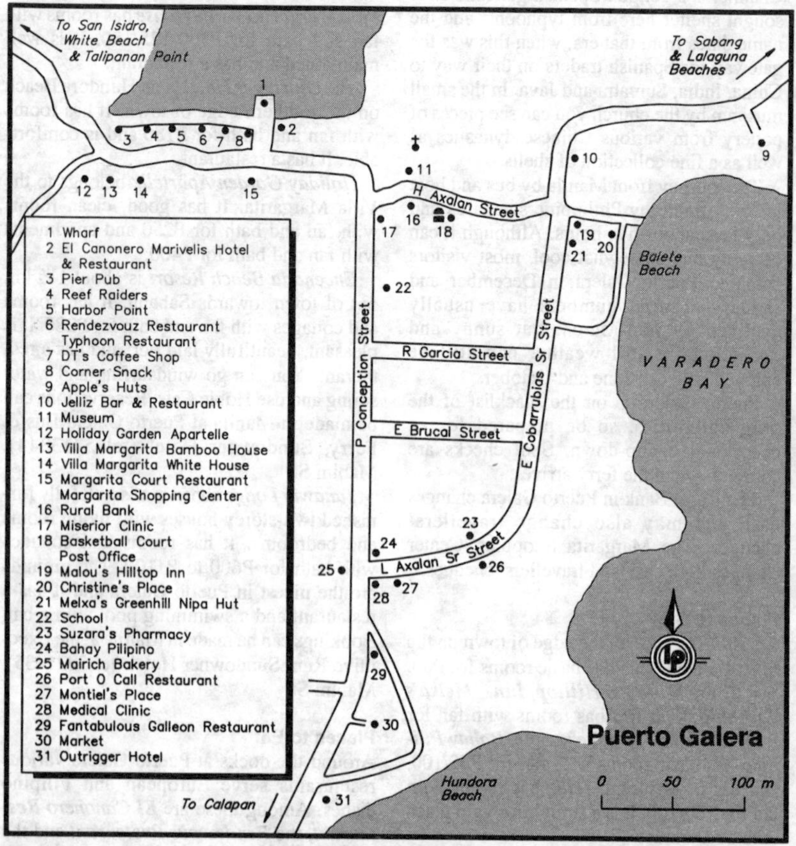

6 and 7 am from the Metro Bank; it's a rough trip of four hours. Alternatively, you could make this part of the trip by outrigger boat, leaving between 8 and 9 am and taking three hours or more. From Bulalacao, you travel by bus to Roxas, a one-hour journey along a road which is bad as far as Mansalay. A big bus takes you from Roxas to Calapan in four hours. The final stage of the journey is done by jeepney and takes two hours. The last jeepney leaves Calapan for Puerto Galera at 4 pm.

Warning The road between Abra de Ilog and Puerto Galera, shown on most maps of the Philippines, was never built.

AROUND PUERTO GALERA

Beaches just outside Puerto Galera, such as Balete Beach and Hundora Beach, are rather undeveloped and may disappoint some pampered beach-lovers. Most travellers prefer the ones a few km further away. In almost every bay with a beach that's at all usable, you'll find cottages for local and foreign tourists. To the east, resorts have sprung up at Sabang Beach, Small Lalaguna Beach and Big Lalaguna Beach. To the south, they go as far as Tabinay Beach. To the west, White Sand Beach and the neighbouring Talipanan Point are about the limit. The main beaches near Puerto Galera have had electricity laid on. However, considering the number of power failures, it's just as well to have a torch handy.

The greatest commercial activity is in Sabang, where restaurants have been built on sites close to the water and the remaining beach is almost completely blocked by outrigger boats. In Sabang visitors apparently prefer living it up at night to lying on the beach by day, so at night near the discos and bars it can get pretty noisy.

The flimsy cottages are packed close together at Big Lalaguna Beach, but the coral reef is worth seeing and is good for snorkelling. Reef Raiders Dive Center conducts diving courses from US$180. As well as day trips throughout the year, this dive centre runs diving tours from February to May with

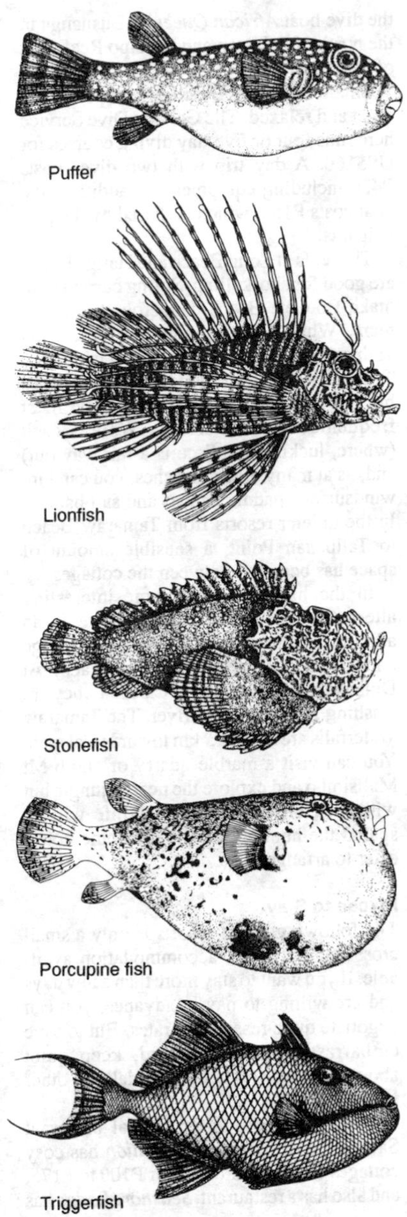

Puffer

Lionfish

Stonefish

Porcupine fish

Triggerfish

the dive boat *African Queen* to Busuanga in the north of Palawan and the Apo Reef west of Mindoro.

Small Lalaguna Beach is comparatively quiet and relaxed. The Galleon Dive Service here runs four or five-day diving courses for US$160. A day trip with two dives costs P420 including equipment. In addition, the boat costs P160, which is shared by the participants.

The reefs at Long Beach and Halige Beach are good for snorkelling. Strong currents can make Boquete Beach dangerous for swimmers. White Beach, Tamaraw Beach and Talipanan Beach, all between San Isidro and Talipanan Point, are good bathing beaches but not so good for snorkelling. The most frequented in this area is White Beach (where, luckily, the disco is a fair way out) and, as at many others beaches, you can hire windsurfers, paddle bancas and sail bancas. In the quieter resorts from Tamaraw Beach to Talipanan Point, a sensible amount of space has been left between the cottages.

In the hinterland are some interesting alternatives to beach living. There is an admittedly fairly civilised Mangyan village barely one km behind White Beach. At Dulangan, six km towards Calapan, they are washing for gold in the river. The Tamaraw Waterfalls are about 15 km towards Calapan. You can visit a marble quarry or climb Mt Malisimbo and explore the nearby jungle but with luck the endangered wildlife will be spared the hunting trips which some hotels offer to arrange.

Places to Stay

The following list of resorts is only a small cross section of the accommodation available. If you want to stay more than a few days and are willing to pay in advance, you can negotiate quite reasonable rates. But to save embarrassing your landlord, keep quiet about the rates you get – especially to other landlords!

You can choose from several places at Sabang Beach. *Traveller's Station* has cosy cottages with fan and bath for P100 to P175, and also has a restaurant. *Seashore Lodge* has basic and good cottages with fan and bath for P150 to P250. It has a restaurant. *John's Place* has clean and good cottages with fan and bath for P200. *Terraces Garden Resort* has rooms with fan and bath for P250. It is clean and good and has a restaurant. The surroundings are pleasant – small houses among tropical plants on a slope above Sabang.

There are various places at Small Lalaguna Beach. *China Moon* has popular cottages with fan and bath for P80. Both *Nick & Sonia's Cottages* and *Full Moon* have plain but well-maintained cottages with fan and bath for P100. Full Moon has a restaurant. *El Galleon Beach Resort* has rooms with fan and bath for P150 to P200. It is comfortable and has a restaurant. *Carlo's Inn* is on the slopes. It has rooms with fan and bath for P150 to P250 and apartments with fan and bath for P250 to P450. It also has weekly and monthly rates, is clean and good and has a restaurant.

Marina's Inn at Big Lalaguna Beach has simple and good cottages with fan and bath for P120 to P150.

Rosita's at Big Lalaguna Beach has cottages with fan and bath for P150 to P250. It is pleasant and has a restaurant.

Coco Beach Resort at Coco Beach has rooms with fan and bath for US$30. It is in nice surroundings and has a restaurant, windsurfing, sailing and diving, and even a barber shop and beauty parlour. Reservations can be made in Manila at the Coco Beach Booking Office, Sundowner Hotel (tel 5215958), Mabini St.

You will find the following places at White Beach. *Lodger's Nook* has simple cottages for P80 and with fan and bath for P100 to P150, and also has a restaurant. *Crystal Garden Beach Resort* has cottages with fan and bath for P120. It is good value and has a restaurant. *White Beach Nipa Hut* has basic and good cottages with fan and bath for P120 to P150. It has a restaurant and is open until midnight. *Summer Connection* has cottages with bath for P150. It is a pretty little place, with a restaurant, pleasantly situated on the slope at the western end of White Beach.

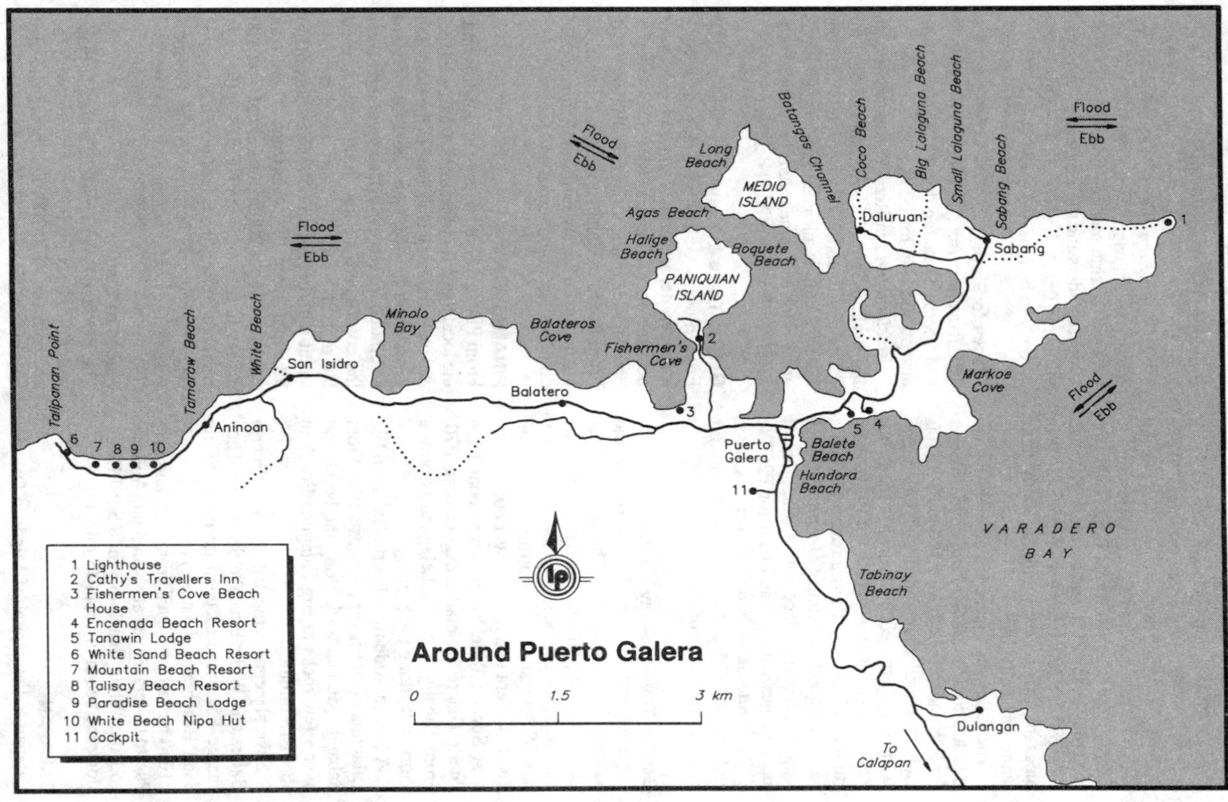
Flood
Ebb
Long Beach
MEDIO ISLAND
Batangas Channel
Coco Beach
Big Lalaguna Beach
Small Lalaguna Beach
Sabang Beach
Agas Beach
Daluruan
Sabang
1
Halige Beach
Boquete Beach
PANIQUIAN ISLAND
Minolo Bay
Balateros Cove
Fishermen's Cove
2
Markoe Cove
Talipanan Point
Tamaraw Beach
White Beach
San Isidro
Balatero
3
5
4
Aninoan
6
7
8
9
10
Puerto Galera
Balete Beach
Hundora Beach
11
VARADERO BAY
Tabinay Beach
1 Lighthouse
2 Cathy's Travellers Inn
3 Fishermen's Cove Beach House
4 Encenada Beach Resort
5 Tanawin Lodge
6 White Sand Beach Resort
7 Mountain Beach Resort
8 Talisay Beach Resort
9 Paradise Beach Lodge
10 White Beach Nipa Hut
11 Cockpit
Around Puerto Galera
0
1.5
3 km
Dulangan
To Calapan

Cherry's Inn has cottages with bath for P150. It is simple but has a good restaurant. *White Beach Lodge* has cosy cottages with fan and bath for P150, and also has a good restaurant.

Tamaraw Beach Resort at Tamaraw Beach has cottages for P120 and cottages with bath for P180 to P200. It has a restaurant and is in pleasant, shady surroundings with table tennis and volleyball.

The following places are all at Talipanan Beach. *Paradise Beach Lodge* has cottages for P75 and with bath for P100 to P120. It is plain but well maintained and has a restaurant. *Talisay Beach Resort* has rooms for P100 and cottages with bath for P150. In an attractive location, it has a restaurant and a bar with good cocktails. *Mountain Beach Resort* is a pretty place with a restaurant. It has cottages with fan and bath for P250 to P300. *White Sand Beach Resort* has basic cottages for P75 and cottages with bath for P100. It has a restaurant.

Getting There & Away

Jeepneys run between Puerto Galera and Sabang. They charge P5. The last one back leaves Sabang in the late afternoon. The unsealed road can be impassable after heavy rain. A Special Ride by outrigger boat from Puerto Galera to Sabang costs P80.

A Special Ride by outrigger boat from Puerto Galera to Small Lalaguna costs P70. From Sabang to Small Lalaguna is only a short walk along the beach.

A Special Ride from Puerto Galera to Big Lalaguna by outrigger boat costs P60. From Sabang, you can walk along the beach and over a few rocks to Big Lalaguna Beach in about 15 minutes.

Several jeepneys run daily between Puerto Galera and White Beach in San Isidro. They charge P5. Some of them go on to White Sand Beach at Talipanan Point. This costs P10. The last one back from San Isidro to Puerto Galera leaves at about 5 pm. You can go from White Beach to White Sand Beach along the beach in about 45 minutes.

CALAPAN

Calapan is the capital of Mindoro Oriental Province. The Sanduguan Festival was held here for the first time from 18 to 21 May 1981. *Sanduguan* means friendship in the Mangyan language. At the festival they re-enacted the first meeting between seafaring Chinese traders and the indigenous Mangyan at Aroma Beach. It was such a success that it is likely to be repeated every year.

Places to Stay

The *Travellers Inn* (tel 1926) in Leuterio St has rooms with fan for P50/70 and with air-con and bath for P250.

Riceland Inn I in Rizal St has rooms with fan for P50-55/65-75, with fan and bath for P95-105/120 and with air-con and bath for P215/225. It is pleasant, the restaurant is good value and some rooms have wide beds. *Riceland Inn II* is in M H del Pilar St.

Getting There & Away

From Puerto Galera to Calapan, several jeepneys depart from 7 am onwards from near the docks. The trip takes two hours. A Special Ride in an outrigger boat costs P350. From Roxas to Calapan is a four-hour trip – big buses run hourly until 3 pm. You can also do it in stages by minibus and jeepney.

PINAMALAYAN

From Pinamalayan boats go to Sibali Island, the local name for Maestro de Campo Island, and on to Banton Island, both in the Romblon group. You can also take a boat from here to Marinduque. You can ask about timetables at the coast-guard station, 200 metres beyond the market. From the coast-guard station a street with houses on both sides runs off to the right along the waterfront. There's an open area about 200 metres along, and 100 metres further on is the beach. On the right are three houses, the last of which is painted bright green and belongs to the Wortner-Perez family, with whom you can stay.

Places to Stay

The *Wortner-Perez House* is a simple place with dorm beds for P50 and rooms with fan and bath for P100/200. Full board can also be arranged for about P250 per person. They serve Filipino and Viennese-style European food. For excursions you can rent rubber boats and motorcycles there.

BONGABONG

From Bongabong boats run to Tablas on Romblon (see the To/from Mindoro section at the end of this chapter).

Mabuhay Lodging House near the market has simple rooms with fan for P30/60.

ROXAS

From Roxas, big outrigger boats run to Tablas on Romblon and Boracay on Panay (see the To/from Mindoro section). That's probably the only reason for staying here. Some of the waiting time can be spent at the nearby Melco Beach.

Places to Stay

Santo Nino Lodging House has basic rooms for P30 per person; it has a restaurant.

Melco Beach Lodge at Dangay has rooms and cottages for P40/60. It is simple and relatively good and has a restaurant. It is a P5 tricycle ride from town and, although the beaches are not terribly good, it's a good place to stay while waiting for boats to Tablas or Boracay.

Getting There & Away

Big buses leave the market at Calapan hourly every day from early morning to 3 pm, bound for Roxas via Pinamalayan and Bongabong. It takes two hours to reach Pinamalayan, three hours to Bongabong and four hours to Roxas.

Minibuses in the market at Calapan go to Bongabong. From Bongabong to Roxas, the last jeepney or minibus goes at about 6 pm from the market. The only reliable information about departure times comes from the drivers; information that the waiting passengers give you will usually be useless.

MANSALAY

This is a good starting point for visits to the Mangyan tribes, but be warned that rubbernecks or camera-happy tourist are not appreciated. Father Antoon Postma, a Dutch missionary who has published a number of books and articles on this peaceful tribe, took care of the Mangyan around Mansalay for many years. A visit without reason is intrusive and unnecessary. If, however, you are genuinely interested in the problems of these minority groups, the members of the mission are informative and cooperative.

Getting There & Away

Several jeepneys run daily from Roxas to Mansalay. If you want to go on into the mountains to visit the Mangyan, go early or you'll be walking in the noon heat.

SAN JOSE

Among other things, San Jose is one of the starting points for diving excursions to Apo Reef. It is in the south-western part of Mindoro Occidental and is handy for people with a bit of time to fit in a boat trip to Palawan. Boats only leave for Coron on Busuanga seldom and very irregularly. In Mindoro Occidental there are many cultural minorities, the most remote tribes having little contact with civilisation. Occasionally some come into town and with luck you may meet Mangyans who will guide you to their village.

Queen's Ranch is a good place for a day trip. It is two hours away by jeepney and you can stay there overnight for P50 per person. From there it takes about eight hours on foot to reach the Mt Iglit Tamaraw Reservation.

Boats can also be hired in San Jose for swimming and snorkelling on the nearby islands like Ilin and Ambulong. On Ambulong is the Ambulong Beach Resort.

Places to Stay

The *Jolo Hotel* (tel 618) in Rizal St has rooms for P40/60, with fan for P45/70 and with fan and bath for P80/100. It is simple and fairly good and has a restaurant.

The *Midtown Pension House* in Raja Soliman St has clean rooms with fan for P40/80 and with fan and bath for P60/120. As it is beside the market, you can be sure of waking early in the morning.

The *Sikatuna Hotel* (tel 697) in Sikatuna

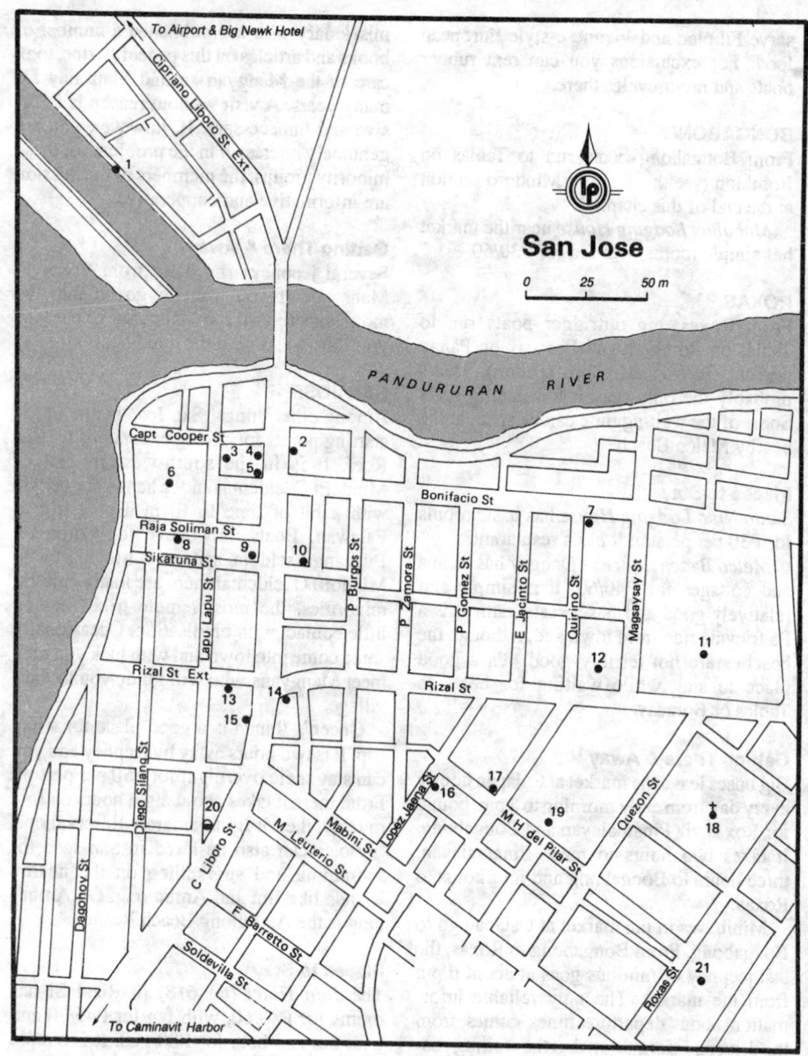

St has rooms with fan for P40/60 and with fan and bath for P75/100. It is homely and good value.

The *Big Newk Hotel* near the airport in Airport Rd has singles/doubles with fan and bath for P100/160-180 and doubles with air-con and bath for P300. It is comfortable and has a restaurant.

Getting There & Away

Few buses make a daily trip from Roxas to Bulalacao, so it's better to go by jeepney to

1 North Pier (Boats to Sablayan)
2 Masagana Shipping Lines
3 Loreto Shipping Lines
4 Golden Hotel
5 Cora's Restaurant
6 Market
7 William Lines
8 Midtown Pension House
9 Mosquera's Hotel
10 Sikatuna Hotel
11 Pilot School
12 High School
13 Gem Hotel
Hong Kong Restaurant
14 Jolo Hotel & Restaurant
15 Philippine Airlines
16 Bachelor's Inn
17 Philippine National Bank
18 Church
19 Police Station
Post Office
Town Hall
20 Ramadel Bus Terminal
21 Divine Word College

Mansalay and then get another jeepney on to Bulalacao. This takes about two hours. Leave early if you don't want to stay in Bulalacao overnight.

A boat leaves Bulalacao for San Jose in the morning any time between 8 and 10.30 am, depending on the tides. The trip takes two hours or more, usually finishing at South Pier, Caminawit Harbor, four km out of San Jose. In the dry season, from December to May, it is also possible to get there by jeepney, leaving at 4 am.

From Mamburao to San Jose via Sablayan, there is at least one jeepney daily, taking eight hours. In the rainy season the jungle track becomes impassable and outrigger boats are the only way to make the journey. Departure is at 8 am, with a midday halt in Sablayan and finishing in San Jose at North Pier. It takes 11 hours.

SABLAYAN & APO ISLAND

Like San Jose, Sablayan is a starting point for excursions to tiny Apo Island, with the wide Apo Reef to the east. Divers, snorkellers and would-be Robinson Crusoes should have a good time here.

The three lighthouse keepers on the island are relieved at the end of the month and there's a good chance of hitching a free lift then. Otherwise you have to charter a boat. A return trip in a big outrigger boat, including a trip round the island, shouldn't cost more than P1400. Arrange a pick-up time beforehand. The only place to camp is at the south-eastern end, but make sure your tent is closed up before sunset or you will be tortured by sandflies. Take your own food and about five litres of water per day. The lighthouse keepers are always happy to get cigarettes.

Places to Stay

The *Emely Hotel* has rooms for P35/70 and with fan for P80. It is a basic place but meals can be arranged. The small restaurants near the pier close at about 7 pm.

MAMBURAO

Mamburao is the capital of Mindoro Occidental Province. It has a daily air connection to and from Manila.

Places to Stay

Traveller's Lodge has rooms with fan for P50/100 and with fan and bath for P75/120. It is a simple place with a restaurant.

Mamburao Beach Resort has rooms and cottages with bath for P1200 per person including meals. It is pleasant and has a restaurant as well as Hobie Cats and windsurfers. It is several km outside Mamburao – P100 by tricycle. Information and reservations can be made in Manila at Mamburao Resort Corporation (tel 8152733), Cityland Condominium III, on the corner of Estaban and Herrera streets, Makati.

Getting There & Away

From Puerto Galera, a boat leaves daily at about noon for Wawa – the landing place for Abra de Ilog – as long as there are enough passengers. It takes two hours or more and should cost P15, not the P50 likely to be

Trees of the Philippines

Screw pine *(Pandanus tectorius)*

Sago palm *(Metroxylon sagu)*

Pitogo palm *(Cycas rumpii)*

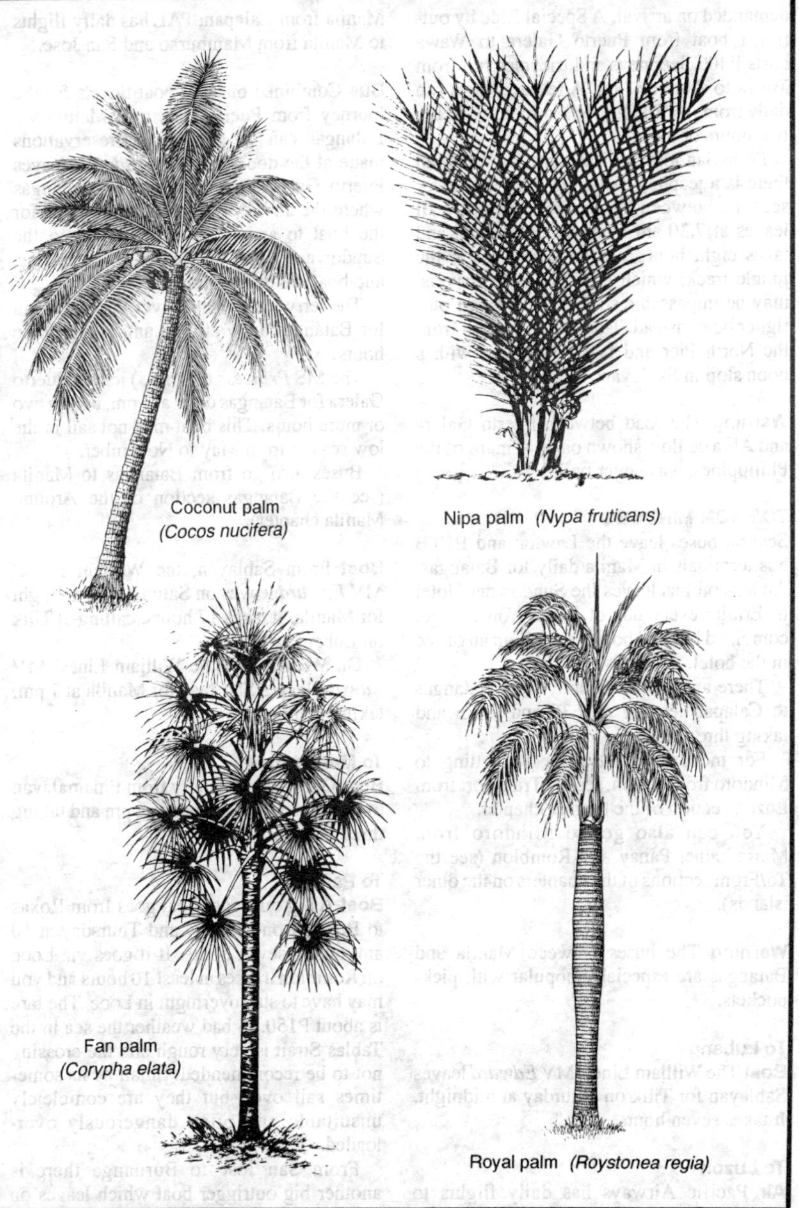
Coconut palm
(*Cocos nucifera*)

Nipa palm (*Nypa fruticans*)

Fan palm
(*Corypha elata*)

Royal palm (*Roystonea regia*)

demanded on arrival. A Special Ride by outrigger boat from Puerto Galera to Wawa costs P400. Jeepneys and tricycles run from Wawa to Abra de Ilog. A few jeepneys run daily from Abra de Ilog to Mamburao, taking two hours or more.

From San Jose to Mamburao via Sablayan there is a jeepney daily, but only in the dry season, between December and May. It leaves at 7.30 am from the Jolo Hotel and takes eight hours. In the rainy season the jungle track, which crosses a lot of rivers, may be impassable so there will be an outrigger boat instead. This leaves at 8 am from the North Pier and takes 11 hours, with a noon stop in Sablayan.

Warning The road between Puerto Galera and Abra de Ilog, shown on most maps of the Philippines, was never built.

TO/FROM MINDORO

Several buses leave the Lawton and BLTB bus terminals in Manila daily for Batangas. An air-con bus leaves the Sundowner Hotel in Ermita every day at 9 am. You can get combined bus and boat tickets from an office in the hotel.

There are two boats daily from Batangas to Calapan leaving at 7.30 and 9 am and taking three hours.

For more information about getting to Mindoro from Luzon, see the Transport from Luzon section of the Manila chapter.

You can also get to Mindoro from Marinduque, Panay and Romblon (see the To/From sections of the chapters on the other islands).

Warning The buses between Manila and Batangas are especially popular with pickpockets.

To Lubang

Boat The William Lines' MV *Edward* leaves Sablayan for Tilik on Saturday at midnight. It takes seven hours.

To Luzon

Air Pacific Airways has daily flights to Manila from Calapan; PAL has daily flights to Manila from Mamburao and San Jose.

Bus Combined bus and boat tickets for the journey from Puerto Galera to Manila via Batangas can be bought and reservations made at the docks. The MB *Sikat II* leaves Puerto Galera daily at 9 am for Batangas where the air-con bus waits at the dock for the boat to arrive, and goes direct to the Sundowner Hotel in Manila. The trip (bus and boat) takes five hours.

The ferry MS *Queen* leaves Puerto Galera for Batangas daily at 7.30 am, taking three hours.

The MS *Princess* (Express) leaves Puerto Galera for Batangas daily at 1 pm, taking two or more hours. This boat may not sail in the low season from May to November.

Buses also go from Batangas to Manila (see the Batangas section of the Around Manila chapter).

Boat From Sablayan, the William Lines' MV *Edward* leaves on Saturday at midnight for Manila. It takes 17 hours, calling at Tilik on Lubang.

On Wednesdays the William Lines' MV *Edward* leaves San Jose for Manila at 7 pm, taking 16 hours.

To Marinduque

Boat One boat goes daily from Pinamalayan to Gasan, leaving at 5 am or 2 pm and taking three hours or more.

To Panay

Boat A big outrigger boat goes from Roxas to Boracay on Monday and Thursday at 10 am, taking seven hours. If it goes via Looc on Romblon it takes at least 10 hours and you may have to stay overnight in Looc. The fare is about P150. In bad weather the sea in the Tablas Strait is very rough and the crossing not to be recommended. Small boats sometimes sail over, but they are completely unsuitable and often dangerously overloaded.

From San Jose to Buruanga there is another big outrigger boat which leaves on

Thursday and Sunday at 9 am. It usually takes eight hours, but sometimes takes as long as 12 hours. This trip is also not recommended when the waves are high in Tablas Strait.

To Romblon

Boat From Bongabong, a big outrigger boat runs to Carmen on Tablas on Wednesday, Friday and Sunday at 9 am. It takes six hours and then goes on from Carmen on Tablas to Romblon on Romblon.

A big outrigger boat runs irregularly from Pinamalayan to Sibali Island and then continues on to Banton Island.

From Roxas to Looc, a big outrigger boat goes on Sunday and Friday at 10 am, sometimes also on Monday and Thursday. It takes four hours. It may possibly go to Odiongan and not Looc.

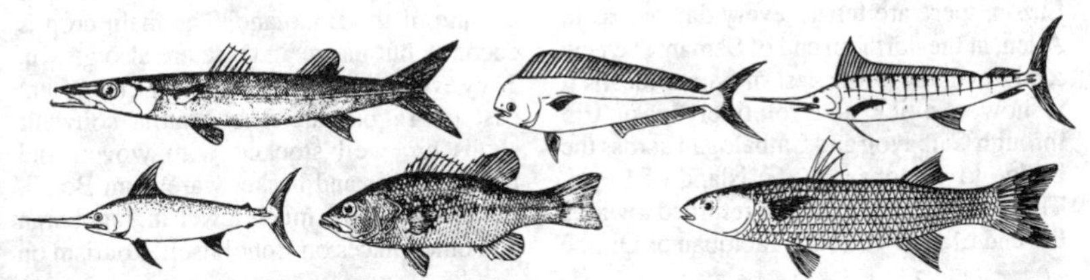

The Visayas

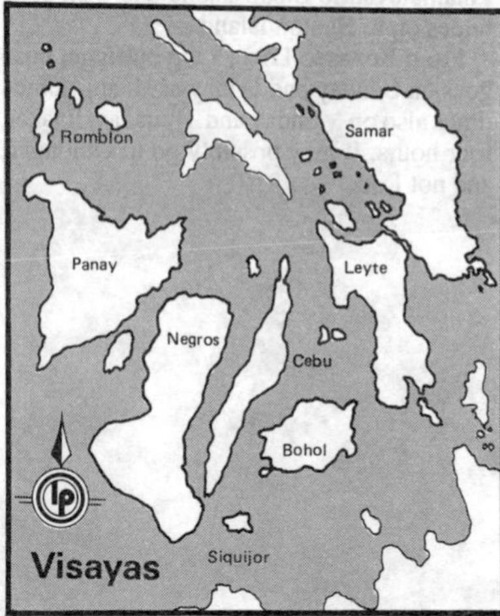

South of the island of Luzon is the main island group of the Philippines, the Visayas. The major islands in this group are Bohol, Cebu, Leyte, Negros, Panay, Romblon, Samar and Siquijor. The Visayas are bordered to the south by Mindanao and to the west by long, narrow Palawan.

Island Hopping

It's in the Visayas that possibilities for island hopping in the Philippines are at their best. A possible circuit of the Visayas could take you to most of the places of interest with minimal backtracking. Starting from Manila, you could travel down to the Bicol region and, from Matnog, at the southern tip of Luzon, there are ferries every day across to Allen, at the northern end of Samar. The new road down the west coast of Samar means it is now a quick and relatively easy trip through Calbayog and Catbalogan across the bridge to Tacloban on the island of Leyte. This was where MacArthur returned towards the end of WW II. From Tacloban or Ormoc there are regular ships to Cebu City or less regularly from Maasin to Bohol.

Cebu was where Magellan arrived in the Philippines and you can still find a number of reminders of the Spanish period. From Cebu there are daily ferries to the neighbouring island of Bohol, famous for its Chocolate Hills. Ferries also cross daily between Cebu and Negros, either in the south of the island to Dumaguete, or closer to Cebu City from Toledo to San Carlos. You can then continue by bus to Bacolod, where you can get a ferry across to Iloilo on Panay.

Panay has the usual assortment of bus and jeepney routes. At the north-west tip you can make the short crossing by outrigger boat to the beautiful and laid-back island of Boracay. After a spell of lazing on the beach there, you can find another boat to cross to Tablas in the Romblon group, usually to Looc in the south. Take a jeepney to Odiongan and a boat from there to Roxas in Mindoro. Another bus ride will take you to Puerto Galera, a popular travellers' beach centre. Finally, there are daily ferries to Batangas, only a few hours by bus from Manila – quite an interesting and adventurous trip.

Bohol

Situated between Leyte and Cebu, in the south of the Visayas, Bohol is the 10th largest island of the Philippines. Another 72 small islands belong to the province of the same name. Agriculture is the main source of income of the Boholano. The main crop is coconut, but maize and rice are also grown. They even have rice terraces near Lila, 25 km east of Tagbilaran. The Manila souvenir shops are well stocked with woven and plaited goods and basket ware from Bohol, but the prices are much lower in Tagbilaran and other places on Bohol itself. Tourism on this attractive island with its friendly people is only just being developed. Its historical significance is due to the blood compact between the Spanish conqueror Legaspi and Rajah Sikatuna. Today most visitors go to Bohol to see the Chocolate Hills. The Swiss author Erik von Daniken had a great time writing about this strange hilly landscape. A few km north of Tagbilaran, near Corella, live the rare, shy tarsier monkeys, the smallest monkeys in the world, with large, round eyes and long tails.

TAGBILARAN

There are no special sights in Tagbilaran, the capital of Bohol Province. The best beach near the city is Caingit Beach, behind the Hotel La Roca, but even it is nothing special. You can take some interesting trips from Tagbilaran to Panglao Island or along the western and eastern coasts of Bohol. The main street is Carlos P Garcia Ave, or CPG Ave for short. Every day there is a never-ending stream of noisy tricycles and the dust and exhausts make for a really thick atmosphere. In this street is the Agora Market, where you can catch buses and jeepneys. In the CPG Ave you will also find restaurants and many shops, including the Tagbilaran Friendly Bazaar, where a moneychanger on the ground floor will give a good exchange rate. The Philippine National Bank has a branch near the plaza and the post office is in a new building next to the City Hall.

The airport is on the northern edge of town and a tricycle from there to the market costs P3. If you are planning to leave Bohol by plane you would be well advised to reconfirm your flight out immediately on arrival and have it entered on a list, as the system may not yet be computerised. Philippine Airlines does not have an office in town.

If you arrive by ship it is only a km from the wharf to the market and costs P2 by tricycle.

Places to Stay

Traveller's Inn in Carlos P Garcia Ave has singles/doubles with fan for P100/120, with fan and bath for P140/160 and with air-con and bath for P250/350. It has a lounge and is simple and reasonably good.

Executive Inn (tel 3254) in J S Torralba St has simple singles/doubles with fan for P50/70, with fan and bath for P80/100 and with air-con and bath for P150/200.

Vista Lodge (tel 3072) in Lesage St has singles/doubles for P40/60, with fan and bath for P70/90 and with air-con and bath for P150/175. It is unpretentious but fairly good.

Vista Lodge Annex (tel 2326) in M H del Pilar St has reasonable rooms for P35/50, with fan for P45/65 and with fan and bath for P60/80. The rooms at the back are noisy from 7 am because of the nearby school.

The *Dagohoy Hotel* (tel 3479) in Cellestino Gallares St has rooms with fan for P60/120 and with fan and bath for P80/160. It is simple and has rooms by the hour.

LTS Lodge (tel 3310) in CPG Ave has clean, good rooms with fan for P100/180 and with air-con and bath for P200/380.

The *Gie Garden Hotel* (tel 3182) in M H del Pilar St has rooms with air-con and bath for P250/380. It is friendly and well kept and has a restaurant.

The *Hotel La Roca* (tel 3179) in Graham Ave, on the northern edge of town near the airport, has rooms with fan and bath for P170/160 and with air-con and bath for P330/380 and suites from P530. It's a comfortable place with a restaurant and a swimming pool.

Island Leisure Inn (tel 2482) in the Ilaw International Center at Bool is about three km east of Tagbilaran. It has dorm beds for P50, rooms with fan and bath for P150/200 and with air-con and bath for P200/265. Some rooms have a balcony. It is nice and tidy and has a restaurant, bar and disco.

Places to Eat

The *Gie Garden Hotel* restaurant has good cheap meals. The food at the seafood restaurants to the right of the wharf can also be recommended.

The *Garden Café*, a bamboo building next to the church, is a pleasant place to sit. Its owners are deaf-mutes. Although the menu is not large, they are happy to do special orders such as mango and banana omelettes.

JJ's Food Stream and the *Rose Restaurant* have reasonably priced meals. The *Leoning Snack Bar & Bakery* serves cake, ice cream and shakes, as well as breakfast. The *Harvest Restaurant* and the *Horizon Restaurant* in the Agora Market Complex are very good but a bit dearer.

Entertainment

The *Ideal Snack Corner* not only serves snacks and cheap daily meals but also shows nonstop feature films on a big screen. The well-run *Park Side Restaurant* serves excellent meals and turns on rock and pop videos and sing-alongs for its guests until midnight. If you want a late beer with billiards and bowling, try the *Marbella Complex*, the *Channel Five Disco* and the *Inner Patio Disco* in Burgos St, about one km out of town going towards Bool.

AROUND TAGBILARAN

There are some some historical sights to the north and east of Tagbilaran. It is best to hire a car and do a round trip, possibly starting from Alona Beach on Panglao Island. There would also be time to include a detour to the Chocolate Hills. The following places can be reached by public transport from Tagbilaran.

About 15 km north of Tagbilaran near Maribojoc stands the old Punta Cruz Watchtower, built in the time of the Spaniards in 1796 to look out for pirates. It gives a good view over other islands of the Visayas.

Loon, a few km to the north-west, has a beautiful old church dating back to 1753. It has noteworthy ceiling frescoes. Various kinds of basket ware are for sale on Sundays in the market at Antequera, about 10 km north-east of Maribojoc. Little more than a km outside this place are the beautiful Inambacan Falls.

A memorial at Bool, barely three km east of Tagbilaran, is a reminder of the blood compact between Legaspi and Rajah Sikatuna. At Bool there is also the Ilaw International Center, with its open-air restaurant,

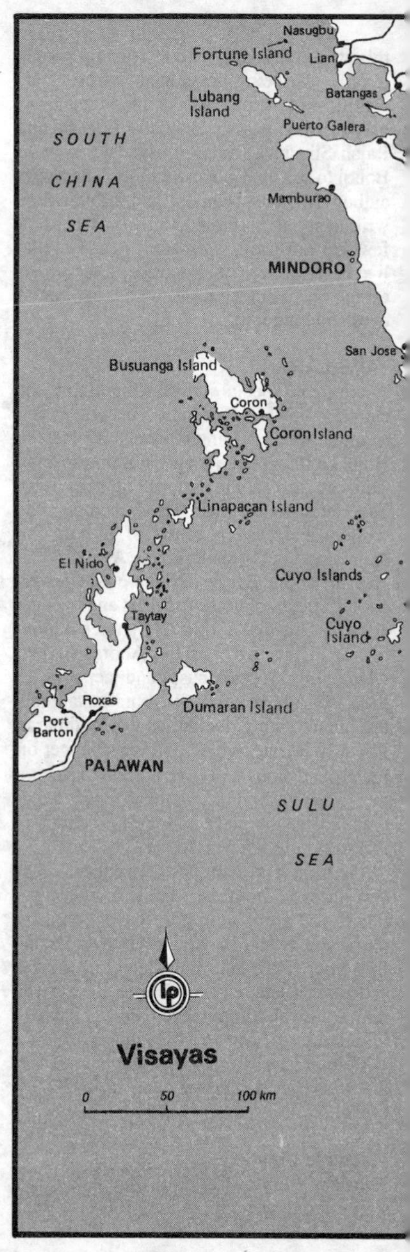

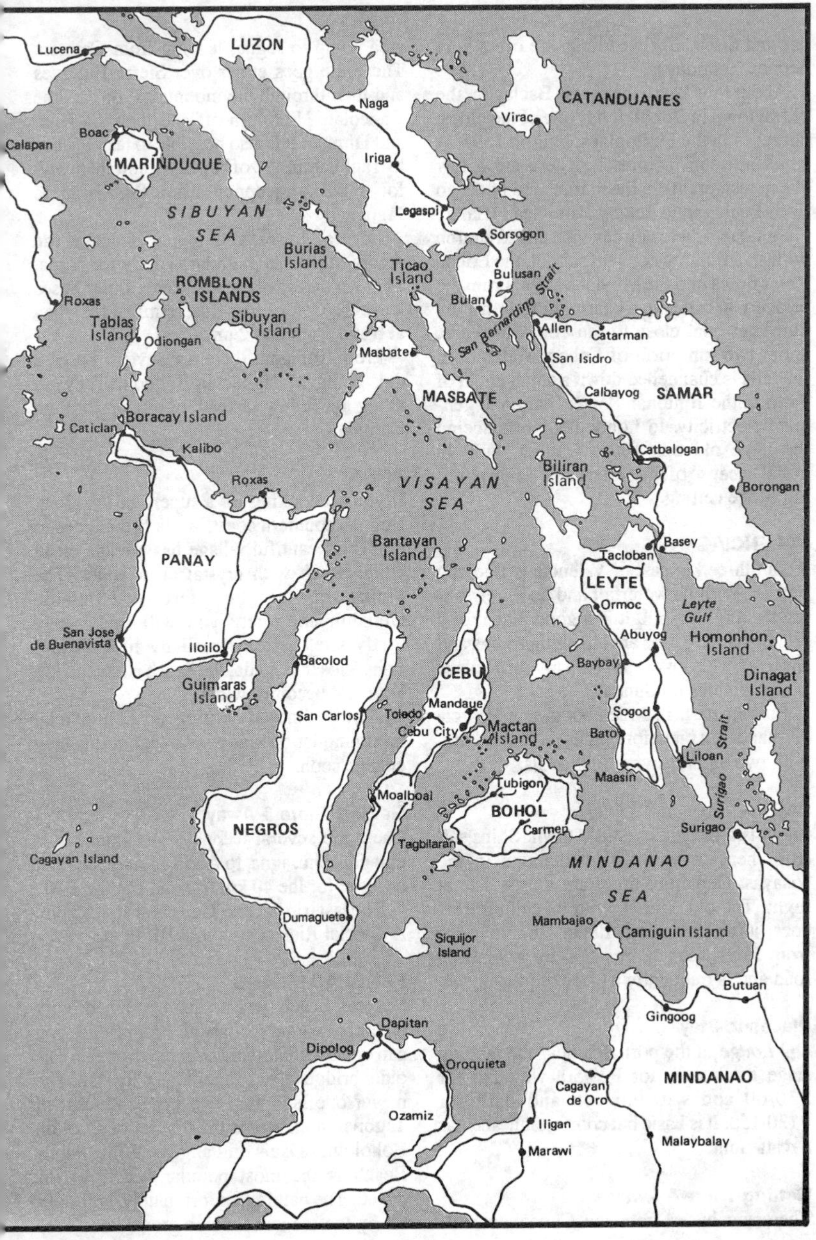
LUZON
Lucena
Naga
CATANDUANES
Virac
Boac
Calapan
MARINDUQUE
Iriga
Legaspi
SIBUYAN
SEA
Sorsogon
Burias
Island
Ticao
Island
Bulusan
ROMBLON
ISLANDS
Roxas
Bulan
San Bernardino Strait
Tablas
Island
Sibuyan
Island
Odiongan
Allen
Catarman
Masbate
San Isidro
MASBATE
Calbayog
SAMAR
Boracay Island
Caticlan
Kalibo
Catbalogan
Biliran
Island
Roxas
VISAYAN
SEA
Borongan
Basey
Bantayan
Island
Tacloban
PANAY
LEYTE
Ormoc
Leyte
Gulf
San Jose
de Buenavista
Iloilo
Abuyog
Homonhon
Island
Bacolod
CEBU
Baybay
Guimaras
Island
Dinagat
Island
San Carlos
Mandaue
Toledo
Sogod
Cebu City
Mactan
Island
Bato
Liloan
Surigao Strait
Maasin
Tubigon
Moalboal
BOHOL
NEGROS
Carmen
Surigao
Tagbilaran
Cagayan Island
MINDANAO
SEA
Dumaguete
Mambajao
Camiguin Island
Siquijor
Island
Butuan
Gingoog
Dapitan
Dipolog
Oroquieta
MINDANAO
Cagayan
de Oro
Ozamiz
Iligan
Malaybalay
Marawi

bar and disco. Big weddings are often held here on Saturdays.

About four km to the east is Baclayon, the oldest town in Bohol. It has one of the oldest churches in the Philippines, built in 1595. A small museum adjoins it. There are a few cheap restaurants in the market and boats go from Baclayon to nearby Pamilacan Island.

At Loay, where you can visit an old church with an adjoining convent school, the Loboc River flows into the Mindanao Sea. From the bridge you can take a charming river trip by outrigger boat close to the Tontonan Falls, about two km north of Loboc. Water from the falls is channelled down a small chain of dams to the Tontonan Power Station to generate electricity. In Loboc it's worth seeing the large old San Pedro Church, built in 1602, because of the remarkable naive painting of the ceiling.

VALENCIA

About three km east of Valencia is Badiang Spring. With its waterfall and cool, refreshing swimming pool, it is a good place for a relaxing stay. There are changing rooms and showers. This lovely spot is a favourite place for excursions on Sundays.

Further east, in Maambong, near Garcia Hernandez, a bit before Jagna, is Roxas Park, with two natural swimming pools.

JAGNA

Jagna is a busy, clean little town. Ships sail from here to various destinations in the Visayas. Departure times are mostly late at night. The old church, with its ceiling frescoes, is worth seeing. Ilihan Hill, four km from Jagna, can be reached by a winding road and is frequently a place of pilgrimage.

Places to Stay

DQ Lodge in the port area near the landing stage has rooms for P25/50, with fan for P30/60 and with air-con and bath for P130/150. It is basic but comfortable and has a restaurant.

Getting There & Away

There are buses from the Chocolate Hills area going to Jagna, leaving from Carmen. The route goes either over Sierra Bullones and then through the mountains, or past the Chocolate Hills turn-off and then via Bilar and Dimiao. It is also possible to take the bus to Tagbilaran, get off in Loay and then wait for a bus or jeepney from Tagbilaran to Jagna.

Several buses and jeepneys leave the Agora Market in Tagbilaran daily for Jagna. The trip takes two hours. Ceres Liner buses leave the Ceres Liner Bus Terminal for Ubay at 6 and 9 am and 2 pm.

From Tubigon, there are several buses a day going to Jagna via Talibon. They go along the coast instead of going through Carmen.

ANDA

If you are looking for a superb beach along Bohol's southern coast, Anda is the place to go. This beautiful village has a wide, clean white beach with crystal clear water. The picturesque scenery starts just outside Guindulman, where you will find lonely sandy stretches separated by rock formations; closer to Anda, the beach is several km long and becomes wider.

At the time of writing no commercial accommodation was available, but this may change soon.

Getting There & Away

There are several jeepneys and mini buses that go from Jagna, to Anda, taking one hour or more for the 40 km trip and costing P10.

The last trip back to Jagna is at about 5 pm. A Special Ride costs about P150 one way.

PANGLAO ISLAND

Several beach resorts have opened very recently on Panglao Island. From Bohol you can cross to this island over two bridges. The older bridge is near Tagbilaran City Hall. The newer one is almost two km south-east of Tagbilaran and joins the district of Bool on Bohol with Dauis on Panglao. White Alona Beach is the most popular beach on the island. The bathing, unfortunately, is spoilt a bit by the sea grass which grows knee deep

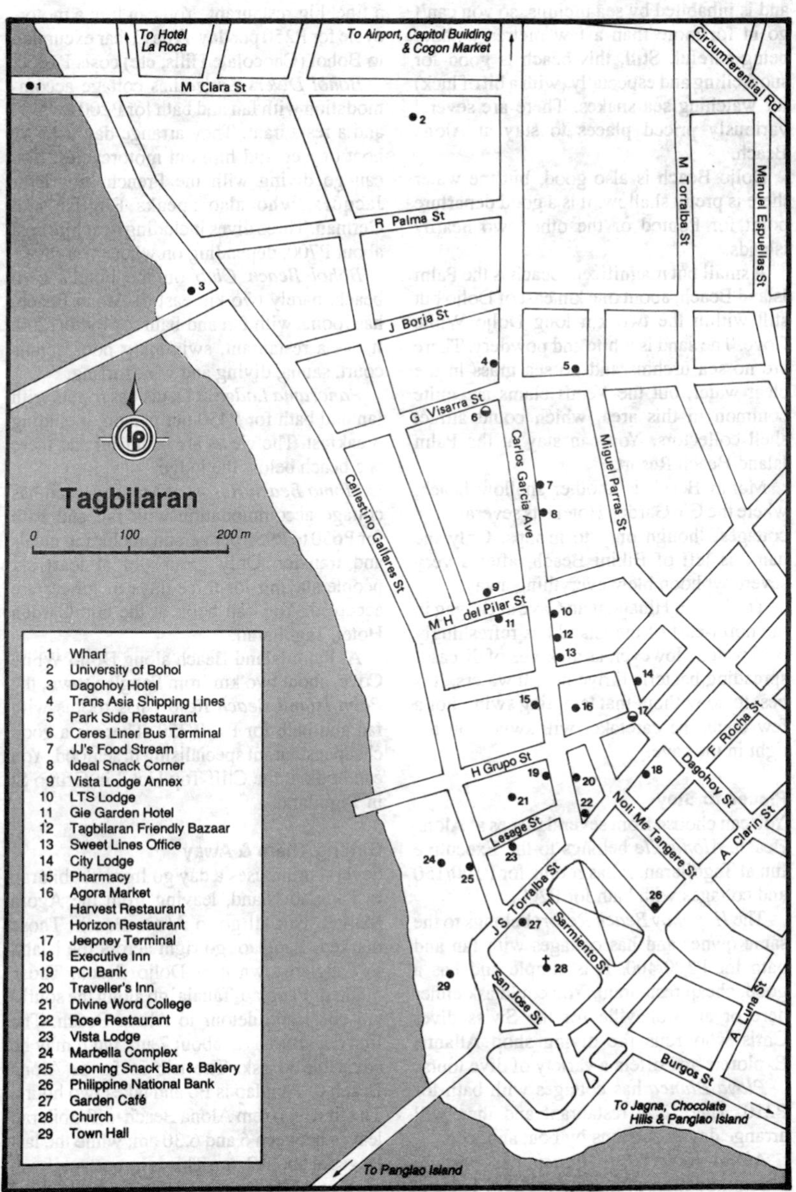
To Hotel La Roca
To Airport, Capitol Building & Cogon Market
M Clara St
Circumferential Rd
M Torralba St
Manuel Espuellas St
R Palma St
J Borja St
G Visarra St
Carlos Garcia Ave
Miguel Parras St
Cellestino Gallares St
M H del Pilar St
F Rocha St
Dagohoy St
H Grupo St
Noli Me Tangere St
A Clarin St
Lesage St
J S Torralba St
F Sarmiento St
San Jose St
A Luna St
Burgos St
To Jagna, Chocolate Hills & Panglao Island
To Panglao Island
Tagbilaran
0
100
200 m
1 Wharf
2 University of Bohol
3 Dagohoy Hotel
4 Trans Asia Shipping Lines
5 Park Side Restaurant
6 Ceres Liner Bus Terminal
7 JJ's Food Stream
8 Ideal Snack Corner
9 Vista Lodge Annex
10 LTS Lodge
11 Gie Garden Hotel
12 Tagbilaran Friendly Bazaar
13 Sweet Lines Office
14 City Lodge
15 Pharmacy
16 Agora Market
Harvest Restaurant
Horizon Restaurant
17 Jeepney Terminal
18 Executive Inn
19 PCI Bank
20 Traveller's Inn
21 Divine Word College
22 Rose Restaurant
23 Vista Lodge
24 Marbella Complex
25 Leoning Snack Bar & Bakery
26 Philippine National Bank
27 Garden Café
28 Church
29 Town Hall

and is inhabited by sea urchins, so you can't go in for more than a few metres without being careful. Still, this beach is good for snorkelling and especially (with a bit of luck) for watching sea snakes. There are several variously priced places to stay at Alona Beach.

Doljo Beach is also good, but the water there is pretty shallow. It is a good departure point for Pontod or the other two nearby islands.

A small but magnificent beach is the Palm Island Beach, about one km east of Doljo but still within the two km long Doljo White Cove. The sand is white and powdery. There are no sea urchins and no sea grass in the clear water, but the Venus clams are quite common in this area, which could attract shell collectors. You can stay at the Palm Island Beach Resort.

Momo Beach is another shallow beach, where the Gie Garden Hotel lets several large cottages, though only to groups. Only the name is left of Bikini Beach, after a very severe typhoon blew everything away.

The lake in Hinagdanan Cave at Bingag in the north-east of the island has refreshingly cool water. However, as all kinds of disease-spreading bacteria thrive in still waters, it is best to do without that tempting swim. For a few coins the caretaker will switch on the light in the cave.

Places to Stay

You can choose from several places at Alona Beach. *Alonaville* belongs to the Executive Inn at Tagbilaran. It has rooms for P100/150 and cottages with bath for P200.

The *Hoyohoy Beach Resort* belongs to the same owner and has cottages with fan and bath for P300/400. It is simple and has a good, cheap restaurant. You could ask either here or at Alonaville for the Swiss diver Chris who runs the diving shop Atlantis Explorers and offers a variety of dive tours.

Playa Blanca has cottages with bath for P210. There is a restaurant and they will arrange day excursions by boat and jeep.

Alona Kew White Beach has cottage accommodation with bath for P250. There is a fine, big restaurant. You can hire a motorcycle for P250 per day. A day's car excursion to Bohol (Chocolate Hills, etc) costs P1000.

Bohol Divers Lodge has cottage accommodation with fan and bath for P200 to P300 and a restaurant. They arrange day trips by boat or jeep and hire out motorcycles. You can go diving with the French proprietor Jacques, who also speaks English and German. Three dives including gear hire cost about P700, depending on where you dive.

Bohol Beach Club on the hotel's own beach, barely two km east of Alona Beach, has rooms with fan and bath for P950/1200. It has a restaurant, swimming pool, tennis court, sauna, diving and windsurfing.

Panorama Lodge at Dauis has rooms with fan and bath for P450 per person, including breakfast. The views are beautiful and there is a beach below the lodge.

Momo Beach Resort at Momo Beach has cottage accommodation with fan and bath for P650 to P950 per person, including meals and transfer. Only groups of at least six people staying for three days or longer are accepted. You can book at the Gie Garden Hotel, Tagbilaran.

At Palm Island Beach along Doljo White Cove, about two km from Panglao town, the *Palm Island Beach Resort* has rooms with fan and bath for P150/250. There is a good cheap restaurant specialising in seafood. You can book at the Cliff Top Hotel in Grupo St in Tagbilaran.

Getting There & Away

Several minibuses a day go from Tagbilaran to Panglao Island, leaving from the Agora Market. Not all go to Alona Beach. Those marked 'Panglao' go right across the island to Panglao town near Doljo Beach. Those marked 'Panglao-Tauala' go along the southern coast and detour to Alona Beach. The first departure is at about 7 am, but it may be advisable to ask. The trip as far as Alona Beach or Panglao is P6 and takes two hours. The first bus from Alona Beach to Tagbilaran leaves between 6 and 6.30 am, while the last leaves at about 2 pm. This is important if you are just making a day trip as normally there

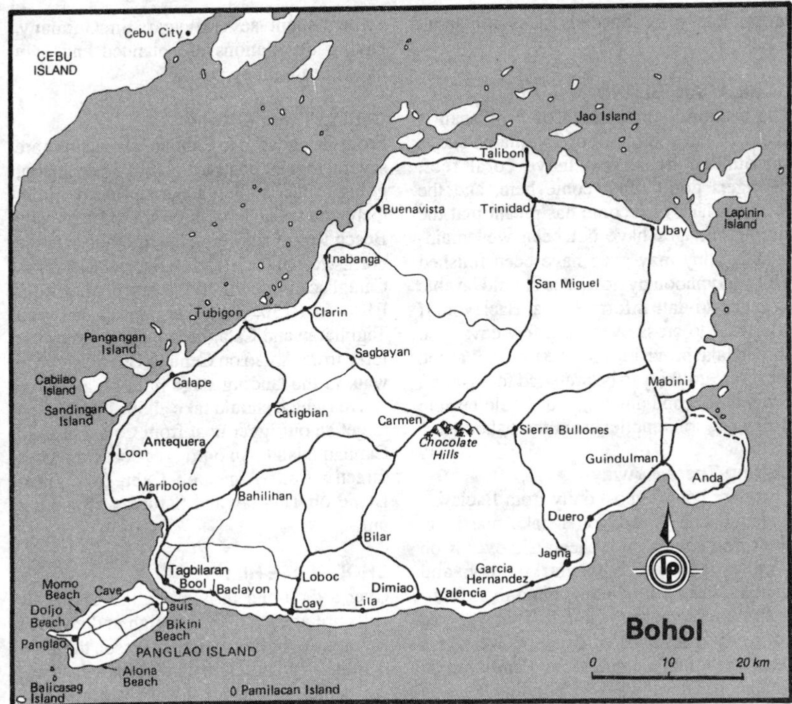

are no tricycles waiting for passengers at the beach.

From Tagbilaran to Doljo Beach or Alona Beach by tricycle costs P80, but P100 is often asked. The trip takes one hour.

BALICASAG ISLAND

The small island of Balicasag lies about 10 km south-west of Panglao Island. It is surrounded by a coral reef which offers excellent diving and snorkelling. This underwater world is a marine sanctuary which the local fishermen know and respect. Strangers have so far been very scarce on this somewhat remote island. One of them didn't want to leave and shot himself at the top of the lighthouse. Since then, the lighthouse has been closed to visitors.

Places to Stay

The *Balicasag Island Dive Resort* has good rooms with fan and bath for P300/400. It has a restaurant and there is diving equipment for hire. Diving tours (two dives) with a guide cost US$25.

You could also ask around for private accommodation on the island. There are basic cottages where you can stay the night for P30. Rice and fish will be prepared on request, but it wouldn't hurt to bring a few tins and maybe a bottle of rum from Tagbilaran.

Getting There & Away

It is proposed to run boats fairly regularly from Tagbilaran to Balicasag Island, which would take two hours. Please make further inquiries. Otherwise the Alona Beach resort proprietors offer Special Rides for about P300.

PAMILACAN ISLAND

The beautiful small island of Pamilacan is about 20 km south-east of Tagbilaran and is surrounded by an extensive coral reef. Strangers don't often come here, and the resultant lack of income has meant that the simple cottages have not been well maintained. They may even have been finished off by a typhoon by now. You should be able to get up-to-date information at Baclayon. If you want to cross over for a few days, you should take provisions for the first day, as the locals are unlikely to be prepared for visitors. From the second day on, you should be able to arrange for supplies from the fishermen.

Getting There & Away

There are boats almost daily from Baclayon to Pamilacan Island which take one hour. Your best chance of a cheap trip over is on Wednesday, which is market day, and Sunday when the fishermen and their families return home from church. That will cost you only a few pesos. Even on weekdays there are often people from Pamilacan in Baclayon. They always anchor their boats on the right-hand side of the landing stage looking towards Pamilacan and leave for home shortly before 3 pm. If you can wait for them, you won't have to pay the P250, which is about what a Special Ride would cost.

CABILAO ISLAND

Cabilao Island is 30 km, as the crow flies, north-west of Tagbilaran in Cebu Strait between Bohol and Cebu. The nearby reef offers excellent snorkelling and diving. Several large beach resorts on Cebu prefer these diving grounds for their guests and send diving boats almost daily.

Places to Stay

La Estrella Beach Resort has dorm beds with bath for P50 and rooms and cottages with bath for P150. There is a restaurant with Filipino and German cuisine, as Babie, the owner, spent several years in Germany. Diving installations are planned and may have been built by now.

Getting There & Away

From Catagbacan to Cabilao Island, there are several regular boats a day for P5 per person, going to the landing stage at Talisay. From there you walk about three km to La Estrella Beach Resort adjoining the lighthouse in the north-west of the island. A Special Ride from Catagbacan directly to the resort costs from P100 to P150. There are buses between Tagbilaran and Catagbacan. If you go by car ferry from Argao on Cebu to Bohol, you can walk to the landing stage in Loon after you arrive (which should take about 10 minutes) to get an outrigger boat from Catagbacan to Cabilao Island. An outrigger boat even goes directly from Argao on Cebu to Cabilao Island on Tuesday and Saturday at about 2 pm.

CHOCOLATE HILLS

Over a thousand in number, the Chocolate Hills are about 30 metres high and covered in grass. At the end of the dry season the grass is quite dry and chocolate coloured, hence the name. If you are not in a hurry, you should spend the night in the Chocolate Hills Complex to experience the strange effect of the sunrise in this mysterious landscape the following morning. Admission to the complex is P3.

There are two legends about the origin of the Chocolate Hills and two geological explanations. The first legend tells of a fight between two giants who threw stones and sand at each other for days, until they were so tired and exhausted they made friends and left the island. They didn't, however, tidy up the battlefield, leaving the Chocolate Hills. The second legend is a lot more romantic. Arogo, a young and unusually strong giant, fell in love with an ordinary mortal, Aloya. After Aloya's death, Arogo cried bitterly. The Chocolate Hills are proof of his grief, for his tears turned into hills.

According to some geologists, Bohol lay under water in prehistoric times. Volcanic eruptions caused unevenness on the bottom of the sea which was gradually smoothed and rounded by the movement of the water. Most serious geologists, however, regard such an explanation as nonsense. Even though the geological origin of the hills has not yet been explained beyond doubt, the consensus is that they are weathered formations of a kind of marine limestone lying on top of impermeable clay soils. Comparisons have been made with the Hundred Islands of North Luzon.

Places to Stay

Hostel Chocolate Hills has dorm beds for P50 and double rooms with bath for P150. It is pleasant and has a restaurant and a swimming pool.

Getting There & Away

Several buses a day leave Tagbilaran for Carmen from the Agora Market. The trip takes two hours. Ceres Liner buses leave the Ceres Liner Bus Terminal for Talibon and Ubay at 6 am and 2 and 3 pm. This takes one hour or more, but you have to get off before Carmen. The other passengers will make sure the bus driver stops at the right place. It is about a 500 metre walk from the main road to the Chocolate Hills Complex. The last bus leaves Carmen for Tagbilaran at about 5 pm.

From Tubigon to Carmen, there are several buses a day. They leave fairly reliably after the arrival of a ship from Cebu and take two hours. The bus may continue beyond Carmen and pass the turn-off to the Chocolate Hills Complex. Otherwise, take the next bus or jeepney going to Bilar, Loay or Tagbilaran to the turn-off. From there it is about a 500 metre walk. You can also take a tricycle from Carmen to the complex, which costs P30 to P40.

TUBIGON

Tubigon is a small place with a wharf for ships to and from Cebu.

Alexandra Reserva Lodging House is near the wharf and bus terminal and has rooms with fan for P40/60. It is simple and the rooms are also let by the hour.

Getting There & Away

There are several buses a day from Carmen to Tubigon, taking two hours. The last bus leaves at about 5 pm. If there is no bus from Tagbilaran which you can take from the turn-off on the main road to Carmen, you can always hitchhike.

From Tagbilaran to Tubigon, there are daily Ceres Liner buses at 6 am and 2 and 3.30 pm, taking an hour or more. A tricycle from the Agora Market to the Ceres Liner Bus Terminal shouldn't cost any more than P2.

UBAY

Ubay is a little place on the eastern coast of Bohol from which boats leave daily for Maasin and Bato on Leyte.

Royal Orchid Pension House has rooms for P50/100 and with fan for P60/120. It's an unpretentious but comfortable place with a common room.

Getting There & Away

From Carmen to Ubay via Sierra Bullones, there are several buses a day. They come either from Tagbilaran (these you can board at the turn-off on the main road) or from Carmen.

From Tagbilaran to Ubay, there are a few Ceres Liner buses a day, leaving from the Ceres Liner Bus Terminal. The buses going via Jagna leave at 6 and 9 am and 2 pm; those travelling via Carmen and Sierra Bullones leave at 3 pm. The trip takes three hours. Additional buses may leave from the Agora Market.

From Ubay to Tagbilaran via Sierra Bullones and Carmen, there is a daily Ceres Liner bus, which might leave at 2 pm or earlier. The buses going via Jagna leave at 4 and 9.30 am and 2 pm.

TALIBON

Talibon is on the northern coast of Bohol and has a wharf for ships to and from Cebu. You can also cross to nearby Jao Island from here.

Lapyahan Lodge has rooms for P30/60 and with fan and bath for P50/100. It is simple with a pleasant, friendly family atmosphere.

Getting There & Away

Ceres Liner buses coming from Tagbilaran leave daily from the Chocolate Hills Complex turn-off to Talibon at about 8 am and 4 pm. The trip takes two hours.

From Tagbilaran to Talibon via Carmen, there are Ceres Liner buses daily at 6 am and 2 pm, taking four hours.

JAO ISLAND

Jao (pronounced 'how') Island is one of the many small islands off the northern coast of Bohol. Unfortunately, a severe typhoon has destroyed the coral reef, so there is nothing for snorkellers to see. Even the swimming is not especially good. At the south-eastern corner of the island the German-Canadian Heinz Kunzemann and his Filipina wife operate a small resort on a lagoon near the beach. Yachts can tie up here and you can hire bancas (outrigger boats). Heinz is a passionate sailor who decided to sell his ship after a long trip from Canada via the South Seas, so he dropped anchor at Jao. He is a radio ham and has contacts around the world.

Places to Stay

Laguna Escondido Resort & Yacht Haven has dorm beds for P50, double rooms for P100 to P120 and cottages with bath for P150. There is a restaurant which serves European-Filipino meals for P60. You can also arrange full board for about P250 to P300 a day.

Getting There & Away

From Talibon, boats leave regularly for Jao Island for P2 per person, taking 20 minutes. Special Rides are offered for P50. Every day at 9 am the 'service boat of Mr Heinz' comes to Talibon and returns to Jao Island after a short stop. The boatman usually has a hand radio transmitter with him with which he can inquire from Talibon about available cottages.

TO/FROM BOHOL

You can get to Bohol from Camiguin, Cebu, Leyte, Luzon, Mindanao, Negros and Siquijor (see the Transport from Luzon section of the Manila chapter and the relevant To/From sections of this chapter and of the chapters on the other islands).

PAL has an office at Tagbilaran Airport. Trans Asia Shipping Lines (tel 3234) is in Carlos P Garcia Ave, Tagbilaran, as is Sweet Lines (tel 3021). Sulpicio Lines (tel 3079) is in Grupo St and William Lines (tel 3048) is in Governor Gallares St.

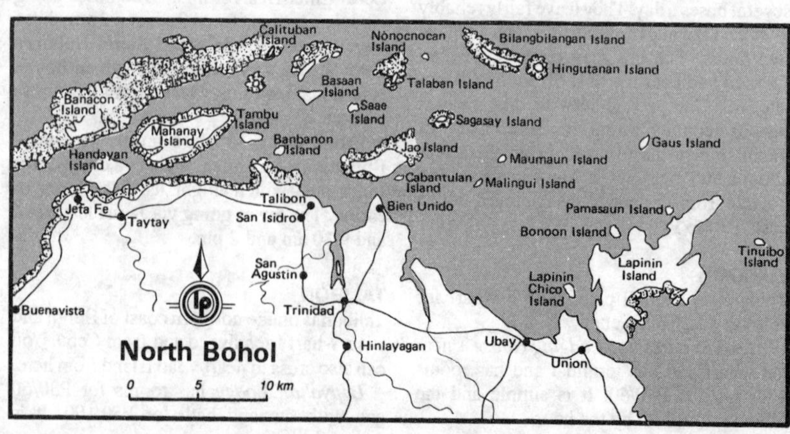

To Cebu

Air PAL flies daily from Tagbilaran to Cebu City. It is advisable to reconfirm at least three days before flying.

Bus The MV *Kanlaon Ferry* leaves Loon for Argao daily at 2 pm and takes one hour. Ceres Liner buses from Carmen, Jagna, Tagbilaran, Talibon and Ubay connect with the ferry at Loon and go from Argao on to Cebu City.

Boat The Sweet Lines' MV *Sweet Time* or MV *Sweet Pearl* leaves Tagbilaran for Cebu City daily at 11 pm and takes three hours or more. The MV *Sweet Time* also leaves on Monday at 2 am. The Trans Asia Shipping Lines' MV *Asia Japan* leaves daily at 8.30 am and takes four hours.

From Tubigon to Cebu City, the MV *Charing* leaves daily at 9 am, taking three hours; the MV *Rayjumar* leaves daily at 11 am, taking two hours or more; the MV *Queen Leonora* leaves daily at 4 pm, taking two hours or more; and the MV *Harvey* leaves daily at midnight, taking three hours.

From Talibon to Cebu City the MV *Talibon Cruiser* leaves daily at 8 am and 6 pm, taking four hours, while the MV *Charisse* leaves daily at 10 am, taking four hours.

To Leyte

Boat To go from Ubay to Bato, you catch the big outrigger boat, which leaves daily at 10 am going via Lapinin Island and taking three hours.

A big outrigger boat leaves Ubay for Maasin daily at 10 am, taking four hours.

From Jagna to Maasin, the Trans Asia Shipping Lines' MV *Asia Thailand* leaves on Wednesday at 8 pm and their MV *Asia Indonesia* leaves on Saturday at 8 pm and on Sunday at 3 pm.

To Luzon

Air Aerolift and PAL fly daily from Tagbilaran to Manila.

Boat From Tagbilaran to Manila via Dumaguete on Negros, the William Lines' MV *Misamis Occidental* leaves on Wednesday at 2 pm, taking 37 hours.

To Mindanao

Boat From Jagna to Butuan, the Trans Asia Shipping Lines' MV *Asia Thailand* leaves on Tuesday at 11 pm and on Friday at midnight, taking six hours, and the Trans Asia Shipping Lines' MV *Asia Indonesia* leaves on Friday at 11 pm, taking six hours. The Sulpicio Lines' MV *Nasipit Princess* leaves on Thursday at 8 pm, taking six hours.

From Tagbilaran to Cagayan de Oro, the Trans Asia Shipping Lines' MV *Asia Thailand* leaves on Monday at midnight, taking eight hours; and the Sweet Lines' MV *Sweet Time* leaves on Tuesday at 6 pm, taking nine hours.

From Jagna to Cagayan de Oro, the Trans Asia Shipping Lines' MV *Asia Indonesia* leaves on Thursday at 7 pm, taking seven hours, and the Trans Asia Shipping Lines' MV *Asia Thailand* leaves on Saturday and Sunday at 11 pm, taking seven hours. The Sulpicio Lines' MV *Cagayan Princess* leaves on Saturday at 9 pm, taking seven hours.

From Tagbilaran to Ozamiz, the William Lines, MV *Misamis Occidental* leaves on Sunday at 1 am, taking eight hours.

From Tagbilaran to Plaridel, the Sweet Lines' MV *Sweet Time* leaves on Saturday at 1 pm, taking 10 hours and travelling via Larena on Siquijor.

To Negros

Boat From Tagbilaran to Dumaguete, the William Lines' MV *Misamis Occidental* leaves on Wednesday at 2 am, taking three hours.

To Siquijor

Boat From Tagbilaran to Larena, the Sweet Lines' MV *Sweet Time* leaves on Saturday at 1 pm, taking three hours.

Cebu

This island, more than 200 km long and just 40 km across at its widest point, is at the centre of the Visayas, locked between Negros, Leyte and Bohol. It is the main island of Cebu Province and home to the capital, Cebu City. Of the smaller islands which are also part of the province, the most important are Mactan, Bantayan and Camotes. Cebu is a hilly island and flat areas are only to be found on the coast and in the north.

When the Spaniards arrived in Cebu, it was called Sugbo and trade was already being carried on with China. Today, many different industries contribute to the province's economic importance. There are large copper mines near Toledo, and coal, iron ore, gold and silver are also mined. Cement has been produced in Cebu for some years, but oil is the hope of the future. At the moment, Cebu supplies the West with fashionable shell and coral jewellery and also with rattan furniture.

The cultivation of maize is the dominant agricultural activity. However, there are also sizeable sugar plantations in the north and more are planned. The mangoes of Cebu are famous; they only cost a few pesos each during the harvest season, which is in March, April and May.

The people of Cebu are all very friendly. They speak Cebuano, the main dialect of the Visayas. Many Chinese live in Cebu City, and they speak Chinese among themselves. Visitors, though, can get by quite well with English.

Cebu has many expensive beach resorts which are always promoted in the island's tourist literature. If you can do without luxury you may prefer some of the beaches as yet undiscovered by most tourists. The coral gardens at Sumilon and at Pescador Island near Moalboal are worth seeing, as are the guitar factories on Mactan Island. Treks into the interior are growing in popularity, as are lazy days near the refreshing waterfalls.

CEBU CITY

Cebu City is the third largest city in the Philippines, with a population of about 575,000. Even so, the 'Queen City of the South' is easy to get to know. The busy city centre, called Downtown, includes Colon St, the oldest street in the Philippines. It has unfortunately lost some of its charm in recent years. The houses and streets are only just being maintained and the easy and natural friendliness of many of the locals has obviously suffered because of their economic difficulties. The many beggars and homeless who camp in the streets and in doorways bear witness to their privations.

In contrast with the depressed Downtown, Uptown – the area north of the Rodriguez St, Fuente Osmena, General Maxilom Ave axis – has obviously gained in prosperity. Smart restaurants, varied places of entertainment and a well-cared-for townscape provide a marked contrast with the very busy Colon area, particularly in the late afternoon. The densely populated outer suburbs and adjoining barrios are gradually joining up with Cebu City. According to the projections of the city's progressive town planners, its appearance will change considerably in the near future. An imposing new city is being planned in the Reclamation Area in the harbour, with numerous skyscrapers, shopping centres and leisure and recreation centres and a new city hall.

Life in Cebu City is more leisurely than in Manila. There are, of course, any amount of jeepneys, PU-Cabs and even a few *tartanillas* (horse-drawn carriages), but you can get almost anywhere in this city on foot. There are plenty of hotels, restaurants and cinemas, while beaches are great for leisure activities. Transport facilities to other islands are excellent.

The colourful and crowded Sinulog Festival takes place in Cebu City every January. (See also the section on Fiestas & Festivals in the Facts about the Country chapter.)

Orientation

Recently several streets in Cebu City were renamed, but people still use the following

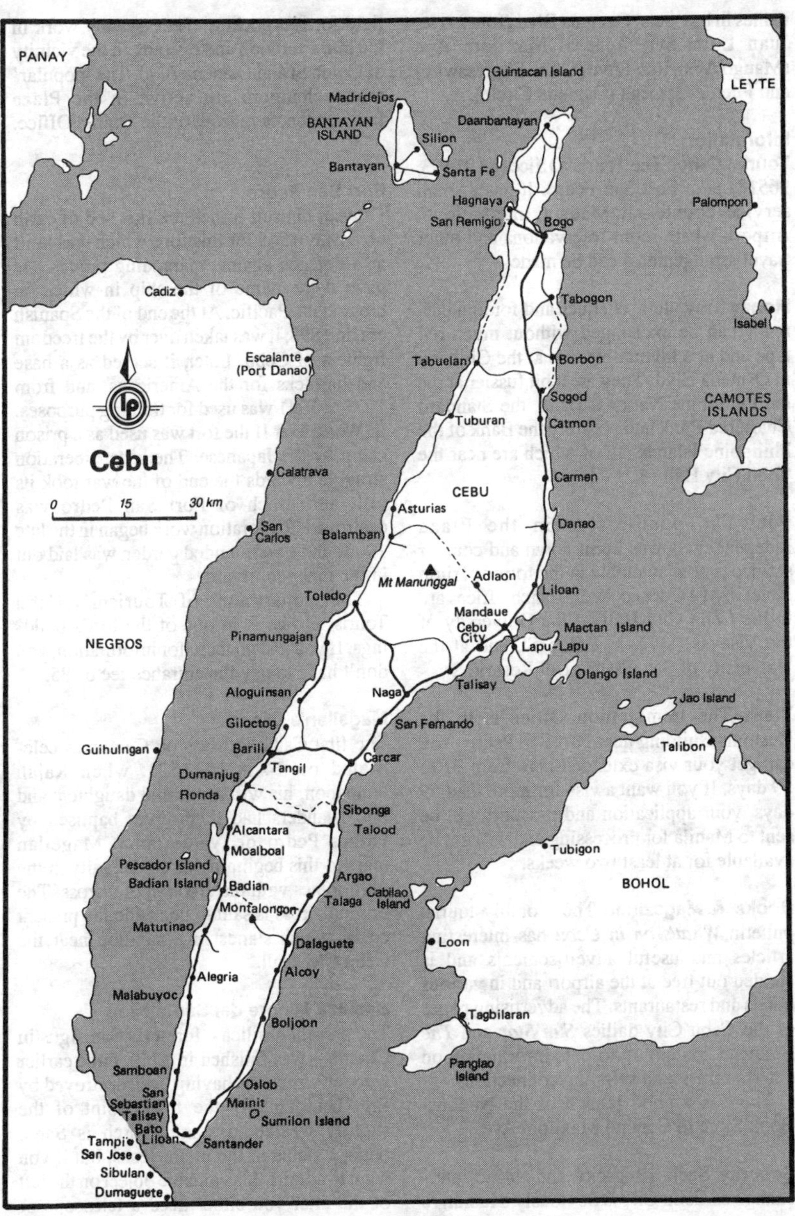
PANAY
Guintacan Island
LEYTE
Madridejos
BANTAYAN ISLAND
Silion
Daanbantayan
Bantayan
Santa Fe
Palompon
Hagnaya
San Remigio
Bogo
Cadiz
Tabogon
Isabel
Escalante (Port Danao)
Tabuelan
Borbon
Sogod
CAMOTES ISLANDS
Tuburan
Catmon
Cebu
Calatrava
Carmen
0
15
30 km
CEBU
Asturias
San Carlos
Danao
Balamban
Mt Manunggal
Adlaon
Toledo
Liloan
Mandaue
Mactan Island
NEGROS
Cebu City
Pinamungajan
Lapu-Lapu
Olango Island
Talisay
Aloguinsan
Naga
Jao Island
Giloctog
San Fernando
Guihulngan
Talibon
Barili
Carcar
Tangil
Dumanjug
Ronda
Sibonga
Talood
Alcantara
Moalboal
Tubigon
Pescador Island
Argao
Badian Island
Badian
BOHOL
Cabilao Island
Talaga
Montalongon
Matutinao
Dalaguete
Loon
Alcoy
Alegria
Malabuyoc
Boljoon
Tagbilaran
Samboan
Panglao Island
Oslob
San Sebastian
Mainit
Talisay
Sumilon Island
Bato
Tampi
Liloan
Santander
San Jose
Sibulan
Dumaguete

names in brackets: Osmena Blvd (Jones Ave, Juan Luna St), General Maxilom Ave (Mango Ave), Rizal Ave (South Expressway) and Fuente Osmena (Osmena Circle).

Information

Tourist Office The Tourist Office (tel 91503, 96518) is in Fort San Pedro. It has a small service counter at Mactan International Airport, where room reservations and other travel arrangements can be made.

Money Travellers' cheques and foreign currency can be exchanged without much red tape and at a favourable rate at the Citibank in Osmena Blvd. They are a bit fussier at the the Philippine National Bank, the Standard Chartered Bank and possibly the Bank of the Philippine Islands, all of which are near the Cebu City Hall.

Post The post office in the Plaza Independencia was burnt down and counter service is now available in the former Triton Hotel in M J Cuenco Ave. Branch offices are in the Cebu City Hall, at the University of the Visayas (UV), in Colon St, and at the University of San Carlos, Del Rosario St.

Visas The Immigration Office is in the Customs Building near Fort San Pedro. You can get your visa extended here from 21 to 59 days. If you want a visa for more than 59 days, your application and passport will be sent to Manila for processing and will not be available for at least two weeks.

Books & Magazines The monthly tourist bulletin *What's on in Cebu* has interesting articles and useful advertisements and is handed out free at the airport and in various hotels and restaurants. The advertising pages of the Cebu City dailies *Sun Star* and *The Freeman* contain up-to-date information on entertainment and shipping connections.

There is a good branch of the National Book Store in General Maxilom Ave.

Security Such a big city and traffic interchange as Cebu City is obviously a lucrative field for pickpockets. They usually work in the late afternoon and evening in the vicinity of Colon St and Osmena Blvd. The 'popular' moneychangers are active in the Plaza Independencia in front of the Tourist Office.

Fort San Pedro

Legaspi himself turned the first sod of earth on 8 May 1565 for this fort, which was built as a defence against marauding pirates. He gave it the name of the ship in which he crossed the Pacific. At the end of the Spanish era, in 1898, it was taken over by the freedom fighters of Cebu. Later, it served as a base and barracks for the Americans, and from 1937 to 1941 was used for training purposes. In World War II the fort was used as a prison camp by the Japanese. The bitter liberation struggle towards the end of the war took its toll, and much of Fort San Pedro was destroyed. Restoration work began in the late 1960s and a well-tended garden was laid out in the inner courtyard.

The Department of Tourism's Cebu Tourist Office is in one of the fort's buildings. If you just go there for information, you don't have to pay the entrance fee of P5.

Magellan's Cross

The first Catholic Mass on Cebu was celebrated on 14 April 1521, when Rajah Humabon, his wife, sons and daughters and 800 islanders had themselves baptised by Father Pedro de Valderrama. Magellan marked this beginning of Christianity in the Philippines with the erection of a cross. The original cross is said to be inside the present cross, which stands in a pavilion near the Cebu City Hall.

Basilica Minore del Santo Nino

The present basilica – formerly San Agustin Church – was finished in 1740, three earlier wooden structures having been destroyed by fire. Undoubtedly the focal point of the slightly weathered stone church is Santo Nino, a statue of the infant Jesus, but if you want to admire this valuable object on the left of the altar you either need a telescope or have to wait in a long queue. In 1565 this treasure, with its jewelled crown and gem-covered clothes, was found undamaged by Juan de Camus, one of Legaspi's soldiers, in a hut near the basilica. Since then Santo Nino has been the patron saint of the Cebuano.

Taoist Temple & Cebu Zoo

Some six km from the city centre lies Beverly Hills, the millionaires' quarter of Cebu City. Here also is the temple of the Taoist religious sect. Its size and architecture indicate that a considerable part of the population of Cebu is Chinese. You can get a good view of the city from this temple.

About two km from the Taoist Temple is Cebu Zoo. Although it contains only a few animals, most of which are housed quite inadequately, it is attractively laid out. Admission costs P5. Attached is a little museum with an amusing collection of grotesque and bizarre stuffed animals.

The taxi fare to the temple from Downtown should be about P20, but fix the fare first. It is cheaper by Lahug jeepney, which will get you fairly close. Catch it on the corner of Jakosalem and Colon streets and get off in Lahug, cross the small bridge, turn right and walk for another km or so.

Cebu Heavenly Temple of Charity

On the way to the Taoist Temple you will see the Cebu Heavenly Temple of Charity on a hill on the left. There is a natural spring underneath it. The middle altar of this beautiful temple houses the statues of the Supreme Gods and of Milagrosa Rosa, the temple's patron saint.

To get there, take a jeepney from Downtown to the Taoist Temple, but when you get to the little bridge, don't turn right but go straight on. One hundred metres further on you will see an iron gate with two guardian lions on the left. Walk through this gate and follow the path until you get to the road about 400 metres away, then turn off to the right. The entrance gate to the temple is 200 metres further on. If it is closed you can go around the temple to the open main gate.

Caretta Cemetery

A visit to this large cemetery is probably only of significance on 1 November – All Saints Day – or perhaps the night before, when everyone is pretty wound up (see the Fiestas & Festivals section of the Facts about the Country chapter). Opposite is the Chinese Cemetery. To get there, catch a jeepney from Colon St going towards Mabolo.

Carbon Market

The agricultural produce and the many and varied handicrafts of Cebu Province are on offer at this big and colourful market. There are also products from other Visayan islands, such as basket ware from Bohol.

Binamira's Collection of Antiques

You will find hand-carved furniture, ornaments and much more in Dr Leocadia Binamira's private antique collection. If you are into antiques you shouldn't miss this treasure house, although it's a private house that is not easy to find and the old lady won't admit everybody.

University of San Carlos Museum

The USC Museum, founded in 1595, was opened in 1967. Its divisions cover ethnography, archaeology, natural sciences and the Spanish colonial period. Filipino objects from different epochs and exhibits from other Asian countries are also displayed. The museum is open Monday to Friday from 9 am to noon and from 2 to 5 pm. (Sometimes it is only open for the afternoon session.) It is closed during vacations.

Casa Gorordo Museum

The Parian district in the Downtown of today was the residential area of the wealthy of Cebu at the turn of the century. Of the remaining four houses, the Gorordo residence has been restored and furnished in the style of the period. The Gorordo family produced the first Archbishop of the Philippines. Apart from furniture, you can see porcelain, liturgical items, clothes and old photographs of Cebu. The museum is

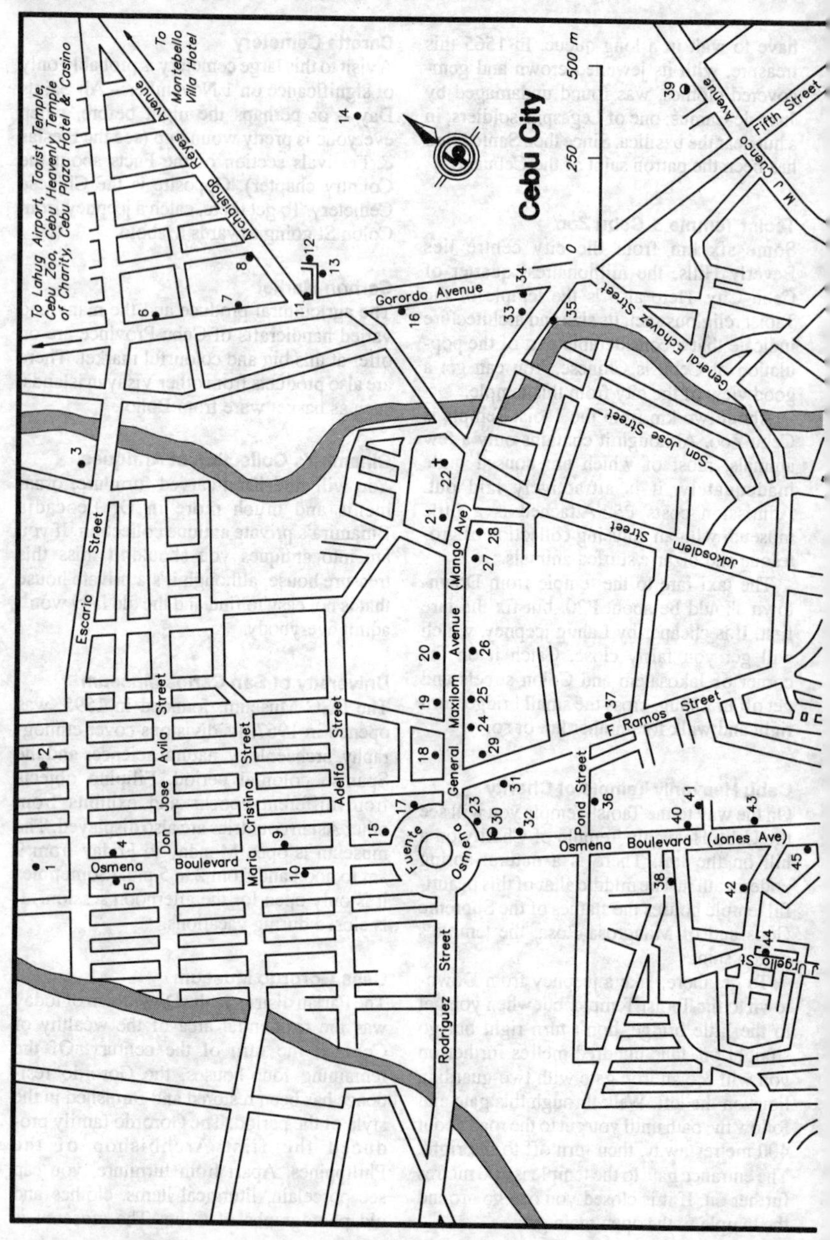
Cebu City
0
250
500 m
To Lahug Airport, Taoist Temple, Cebu Zoo, Cebu Heavenly Temple of Charity, Cebu Plaza Hotel & Casino
To Montebello Villa Hotel
Archbishop Reyes Avenue
Gorordo Avenue
General Echavez Street
San Jose Street
Jakosalem Street
M J Cuenco Avenue
Fifth Street
F Ramos Street
Pond Street
Osmena Boulevard (Jones Ave)
Fuente Osmena
General Maxilom Avenue (Mango Ave)
Rodriguez Street
Adelfa Street
Maria Cristina Street
Don Jose Avila Street
Escario Street
Osmena Boulevard
Urgello St

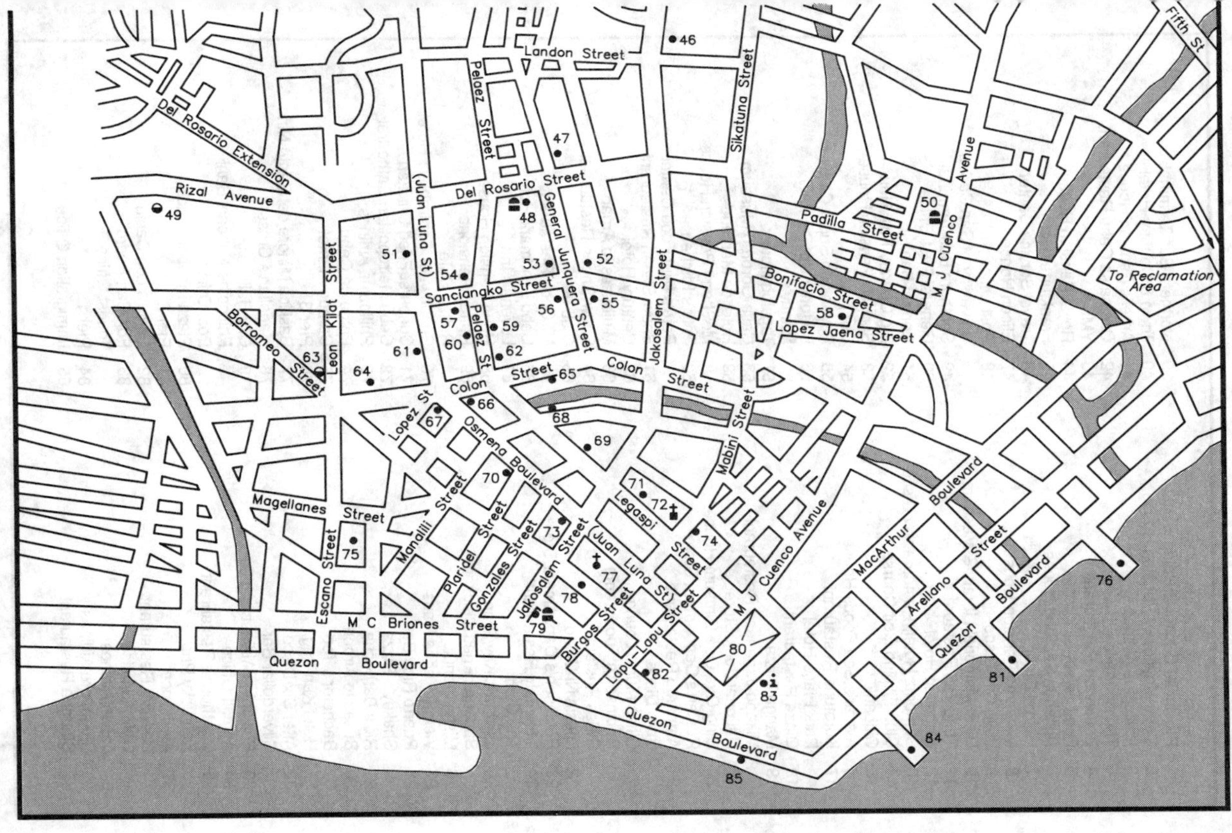
Fifth St
To Reclamation Area
M J Cuenco Avenue
Padilla Street
Bonifacio Street
Lopez Jaena Street
Sikatuna Street
Landon Street
Del Rosario Street
General Junquera Street
Pelaez Street
Sanciangko Street
Pelaez St
(Juan Luna St)
Leon Kilat Street
Rizal Avenue
Del Rosario Extension
Borromeo Street
Colon Street
Jakosalem Street
Mabini Street
Osmena Boulevard
Lopez St
Legaspi Street
(Juan Luna St)
Lapu-Lapu Street
Burgos Street
Jakosalem Street
Gonzales Street
Plaridel Street
Manalili Street
Magellanes Street
Escano Street
M C Briones Street
Quezon Boulevard
Arellano Boulevard
MacArthur Boulevard
M J Cuenco Avenue
46
47
48
49
50
51
52
53
54
55
56
57
58
59
60
61
62
63
64
65
66
67
68
69
70
71
72
73
74
75
76
77
78
79
80
81
82
83
84
85

1 Provincial Capitol Building
2 Cebu Mayflower Pension House
3 Philippine Airlines
The Apartelle
4 Boulevard Restaurant
5 Food Street
6 Pistahan Seafood House
7 Hotrod Diner
8 Maanyag Pension House
9 Love City Disco
10 Rizal Memorial Library & Museum
11 Tung Yan Restaurant
12 Magellan Hotel
13 St Moritz Hotel, Restaurant & Disco
14 Club Filipino Golf Course
15 Citibank
16 Alavar's Sea Foods House
17 Kurofune Restaurant
Park Place Hotel
18 Ginza Restaurant
19 Mango Plaza
Mikado Japanese Restaurant
National Book Store
20 Ding Qua Qua Dimsum House
Rustan's Department Store
21 Amparito Restaurant
Balls Disco
Cities Music Lounge
Robinson's Foodorama
Swiss Restaurant
22 Iglesia Ni Cristo
23 Robinson's Department Store
24 Little Italy Restaurant
The Club
25 Lawiswis Kawayan
Sunburst Fried Chicken
26 Mister Donut
27 Vienna Kaffee-Haus
28 Puerto Rico Bar
Shakey's Pizza
29 Ric's Barbecue
30 Buses to Airport
31 Bachelor's Too
Hotel Kan-Irag
32 After Six Disco
Silverdollar Bar
33 Philippine Airlines
34 Aerolift Office
35 Lighthouse Restaurant
36 Kentucky Pub
37 Air France
Beehive Restaurant
Café Adriatico
Japan Airlines
Singapore Airlines
38 Sinugba Restaurant
39 Northern Bus Terminal
40 Town & Country Hotel
41 Arbel's Pension House
42 Cosina sa Cebu Restaurant
43 YMCA
44 Royal Pension House
45 Frankfurter Hof
46 Travel Service Center
47 Elicon House
48 Post Office
University of San Carlos
49 Southern Bus Terminal
50 General Post Office
51 Central Bank
52 Big Country Folk House
53 Surigao Pension House
54 Our Place
55 Bayanihan Super Club
56 Bottoms Up
Manny's
57 Tagalog Hotel
58 Casa Gorordo Museum
59 Hotel de Mercedes
McSherry Pension House
60 Pete's Kitchen
Pete's Mini Food Center
61 Snow Sheen Restaurant
62 Century Hotel
63 Minibuses to Argao
64 Snow Sheen Restaurant
65 Club 99
Mr Cook Restaurant
66 Cebu Landmark Hotel
67 Lovena's Inn
68 Hope Pension House
69 Ruftan Pensione
Ruftan Café
70 Sundowner Centrepoint Hotel
71 Sunburst Fried Chicken
72 Cebu Metropolitan Cathedral
73 Philippine Airlines
74 Patria de Cebu
75 Carbon Market
76 Pier 3
77 Basilica Minore del Santo Nino
78 Magellan's Cross
79 City Hall
Philippine National Bank
Post Office
80 Plaza Independencia
81 Pier 2
82 Eddie's Log Cabin
83 Fort San Pedro
Tourist Office
84 Pier 1
85 Immigration Office

open daily except Sunday from 9 to noon and from 2 to 6 pm. Admission is P5.

Places to Stay – bottom end

Patria de Cebu (tel 72084) in P Burgos St has rooms with fan for P45/90. It is a simple place and has a restaurant, billiards and bowling.

Royal Pension House (tel 93890) at 165 J Urgello St has good rooms with fan for P75.

The *YMCA* (tel 90125) at 61 Osmena Blvd has rooms with fan for P90/140, with fan and bath for P110/180 and with air-con and bath for P190/380. Couples may be accepted. It is simple but good and has a restaurant, swimming pool, billiards, table tennis and bowls. YMCA members get a discount and temporary membership is obtainable for a few pesos.

Arbel's Pension House (tel 62393) at 57E Osmena Blvd has rooms with fan for P80/120. It is clean and simple, with a restaurant. Some of the rooms have no windows.

The *Town & Country Hotel* (tel 78190) in Osmena Blvd has rooms with fan for P80/120, with fan and bath for P130/170 and with air-con and bath for P230/300. It is homely and good value and has a restaurant. The upstairs rooms are comfortable.

Ruftan Pensione (tel 79138) in Legaspi St has rooms with fan for P85/110. It's basic but habitable and has a restaurant. The rooms looking out on to the courtyard are the quietest.

The *Cebu Mayflower Pension House* (tel 72948) on the Capitol site has rooms with fan for P84/112 and with air-con and bath for P168/202. It is quiet and clean and is near the Provincial Capitol Building.

Surigao Pension House (tel 97857) in General Junquera St, on the corner of Sanciangko St, has rooms with fan and bath for P120/150 and with air-con and bath for P200. It has a restaurant and is centrally located but is surrounded by noisy discos.

Lovena's Inn (tel 99212) in Osmena Blvd has rooms with fan and bath for P58/85 and with air-con and bath for P88/118. It is simple and fairly clean but the rooms vary in quality.

Hope Pension House (tel 93371) in Manalili St has rooms with fan and bath for P90/120 and with air-con and bath for P110/140. It is simple but fairly clean and good.

Frankfurter Hof (tel 54192) in Osmena Blvd has rooms with fan and bath for P150/250. It is nice and tidy and has a restaurant. If you stay for longer than a week you get a discount.

The *McSherry Pension House* (tel 52749, 96772) in Pelaez St has rooms with fan and bath for P150 and with air-con and bath for P200/300. It's a good central place in a quiet lane off Pelaez St, next to the Hotel de Mercedes.

Places to Stay – middle

The *Century Hotel* (tel 97621) in Pelaez St has good, clean rooms with air-con and bath from P240/290. The single rooms on the 4th floor are good for two. The budget rooms are on the 5th floor, next door to the noisy disco nightclub.

The *Cebu Landmark Hotel* (tel 77671-75) in Osmena Blvd has rooms with fan and bath for P200/250 and with air-con and bath for P330/390. It's fairly well kept with a restaurant. Not all rooms have windows.

Elicon House (tel 73653; fax 73507) in General Junquera St has rooms with air-con and bath from P180/190. It is fairly clean and good. Downstairs is the Elicon Café.

The *Tagalog Hotel* (tel 72531) in Sanciangko St has fairly good rooms with fan and bath for P190/250 and with air-con and bath for P235/266.

The *Maanyag Pension House* (tel 95056, 75573) in 255 Archbishop Reyes Ave has rooms with fan for P200 and with air-con and bath for P300/350-450. It's reasonable but the rooms are small. There is a coffee shop.

The *Kan-Irag Hotel* (tel 97611) in F Ramos St has rooms with air-con and bath for P408/498. It is homely and good value and has a restaurant.

The *Hotel de Mercedes* (tel 97631-39) in Pelaez St has rooms with air-con and bath from P490/565. It has a restaurant and is probably the best hotel in Downtown.

The *Park Plaza Hotel* (tel 211131; fax 210118; tlx 6680 PARKHO PU) in Fuente Osmena has rooms with air-con and bath from P510/600. It is friendly and well kept and has a restaurant.

Places to Stay – top end

The *St Moritz Hotel* (tel 74371-74; tlx 48142 MORITZ PM) in Gorordo Ave has rooms with air-con and bath for P850/1130 and suites for P1725. It's very good quality and has a restaurant and a nightclub.

The *Sundowner Centrepoint Hotel* (tel 73030-49; fax 210695; tlx 63460 SUNCEB PN) in Plaridel St, on the corner of Osmena Blvd, has rooms with air-con and bath from P900/1150 and suites for P1975. It's well maintained and has a restaurant.

The *Montebello Villa Hotel* (tel 85021) at Banilad has rooms with air-con and bath from P666/743 and suites for P1332 to P3203. It's attractive and well kept, with a restaurant, coffee shop and swimming pool and is in a lovely position on the edge of town.

The *Magellan Hotel* (tel 74613-20; fax 8176423; tlx 24729 MIH PH) in Gorordo Ave has rooms with air-con and bath from P900 and suites for P2000 to P7000. It is pleasant, with a restaurant, coffee shop and swimming pool.

The *Cebu Plaza Hotel* (tel 212141; fax 52196; tlx 24861 CEPLAPH) at Nivel Hills, Lahug, has rooms with air-con and bath from P2600/2850 and suites for P5570 to P24,360. It has a restaurant, coffee shop, disco, swimming pool and tennis court. It is on a rise a little out of town and is the best hotel in Cebu City. From Downtown, take a Lahug jeepney marked 'Plaza'.

Apartments It is possible to get apartments for a longer stay in Cebu City – look at the ads in the local dailies *Sun Star* and *The Freeman.*

The *Tourists Garden Lodge* (tel 84832, 62124) at 27 Eagle St in Santo Nino Village, Banilad, has apartments to let for P650 a day, P4550 a week and P16,500 a month.

The *Apartelle* (tel 76271) in Escario St has apartments to let by the week and by the month.

Places to Eat

The *Snow Sheen Restaurant*, on the corner of Colon St and Osmena Blvd, has good Chinese and Filipino meals.

Pete's Kitchen in Pelaez St has Chinese and Filipino meals. It is clean and remarkably cheap.

Pete's Mini Food Center in Pelaez St is a large, partly undercover restaurant serving good, cheap Filipino meals.

Ric's Barbecue in F Ramos St has good and cheap Filipino meals.

The *Ruftan Café* in Legaspi St is good for breakfasts and also serves Filipino meals.

El Garaje in Gorordo Ave is a beer garden in front of the Magellan Hotel. It serves good, cheap Filipino meals.

The *Boulevard Restaurant* in Osmena Blvd is a popular garden restaurant with cheap Filipino meals. It shows video clips.

Food Street in Osmena Blvd consists of several small, cheap restaurants opposite the Boulevard Restaurant.

Cosina sa Cebu in Ascension St is a clean restaurant serving cheap Filipino meals. It is popular with students.

Sunburst Fried Chicken in General Maxilom Ave serves different kinds of excellent roast chickens and also good Filipino meals. It is open daily from 9 am to 11 pm. There is another Sunburst Fried Chicken in Legaspi St.

The *Golden Cowrie* in Salinas Drive, Lahug, is recommended as a seafood restaurant in the medium price range. It is open between 11 am and 2 pm and between 6 and 10 pm.

Mister Cook in Colon St is a restaurant where guests choose their own pieces of fish or meat and have them done to their own taste. It also serves fast food. It is open daily from 9 am to 9 pm.

Sinugba Seafood House in J Urgello St specialises in grilled fish. It is open daily between 11 am and 3 pm and between 6 and 10 pm.

The *Alavar's Sea Foods House* in Gorordo Ave is an excellent restaurant specialising in food from Zamboanga on Mindanao, such as blue marlin. It's open daily from 11 am to 2.30 pm and from 5 to 10.30 pm.

The *Lighthouse Restaurant* in General Maxilom Ave serves Filipino food which you eat with your fingers. It is a good restaurant, with restrained live music. It is open daily between 10.30 am and 2 pm and between 5.30 and 10.30 pm.

Downstairs in Robinson's Department Store in Fuente Osmena, there are a couple of cheap dim sum and fast food restaurants which are worth trying.

The *Tung Yan Restaurant* in Gorordo Ave is probably the best Chinese restaurant in Cebu. It is relatively expensive and is near the Magellan Hotel. It is open daily between 11 am and 2 pm and between 6 and 10 pm.

The *Ginza Restaurant* in General Maxilom Ave is a good Japanese restaurant.

The *Kurofune Restaurant* in Fuente Osmena is a Japanese restaurant next to the Park Plaza Hotel. It is open on Monday from 7 to 11 pm and Tuesday to Sunday from 11 am to 2 pm and from 5 to 11 pm.

The smart *Café Adriatico* in F Ramos St features steaks, seafood and salads as well as a good choice of cocktails. It is open daily from noon to 2 am.

The *Beehive Restaurant* in F Ramos St is well known for its good steaks. It's open daily from 10.30 am to 10 pm.

The *Hotrod Diner* in Gorordo Ave has good and reasonably priced fast food in the style of a US snack bar of the 1950s, very similar to Rosie's Diner in Manila. It's open daily from 9 am to 1 am.

Shakey's Pizza in General Maxilom Ave is a favourite local rendezvous for pizzas and live music.

Eddie's Log Cabin in M C Briones St has good US and Filipino meals and cheap daily dishes. It is open daily from 7 am to 2 am.

Our Place is a pub in Pelaez St with European, US and Filipino meals. It's open Monday to Saturday from 9 am to 10 pm.

Frankfurter Hof in Osmena Blvd has good, cheap European and Filipino cuisine. The menu changes regularly.

The *Swiss Restaurant* in General Maxilom Ave serves good European and Filipino meals. It is well run and you can also sit outside. It is open Monday to Friday from 11 am to 11 pm and Sunday from 11 am to 2 pm and from 5 to 11 pm.

Vienna Kaffee-Haus in General Maxilom Ave has good European meals. Although its coffee and cakes are European in price, they are excellent. It's open from 8.30 am till midnight.

The *St Moritz Restaurant* in Gorordo Ave has good European and Filipino meals. It is open daily between 8 am and 10.30 pm.

Entertainment

There are nightclubs dotted all over the town and their number is constantly growing. There are still some good pubs left like *Our Place* in Pelaez St, *The Club* in General Maxilom Ave and the *Kentucky Pub* in Pond St, all favourite haunts of the resident Europeans. The youth of Cebu City often meet in the *Boulevard* in Osmena Blvd where the beer is cheap and they show new video clips on a big screen. In the afternoon the 'kids' drink in *Club 99* in Colon St, which is open from 2 pm. The clientele at the *El Garaje Beer Garden* at the Magellan Hotel is pretty mixed in the small hours.

There is varied entertainment on offer in General Maxilom Ave, such as at the *Puerto Rico Bar*, which is a show disco; *Balls*, which is a sports bar, theatre lounge and disco all in one; the *Cities Music Lounge*, which features good live music and widescreen videos; and *Lawiswis Kawayan*, a big bamboo house with live music.

In Osmena Blvd the go-go girls of the *Silver Dollar Bar* attract numerous guests. Next door at the *After Six* there are disco songs from 7 pm. The Uptown clubs have shows in the *Love City Disco* and *Paradise*, with an admission of P50.

Among the most popular discos are *Bai* in the Cebu Plaza Hotel and *St Gotthard* in Fulton St in Lahug where drinks are served by waitresses on roller skates. The adjoining restaurant offers 20 kinds of breakfast from 5 am.

If you want to eat cheaply with entertainment and fun thrown in, you should go for one of the sing-along restaurants. There are several of these in the city centre as well as some further out, like *Adventure Galley* in Anihan St, Gentle Breeze Subdivision, Mandaue City, which is a few km from Cebu City. Every night from 9 pm until at least 1 am, guests are invited to sing a solo, accompanied by an organist. But don't worry, you don't have to join in.

Getting There & Away

See the To/From Cebu section of this chapter.

Getting Around

Airport Transport Pacific Airways and Aerolift flights using light aircraft use Lahug Airport. This small airport is on the northern edge of town. A PU-Cab from Lahug Airport to Downtown shouldn't cost more than P20.

Mactan International Airport is on Mactan Island, about 15 km from Cebu City. The PAL inland flights use this airport, as do the few international flights from places such as Singapore and Japan.

If they are still running, there is at least one airport shuttle bus an hour from the Loveburger fast-food outlet in Robinson's Department Store in Fuente Osmena going to Mactan International Airport on Mactan Island. The trip costs P10 and can take up to an hour, as road blockages often create delays and have sometimes caused passengers to miss their plane. If you have an early plane to catch, it could pay to spend the night near the airport instead of in town (see the following Lapu-Lapu section).

A PU-Cab from Mactan International Airport to the city should not cost more than P50, but make sure the price is agreed upon before departure. Air-conditioned limousines which you can book in the air terminal near the main exit hardly cost any more.

Tricycles are prohibited in the airport area. You will find them within sight of the taxis in front of the Silangan Hotel. They cost P2 per person as far as the Mandaue-Mactan Bridge or the jeepney terminal, where you can board a jeepney to Cebu City for P2.50.

Taxi The wharves are not far from the city centre and P10 should get you to one of the Downtown hotels by PU-Cab. A fare of P10 within the city area is reasonable, although much more is often demanded. It is therefore important to agree on the price beforehand to avoid argument later.

Jeepney The following jeepney routes should be the most important for tourists: Capitol (Uptown at the end of Osmena Blvd), Lahug (Lahug district in the north of the city), Carbon (Carbon Market, Downtown), and Colon (Colon St, Downtown).

Car & Motorcycle The most reliable car hire would be Avis Rent-a-Car, whose office is at the Magellan Hotel (tel 74611, 99823) in Gorordo Ave. Motorcycles can be hired in the Travel Service Center (tel 54960) in Jakosalem St. A 125 cc bike costs P250 per day.

MT MANUNGGAL NATIONAL PARK

Each year on 17 March the Cebu City Tourist Office organises a big trek to nearby Mt Manunggal. That is the anniversary of the death of President Magsaysay, who, in 1957, crashed to his death here in his private plane. This trek includes an overnight stay, so take a tent, provisions and water. Share of jeep transport to Adlaon costs about P50.

LAPU-LAPU

Lapu-Lapu, on the island of Mactan, was founded in 1730 by Augustinian monks. The island is connected with Cebu by the 864 metre long Mandaue-Mactan Bridge. About 105,000 people live today in the former administrative centre of Opon. There is a memorial to Chief Lapu-Lapu, who killed Ferdinand Magellan in the battle of Mactan Island on 27 April 1521.

Places to Stay

The *Heidelberg* (tel 88569) at the Mandaue-Mactan Bridge has rooms with fan for P180, with air-con for P320 and apartments with air-con and bath for P500. It's a relatively good place with a restaurant and beer garden. It also has cars and motorcycles for hire and a tricycle service to the airport.

The *Silangan Hotel* (tel 88462) at the airport has rooms with air-con and bath for P185/250. It's fairly good value and has a restaurant. Both it and the Heidelberg are ideal if you have to take an early plane out.

The *Hotel Cesario* near the Mandaue-Mactan Bridge has very comfortable rooms with air-con and bath from P1100 and also has a restaurant.

Places to Eat

The *Heidelberg* at the Mandaue-Mactan Bridge serves good European meals. You can get various snacks at the little *1890* pub on the way from the centre of town to the jeepney terminal. Near the markets are two *Lechon* restaurants. Try them if you like pork.

The *Silangan Restaurant* in the hotel of the same name at the airport is rather expensive. On the other hand, you can get cheap meals in the nearby open-air *El Garaje*, which is a favourite among the locals.

Entertainment

You can dance in the *Phoenix Disco* in the former Imperial Hotel, where the women workers from the TMX factory opposite now live. Other night spots are *Blitz Disco*, *Starfire* and *Lucky Five*.

Getting There & Away

A lot of jeepneys go daily from Cebu City to Lapu-Lapu – just listen for the 'opon-opon' call. All go through Manalili St, where a few passengers get on. The seats next to the driver are best, as the ones behind get very crowded. The fare is P2.50.

At the Lapu-Lapu Market the tricycles wait for passengers going further, perhaps to the beaches.

A PU-Cab from Cebu City to Lapu-Lapu costs about P40, but if you want to go to the beach you have to pay another P10.

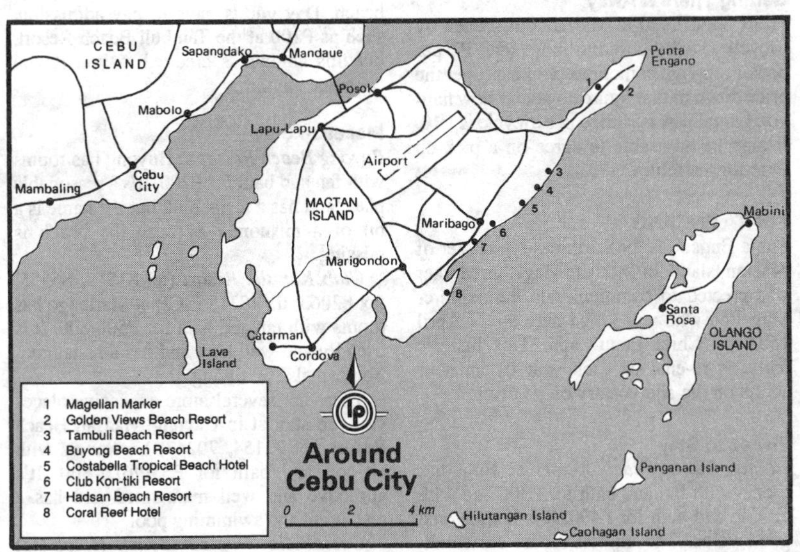

The last jeepney from Lapu-Lapu to Cebu City leaves at 11 pm, and the next does not go till about 4 am the following morning. The jeepney terminal is a bit outside the city, towards Cebu City.

MARIGONDON

The nearest best public beach beyond Cebu City is Marigondon Beach. It is a favourite with the locals and is especially popular at the weekend. There is ample roofed seating where day visitors can eat freshly grilled fish at low prices and drink beer and tuba. The beach itself is only just acceptable, but you can hire a boat and get out to Olango Island for a bit of snorkelling. Fix the price beforehand.

Places to Stay

On the right, behind some dense shrubs on the way from Lapu-Lapu to Marigondon, is the *Hawaiian Village*. A cottage with a wide bed and running water costs about P100 per day. There are some basic cottages right on the beach for an extra P50.

Getting There & Away

From Lapu-Lapu to Marigondon Beach by tricycle usually costs no more than P2 per person, though sometimes you can't get the price down to that figure no matter how hard you bargain. A fair price per tricycle is P10. It may be advisable to agree on a pick-up time for the return.

PUNTA ENGANO

Punta Engano is the north-eastern corner of Mactan Island. In 1866 the Magellan Marker was erected to commemorate the explorer Magellan who was killed here on 27 April 1521 by Chief Lapu-Lapu. This historic battle is re-enacted each year by amateur actors on the anniversary of his death.

Places to Stay

Golden Views Beach Resort at Buot has rooms with fan and bath for P300 and with air-con and bath for P400. It is homely and good value. The air-con rooms are subdivided into sleeping and living areas. There is also a restaurant.

Getting There & Away

A tricycle from Lapu-Lapu to Punta Engano costs P3 per person. You should be able to get a Special Ride for P15 by skilful bargaining.

MARIBAGO

At Maribago, between Marigondon and Punta Engano, you can inspect some guitar factories. The biggest is probably Lilang's Guitar Factory, but the smaller factories also make quite good and well-priced guitars; it pays to compare them. If you want a guitar that will last, it is worth spending a few pesos more and buying an export guitar, as the ones that are made for the local market are dirt cheap but perish quickly once out of the tropics. You can get a good export guitar from P2000. Since PAL will not accept them as hand luggage, at least beyond Cebu, they have to go in the hold, so have them well packed. It is even better to invest in a strong guitar case.

Maribago has several fine hotels by the beach. Day guests have to pay admission, such as P100 at the Tambuli Beach Resort, but this amount is credited to you if you consume anything.

Places to Stay

Buyong Beach Resort at Buyong has rooms with fan and bath for P200. It's a reasonable place and has a restaurant, but the name is a bit of a misnomer because the beach is missing.

Club Kon-tiki Resort (tel 81519, 86555; fax 82063; tlx 48315 FICI) at Maribago has rooms with fan and bath for P500/600. It is friendly and well kept and has a restaurant. You can also go diving.

There are several more expensive places you can stay at in Buyong. Hadsan Beach Resort (tel 92154, 70247) has rooms with air-con and bath for P550/620-800. It's attractive and well maintained and has a restaurant and swimming pool.

Costabella Tropical Beach Hotel (tel

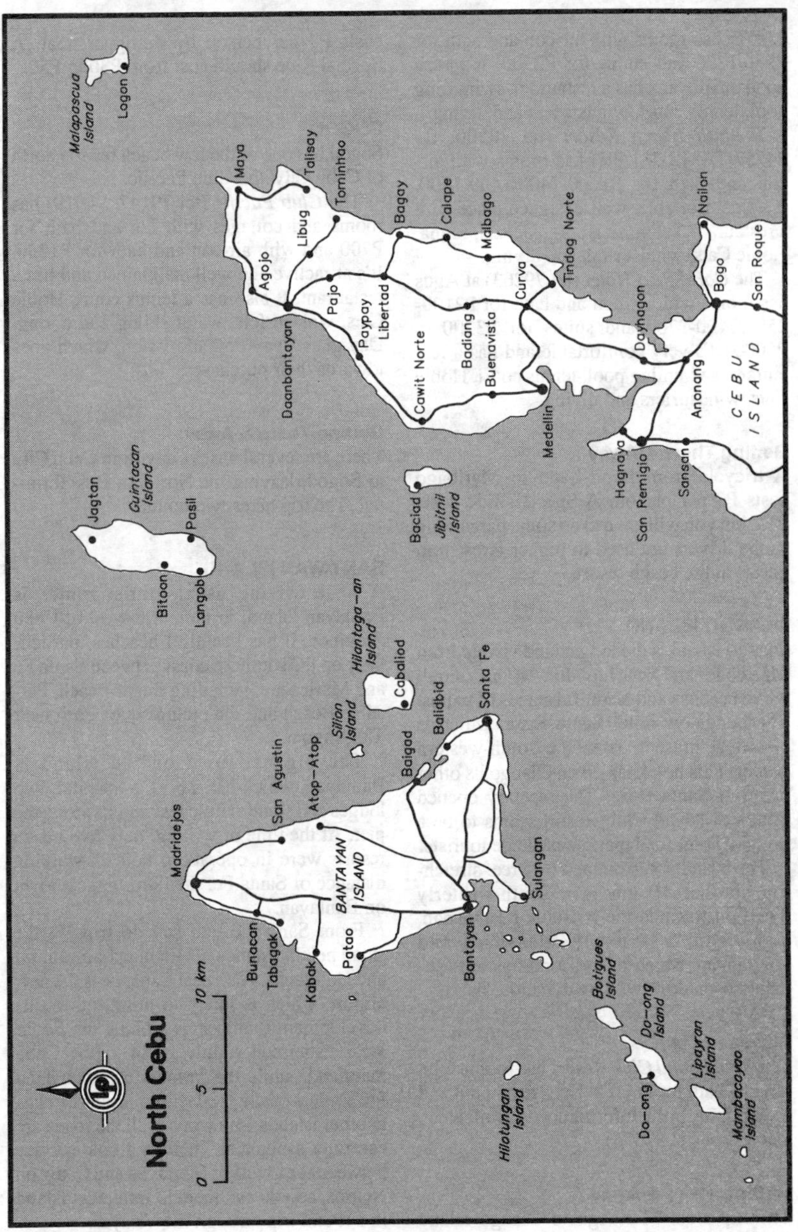
North Cebu
0
5
10 km
Malapascua Island
Logon
Maya
Talisay
Tominhao
Libug
Agojo
Daanbantayan
Pajo
Paypay
Libertad
Bagay
Calape
Malbago
Tindog Norte
Curva
Badiang
Buenavista
Cawit Norte
Medellin
Nailon
Bogo
San Roque
Dayhagon
Anonang
CEBU ISLAND
Hagnaya
San Remigio
Sansan
Guintacan Island
Jagtan
Pasil
Bitoon
Langob
Baciad
Jibitnil Island
Hilantaga-an Island
Caballod
Silion Island
Santa Fe
Balidbid
Baigad
Atop-Atop
San Agustin
Madridejos
BANTAYAN ISLAND
Bunacan
Tabagak
Kabak
Patao
Bantayan
Sulangan
Botigues Island
Do-ong Island
Do-ong
Lipayran Island
Mambacayao Island
Hilotungan Island

85475) has rooms with air-con and bath for P980/1200 and suites for P2300. It's very good quality and has a restaurant, swimming pool, tennis court, windsurfers and diving.

Tambuli Beach Resort (tel 70200; tlx 24757 TAMBULI PH) has rooms with air-con and bath for P1200-1400/1400-1500. It's a comfortable, well-designed place with a restaurant, swimming pool, jacuzzi, sauna, Hobie Cats, windsurfers and diving.

The *Coral Reef Hotel* (tel 79203) at Agus has rooms with air-con and bath for P2100-2500/2400-2700 and suites for P3200 to P5000. It's very comfortable and has a restaurant, swimming pool, tennis court, Hobie Cats, windsurfers and diving.

Getting There & Away

A tricycle from Lapu-Lapu to Maribago costs P3 per person. A Special Ride costs P15, but you will have to do some bargaining as the drivers are used to higher fares from guests at the beach resorts.

OLANGO ISLAND

Olango Island is the long island visible from Maribago and Marigondon. It has small white beaches and beautiful stands of palms. The bungalow hotel Santa Rosa, which is closed at present, is in the south-western corner. This hotel has given Olango its other name of Santa Rosa. The recently opened Southern Island Club Resort seems to be a holiday hotel for Japanese package tourists.

The island is surrounded by a reef stretching another 10 km in a south-westerly direction towards the islands of Panganan, Caohagan, Lassuan (Kalassuan) and Hilutangan. Much of the coral has unfortunately been destroyed by dynamite fishing.

Places to Stay

Southern Island Club Resort has rooms with fan and bath for P600. It has a restaurant and a swimming pool. Information is available in Cebu City (tel 82095).

Getting There & Away

The trip from Maribago to Olango Island costs P3 per person by outrigger boat. A Special Ride should cost from P30 to P50.

SOGOD

Sogod has one of the few beach resorts north of Cebu City, the Club Pacific.

The *Club Pacific* (tel 79147, 94019) has rooms and cottages with fan and bath for P700 and with air-con and bath for P1250. It's attractive and well maintained and has a restaurant. It also has a tennis court, Hobie Cats, windsurfers, water skiing and diving. Day guests pay P50 admission, which goes towards their purchases.

Getting There & Away

There are several buses a day from Cebu City to Sogod, leaving the Northern Bus Terminal. The trip takes two hours.

BANTAYAN ISLAND

A little off the usual tourist routes is Bantayan Island, in the north-west of Cebu Province. It has beautiful beaches, particularly on the southern coast between Santa Fe and Maricaban, including Sugar Beach, Paradise Beach and the picturesque beach near Tingtingon.

The biggest town on the island is Bantayan, which has a port, a hospital, two lodges and some simple restaurants along the pier. At the time of writing, only two beach resorts were in operation, both in walking distance of Santa Fe, the third biggest town on Bantayan.

From Santa Fe you can do trips to the small nearby islands of Hilantaga-an, Jibitnil and Guintacan. Also near Santa Fe is the new airport, which is likely to bring the tourist development Bantayan is looking for. So far local fishermen supply squid to the Cebu mainland, while the farmers use their land for poultry raising and ship millions of eggs to other islands – no wonder all the roads are carefully asphalted. There is a boat service between the towns of Bantayan and Cadiz on Negros, so you can include Bantayan Island in a round trip through the Visayas.

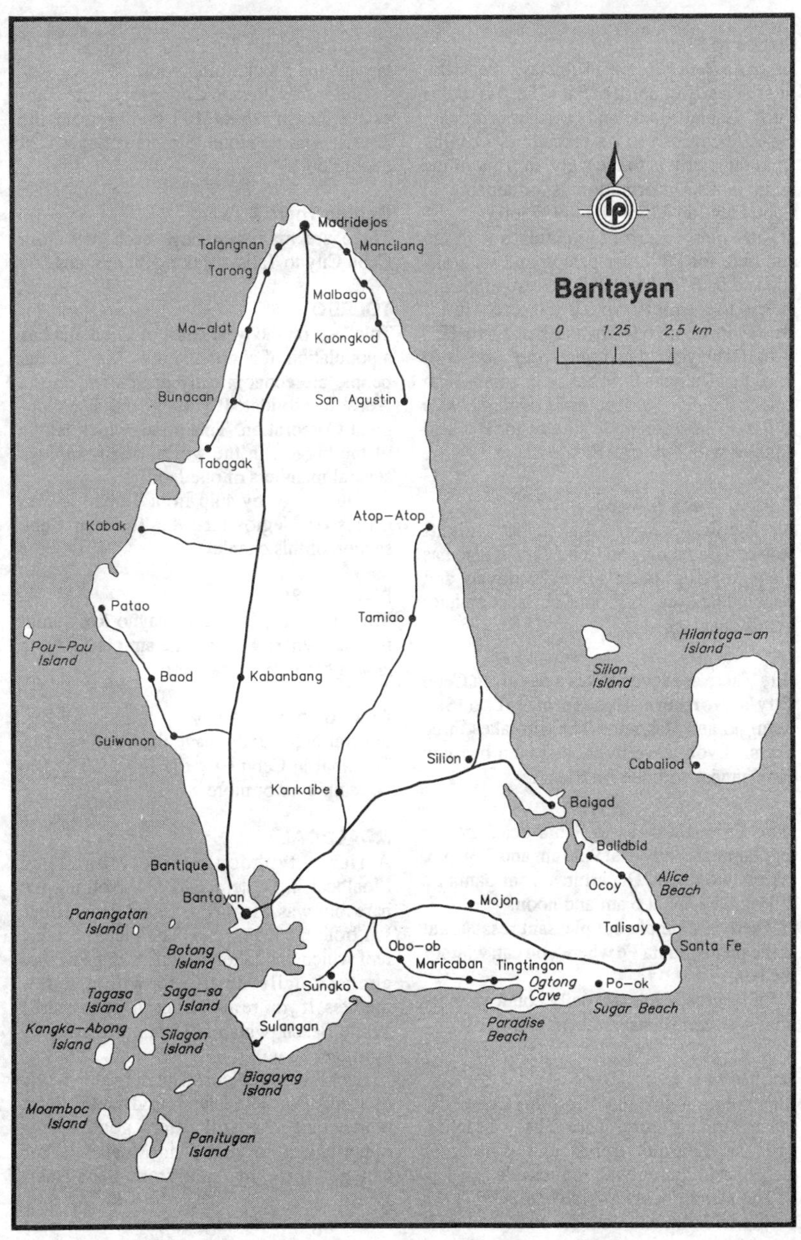
Bantayan
0 1.25 2.5 km
Madridejos
Talangnan
Mancilang
Tarong
Malbago
Ma-alat
Kaongkod
Bunacan
San Agustin
Tabagak
Atop-Atop
Kabak
Patao
Tamiao
Pou-Pou Island
Hilantaga-an Island
Silion Island
Baod
Kabanbang
Guiwanon
Silion
Cabaliod
Kankaibe
Baigad
Balidbid
Bantique
Alice Beach
Ocoy
Bantayan
Mojon
Panangatan Island
Talisay
Santa Fe
Botong Island
Obo-ob
Maricaban
Tingtingon
Ogtong Cave
Po-ok
Tagasa Island
Saga-sa Island
Sungko
Sugar Beach
Paradise Beach
Sulangan
Kangka-Abong Island
Silagon Island
Biagayag Island
Moamboc Island
Panitugan Island

Places to Stay

Santa Fe Beach Resort in Talisay, a beautiful little village just north of Santa Fe, has rooms for P120 and rooms and cottages with bath for P200. It also has a restaurant. Coming from the pier it is to the right, in front of the large tanks. Information is obtainable in Cebu City (tel 82568, 83489, 73603).

Kota Beach Resort has cottages with fan and bath for P300 per person and with air-con and bath for P600. It has a restaurant and is on the lonely south-eastern tip of Bantayan, about one km south of Santa Fe.

In Bantayan, the *Saint Josef Lodge* in President Osmena Sr St has basic rooms with fan for P30/55. The *Admiral Lodging House* in Rizal Ave has simple singles for P75 and doubles with fan for P120.

Getting There & Away

Air Pacific Airways plans to have flights between Bantayan and Cebu City. It also has plans for flights between Bantayan and Bacolod (see the To/From Cebu section later in this chapter).

Bus There are seven buses a day from Cebu City's Northern Bus Terminal to San Remigio and Hagnaya. The trip takes three hours. If you leave by the 6.30 am bus you can connect with the first ferry.

Boat From Hagnaya to Santa Fe, there are regular boats daily at at 9.30 am and 9.30 pm, taking two hours. Departures from Santa Fe to Hagnaya are at 6 am and noon.

There is a simple but pleasant resataurant at the pier in Santa Fe where you can wait for the boat.

To Negros, there is a daily connection by boat between Bantayan town and Cadiz.

TALISAY

This makes a nice day trip from Cebu City but not much more. The Talisay beaches, such as Tangque Beach and Canezares Beach, are anything but impressive.

The *Tourist Seaside Hotel* (tel 97011) has rooms with fan and bath for P150 and with air-con and bath for P280. There is a restaurant and a swimming pool.

Canezares Beach Cottages is on Canezares Beach, about 100 metres from the Tourist Seaside Hotel. Simple cottages cost about P60.

Getting There & Away

There are many jeepneys each day from Cebu City to Talisay, taking 30 minutes.

TOLEDO

Toledo is on the west coast of Cebu and has a population of about 105,000. Many of the people are economically dependent on the Atlas Consolidated Mining and Development Corporation. This mine, which is one of the biggest in the world, often employs several members of one family.

You can go by ship from Toledo to San Carlos on Negros (see the To/From Cebu section of this chapter).

Places to Stay

You can inquire at the Vizcayno Restaurant near the wharf whether the simple *Lodging House* has rooms available.

Getting There & Away

Several buses daily leave the Southern Bus Terminal in Cebu City for Toledo. The trip takes an hour or more.

MOALBOAL

A fierce typhoon severely damaged Moalboal in September 1984. Nothing but bare rock was left of Panagsama Beach, three km from the main road. The fabulous coral reef which had taken centuries to grow was almost totally destroyed within a few minutes. If you're after a beach, go to nearby White Beach, which is 15 minutes away by outrigger boat.

Luckily, the colourful underwater world of nearby Pescador Island survived the fierce whirlwinds and still offers good diving opportunities to visitors in Moalboal. You can get there by boat from Panagsama Beach.

Diving and diving instruction are very

cheap in Moalboal, even by Philippine standards. You pay about P200 for a diving trip, which includes the hire of a boat. They have diving equipment at the various diving centres, but as usual, it is best to have your own. You can hire a mask, snorkel and flippers for P50 per day. A week's diving course will cost you about US$170. Inquire from Nelson of Ocean Safari Philippines at Nelson's Dive Shop, next to Eve's Kiosk; from Bert Schaap of Aquarius Watersports in the Sumisid Lodge; or from Oscar Regner in the Moalboal Reef Club.

To hire a motorcycle will cost around P300 per day, although you may be able to bargain in some places.

A little south-east of Pescador Island is the small Badian Island, with its beautiful white beach and the Badian Beach Resort (temporarily closed), which more and more travel agents are including in their brochures.

Places to Stay

Pacita's Nipa Hut has cottages with bath for P75, and also has a restaurant. *Eve's Kiosk* has rooms with fan for P30/60 and with fan and bath for P80/100. There are also cottages with fans, a restaurant and a disco-bar.

Norma's Travellers Resthouse has rooms and cottages with bath for P50 as well as a restaurant. *Pacifico's Cottages* has singles/doubles for P40/70, with fan for P100/125 and doubles with fan and bath for P150. *Cora's Palm Court* has rooms with fan and bath for P65/100. There is also a restaurant.

Moalboal Reef Club has very comfortable rooms with fan for P475, with fan and bath for P600 and with air-con and bath for US$110. *Sumisid Lodge* offers full board. The fee charged must be arranged with the proprietor.

Badian Beach Resort on Badian Island has rooms with bath for US$110. It is a lovely place, with a restaurant, swimming pool and windsurfing. Unfortunately, this resort was badly damaged by Typhoon Ruping in November 1990 and it has been closed temporarily.

Places to Eat

You can eat cheaply at Pacita's Nipa Hut, Eve's Kiosk, *Lucy's Restaurant*, Cora's Palm Court and Norma's Travellers Resthouse. A bit more expensive, but delicious, are the garlic dishes at *Hannah's Place*. *Divina's Restaurant* has a nice atmosphere at its nightly sing-alongs.

Getting There & Away

Several buses leave the Southern Bus Terminal in Cebu City for Moalboal daily, taking over two hours. If in a good mood, your driver may even take you straight to the beach. Otherwise you will have to take a tricycle from the main street to Panagsama Beach, at a cost of P15. Hardly any buses leave Moalboal for Cebu City between 10.30 am and 3 pm.

The connection between Toledo and Moalboal along the west coast is a bit frustrating. You have to allow for changing three times and waiting. It is better to go from Toledo to Naga and there get the next bus from Cebu City to Moalboal.

MATUTINAO

In the midst of lush tropical vegetation in the mountains near Matutinao you can find the refreshingly cool, crystal-clear Kawasan Falls. They are probably the best waterfalls on Cebu. The natural pools are great for swimming in. This really idyllic place is a good starting point for mountain treks. There is a P5 entrance fee.

Places to Stay & Eat

There are a few cottages near the waterfalls which you can rent for P30 per person. There is also a small restaurant which serves cold drinks as well as meals. As these few cottages may be booked out, it is probably a good idea to do a day trip first to check them out.

Getting There & Away

There are no problems getting from Moalboal to Matutinao by jeepney or bus by day, but you could have trouble getting transport in the late afternoon. The trip takes 45 minutes. Get off at the church in Matutinao

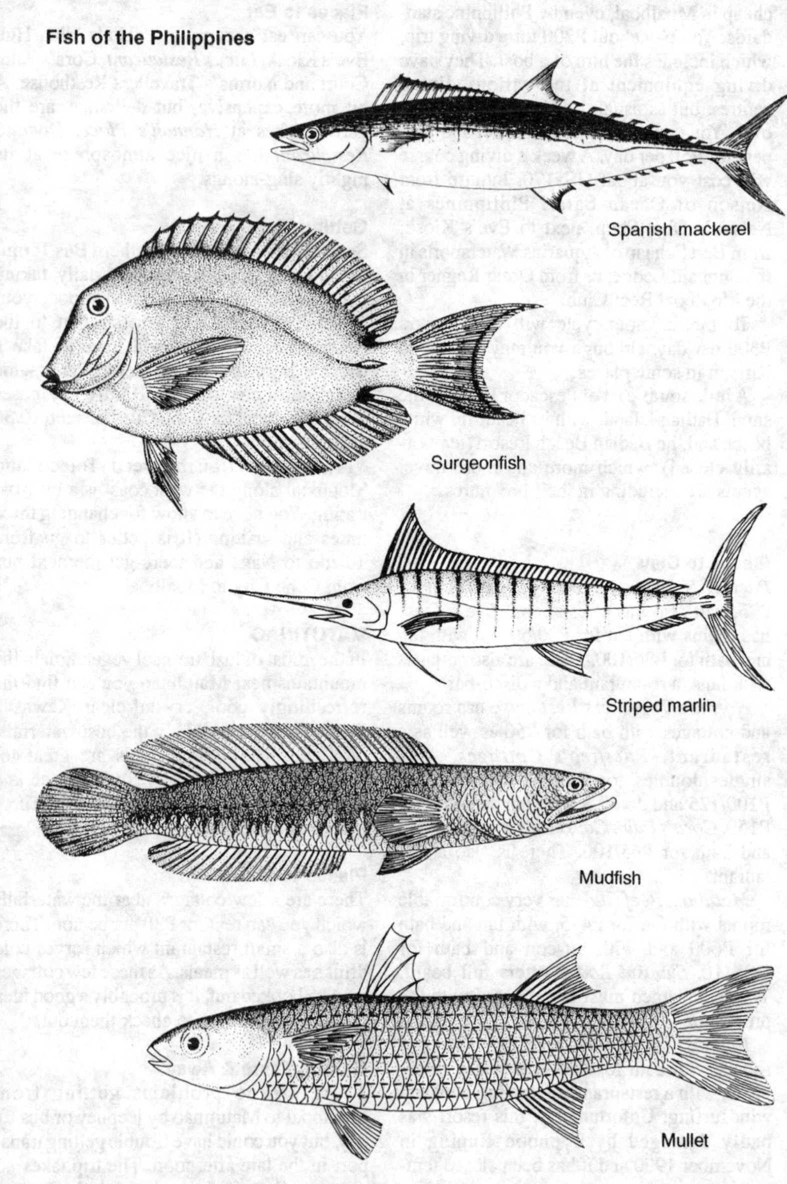
Fish of the Philippines
Spanish mackerel
Surgeonfish
Striped marlin
Mudfish
Mullet

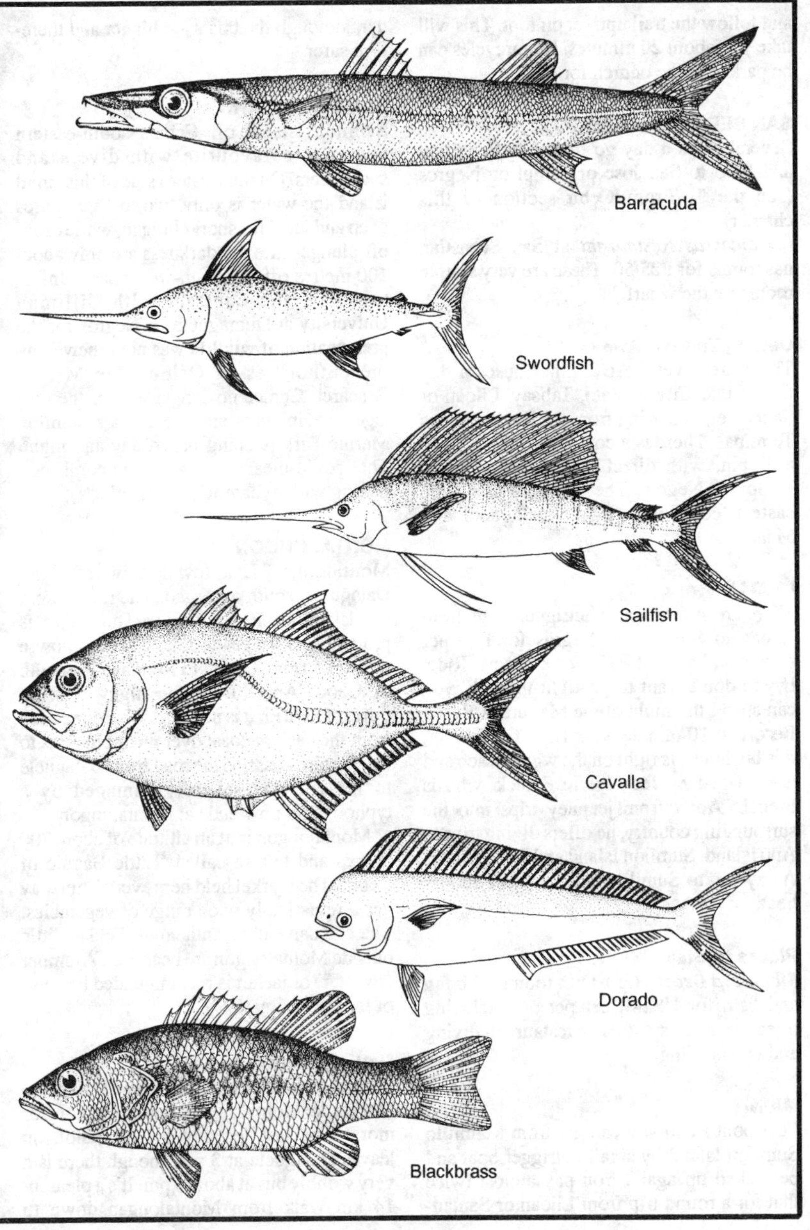
Barracuda
Swordfish
Sailfish
Cavalla
Dorado
Blackbrass

and follow the trail upriver on foot. This will take you about 20 minutes. Motorcycles can be parked at the church for P5.

SAN SEBASTIAN & BATO

Several ships a day go from San Sebastian and Bato to San Jose or Tampi on Negros (see the To/From Cebu section of this chapter).

Contessas Restaurant at San Sebastian has rooms for P25/50. These are very simple rooms by the wharf.

Getting There & Away

There are several ABC Liner buses a day from Cebu City to Bato, Talisay, Liloan or Santander, departing from the Southern Bus Terminal. There is a convenient air-con bus at 1 pm, with direct boat connections to Tampi on Negros. The bus goes along the eastern coast via Argao, Dalaguete and Mainit.

LILOAN

There are several daily outrigger boats from Liloan to Sibulan on Negros for P10 per person and at least P150 for a Special Ride. If you don't want to go right through, you can spend the night at the Manureva Beach Resort. A 10 minute walk from Liloan pier, this big house is right on the white beach and is managed by Jean-Pierre Franck, who is French. Apart from jeepney trips into the surrounding country, he offers diving trips to Apo Island, Sumilon Island and Dako Island. A day trip to Sumilon Island costs P500 by boat.

Places to Stay

Manureva Beach Resort has rooms with fan and bath for US$40 per person, including three meals a day. It has a restaurant, diving and windsurfing.

MAINIT

For about P200 you can get from Mainit to Sumilon Island by small outrigger boat and be picked up again. You pay almost twice that for a round trip from Liloan or Santander, although the boats are bigger and therefore safer.

SUMILON ISLAND

Sumilon Island, off Cebu's south-eastern coast, is a favourite with divers and snorkellers. On the western side of this small island the water is only two to five metres deep and ideal for snorkelling in, while drop-off plunges into the darkness are only about 100 metres off the south-west coast. Unfortunately, the contract with Silliman University at Dumaguete on Negros for the preservation of wildlife was not renewed by the authorities in Oslob. The Marine Research Center no longer exists, the cottages are in ruins and the former Sumilon Marine Park is being fished day and night. That could mean the end of the coral reef: fishing with dynamite is so easy!

MONTALONGON

Montalongon is a few km inland from Dalaguete, south of Argao. The road across the island from Sibonga to Dumanjug is probably no longer usable. There is now a new road from Talood to Ronda in the south of Cebu. Apart from the highway from Carcar to Barili, it is now the only connection from the eastern coast over the mountains to the western coast, as the road from Dalaguete to Badian was severely damaged by a typhoon and now ends at Montalongon.

Montalongon is at an altitude of about 700 metres and is also called 'Little Baguio of Cebu'. The market held here every Thursday has a remarkably wide range of vegetables. The extensive chrysanthemum fields a little outside Montalongon are beautiful. A jumper (sweater) or jacket is recommended because of the cool climate.

Getting There & Away

Several jeepneys go daily from Dalaguete Market to Montalongon, taking an hour or more. The last jeepney for Montalongon leaves Dalaguete at 3 pm, though there is a very wobbly bus at about 4 pm. It's a pleasant 14 km walk from Montalongan down to

Dalaguete, with good views and almost no sound of traffic.

ARGAO

Argao is a small provincial town on the southern coast of Cebu which became known when the exclusive Argao Beach Club opened at the beginning of the 1980s, a few km from the centre. Nonresidents pay P50 admission, but this is credited towards anything consumed. Next door is Dalaguete Public Beach, which is free. Showers are available and the daily rent for sun shelters is P15, or P25 on Sundays and holidays. The meals are cheap here. There is a daily connection by car ferry between Argao and Loon on Bohol (see the To/From Cebu section of this chapter).

Places to Stay

Four Brothers Inn has doubles for P80. It is basic and a bit noisy and has a restaurant. *Sunshine Club* has rooms for P150. It is simple and good and has a restaurant. *Luisa's Place* has rooms with fan and bath for P150. It's a comfortable place and has a restaurant.

Bamboo Paradise has rooms with fan and bath for P250/300 including breakfast. It is homely and good value and has a restaurant. The owners, Carola, who is German, and Rey Rubia, run day trips.

Mahayahay Beach Resort has rooms with fan and bath for P300 and with fan, bath and kitchen for P350. It is friendly and well kept, with big rooms and a restaurant.

Argao Beach Club (tel 70200) has rooms with air-con for P1100-1400/1400-1600. It's excellent and has a restaurant, swimming pool, tennis court, Hobie Cats, windsurfers and diving.

Places to Eat

You can eat well and cheaply at Luisa's Place and at the Four Brothers Inn. In *Carmen's Kitchen* it's no problem to have a fish you've brought from the market prepared for the table. The Bamboo Paradise has German and Filipino cuisine, while the cuisine in the Mahayahay Beach Resort is both Filipino and Swiss.

The *Tan-awan Restaurant* at the Argao Beach Club is mainly geared to international guests.

Getting There & Away

There are several ABC Liner buses a day from Cebu City going to Argao. They leave from the Southern Bus Terminal bound for Santander, Bato or Talisay. The trip takes an hour or more. There is a somewhat faster air-con bus at 1 pm. A Ceres Liner bus leaves at 8 am and connects with the ferry from Argao to Loon on Bohol.

Several minibuses a day also leave from the Argao bus terminal but they are pretty uncomfortable.

TO/FROM CEBU

You can get to Cebu from Bohol, Leyte, Luzon, Masbate, Mindanao, Negros, Palawan, Panay, Samar and Siquijor (see the Transport from Luzon section of the Manila chapter and the relevant To/From sections of this chapter and of the chapters on the other islands).

Air

Following are the addresses and telephone numbers of the major airline offices in Cebu City:

Aerolift
- Gorordo Ave (tel 72786)
- Mactan International Airport (tel 88100, 88165)

Pacific Airways
- Lahug Airport (tel 92854)

Philippine Airlines
- Osmena Blvd (tel 90006, 91207)
- General Maxilom Ave (tel 79154, 94664)
- Escario St/Capitol (tel 52918, 53146)
- Mactan International Airport (tel 84811, 88459)

Boat

The shipping lines in Cebu are pretty relaxed about keeping to the timetables. Ships are cancelled and others put on without any notice. Even the people on the ticket counters seem to be quite clueless. The announcements in the dailies *The Freeman* and *Sun Star* are more or less reliable. Information from the shipping lines is more accurate, but probably only if you phone and say you are a foreign tourist.

The following are the addresses and telephone numbers of the major shipping lines in Cebu City:

Aboitiz Lines
Osmena Blvd (tel 75440, 93075)
Escano Lines
Reclamation Area (tel 93311, 62122)
George & Peter Lines
Jakosalem St (tel 75508, 74098)
Georgia Shipping Lines
Corner Arellan Blvd and Sotto St (tel 79276, 210680)
Carlos Gothong Lines
Reclamation Area (tel 73107, 95545)
K & T Shipping Lines
MacArthur Blvd (tel 92681)
Roble Shipping Lines
Sotto St (tel 97136, 79632)
Sulpicio Lines
Reclamation Area (tel 73839, 79956)
Sweet Lines
Arellano Blvd (tel 97415, 77431)
Trans Asia Shipping Lines
Briones St (tel 96909, 92022)
Western Samar Shipping Lines
MacArthur Blvd (tel 91229, 74050)
William Lines
Reclamation Area (tel 92471, 736619)

To Bohol

Air PAL flies daily from Cebu City to Tagbilaran.

Bus The MV *Kanlaon Ferry* leaves daily from Argao for Loon at 11 am. The trip takes an hour. There is a daily Ceres Liner bus from Cebu City to Argao, leaving at 8 am from the Southern Bus Terminal and going to the ferry and on from Loon to Tagbilaran.

Boat A large outrigger boat goes from Argao to Cabilao Island on Tuesday and Saturday at 2 pm, taking an hour or more.

The journey from Cebu City to Tagbilaran takes four hours. The Sweet Lines' MV *Sweet Time* or MV *Sweet Pearl* leaves daily at noon and on Friday at 10 pm. The Trans Asia Shipping Lines' MV *Asia-Japan* leaves daily at 6.30 pm. The Sulpicio Lines' MV *Bohol Princess* leaves on Saturday at noon.

From Cebu City to Talibon, the MV *Charisse* leaves daily at 9 pm, taking four hours or more, and the MV *VG Express* leaves on Monday, Wednesday and Friday at 9 pm, also taking four hours. You can sleep on the boat.

From Cebu City to Tubigon, the MV *Tubigon* leaves daily at 6 am, noon and 4 and 10 pm; the MV *Harvey* leaves daily at noon; and the MV *Charing* leaves daily at 4 pm. All take two hours.

There are also some ships sailing from Cebu City to Tubigon.

To Camiguin

Air PAL is planning to set up a service from Cebu City to Mambajao. At present the fastest connection is from Cebu City via Cagayan de Oro or Butuan by air, then on by bus to Balingoan and on by ship to Binone, where jeepneys wait at the wharf for passengers to Mambajao.

Boat There are also ships from Cebu City to Cagayan de Oro and Butuan. The Georgia Shipping Lines' MV *Luzille* leaves Cebu City for Mambajao on Wednesday and Friday at 7 pm, taking eight hours.

To Leyte

Air Pacific Airways flies daily from Cebu City to Maasin. PAL flies from Cebu City to Ormoc on Tuesday and Friday, and daily from Cebu City to Tacloban.

Boat A large outrigger boat leaves Carmen for Isabel daily at 8 am, taking four hours.

The Roble Shipping Lines' MV *Guada Cristy* leaves Cebu City for Hilongos on Monday, Wednesday and Friday at 10 pm, taking six hours.

The K & T Shipping Lines' MV *Guiuan* and MV *Cebu Queen* leave Cebu City for Liloan on Monday and Friday at 10 pm, taking six hours.

The Escano Lines' MV *Escano* leaves Cebu City for Maasin on Monday at 10 am, taking seven hours.

The Sulpicio Lines' MV *Cebu Princess* leaves Cebu City for Ormoc on Monday at

Top: Rainbow over the Chocolate Hills, Bohol (JPk)
Bottom: Filipino house and tropical flowers (JP)

Top: Panning for gold in Negros (JP)
Bottom: A steam-age dinosaur brings in the sugar cane in Negros (JP)

10 pm. The Aboitiz Lines' MV *Aklan* makes the same journey from Monday to Saturday at 10 pm. Both take seven hours.

The Carlos Gothong Lines' MV *Dona Cristina* leaves Cebu City for Palompon on Monday at 10 pm. The MV *Our Lady of Fatima* leaves on Wednesday at noon. The MV *Our Lady of Guadalupe* leaves on Friday at 10 pm. All take five hours.

The K & T Shipping Lines' MV *Leyte Queen* leaves Cebu City for Tacloban on Tuesday, Thursday and Saturday at 6 pm, taking 12 hours.

To Luzon

Air PAL flies daily from Cebu City to Legaspi. Both Aerolift and PAL fly daily from Cebu City to Manila.

Boat From Cebu City to Manila, the William Lines' MV *Dona Virginia* leaves on Monday at 8 pm and on Friday at 10 am, taking 23 hours; the Sweet Lines' MV *Sweet Baby* leaves on Tuesday at 10 am and on Friday at 6 pm, taking 22 hours; the Sulpicio Lines' MV *Filipina Princess* leaves on Wednesday at 8 pm and on Sunday at 10 am, taking 21 hours; and the Sulpicio Lines' MV *Davao Princess* leaves on Friday at 10 am, taking 23 hours.

To Masbate

Boat The Escano Lines' MV *Augustina* leaves Cebu City for Masbate on Monday at 10 am and on Friday at 7 pm, taking 13 hours.

The Georgia Shipping Lines' MV *Princess Joan* leaves Cebu City for Cataingan on Monday, Wednesday and Friday at 10 pm, taking 10 hours.

To Mindanao

Air From Cebu City, PAL flies daily to Butuan, Cagayan de Oro, Cotabato, Davao, Dipolog, General Santos City, Ozamiz, Pagadian and Surigao. It also has flights on Wednesday and Sunday to Iligan; on Monday and Friday to Bislig; on Tuesday, Thursday and Saturday to Tandag; and from Monday to Thursday, Saturday and Sunday to Zamboanga.

Boat From Cebu City to Butuan, the Sulpicio Lines' MV *Nasipit Princess* leaves on Monday, Wednesday and Saturday at 8 pm, taking 12 hours and arriving at Nasipit; the Carlos Gothong Lines' MV *Don Calvino* leaves on Tuesday, Thursday and Saturday at 6 pm, taking 12 hours; the Trans Asia Shipping Lines' MV *Asia Indonesia* leaves on Tuesday, Thursday and Saturday at 6 pm, taking 14 hours; and the Carlos Gothong Lines' MV *Our Lady of Lourdes* leaves on Friday at 6 pm, taking 11 hours.

From Cebu City to Cagayan de Oro, the Sulpicio Lines' MV *Cagayan Princess* leaves on Monday, Wednesday and Friday at 7 pm, taking 10 hours; the Sweet Lines' MV *Sweet Time* leaves on Monday at 10 pm, taking nine hours; the Trans Asia Shipping Lines' MV *Trans Asia* leaves on Tuesday to Sunday at 7.30, taking nine hours; and the Carlos Gothong Lines' MV *Dona Lili* leaves on Tuesday, Thursday and Saturday, taking 10 hours.

From Cebu City to Davao, the Sulpicio Lines' MV *Davao Princess* leaves on Monday at noon, taking 24 hours.

From Cebu City to Dipolog, the George & Peter Lines' MV *Jhufel*, MV *Don Joaquin* or MV *Don Victoriano* leaves daily at 10 pm, taking 12 hours and possibly going via Dumaguete.

From Cebu City to Iligan, the William Lines' MV *Ozamiz City* or MV *Iligan City* leaves on Monday, Wednesday and Friday at 7 pm, taking 12 hours, and the Carlos Gothong Lines' MV *Don Benjamin* leaves on Monday, Thursday and Saturday at 7 pm, taking 11 hours.

From Cebu City to Ozamiz, the William Lines' MV *Ozamiz City* or MV *Iligan City* leaves on Monday, Wednesday and Friday at 7 pm, taking 10 hours, and the Carlos Gothong Lines' MV *Dona Cristina* leaves on Tuesday, Thursday and Saturday at 7 pm, taking 12 hours.

From Cebu City to Plaridel, the Sweet Lines' MV *Sweet Time* leaves on Friday at 10 pm, taking 12 hours; the Georgia Shipping Lines' MV *Luzille* leaves on Sunday at 7 pm, taking 10 hours.

From Cebu City to Surigao, the Sweet Lines' MV *Sweet Home* or MV *Sweet Heart* leaves daily at 7 pm, taking 16 hours.

From Cebu City to Zamboanga, the George & Peter Lines' MV *Jhufel* leaves on Monday and Wednesday at 10 pm, taking 24 hours and possibly going via Dumaguete; and the MV *Don Joaquin* leaves on Wednesday at 10 pm, also taking 24 hours and going via Dumaguete.

To Negros

Air Pacific Airways flies daily from Cebu City to Bacolod via Calatrava. PAL flies daily from Cebu City to Bacolod and to Dumaguete.

Pacific Airways is also planning a service from Bantayan Island to Bacolod.

Bus Ceres Liner buses leave Cebu City daily for Bacolod at 6 and 7 am from the Southern Bus Terminal. They meet the ferry going from Tuburan to Escalante (Port Danao) and go on to Bacolod. The trip, including the ferry ride, takes seven hours.

Boat Several ferries a day leave Bato for Tampi, taking 45 minutes. The last departure is at about 4.30 pm. A boat may go from Talisay to San Jose, where jeepneys for Dumaguete wait at the wharf.

From Cebu City to Dumaguete, you can go by the George & Peter Lines' MV *Jhufel*, MV *Don Joaquin* or MV *Don Victoriano*. The boats leave daily at 10 pm and possibly at 8 pm on Thursday and Sunday, taking six hours.

From Liloan to Sibulan, you travel by big outrigger boat. There are several trips daily, taking 20 minutes.

Boats leave Tangil daily for Guihulngan at 6.30 and 8 am, taking two hours.

A ferry from Toledo to San Carlos leaves daily at 9 am and 4 pm, from Monday to Saturday, and at 1.30 pm on Sunday. There may be different departure times on holidays. Only one boat goes on Holy Thursday and none on Good Friday. The timetable on this route changes frequently. Buy your ticket from the kiosk at the entrance to the pier and not from the shady men offering you a ticket. The trip takes 1¾ hours.

The last bus from San Carlos to Bacolod waits for the last boat from Toledo. A combined bus and boat ticket is cheaper than two single tickets.

From Bantayan town on Bantayan Island, a boat leaves daily at 11 am for Cadiz on the northern coast of Negros, taking three hours or more.

To Palawan

Air PAL flies daily from Cebu City via Iloilo on Panay to Puerto Princesa.

To Panay

Air PAL flies daily from Cebu City to Iloilo. Pacific Airways also flies daily via Calatrava and Bacolod on Negros to Iloilo and probably twice a week via Bacolod to Caticlan (near Boracay).

PAL also flies from Cebu City to Kalibo on Monday, Wednesday, Friday and Saturday.

Boat The Carlos Gothong Lines' MV *Our Lady of Guadalupe* leaves Cebu City for New Washington via Palompon on Leyte on Friday at 10 pm, taking 28 hours.

To Samar

Boat The Western Samar Shipping Lines' MV *Helen* leaves Cebu City for Catbalogan on Tuesday and Saturday at 6 pm, taking 14 hours.

To Siquijor

Air PAL is planning a service from Siquijor to Cebu City.

Boat The George & Peter Lines' MV *Dona Rosario* leaves Cebu City for Larena on Monday and Saturday at 8 pm, taking six hours. The Sweet Lines' MV *Sweet Time* leaves on Friday at 10 pm, going via Tagbilaran on Bohol and taking eight hours.

The George & Peter Lines' MV *Dona Rosario* leaves Cebu City for Lazi on Monday at 8 pm, taking six hours.

Leyte

Leyte is one of the Visayan Islands and lies between Samar, Cebu, Bohol and Mindanao. The San Juanico Bridge, which is over two km long and joins the islands of Leyte and Samar across the San Juanico Strait, is probably the most beautiful bridge in South-East Asia. Central and southern Leyte are somewhat mountainous with plains in the northern and western parts of the island. Administratively, it is divided into the province of Leyte, whose capital is Tacloban, and Southern Leyte, whose capital is Maasin.

Copra is Leyte's most important export product. More than 30% of cultivable land is planted with coconut palms. Other important agricultural exports are rice, maize, sugar cane and abaca. These are mostly shipped directly from Tacloban, making it unnecessary to send exports via Manila.

Leyte is particularly remembered as the place where General MacArthur's fulfilled his 'I shall return' pledge. In October 1944, US troops landed at Red Beach in Palo, a little south of Tacloban, and started pushing the Japanese out of the Philippines. A little further south is Tolosa, the birthplace of former first lady Imelda Marcos.

The main dialect in and around Tacloban is Waray-Waray, whereas in the north-west and the south it is Cebuano. You can get by quite well with English.

TACLOBAN

The capital of Leyte is a port town with about 105,000 inhabitants. It has an excellent harbour with facilities for handling large ships and overseas trade. The colourful market at the western end of the wharf is full of life. A large relief on the wall of the Provincial Capitol Building depicts MacArthur's return to the Philippines. This historic event is celebrated each year on 19 and 20 October with cockfights and parades.

The museum in Tacloban's Divine Word University has rare and priceless artefacts from Leyte and Samar, which date from the early trade with China, and from the Sohoton Cave diggings. Another good museum is the colonial-style Santo Nino Shrine and Heritage Museum, which was developed by Imelda Marcos and houses a collection of works of art and antiquity from around the world; it also has a swimming pool behind it. Next door is the equally large People's Center, with a library for Samar and Leyte.

As a reward for climbing the many steps (decorated with 14 statues representing the Stations of the Cross) to the base of the statue of Christ, you will get a beautiful view over Tacloban and its busy port. You can get there from the market along Torres St. You can also get a good view over San Pedro Bay from the veranda café of the exclusive Leyte Park Hotel, which has two swimming pools, one of them heart-shaped.

The small island of Dio with its white beach lies south-east of Tacloban in San Pedro Bay, about 15 minutes by outrigger boat. It used to belong to the Marcos clan, whose members and special guests spent their holidays here. Apart from luxury cottages and a swimming pool, there is also supposed to be a secret tunnel, which became known only after Marcos's fall. Part of Dio Island Beach Resort, which today is open to all guests, is Baluarte Beach Resort in San Jose, a little south of Tacloban, on the way to Palo. If you are keen on history, you should visit MacArthur Park on Red Beach, where General MacArthur landed. Nature lovers will enjoy a day trip to Sohoton National Park near Basey on the island of Samar.

Information

Money The Philippine National Bank in Justice Romualdez St changes travellers' cheques but you will need a photocopy of your passport.

Places to Stay – bottom end

San Juanico Travel Lodge at 104 Justice Romualdez St is a comfortable place with rooms with fan for P50/60 and with fan and bath for P60/80.

Manabó Lodge (tel 3727) in Zamora St

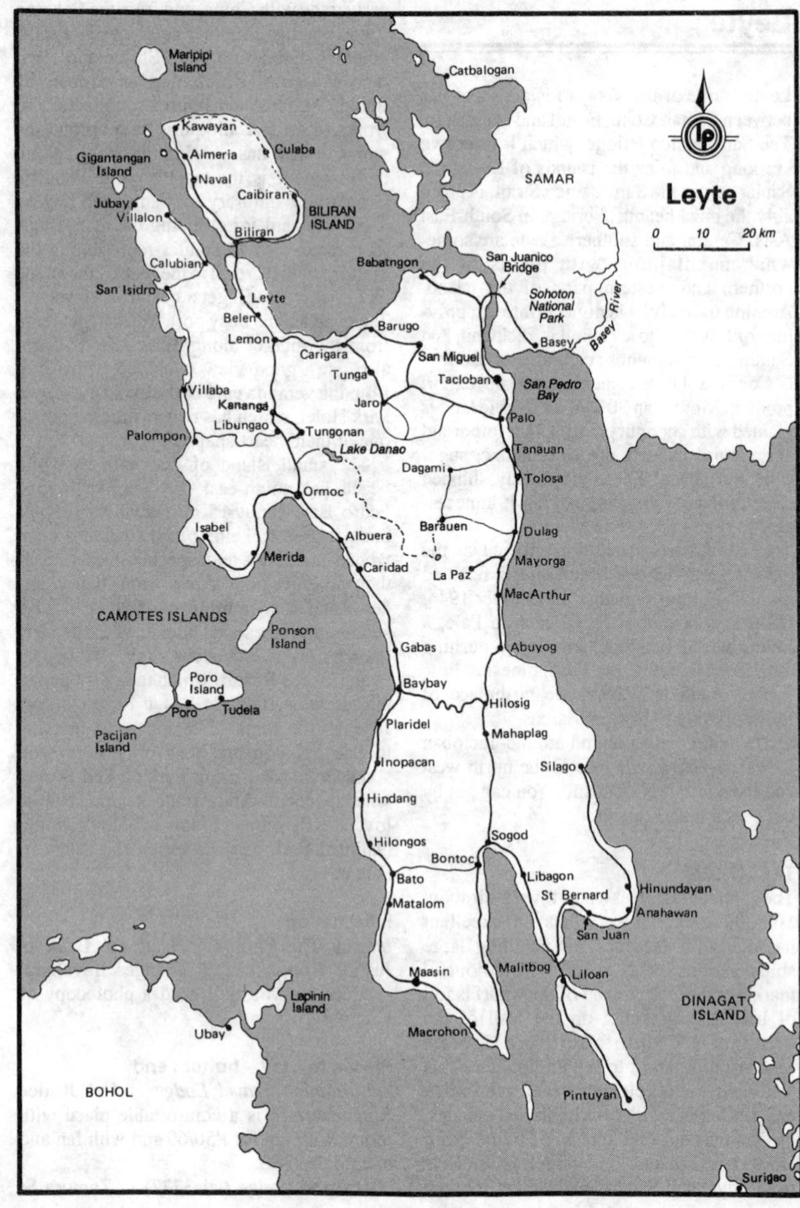
Leyte
0 10 20 km
Maripipi Island
Catbalogan
Kawayan
Gigantangan Island
Almeria
Culaba
Naval
Caibiran
BILIRAN ISLAND
SAMAR
Jubay
Villalon
Biliran
Calubian
Babatngon
San Juanico Bridge
San Isidro
Sohoton National Park
Leyte
Belen
Basey River
Lemon
Barugo
Basey
Carigara
San Miguel
Tunga
Tacloban
San Pedro Bay
Villaba
Jaro
Kananga
Palo
Libungao
Palompon
Tungonan
Lake Danao
Tanauan
Dagami
Tolosa
Ormoc
Barauen
Isabel
Albuera
Dulag
Merida
Mayorga
Caridad
La Paz
MacArthur
CAMOTES ISLANDS
Ponson Island
Gabas
Abuyog
Poro Island
Baybay
Poro
Tudela
Hilosig
Pacijan Island
Plaridel
Mahaplag
Inopacan
Silago
Hindang
Sogod
Hilongos
Bontoc
Bato
Libagon
St Bernard
Hinundayan
Matalom
Anahawan
San Juan
Malitbog
Liloan
Maasin
Lapinin Island
DINAGAT ISLAND
Ubay
Macrohon
BOHOL
Pintuyan
Surigao

has reasonable rooms with fan for P100/140 and with fan and bath for P120/160. *Allee Lodge* (tel 3280) in Burgos St, on the corner of M H del Pilar St, has very basic rooms with fan for P40, with fan and bath for P60 and with air-con and bath for P200.

LSC House (tel 3175), also known as Leyte State College Mini Hotel, in Paterno St, has rooms with fan and bath for P150, and rooms with air-con and bath for P175/265. It's a reasonable place with a cafeteria and a tearoom.

Cecilia's Lodge (tel 2815) at 178 Paterno St is a simple but fairly good place. It has rooms with fan for P70/100, with fan and bath for P100/150 and with air-con and bath for P180/250.

Places to Stay – middle

Primerose Hotel (tel 2248) in Zamora St, on the corner of Salazar St, has rooms with fan and bath for P180/220 and with air-con and bath for P260/400. It is not very clean and some of the rooms smell rather musty.

Tacloban Plaza Hotel (tel 2444) in Justice Romualdez St has rooms with air-con and bath for P180/300. It is nice and tidy and has a restaurant. Some of the rooms are above the bowling alley and could be a bit noisy.

Tacloban Village Inn (tel 2926) in Veterano St has rooms with air-con and bath for P180/300. It is quite comfortable and has a restaurant.

Baluarte Beach Resort (tel 2811, 2705) in San Jose has rooms with fan and bath for P200 and with air-con and bath for P340. It has a restaurant and a swimming pool.

Places to Stay – top end

Leyte Park Hotel (tel 3300-04) on Magsaysay Blvd is the best hotel in town and is directly on San Pedro Bay. Singles/doubles with air-con and bath cost P1260/1400. It has a restaurant, swimming pool and tennis court.

Places to Eat

The *Good Morning* Restaurant in Zamora St has an adjoining bakery where you can get a decent breakfast.

There is a good variety of chicken and Filipino dishes at the *Sunburst Fried Chicken* in Burgos St. Good Chinese and Filipino meals can be had in the *Asiatic Restaurant* and the *Savory Steak House*, both in Zamora St.

The *Rovic Restaurant* in Zamora St and the *Veranda Café* in the Leyte Park Hotel both have a more or less international cuisine. At the *Lapyahan House of Seafood* in Real St, you eat with your fingers – an excellent culinary experience. A window seat looking out on the sea will make your dinner complete.

Entertainment

You can enjoy live music every evening in the open-air restaurant *Sinugba Fiesta* in M H del Pilar St. Among the most popular dance restaurants are the *Stone Age Disco* at the Tacloban Village Inn, the *Disco at the Park* at the Leyte Park Hotel and the *Spacer Disco* in Real St. The night clubs *Olongapo Disco* and *La Azotea*, both at the corner of M H del Pilar and Zamora streets, have nightly shows and live music.

Getting Around

A shuttle bus between Romualdez Airport and Tacloban leaves Tacloban from the Tacloban Plaza Hotel in Justice Romualdez St but does not run regularly. The fare is P7. A jeepney from the airport to Tacloban costs P10, but the fare is less in the opposite direction. A taxi from the airport to the centre of town should not cost more than P40.

AROUND TACLOBAN

Sohoton National Park & Basey

Although Sohoton National Park is on the island of Samar, the simplest way to get there is from Tacloban, either direct or via Basey. It has waterfalls, underground waterways and a labyrinth of caves, which are also called 'wonder caves' because of their glittering stone formations. The biggest and most beautiful are Panhulugan I, Bugasan III and Sohoton. A park ranger lives at the entrance to the park and will, on request, guide you through the caves with a kerosene lamp. You can stay overnight with the ranger, but you have to take your own provisions. The best time to see the caves is from March to July, as you can only visit them when the water level is low, not after prolonged rainfall.

Basey is well known for its colourful mats and other woven goods, which are sold in the markets in Tacloban.

Getting There & Away Staff at the Tacloban Tourist Office should be able to help you arrange some of these trips and they should also know about possible NPA (New People's Army) activities in the national park.

You can hire an outrigger boat with 16 hp motor at the wharf at Tacloban for about P350 to P400. It's a bit cheaper if you go by jeepney from Tacloban to Basey and then hire a boat for about P300. Make sure first, though, that the cost of a guide (P30) and a kerosene lamp (P20) are included. The first jeepney leaves Tacloban for Basey at about 7 am, the second not till 9.30 am, each taking over an hour. A day trip from Basey to the Sohoton National Park is only worthwhile if you arrive early in Basey, as the last jeepney leaves for Tacloban at about 3 pm and then only if there are enough passengers.

The beautiful trip upriver to the park takes about one hour.

PALO

A monument and a plaque on Red Beach at Palo commemorate the return of General MacArthur to the Philippines on 20 October 1944 after a major naval battle. He liberated the country from Japanese occupation roughly two years after fleeing from the island fortress of Corregidor in Manila Bay.

Palo Cathedral, built in 1596 with an altar covered in gold leaf, was temporarily converted to a hospital by the Americans in 1944.

Places to Stay

City Lodge Pension has rooms with air-con and bath for P240. It's comfortable, clean and you can rent rooms by the hour.

1 Children's Park
2 Leyte Park Hotel
3 Plaza Libertad
4 Provincial Capitol Building
5 Wharf
6 K&T Shipping Lines
7 William Lines
8 Botanical Garden
9 Buses & Jeepneys
10 Sulpicio Lines
11 Market
12 San Juanico Travel Lodge
13 Primerose Hotel
14 Asiatic Restaurant
15 Good Morning Restaurant
Savory Steak House
16 Rovic Restaurant
17 Manabo Lodge
18 La Azotea
Olongapo Disco
19 Airport Bus
Tacloban Plaza Hotel
20 Philippine National Bank
21 Stations of the Cross
22 Minibuses to Samar
23 Town Hall
24 Allee Lodge
25 Tacloban Village Inn
26 Philippine Airlines
27 Sunburst Fried Chicken
28 Santo Nino Church
29 Lapyahan House of Seafood
30 Cecilia's Lodge
31 Divine Word University
32 LSC House
33 Spacer Disco
34 Library for Samar & Leyte
People's Centre
Santo Nino Shrine & Heritage
Museum
35 Philtranco Bus Terminal

MacArthur Park Beach Resort (tel 3015, 3016) has rooms with fan and bath for P460/545, with air-con and bath for P680/820, and suites for P1090. It is pleasant and has a restaurant. You may be able to negotiate about the prices.

Getting There & Away

Several jeepneys a day leave Tacloban wharf for Palo, but not all make the detour to MacArthur Park (formerly Imelda Park), about 1½ km from the main road.

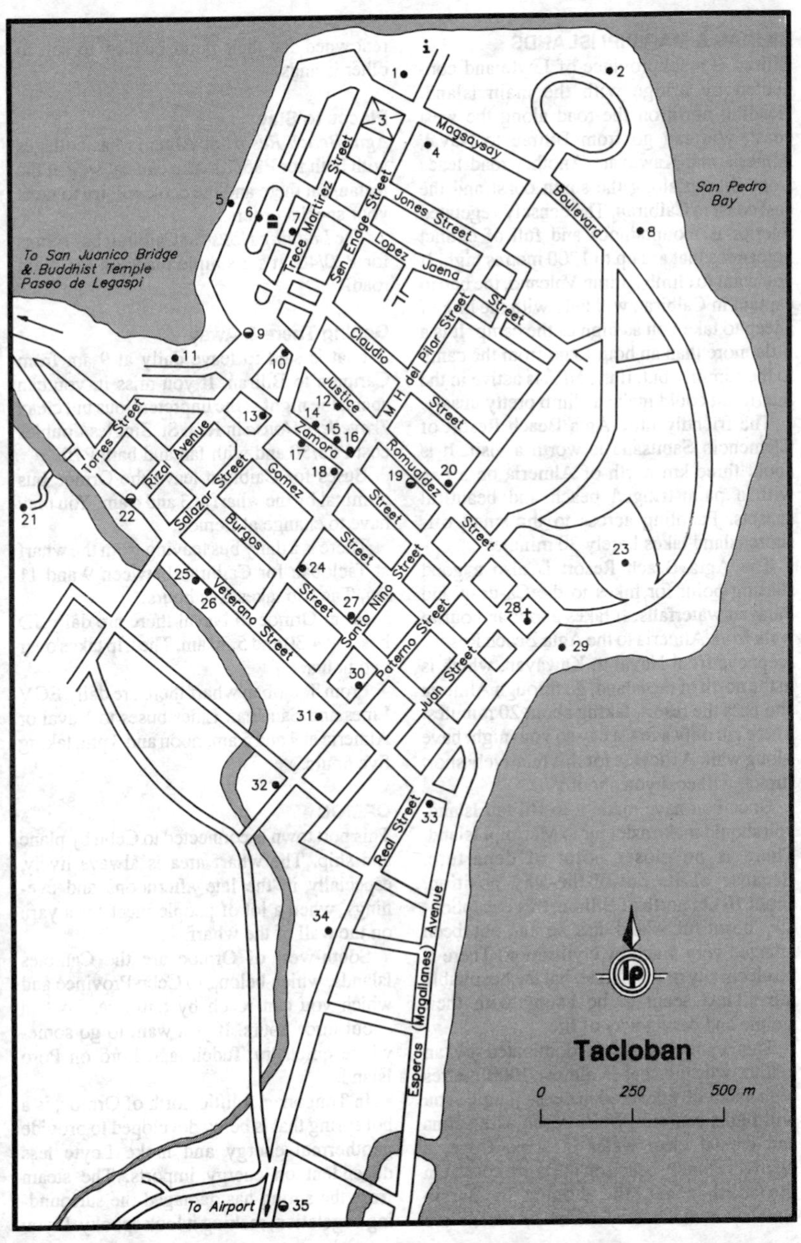
San Pedro Bay
To San Juanico Bridge & Buddhist Temple Paseo de Legaspi
Magsaysay Boulevard
Trece Martirez Street
Sen Enage Street
Jones Street
Lopez Jaena Street
Claudio
M H del Pilar Street
Justice
Zamora
Romualdez Street
Torres Street
Rizal Avenue
Salazar Street
Gomez Street
Burgos Street
Santo Nino Street
Veterano Street
Paterno Street
Juan Street
Real Street
Avenue (Magallanes) Esperas
To Airport
Tacloban
0 250 500 m

BILIRAN & MARIPIPI ISLANDS

Biliran is a subprovince of Leyte and connected by bridge with the main island. Heading north on the road along the west coast, you can go from Biliran to Naval, Almeria and Kawayan. Another road leads from Biliran along the south coast and the east coast to Caibiran. The densely vegetated interior is mountainous and full of extinct volcanoes that are up to 1200 metres high. If you want to climb Biliran Volcano, the barrio captain in Caibiran will help with the hire of a jeep to take you as high as the camp. It is a little more than an hour to go from the camp to the summit, but, if the NPA is active in the interior, it could make a climb pretty unsafe.

The friendly little Agta Beach Resort of Clemencio Sabitsana is worth a visit. It is about three km north of Almeria on a bay with a palm-fringed beach and beautiful sunsets. Paddling across to the small offshore island takes barely 30 minutes.

The Agta Beach Resort is also a good starting point for hikes to the Ca-ucap and Palayan waterfalls. It takes about an hour to walk from Almeria to the Agta Beach Resort. Jeepneys from Naval to Kawayan, which is in the north of the island, go through Almeria and pass the resort, taking about 20 minutes. There are only a few a day so you might have a long wait. A tricycle for this relatively short stretch will cost you about P70.

Once you have made it to Biliran Island, you should make a detour to Maripipi Island. There is no closer point of departure. Because of its out-of-the-way position, about 10 km north of Biliran, this exceptionally beautiful island has so far not been affected very much by civilisation. There is no electricity or telephone, but the hospitable inhabitants seem to be happy with their simple and caring way of life.

This exotic island is dominated by an extinct volcano that is almost 1000 metres high and partly covered in dense jungle. You will find a beautiful white beach with palms and crystal clear water in Napo Cove, a relatively lonely beach on the north coast. On the south coast, the women in Barrio Binalayan make clay utensils, which are renowned for their good quality, to sell to other islands.

Places to Stay

Agta Beach Resort at Almeria has cottages with bath for P35/70. You can eat well at the restaurant there and the cook will try to meet your special orders.

The *Lodging House* at Caibiran has rooms for P20/40. It's a simple place on the main road.

Getting There & Away

A boat is said to leave daily at 9 am from Carigara to Biliran. If you miss it, you can spend the night at the unpretentious but clean *Travellers House* in Real St. Singles/doubles cost P25/50 and with fan and bath P70.

Buses for Caibiran leave the Ormoc bus terminal by the wharf at 3 and 4 am. You may have to change at Lemon.

There is a daily bus leaving from the wharf at Tacloban for Caibiran between 9 and 11 am. The trip takes five hours.

From Ormoc to Naval there are daily JD buses at 4.30 and 5.30 am. The trip takes over two hours.

From Tacloban wharf there are daily EGV Lines and San Juan Lines buses to Naval or Almeria at 4 and 5 am, noon and 3 pm, taking five hours.

ORMOC

This port town is connected to Cebu by plane and ship. The wharf area is always lively, especially in the late afternoons and evenings, when a lot of people meet for a yarn on the wall of the wharf.

South-west of Ormoc are the Camotes Islands, which belong to Cebu Province and which you can reach by outrigger boat in about three hours. If you want to go somewhere quiet, try Tudela and Poro on Poro Island.

In Tungonan, a little north of Ormoc, is a hot spring that is being developed to provide geothermal energy and make Leyte less dependent on energy imports. The steam from the spring has damaged the surrounding vegetation, making it look spooky. If you want to visit the geothermal project, you need a permit which you have to apply for in writing two weeks beforehand to the Project Manager at the following address: PNOC EDC Geothermal Project, Tungonan, Ormoc City.

North-east of Ormoc City is Leyte National Park, the northern beginning of the Leyte Nature Trail, which is about 50 km long, and leads through mountainous Central Leyte, connecting Danao and Mahagnao lakes. Because of increased NPA activity in this region, the Tacloban Tourist Office at present strongly advises against a stay in the national park.

Palompon is a coastal town north-west of Ormoc and three hours away by jeepney. Ships go from Palompon to Cebu and Panay. If you follow the road from Palompon northwards along the coast, you will reach Jubay (pronounced Hubye), where you can get a boat to small Gigantangan Island, which is off the usual routes.

Places to Stay & Eat

There are several good, cheap hotels in Ormoc. *Eddie's Inn* (tel 2499), on the corner of Rizal and Lopez Jeana streets, is simple with rooms for P25/50. *Pongos Hotel* (tel 2482) in Bonifacio St has rooms with fan and bath for P70/100 and with air-con and bath for P110/150. It is basic, but clean and good.

The *Shalom Pensione* (tel 2208), on the corner of Bonifacio and Cataag streets, has rooms with fan for P35/70 and with fan and bath for P55/110. It's simple, reasonably good and has a restaurant.

The best hotel in Ormoc is the *Hotel Don Felipe* (tel 2460, 2007) in Bonifacio St, beside the wharf. It has rooms with fan and bath for P70/110 and with air-con and bath for P135-325/170-366. It also has a good restaurant. Another good restaurant with excellent food is the *Magnolia Sizzler* on the corner of Bonifacio and Lopez Jaena streets.

Getting There & Away

Buses for Ormoc leave Tacloban wharf daily from 4 am until the early afternoon. The trip takes three hours. A JD express bus leaves at 3 pm from the corner of Veterano and Santo Nino streets, opposite the Divine Word University.

Buses for Ormoc leave Naval on Biliran Island at 8 am, noon and 3 pm, taking three hours.

The first bus leaves Ormoc for Tacloban from the wharf at around 5.30 am, straight after the ship from Cebu arrives.

BAYBAY

Ships go from Baybay to Cebu and other islands. With mountains in the background and an old Spanish church dominating the town, it makes a most attractive picture seen at dawn from a ship just arriving in port.

About seven km north of Baybay is the modern Visayan State College of Agriculture (VISCA for short) which was financed by the World Bank.

Places to Stay

Ellean's Lodge is an unpretentious place with rooms for P35/60 and with fan for P45/90.

Getting There & Away

Several buses a day go from Tacloban wharf to Baybay, taking over two hours.

BATO & HILONGOS

Bato is a small port between Baybay and Maasin with sea links to Cebu and Bohol. Ships also leave for Cebu from Hilongos, a little north of Bato, where there is a tall belfry dating from the Spanish conquest.

Hilongos is more pleasant than Bato, especially as it has a couple of nice restaurants, such as Liberte Snack Haus by the public market. It costs P2 to go by tricycle from Bato to Hilongos.

Places to Stay

Green House Lodging at Bato is a simple place with rooms for P30/60 and with fan for P35/70.

Getting There & Away

Several buses a day go from Tacloban wharf to Bato, taking three hours.

MAASIN

Maasin is the capital of Southern Leyte Province. There are connections by plane and ship from here to Cebu as well as by ship to Bohol and Mindanao.

The *Ampil Pensione* in Abugao St is fairly reasonable with rooms for P35/60.

Getting There & Away

Several buses leave the Tacloban wharf for Maasin, taking over three hours for the trip.

LILOAN

The waters around Liloan offer good diving and snorkelling opportunities. The cottages on Bitoon Beach were almost totally destroyed by a typhoon, but they may have been restored by now.

A ferry service operates between Liloan and Surigao in north-east Mindanao.

Places to Stay

C & S Lodge has rooms for P20/40, which are simple and fairly good. *Liloan Hillside Lodge* behind the ferry terminal has rooms for P25/50. This place is homely and has a restaurant.

Getting There & Away

There are several buses daily from Tacloban to Liloan, leaving from the wharf. The trip takes three hours and over four hours via Maasin.

TO/FROM LEYTE

To reach Leyte you can go from Bohol, Cebu, Luzon, Mindanao, Panay and Samar (see Transport from Luzon section of the Manila chapter and the relevant To/From sections of this and the Mindanao & Palawan chapter).

To Bohol

Boat A big outrigger boat leaves Bato daily for Ubay at 10 am via Lapinin Island, taking four hours.

The MV *Asia Thailand* of Trans-Asia Shipping Lines leaves Maasin for Jagna on Thursday at 10 am, taking four hours.

A big outrigger boat leaves Maasin daily for Ubay at 10 am, taking four hours.

To Cebu

Air Pacific Airways has daily flights from Maasin to Cebu City. PAL flies from Ormoc to Cebu City on Tuesday and Friday, and daily from Tacloban to Cebu City.

Boat There are numerous ships to Cebu City, leaving from various towns in Leyte. The MV *Bato* of Aboitiz Lines leaves Bato on Tuesday, Thursday and Sunday at 9 pm and takes over five hours.

The MV *Ormoc* of Aboitiz Lines leaves Baybay on Tuesday, Thursday and Sunday at 10 pm; it takes over five hours.

The MV *Guada Cristy* of Roble Shipping Lines leaves Hilongos on Tuesday, Thursday and Sunday at 10 pm, taking six hours.

From Isabel, the MV *Our Lady of Fatima* of Carlos Gothong Lines leaves on Monday at 10 am, taking five hours.

The MV *Guiuan* or the MV *Cebu Queen* of K & T Shipping Lines leaves Liloan on Thursday and Sunday at 6 pm; the trip takes six hours.

The MV *Asia Thailand* of Trans-Asia Shipping Lines leaves Maasin on Thursday at 9 pm, taking six hours.

The MV *Aklan* of Aboitiz Lines leaves Ormoc on Tuesday, Friday and Saturday at noon, Wednesday at 11 pm and Thursday at 10 pm. The trip takes six hours.

The MV *Dona Cristina* of Carlos Gothong Lines leaves Palompon on Tuesday at 8 am, and the MV *Our Lady of Guadalupe* leaves on Friday at 8 am. Both take five hours.

The MV *Leyte Queen* of K & T Shipping Lines leaves Tacloban on Wednesday, Friday and Sunday at 5 pm, taking 12 hours.

If you're not heading for Cebu City, there is a large outrigger boat that leaves Isabel daily at 4 pm for Carmen, taking four hours.

To Luzon

Air PAL flies daily from Tacloban to Manila. Aerolift has flights daily except Wednesday and Sunday from Ormoc to Manila.

Bus Philtranco Company air-con buses leave Tacloban daily for Manila at 6 am and 5 pm. Travel time is 25 hours, including the ferry from San Isidro to Matnog. It is advisable to reserve a seat.

Boat The MV *Tacloban City* of William Lines leaves Tacloban for Manila on Wednesday at 1 pm and Saturday at 7 pm, taking 24 hours.

To Mindanao

Bus An air-con Philtranco bus leaves Tacloban for Cagayan de Oro daily at 11 pm, but is sometimes a few hours late when the bus comes from Manila. The trip takes 13 hours, including the ferry from Liloan to Lipata, 15 km north of Surigao. You can also get an air-con Philtranco bus from Tacloban to Davao daily. The trip takes 16 hours, including the ferry from Liloan to Lipata.

Boat MV *Maharlika II* leaves Liloan for Lipata, 15 km north of Surigao, at 8.30 am, taking three hours. The MV *Surigao Princess* of Sulpicio Lines leaves Maasin for Surigao on Sunday at 1 am, taking four to five hours. A ship also goes daily from Maasin to Surigao, leaving around midnight.

To Panay

Boat The MV *Our Lady of Guadalupe* of Carlos Gothong Lines leaves Palompon for New Washington on Saturday at 8 am or 8 pm. The trip takes 12 hours. The MV *Our Lady of Fatima* of Carlos Gothong Lines leaves Palompon for Roxas on Wednesday at 8 pm, taking 11 hours.

To Samar

Bus Air-con Philtranco buses leave Tacloban for Manila daily at 6 am and 5 pm going through Catbalogan and Calbayog. Travel time to Catbalogan is two hours and four hours to Calbayog. It is advisable to book. Several regular buses leave daily from the wharf for Catbalogan, taking three hours.

Boat The MV *Cebu Princess* of Sulpicio Lines leaves Ormoc for Calbayog on Tuesday at 7 am, taking eight hours. The MV *Stacey* of K & T Shipping Lines leaves Tacloban for Guiuan on South Samar every second day at 11 pm. The trip takes six hours.

Negros

Lying between Cebu and Panay in the southwest of the Visayas, Negros consists of the provinces of Negros Occidental and Negros Oriental, which are separated by mountain chains in the centre of the island. The south takes its character from the extended Tablas plateau and the wide plains west of an imaginary line from Ilog to Cadiz.

Negros is the sugar island of the Philippines. Around 450,000 ha, or more than half of the total land area, is used for the production of sugar. About 60% of the total sugar production of the country comes from here. There are big sugar-cane plantations and refineries in Victorias and Binalbagan.

Sugar exportation began in the middle of the 19th century, when the production of the first plantations was shipped to Japan, China, Australia, the UK, Canada and the USA. From then on it brought great wealth and political power to the few sugar barons living on their haciendas. During the years of the sugar boom the seasonally employed field workers were at least able to earn enough to keep their families. This irresponsible system of exploitation and social indifference existed until 1985, when the world market price of sugar fell so drastically that it wasn't even worth cutting the cane.

Negros, with its single product economy, was economically at rock bottom. About a quarter of a million Sacada (the name of the plantation workers) were out of work. Because of the absence of any government relief programme and the unwillingness of most *hacienderos* to make some land available for grain planting by their needy workers, many desperate Negrenses took to the mountains to join the antigovernment NPA in its underground fighting.

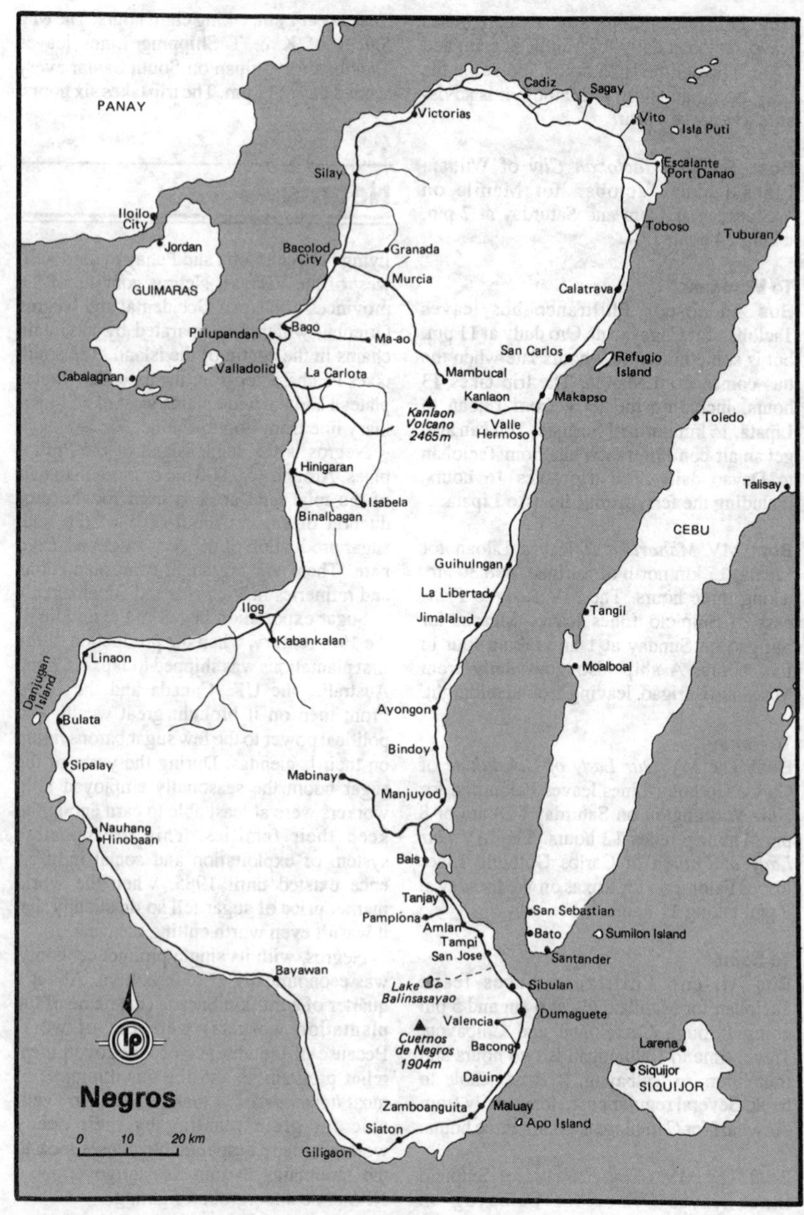
PANAY
Iloilo City
Jordan
GUIMARAS
Cabalagnan
Pulupandan
Bago
Valladolid
La Carlota
Ma-ao
Bacolod City
Granada
Murcia
Silay
Victorias
Cadiz
Sagay
Vito
Isla Puti
Escalante
Port Danao
Toboso
Tuburan
Calatrava
San Carlos
Refugio Island
Mambucal
Kanlaon Volcano 2465m
Kanlaon
Makapso
Valle Hermoso
Toledo
Talisay
CEBU
Hinigaran
Isabela
Binalbagan
Guihulngan
La Libertad
Jimalalud
Tangil
Moalboal
Ilog
Kabankalan
Linaon
Danjugan Island
Bulata
Sipalay
Ayongon
Bindoy
Mabinay
Manjuyod
Nauhang
Hinobaan
Bais
Tanjay
Pamplona
Amlan
Tampi
San Jose
San Sebastian
Bato
Sumilon Island
Santander
Bayawan
Lake Balinsasayao
Sibulan
Dumaguete
Valencia
Cuernos de Negros 1904m
Bacong
Dauin
Larena
Siquijor
SIQUIJOR
Negros
Zamboanguita
Maluay
Apo Island
Siaton
Giligaon
0 10 20 km

If government figures are to be believed, conditions on Negros since 1988 have improved with rising sugar prices. An important part in this improvement is due to the new extensive prawn culture (Black Tiger Prawn, *Penaeus monodon)* and the successful selling of these delicacies, especially to Japan.

'Sugarland', of course, also aims to develop tourism. Resorts such as Mambucal Summer Resort, Santa Fe Resort and Taytay Beach Resort have already been set up. Kanlaon Volcano may, it is hoped, become a similar attraction to the famous Mayon Volcano in South Luzon. Pretty good beaches can be found in the south-west of the island; this is also where adventurers are panning for gold in the mountains.

Among the main attractions of Negros are the old steam locomotives, some of which were still being used until recently to bring home the sugar cane, side by side with modern diesel locomotives. During the milling season between October and April, you may still be able to hitch a ride for a few km on one of these working museum pieces. There are only a few steam locomotives left today, but you can see them near the sugar mills. The best of these old-timers belong to the Hawaiian-Philippine Sugar Co in Silay; Vicmico in Victorias; Central Azucarera de la Carlota in La Carlota; and the Ma-ao Sugar Central in Bago. Also worth seeing are the ones that belong to Biscom in Binalbagan, Sagay Sugar Central and Lopez Sugar Central in Toboso, and San Carlos Milling Co in San Carlos. Colin Carraf describes them all in his book *Iron Dinosaurs*.

The aborigines of Negros are called the Negrito, hence the name of the island. Some tribes of this cultural minority still live in the mountain regions. The main dialect in Negros Occidental is Ilongo, whereas Cebuano is spoken in Negros Oriental.

BACOLOD

The capital of Negros Occidental province, Bacolod has about 260,000 inhabitants and is the sugar capital of the Philippines. The name Bacolod is derived from the word *buklod*, or hill, which refers to a rise on which the town's first church stood. Next to the old San Sebastian Cathedral is the Bacolod City Plaza, with benches under shady trees, where cultural events are held on Sunday afternoons and special occasions.

Bacolod is a leading producer of ceramics in the Philippines. Most of the workshops, such as NLS Ceramics and Bilbao Ceramics, are on the edge of town. Only MDS Ceramics, at 26 Rosario St, has a central location.

Places to Stay – bottom end

There is a wide variety of accommodation in Bacolod. The *YMCA* (tel 26919) in Burgos St has rooms with fan for P80/100. It's basic, good and fairly clean. YMCA members receive a 10% discount.

Halili Inn (tel 81548) in Locsin St has rooms with fan for P50/70, with fan and bath for P100/110 and with air-con and bath for P150/200. There are narrow beds in the cheaper rooms and the place could do with a renovation.

Best Inn (tel 23312) in Bonifacio St has rooms with fan for P70/100, with fan and bath for P90/120 and with air-con and bath for P160/230. It's basic and relatively clean but fairly noisy. Each bathroom is shared between two rooms.

Places to Stay – middle

The *Family Pension House* (tel 81211) at 123 Lacson St Extension is fairly clean and comfortable, has a restaurant and is in a quiet location on the southern edge of town. Rooms with fan and bath cost P123 and with air-con and bath cost P180.

Las Rocas Inn (tel 27011) in Gatuslao St has singles with fan for P93, rooms with fan and bath for P163/226 and with air-con and bath for P310/360. It has seen better days but is to be renovated and also has a restaurant.

Bascon Hotel (tel 23141, 23143) in Gonzaga St is nice and clean and has a restaurant. Singles/doubles with air-con and bath cost P280/345 and suites cost P530.

Sea Breeze Hotel (tel 24571-75) in San Juan St has rooms with air-con and bath from

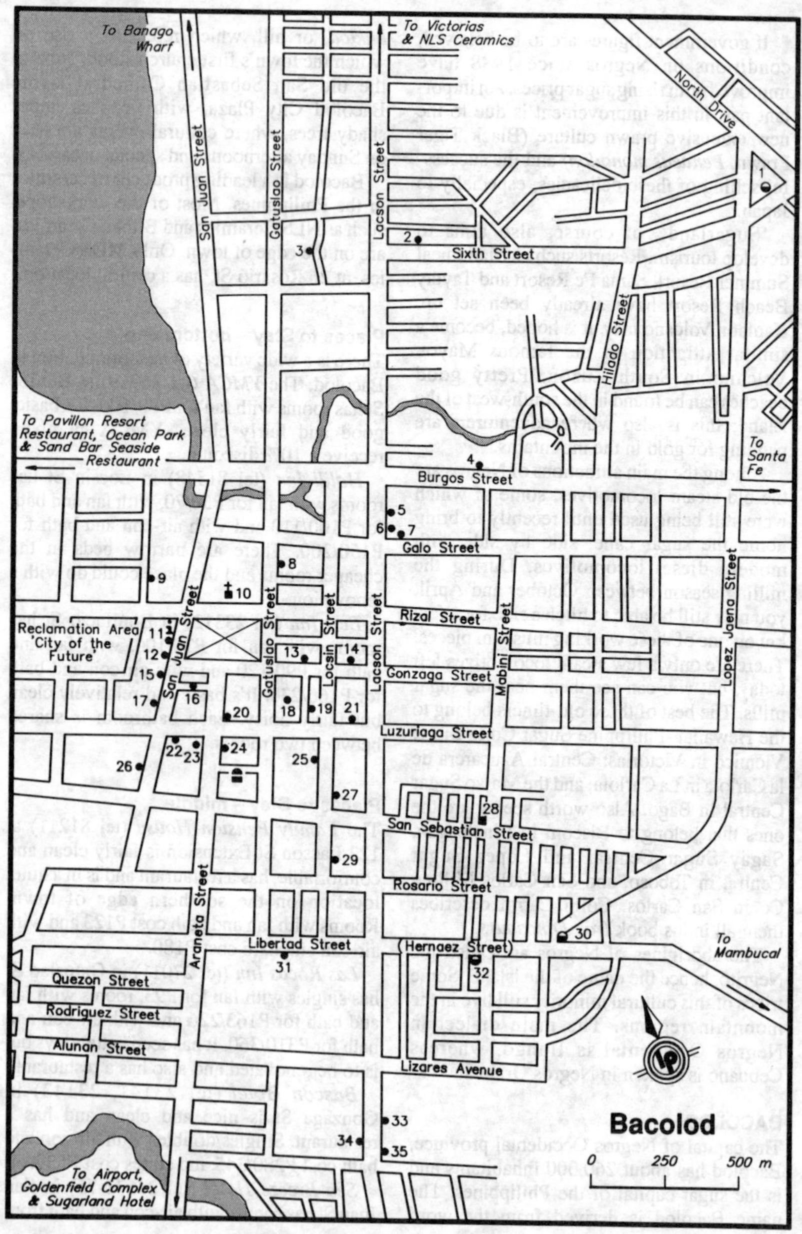
To Banago Wharf
To Victorias & NLS Ceramics
North Drive
San Juan Street
Gatusiao Street
Lacson Street
Sixth Street
Hilado Street
To Pavillon Resort Restaurant, Ocean Park & Sand Bar Seaside Restaurant
To Santa Fe
Burgos Street
Galo Street
Rizal Street
Reclamation Area 'City of the Future'
Locsin Street
Gonzaga Street
Mabini Street
Lopez Jaena Street
Luzuriaga Street
San Sebastian Street
Araneta Street
Rosario Street
(Hernaez Street)
Libertad Street
To Mambucal
Quezon Street
Rodriguez Street
Alunan Street
Lizares Avenue
Bacolod
0 250 500 m
To Airport, Goldenfield Complex & Sugarland Hotel

1 Northern Bus Terminal
2 Negros Navigation Lines
3 Provincial Capitol Building
4 YMCA
5 Small Bars
6 Peninsula Disco
7 Macho Disco
8 Las Rocas Hotel
9 Manokan Country
10 San Sebastian Cathedral
11 Reming's & Sons Restaurant
Tourist Office
12 Tita's Food Centre
13 International Restaurant
14 Bascon Hotel
15 Sea Breeze Hotel
16 Fantasy Food
Shopping Centre
17 Coney Island Ice Cream
18 Market
19 Best Inn
Kong Kee Diners & Bakery
20 Philippine National Bank
21 Roofdeck Disco
22 Gaisano Department Store
Gaisano Food Plaza
23 Town Hall
24 Barrio Fiesta Restaurant
25 Mira's Café
26 Nena's Chicken Barbecue
27 Halili Inn
28 Ang Sinugba Restaurant
29 Deja Vue Hotel & Disco
30 Jeepneys to Mambucal & Ma-ao
31 Sports Complex
32 Southern Bus Terminal
33 Cactus Room Restaurant
Family Pension House
34 Sugbahan Restaurant
35 Alavar's Sea Food's House

P495/540. It's a pleasant place with a restaurant.

Places to Stay – top end

Sugarland Hotel (tel 22460-69) in Araneta St, Singcang, has rooms with air-con and bath from P447/502 and suites for P755. It has a restaurant, swimming pool and roof garden.

The *Goldenfield Garden Hotel* (tel 83541; fax 22356), in the Goldenfield Commercial Complex, near the airport, has rooms with air-con and bath for P840 and suites for P1400. It has a restaurant and a disco and is the best hotel in Bacolod.

Places to Eat

The *Reming's & Sons Restaurant* in the city plaza serves good Filipino fast food. Another favourite for fast food is the air-conditioned *Gaisano Food Plaza* in Luzuriaga St, which also has videos and live music.

For cheap Filipino dishes, try the *Ihaw-Ihaw Restaurant* in Las Rocas Hotel in Gatuslao St. The *Kong Kee Diners & Bakery* in Bonifacio St, next door to the Best Inn, serves good, cheap Filipino and Chinese meals and fresh bread rolls.

The clean, well-kept *Ang Sinugba Restaurant* in San Sebastian St is well known for its native food. In the cosy *Cactus Room Restaurant*, at the Family Pension House in Lactos St Extension, you will find a wide choice of cheap steaks. Nearby is the Bacolod branch of the popular *Alavar's Sea Foods House* with excellent dishes in the Zamboanga style.

Mira's Café in Locsin St serves native coffee. If you want cakes to go with it, you can get them at the bakery on the corner.

There are three good restaurants in the Sugarland Hotel near the airport. They are the *Café Hacienda*, which serves international dishes, the *Poolside Bar-B-Q's*, which has Filipino food, and the *Caribbean Grill Restaurant*, which has seafood dishes.

Just 200 metres further south, within the Goldenfield Commercial Complex, are the *Old West Steakhouse*, with its cosy atmosphere, *Shakey's Pizza* and *Carlo Pizza Garden*, the open-air *Foodland* and the more expensive *Seafood Market Restaurant*.

Jumbo's Food Circus in the city plaza is a favourite rendezvous for snacks at night. Among other things it has pasta dishes, hamburgers and pancakes. You can get barbecues and beer at the many all-night restaurants at the *Manokan Country* in the Reclamation Area.

Also in the Reclamation Area, at the western end of Burgos St Extension, you can spend a breezy evening in the *Sand Bar*

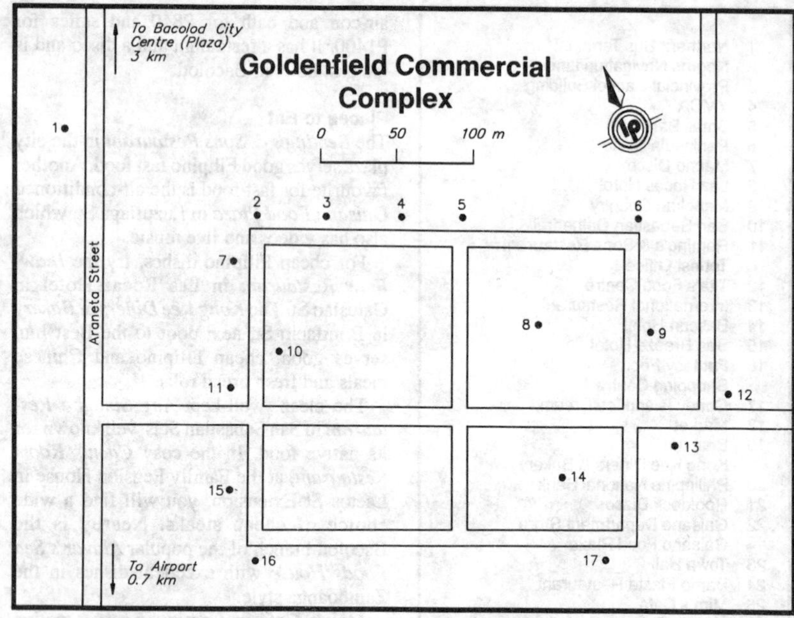

1 Sugarland Hotel
2 Alice Log Cabin
Popeye's Ice Cream Parlour
3 Nova Park Restaurant
Old West Bar
4 Alfonso Pub
Disco 2000
5 Franky's Restaurant
6 Carlo Pizza Garden
7 Square Circle Pub
8 Car Park
9 Cinema
10 Limelight Pub
11 Shakey's Pizza
12 Seafood Market Restaurant
13 Goldenfield Garden Hotel
14 Foodland
15 Casino
16 Senyang Restaurant
17 Super Bowling Lanes

Seaside Restaurant and the *Pavillion Resort Restaurant*. Make sure a taxi will pick you up afterwards as there is almost no transport back to the city at night.

Entertainment

There are a couple of small bars in Lacson St, and not far away are the *Peninsula Disco* and the *Macho Disco,* which have shows in between the dancing. Similar nightclubs are the *Roofdeck Disco* in Luzuriaga St and the *Deja Vue Disco* in Locsin St. The latter is still known by its former name of Rose Disco.

Among the most popular in the Goldenfield Commercial Complex are *Disco 2000* and the big *Limelight Pub* with live music nightly. Within the complex, there are also entertainment places like the *Casino,* the 40 lane *Super Bowling Lanes*, the biggest in the Visayas, and the *Quorum Disco* in the

Goldenfield Garden Hotel which opens at 9 pm.

Getting There & Away

Ceres Liner express buses leave Dumaguete for Bacolod daily at 6.45, 8.30 and 10.30 am and noon, taking nine hours. You can book seats.

A few Ceres Liner buses travel from Hinobaan to Bacolod daily. The last departure is generally in the early afternoon. The bus terminal is in Nauhang, a little north of Hinobaan. The trip takes seven hours.

Several Ceres Liner buses a day go from San Carlos to Bacolod. The last one leaves after the last ship arrives from Toledo, Cebu. The trip takes four hours.

There are jeepneys to Mambucal, Ma-ao, Silay and Victorias (see the Getting There & Away sections for these towns).

Getting Around

Airport Transport Bacolod's airport is about five km south of the city. On leaving the terminal, turn left to go towards the city. You can stop a passing jeepney, as they all go to the city plaza.

A PU-Cab from the airport to the city centre should cost no more than P15, but it is best to agree on a price with the driver beforehand.

Boat Banago Wharf is about seven km north of the city. A jeepney will cost you P5 and a PU-Cab about P20, but determine the price first.

Bus Buses from Dumaguete and San Carlos arrive at the Northern Bus Terminal. Jeepneys marked 'Libertad' leave the Northern Bus Terminal for the city centre and cost P1.

MAMBUCAL

With its hot sulphur springs, Mambucal is the best known resort on Negros, yet it's not overcrowded. The Summer Resort has swimming pools, waterfalls and accommodation. You can't go from Mambucal across the island to the east coast as, in the central area of Negros, all roads end at the Kanlaon Massif.

It's about five km from the edge of town to Mt Kanlaon National Park. If you want to climb Kanlaon, you need to allow three to four days for the round trip. Edwin Gatia of the Bacolod Tourist Office can organise guides from the Negros Mountaineering Club (tel 23807, 21839). An excellent guide, he himself advises those who intend to climb the volcano or visit the national park for bird-watching or other activities to inform the club for coordination and safety purposes.

You can also find knowledgeable guides in Mambucal, such as Chris Garzon, who will also provide a tent and cooker. The tour will cost you about P700.

Places to Stay

Pagoda Inn has rooms for P50. It is simple and good, even if the showers are on the other side of the road. The food is good, especially the chicken with vegetables, and Grandma brews an excellent native coffee.

Mambucal Health Resort has rooms from P25/50 and with bath from P50/60 and also has a swimming pool.

Getting There & Away

Several jeepneys a day go from Bacolod to Mambucal, leaving from Libertad (Hernaez) St. The trip takes one hour, but the morning trip from Mambucal to Bacolod can take up to two hours because of the many stops. The last jeepney back leaves at about 4.30 pm.

MA-AO

The sugar-cane fields of Ma-ao stretch to the foot of the Kanlaon Volcano, crisscrossed by about 280 km of railway tracks. Just as exciting as the bridges that cross the rivers and ravines are the old steam locomotives, which were used until recently to bring in the harvest.

These old-timers were recently pensioned off and pushed on to the 'old-timer tracks' of the MSC (Ma-ao Sugar Central), where they are open to inspection. There are two Alco (American Locomotive Company) 2-6-0s:

one is the TS 1-3, dated 1921, and the other is the BM 5, dated 1924.

Getting There & Away

Several jeepneys go daily from Libertad St in Bacolod to Ma-ao, taking one hour. The last trip back is at 4 or 5 pm.

SILAY

A little outside Silay is the Hawaiian-Philippine Sugar Company, one of the largest plantations on Negros, which has a rail network that is about 180 km long.

Nicknamed 'Red Dragons', the steam engines used here are in excellent condition. The name goes back to the time when they were bright red, but today they are blue-black in colour. In World War II, most of them were hidden from the Japanese by being run on special rails into the wooded mountains. They include a 1920 Henschel 0-6-0 and six Baldwin 0-6-0s built in 1919, 1920 and 1928.

Getting There & Away

Several jeepneys a day leave from Lacson St, on the corner of Libertad St, in Bacolod for Silay. They take 30 minutes. Buses and jeepneys from the Northern Bus Terminal also go through Silay.

Jeepneys leave from the market in Silay to go to the Hawaiian-Philippine Sugar Company.

VICTORIAS

The Victorias Milling Company, Vicmico, is open for inspection from Tuesday to Friday. It's part of a large industrial complex where sugar is processed in several stages for the consumer. Guided tours start at the porter's lodge, which is at the main entrance, where the jeepneys from Victorias stop. Men wearing shorts, and women wearing shorts or miniskirts will be refused admission. Sandals and thongs (flip-flops) are not permitted for safety reasons.

Vicmico's 349 km railway track is the longest on Negros and possibly the longest two-foot gauge track in the world. As with the Hawaiian-Philippine Sugar Company on Silay, the diesel and steam locomotives are directed by radio remote control from a central point, but the dark-green old-timers are now used only during the peak season from January to February. The rolling stock includes eight Henschel 0-8-0Ts, dating back to 1926 to 1928, and two Bagnall 0-4-4Ts, which were built for the Kowloon (Hong Kong) to Canton Line in China.

Apart from the sugar mill, the St Joseph the Worker Chapel is worth seeing. The unusual coloured mural showing an angry Filipino Jesus, the 'Angry Christ' has received international attention after an article about it appeared in *Life* magazine.

Getting There & Away

Several jeepneys and buses a day run from the Bacolod Northern Bus Terminal to Victorias. They take one hour. Several jeepneys go daily from Victorias to the Vicmico sugar mill, taking 15 minutes.

SAN CARLOS

There is a shipping service between San Carlos and Toledo, Cebu. The offshore Sipaway (or Refugio) Island is supposed to have a few beautiful beaches and walking tracks. There are several Sari-Sari stores, but their stock is limited, so it's advisable to bring your own provisions from San Carlos.

Places to Stay

Van's Lodging House near the wharf is basic with rooms for P30/60. *Papal Lodge* (tel 455) in V Gustilo St has simple rooms for P40/80 and there is a restaurant on the corner.

Coco Grove Hotel (tel 432) in Ylagan St is the best hotel in San Carlos. It has rooms for P60/120, with fan for P75/140, with fan and bath for P140/220, and with air-con and bath for P350/380-420. It also has a restaurant.

Getting There & Away

Several Ceres Liner express buses leave the Northern Bus Terminal at Bacolod for San Carlos daily, some going on to Dumaguete. The trip takes four hours.

From Dumaguete there are Ceres Liner

express buses going to Bacolod via San Carlos, leaving daily at 6.45, 8.30 and 10.30 am and at noon. The trip takes five hours.

DUMAGUETE

Dumaguete, the capital of Negros Oriental Province, is also a pleasant university town. Silliman University, whose extensive campus is on the northern edge of town, is the only Protestant university in the Philippines and was named after its founder Dr Horace B Silliman. It has a small anthropological museum and also a cafeteria which has cheap meals. For further information about the university, ask at the administration building.

Silliman Beach is not good for swimming and is also in a flight path, but members of the nearby marine laboratory run diving courses there twice a year. They also use a boat that you can charter for diving excursions. Favourite destinations are South Cebu, Sumilon Island and Apo Island, south of Dumaguete.

Every year between 21 and 25 January, Dumaguete celebrates Negros Oriental Founders Day. The folkloric dances in the Aquino Freedom Park are among the best of the many attractions of this important festival.

Places to Stay – bottom end

Jo's Lodging (tel 2160) in Silliman Ave is unpretentious, fairly clean and has a restaurant. Singles/doubles with fan cost P30/60. *Casa Lona Hotel* (tel 3384), in the market in Real St, has rooms with fan and bath for P100/150. It is clean, pleasant and has spacious rooms.

Places to Stay – middle

Opena's Hotel (tel 3462) in Katada St has singles with fan for P62, rooms with fan and bath for P135/174 and with air-con and bath for P207/230. It's comfortable and has a restaurant. The owners have recently opened the *Summerland Resort*, which has cheap cottages on the black beach of Amlan, 23 km north-west of Dumaguete.

Al Mar Hotel (tel 3453) in Rizal Ave, on the corner of San Juan St, is a homely place. It has singles with fan for P73, singles/doubles with fan and bath for P78/134 and doubles with air-con and bath for P224.

Hotel El Oriente (tel 3486, 2539) in Real St is pleasant. Singles with fan and bath cost P106 and rooms with air-con and bath cost P285/330.

El Oriente Beach Resort in Mangnao, south of Dumaguete has rooms with fan and bath for P95/140 and with air-con and bath for P255/295. It is clean and comfortable.

Panorama Hotel is an attractive, large house by the sea on Cangmating Beach at Sibulan, about six km north of Dumaguete – a P20 tricycle ride away. It has singles/doubles with fan for P100/200 and doubles with fan and bath for P300. It's homely and good value and has a restaurant. Charlie, the owner, is Swiss.

Places to Stay – top end

Santa Monica Beach Resort (tel 3441) in Banilad, south of Dumaguete, has rooms with fan and bath for P210/235 and with air-con and bath for P270/330. It's a pleasant place with a restaurant and diving.

Insular Hotel (tel 3495) in Silliman Ave, near the university, has rooms with fan and bath for P275/297 and with air-con and bath for P308/353. It's friendly and well kept and has a restaurant.

The best hotel in Dumaguete is the *South Sea Resort Hotel* (tel 2857, 3683) in Bantayan, near Silliman Beach. It has rooms with fan and bath for P245-280/330-365 and with air-con and bath for P336-392/448-504. It also has a restaurant and swimming pool.

Places to Eat

You can eat well at a reasonable price at *Opena's Restaurant*, downstairs in the hotel of the same name. Also good and cheap are *Ree's Restaurant* in Alfonso St, on the corner of Legaspi St, and the *Orient Garden Restaurant* in Alfonso St, on the corner of San Juan St. The cuisine at the Chinese *Chin Lun Restaurant* on Rizal Blvd is excellent.

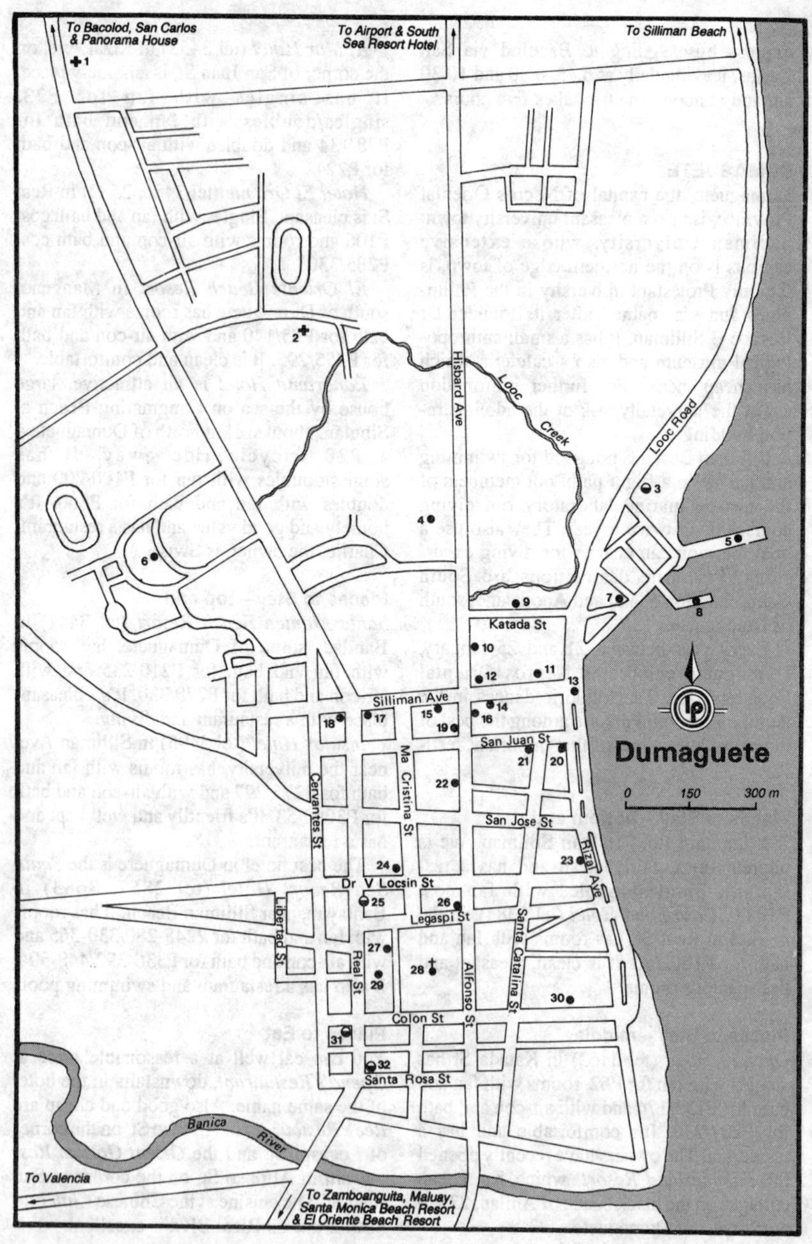
To Bacolod, San Carlos & Panorama House
To Airport & South Sea Resort Hotel
To Silliman Beach
Hisbard Ave
Looc Creek
Looc Road
Katada St
Silliman Ave
San Juan St
Ma Cristina St
Cervantes St
San Jose St
Rizal Ave
Dr V Locsin St
Legaspi St
Libertad St
Real St
Santa Catalina St
Alfonso St
Colon St
Santa Rosa St
Banica River
To Valencia
To Zamboanguita, Maluay, Santa Monica Beach Resort & El Oriente Beach Resort
Dumaguete
0 150 300 m

1	Provincial Hospital
2	New Silliman Medical Center
3	Northern Bus Terminal
4	Silliman University
5	Pier 1
6	Provincial Capitol Building
7	George & Peter Lines William Lines
8	Pier 2
9	Opena's Hotel
10	University Cafeteria
11	Administration Building Museum
12	Silliman Cooperative Store
13	Aquino Freedom Park Barbecue Stands
14	Jo's Lodging
15	Insular Hotel
16	Jo's Cake House & Restaurant
17	Philippine National Bank
18	Hotel El Oriente
19	Orient Garden Restaurant
20	Al Mar Hotel
21	Kamay Kainan Seafood House Post Office
22	Plaza Department Store
23	Chin Lun Restaurant
24	Kamagong Restaurant
25	Jeepneys & Minibuses to San Jose & Tampi
26	Ree's Restaurant
27	Casa Lona Hotel
28	Church
29	Market
30	City Hall
31	Jeepneys to Valencia, Maluay & Zamboanguita
32	Southern Bus Terminal

At *Jo's Cake House & Restaurant* you get healthy fruit juices, several different cakes and Chicken Inato, which is reputed to be the best chicken dish in town.

The open-air restaurant at the South Sea Resort Hotel is pleasant, as is the partly open-air *Kamagong Restaurant*, on the corner of Locsin and Ma Cristina streets, which is popular with students.

The *Kamay Kainan Seafood House*, on the corner of San Juan and Santa Catalina streets, has folk music, and there are barbecue stands after dark on Rizal Blvd, near Aquino Freedom Park and the church.

Getting There & Away

Several Ceres Liner express buses go daily to Dumaguete via San Carlos from the Northern Bus Terminal in Bacolod. The trip takes nine hours from Bacolod and five hours from San Carlos.

A few buses go daily to Dumaguete via Hinobaan, leaving from the Southern Bus Terminal in Bacolod. The last departure is at 8 am and the trip takes 12 hours.

A few buses go daily to Dumaguete from the Nauhang bus terminal near Hinobaan. The last bus is supposed to leave at 2.45 pm, possibly earlier. The trip takes six hours with a one-hour stop in Bayawan. If you're in a hurry, buy a ticket only as far as Bayawan because you will usually find buses ready to leave for Dumaguete.

Getting Around

A tricycle from the airport into town should not cost more than P3 per person, but considerably more is often demanded.

AROUND DUMAGUETE

Twin Lakes

About 25 km west of Dumaguete are two crater lakes surrounded by dense rainforest: Lake Balinsasayao and the smaller adjoining Lake Danao, at a height of about 800 metres. There is a basic nipa hut where you can stay overnight, but you have to bring your own provisions.

Getting There & Away You can get there from Dumaguete by bus or jeepney going north. Get off about two km before San Jose, or travel back from San Jose by tricycle to the small track leading from the road up to Twin Lakes. You have to walk the remaining 15 km or so as it is impossible for jeepneys or tricycles. Motorcyclists without cross-country experience would have great difficulty too because of the steep slope and rough track.

San Jose & Tampi

Ships for San Sebastian, Talisay and Bato on Cebu leave from San Jose and Tampi (see the To/From Negros section of this chapter).

Getting There & Away Jeepneys and minibuses for San Jose and Tampi leave Dumaguete from the corner of Real and Locsin streets.

VALENCIA

From Valencia you can take a tricycle to Camp Lookout at the extinct volcano Cuernos de Negros. This should cost about P40 but it's a hard trip by tricycle so you might find it better to walk. The trip is between eight to 12 km, according to different reports. Unfortunately, the views of Dumaguete, Cebu and Siquijor Island are now partly obstructed by the vigorously growing vegetation.

In Terejo, about two km out of Valencia, is the Banica Valley Resort, which has a small creek, a swimming pool and a few resthouses. It's popular with the locals, especially at weekends. If you want to go there on foot, ask for the swimming pool, which is near a shrine.

Getting There & Away

Several jeepneys run daily to Valencia from Real St, on the corner of Colon St, in Dumaguete.

MALUAY & ZAMBOANGUITA

Probably the best beaches in the Dumaguete area are those near Maluay (Malatapay) and Zamboanguita. Although the sand is black, the water is clean and clear. You can get to offshore Apo Island from either place. The friendly and well-maintained Salawaki Beach Resort, about two km south-west of Zamboanguita, is an excellent place to stay in this area.

Quite close to the Beach Resort, is a centre for the World Peace & Life's Survival organisation called The Lamplighter. Among other activities, it looks after the Cebu City Zoo. Its members are concerned with reafforestation and trying to restore the ecological balance. Father Eleuterio Tropa, the founder and president of the Lamplighter, is very forthcoming and is happy to show visitors around Spaceship 2001 as he calls his establishment.

Maluay has a large market on Wednesdays which is worth seeing. Farmers come from the mountains, and fishermen from the coast and nearby islands tie their boats up here. The market trades in agricultural produce, livestock and seafood. Chickens and fish are grilled, and whole pigs roasted on the beach, amid much chattering, gossiping, laughing, eating and drinking.

Places to Stay

Salawaki Beach Resort, two km beyond Zamboanguita coming from Dumaguete, has dorm beds for P40 and cottages with bath for P150 to P250. The rooms are spacious and well furnished and there is a restaurant with good cheap meals and native coffee. The resort is on the beach, about 200 metres from the large sign on the road. A boat to Apo Island costs P300.

Getting There & Away

Several jeepneys a day leave for Maluay and Zamboanguita, from the corner of Real and Colon streets in Dumaguete. You can also take a Ceres Liner bus bound for Bayawan and Hinobaan. The trip takes 40 minutes.

APO ISLAND

Little Apo island, about eight km south-east of Zamboanguita, is barely 120 metres high and has a five-metre-deep lagoon separated by a white beach from the sea. To protect some unusual coral formations and rare fish, part of the waters around Apo Island have been declared a sanctuary and placed under the protection of Silliman University in Dumaguete. As a result, the 'fish sanctuary' offers excellent diving and snorkelling conditions.

There is now said to be overnight accommodation for P50 per person on the island.

Getting There & Away

You can hire boats in Zamboanguita and Maluay for about P300 to go to offshore Apo Island. It's better to leave before 8 am and return after 4 pm because of the swell. You can cross from Maluay fairly cheaply on Wednesday afternoons, when Apo Island fishermen return to their island after the market.

HINOBAAN

As an interesting alternative to the usual route from Bacolod to Cebu via San Carlos and Toledo, you can travel along the west and south coasts via Hinobaan and Dumaguete. However, the roads are rather difficult, so you will need to take two days to do this route. The last section from Bayawan to Zamboanguita is particularly attractive, but the road is in poor condition.

Early in 1982 Hinobaan experienced a real gold rush. Both the national and international press published daily reports about new finds which brought numerous adventurers and optimists. Gold fever broke out in earnest when it was reported that a Filipino had found gold to the value of P23,000 in a single day. Soon afterwards an estimated 20,000 people were trying their luck along a 17 km stretch of the Bacuyongan River and many did find gold. The average daily yield at the peak of the rush is said to have been one gram per person; this sold at P80.

Unfortunately, there were untoward events, too. Within eight weeks one digger died in a landslide and another three in fighting over claims. Altogether, 17 victims were counted in two months. The most lucrative yields were those won by the buyers, merchants and traders, who soon made the sleepy village of Nauhang into a lively trading centre with a wild west character. From the Crossing Golden Southbend (a junction near Nauhang), jeepneys ran about seven km inland to Spar III at Sitio Sangke, where the well-trodden path to the promising river begins.

Government drilling to a depth of 300 metres was not completed until the end of 1982. The result surpassed all expectations, indicating a probable 10 million tonnes of rock with a content of three grams of gold per tonne. That could have been the discovery of the century. The government put an embargo on freelance gold prospecting, ending the adventurous wild times.

Places to Stay

Gloria Mata Lodging House in Hinobaan is reasonably good with rooms for P10/20. *Mesajon Lodging House* in Gatuslao St, Hinobaan, has good, clean rooms with fan for P30/60. Mrs Mesajon is very skilled in preparing an excellent Chicken Binakol. Made with onions and lemon grass in young coconut, this chicken dish is a speciality of south-west Negros.

About 25 km north of Hinobaan is *Dalula's Lodging House* in San Jose/Sipalay. It's a comfortable place; rooms with fan cost P50/90.

Getting There & Away

Several Ceres Liner buses go from Bacolod to Hinobaan daily from the Southern Bus Terminal. They are either direct or continue on to Dumaguete. The road is good until Kabankalan, after which it deteriorates, but the views are much better. The trip takes six hours. Some buses only go to Nauhang, and a tricycle from there to Hinobaan costs P2 per person.

The last bus from Bacolod to Dumaguete via Hinobaan leaves at 8 am, taking 12 hours.

A few Ceres Liner buses run daily from Dumaguete to Hinobaan, taking six hours. The bus stops for an hour at Bayawan.

BINALBAGAN

On the way to Hinobaan, you will go past Binalbagan, which is about 80 km south of Bacolod. This is where you will find the biggest sugar refinery and plantation in the world. It is called Biscom, which is short for Binalbagan Sugarmill Company. The two Baldwin locomotives 2-6-2T No 6, dated 1924, and Davenport 0-4-0T No 28, dated 1929, are no longer used, but may be inspected.

KABANKALAN

Kabankalan is about 40 km south of Binalbagan. This small town celebrates the Sinulog Festival on the third weekend (Friday, Saturday and Sunday) in January with parades, cultural events and horse fights. The Kabankalanons maintain that their Sinulog Festival is older and more authentic than the better known one in Cebu City.

Places to Stay

Friends Inn has double rooms with fan and bath for P80 and with air-con and bath for P120. It's basic but comfortable, and is about two km north of Kabankalan.

TO/FROM NEGROS

You can get there from Bohol, Cebu, Luzon, Mindanao, Panay and Siquijor (see the Transport from Luzon section of the Manila chapter and the relevant To/From sections of this and the Mindanao & Palawan chapter).

To Bohol

Boat The William Lines' MV *Misamis Occidental* goes from Dumaguete to Tagbilaran on Saturday at 6 pm, taking three hours.

To Cebu

Air PAL flies daily to Cebu City from Bacolod and Dumaguete, and Pacific Airways flies daily to Cebu City from Bacolod via Calatrava.

Pacific Airways is planning a service from Bacolod to Bantayan Island.

Bus Ceres Liner buses leave Bacolod's Northern Bus Terminal daily at 7.45 and 9 am for the ferry from Escalante (Port Danao) to Tuburan and on to Cebu City. The trip takes over seven hours, including the ferry.

Boat The MV *Jhufel*, the MV *Don Joaquin* or the MV *Don Victoriano* of George & Peter Lines leaves Dumaguete for Cebu City daily at 10 pm and at 8 pm (usually) on Thursday and Sunday. The trip takes six hours.

The boats leave Guihulngan for Tangil daily at 6.30 and 8 am, taking two hours. The connection from Tangil to Moalboal is better than the one from Toledo to Moalboal.

A ferry from San Carlos to Toledo leaves daily at 5.30 am and 1.30 pm, and on Sunday usually at 10.30 am. The departure times may be different on holidays. On Easter Thursday there may only be one boat and on Good Friday there are none. The times of departure are liable to change. For reliable information ask at the wharf rather than the trishaw drivers in town. The trip takes 1¾ hours.

A large outrigger boat goes daily from Sibulan to Liloan, taking 20 minutes.

The ferry from Tampi to Bato runs several times a day, the last trip leaving at about 3.30 pm. The trip takes 45 minutes. The boat from San Jose may also go to Talisay. Jeepneys and minibuses run from Real St, on the corner of Locsin St, in Dumaguete, to the wharf. Buses meet the boat in Bato or Talisay for Cebu City; an air-con bus leaves at 8.30 am.

From Cadiz to Bantayan town, north-west of Cebu, a boat leaves daily at 11 am, taking three hours or more. The river port in Cadiz is several km long and the boat for Bantayan anchors in the Reclamation Area, near the Hitalon Bridge, where you have to get off the jeepney or bus.

To Luzon

Air PAL flies daily to Manila from Bacolod and Dumaguete.

Boat To go from Bacolod to Manila, you can take several Negros Navigation Lines' ships. The MV *Don Claudio* leaves on Monday at 4 pm, taking 24 hours; the MV *Don Julio* leaves on Wednesday at 4 pm, taking 21 hours; and the MV *Santa Florentina* leaves on Friday at 6 pm, taking 24 hours.

The MV *Misamis Occidental* of William Lines leaves Dumaguete for Manila on Wednesday at 9 am, taking 30 hours.

To Mindanao

Air PAL flies from Dumaguete to Dipolog on Tuesday and Thursday.

Boat The MV *Jhufel*, the MV *Don Joaquin* and the MV *Don Victoriano* of George & Peter Lines all go from Dumaguete to Dipolog, leaving daily at 7 or 8.30 am. The trip takes over five hours. The boat sometimes continues on to Zamboanga.

The MV *Misamis Occidental* of William

Lines runs from Dumaguete to Ozamiz via Tagbilaran, Bohol, leaving on Saturday at 6 pm and taking 14 hours.

To Panay

Air Pacific Airways flies daily from Bacolod to Iloilo, and probably twice a week from Bacolod to Caticlan.

Bus As an alternative to the popular connection by boat from Bacolod to Iloilo, you can go via Guimaras Island. Go by jeepney or bus to Valladolid, about 30 km south of Bacolod and get off at the first bridge. A boat goes daily from Valladolid to Cabalagnan, on Guimaras, at about 11 am, stopping at several small islands on the way, including Nagarao Island. From Cabalagnan a jeepney leaves in the morning for Jordan, where you can catch a connecting ferry to Iloilo.

Twice a week a boat sails from Pulupandan, a little north of Valladolid, to Suclaran on Guimaras.

For further information about Guimaras Island, see the section on Panay in this chapter.

Boat The MV *Don Vicente* and the MV *Princess of Negros* of Negros Navigation Lines sail from Bacolod to Iloilo from Monday to Thursday and Saturday at 7 and 10 am and 3 pm, and on Friday and Sunday at 8 and 11 am and 4 pm. The trip takes over two hours. Warning: these times are subject to change.

Banago Wharf is about seven km north of Bacolod. To go there, a jeepney takes about 30 minutes and costs P5, and a PU-Cab costs about P20.

The MV *Santa Maria* of Negros Navigation sails from Bacolod to Roxas on Sunday at 7 am, taking seven hours.

From Victorias's port Da-an Banwa, the MV *Queen Rose* or the MV *Princess Jo* leaves daily between 9 and 11 am for Culasi, and the MV *Seven Seas* or the MV *San Vicente* leaves daily between 9 and 11 am for Malayu-an, both near Ajuy on the east coast of Panay, taking two hours.

To Siquijor

Boat A big outrigger boat leaves Dumaguete for Larena daily at 1 pm, taking over two hours. For safety reasons, this trip is not recommended in bad weather.

The MV *Catherine* leaves Dumaguete daily for Siquijor at 2 pm, taking over two hours. A tricycle from Siquijor to Larena costs P3 per person.

Panay

Panay is the large triangular island in the west of the Visayas. It is subdivided into the provinces of Iloilo, Capiz, Aklan and Antique. Iloilo City, with about 250,000 inhabitants is the biggest town on the island. The economy is predominantly agricultural, although there is also a textile industry in Iloilo City. Fabric made from pina, the fibres of the pineapple leaf, is used to make Filipino barong tagalog shirts.

Among the main tourist attractions in Panay are the Ati-Atihan Festival in Kalibo and the Dinagyang Festival in Iloilo. There are also several beautiful old churches along the south coast.

Sicogon Island has been open to tourists since the 1970s, so this beautiful tropical island is well known to foreigners. Now Boracay, another dream island, off the north-western tip of Panay, has developed into a favourite on the international travel scene. Before and after the Ati-Atihan Festival in Kalibo, Boracay is full!

ILOILO CITY

The name Iloilo is derived from the description 'Ilong-Ilong', meaning 'like a nose'. This refers to the outline of the city centre, which lies between the mouths of the Iloilo and Batiano rivers. Iloilo is not markedly different from other Philippine port towns of a similar size, but the image of this capital of Iloilo Province has recently been improved. What attracts attention apart from the lovely old houses in the side streets are the modern jeepneys and those like the American street

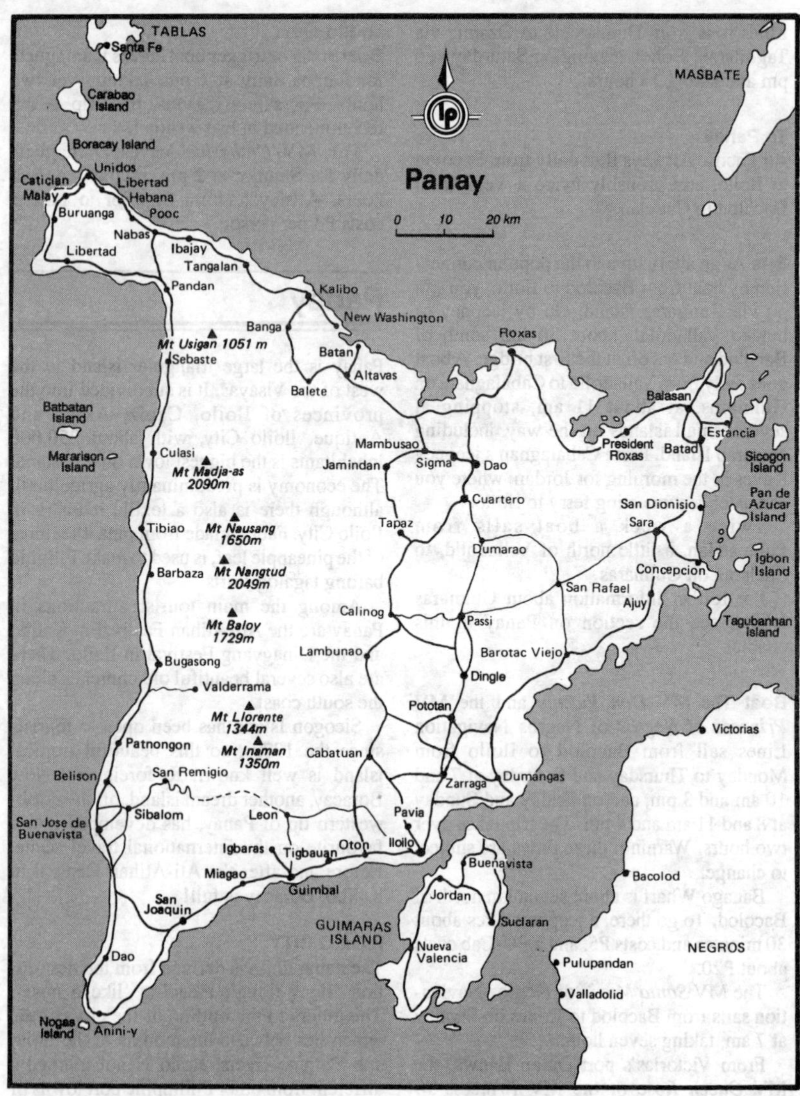

cruisers of the 1950s. The 'Window on the Past' is a little museum worth seeing. It's open daily from 8 am to noon and from 1 to 5 pm.

Six km west of the city is the suburb of Arevalo. Until a few years ago, it was well known for its cottage industry of making woven fabrics from *jusi* and *pina*. Today only one loom still exists at the Sinamay Dealer in Osmena St. You can still buy clothes and fabrics here. It is in a beautiful old house partly furnished with valuable carved furniture – something that only wealthy Filipinos can afford. On the way to Arevalo, you pass through Molo, which has a 19th century church built of coral.

Every year on the weekend after the Ati-Atihan Festival in Kalibo, the people of Iloilo celebrate the city's greatest festival, the Dinagyang. The *paraw* regatta, a race between outrigger sail boats in the Iloilo Strait, between Iloilo and Guimaras Island, is held on the second Saturday or Sunday in February.

In Pavia, a little north of Iloilo, water buffalo races take place each year on 3 May from 8 am. To get there, take a jeepney from the Shoemart.

Information

Money The Central Bank does not accept travellers' cheques. The Chartered Bank gives a good rate but charges P33 handling fee per cheque. Your best bet is to go to the Philippine National Bank (PNB), on the corner of General Luna and Valeria streets.

Places to Stay – bottom end

The *New Iloilo International House* (tel 72865), a simple place in J M Basa St, has rooms with fan for P70/90, with fan and bath for P90/110 and with air-con and bath for P160/180.

D'House Pensione (tel 72805) at 127 Quezon St is a homely place with a restaurant. Rooms with fan cost P70/140.

Iloilo Lodging House (tel 72384) in Aldeguer St has rooms with fan for P70/120, with fan and bath for P100/150 and with air-con and bath for P140/200. The rooms are small and bathrooms are shared between two rooms.

Eros Travellers Pensionne (tel 76183) in General Luna St has singles with fan and bath for P90 and rooms with air-con and bath for P140/170. It's comfortable and has a restaurant. A similar place is the *Family Pension House* (tel 72047, 79208) in General Luna St; it has rooms with fan and bath for P85/120 and with air-con and bath for P180.

Places to Stay – middle

You may have trouble finding *Madia-as Hotel* (tel 72756) in Aldeguer St as the entrance is hidden away in a lane off the street. Singles/doubles with fan and bath are P160/175 and with air-con and bath P240/250. It's clean and comfortable and has a restaurant.

Situated in a lane between J M Basa and Iznart streets, *Centercon Hotel* (tel 73431-33) is very central; it has rooms with fan for P150 and with air-con and bath for P217/277. It's a quiet place, apart from the rooms with fans on the sixth floor, and it has a restaurant.

New River Queen Hotel (tel 79997, 76443) in Bonifacio Drive has rooms with fan and bath for P160/195 and with air-con and bath for P250/290. It's fairly clean and has a restaurant.

Casa Plaza Pension House (tel 73461-67) in General Luna St is reasonably good and has a restaurant. Singles/doubles with air-con and bath cost 340/450, including breakfast.

If you're on a waiting list for a flight, you can stay at the *Bayani Hotel* (tel 72954) at the airport, which has rooms with fan and bath for P100/120 and with air-con and bath for P150/200. The airport opens at 3.30 am.

Places to Stay – top end

The best hotel in the centre of town is the *Amigo Terrace Hotel* (tel 74811-19) in Iznart St. It has rooms with air-con and bath for P436/470 and suites from P570. It has a restaurant and a swimming pool.

Similar, but more expensive, is the *Sarabia Manor Hotel* (tel 72731-35) in General Luna St; rooms with air-con and bath cost from P400/460 and suites from P800.

Hotel del Rio (tel 75585) in M H del Pilar St is a lovely place with a restaurant and swimming pool a little outside the centre of town on the Iloilo River. It has rooms with

1	Marina's Restaurant	30	Ships to Bacolod
2	New River Queen Hotel	31	Negros Navigation Lines
3	Nena's Manokan Restaurant	32	Sulpicio Lines
4	The Key Steambath & Barber Shop	33	Fountain Head Disco
5	Yokpek Restaurant	34	Buses to Roxas & Estancia
6	Museum	35	Kuweba Disco Theater
7	Provincial Capitol Building	36	Boats to Jordan
8	St Paul's Hospital	37	Iloilo Lodging House
9	Bistro sa Iloilo		King Ramen Restaurant
	Family Pension House	38	Mansion House Restaurant
	Tree House Restaurant	39	The Summer House Restaurant
10	Nena's Manokan Restaurant	40	Centercon Hotel
11	Casa Plaza Pension House	41	Love City Disco
12	Philippine National Bank	42	Swan Restaurant
13	Eros Travellers Pensionne	43	Aldous Snack Bar
14	Universidad de San Agustin	44	Madia-as Hotel
15	Philippine Airlines	45	New Iloilo International House
16	Bistro Valeria	46	Immigration Office
17	Bank of the Philippine Islands		Post Office
18	LBC Office	47	Springhead Disco Bar
19	William Lines	48	Plaza
20	Base Disco	49	S'Table Restaurant & Snack Bar
	Sarabia Manor Hotel	50	Plaza Libertad
21	Jeepneys to Pavia	51	Buses to San Jose de Buenavista
	Shoemart	52	Market
22	Batchoy Restaurants	53	Central Market
23	Amigo Plaza Shopping Centre	54	Gaisano Department Store
	Amigo Terrace Hotel	55	Buses to Kalibo & Caticlan
24	Jefferson's Restaurant	56	Lighthouse
25	The Tavern Pub		Rotary Park
26	Ang Kamalig Restaurant	57	Boats to Buenavista
27	Bayani Super Nightclub	58	Boats to Jordan
28	Ihawan Garden Restaurant	59	Wharf
29	Magnolia Icecream & Pancake House	60	Fort San Pedro Drive Inn

air-con and bath for P400/470 and suites from P780.

Another attractive hotel is the *Villa Rosa by the Sea* (tel 76953) in Calaparan, Villa, six km west of Iloilo. Singles/doubles with air-con and bath cost P365/420. It also has a restaurant and a swimming pool.

Places to Eat

You can get good Chinese and Filipino meals, as well as a proper Western breakfast, in J M Basa St, upstairs in the *Mansion House Restaurant* and in *The Summer House*. *Angelina* in Iznart St can also be recommended. The *Ang Kamalig Restaurant* in Delgado St serves good and fairly cheap Filipino meals.

Valeria St has several Batchoy restaurants – one of the best is the *Oak Barrel*. (Batchoy is a speciality of the western Visayas and consists of beef, pork and liver in noodle soup).

The two *Nena's Manokan* restaurants in Bonifacio Drive and General Luna St serve Filipino food that you have to eat with your fingers. In *Marina's Restaurant* Filipino food is served outside in lovely native surroundings. The *Yokpek Restaurant* in Bonifacio Drive offers Chinese dim sum.

The Tavern Pub, on the corner of Quezon and Delgado streets, is air-conditioned, well kept and cosy. Prices are slightly higher than usual, but there is a remarkable range of cocktails.

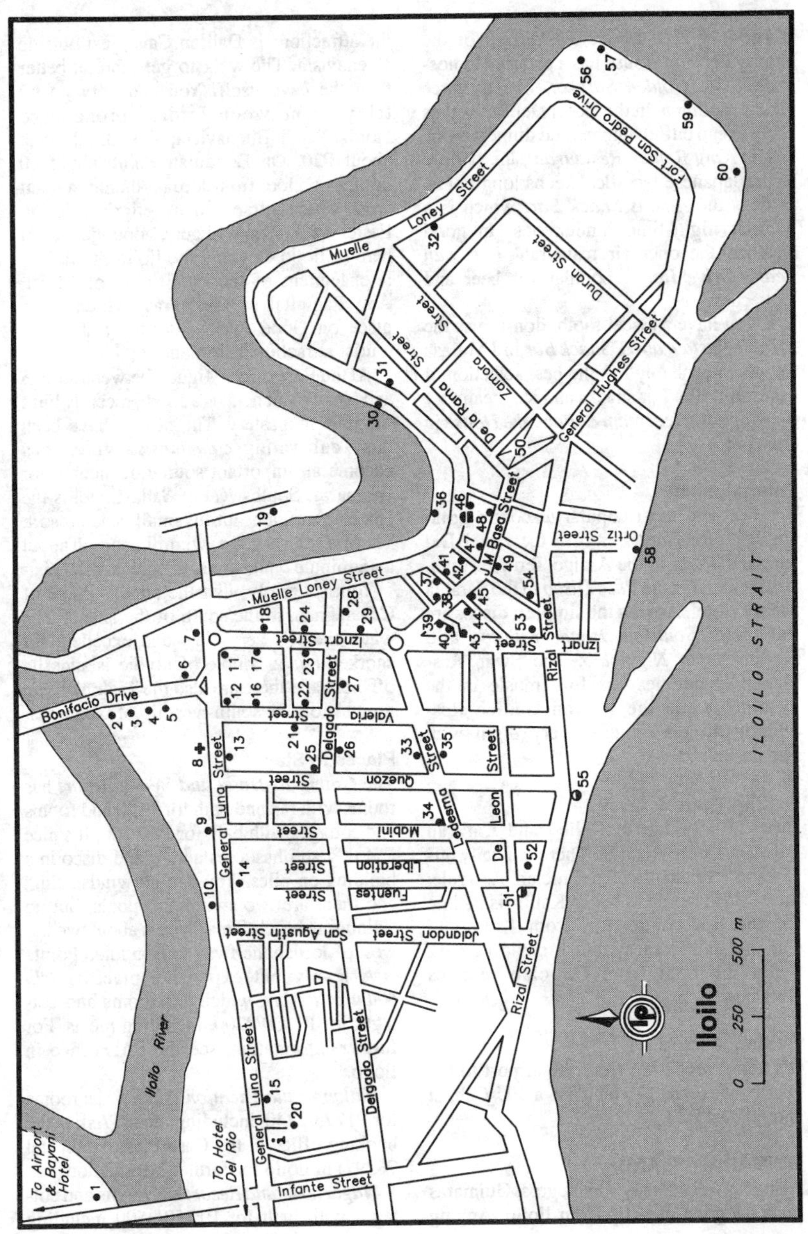
Iloilo
Iloilo River
ILOILO STRAIT
To Airport & Bayani Hotel
To Hotel Del Rio
Bonifacio Drive
General Luna Street
Infante Street
Delgado Street
San Agustin Street
Jalandon Street
Rizal Street
Fuentes Street
Liberation Street
Mabini Street
Quezon Street
Ledesma Street
De Leon Street
Valeria Street
Iznart Street
Muelle Loney Street
J M Basa Street
Ortiz Street
General Hughes Street
De la Rama Street
Zamora Street
Duran Street
Muelle Loney Street
Fort San Pedro Drive
0 250 500 m

The airy *Tree House Restaurant* of the Family Pension House has a pleasant atmosphere. The *Golden Salakot*, one of three good restaurants in the Hotel Del Rio serves fairly cheap buffet lunches and dinners daily.

The *King Ramen Restaurant*, the 'House of the Japanese Noodles' keeps long hours, as does the *Aldous Snack Bar*, which is a popular night-time rendezvous. In good weather, the open-air restaurant *Fort San Pedro Drive Inn* is popular for beer and barbecues.

If you have a sweet tooth, don't miss the *S'Table Restaurant & Snack Bar* in J M Basa St, which probably has the best selection of cakes in Iloilo. For snacks and ice cream, try the *Magnolia Icecream & Pancake House* in Iznart St.

Entertainment

The best and most popular discos in Iloilo are *Treasure Hunt Disco* in the Hotel Del Rio, and *Tivoli* in the Amigo Terrace Hotel. Also popular is the *Base Disco* in the Sarabia Manor Hotel. Among the simplest discos are the rustic *Fountain Head*, *Kuweba* and *Bayani Super Nightclub*. The Swan Restaurant sometimes has folk music in the evening, while the Ihawan Garden Restaurant attracts crowds every night with popular live music.

Getting There & Away

Buses from Iloilo to Kalibo and Caticlan now leave from Rizal St. There is a daily bus at 4 and 9.15 am direct to Caticlan. As a rule, the 11.30 am express bus to Kalibo is in time for the last connection from Kalibo to Caticlan and Boracay, but it could be dark when the boat from Caticlan reaches Boracay.

Getting Around

It's about seven km from the airport to the centre of town. If you take a PU-Cab, it should cost P20.

GUIMARAS ISLAND

Lying between Panay and Negros, Guimaras makes a good day trip from Iloilo. Among the attractions is Daliran Cave, just outside Buenavista. The walk to get there is better than the cave itself. You can only go by tricycle between Jordan (pronounced Hordan) and Buenavista; this should cost about P20. On Bondulan Point, about 40 minutes on foot from Jordan, there is a giant cross which attracts many pilgrims during Easter week. You will get a good view from here of Iloilo City and the Iloilo Strait. The re-enactment of the crucifixion of Christ, Ang Pagtaltal sa Guimaras, which takes place on Good Friday, is now a growing tourist attraction in Jordan.

At the Barrio San Miguel, between Jordan and Nueva Valencia, is a small, recently built Trappist monastery. The monks have been busy cultivating *calamansis*, which has become an important source of income for Guimaras. South-west of San Miguel is the Isla Naburot, a beautiful small beach resort. There is a fairly good swimming beach about a 45 minute walk south of Nueva Valencia.

Tourists rarely visit the small village of Cabalagnan, in the south of the island. The water there is very clear and excellent for snorkelling. A couple of idyllic islands lie offshore and there are also the Taclon diving grounds off the south-west tip of Guimaras.

Places to Stay

The *Guimaras Hotel and Beach Resort* has rooms with fan and bath for P120 and rooms and cottages with bath for P80/160. It's nice and tidy and has a restaurant and disco in a building on piles. You can go windsurfing, and there are two swimming pools, but no swimming beach. This place is about two km west of Jordan, halfway to Bondulan Point.

A lovely but expensive place is *Isla Naburot Resort*, which has rooms and cottages for P1100/2200, including meals. For further information, see the PAL office in Iloilo.

Tatlong Pulo Vacation Islands has rooms for P1275/2240, including meals. Ask at the booking office in the Casa Plaza Hotel (tel 78297) in Iloilo for further information.

Nagarao Island Resort has rooms and cottages with bath for P1250/2500 including meals. It has a restaurant and you can go windsurfing there. For further information, ask at the Nagarao Island Office (tel 78613, tlx 5910 AISCPU) at 113 Seminario St, Jaro, in Iloilo.

Getting There & Away

Several small ferries run daily from Iloilo to Guimaras almost hourly between 5 am and 5 pm. They leave for Jordan from the wharf near the post office and for Buenavista from Rotary Park. The last return ferry leaves at 5 or 6 pm. Several small boats go daily from the Ortiz wharf, near the central market, to Jordan.

The service charge in the resorts usually includes transfers, but it can cost up to P1000.

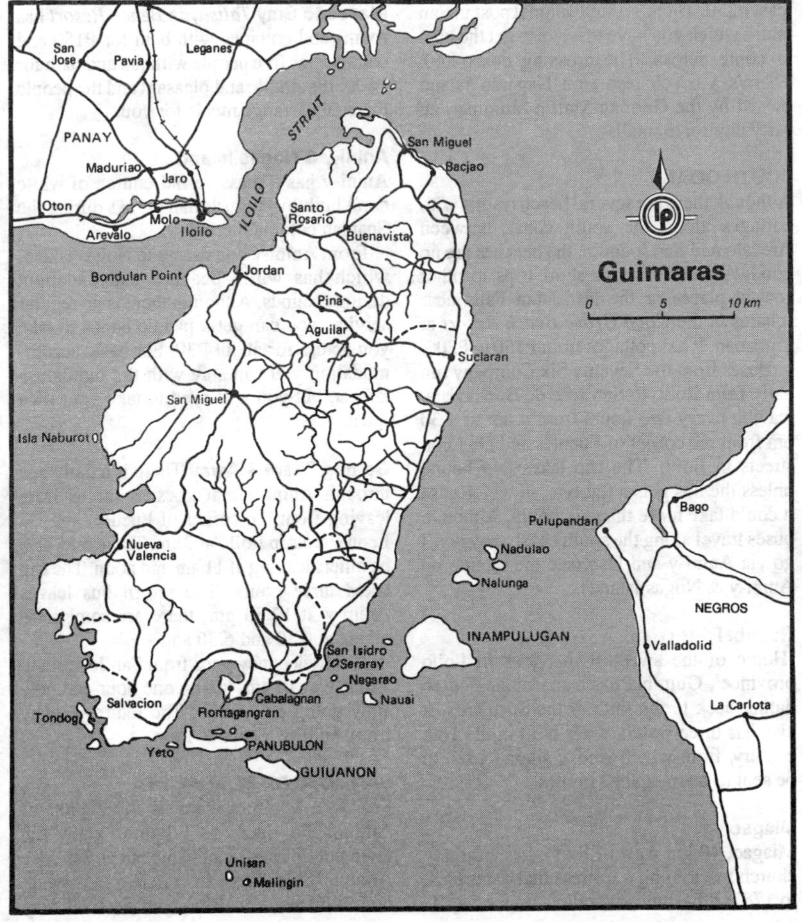

Getting Around

Jeepneys run between Jordan and Nueva Valencia, a few going as far as Cabalagnan. They return to Jordan only in the morning. You can go to Valladolid on Negros on a daily boat. It leaves Cabalagnan at 3 or 4 am and stops at several islands. You can also board the boat on Nagarao Island.

Once a day at about noon, a jeepney runs from Jordan to San Isidro, where you can cross to Nagarao Island. The ride costs P10, but the asking price for a Special Ride is at least P250. There's a small signal post in San Isidro which you have to wave to get the boat to come across. The crossing costs P40. There's a beach resort on Nagarao Island owned by the German Martin Stummer, an early environmentalist.

SOUTH COAST

Although there are several beach resorts with cottages along the south coast, between Arevalo and San Joaquin, the beaches are no good. A good base for short trips to other coastal places or the Nadsadan Falls near Igbaras is the *Coco Grove Beach Resort* at Tigbauan. It has cottages from P150 to P200.

Buses from the Seventy Six Company run daily from Iloilo to San Jose de Buenavista, leaving every two hours from 4 am to 4.30 pm from the corner of Fuentes and De Leon streets in Iloilo. The trip takes two hours, unless the bus gets a flat tyre, in which case it could take more than six hours. Although buses travel along the south coast, they don't go via Anini-y and Dao (see the section on Anini-y & Nogas Island).

Guimbal

'Home of the sweetest mangoes in Iloilo province', Guimbal has a sandstone church dating back to the time of the Spaniards. It also has three watchtowers built in the 16th century, from which smoke signals used to be sent to warn against pirates.

Miagao

Miagao, 40 km west of Iloilo, has a mighty church resembling a fortress that dates back to 1787. It has unusual reliefs on the façade mixing European elements (St Christopher) and Philippine plants (coconut palms and papaya trees).

San Joaquin

The most military church in the Philippines is in San Joaquin. The façade, built of blocks of coral, shows the battle of the Spanish against the Moors in Tetun, Morocco, in 1859. Every second Saturday in January, water buffalo fights are held in San Joaquin.

Places to Stay *Talisayan Beach Resort* has rooms and cottages with bath for P150 and cottages for five people with fan and bath for P500. It's simple and pleasant and the people there can arrange meals for you.

Anini-y & Nogas Island

Anini-y has a massive old church of white coral built by Augustinian monks during the Spanish colonial period.

From Anini-y you can go to Nogas Island, which has white beaches and excellent diving grounds. Although there is no regular service, you can get a paddle banca to take you across for about P30. For basic accommodation you can stay with the lighthouse keeper, but you will need to take your own linen.

Getting There & Away There is a daily bus through Anini-y that goes as far as Dao, leaving from the corner of Fuentes and De Leon streets in Iloilo at 7 am. There may also be others leaving at 11 am and noon. The trip takes three hours. The return bus leaves Anini-y at 12.30 pm; there are sometimes others at 4.30 and 6.30 am.

A daily jeepney goes from San Joaquin to Anini-y at 10 am, taking one hour and possibly going on to Dao. The return jeepney from Anini-y leaves at 1 pm.

SAN JOSE DE BUENAVISTA

San Jose de Buenavista is the capital of Antique Province, so Filipinos know the town not by its official name but as San Jose Antique. Ships leave from here for Palawan. Unfortunately, the Binirayan Festival may

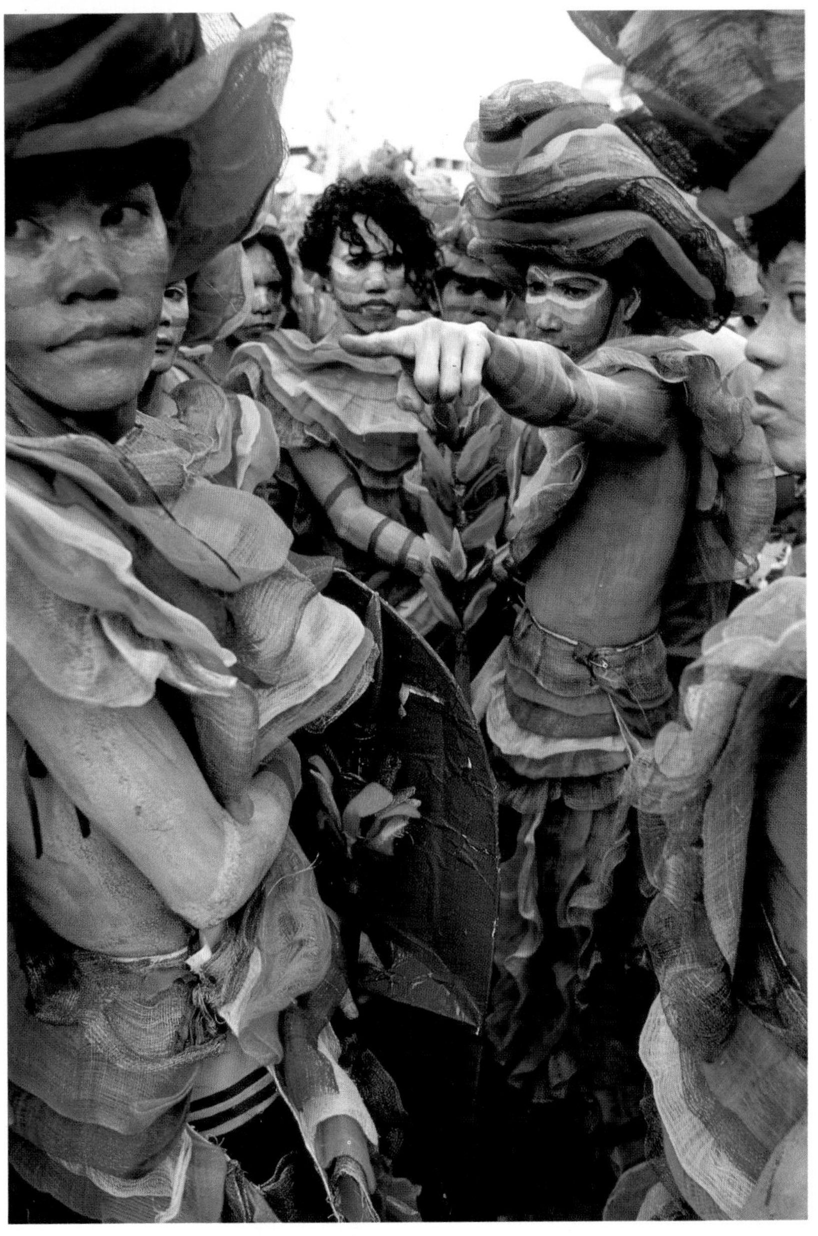

Colourful costumes abound in the Ati-Atihan Festival in Kalibo, Panay (JPk)

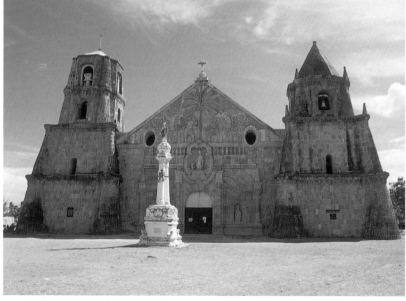

Top: Scene from the Ati-Atihan Festival in Kalibo, Panay (JP)
Bottom: Fortress Church in Miagao, south-east of Iloilo, Panay (JP)

no longer be held because of financial problems.

Places to Stay

G & G Lodge (tel 446) is a simple place with a restaurant in J C Zaldivar St, in the market, which has rooms for P40/80 and a restaurant. *Binirayan Hotel* (tel 226) has rooms with fan and bath for P88/132. It is simple and fairly clean.

Getting There & Away

There are few jeepneys and buses from San Jose de Buenavista to Culasi and Pandan. As the road is in poor condition, it takes four hours to reach Culasi and seven hours to reach Pandan. Some jeepneys only go as far as Culasi. From Pandan you can get connections to Malay and Kalibo.

CULASI

You may like to break the trip along the west coast of Panay at Culasi and spend a few days on Mararison Island. The crossing by daily outrigger boat from Culasi takes about 30 minutes.

Balestramon Lodging House is a simple place and has rooms for P30/60.

SAN DIONISIO & PAN DE AZUCAR ISLAND

San Dionisio is a small place on the coast with a big waterfront market. There is a string of beautiful islands lying offshore which you can reach quickly by outrigger boat. A Special Ride costs P70 and a regular ride costs P25.

The most conspicuous island is Pan de Azucar – its 575 metre high 'sugar loaf' can be seen a long way off. Because of its scenic attractions and friendly people, this island promises to become very popular before long. For the time being, it will only attract visitors who are prepared to put up with basic amenities. Little Agho Island, too, a little further south-east, is among the more attractive of the islands. Surprisingly, there is not even the beginning of any tourist development here. There is still no commercial accommodation available. You either have to get an invitation to stay or bring a tent.

Places to Stay

You can only stay in private houses in San Dionisio, for example, with the Esteban Juanico family, or at the Chinese store, next to the petrol station.

On Pan de Azucar Island you also have to depend on private hospitality, but as the locals are friendly, this should not be too difficult. You could ask for Anidlina and Avelino de Julian who like to accommodate travellers. They run a small store and don't mind preparing the fish you bought from the fishermen at the beach for the table. It's up to you how much you pay.

Getting There & Away

There is no direct bus from Iloilo to San Dionisio. The best way to get there is by Garnet Express bus to Estancia from Mabini St. They leave hourly from 2.30 am to 3 pm. To go to San Dionisio, get off no later than the turn-off in Deveria and wait for a jeepney coming from the larger town of Sara. As an alternative, you can get off at Sara, which is more pleasant than Deveria.

ESTANCIA

This unattractive little town serves mainly as a jumping-off point for the islands. Boats cross from here to the Sicogon and Gigante Islands and other destinations.

Fuentes Lodging House in Inventor St in Estancia offers basic accommodation with rooms for P30/60.

Estancia's few restaurants close very early. Only *Melbert Restaurant* in Reyes Ave stays open after 8 pm.

Getting There & Away

Garnet Express buses go daily from Iloilo to Estancia more or less on the hour between 2.30 am and 3 pm. They leave from Mabini St and take over five hours.

From Roxas to Estancia, there are several jeepneys or minibuses every morning. You may have to change at President Roxas. The trip takes three hours.

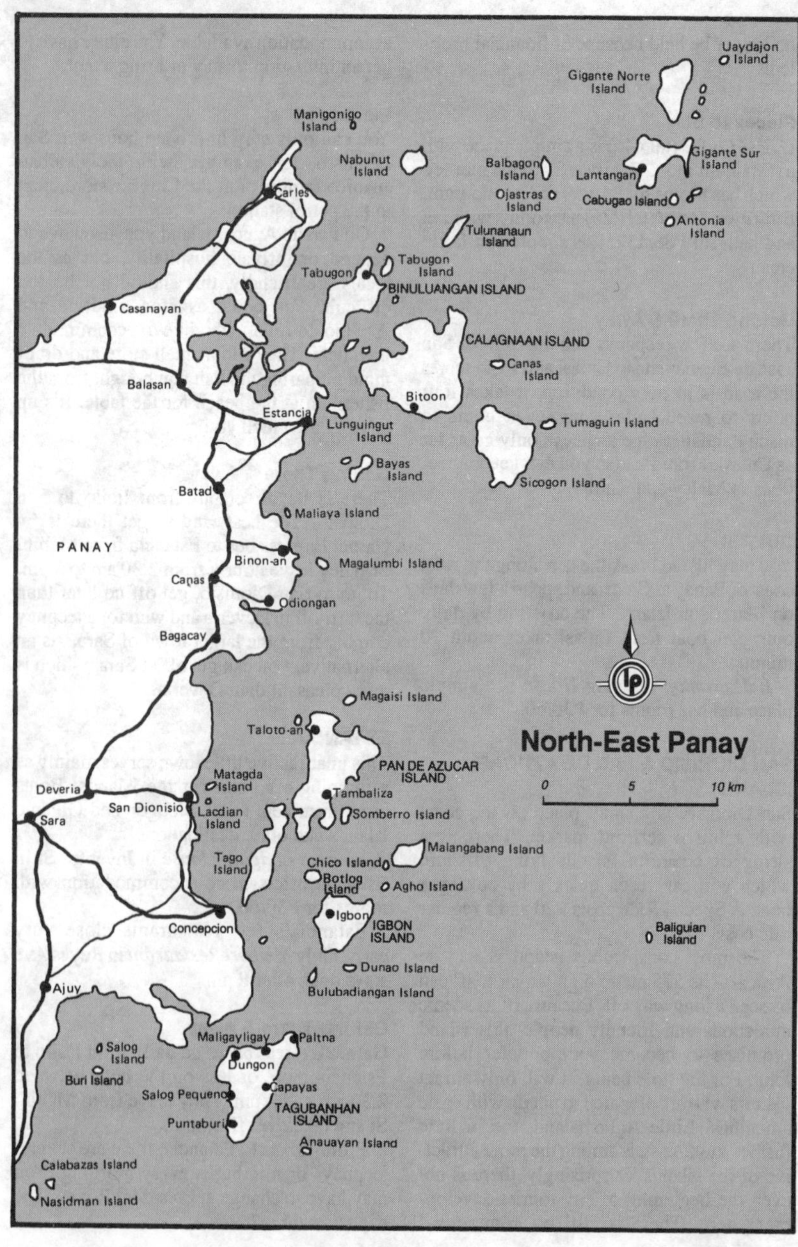
North-East Panay
0
5
10 km
Uaydajon Island
Gigante Norte Island
Manigonigo Island
Nabunut Island
Balbagon Island
Lantangan
Gigante Sur Island
Ojastras Island
Cabugao Island
Antonia Island
Carles
Tulunanaun Island
Tabugon
Tabugon Island
BINULUANGAN ISLAND
Casanayan
CALAGNAAN ISLAND
Canas Island
Balasan
Bitoon
Estancia
Lunguingut Island
Tumaguin Island
Bayas Island
Sicogon Island
Batad
Maliaya Island
PANAY
Binon-an
Magalumbi Island
Capas
Odiongan
Bagacay
Magaisi Island
Taloto-an
PAN DE AZUCAR ISLAND
Matagda Island
Deveria
Tambaliza
San Dionisio
Lacdian Island
Somberro Island
Sara
Malangabang Island
Tago Island
Chico Island
Botlog Island
Agho Island
Igbon
Concepcion
IGBON ISLAND
Baliguian Island
Dunao Island
Ajuy
Bulubadiangan Island
Maligayligay
Paltna
Salog Island
Dungon
Buri Island
Salog Pequeno
Capayas
TAGUBANHAN ISLAND
Puntaburi
Anauayan Island
Calabazas Island
Nasidman Island

SICOGON & GIGANTE ISLANDS

These islands are off the north-eastern tip of Panay. Sicogon Island is very beautiful and the exclusive Sicogon Island Club was one of the first internationally known beach resorts of the Philippines. This is the only place where tourists can stay the night, as the 3000 inhabitants are strictly forbidden to let rooms to tourists. They are not allowed to sell anything either, so the only restaurant is that belonging to the resort. To cap it all, locals are not even allowed to bring strangers to the island unless they are guests of the resort.

Gigante Norte and Gigante Sur islands are both very rugged. Massive rocks, commonly known as the 'enchanted rocks', contain lots of caves which have given rise to many mysterious tales. It is rumoured that the complex system of tunnels between the caves used to serve as a hide-out for pirates.

Of the 10 caves on Gigante Sur, only three have been explored. Most islanders are too scared and superstitious to enter them and many are just not interested. Turtle Cave, also called Pawikan, has a huge antechamber where white monkeys swing on roots hanging down from the top of the opening. Tiniphagan and Elephant Caves have been even less explored than Turtle Cave and they may have connecting tunnels to other caves. A good departure point for visiting the caves is Barrio Lantangan. It's recommended that you hire a guide and take stout shoes, torches, candles and drinking water. There is a natural swimming pool near the caves.

On Gigante Norte you can easily get to Langub Cave from the Barrio Piagao. A beautiful beach with crystal clear water stretches all along the barrio.

Just south of the two Gigante Islands are the small islands of Cabugao Norte and Cabugao Sur. Cabugao Norte has a few huts and a small cave and a pretty good swimming beach. The settlement on Cabugao Sur is slightly larger and there is a good swimming beach with very fine sand.

Places to Stay

Sicogon Island Club has doubles and cottages from US$45. There are Hobie Cats and you can play tennis and go windsurfing.

On the Gigante Islands you have to find your own accommodation – possibly at the Barrio Lantangan – but this shouldn't be a problem. It's up to you how much you pay.

Getting There & Away

If you go to the islands from Estancia, you will find that the Special Rides on offer are very expensive, as strangers are usually presumed to be going to Sicogon – and are also thought to be very rich. To go to the Gigantes from Estancia, you'd best get in touch with Mr Rustum Tan and his family. They have relatives on the islands and can negotiate a reasonable price for the Special Ride to Gigante Sur. The trip takes over two hours.

ROXAS

Roxas City is the capital of Capiz Province. There are no tourist attractions and the only reason for going there is as a stopping point on the way to Manila or Romblon. The best time of year to be there is in October, when the locals celebrate the Halaran Festival with music and dancing in the streets.

Places to Stay

The *Beehive Inn* (tel 418) in Roxas Ave is a simple place which has rooms with fan for P35/50, with fan and bath for P60/80 and with air-con and bath for P135.

The *River Inn* (tel 809) in Lapu Lapu St has rooms with fan for P50/60 and with air-con for P150. It's unpretentious and homely, but the doors close at 9 pm.

Halaran House (tel 675) in Roxas Ave has singles with fan for P70, rooms with fan and bath for P95/125 and with air-con and bath for P125/160. It's a pleasant place with a restaurant.

Halaran Plaza (tel 649) in Rizal St, opposite the City Hall, is also quite good and has a restaurant. Singles/doubles with fan and bath cost P110/130 and with air-con and bath P135/165.

Well located on Baybay Beach between the airport and the harbour is *Marc's Beach Resort* (tel 103). It has cottages for P50, with fan and bath for P150, and doubles with air-con and bath for P185. It's a comfortable place with a restaurant and a tennis court. Another good place in Baybay is *Villa Patria Cottages* (tel 180). Rooms with fan and bath cost P200/225-250 and with air-con and bath P285/385.

Places to Eat

Of the few restaurants in Roxas only two are worth mentioning. *John's Fast Foods* in Roxas Ave, opposite Halaran House, is remarkably cheap and has a large selection of Filipino and Chinese dishes. *Halaran House Restaurant* serves well-priced meals of the day *(comida)* but no beer.

Getting There & Away

Several R&K Transit buses run daily from Iloilo to Roxas, leaving from Ledesma St, on the corner of Mabini St, or Rizal St at about 8.30, 10 and 11 am and 1 and 3 pm. The trip takes over four hours. A Nandwani's Tourist Transport air-con bus leaves from the corner of Mabini and Delgado streets at 10.30 am and 3.30 pm.

The last bus for Iloilo usually leaves Roxas at about 11.30 am.

Several buses a day go from Roxas to Kalibo, departing between 5 am and noon, and taking over three hours.

KALIBO

The oldest town in Aklan, Kalibo is also the capital of the province. Well known for the pina textiles and intricately woven abaca shoes and handbags it manufactures, Kalibo is even more renowned for the annual Ati-Atihan Festival held in January. This is the Mardi Gras of the Philippines. Long before the show begins, the people of Aklan think of nothing but the vibrant *Tam-Tam*. Other villages in the Philippines hold similar festivals but the one in Kalibo is the most popular.

About 20 km north-west of Kalibo are the Jawili Falls, which cascade down the valley, forming several basins where you can have a refreshing swim. To get there, take a bus or jeepney from Kalibo going to Nabas or Caticlan, get off at Tangalan and go on by tricycle.

In Banga, few km south of Kalibo, you can visit the Aklan Agricultural College with its well-equipped experimental station. If you want to stay, there is a guesthouse.

Places to Stay

Gervy's Lodge (tel 3081) in R Pastrada St has simple rooms for P35/70. *RB Lodge* (tel 2604), in the same street, has rooms with fan for P35/70 and with air-con and bath for P175.

The *Apartel Marietta* (tel 3302) in Roxas Ave has rooms with fan for P50/100. It's comfortable and also has a restaurant.

The Green Mansions (tel 2244) in M Laserna St has dorm beds with fan for P50, rooms with fan for P60/120 and with fan and bath for P100/200. It's reasonably good.

There are a few good hotels in S Martelino St. The *Glowmoon Hotel* is a pleasant place; singles/doubles with fan cost P50/80, doubles with fan and bath cost P150 and singles/doubles with air-con and bath cost P180/250. It also has a restaurant.

The *Hotel Casa Felicidad* (tel 3146) has dorm beds with fan for P50, rooms with fan and bath for P150/200 and with air-con and bath for P200/300.

Casa Alba Hotel (tel 3146) has dorm beds with fan for P75, rooms for P75/100, with fan for P150/200 and with air-con and bath for P250/350.

LM Plaza Lodge in Martyrs St has fairly good rooms with fan for P50/80, with fan and bath for P70/90 and with air-con and bath for P250/270.

A little outside town is the *Bayani Resort Hotel* in Old Busuang; rooms with air-con and bath cost P150/190-200. It's pleasant with a restaurant and swimming pool, but you could have trouble getting to town in the evening.

During the Ati-Atihan Festival, prices in Kalibo may be tripled and it can be almost impossible to find a hotel room.

Places to Eat

You can enjoy good Chinese meals at the

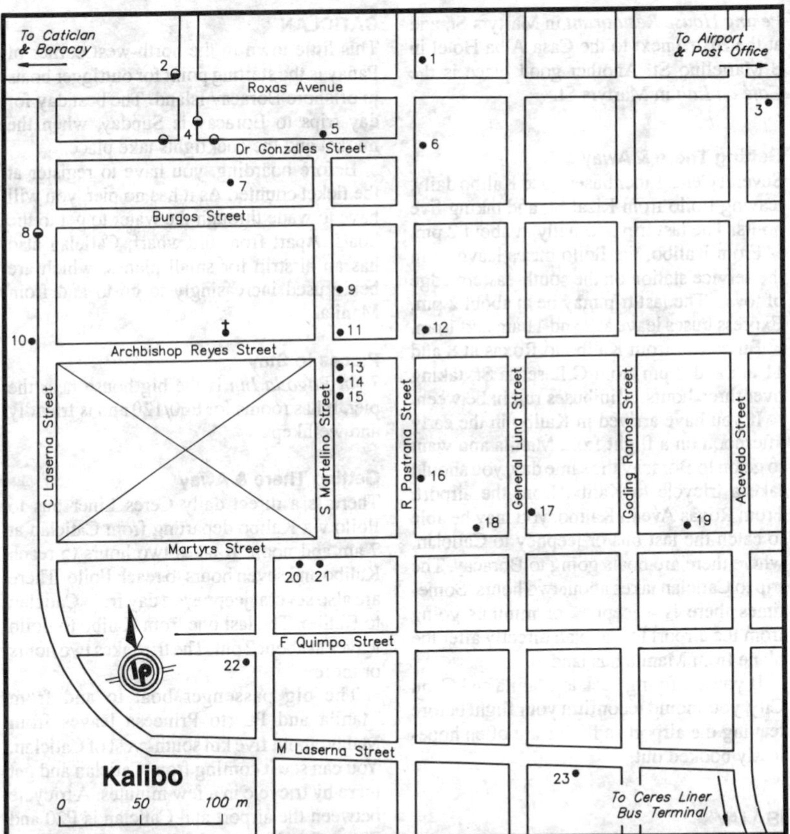

1 RB Lodge	13 Hotel Casa Felicidad
2 Jeepneys & Buses to Caticlan & Malay	14 Casa Alba Hotel
3 Apartel Marietta	PT&T Office
4 Jeepneys to Dumaguit & New Washington	15 Bistro
5 Gothong Lines	16 Gervy's Lodge
6 William Lines	17 Lemon Lodge
7 Market	18 Peking House Restaurant
8 Buses to Roxas	19 Great Minds Pub
9 Glowmoon Hotel	20 Café au Lait
10 Aboitiz Lines	21 LM Plaza Lodge
11 Aklan Museum	22 Glowmoon Pension House
12 Philippine National Bank	LM Lodge
	23 The Green Mansions

Peking House Restaurant in Martyrs St, and at the *Bistro* next to the Casa Alba Hotel in S Martelino St. Another good place is the *Café au Lait* in Martyrs St.

Getting There & Away

Several Ceres Liner buses go to Kalibo daily, leaving Iloilo from Rizal St, and taking five hours. The last trip is usually at about 2 pm.

From Kalibo, the Iloilo buses leave from the service station on the south-eastern edge of town. The last trip may be at about 2 pm. Express buses leave at 7 and 11 am and 1 pm.

Buses run from Kalibo to Roxas at 8 and 11 am and 2 pm from C Laserna St, taking over three hours. Minibuses run in between.

If you have arrived in Kalibo in the early afternoon on a flight from Manila and want to go on to Boracay the same day, you should take a tricycle to Kalibo from the airport. From Roxas Ave in Kalibo, you may be able to catch the last bus or jeepney to Caticlan, where there are boats going to Boracay. The trip to Caticlan takes about two hours. Sometimes there is a jeepney or minibus going from the airport to Caticlan directly after the plane from Manila has landed.

If you are flying back to Manila and Cebu City, you should reconfirm your flight before leaving the airport as flights are often hopelessly booked out.

IBAJAY

Ibajay, pronounced Ibahay, is a small village halfway between Kalibo and Caticlan. Each year on the weekend after the Kalibo festival, the 'really original' Ati-Atihan Festival (according to the locals) is held here. It is more authentic and traditional than the commercialised Kalibo festival. Sunday is the main day. The festival is very colourful and offers great opportunities for photos.

Places to Stay

The *Western Horizon Hotel,* opposite the service station is a basic, clean place. Singles/doubles with fan cost P50/100. It may be necessary to stay in Kalibo.

CATICLAN

This little town in the north-west corner of Panay is the starting point for outrigger boats to offshore Boracay Island. The best day for day trips to Boracay is Sunday, when the market and the cockfights take place.

Before boarding, you have to register at the ticket counter. As it has no pier, you will have to wade through the water to get to the boats. Apart from the wharf, Caticlan also has an airstrip for small planes, which are being used increasingly to go to and from Manila.

Places to Stay

Twin Pagoda Inn is the big house near the pier. It has rooms for P60/120 and is friendly and well kept.

Getting There & Away

There is a direct daily Ceres Liner bus to Iloilo via Kalibo departing from Caticlan at 7 am and noon. It takes two hours to reach Kalibo and seven hours to reach Iloilo. There are also several jeepneys a day from Caticlan to Kalibo. The last one from Kalibo to Iloilo leaves at about 2 pm. The trip takes two hours or more.

The big passenger boat to and from Manila and Puerto Princesa leaves from Malay, about five km south-west of Caticlan. You can see it coming from Caticlan and get there by tricycle in a few minutes. A tricycle between the airport and Caticlan is P20 and P20 to P30 between Malay and Caticlan.

BORACAY

Boracay Island is a great place for just lazing around. Seven km long, it is only one km wide at its narrowest point. Boracay's largest villages or *barangays* are Yapac, Balabag and Manoc Manoc. They, and several smaller hamlets called *sitios*, are connected by a confusing network of paths and tracks, so the map of Boracay can only serve as a general guide.

There is a beautiful beach on the west coast with very fine white sand, particularly near Balabag. The water is quite shallow, however. For snorkelling the east coast is

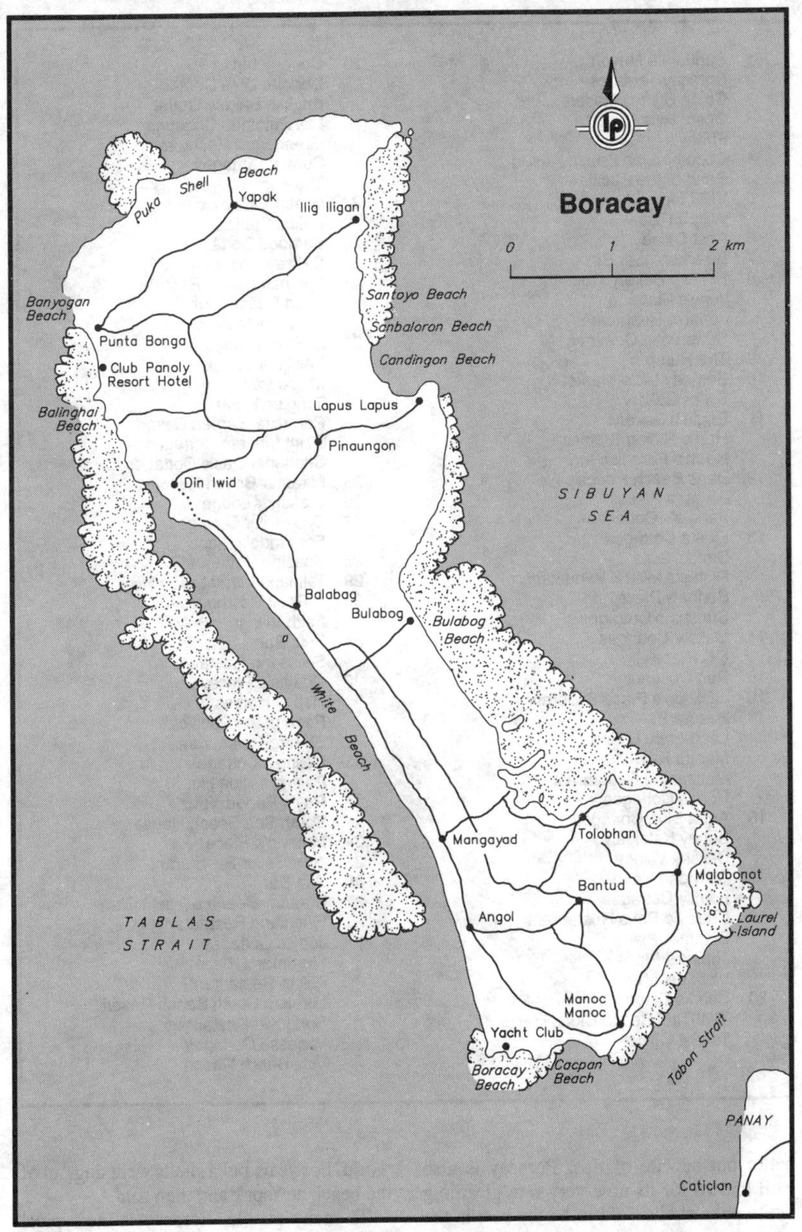
Boracay
0
1
2 km
Puka Shell Beach
Yapak
Ilig Iligan
Banyogan Beach
Punta Bonga
Club Panoly Resort Hotel
Santoyo Beach
Sanbaloran Beach
Candingon Beach
Balinghai Beach
Lapus Lapus
Pinaungon
Din Iwid
SIBUYAN SEA
Balabag
Bulabog
Bulabog Beach
White Beach
Mangayad
Tolobhan
Malabonot
Bantud
Angol
Laurel Island
TABLAS STRAIT
Manoc Manoc
Yacht Club
Boracay Beach
Cacpan Beach
Tabon Strait
PANAY
Caticlan

1	Sundance Resort
2	Boracay Terraces
3	Costa Blanca Resort
	Costa Hills Resort
	Friday's
4	Cocomangas Beach Resort
	Pearl of the Pacific
5	VIP Lingau
	Willy's Place
6	Post Office
7	Beachcomber Bar
8	English Bakery Outlet
	Jony's Place
	Jonah's Restaurant
	Seabreeze Cottages
9	The Hump
10	Boracay Little Market
	Swiss Bakery
11	English Bakery
	Horse Riding Stables
	Nena's Paradise Inn
12	Bans Beach House
	Jomar's Place
	Vangie's Cottages
13	Fiesta Cottages
	Sand Castle
	Richie's Mistral Windsurfing
	Serina's Place
	Sunshine Cottages
14	Galaxy Cottages
	6 C Place
15	Red Coconut
16	Jackson's Place & Library
17	Bazura Bar
	Lapu-Lapu Diving
	Mango Ray
	Mezzanine Restaurant
	Nora's Cottages
18	Aqua Blue Cottages
	Bahay Kaibigan
	Dalisay Village
	Diamond Head
	Family Cottages
19	Chez de Paris Restaurant
	Summer Place
	Jopine's Place
	Vista del Mar
20	Sharks Disco
	Tirol-Tirol Beach Club
	Tourist Office
21	Country Inn
	Donaire Dive Center
	English Bakery Outlet
	Las Palomas Cottages
	Green Yard Restaurant
	Sunset Cottages
	Tito's
22	Green Valley Homes
	Police Station
23	Bamboo Cottages
	Dalisay Cottages
	Lorenzo Beach Resort
	Palm Beach Club
	Titay Restaurant
24	Holiday Homes
	Lea Homes
	Magic Palm
	Tonglen Homes
	Paradise Garden Resort
	Saint Vincent Cottages
	Shangrila Oasis Cottages
25	Miramar Beach Resort
26	Trafalgar Lodge
27	Casa Pilar Cottages
	Fernando's Place
28	Seaside Cottages
29	Talipapa Market
30	A-Rock Resthouse
	Faith Village
31	Sulu Bar
	Swiss Inn Restaurant
32	Charlie's Place
	Happy Homes
	Pearl of the Pacific
	Starfire Restaurant
33	Deling's Cottages
	Pacing's Nipa Hut
	Roy's Rendezvouz
	South Sea Beach House
34	Moreno's Place
35	Jolly Sailor Restaurant
36	Sun Bar
37	Boracay Beach & Yacht Club
	Fischfang Restaurant
	Judy's Cottages
	Floremar's Place
	Italian Restaurant
	Lorenzo South Beach Resort
	Sundown Restaurant
	Vanessa Cottages
	Villa Beach Resort

better but beware of rips. Boracay is also well known for its now very rare gleaming white puka shells, said to be the best in the world. For years puka shells were dug out of the beach at Yapak and then sold.

To many people, Boracay is the typical

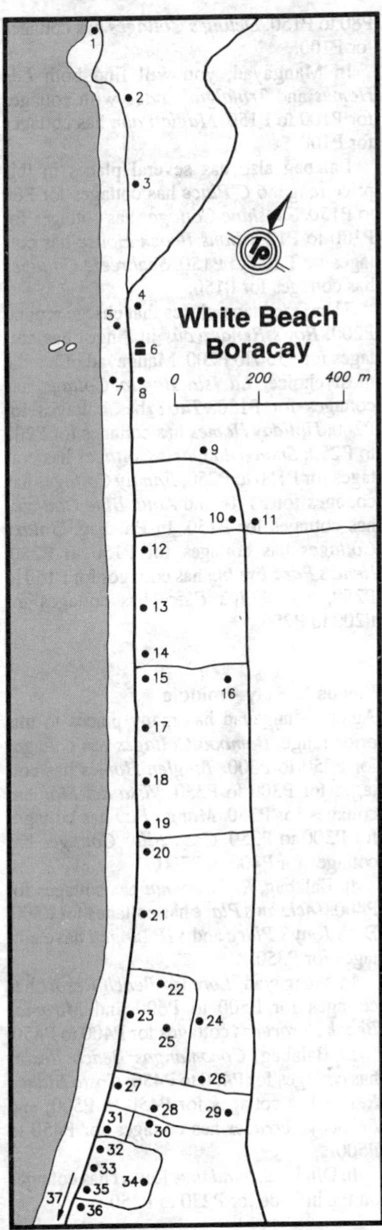

Pacific island paradise. But, although the friendly islanders are surprisingly tolerant, there are local customs that travellers should be aware of. For instance, although they don't protest openly, many of the locals find topless women tourists on the beaches offensive.

Tourism only came to the island at a time when the price of copra hit rock bottom. Today, the people of Boracay are earning money again, most of which, fortunately, stays on the island instead of disappearing into the coffers of foreign companies. Whether this will change in the foreseeable future depends on the Department of Tourism, which is thinking of making Boracay into South-East Asia's leading beach resort with all the usual luxuries. The mind boggles, especially when you think of the irreparable damage caused by similar developments in other countries. The fact that Boracay is an attraction because of its lack of development does not seem to impress the powers that be. So far these plans are still in the discussion stages and the inhabitants and guests of the island hope they will go no further.

Every day seems to be a holiday on Boracay – all you need to do is relax and enjoy yourself. Long before you get up, someone has swept around the cottages and put thermos flasks with hot water on the balcony tables. You can even have fresh bread rolls delivered in the morning. Just make some coffee and decide whether to go sailing, windsurfing, or perhaps snorkelling and looking at corals. If you're curious you may get as far as the Yapak Caves or the other side of the island, where there are still fishermen who have nothing to do with tourism, except that they too have to pay higher prices in the stores.

At sunset, everyone gathers on the white sandy beach to admire the changing colours of the sky. Unfortunately, this is also where the sandflies lie in wait. Only the newcomers and the macho men lie on the sand without protection. Those who know how itchy the bites of this silent plague can be, coat themselves in coconut oil or keep their distance.

A glass of piña colada or palm wine completes the picture.

Things to Do

There are lots of opportunities for leisure and diversion on Boracay. For P150 a day, you can hire a *paraw*, a small, fast outrigger sail boat given to capsizing. A paddle outrigger boat costs only P10 per hour or P50 per day. Windsurfing and horse riding both cost P100 to P150 per hour. You can now also take a course in diving and go snorkelling on the coral reefs of the neighbouring islands. A diving trip, including one dive, the boat and equipment, will cost you P350. For further information, see Wally in the Sulu Bar in Angol or the guys from Lapu-Lapu Diving.

To the south of Balabag, in Jackson's Place, behind the Red Coconut Restaurant and just off the beach, is the library, where you can borrow reading matter from around the world for a few pesos.

Places to Stay

In the last few years, many fine cottages have been added to the available accommodation. Most of them are on White Beach, between Balabag and Angol. They are all equipped with either two single beds or a double bed and nearly always have their own terrace and bathroom. If you are staying on your own, you may get the price lowered in the off season.

The influx of tourists has attracted a few shady characters who want their share in the boom. Keep an eye on your valuables and lock your cottage, especially at night. If possible, use your own lock.

Out of about 100 beach resorts, a selection has been made of some 40 clean and comfortable places to stay. Each of the towns along White Beach is represented in the different price brackets. The prices shown are for cottages or rooms with a bathroom for two people.

Places to Stay – bottom end

There are several good, cheap places in Angol. *Moreno's Place* has cottages for P80 to P120. *Pacing's Nipa Hut* has cottages for P80 to P150. *Deling's Cottages* has cottages for P100.

In Mangayad, you will find both *Lea Homes* and *Trafalgar Lodge* with cottages for P100 to P150. *Magic Palm* has cottages for P100.

Balabag also has several places in this price range. *6 C Place* has cottages for P80 to P150. *Sunshine Cottages* has cottages for P100 to P120. *Bans Beach House* has cottages for P100 to P150. *Seabreeze Cottages* has cottages for P150.

There are many places that charge around P200. *Roy's Rendezvous* in Angol has cottages for P150 to P200. Mangayad offers the most choice. *La Isla Bonita Cottage* has cottages for P150; *Tito's* has cottages for P200; *Holiday Homes* has cottages for P200 to P250; *Shangrila Oasis Cottages* has cottages for P150 to P250; *Family Cottages* has cottages for P170; and *Aqua Blue Cottages* has cottages for P150. In Balabag, *Galaxy Cottages* has cottages for P150 to P250; *Nena's Paradise Inn* has cottages for P150 to P250; and *Willy's Place* has cottages for P200 to P250.

Places to Stay – middle

Again, Mangayad has many places in this price range. *Bamboo Cottages* has cottages for P250 to P300. *Tonglen Homes* has cottages for P300 to P350. *Vista del Mar* has cottages for P350. *Mango Ray* has cottages for P300 to P350. *Casa Pilar Cottages* has cottages for P400 to P500.

In Balabag, *Red Coconut* has cottages for P400. *Jackson's Place* has cottages for P300. Both *Jony's Place* and *VIP Lingau* have cottages for P350.

In Mangayad, *Lorenzo Beach Resort* has cottages for P500 to P600 and *Miramar Beach Resort* has cottages for P400 to P450.

In Balabag, *Cocomangas Beach Resort* has cottages for P400 to P450; *Costa Blanca Resort* has cottages for P450 to P500; and *Boracay Terraces* has cottages for P450 to P500.

In Din Iwid, *Sundance Resort* has cottages on the hillside for P250 to P350.

Places to Stay – top end

Pearl of the Pacific in Angol and Balabag has cottages for P600 to P900 including breakfast. In Balabag, *Friday's* has cottages for P650 to P800 and *Costa Hills Resort* has cottages for P600 to P1200, including breakfast. In Mangayad, *Paradise Garden Resort* has rooms with bath for P900/1000, and *Palm Beach Club* has cottages for P500 to P800 and with air-con and bath for P1200 to P1400, including breakfast.

Boracay Beach & Yacht Club in Manoc Manoc has cottages for P2400, including meals.

The *Club Panoly Resort Hotel* in Punta Bonga has cottages from P3000 to P4000.

Places to Eat

There are now plenty of restaurants. They are often busy in the evening and you may have to wait for up to an hour to be served. If you want to avoid this, book ahead or go before 8 pm. Thanks to gas or kerosene refrigerators, you can now get cold drinks pretty well everywhere.

In Balabag, you can enjoy a great paella at the *Red Coconut*, and Mexican dishes at *Jony's Place*. *Jonah's*, opposite the Beachcomber Bar, has excellent fruit juices.

The garden restaurant *Mango Ray* in Mangayad is set in beautiful surroundings, and you can get both Filipino and Swiss meals at the *Bamboo Restaurant*. The *Green Yard* has good wiener schnitzel and veal cordon bleu.

In Angol, the *Starfire* and *Happy Homes* serve cheap meals and the *Sundown Restaurant* has good European cuisine. Fruit salads are a speciality at the *Jolly Sailor*, where you can also pick up useful travel hints.

Entertainment

After dinner many guests like to listen to music (powered by generators) or go dancing at their favourite place. Many like the *Beachcomber* at Balabag, where the dancing can become very animated when things warm up. Others prefer the *Bazura Bar* one km further south, *Sharks Disco* in Mangayad or the *Sulu Bar* in Angol. At the *Sun Bar*, also in Angol, you can sip a cocktail while lying on thick cushions, playing chess or backgammon and whiling the balmy night away.

Getting There & Away

Air The quickest (and dearest) connection between Manila and Boracay via Caticlan is by Aerolift and Pacific Airways.

PAL flies from Manila to Kalibo on Panay and Tugdan on Tablas Island, in the province of Romblon. The connection from Kalibo to Boracay via Caticlan is better than the one from Tugdan to Boracay via Santa Fe.

Boat Many boats cruise along White Beach heading for Caticlan; just wait at one of the signposted boat stops and wave one down if you want to go there. The first boat comes along at about 6.30 am. On arrival in Caticlan, you can get a jeepney or bus to Kalibo. The trip takes two hours or more.

From June to November, during the southwest monsoons, the sea on the west side of Boracay can grow too rough for outrigger boats. They then have to tie up on the east coast, at or near Bulabog.

There are shipping services between Manila and Malay, New Washington and Dumaguit. Dumaguit and New Washington are near Kalibo on Panay, and Malay is near Boracay. (See the section on getting to Panay in the Transport from Luzon section of the Manila chapter.)

TO/FROM PANAY

You can get to Panay from Cebu, Leyte, Luzon, Mindanao, Mindoro, Negros, Palawan and Romblon (see the Transport from Luzon section of the Manila chapter and the relevant To/From sections of this chapter and of the chapters on the other islands.)

To Cebu

Air PAL flies daily from Iloilo and Kalibo to Cebu City on Monday, Wednesday and Saturday.

Pacific Airways flies daily from Iloilo to

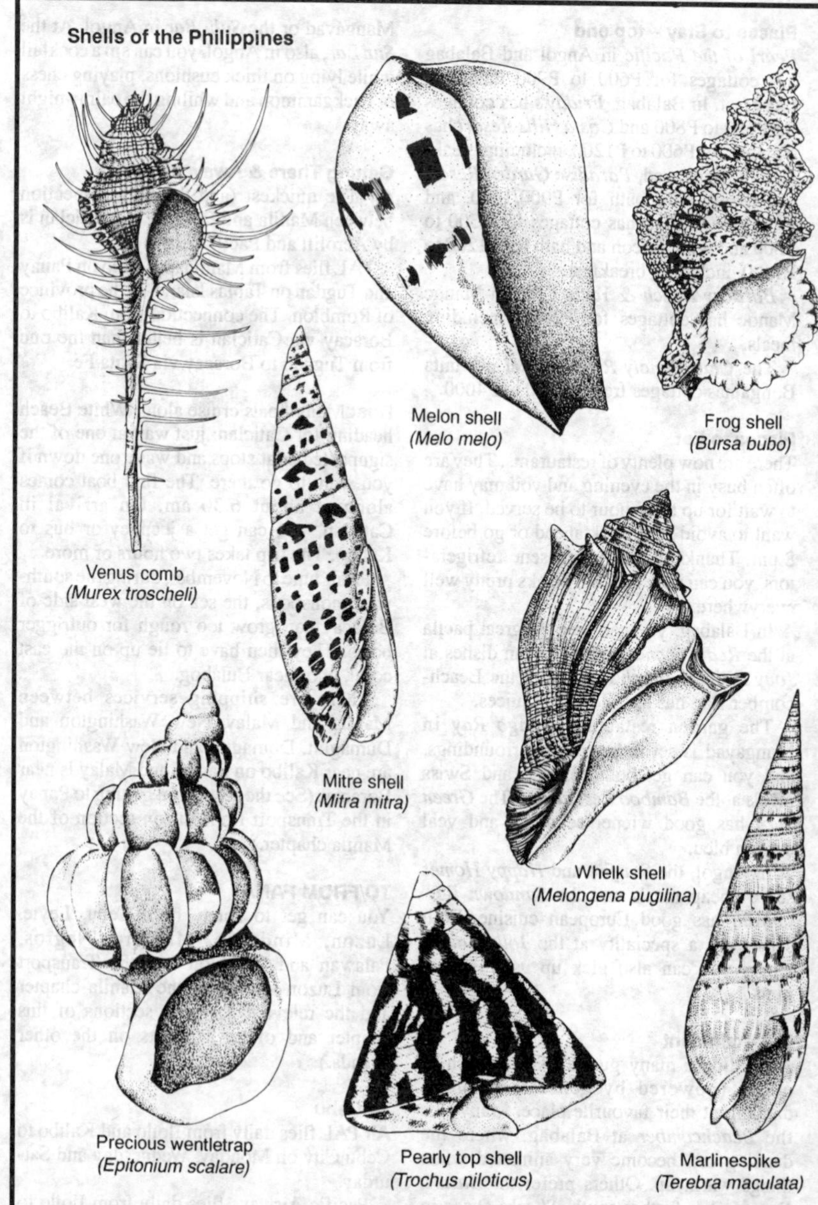
Shells of the Philippines
Venus comb
(Murex troscheli)
Melon shell
(Melo melo)
Frog shell
(Bursa bubo)
Mitre shell
(Mitra mitra)
Whelk shell
(Melongena pugilina)
Precious wentletrap
(Epitonium scalare)
Pearly top shell
(Trochus niloticus)
Marlinespike
(Terebra maculata)

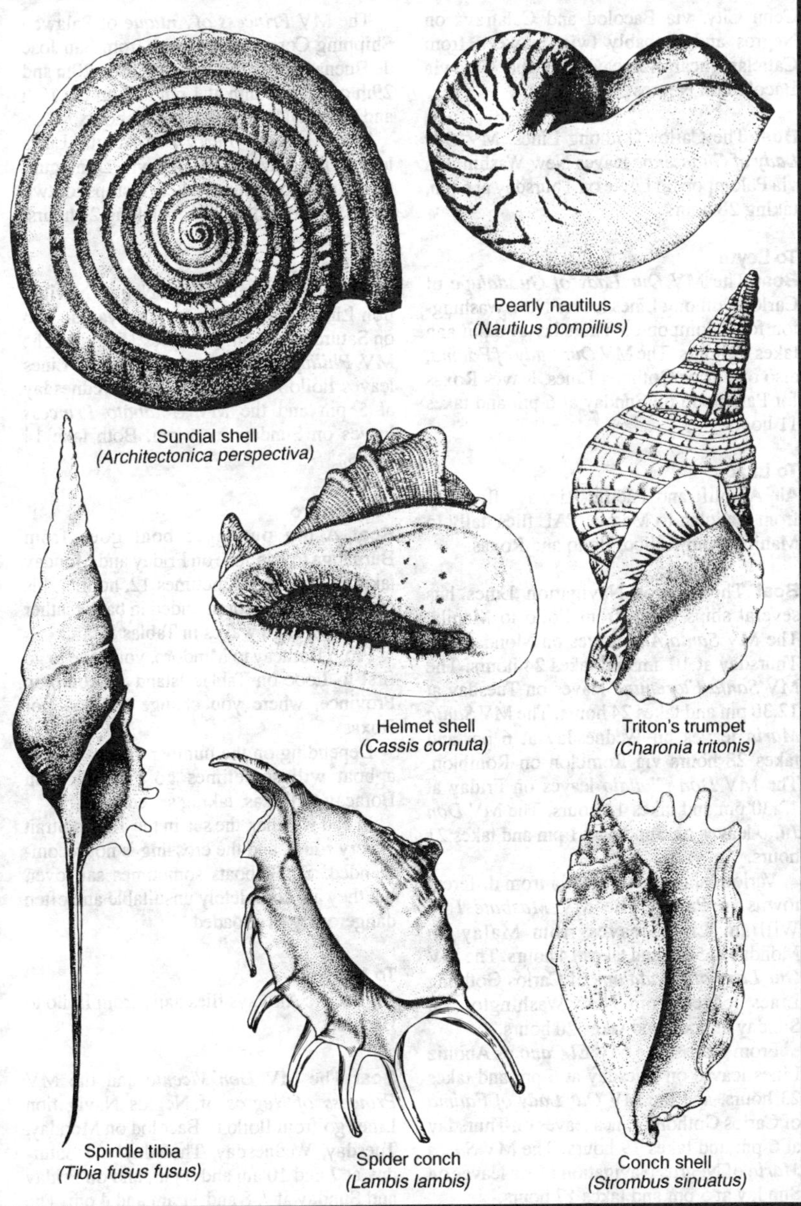
Sundial shell
(Architectonica perspectiva)
Pearly nautilus
(Nautilus pompilius)
Helmet shell
(Cassis cornuta)
Triton's trumpet
(Charonia tritonis)
Spindle tibia
(Tibia fusus fusus)
Spider conch
(Lambis lambis)
Conch shell
(Strombus sinuatus)

Cebu City, via Bacolod and Calatrava on Negros and probably twice a week from Caticlan (near Boracay) to Cebu City via Bacolod on Negros.

Boat The Carlos Gothong Lines' MV *Our Lady of Guadalupe* leaves New Washington via Palompon on Leyte on Thursday at 6 pm, taking 28 hours.

To Leyte

Boat The MV *Our Lady of Guadalupe* of Carlos Gothong Lines leaves New Washington for Palompon on Thursday at 6 pm and takes 12 hours. The MV *Our Lady of Fatima*, also of Carlos Gothong Lines, leaves Roxas for Palompon on Sunday at 6 pm and takes 11 hours.

To Luzon

Air Aerolift and Pacific Airways fly daily from Caticlan to Manila. PAL flies daily to Manila, from Kalibo, Iloilo and Roxas.

Boat The Negros Navigation Lines has several ships going from Iloilo to Manila. The MV *Santa Ana* leaves on Monday and Thursday at 10 am and takes 24 hours. The MV *Santa Florentina* leaves on Tuesday at 12.30 pm and takes 24 hours. The MV *Santa Maria* leaves on Wednesday at 6 pm and takes 28 hours via Romblon on Romblon. The MV *Don Claudio* leaves on Friday at 12.30 pm and takes 14 hours. The MV *Don Julio* leaves on Sunday at 1 pm and takes 21 hours.

Various ships go to Manila from different towns in Panay. The MV *Masbate I* of William Lines leaves from Malay on Monday at 5 am and takes 14 hours. The MV *Our Lady of Guadalupe* of Carlos Gothong Lines leaves from New Washington on Sunday at noon and takes 20 hours.

From Roxas, the MV *El Cano* of Aboitiz Lines leaves on Tuesday at 6 pm and takes 23 hours, and the MV *Our Lady of Fatima* of Carlos Gothong Lines leaves on Thursday at 6 pm and takes 19 hours. The MV *Santa Maria* of Negros Navigation Lines leaves on Sunday at 5 pm and takes 17 hours.

The MV *Princess of Antique* of Palawan Shipping Corporation leaves from San Jose de Buenavista on the 2nd, 6th, 16th, 20th and 29th of each month at 1 pm and on the 10th and 26th at 11 am and takes 23 hours.

The MV *Super Ferry 1* of Aboitiz Lines leaves Boracay for Manila via Dumaguit, near Kalibo on Panay (where it stops for two hours), on Tuesday at noon, taking 22 hours.

To Mindanao

Boat The MV *Santa Ana* of Negros Navigation Lines leaves Iloilo for Cagayan de Oro on Saturday at 5 pm and takes 15 hours. The MV *Philippine Princess* of Sulpicio Lines leaves Iloilo for Zamboanga on Wednesday at 5 pm and the MV *Cotabato Princess* leaves on Sunday at 11 pm. Both take 14 hours.

To Mindoro

Boat A big outrigger boat goes from Buruanga to San Jose on Friday and Monday taking eight, and sometimes 12, hours. This crossing is not recommended in bad weather because of high waves in Tablas Strait.

From Boracay to Mindoro, you have to go first to Looc on Tablas Island in Romblon Province, where you change the boat for Roxas.

Depending on the number of passengers, a boat will sometimes go directly from Boracay to Roxas, taking seven hours.

In bad weather, the sea in the Tablas Strait is very rough and the crossing is not recommended. Small boats sometimes sail over, but they are completely unsuitable and often dangerously overloaded.

To Negros

Air Pacific Airways flies daily from Iloilo to Bacolod.

Boat The MV *Don Vicente* and the MV *Princess of Negros* of Negros Navigation Lines go from Iloilo to Bacolod on Monday, Tuesday, Wednesday, Thursday and Saturday at 7 and 10 am and 3 pm, and on Friday and Sunday at 7, 8 and 11 am and 4 pm. The trip takes over two hours. Note that these times change frequently.

The fully air-conditioned *Bacolod Express* leaves Iloilo for Bacolod daily at 7 am and 2 pm, taking one hour. Tickets are available at Negros Navigation Offices and cost about twice as much as for the regular ferries.

From Culasi, the MV *Queen Rose* or the MV *Princess Jo* leaves for Victorias's port Da-an Banwa daily between 9 and 11 am, and the MV *Seven Seas* or MV *San Vicente* leaves from Malayu-an for the same destination daily between 9 and 11 am. Either trip takes two hours. Culasi and Malayu-an are two small places near Ajuy on the east coast of Panay.

The MV *Santa Maria* of Negros Navigation Lines leaves on Saturday at 11 pm from Roxas for Bacolod and takes seven hours.

To Palawan

Air PAL flies daily from Iloilo to Puerto Princesa.

Boat The MV *Masbate I* of William Lines leaves Malay for Puerto Princesa on Saturday at 1 pm, taking 15 hours.

The MV *Princess of Antique* of Palawan Shipping Lines leaves San Jose de Buenavista for Cuyo and Puerto Princesa on the 7th and 21st of the month at midnight. It takes six hours to reach Cuyo and 28 hours to reach Puerto Princesa.

To Romblon

Boat A large outrigger boat leaves Boracay for Looc on Tablas twice a week, taking two hours, and for Santa Fe on Tablas daily at 6.30 am, taking over an hour. At Santa Fe, you can get a jeepney to Tugdan, Tablas Island's airport.

The MV *El Cano* of Aboitiz Lines leaves Dumaguit (Kalibo) for Romblon town on Saturday at 4 pm, taking six hours.

The MV *Santa Maria* of Negros Navigation Lines leaves Iloilo for Romblon town on Wednesday at 6 pm and takes 11 hours.

Romblon

Almost in the centre of the Philippine archipelago, Romblon Province is made up of about 20 islands and islets, the largest of which are Tablas, Sibuyan and Romblon. All three are hilly and Sibuyan is thickly forested.

Because of its large marble deposits, Romblon is also called 'Marble Country'. Experts consider that Romblon marble is at least equal in quality to Italian marble. It is usually sold as large blocks, but several families make a few pesos by selling handmade ashtrays, chess pieces, vases and statues. When passenger ships visit, people set up stalls on the wharf of Romblon town to sell marble souvenirs.

ROMBLON ISLAND

Romblon

The small port town of Romblon is the capital of Romblon Province. In the typhoon season, ships often take cover in its sheltered bay. The two forts of San Andres and Santiago Hill were built by the Spaniards in 1640 and are said to have underground passages leading to the coast. Today, San Andres is used as a weather station. From the forts there is a good view of San Joseph's Cathedral and the town with its Spanish-style houses. Dating back to 1726, the cathedral houses a collection of antiques that you can see on request.

A trip to one of the two lighthouses, Sabang and Apunan, makes a good outing. If you don't mind heights and trust in the stability of the lighthouse, you can climb to the top and enjoy the view over palm forests, rocky cliffs and marble quarries.

A round trip of the island by tricycle, including a vista of marble quarries and works, can be arranged for P150 in Romblon town.

The bay of Romblon is sheltered by small Lugbon Island, which you can quickly reach by outrigger boat from the harbour. The island has a beautiful white beach and a few cottages, but you should bring your own provisions.

Places to Stay *Sea Side Lodge* by the harbour has rooms for P30/60. It is unpretentious and fairly good. *Fest Inn* near the church has simple rooms for P35/70. *Marble Hotel* is a reasonable place with rooms for P50/100.

Places to Eat The *Kawilihan Food House* by the harbour is probably the best restaurant in Romblon. The landlord, Arturo Fabillon, will arrange island and diving trips on request.

Getting There & Away A boat does about four trips a week between Romblon town and Magdiwang on Sibuyan Island. This takes two hours. Outrigger boats leave daily from San Agustin on Tablas for Romblon town at 8 am and 1 pm, taking 45 minutes.

Agnay

About six km south-west of Romblon before Mapula, Agnay has a few wonderful large tree houses directly above the water on a beautiful beach. A tricycle there should not cost more than P4 per person, but agree on the fare beforehand.

Places to Stay The *Selangga Tree House* costs P50 per person with shower and cooking facilities but bring your own provisions from Romblon. Full board can be arranged. For information, ask Reynaldo Festin in Romblon. The *Villa del Mar*, outside Agnay, has rooms with fan and bath for P300 and with air-con and bath for P500.

TABLAS ISLAND

Tablas is the largest island in the Romblon archipelago. Travel is comparatively dear and it seems as if tourists are being exploited.

Outrigger boats go daily from Romblon harbour to San Agustin on Tablas Island, at 8 am and 1 pm, taking 45 minutes.

San Agustin

San Agustin is a nice little town and has a wharf for boats to and from Romblon town. You can also do day trips to the Bitu Falls near Dabdaban and the Cajbo-aya Ruins. The *S & L Lodge* is a simple place which has rooms for P20/40.

Getting There & Away Several jeepneys a day run from Looc to San Agustin, taking two hours. The 6 am jeepney from Looc connects with the boat to Romblon.

Calatrava & San Andres

At Kabibitan near Calatrava, the Tinagong Dagat is a 'hidden lake', which is really two lakes with diameters of 80 and 100 metres. A track runs from San Andres (Despujols) to the high Mablaran Falls.

Odiongan

Tricycles run a shuttle service to the small harbour which lies just outside the town of Odiongan. There are shipping services to Manila, Puerto Princesa (Palawan) and Roxas (Mindoro). Only large outrigger boats run to Mindoro. The *Shellborne Hotel* has rooms for P40/80 and with fan and bath for P45/90.

Getting There Several jeepneys run daily from San Agustin wharf to Odiongan, via Calatrava and San Andres, taking two hours.

Looc

Boats connecting with the jeepney from the airport sail from Looc to Boracay, at a cost of P50 per person, but the operators will demand P80. If you want to charter a boat it will cost P300 to 400. The trip takes two hours or more.

Places to Stay The *Plaza Inn* has rooms for P30/60 and with fan and bath for P40/80. There is a boat service to Boracay. *Tablas Pension House* has rooms with fan for P45/80. It is basic, but comfortable.

Getting There & Away Several jeepneys a day run from Odiongan to Looc, taking one hour.

Santa Fe

There is a daily outrigger boat from Santa Fe to Caticlan on Panay, via Carabao and Boracay islands. It picks up passengers who are coming from the airport in Tugdan and takes two hours. The fare to Boracay is P70 per person. If you charter a boat, it should not cost more than P300, but up to P700 may be demanded. This smacks of highway robbery, especially as the boat operators are very reluctant to bargain.

Places to Stay You can stay in private houses for about P25 per person. One possibility is with the tricycle rider Jonny and his wife, Sandra, who will also prepare simple meals.

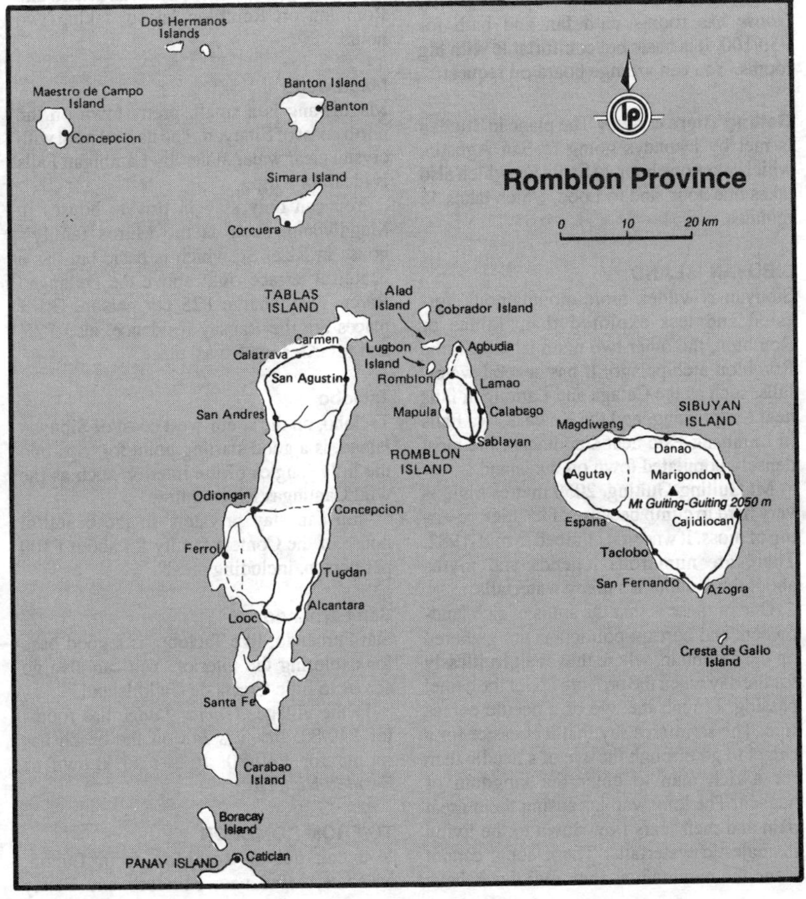

Getting There & Away There are several jeepneys a day from Looc to Santa Fe. They leave from the plaza and take 45 minutes.

Tugdan

You can get flights to and from Manila at Tugdan's airport. The planes to Manila are almost always booked out and it takes several days in Tugdan to get to the top of the waiting list.

Places to Stay The *Gutierrez Cool Spot* has simple rooms for P25/50. *Airport Pension House* has rooms with fan and bath for P50/100. It is basic but comfortable with big rooms. You can arrange board on request.

Getting There & Away The plane in Tugdan is met by jeepneys going to San Agustin, which takes one hour, to Santa Fe, which also takes one hour, and to Looc, which takes 45 minutes.

SIBUYAN ISLAND

Sibuyan is wilder, more mountainous, forested and less explored than Tablas or Romblon, the other two main islands in the Romblon archipelago. It has several waterfalls, such as the Cataga and Lambigan falls near Magdiwang, and the Kawa-Kawa Falls in Lumbang Este near Cajidiocan, the most densely populated town on the island.

Mt Guiting-Guiting, 2050 metres high, is very hard to climb because of its thick covering of moss. It was first climbed in mid-1982. There are numerous legends and myths about the mountain's many waterfalls.

One of these is that the souls of rich landowners and corrupt politicians are gathered on the mountain, where they wait fruitlessly for the day when the proverb about the camel passing through the eye of a needle comes true. The scriptures say that it is easier for a camel to go through the eye of a needle than for a rich man to enter the kingdom of heaven. The long wait is causing them great pain and their tears flow down to the living in majestic waterfalls. These souls cannot leave the mountain as their evil deeds have encouraged the growth of impenetrable moss and mud.

Another myth says that a giant magnet inside the mountain attracts climbers who then get caught in the moss and die of hunger. It also makes the instruments of aircraft go haywire, causing them to crash on the mountain.

Offshore, the coral reefs around Cresta de Gallo Island with its white sands are well known for the good diving they offer.

A boat runs about four times a week between Magdiwang on Sibuyan Island and Romblon on Romblon Island, taking two hours.

Magdiwang

Magdiwang is a small, pretty town on the north coast of Sibuyan. The natural pool with crystal clear water at nearby Lambigan Falls is ideal for a dip.

You can only stay in private houses in Magdiwang, such as the Muros family's house in Rizal St, which is basic but has a beautiful terrace right above the Dulangan River. They charge P25 per person. Other places are the Ransay residence, also P25, and Mrs Geneva Rivas' place.

Taclobo

Taclobo, on the south-west coast of Sibuyan Island, is a good starting point for trips into the hilly jungles of the interior, such as the wild Cantingas River valley.

You can stay privately in the beautiful house of the Cometa family for about P100 per person, including meals.

San Fernando

San Fernando, like Taclobo, is a good base for exploring the interior. You can also go across to little Cresta de Gallo Island.

In the village, *Jenmar Lodge* has rooms for P40/80. *Bernie's Inn* on the beach has rooms for P40/80. It is also known as *Bernie's Nipa Huts*.

TO/FROM ROMBLON

You can get to Romblon from Luzon, Masbate, Mindanao, Mindoro and Panay (see the Transport from Luzon section of the Manila chapter and the relevant To/From sections of this chapter and the chapters on the other islands).

To Luzon

Air PAL flies daily except Sunday from Tugdan on Tablas Island to Manila.

Boat There is a boat four times a week from Magdiwang on Sibuyan Island to Lucena which takes 12 hours.

The William Lines' MV *Masbate I* runs from Odiongan on Tablas Island to Manila on Thursday at 4 pm, taking 12 hours.

A boat sails daily from Romblon town to Lucena and takes 12 hours.

From Romblon town to Manila, the Negros Navigation Lines' MV *Santa Maria* sails on Thursday at 9 am, taking 13 hours, and the Aboitiz Lines' MV *El Cano* leaves on Saturday at midnight, taking 16 hours.

To Masbate

Boat A large outrigger boat sails from Cajidiocan (on Sibuyan) to Mandaon three times a week, taking five hours.

To Mindoro

Boat A large outrigger boat sails from Romblon town to Bongabong on Tuesday, Thursday and Saturday at 7 am, taking six hours, and from Looc on Tablas Island to Roxas on Saturday at 10.30 am, taking four hours. Additional trips may be run on Monday and Thursday and even daily if required. Sometimes they may run from Odiongan, also on Tablas Island, instead of Looc.

To Palawan

Boat The William Lines' MV *Masbate I* sails from Odiongan on Tablas to Puerto Princesa on Tuesday at 8 pm, taking 17 hours.

To Panay

Boat A big outrigger boat runs from Looc on Tablas to Boracay about twice a week, at around 2 to 3 pm, taking two hours.

The Negros Navigation Lines' MV *Santa Maria* sails from Romblon town to Iloilo on Tuesday at 9 am and takes 11 hours.

The Aboitiz Lines' MV *El Cano* sails from Romblon town to Roxas on Friday at 3 pm and takes five hours.

A big outrigger boat sails from Santa Fe to Boracay daily, soon after the Manila plane's arrival in Tugdan. The boat waits for the jeepney from the airport and goes on to Caticlan. The trip takes an hour or more.

Samar

The second biggest island in the Visayas, Samar lies between South Luzon and Leyte and is connected with Leyte by the two-km long San Juanico Bridge, which spans the San Juanico Strait. The island is divided into the three provinces of Eastern, Northern and Western Samar and is surrounded by about 180 small islands. One of these is Homonhon, where Ferdinand Magellan is reputed to have set foot for the first time on Philippine soil on 16 March 1521. Samar's landscape is hilly and steep and the greater part of the island is thickly wooded. Plains exist only along the coast and in the north, around Catarman.

Samar's climate is different from that of other islands in the Philippines, with dry periods only occurring occasionally in May and June. Apart from these, it rains the whole year, with most rain falling from November to February. In early October to December there are fierce typhoons. The best and sunniest time to visit Samar is from May to September.

The main crops are rice, maize and sweet potatoes, but Samar does not produce enough of these to be self-sufficient. On the other hand, there are plentiful harvests of abacas and coconuts, and Borongan, in Eastern Samar, is the leading copra producer.

Sohoton National Park, near Basey in Southern Samar, is Samar's outstanding natural attraction. The best way to reach it is from Tacloban on Leyte (see the section on the park in the chapter on Leyte). Rather less

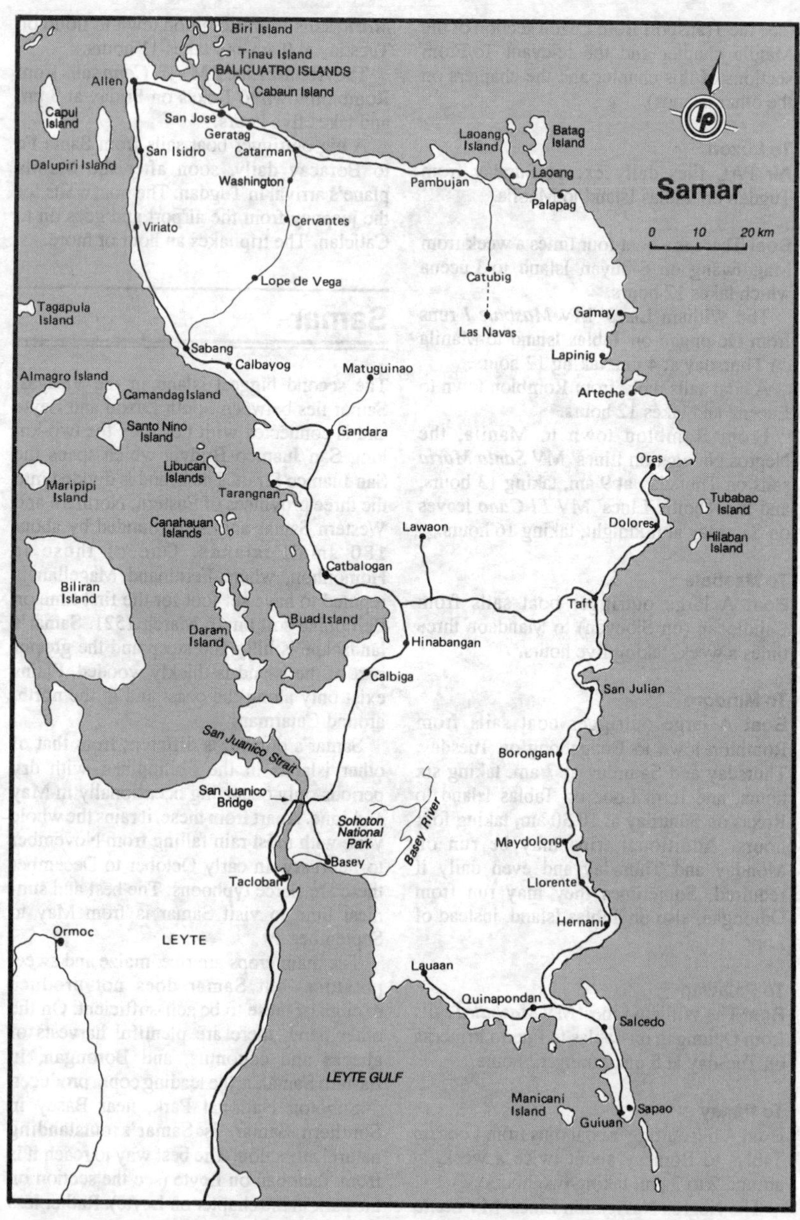
Samar
0 10 20 km
Biri Island
Tinau Island
BALICUATRO ISLANDS
Cabaun Island
Allen
Capul Island
San Jose
Geratag
Catarman
San Isidro
Dalupiri Island
Washington
Cervantes
Viriato
Lope de Vega
Laoang Island
Batag Island
Laoang
Pambujan
Palapag
Catubig
Las Navas
Gamay
Lapinig
Arteche
Tagapula Island
Sabang
Calbayog
Matuguinao
Almagro Island
Camandag Island
Santo Nino Island
Gandara
Libucan Islands
Maripipi Island
Tarangnan
Canahauan Islands
Oras
Tubabao Island
Dolores
Hilaban Island
Lawaon
Biliran Island
Catbalogan
Buad Island
Taft
Daram Island
Hinabangan
Calbiga
San Julian
San Juanico Strait
Borongan
San Juanico Bridge
Sohoton National Park
Basey River
Maydolong
Basey
Tacloban
Llorente
Hernani
Ormoc
LEYTE
Lauaan
Quinapondan
Salcedo
LEYTE GULF
Manicani Island
Sapao
Guiuan

exciting are the Blanca Aurora Falls near Gandara, between Calbayog and Catbalogan.

The inhabitants of Samar are Visayans who call themselves Waray and speak the Waray-Waray dialect.

Central and Eastern Samar are regarded as problem areas as fighting often breaks out there between government troops and the NPA. Find out what the situation is before you venture there although Northern Samar and the west coast are OK.

ALLEN

Allen has a wharf for ferries to and from Matnog on Luzon. There are also boats for Capul and Dalupiri islands, which lie offshore to the west.

La Suerte Lodging House, *Bicolana Lodging House* and *El Canto Lodging House* all have simple rooms for P25/50.

Getting There & Away

Several buses a day go from Catbalogan to Allen via Calbayog, such as the Golden Eagle buses at 9 and 10 am, which continue on to Catarman. The trip takes three or more hours from Catbalogan and over an hour from Calbayog.

GERATAG & SAN JOSE

Three km west of Geratag lies San Jose, from where several boats leave daily for the Balicuatro Islands offshore. They go to San Antonio on Tinau Island and Biri on Biri Island, and possibly other islands as well. If you want to spend a few days in the picturesque village of San Antonio on Tinau Island, you can organise an overnight stay at House Mendoza in Geratag.

Places to Stay

House Mendoza by the beach at Geratag has good, clean rooms for P25/50.

Getting There & Away

Several buses and jeepneys depart from Allen daily and go through San Jose and Geratag on the way to Catarman and Rawis (for Laoang). The trip takes one hour.

CATARMAN

Catarman, the capital of Northern Samar Province, is the starting point for travel in the north-east. Attractions are the Laoang or Batag islands, or, on the edge of the jungle near Las Navas, south of Catubig, a logging camp with the atmosphere of a gold diggers' camp. The best way to get there is by boat. You follow the mangrove river upstream from the hamlet of Laoang, on Laoang Island, until you get to Catubig. Then continue onwards through a beautiful landscape via Las Navas to an impressive waterfall where the loggers are.

An easy river cruise is to go along the Catarman River from Catarman as far as Washington. A boat leaves at 1 pm and takes less than two hours for the nine-km trip. You can go back to Catarman by jeepney. The airport manager has tourist information about the sights of Northern Samar and photos of the most attractive places in this province.

Places to Stay

The *Sanitary Lodging House* in Bonifacio St has simple rooms for P20/40. *Rendezvous Lodging House* in Jacinto St has basic rooms for P25/50. *Island Hotel* in Rizal St has fairly good rooms with bath for P35/70.

Getting There & Away

Several minibuses a day run from Catarman to Rawis (for Laoang) until about 5 pm. The trip takes an hour or more.

CALBAYOG

Calbayog is at one end of what is probably the most scenic coastal road in the Philippines; at the other end is Allen. The road runs along almost the entire length of the coast and is especially impressive near the village of Viriato (about halfway between Calbayog and Allen), with mountains, steep cliffs, distant islands and little bays with colourful boats.

There is a large waterfall near Viriato that can be seen as far back as the bridge near the river mouth. The area around Viriato is good for a day trip and could include a hike along the coast. It is no problem getting back to Calbayog as there are plenty of jeepneys on the road.

Approximately 50 km south-east of Calbayog are the Blanca Aurora Falls, the best known on Samar. To get there take the bus going to Catbalogan from Calbayog. Get off at the small village a few km beyond Gandara. A river boat for Buenavista leaves at 10 am and noon, taking one hour. From Buenavista it is three km on foot to the village of Blanca. Keep on walking and after about 10 minutes you will get to the falls. It's best to check in Gandara whether the waterfall area is still a stronghold of the NPA.

Places to Stay

Wayside Lodging House has good, simple rooms with fan for P20/40. *Calbayog Hotel* has rooms with fan for P35/70 and also has a restaurant. *San Joaquin Inn* (tel 386, 387) in Nijaga St has rooms with fan for P40/80, with fan and bath for P70/140, and with air-con and bath for P250. The common bathrooms aren't clean, however. It also has a restaurant.

The best hotel in Calbayog is the *Seaside Drive Inn* (tel 234) in Rawis. It has rooms for P40/80, with fan and bath for P110 and with air-con and bath for P220. It is nice and tidy and has a restaurant.

Getting There & Away

Golden Eagle buses run daily at 5 and 9 am from Catarman to Calbayog via Allen. The trip takes over two hours to Catarman and over an hour to Allen. The buses go on to Ormoc on Leyte.

There are also several jeepneys daily, taking over three hours to Catarman and two hours to Allen.

Several buses a day go from Catbalogan to Calbayog. You can get a Golden Eagle bus at 9 or 10 am going to Allen and Catarman. The trip takes two hours.

There are also several jeepneys daily, taking an hour or more.

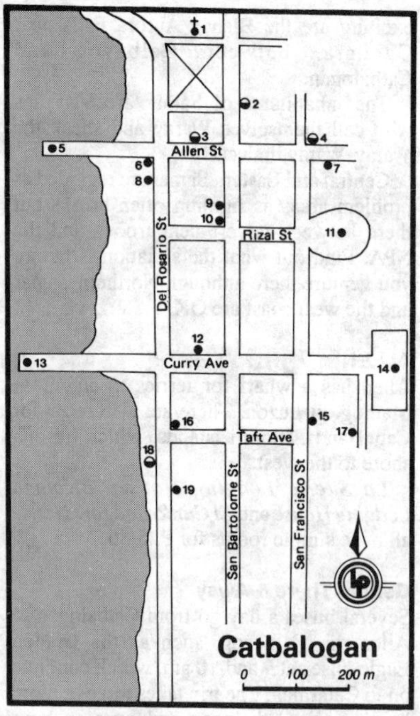

1 Church
2 Philtranco Buses to Manila & Tacloban
3 Buses to Calbayog
4 Buses to Tacloban
5 Pier 2
6 William Lines
7 Amparo's Hotel
8 Fortune Hotel & Restaurant
9 Town Hotel
10 D'Swing Beer Inn
11 Statue
12 Kikay's Hotel
13 Pier 1
14 Provincial Capitol Building
15 Samar National School
16 Lee's Kitchenette
17 Philippine National Bank
18 Minibuses to Tacloban
19 Western Samar Shipping Lines

CATBALOGAN

Catbalogan, the capital of Western Samar Province, hasn't all that much to offer travellers, so most people head straight for

Tacloban. You can, however, get buses from here that go across the island to the east coast. You can change US dollars and travellers' cheques at the Philippine National Bank.

Places to Stay

Town Hotel in San Bartolome St has simple rooms for P20/40 and with fan for P25/50. *Amparo's Hotel* in Allen St has rooms for P20/40. It's basic but habitable and has a restaurant.

Kikay's Hotel (tel 664) in Curry Ave has singles/doubles for P25/50, doubles with air-con for P150 and with air-con and bath for P170. It is fairly clean and good and has a restaurant, but only two rooms have air-con.

Fortune Hotel (tel 680) in Del Rosario St has rooms with fan for P60/100, with fan and bath for P130 and with air-con and bath for P200. It is simple and good and has a restaurant. *Tony's Hotel*, also in Del Rosario St, has rooms with fan and bath for P60/120. It's fairly well kept and has a restaurant.

Places to Eat

You can get good meals in the *Fortune Restaurant* in the hotel of the same name. *Tony's Kitchen* is another cheap restaurant where you can eat well.

Getting There & Away

Several buses and jeepneys run daily from Catarman to Catbalogan via Allen and Calbayog, such as the Golden Eagle buses, which leave at 5 and 9 am. Going to Catbalogan, the trip takes five hours from Catarman, four hours from Allen and two hours from Calbayog.

BORONGAN

Borongan, the capital of Eastern Samar, is an important trading post for copra, timber, rattan and bamboo.

Domsowir Hotel in Real St has singles for P55, with fan for P65 and doubles with fan and bath for P110. It also has a restaurant.

Getting There & Away

A daily SBL Lines bus runs from Catbalogan to Borongan at 9 am from Pier 1. The trip takes five hours.

Guiuan

A friendly little town on a peninsula in south-east Samar, Guiuan is fairly easy to reach by boat from Tacloban on Leyte. The Americans started their aerial attacks on the Japanese from here and the giant airport at the eastern edge was once one of the biggest US bases in the Pacific. Today grass grows on the unused runways.

Near Guiuan are a couple of beautiful beaches which are hardly ever visited, as well as numerous small islands west of Guiuan in Leyte Gulf.

Places to Stay

Arcenos Boarding House in Managantan St has simple rooms for P40/80 and with fan for P50/100.

Blue Star Lodging House in Concepcion St has rooms for P35/70 and with fan for P40/80. It's a reasonable place with a sing-along disco. The *Villa Rosario Lodging House* in Concepcion St has dorm beds with fan for P45, rooms for P50/100 and with fan for P65/125. It is basic, clean and good.

Places to Eat

You can get very cheap meals at the clean *Sherly Tan Restaurant* in Concepcion St. The *Blue Star Lodging House* serves meals if you order them in advance.

TO/FROM SAMAR

You can get to Samar from Cebu, Leyte, Luzon and Masbate (see the Transport from Luzon section of the Manila chapter and the relevant To/From sections of this and the Around Luzon chapter).

To Bohol

Boat The Sulpicio Lines' MV *Bohol Princess* runs from Calbayog to Tagbilaran on Thursday at 2 pm, taking 14 hours.

To Cebu

Boat The Western Samar Shipping Lines' MV *Helen* runs from Catbalogan to Cebu

City twice weekly, usually on Thursday and Monday at 6 pm, taking 14 hours.

To Leyte

Bus Several Philtranco and Golden Eagle buses run daily from Catarman, Calbayog and Catbalogan to Tacloban along the west coast of Samar, either to Tacloban only or on the way to Ormoc or Mindanao. The buses leave Catbalogan at 4, 10 and 11 am and 2 pm from the Petron service station. In between, other buses leave about every 30 minutes.

The trip takes two hours from Catbalogan to Tacloban.

Boat The William Lines' MV *Cebu Princess* leaves Catbalogan for Ormoc on Saturday at midnight, taking seven hours.

The K & T Shipping Lines' MV *Stacey* leaves Guiuan for Tacloban every second day at 10 pm, taking six hours.

To Luzon

Air PAL flies daily from Calbayog to Manila and from Catarman to Manila.

Bus An Inland Trailways air-con bus runs from Catarman to Manila daily at 8 am. It takes 23 hours, including the Allen-Matnog ferry. The trip finishes at Pasay (E de los Santos Ave) in Manila. There is also a Philtranco bus.

Philtranco air-con buses run daily from Catbalogan and Calbayog to Manila. The bus comes from Mindanao or Leyte and is mostly full. The trip takes 23 and 25 hours respectively, including the San Isidro-Matnog ferry.

Boat Depending on the season, two to four ferries a day run from Allen and San Isidro to Matnog, usually leaving between 5 and 8 am. Further trips are likely between 10 am and 1 pm and during the afternoon. The trip takes one to two hours.

The Sulpicio Lines' MV *Cebu City* leaves Calbayog for Manila on Wednesday at 10 am. The trip takes 27 hours via Masbate on Masbate.

The William Lines' MV *Tacloban City* leaves Catbalogan for Manila on Wednesday at 7 pm and takes 18 hours.

To Masbate

Boat The Sulpicio Lines' MV *Cebu Princess* leaves Calbayog for Masbate on Masbate on Wednesday at 10 am. It takes four hours.

Siquijor

The island of Siquijor is about 20 km east of southern Negros and is one of the smallest provinces in the Philippines. The main towns of this pleasant province are Siquijor, Larena, Maria and Lazi. Siquijor is the capital and Larena and Lazi have ports with connections to other islands. A surfaced road encircles this hilly island, connecting its well-kept villages and small towns; jeepneys and tricycles are the main means of transport. The 70,000 inhabitants are both friendly and pleasantly unobtrusive. The main industries are agriculture and fishing. Manganese mining north-west of Maria reached its peak before World War II, and deposits of copper and silver have not yet been mined.

When the Spaniards discovered the island, they called it Isla del Fuego, which means island of fire. This suggests that they saw a large fire as they sailed past. It is believed that what they saw were countless glow-worms.

There is a legend that millions of years ago Siquijor lay completely under water. It emerged from the sea amid crashing thunder and flashing lightning. Fossils of mussels, snails and other underwater creatures can still be found in the mountainous interior and are quoted as evidence for this belief.

You can tell that there is something mysterious about Siquijor when you tell Filipinos that you intend to travel there. They will tell you about witches and magicians and healers with wondrous powers. Many strange events take place on this singular island and are enhanced by the practice of voodoo and black magic. Filipinos will warn

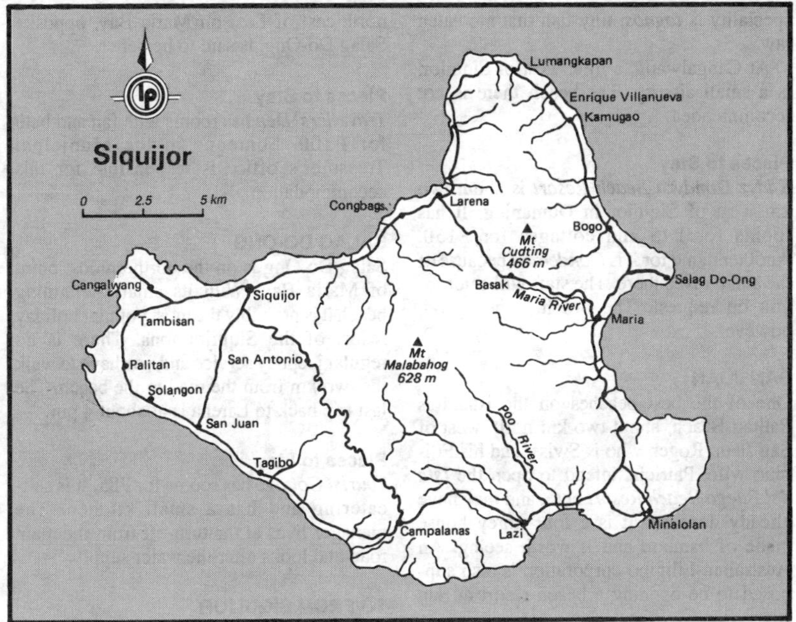

you that it is better to avoid it for your own safety's sake.

LARENA

Larena is a pretty little place with a few beautiful houses. The place comes to life only when a boat docks or departs or when the locals get together for their twice weekly festivals and dance uninhibitedly in the streets.

If you walk to Congbagsa and go on along the road that branches off to the right, past the large white building of the National Food Authority, you will reach a beautiful bay with a white beach. If there weren't so many sharp-edged stones in the water, the place would be perfect. There is a very refreshing spring in the rocks here.

Places to Stay

The *Tourist Guest House*, just a few minutes' walk uphill from the wharf, has unadorned rooms for P40/80. *Louisa & Son's Lodge* at the wharf has rooms for P25/50. Louisa and Douglas are very helpful and have some good information. You can hire a motorbike for about P100.

Sandugan White Beach Nipa Hut, some 400 metres off the ring road, about six km north of Larena, has cottages with rooms with bath for P120/240. It is a beautiful place to stay at, and has cooking facilities, but the staff will prepare meals for you if you arrange it first with the owner, Nick Buca.

Places to Eat

There is a fairly large restaurant near the market, where the jeepneys wait for passengers. A few smaller places are near the wharf.

SIQUIJOR

The small town of Siquijor is the capital of the island. It has a Provincial Capitol Building, a church, a hospital and a post office. You can get Filipino sardines, called *ihalason*, cheaply at the market. Another speciality is *tognos*, tiny fish that are eaten raw.

At Cangalwang, a little west of Siquijor, is a small airstrip. The beach there is not recommended.

Places to Stay

Eddyz Dondyza Beach Resort is about two km west of Siquijor in Dumanjug. It has rooms for P75 and cottages for P150. Another name for it is *Dondeezco* because of the small disco there. The staff will cater for you on request. The beach is not good, however.

SAN JUAN

One of the best beaches on the island is Palitan Beach, about two km north-west of San Juan. Roger, who is Swiss, and his Filipino wife, Patricia, intend to open the *Isla del Fuego Beach Resort* here, and may have already done so. It is a four-storey house made of bamboo and is worth seeing. An Australian-Filipino corporation is also supposed to be opening a beach resort at San Juan.

SAN ANTONIO

San Antonio is in the mountainous centre of the island and is supposed to be the place for the nature healers, also known as *mananambals*. The road there is bad and not easy for tricycles to pass through. Don't expect to find a devil's kitchen there. The work of these healers has nothing to do with magic, but is an original attempt to effect cures through the use of herbs and other natural ingredients. A visit during Holy Week would be interesting, as this is when the quacks and 'druids' of the southern Philippines gather to exchange information and create dubious herbal mixtures after performing mysterious rites.

LAZI

Lazi has a small wharf and is similar to Larena. On Sundays, popular cockfights are held in the rustic cockpit. The coral beaches, a little to the east, are unsuitable for either swimming or snorkelling. Lapac Beach, north-east of Lazi on Maria Bay, opposite Salag Do-Ong, is said to be better.

Places to Stay

Travellers' Den has rooms with fan and bath for P100. Someone in the Municipal Treasurer's office is responsible for this accommodation.

SALAG DO-ONG

Salag Do-Ong is on the northernmost point of Maria Bay. With its small swimming beach it is probably the most popular holiday resort of the Siquijodnons. There is no regular jeepney service and you have to walk the two km from the road to the beach. The last trip back to Larena is at about 4 pm.

Places to Stay

Tourist Cottage has rooms for P85. It is self-catering and has a small kitchen. The manager lives at the turn-off from the main road and looks after the water supply.

TO/FROM SIQUIJOR

You can get to Siquijor from Bohol, Cebu, Mindanao and Negros (see the relevant To/From sections of this and the Mindanao & Palawan chapter).

To Bohol

Boat The Sweet Lines' MV *Sweet Time* sails from Larena to Tagbilaran on Sunday at midnight. The trip takes three hours.

To Cebu

Air PAL is planning a service from Siquijor to Cebu City.

Boat The George & Peter Lines' MV *Dona Rosario* sails from Larena to Cebu City on Tuesday and Sunday at noon and takes six hours.

The Georgia Shipping Lines' MV *Luzille* leaves from Lazi to Cebu City twice a week, taking six hours.

To Mindanao

Boat The George & Peter Lines' MV *Dona*

Rosario sails from Lazi to Oroquieta on Tuesday at noon. The trip takes four hours.

To Negros

Boat A large outrigger boat sails from Larena to Dumaguete daily at 7 am and takes two or more hours. For safety reasons, this service is not recommended in bad weather.

The MV *Catherine* sails daily at 7 am from Siquijor to Dumaguete and takes two or more hours.

GETTING AROUND

Numerous jeepneys leave from the market in Larena to go to various places around the island. Always ask about the last trip back or you may have to walk, hire a tricycle or stay the night. A tricycle should not cost more than P150 a day.

Mindanao & Palawan

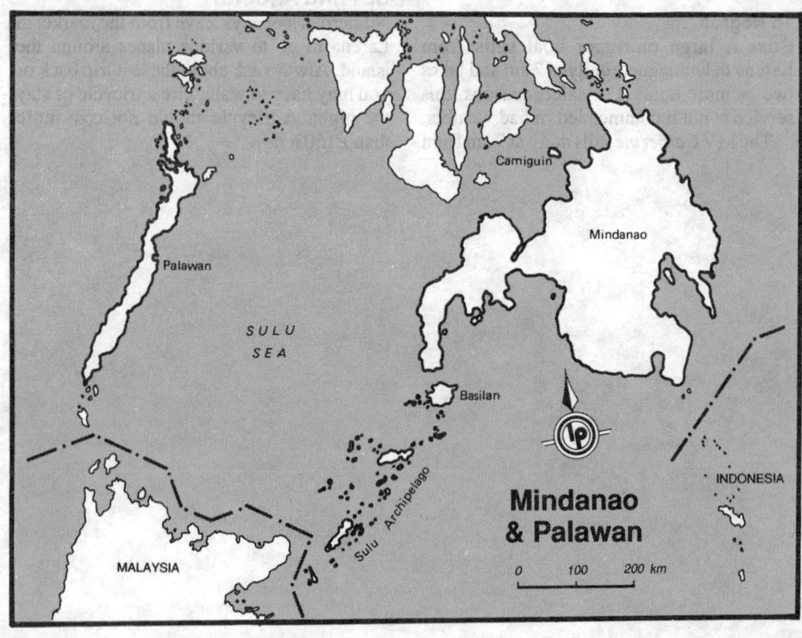

South of the Visayas is the large island of Mindanao, second in size only to Luzon. Smaller islands associated with Mindanao include the tiny island of Camiguin, off the north coast, the island of Basilan, off Zamboanga, and the archipelago pointing towards Borneo – the Sulu Islands. To the west is the long narrow island of Palawan.

Camiguin

Camiguin lies off the north coast of Mindanao. Though relatively small, it has no less than seven volcanoes, as well as springs and waterfalls. The best known volcano is Hibok-Hibok, which last erupted in 1951. The volcanoes tend to attract the clouds and especially in the wet season from December to February there can be a lot of rain. The sunniest months are April, May and June. Camiguin is well known for its *lanzones* fruit, which grows on Hibok-Hibok's slopes and is the best in the Philippines. The colourful Lanzones Festival takes place every year in late October, usually 24 and 25 October, in Mambajao.

The Camiguinos are well known for their hospitality. Certainly it is one reason why the comparatively few visitors who have so far discovered it like to come back. The word Camiguin is pronounced like 'Come again'.

While it is possible to travel around the island on jeepneys and tricycles, which the locals call motorellas, there are very few vehicles between Yumbing and Catarman.

MAMBAJAO

The little town of Mambajao is the capital of Camiguin, which has been a province since 1966. There is a tourist information centre in the Provincial Capitol Building. Mambajao also has a branch of the Philippine National Bank (PNB); you can change travellers' cheques there, although the rate is not as good as in Cagayan de Oro or Cebu City, for instance. You might find a bit of social life in the Parla and Sunriser discos.

Places to Stay

Tia's Pension House is a nice big house near the Town Hall. It has singles/doubles for P35/60, with fan for P110/120 and is quite good. You can have meals cooked there or use the kitchen for a small charge.

Camiguin Travel Lodge is a basic place with singles/doubles for P35 per person. It has a restaurant, but is a bit noisy, as it is near the market.

Tia's Beach Cottages in Tapon, a few minutes from the centre, has cottages with bath for P150. They are clean and quiet and have electricity from 6 to 11 pm.

Gue's Cottages, a few minutes' walk south-east of the town on Cabua-an Beach, has cottages at P60 to P70 and is clean and quiet.

The *Tree House* at Bolokbolok, about a km north-west of Mambajao, has rooms for P40/70, with bath for P80/100 and cottages with bath for P100 to P120. They are planning to build more tree houses. There is a restaurant, a tennis court, windsurfing and paddle bancas, and you can hire motorbikes for P200 a day.

HIBOK-HIBOK VOLCANO

Standing 1320 metres high, Hibok-Hibok is the most active of Camiguin's seven volcanoes. On 5 December 1951 it erupted without warning, killing over 2000 people. A small collection of photos and newspaper cuttings can be seen at the Comvol Station which monitors volcanic activity. This is about 400 metres up the mountain and takes a good hour to reach on foot. The team from the station are happy to show you around and explain the use of the seismographic instruments. They appreciate small gifts like bread, sweets and cigarettes from outside.

The Comvol staff can no longer organise trips up the volcano. The guides arranged by the Provincial Tourism Office in the Provincial Capitol Building charge about P200 and go up through Esperanza. It is not practical to do the trip without a guide as there is no well-defined path. There are times when you have to walk through metre-high grass and there are no landmarks so that the whole area looks much the same. Once at the top, you can climb down to a moss-encircled crater lake. This takes about 45 minutes. If you start early, you won't need to spend the night up there, but if you decide to go down to the lake, it would be wise to spend the nights before and after the trek at the Comvol Station, which gives you much more time. Alternatively, you can take a tent and camp beside the lake.

AROUND MAMBAJAO

Katibawasan Falls

These falls are a great place to swim; they are about 50 metres high and have refreshingly cool water. There is a resthouse, but you have to take your own food. The best time to go there is from 10 am to 2 pm, when the sun is high. Admission costs P3.

Getting There & Away To go to the falls, go from Mambajao to Pandan, which is on the edge of town, by tricycle. You have to do the remaining two km to the falls on foot.

Ardent Hot Springs

A natural swimming pool with water at least 50°C, this beauty spot is soon to have its tourist facilities upgraded. Entrance is P2.

The *Ardent-Esperanza Mountain Resort* has dorm beds for P25 and cottages for P150.

Getting There & Away Go from Mambajao by tricycle to Kuguita; from there the springs are about 2½ km on foot. A jeepney service from Mambajao has been planned.

WHITE ISLAND

White Island is a small island about three km north of Agoho. It is simply coral and sand and offers good diving but no shade. To stay there overnight, you need to take firewood, food, sunscreen lotion and a sleeping bag. A tarpaulin or tent is needed as shelter from the constant winds. You can find most of the equipment you need in Mambajao. You are seldom alone as most of the local fishermen visit the island; in the mornings you can buy any quantity of fresh fish from them. Almost every day around 5 pm small parties start arriving to watch the sunset. There's always the chance of a lift if you need it. Later, as it gets dark, local people make for the island to catch crabs, which are then thrown alive onto the coals and eaten.

Getting There & Away

To get there, go by tricycle or jeepney from Mambajao to Yumbing, Naasag or Agoho, then charter a boat. At the White Island Terminal in Agoho and in the resorts there, you can organise a round trip for P80.

AROUND THE ISLAND

You can travel right around the island, which has a circumference of about 65 km, in about three hours, if you don't make too many stops. For the best connections, go in an anticlockwise direction, as the road between Binone and Mambajao is most travelled by jeepneys and buses and is your best prospect for getting transport on the return trip. Plenty of jeepneys also travel between Catarman, the second largest town on the island, and Binone. Along the west coast, however, be prepared to walk a few km, as only a few jeepneys run from Mambajao to Catarman and back, and the last jeepney from Catarman leaves at about 3 or 4 pm. For short distances you may be able to use tricycles but the service is only good in and around Mambajao. You are more independent of public transport with a hired motorbike and, although there is no commercial hiring, some motorbike owners in Mambajao are willing to hire out their machines for P150/200 a day. In the resorts you will be charged P200 a day.

Agoho & Bugong

A few km west of Kuguita are Agoho and Bugong, two small coastal towns which are popular with most travellers and which have accommodation. At Agoho you can get a boat to the offshore White Island for P80; every few days, a boat goes from Agoho to Jagna on Bohol to deliver fish so they might take you with them (see To/From Camiguin in this chapter).

Places to Stay *Camiguin Seaside Lodge* is also known as Agohay Cottage and is in Agoho. It has dorm beds for P30, rooms for P80 and cottages with bath for P150. It is clean and good and has a restaurant.

Morning Glory Cottages in Agoho has dorm beds for P35, rooms for P75 and cottages with bath for P125/180. It is comfortable and has a restaurant as well as good cooking facilities.

The simple *Caves Resort* in Agoho has singles/doubles for P40/70, with bath for P80/100 and cottages with bath for P100/120. It is homely and has a restaurant. There is also a tennis court and windsurfing, and you can hire motorbikes for P200 a day.

Jasmine by the Sea in Bugong has doubles with bath for P110 and windsurfing. It is good but relatively expensive.

Naasag

About an hour's walk from Naasag, three km south-west of Yumbing, you will find the Tangub Hot Springs. A winding road leads down towards the sea. The hot springs are considered unsuitable for swimming in, but you can sit on a rock in the sea and enjoy the mixture of spring and sea water at a pleasant bath temperature. You will also find good corals here.

Bonbon

Bonbon has some interesting ruined churches and a cemetery sunk under the sea.

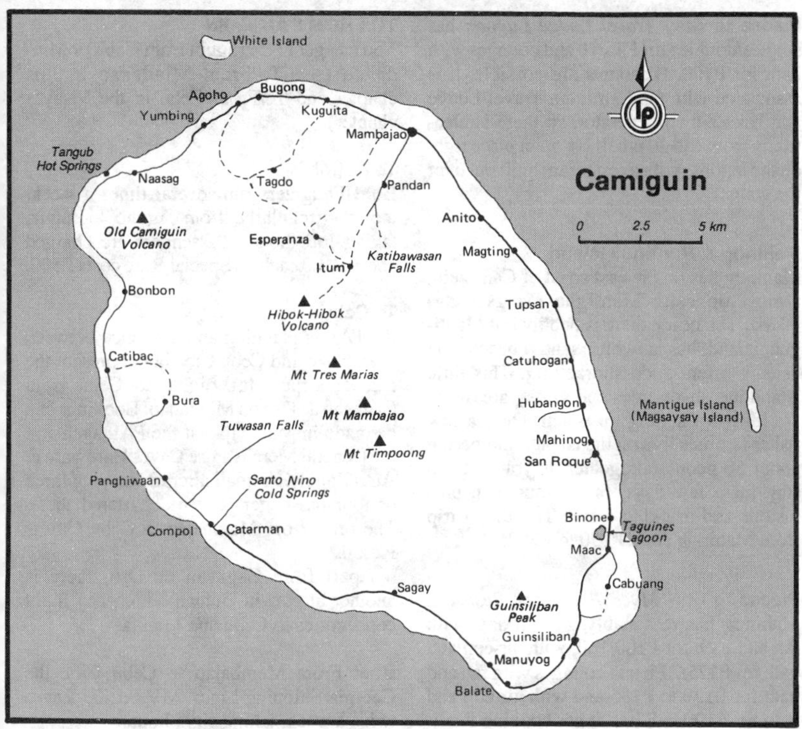

Some years ago grave stones could be seen at low tide; today a cross stands in the sea to mark the site of the submerged graves. Snorkelling is good in this area.

Catarman

Just outside Catarman is a track which leads to the Tuwasan Falls. The local people compare the two main falls with two different women: one, Katibawasan, wears lots of make-up; the other, Tuwasan, has a natural, unspoilt beauty. A hydroelectric plant has been planned but has not yet been built.

The nearby Santo Nino Cold Springs are refreshingly cool and you can swim in a nice large pool that is one to two metres deep. There are toilets and a picnic shelter. The place is also known as the Kyab Pool and is over two km off the main road.

You can stay in pleasant rooms at the high school for P30 per person.

Guinsiliban

This village in the south of the island has a 300-year-old Moro watchtower behind the elementary school. The planned Tamula Beach Cottages may be open by now.

Binone

Binone (Benoni) is the port for ferries going to and from Balingoan on Mindanao and is also a favourite diving place. From here boats go to Mantigue (Magsaysay) Island, which lies offshore. South of Binone is a beautiful artificial lake, Tanguines Lagoon, which is 10 minutes' walk from Binone and about two km from the wharf.

Places to Stay *Travel Lodge Lagoon* has singles/doubles for P35/70 and cottages with bath for P100. Discounts are possible. It is associated with the Camiguin Travel Lodge and has its own generator, so there is electricity from 6 to 10 pm. It is a quiet place right on the lagoon, with a restaurant built out over the water.

Mahinog & Mantigue Island

Mahinog lies on the east coast of Camiguin, almost opposite Mantigue (Magsaysay) Island. The beach there is pebbly but Mantigue Island has a white sandy beach and usually offers good snorkelling. This little island has shady trees and grassy areas that are ideal for setting up a tent. Only a few fisher families live on the island, numbering about 50 people altogether. If you want to stay for a few days, bring your own provisions and drinking water. The round trip from Mahinog costs P150 to P200.

Places to Stay *Mychellin Beach Resort* in Mahinog has reasonably good rooms with fan and bath for P100/160; with air-con and bath for P175/275; and cottages with fan and bath for P120 to P185 and with air-con and bath for P190 to P300. It has cooking facilities and motorbike hire.

Magting

It is claimed that there are million-year-old caves in Magting, where tools and skeletons of ancient humans have been unearthed. Unfortunately, a landslide caused by a minor earthquake blocked the entrance, so it is not recommended (and may not be possible) to go cave exploring. The only beach here is pebbly and not very good. Magting is about seven km from Mambajao; the trip costs P2 by jeepney.

Places to Stay *Padilla's Beach Cottages* has rooms for P25/50 and cottages with bath for P80. There are cooking facilities, and motorbikes, outrigger boats, masks and snorkels are available for hire.

TO/FROM CAMIGUIN

You can get to Camiguin from Cebu or Mindanao (see To/From Mindanao in this chapter and To/From Cebu in the Visayas chapter).

To Bohol

Boat Freighters run several times a week, though irregularly, from Agoho to Jagna, taking four hours. Passengers are charged about P100 each. A Special Ride costs P500.

To Cebu

Air PAL is planning an air service between Mambajao and Cebu City, but at present the nearest airport for flights to Cebu is in Cagayan de Oro on Mindanao. Bookings can be made in Mambajao at the PAL agents in the General Merchandise Caves Hardware & Auto Supply. A small aircraft carrying three or four passengers can be chartered there. The price from Mambajao to Cebu City is P2000.

Apart from Cagayan de Oro, there is another airport in Butuan which has flight connections to Cebu and Manila.

Boat From Mambajao to Cebu City, the Georgia Shipping Lines' MV *Luzille* leaves twice a week, taking eight hours.

From Binone to Cebu City, the Tamula Shipping Lines' MV *Ruperto* leaves twice monthly, taking 14 hours.

To Mindanao

Boat From Binone to Balingoan, the Tamula Shipping Lines' MV *Ruperto Jnr*, MV *Hijos* and MV *Anita* leave at 5.30, 6.30, 10.30 am, noon and 2 pm, taking an hour or more. It's possible that the 6.30 and 10.30 am departures may leave from Guinsiliban, south of Binone.

Mindanao

Mindanao is the second largest island of the Philippines. Its landscape is dominated by mountain chains running north-south. Close

Top: Mosque on Lake Lanao, Mindanao (JP)
Bottom: Maranao brass ware on display in Marawi, Mindanao (JP)

Top: Changing a flat tyre: a recurring problem in the Philippines (JP)
Bottom: Basligs (fishing craft) anchor off Zamboanga, Mindanao (TW)

to Davao is Mt Apo, the highest mountain in the Philippines. Mindanao is one of the Philippines' richest islands, even though little of its mineral wealth has yet been tapped. There is an occasional gold rush sparked off by rumours of a sizeable find, but at present most of the island's income comes from agriculture, with large pineapple plantations in the north near Cagayan de Oro and banana groves in the south near Davao.

It is not quite true that all of the Mindanao population is Muslim but certainly most of the Muslim Filipinos live there and on the neighbouring Sulu Islands. The area around Lake Lanao in central Mindanao is predominantly Muslim. There has been an on-going struggle for an autonomous Muslim state on the island for some years. The struggle between the MNLF (Moro National Liberation Front) and government troops can present some dangers to travellers, although, as usual, the situation is often portrayed as worse than it is. Nevertheless, you should inquire about possible disturbances before making overland trips in western Mindanao. Avoid buses carrying soldiers as these are especially likely to be shot at.

Rebel soldiers have recently caused further unrest on the island. On 3 October 1990, backed by a group of about 300 rebels, Alexander Noble launched an insurrection to establish Mindanao as a separate republic. Noble took control of Butuan, Cagayan de Oro and Iligan without a shot being fired. The rebellion attests general discontent on the island, which still does not have basic services such as water, electricity and rubbish collection. It was seen by many as an attempt to destabilise the government and oust Mrs Aquino. Unaided, however, by other rebel groups on Mindanao, such as the NPA or Muslim secessionists, Noble and his group were soon overrun by government troops and forced to surrender.

SURIGAO

Surigao, in north-east Mindanao, is the starting point for trips to Lake Mainit, the Placer gold fields and offshore islands like Dinagat and Siargao. It's always a bit rainy in north-east Mindanao and in December and January you have to reckon on heavy downpours. If you can put up with a few drops, however, you will be well rewarded by the magnificent landscape of the east coast. The best time to visit Surigao and its surroundings is from April to May.

The best beach with overnight cottage accommodation is Mabua, 12 km outside the city, a favourite weekend resort. Here the water is clear and the swimming is great, although the beach itself has black pebbles instead of sand.

Places to Stay

Flourish Lodge in Borromeo St, Port Area, has simple but relatively good rooms with fan for P50/60. *Litang Lodge* (tel 667) at 100 Borromeo St has rooms for P30/60-80, with fan and bath for P80/100 and with air-con and bath for P150/180. It is unadorned and the rooms are small, but it does have a restaurant.

Garcia Hotel (tel 658) on 311 San Nicolas St has rooms with fan for P60/100, with air-con for P200/240 and with air-con and bath for P200/220. It is relatively clean and good.

The Tavern Hotel (tel 293) on Borromeo St is the best place in town. It has rooms with fan for P50/100, with fan and bath for P100/140, with air-con and bath for P200/250, and suites for P500. It is pleasant and attractive and has a restaurant. You can arrange for the hotel boat to take you to the offshore islands.

Places to Eat

The restaurant at the *Tavern Hotel* in Borromeo St, where you can sit outside, right on the water, is exceptionally pleasant. The *Cherry Blossom Restaurant*, on the corner of San Nicolas and Vasques streets, has good food and live music. More small, reasonably priced restaurants are to be found on the waterside of the market near City Hall.

A little outside the city, in Rizal St, going in the direction of the airport, the dance enthusiasts gather every evening in the very

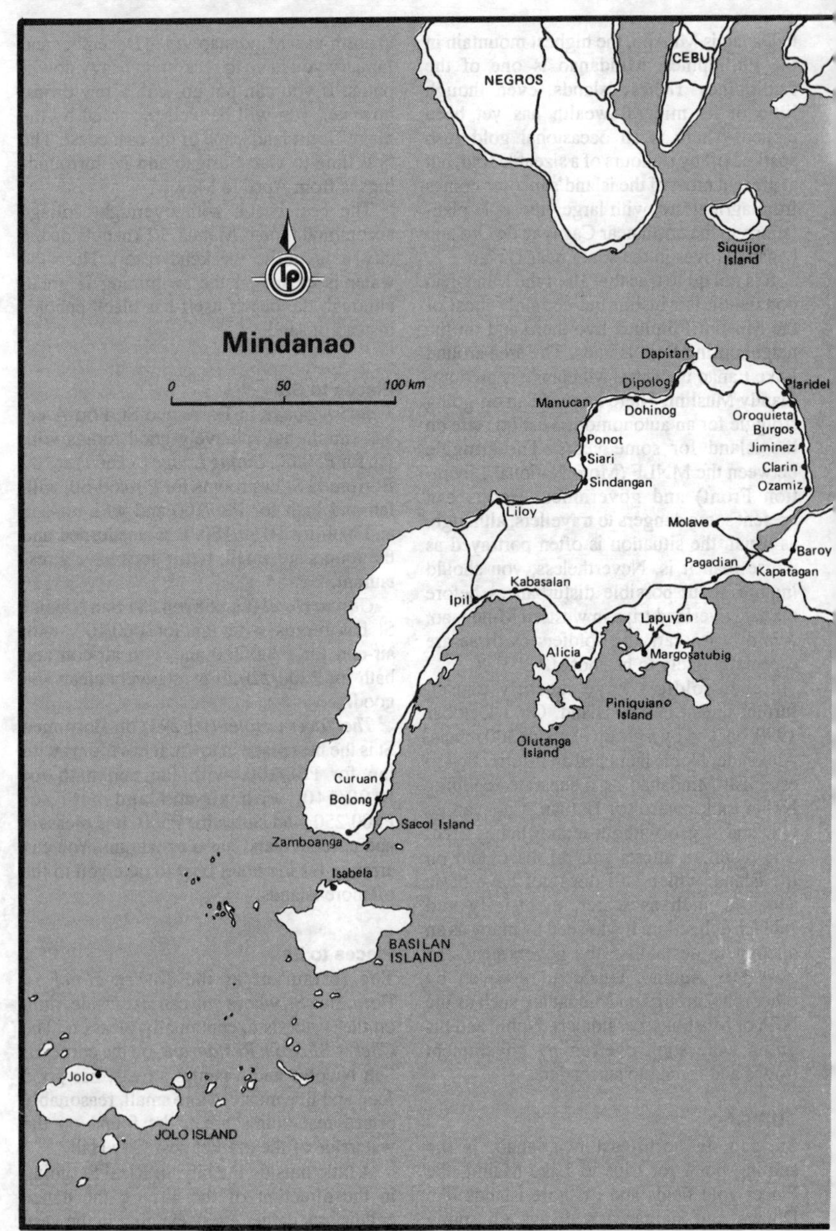
Mindanao
0
50
100 km
NEGROS
CEBU
Siquijor Island
Dapitan
Dipolog
Manucan
Dohinog
Ponot
Siari
Sindangan
Plaridel
Oroquieta
Burgos
Jiminez
Clarin
Ozamiz
Liloy
Molave
Baroy
Pagadian
Kapatagan
Kabasalan
Ipil
Lapuyan
Alicia
Margosatubig
Piniquiano Island
Olutanga Island
Curuan
Bolong
Sacol Island
Zamboanga
Isabela
BASILAN ISLAND
Jolo
JOLO ISLAND

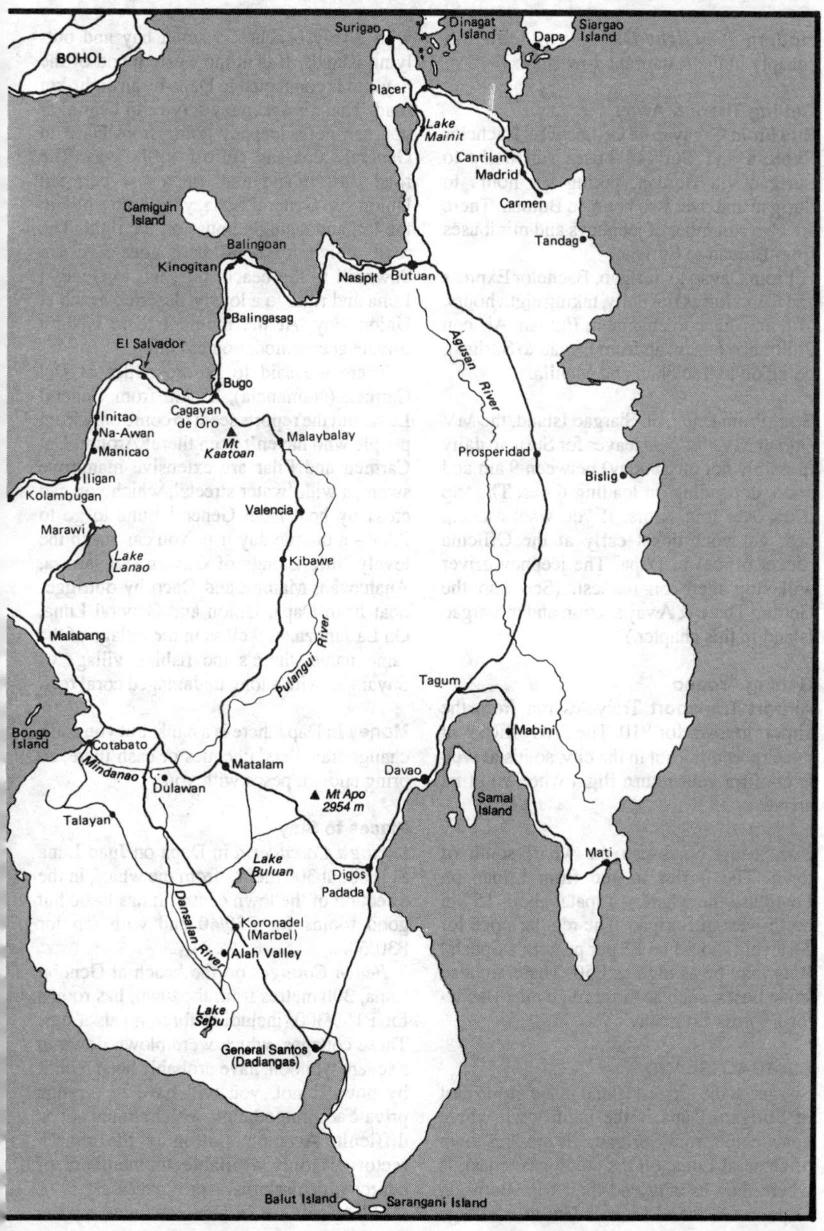
Surigao
Dinagat Island
Dapa
Siargao Island
BOHOL
Placer
Lake Mainit
Cantilan
Madrid
Carmen
Tandag
Camiguin Island
Balingoan
Kinogitan
Nasipit
Butuan
Balingasag
El Salvador
Agusan River
Bugo
Cagayan de Oro
Initao
Na-Awan
Manicao
Mt Kaatoan
Malaybalay
Prosperidad
Bislig
Iligan
Kolambugan
Valencia
Marawi
Lake Lanao
Kibawe
Malabang
Pulangui River
Tagum
Bongo Island
Cotabato
Mindanao
Mabini
Matalam
Davao
Dulawan
Mt Apo 2954 m
Samal Island
Talayan
Lake Buluan
Mati
Digos
Padada
Dansalan River
Koronadel (Marbel)
Alah Valley
Lake Sebu
General Santos (Dadiangas)
Balut Island
Sarangani Island

modern *Limelight Disco*; you can eat cheaply in the restaurant downstairs.

Getting There & Away

Bus From Cagayan de Oro, several Bachelor Express and Surigao buses run daily to Surigao via Butuan, taking six hours to Surigao and over two hours to Butuan. There are also a number of jeepneys and minibuses from Butuan to Surigao.

From Davao to Surigao, Bachelor Express and Ceres buses run daily, taking eight hours. You may have to change in Butuan. Air-con Philtranco buses run from Davao to Surigao, going on to Tacloban and Manila.

Boat From Dapa, on Siargao Island, the MV *Dua* or MV *Philippe* leaves for Surigao daily (possibly not on Sunday) between 9 am and noon, depending on loading times. The trip takes over four hours. If you want a camp bed, get your ticket early at the Officina (ticket office) in Dapa. The jeepney driver will stop there on request. (See also the Getting There & Away section under Siargao Island in this chapter.)

Getting Around

Airport Transport Tricycles run from the airport to town for P10. The PAL office is at the airport now, not in the city, so it's as well to confirm your return flight when you first arrive.

Boat Most boats use the wharf south of town. The ferries to and from Liloan on Leyte use the wharf at Lipata, about 15 km north-west of Surigao. The regular price for a tricycle should be P3 per person; a Special Ride may be as high as P50. There are also some buses, such as those run by the Bachelor Express Company.

SIARGAO ISLAND

Siargao is the biggest island in the group east of Surigao. Dapa is the main town where boats come from Surigao; the smaller town of General Luna, on the south-east coast, is where they usually end their trip. Between Dapa and General Luna is Union, a village with lovely beaches, a small bay and outlying islands. It is at the western end of the bay and is connected to Dapa by an eight-km road. There is a jeepney service to Union, or you can get a jeepney going from Dapa to General Luna and get off on the way. The road runs inland and, on a rise between Union and General Luna, you'll see a hill on the left and a single house on the right. The road which forks off here goes five km downhill to the beach, then left to General Luna and right to a lovely, deserted beach at Union Bay. At the moment there is only private accommodation at Union.

There are said to be crocodiles at Del Carmen (Numancia), 25 km from General Luna, but the reports seem to come only from people who haven't been there! Around Del Carmen and Pilar are extensive mangrove swamps with 'water streets', which you can cross by boat from General Luna to go to Pilar – a unique day trip. You can reach the lovely little islands of Guyam, La Janoza, Anahawan, Mamon and Daco by outrigger boat from Dapa, Union and General Luna. On La Janoza, as well as in the village of the same name, there's the fishing village of Suyangan with a long undamaged coral reef.

Money In Dapa there is a bank, but you can't change travellers' cheques or cash there, so bring enough pesos with you.

Places to Stay

Lucing's Carenderia in Dapa on Juan Luna St is about 300 metres from the wharf, in the direction of the town centre. It has basic but good rooms for P20/40 and with fan for P30/60.

Beach Cottages on the beach at General Luna, 300 metres from the town, has rooms for P150/300, including three meals a day. These cottages, which were blown down in a severe typhoon, have probably been rebuilt by now; if not, you will have to arrange private accommodation, which should not be difficult. Accommodation in the church rectory is only available to members of church organisations. Ask if necessary.

When you are in General Luna, try the

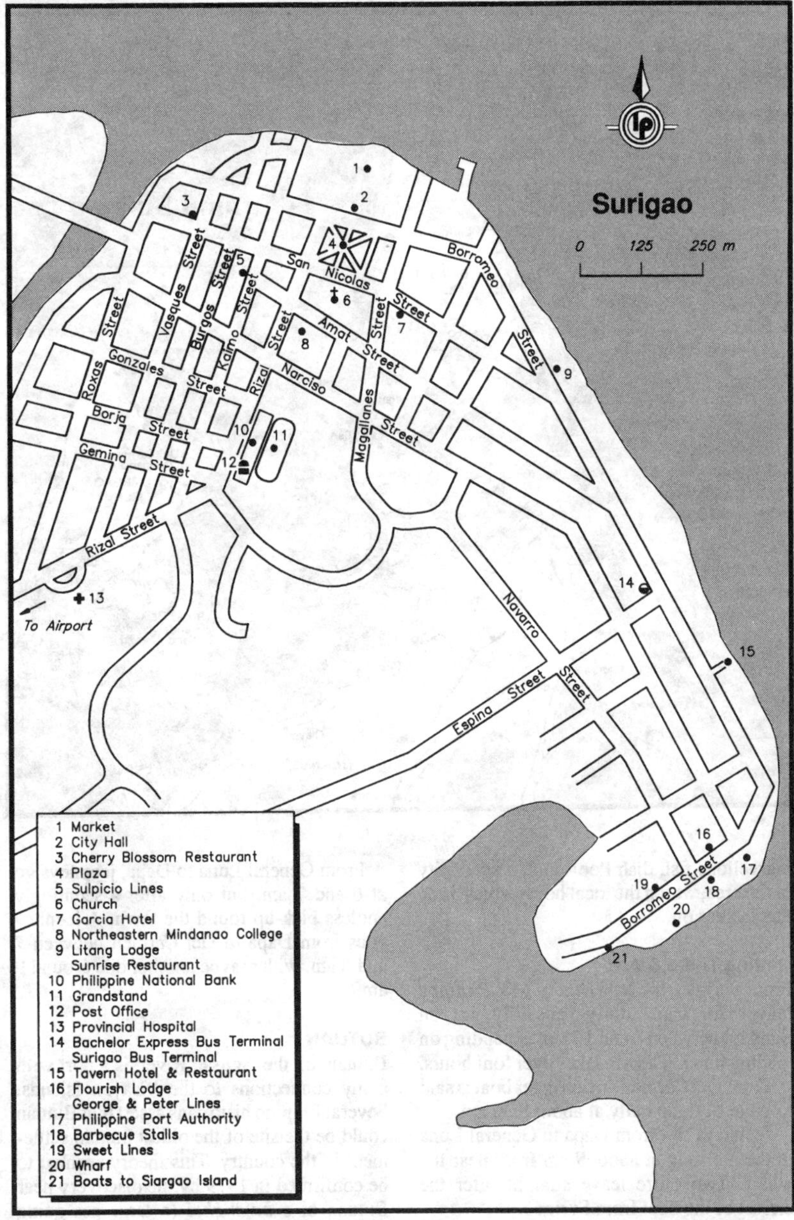
Surigao
0 125 250 m
Borromeo Street
San Nicolas Street
Amat Street
Vasques Street
Burgos Street
Kaimo Street
Rizal Street
Roxas Street
Gonzales Street
Borja Street
Gemina Street
Narciso Street
Magallanes Street
Rizal Street
Navarro Street
Espina Street
Borromeo Street
To Airport
1 Market
2 City Hall
3 Cherry Blossom Restaurant
4 Plaza
5 Sulpicio Lines
6 Church
7 Garcia Hotel
8 Northeastern Mindanao College
9 Litang Lodge
Sunrise Restaurant
10 Philippine National Bank
11 Grandstand
12 Post Office
13 Provincial Hospital
14 Bachelor Express Bus Terminal
Surigao Bus Terminal
15 Tavern Hotel & Restaurant
16 Flourish Lodge
George & Peter Lines
17 Philippine Port Authority
18 Barbecue Stalls
19 Sweet Lines
20 Wharf
21 Boats to Siargao Island

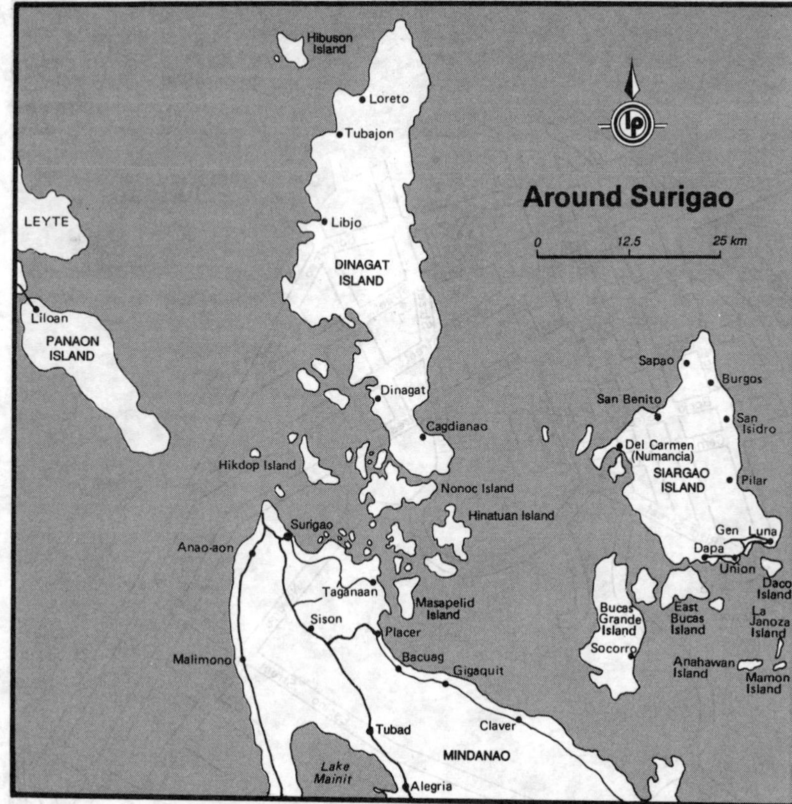

marvellous fish dish Poot-poot, a speciality of the area, which the local housewives pride themselves on.

Getting There & Away

From Surigao, the MV *Dua* or MV *Philippe* leaves for Dapa daily (possibly not on Sunday) between 8 and 10 am, depending on loading times. The trip takes over four hours.

From Del Carmen an outrigger boat is said to go to Surigao daily at about 8.30 am.

Jeepneys run from Dapa to General Luna in the morning at about 9 am from near the wharf. Two more leave straight after the arrival of the boat from Surigao.

From General Luna to Dapa, jeepneys go at 6 and 7 am, but only after a seemingly endless pick-up round the town. A jeepney goes from Dapa to Del Carmen between 7 and 8 am, with maybe another one around 9 am.

BUTUAN

Butuan, on the Agusan River, is a port with many connections to the Visayan Islands. Several Filipino historians assert that Butuan could be the site of the oldest human settlement in the country. This theory seemed to be confirmed in 1979 by the discovery near Butuan of a *balanghai* (a large sea-going outrigger boat) thought to be over 1000 years old. In 1984, not far from the Agusan River, human bones, including skulls, were found together with death masks, porcelain, pottery and jewellery, which indicated an even earlier occupation of Butuan. You can see the balanghai in a specially made glass showcase in the place it was found outside the town. The 1984 finds are displayed in a museum on the edge of town.

Balanghai

Places to Stay – bottom end
A & Z Lowcost Lodging House I in Langihan Rd has basic rooms for P25/50 and with fan for P35/60. *A & Z Lowcost Lodging House II* is on the corner of Burgos and San Francisco streets.

Elite Hotel (tel 3133), on the corner of San Jose and Concepcion streets, has rooms for P40/60, with fan for P60/75, with fan and bath for P89/100 and with air-con and bath for P120/150. It is unadorned but relatively clean and good.

Imperial Hotel (tel 2199) in San Francisco St has singles/doubles with fan for P40/70, singles with fan and bath for P70 and rooms with air-con and bath for P100, P140/160 and P180. It is clean and relatively good.

The *New Narra Hotel* (tel 3145) at 1100 R Calo St, in the suburb of Bading, has rooms with fan and bath for P100/120 and with air-con and bath for P150/200. It is homely and has a restaurant. It is in a quiet location slightly outside the city centre and has transport to the airport.

Century Hotel (tel 2547) in Villanueva St has good, clean rooms with fan and bath for P100/170 and with air-con and bath for P250/290.

Places to Stay – top end
Almont Hotel (tel 3332) in San Jose St has rooms with air-con and bath for P300/420 and 580. It is clean and good and has a restaurant.

Getting There & Away
From Surigao several Philtranco and Bachelor Express buses run to Butuan daily; they also go to Davao, Cagayan de Oro or Iligan via Butuan. It takes two hours and the last bus usually leaves at about 6 pm.

From Davao, Bachelor Express and Ceres Liner buses run daily to Butuan, the last leaving at about 1.30 pm. They take over six hours. Air-con Philtranco buses also run from Davao to Butuan and go on to Tacloban and Manila via Surigao.

From Cagayan de Oro, several Bachelor Express buses run daily to Butuan, taking three hours or more.

Getting Around
Airport Transport The road from Butuan to Cagayan de Oro is about 200 metres from the airport. To the left it goes to Butuan and to the right it goes to Balingoan (for Camiguin) and Cagayan de Oro. Buses pass along here. A taxi from the airport to Butuan costs about P25; a jeepney costs P2.

Boat Not all boats from other islands come to the river port of Butuan. Trans-Asia Shipping Lines' vessels to and from Bohol use the seaport of Nasipit/Lumbacan. Jeepneys run between Nasipit/Lumbacan and Butuan, taking 30 minutes. They leave Butuan from the shipping agencies in R Calo St.

BALINGOAN
A small coastal town on the road from Butuan to Cagayan de Oro, Balingoan is the

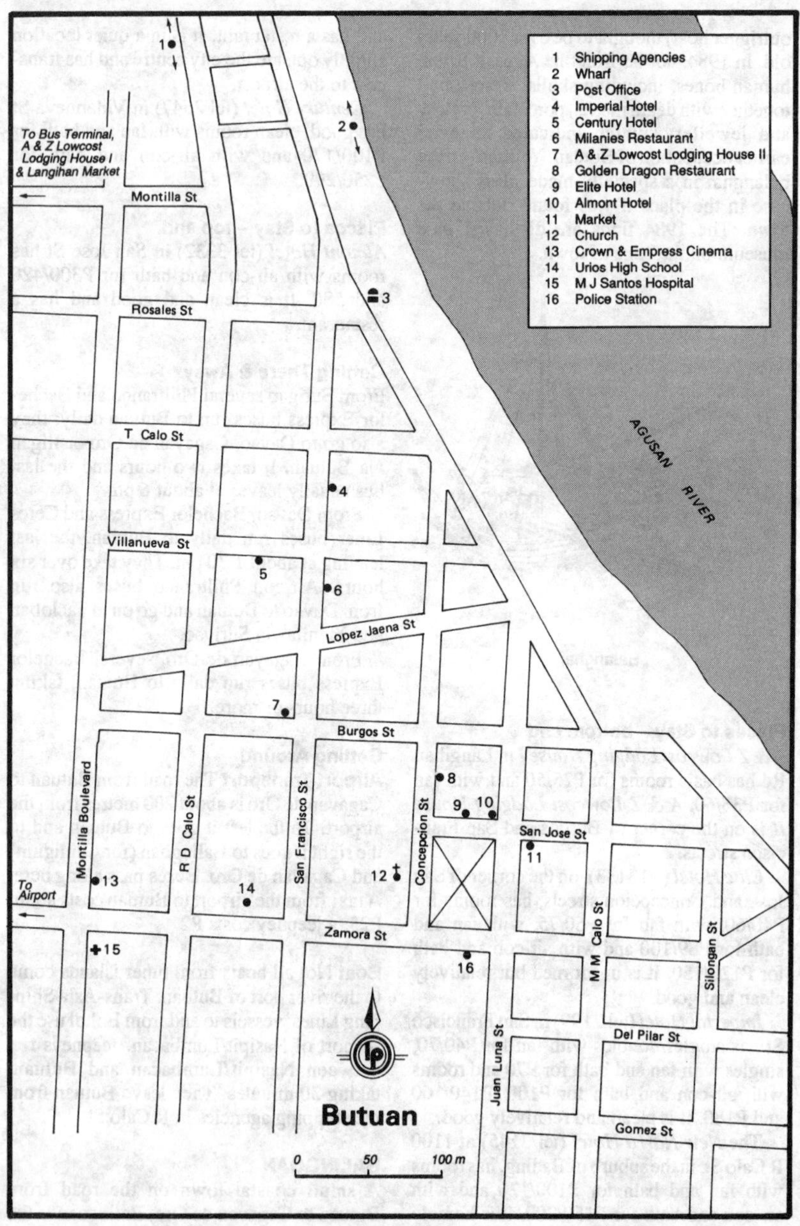
1 Shipping Agencies
2 Wharf
3 Post Office
4 Imperial Hotel
5 Century Hotel
6 Milanies Restaurant
7 A & Z Lowcost Lodging House II
8 Golden Dragon Restaurant
9 Elite Hotel
10 Almont Hotel
11 Market
12 Church
13 Crown & Empress Cinema
14 Urios High School
15 M J Santos Hospital
16 Police Station
To Bus Terminal, A & Z Lowcost Lodging House I & Langihan Market
Montilla St
Rosales St
T Calo St
Villanueva St
Lopez Jaena St
Burgos St
Zamora St
San Jose St
Del Pilar St
Gomez St
Montilla Boulevard
R D Calo St
San Francisco St
Concepcion St
Juan Luna St
M M Calo St
Silongan St
To Airport
AGUSAN RIVER
Butuan
0
50
100 m

departure point for ships going to nearby Camiguin Island. (See also To/From Mindanao in this chapter.)

Ligaya's Restaurant & Cold Spot has simple rooms with fan for P20/30. There is a similar lodging place opposite.

CAGAYAN DE ORO

This is a clean and friendly university city with numerous schools. An old legend tells how the name Cagayan is derived from the word 'kagayha-an', which means shame. The legend tells of an attack on a Manobo tribe by another tribe. The defeated villagers planned to retaliate, but, before they could, their chieftain fell in love with the daughter of the enemy chieftain and married her. His disgusted subjects referred to their village as a place of shame or 'kagayha-an'. The Spaniards pronounced it Cagayan and, after they discovered gold in the river, it became Cagayan de Oro.

The Xavier University Folk Museum in Corrales Ave is worth seeing.

Places to Stay

Casa Filipina Lodge (tel 3383) in Borja St has rooms with fan for P37/54 and with fan and bath for P50/70. The annexe rooms are nice and quiet.

Mabini Lodge (tel 3539) in Mabini St, on the corner of Velez St, has rooms with fan for P55/100 and with air-con and bath for P200. It is clean and good and has a restaurant.

City Pension (tel 2843), on the corner of Capistrano and Yacapin streets, has reasonable rooms with air-con for P120.

The *New Golden Star Inn* (tel 4079) at 129 Borja St has rooms with fan for P80/120, with fan and bath for P100/130, and with air-con and bath for P200. It is relatively good, with a pleasant balcony.

Sampaguita Inn (tel 2640, 2740) in Borja St has rooms with fan and bath for P100/115, and with air-con and bath for P125/145. It is basic and relatively good, but the bedrooms don't live up to the standard of the lobby.

Oro United Inn (tel 4884) in Gomez St has rooms with fan and bath for P110/155 and with air-con and bath for P165/210.

Bonair Inn (tel 5431) in Don Sergio Osmena St has singles with fan and bath for P110 and rooms with air-con and bath for P150/220.

Hotel Tropicana (tel 3494, 3949) has good rooms with air-con and bath for P235/495.

VIP Hotel (tel 3629, 3892; tlx 48404 ITT VIPHTL PM) in Velez St is the best hotel in town. It has rooms with air-con and bath for P430-590/490-700, and suites from P715. It has a restaurant and the dearer rooms have a fridge and TV.

Places to Eat

The *Spoon Restaurant* in Capistrano St has good, reasonably priced menus that change daily. The *Ice Cream Palace* opposite has a good chop suey but it's fairly expensive. In the same street, opposite the Kairo Movie House, is a clean place called *Thrive's Chicken House*.

You get big meals which are very good value at the *Bagong Lipunan Restaurant* in Velez St, between the VIP Hotel and the Hotel Tropicana. The *Patio Restaurant* downstairs in the VIP Hotel is open 24 hours a day and the lunch and dinner specials are pretty good value.

A little further north is the air-conditioned *Caprice Steak House* and the small *Salt & Pepper Restaurant*, which has a limited menu but cheap beer.

Entertainment

If you want nightlife, Cagayan de Oro has plenty of discos, as well as 20 bars and eight cinemas. The most popular are the *Alabama Disco* in Capistrano St and the *On Deck Disco* in Taal St which has live music. The *Love City Disco*, also in Taal St, has live shows. So does the Garden Restaurant near Gaston Park, but bands appear there as well. In the *Ice Cream Palace Disco* in Capistrano St you can watch go-go dancers.

The Pelaez Sports Complex in Don Apolinario St is well equipped; its facilities include a large swimming pool.

Getting There & Away

Air PAL has return flights from Davao to

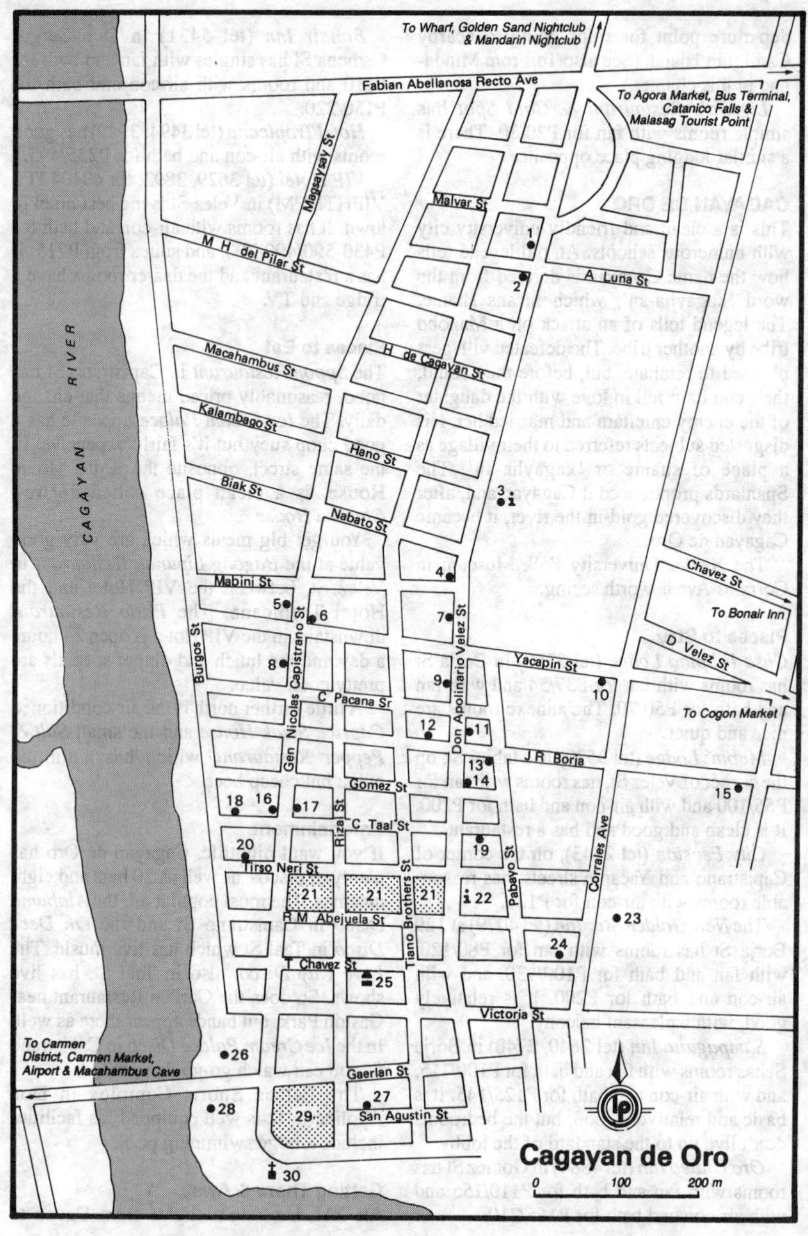
To Wharf, Golden Sand Nightclub & Mandarin Nightclub
Fabian Abellanosa Recto Ave
To Agora Market, Bus Terminal, Catanico Falls & Malasag Tourist Point
Magsaysay St
Malvar St
M H del Pilar St
A Luna St
CAGAYAN RIVER
Macahambus St
H de Cagayan St
Kalambago St
Hano St
Biak St
Nabato St
Chavez St
Mabini St
To Bonair Inn
Burgos St
Gen Nicolas Capistrano St
Don Apolinario Velez St
D Velez St
Yacapin St
C Pacana Sr
To Cogon Market
J R Borja
Gomez St
Rizal St
C Taal St
Tirso Neri St
Tiano Brothers St
Pabayo St
Corrales Ave
R M Abejuela St
T Chavez St
Victoria St
To Carmen District, Carmen Market, Airport & Macahambus Cave
Gaerlan St
San Agustin St
Cagayan de Oro
0 100 200 m
1
2
3
4
5
6
7
8
9
10
11
12
13
14
15
16
17
18
19
20
21
22
23
24
25
26
27
28
29
30

1 Caprice Steak House
2 Salt & Pepper Restaurant
3 Pelaez Sports Complex
Tourist Office
4 Mabini Lodge
5 The Bungalow Restaurant
6 City Pension
7 Hotel Tropicana
8 Alabama Disco
9 Bagong Lipunan Restaurant
10 Magnolia Ice Cream
Shakey's Pizza Parlour
11 VIP Hotel
12 New Golden Star Inn
13 Sampaguita Inn
14 Oro United Inn
15 Casa Filipina Lodge
16 Ice Cream Palace
17 Spoon Restaurant
18 On Deck Disco
19 Love City Disco
20 Philippine Airlines
21 Golden Friendship Park (Divisoria)
22 Tourist Office
23 Xavier University Folk Museum
24 Philippine National Bank
25 Post Office
26 Town Hall
27 Garden Restaurant
28 Riverside Park
29 Gaston Park
30 San Agustin Cathedral

Cagayan de Oro on Monday, Wednesday, Friday and Sunday. The trip takes 35 minutes.

Bus Bachelor Express buses leave Butuan almost hourly from 4.30 to 11 am for Cagayan de Oro; after that the intervals are longer. The buses go via Balingoan, which is the berth for boats to and from Camiguin. The trip takes over an hour to Balingoan and over three hours to Cagayan de Oro.

From Davao several Ceres Liner, Bachelor Express and Fortune Liner buses run daily to Cagayan de Oro, taking 10 hours. Fortune Liner also has air-con buses, taking eight hours.

Several Bachelor Express and Fortune Liner buses go daily between Iligan and Cagayan de Oro, taking an hour or more. Jeepneys and minibuses also cover this route.

From Pagadian, Bachelor Express and Fortune Liner buses leave daily for Cagayan de Oro, hourly between 4.30 am and 1 pm, taking over four hours.

From Zamboanga four or five Fortune Liner and Almirante buses leave daily for Cagayan de Oro, between 4.30 and 6.45 am. Each one leaves as soon as it's full, so you have to get to the bus terminal in good time or even book the day before. It's a 16 hour trip. Express buses – the ones with indicators saying 'Non Stop' or 'Five Stops' – are about three hours faster and only a little dearer.

Getting Around

Airport Transport The airport is barely 10 km from the town. Pu-Cabs may ask up to P100, but you can do the trip for P50. Hard bargaining may bring the fare down to as low as P25, but in that case the vehicle will be packed with extra passengers.

Bus The bus terminal is on the edge of the town beside the Agora Market. There is a jeepney service to the centre. The centrally located Golden Friendship Park is also called Divisoria, so jeepneys with this sign are going there. Jeepneys going from the town to the bus terminal will have the sign 'Gusa/Cugman'.

Boat The wharf is five km from the town centre. There is a jeepney service, which usually goes direct to the bus terminal. The trip by taxi shouldn't cost more than P10.

Tricycle Tricycles here run on a sort of fixed route and they usually leave only when they're full. The most central interchange is Cogon Market. If you go somewhere that isn't on the fixed route, for instance, from the bus terminal to a hotel off the route, it always counts as a Special Ride.

Warning The jeepneys and tricycles travelling from the bus terminal to the city are favourite haunts of pickpockets who travel in twos and often change seats to make the most of their opportunities.

AROUND CAGAYAN DE ORO

The Macahambus Cave is about 14 km south of Cagayan de Oro and can be reached by jeepneys going to Talacag. Make sure you take a powerful torch with you.

Even visitors who are not remotely interested in agriculture will enjoy a trip to the huge pineapple plantations at Camp Phillips, 34 km out of Cagayan. Bachelor minibuses go there and, with any luck, you may get to go on a tour of the plantations. On Wednesday and Saturday, jeepneys run the extra five km from Camp Phillips to the Del Monte Club House, where you can get very good, if not exactly cheap, meals in the Golf Club. The Del Monte Canning Factory is at Bugo, 15 km east of Cagayan de Oro, where the finished products are shipped away.

For a day at the beach, try Raagas Beach near Bonbon and San Pedro Beach in Opol, seven km west of Cagayan de Oro. They're nothing special but are OK for a quick dip.

MALAYBALAY

The capital of Bukidnon, which is the largest province in the northern Mindanao region, Malaybalay lies surrounded by mountain ranges in the valley of a tributary of the Pulangi River. Once a year there's the Kaamulan Festival, usually in November, but, if the weather's bad, it may be held in February or May. The members of the various cultural minorities living in and around Malaybalay get together to celebrate. They meet in Pines View Park, dressed in traditional costumes and play music, dance, and put on craft demonstrations.

Places to Stay

Panama Inn is in a central location in Fortich St and has rooms for P60/70 and with fan and bath for P70/90. The *Haus Malibu* (tel 5714), on the corner of Bonifacio Drive and Comisio St, has rooms for P100 and with bath for P180. It has a coffee shop, is comfortable and the staff offers real hospitality.

Getting There & Away

Bachelor Express and Ceres Liner buses run daily between Cagayan de Oro and Malaybalay, leaving hourly. The trip takes two hours.

ILIGAN

Iligan is an industrial town surrounded by factories. The nearby Maria Christina Falls will be the main source of power for the surrounding districts as far as Zamboanga, once the plant there is at full capacity. The power station so dominates the landscape that it's more likely to appeal to the technically minded than to nature lovers. To get to the falls, take a jeepney from Pier Terminal to Agus Bridge, about seven km away, turn left behind the bridge and walk for about half an hour. You can't swim in the pool and, as the river is a raging torrent, it's too dangerous; the attraction is to look down on the falls from above by going about 200 metres back towards Iligan from the Agus Bridge, where

1 Jade Tourist Inn
2 New Wharf
3 North Wharf
4 South Wharf
5 George & Peter Lines
William Lines
6 Bachelor Express Bus Terminal
Fortune Liner Bus Terminal
7 Marawi Terminal
8 SK Disco
9 Church
10 Maxim Inn
11 Maranao Handicraft
12 Canton Restaurant
13 Philippine Airlines
14 Bar-B-Q Inn
Maharaja Restaurant
15 Police Station
16 Bahayan Restaurant
Iceberg Café & Restaurant
17 Jelo's Ice Cream House
18 J&L Supermart
19 Niga Restaurant
20 Maria Christina Hotel
21 Market
22 Philippine National Bank
23 Post Office

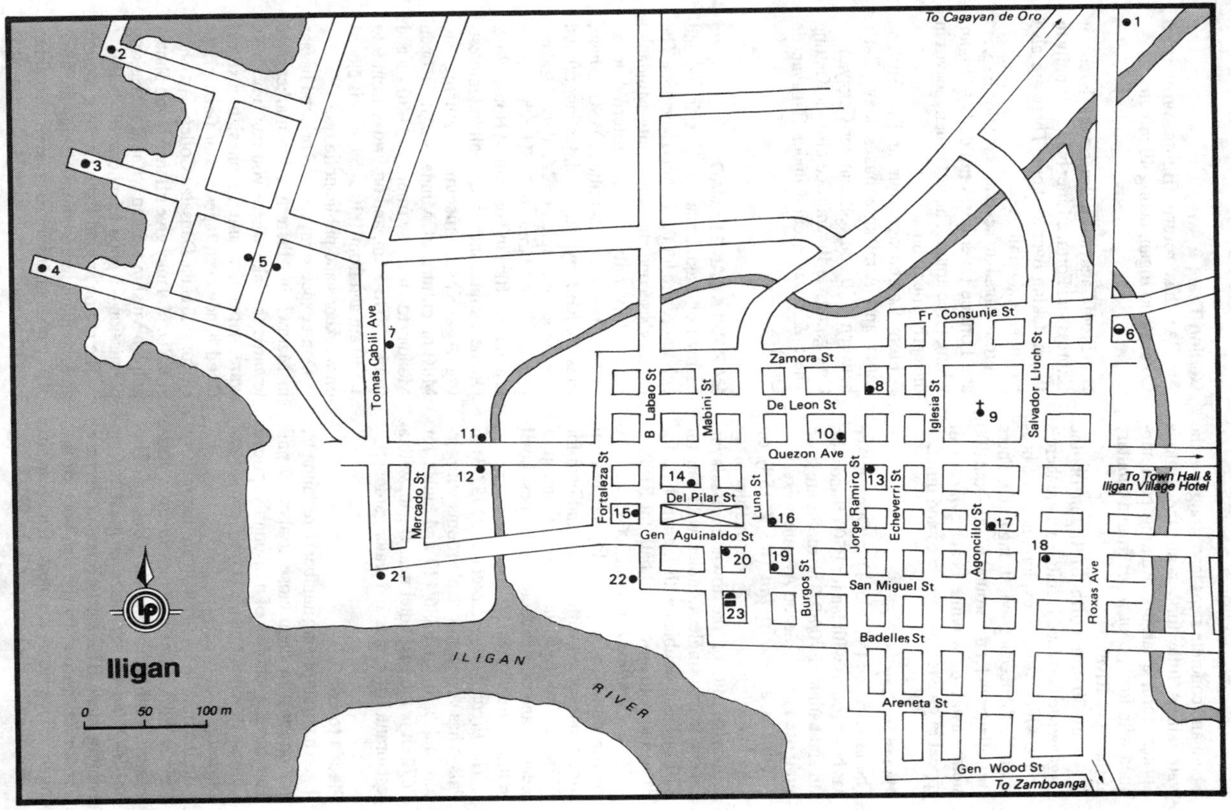
To Cagayan de Oro
1
2
3
4
5
6
7
Tomas Cabili Ave
Zamora St
Fr Consunje St
B Labao St
Mabini St
De Leon St
8
Iglesia St
9
Salvador Lluch St
10
11
Quezon Ave
12
Mercado St
Fortaleza St
14
Del Pilar St
Luna St
Jorge Ramiro St
13
Echeverri St
To Town Hall & Iligan Village Hotel
15
16
Gen Aguinaldo St
Agoncillo St
17
18
20
19
21
22
Burgos St
San Miguel St
Roxas Ave
23
Badelles St
Iligan
ILIGAN RIVER
0
50
100 m
Areneta St
Gen Wood St
To Zamboanga

a path and concrete steps lead straight to the waterfall. A little further on, the Timoga Springs form a large swimming pool supplied with fresh, cool water from a tributary of the Agus River.

About 30 km north of Iligan on the Cagayan de Oro road is Initao, where there's a cave which you can explore, near the hospital. You'll need a good, strong torch. There are cottages to let for around P100 about 300 metres away on a white beach which will appeal to guests wanting peace and quiet.

Places to Stay

The *Maxim Inn* (tel 20601) in Quezon Ave has basic rooms with fan for P50/60 and with fan and bath for P70/80. The rooms are good but those facing Quezon Ave are noisy.

The *Jade Tourist Inn* (tel 21158) on Tibanga Highway is a reasonable place somewhat out of the town on Baslayan Creek. It has singles/doubles with fan for P70/140, and doubles with fan and bath for P150 and with air-con and bath for P190.

Maria Christina Hotel (tel 20645, 21082), on the corner of Aguinaldo and Mabini streets, has rooms with air-con and bath for P238/322, and also has a restaurant. It is pleasant and attractive and is the best hotel in the centre of town.

The *Iligan Village Hotel* (tel 21752-3) in Pala-o has very comfortable rooms with air-con and bath for P336/420 and suites for P672. It is the best hotel near Iligan, with a restaurant, fish ponds and water gardens.

Places to Eat

Iligan has a surprising number of restaurants, though most of them close at about 9 pm. You have a choice of reasonably priced Chinese or regular meals at the *Canton Restaurant*.

In the middle price range are the *Iceberg Café & Restaurant* and the *Bahayan Restaurant*, both with Filipino cooking. The *Bar-B-Q Inn* on the plaza is great for an evening meal. The partly open-air *Terrace Garden Restaurant*, by the fish pond of the Iligan Village Hotel, is a pleasant place to sit.

For nightlife the best spot is the *SK Disco*.

Getting There & Away

Air PAL has return flights daily from Cotabato to Iligan, taking 40 minutes.

Bus From Cagayan de Oro, several Bachelor Express and Fortune Liner buses run daily to Iligan, taking over an hour. There are also jeepneys and minibuses.

From Pagadian several Bachelor Express and Fortune Liner buses run daily to Iligan, taking three hours. The last usually leaves in the early afternoon.

From Zamboanga four or five Fortune Liner and Almirante buses leave daily between 4.30 and 6.45 am for Cagayan de Oro, going via Iligan. (See also the Getting There & Away section under Cagayan de Oro.)

MARAWI & LAKE LANAO

Marawi on Lake Lanao is the spiritual and cultural centre for the Filipino Muslims. The country's second state university, Mindanao State University, usually referred to as 'Misyu' because of its initials, MSU, is here, as is the RP-Libya Hospital, the biggest and most modern hospital on Mindanao. Take a jeepney from Marawi to MSU, where there is a tourist office in Ford Guest House No 2. On the campus, there is a small but interesting Aga Khan Museum, featuring the Muslim culture of Mindanao. It is open Monday to Thursday from 9 to 11.30 am and from 1.30 to 5 pm, and on Friday from 9 to 10.30 am and from 1.30 to 5 pm. It is closed on weekends and public holidays.

Don't expect a mysterious oriental bazaar in Marawi, but there is a big market over towards the lake where you can buy brass ware, tapestries and Indonesian textiles. Good handwoven tapestries at fixed prices are for sale at the Dansalan College Art Shop at MSU. You may give offence if you photograph a Muslim woman without first asking permission – a good telephoto lens helps!

The region around Lake Lanao is a crisis area, so think twice before visiting the town of Tugaya, famous for its brass ware, making boat trips to the small islands of Nusa-Nusa and Silangan, or going south through Muslim territory to Cotabato.

Places to Stay

Marawi Resort Hotel on the MSU campus has very comfortable singles/doubles and cottages with bath for P274/333. The low-priced student guesthouse at MSU no longer accommodates tourists, but it doesn't hurt to ask.

Getting There & Away

Several jeepneys and shared taxis, costing P18 each for four to six people, leave the Marawi Terminal in Iligan daily for Marawi. The jeepneys cost P10 and go to the MSU campus. They wait opposite the Marawi Terminal in Iligan and have a sign with 'Iligan-MSU'. The last departure from Marawi to Iligan is at about 4 pm.

From Marawi a minibus leaves daily for Cotabato at 7 am, but if the trip seems likely to be dangerous, or even impossible, you will have to go back through Iligan.

OZAMIZ

There's not much for the traveller in Ozamiz, a seaport in the south-east of Misamis Occidental Province. It is simply the port for ships to Cebu. (See also To/From Mindanao in this chapter.)

Places to Stay

Cebuana Lodge on the Port Rd has basic rooms for P25/50. The *Grand Hotel*, opposite the post office at 55 Abanil St, on the corner of Ledesma St, has singles with fan for P60 and rooms with fan and bath for P80/100. It is clean and fairly good.

Country Lodge, near the Lilian Liner Bus Terminal on the Ledesma St Extension, has rooms with fan and bath for P50/80 and with air-con and bath for P100/150. It is clean, quiet and good.

The *Holiday Tourist Inn* (tel 20073) in Blumentritt St has homely rooms with fan and bath for P60/80 and with air-con and bath for P150/180.

Getting There & Away

From Dipolog, Lilian Liner buses go daily to Ozamiz via Oroquieta, leaving almost hourly. The trip takes over two hours to Dipolog and one hour to Oroquieta.

From Pagadian several Lilian Liner buses run daily to Ozamiz taking two hours. The last one leaves in the early afternoon.

From Iligan several Bachelor Express and Fortune Liner buses run daily to Kolambugan, some finishing there and some going on to Pagadian. It takes one hour. There is a ferry service between Kolambugan and Ozamiz almost hourly, between 7 am and 5 pm.

OROQUIETA

Oroquieta, on Iligan Bay, in the north-east of the Zamboangan Peninsula, is the provincial capital of Misamis Occidental, but most of the region's trade and industry is centred further south in Ozamiz City.

Places to Stay

Joy Lodge in Oroquieta has rooms with fan for P30/60 and with air-con and bath for P80/150.

The *Beach Resort Elvira* in Orbita St, on the beach at Plaridel, about 20 km north of Oroquieta, has cottages for P80/110. It's homely and you can use the kitchen.

Getting There & Away

Several Lilian Liner buses run daily from Dipolog to Oroquieta, either finishing there or going on to Ozamiz or Plaridel. The trip takes an hour or more.

From Ozamiz several Lilian Liner buses run daily to Oroquieta, some going on to Dipolog. They take one hour.

DIPOLOG & DAPITAN

Dipolog, the capital of Zamboanga del Norte Province, seems very clean and neat. The offshore Aliguay Island has white beaches and extensive undamaged coral reefs good for snorkelling and diving; you can reach it in about 45 minutes by outrigger boat. There's a chance of getting a lift out there with the boats that come in daily to Dipolog and Dapitan to get fresh water.

Minibuses travel the 15 km north-east from Dipolog to Dapitan, a quiet place where the national hero, Jose Rizal, lived in exile from 1892 to 1896. He made the big relief map of Mindanao in the town plaza, near St James Church. From the bridge over the river on the way to Rizal Park, you can catch a boat every 20 minutes going to Dakak Bay, which has a white beach and the luxurious, well-designed Dakak Park & Beach Resort. There is also a very bad road from Dapitan to the bay, but it's better to use the resort's boat service, which is free to hotel guests, and pay the P30 for admission, plus P60 if you want to use the swimming pool.

Places to Stay

There are several places you can choose from in Dipolog. *Ranillo's Pension House* (tel 3030) in Bonifacio St has quite good rooms with fan for P50/70, with fan and bath for P100/120 and with air-con and bath for P180/220.

Ramos Hotel (tel 3299) in Magsaysay St, has rooms with fan for P65/85, with fan and bath for P75/110 and with air-con and bath for P240.

The *Hotel Arocha* (tel 3397, 2332) on Quezon Ave, has singles/doubles with fan for P130/150, doubles with fan and bath for P185 and singles/doubles with air-con and bath for P300/360. It is clean and good and has a restaurant and coffee shop.

Dakak Park & Beach Resort (tel 3147; fax 7222463; tlx 29001 PXO PH) on Dakak Bay has rooms with air-con and bath for P2000 and P2350. It has tastefully furnished cottages in well-organised grounds, and also has a restaurant, open-air bar, swimming pool, whirlpool, sauna, and tennis court, and there is diving and horse riding.

Getting There & Away

Air PAL has return flights daily from Zamboanga to Dipolog, taking 50 minutes.

Bus From Pagadian several Lilian Liner buses run daily to Dipolog via Ozamiz and Oroquieta. It takes five hours from Pagadian, over an hour from Ozamiz and one hour from Oroquieta.

From Zamboanga a few Fortune Liner or

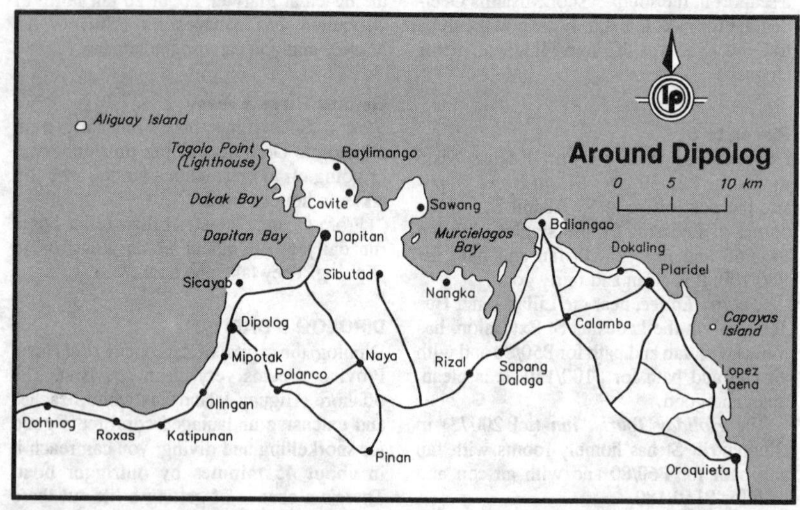

Almirante buses run daily to Dipolog via Ipil or Pagadian. At Pagadian you may have to change to a Lilian Liner bus. The trip takes 13 hours.

PAGADIAN

The image of the province of Zamboanga del Sur is best captured by the DOT's description of Pagadian and the surrounding countryside as a 'land of lakes, caves and waterfalls'. What may also interest the traveller is that the small town of Lapuyan, 40 km from Pagadian, and other parts of the two Zamboangan provinces, are the home of the Subanon, which means 'river people'. American Protestant missionaries brought Christianity and the English language to this isolated mountain world.

Places to Stay

Sea View Hotel (tel 2755) on the National Highway has simple rooms for P60/80, with fan for P70/90, with fan and bath for P90/120 and with air-con and bath for P160/180.

Zamboanga Hotel (tel 437) in Jamisola St has nice rooms with fan and bath for P85/100 and with air-con and bath for P155/200.

Peninsula Hotel (tel 557) also in Jamisola St has clean, good rooms for P50/100, with fan and bath for P100/150 and with air-con and bath for P180/280.

Pagadian City Hotel (tel 285) in Rizal Ave has comfortable rooms with air-con and bath for P200/220.

Getting There & Away

Air PAL flies daily from Zamboanga to Pagadian and back, taking 45 minutes.

Boat Three SKT Shipping Lines' ships sail from Zamboanga to Pagadian and take 12 hours. MV *Lady Helen* leaves on Monday at 7 pm, MV *Dona Isabel II* on Thursday at 7 pm, and MV *Lady Ruth* on Saturday at 7 pm.

The road from Cotabato to Pagadian passes through a crisis area and can be interrupted by broken bridges. It's better to take the daily ship that leaves Cotabato at about 6 pm and takes eight hours.

Bus From Ozamiz several Lilian Liner buses run daily to Pagadian, taking two hours.

From Zamboanga, Almirante and Fortune Liner buses leave hourly from 5 to 10 am for Pagadian, taking eight hours.

From Iligan several Bachelor Express and Fortune Liner buses run daily to Pagadian, taking three hours. The last one leaves at about 2 pm.

ZAMBOANGA

It's hard to see why Zamboanga has been praised as 'the exotic pearl of the south Philippines'. A few Muslims in an otherwise Filipino-populated city hardly make it exotic, and the colourful – and very expensive – sails of the Vintas are only seen at festivals or when one of these boats is chartered. Plain sails are normally used. The popular description of City of Flowers comes from the Malay word 'jambangan', meaning 'land of flowers' and may have been used when the first Malays settled here. It is more likely that the name comes from 'samboangan', a word made up of 'samboang', meaning 'boat pole', and 'an', meaning 'place'.

As well as speaking English, Filipino, Cebuano, Tausug and Samal, the locals in Zamboanga also speak Chavacano, a mixture of Spanish and Philippine languages ironically known as Bamboo Spanish.

Fort Pilar & Rio Hondo

On the outskirts of town, to the east of Zamboanga, are Fort Pilar and the Muslim water village of Rio Hondo. The fort was built in 1635 by Jesuit priests as protection against Muslim, Dutch, Portuguese and English attacks. It was then called Real Fuerza de San Jose, but was renamed Fort Pilar after its overthrow by the Americans at the end of last century. For many years the only part of the ruins worth seeing was the altar on the outside, but in 1986 restoration was begun to make the building usable, and today the Marine Life Museum is already open. Perhaps by now the botany, anthropology and history sections will also be open to the public. The fort may be closed on weekends and holidays.

About 200 metres east of Fort Pilar, past a shining silver mosque, is a bridge leading to a village built on piles in the mouth of the river. This is Rio Hondo. The houses are linked by footbridges, many looking none too secure. For safety reasons, don't visit Rio Hondo after dark.

Markets & Shops

The Barter Trade Market takes place in halls near the Lantaka Hotel. Smuggled goods from Borneo can now no longer be sold here, but only in the new Barter Trade Market in Jolo. However, this isn't taken too seriously. You can shop cheaply at the market in the Alta Mall Building, Governor Alvarez Ave Extension, in the suburb of Tetuan. Receipts are checked at the exits.

The fish market at the docks is very lively and colourful in the late afternoons. In the alleys of the public markets next door, between the fish market and J S Alano St, there are lots of little shops – flea-market style. Here and on the waterside of the Lantaka Hotel, you can buy shells, but you will get a better deal from a wholesaler like the Rocan Shell Shop in San Luis St.

Salva's Orchids (tel 2613) at 300 Tumaga Rd will appeal to flower lovers.

Places to Stay – bottom end

Unique Hotel (tel 3598) on Corcuera St, near the wharf, has rooms with fan for P62/112 and is basic and quite good.

Josefina's Pension House (tel 4142) is in a central position on Governor Lim Ave. It has rooms with fan for P50 and with fan and bath for P85. It is unadorned and quite good.

New Pasonanca Hotel (tel 4579), on the corner of Almonte and Tomas Claudio streets, has singles with fan and bath for P105 and singles/doubles with air-con and bath for P150/210. The rooms are small, but it is homely and has a restaurant and disco.

Atilano's Pension House (tel 4225) in Mayor Jaldon St has rooms with fan and bath for P100/120 and with air-con and bath for P150/185. It's a comfortable place with big rooms and spacious grounds. The food is good – the family run a catering service.

Places to Stay – middle

Mag-V Royal Hotel (tel 4614), on the corner of San Jose Rd and Don Basilio Navarro St, slightly out of town, has singles with fan for P70; singles/doubles with fan and bath for P90/104; with air-con for P135/165; and

1 Santa Cruz Market (New Market)
2 Bus Terminal
3 Airport
4 Alta Mall Building
5 Lutong Pinoy
6 Village Zamboanga
7 Atilano's Pension House
8 Hospital
9 GM's Super Disco
10 Zamboanga Hermosa Hotel
11 New Astoria Hotel & Seafood Restaurant
12 New Pasonanca Hotel
13 King's Palace Disco
14 Paradise Pensionhouse
15 Mag-V Royal Hotel
16 Food Paradise
Hotel Paradise
17 Sulpicio Lines
18 Athletic Field
19 SKT Shipping Lines
20 George & Peter Lines
Immigration Office
21 Sunflower Luncheonette
22 Buses to San Ramon
23 Josefina's Pension House
24 Barter Trade Market
25 Philippine National Bank
26 Town Hall
27 Basilan Shipping Lines
Sweet Lines
28 Philippine Airlines
29 Lantaka Hotel
Tourist Office
30 Boulevard Restaurant by the Sea
31 Market
32 Jeepneys to Pasonanca Park & Taluksangay
33 Unique Hotel
34 Post Office
35 Fish Market
36 Alavar's House of Seafoods
37 Casa de Oro
38 Wharf

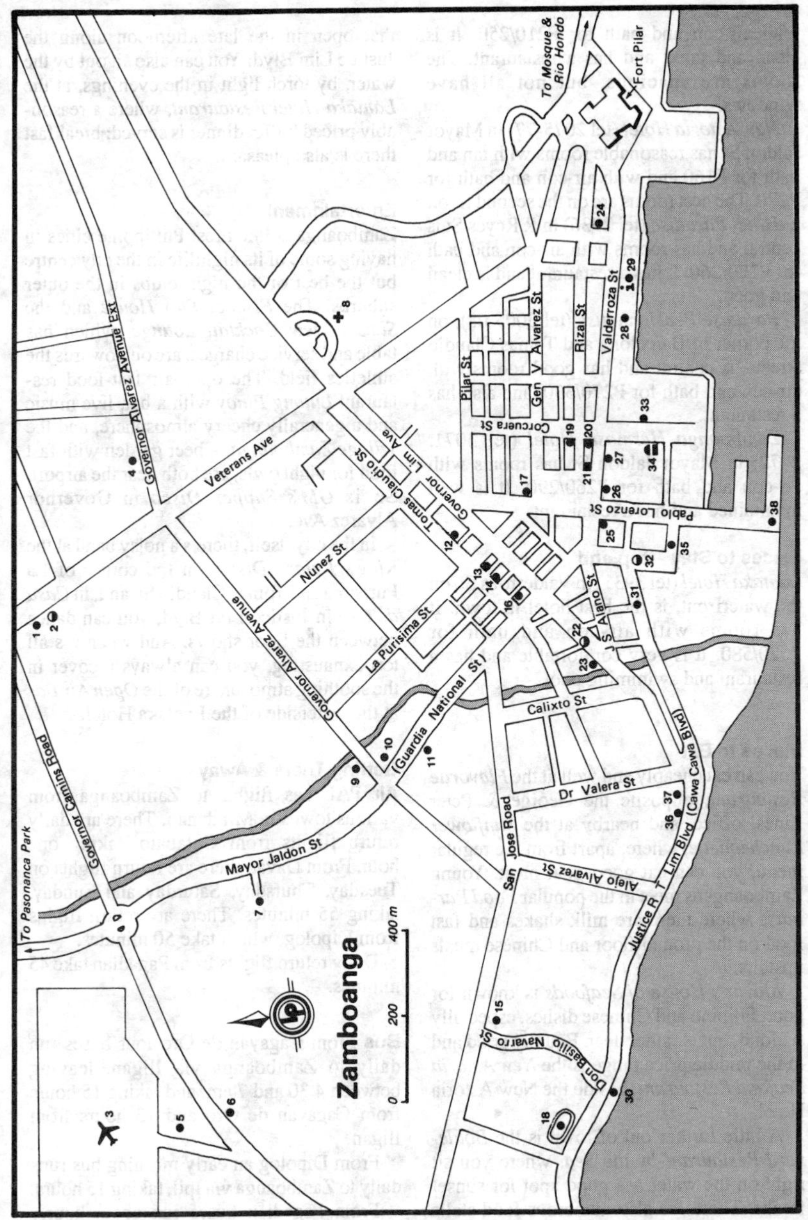
Zamboanga
0
200
400 m
To Pasonanca Park
Governor Camins Road
Governor Alvarez Avenue Ext
Veterans Ave
Governor Lim Ave
Tomas Claudio St
Nunez St
Governor Alvarez Avenue
La Purisima St
(Guardia National St)
Mayor Jaldon St
San Jose Road
Dr Valera St
Alejo Alvarez St
Calixto St
J S Alano St
Pablo Lorenzo St
Corcuera St
Pilar St
Gen V Alvarez St
Rizal St
Valderroza St
Justice R T Lim Blvd (Cawa Cawa Blvd)
Don Basilio Navarro St
Fort Pilar
To Mosque & Rio Hondo

with air-con and bath for P210/250. It is clean and good and has a restaurant. The rooms are spacious, but not all have windows.

New Astoria Hotel (tel 2075-77) in Mayor Jaldon St has reasonable rooms with fan and bath for P160 and with air-con and bath for P270. The best rooms are on the second floor.

Hotel Paradise (tel 2936) in R Reyes St is central and has rooms with air-con and bath for P220/260. It has a restaurant and is clean and good.

Paradise Pensionhouse (tel 3005-08), on the corner of Barcelona and Tomas Claudio streets, is central and has good rooms with air-con and bath for P270/330, and also has a restaurant.

Zamboanga Hermosa Hotel (tel 2071, 2072) in Mayor Jaldon St has rooms with air-con and bath for P260/290. It is well maintained and has a restaurant.

Places to Stay – top end

Lantaka Hotel (tel 3931) in Valderroza St, on the waterfront, is the best hotel in town. It has rooms with air-con and bath for P520/580. It is very comfortable and has a restaurant and swimming pool.

Places to Eat

You can eat cheaply and well at the *Flavorite Restaurant*, opposite the George & Peter Lines' office, and nearby at the *Sunflower Luncheonette*, where, apart from the regular menu, you can eat good goat meat. Young Zamboangans meet in the popular *Food Paradise* where there are milk shakes and fast food on the ground floor and Chinese meals upstairs.

Alavar's House of Seafoods is known for good Filipino and Chinese dishes, especially seafood, but is rather dear. Equally good and in the middle price range is the *New Astoria Seafood Restaurant*, beside the New Astoria Hotel.

A little further out of town is the *Boulevard Restaurant by the Sea*, where you sit right on the water – a good spot for sunset freaks. There are also numerous food stalls that open in the late afternoon along the Justice Lim Blvd. You can also sit out by the water, by torch light in the evenings, at the *Lantaka Hotel Restaurant*, where a reasonably priced buffet dinner is served; breakfast there is also pleasant.

Entertainment

Zamboanga is like most Philippine cities in having some of its nightlife in the city centre but the best of the night clubs in the outer suburbs. The *Fishnet Pub House* and the *Sunset View Cocktail Lounge*, which has table and service charges, are out towards the athletics field. The open-air fast-food restaurant *Lutong Pinoy* with a bar, live music and a generally cheery atmosphere, and the *Village Zamboanga*, a beer garden with fast food for night owls, are both near the airport. So is *GM's Supper Disco* in Governor Alvarez Ave.

In the city itself, there's a noisy band at the *King's Palace Disco*, on the corner of La Purisima and Tomas Claudio St, and, in *Casa de Oro* in Justice Lim Blvd, you can dance between the floor shows. And when it's all too exhausting, you can always recover in the soothing atmosphere of the *Open Air Bar* at the waterside of the Lantaka Hotel.

Getting There & Away

Air PAL has flights to Zamboanga from various towns in Mindanao. There are daily return flights from Cotabato, taking one hour. From Davao there are return flights on Tuesday, Thursday, Saturday and Sunday, taking 55 minutes. There are return flights from Dipolog, which take 50 minutes.

Daily return flights from Pagadian take 45 minutes.

Bus From Cagayan de Oro four buses run daily to Zamboanga via Iligan, leaving between 4.30 and 7 am, and taking 15 hours from Cagayan de Oro and 13 hours from Iligan.

From Dipolog an early morning bus runs daily to Zamboanga via Ipil, taking 15 hours.

From Pagadian buses run about hourly

from 4.30 to 10 am to Zamboanga, taking eight hours.

Boat The Sulpicio Lines' MV *Cotabato Princess* leaves Cotabato for Zamboanga on Tuesday at 10 pm, taking nine hours.

The Sulpicio Lines' MV *Philippine Princess* leaves General Santos City on Friday at 8 pm for Zamboanga, taking 14 hours.

The Sweet Lines' MV *Sweet Glory* leaves Davao for Zamboanga on Saturday at 8 am, taking 23 hours.

The William Lines' MV *Manila City* leaves Davao for Zamboanga on Sunday at 10 pm. It goes via General Santos City and takes 30 hours.

The William Lines' MV *Manila City* leaves General Santos City on Monday at 3 pm for Zamboanga, taking 13 hours.

Three SKT Shipping Lines' ships sail from Pagadian to Zamboanga, all leaving at 7 pm and taking 12 hours. The MV *Lady Helen* goes on Tuesday, the MV *Dona Isabel II* on Friday and the MV *Lady Ruth* on Sunday.

Getting Around

Airport Transport The airport is two km from the city centre. The regular price by jeepney is P1, or P5 by tricycle, but you rarely get a tricycle under P10, and up to P40 is sometimes asked. Taxi drivers, presumably without a licence, demand up to P60.

AROUND ZAMBOANGA

Pasonanca Park & Climaco Freedom Park

If the houses of the early settlers were really surrounded by a carpet of flowers, the nickname City of Flowers can today only belong to Pasonanca Park, about seven km, or 15 minutes by jeepney, north of the city centre.

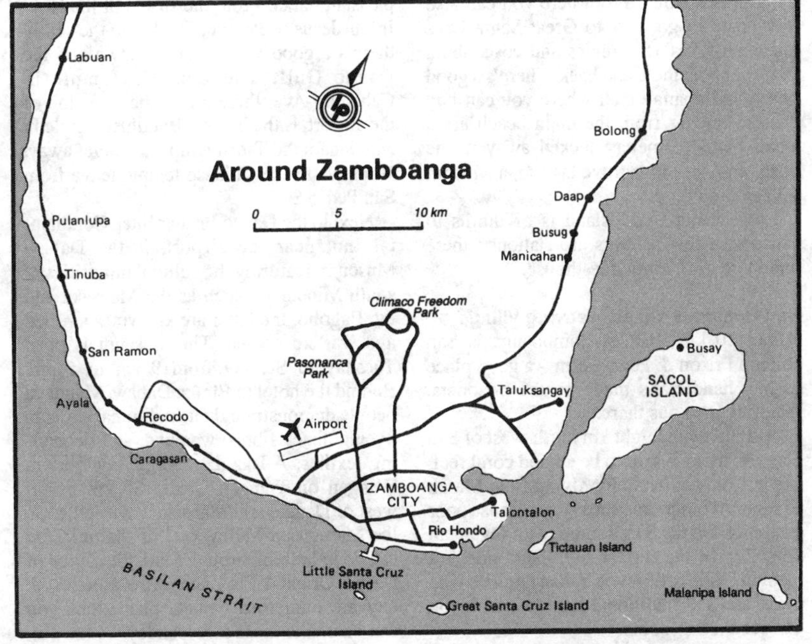

On the way there you pass prize-winning gardens, and in the 58 hectare park itself there are three swimming pools, an amphitheatre and a tree house, where honeymooners can spend one night free. Since the demand is not great, tourists can also stay there by applying to the City Mayor's Office. It's complete with two beds, a stereo, fridge, fan, bath and telephone, but remember, it's for one night only and open to all visitors during the day.

Not far from Pasonanca Park is Climaco Freedom Park, which used to be called Abong-Abong Park. It is now named in memory of a popular mayor, Cesar Climaco, who was murdered by political opponents. From the big cross on Holy Hill, you get a wonderful view over Zamboanga and the Basilan Strait.

Santa Cruz Islands

Sea gypsies try to sell shells and coral to tourists from their outrigger canoes beside the Lantaka Hotel. From here you can also hire boats to go over to Great Santa Cruz Island. It takes 15 minutes and costs about P100 per boat there and back. There's a good beach and a small stall where you can buy drinks. Not far from the main beach are a small Samal cemetery tucked away in the bush, and, in a mangrove lagoon, a Muslim village built on piles.

Little Santa Cruz Island is off limits to visitors. A few soldiers are stationed there and there is an army guesthouse.

San Ramon & Yakan Weaving Village

About 20 km west of Zamboanga is San Ramon Prison & Penal Farm – a good place to buy handicrafts made by the prisoners. You can get a bus there.

At Pulanlupa, eight km north-west of San Ramon, there is said to be a good coral reef, but it is only suitable for diving from March to June. At other times heavy seas cause poor visibility. On the San Ramon road, seven km from Zamboanga on the right-hand side, is a weaving village of seven Yakan families who make and sell traditional fabrics, which you can see on the looms.

Taluksangay

This Muslim town, 19 km north-east of Zamboanga, is partly built over the water. The Badjao live in houses on piles, while the Samal have settled on land centred around a minareted mosque. Their modest income comes mainly from fishing and collecting firewood. The children can get quite aggressive if their begging doesn't produce results. Jeepneys leave Zamboanga for Taluksangay from the public market and the last one back is likely to leave before dark.

DAVAO

The fastest growing city in the Philippines after Manila, Davao, with its population of 800,000, is also the second largest. Its cosmopolitan population of settlers from all over the country is spread over 244 sq km, one of the most sprawling cities in the world. Most people are concentrated in the centre known as 'City Town'.

Davao has a Chinatown and a number of pleasant parks. From the shrine of the Holy Infant Jesus of Prague, five km to the south, there's a good view over the town and the Davao Gulf. The Lon Wa Temple in Cabaguio Ave, three km in the direction of the airport, is the biggest Buddhist temple in Mindanao; the Taoist temple is not far away. Jeepneys to the Chinese temple leave from San Pedro St.

Next to the Davao Insular Inter-Continental Inn, near the airport, is the Dabaw Museum, featuring the cultural minorities of south Mindanao, such as the Mansaka and the Bagobo; the latter are known as a proud and warlike people. The museum is open Tuesday to Sunday from 9 am to 5 pm. Behind the hotel in Etnika Dabaw, Mandaya people demonstrate their traditional skills in dyeing abaca fibres, weaving, and decorating textiles. A Bagobo community lives in Wangan on Wangan Creek, 30 km north-west of Davao, and Mansaka have settled in the Maragusan Valley, east of Mabini. You can go to Mabini through Mati, the capital of Davao Oriental Province. Also around the city are numerous banana plantations you can visit, like those at Lapanday, 14 km out.

Davao is noted for its tropical fruits – including the infamous *durian*. This fruit that 'stinks like hell and tastes like heaven', smells so bad that it is banned from most hotel rooms, and PAL won't allow it on its planes.

The black sand of Tamolo Beach and Times Beach, south-west of Davao, is not worth a visit, but the white Paradise Island Beach on Samal Island makes a good day trip from Davao, as do Talikud Island and Eagle Camp.

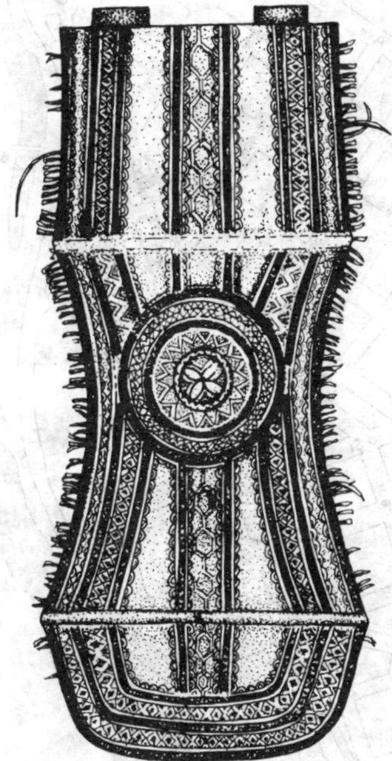

Bagobo shield

Places to Stay – bottom end

Tourist Lodge (tel 78760), on the edge of town, at 55 MacArthur Highway, has singles/doubles with fan for P40/70 and doubles with fan and bath for P110. The rooms are small but there is a restaurant.

Sunny View Inn (tel 78859) in Lizada St, near the wharf, has singles with fan for P40, singles/doubles with fan and bath for P90/110 and with air-con and bath for P110/130. It is basic but habitable.

El Gusto Family Lodge (tel 63832) at 51 A Pichon St (Magellanes St) has rooms with fan for P50/90, with fan and bath for P70/120, and with air-con and bath for P180. It's a clean, quiet place with a nice enclosed garden.

Le Mirage Family Lodge (tel 63811) in San Pedro St is a good place. It has singles with fan for P60, singles/doubles with fan and bath for P100/130 and with air-con and bath for P160/200.

Fortune Inn (tel 76688, 76703) in Magsaysay Ave has cosy singles with fan for P70, with fan and bath for P90, and singles/doubles with air-con and bath for P140/250.

Men Seng Hotel (tel 75185, 73101; fax 64994) in San Pedro St has rooms with fan and bath for P110/140 and with air-con and bath P150/195. It is basic, fairly clean and has a restaurant.

Pension Felisa (tel 79937) in A Pichon St has fairly comfortable rooms with fan and bath for P120/140 and with air-con and bath for P190/220.

B S Inn (tel 79041-46) in Monteverde St has singles with fan for P168, and singles/doubles with air-con and bath for P224/280. It is clean and good.

Royale House (tel 73630, 64537) at 34 Claro M Recto St has rooms with fan for P85/140 and with air-con and bath for P198/255-332. It is clean and good and has a restaurant.

Places to Stay – top end

The *Hotel Maguindanao* (tel 78401-05) at 86 Claro M Recto St, opposite the cathedral, has rooms with air-con and bath from P390 to P470. It's pleasant, comfortable and has a restaurant.

Apo View Hotel (tel 74861-65) on J Camus St has excellent rooms with air-con and bath for P795/965. There is a restaurant and swimming pool. There's a tourist office in the same building.

Durian Hotel (tel 72721-15) on J P Laurel

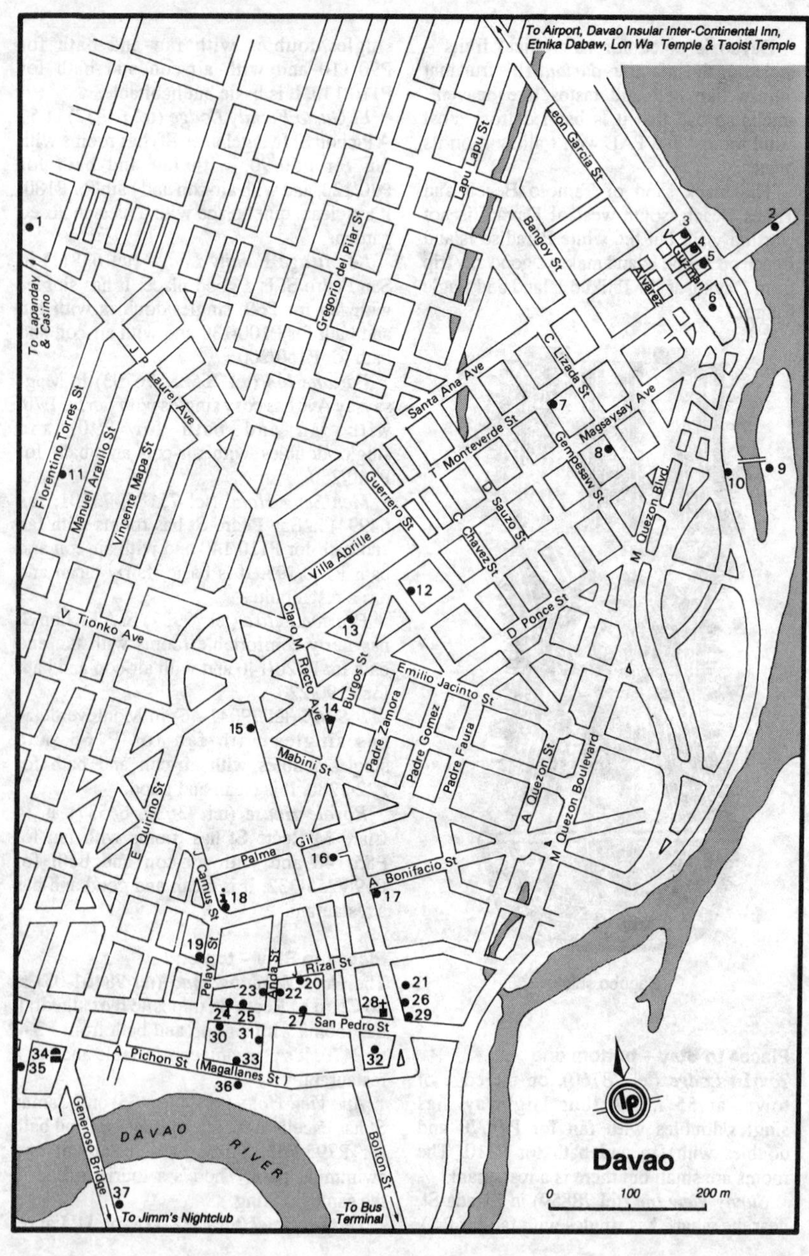

To Airport, Davao Insular Inter-Continental Inn, Etnika Dabaw, Lon Wa Temple & Taoist Temple
To Lapanday & Casino
Leon Garcia St
Lapu Lapu St
Bangoy St
Gregorio del Pilar St
Guzman
Alvarez
J P Laurel Ave
Santa Ana Ave
C Lizada St
Magsaysay Ave
T Monteverde St
Gempesaw St
Florentino Torres St
Manuel Araullo St
Vincente Mapa St
Guerrero St
D Sauzo St
C Chavez St
M Quezon Blvd
Villa Abrille
Claro M Recto Ave
D Ponce St
V Tionko Ave
Burgos St
Emilio Jacinto St
Padre Zamora
Padre Gomez
Padre Faura
Mabini St
A Quezon St
M Quezon Boulevard
E Quirino St
Palma Gil
J Camus St
A Bonifacio St
Pelayo St
Anda St
Rizal St
San Pedro St
A Pichon St (Magallanes St)
Generoso Bridge
DAVAO RIVER
Bolton St
To Jimm's Nightclub
To Bus Terminal
Davao
0 100 200 m

Ave has rooms with air-con and bath for P860/925 and suites for P1345. It is very comfortable, tastefully decorated and also has a restaurant.

Davao Insular Inter-Continental Inn (tel 76051, 76061; fax 62959; tlx DAVINS PM 48209) at Lanang has rooms with air-con and bath for P1450/1740 and suites from P2200. The hotel complex of several two-storey houses in a beautiful garden setting has its own beach, boats to Samal and Talikud Islands, swimming pool, basketball, tennis and squash courts and golf. It is on the edge of the city towards the airport.

1 Durian Hotel
2 Wharf
3 William Lines
4 Sweet Lines
5 Sulpicio Lines
6 Magsaysay Park
7 B S Inn
8 Sunny View Inn
9 Muslim Fishing Village
10 Eateries
11 Harana II Restaurant
Sarung Banggi II Restaurant
12 Trader's Inn
13 Fortune Inn
Shanghai Restaurant
14 Aldevinco Shopping Center
15 Kamayan Restaurant
16 Small Bars
17 Philippine Airlines
18 Apo View Hotel
Tourist Office
19 Dencia's Kitchenette
20 Bronco Disco
21 Royale House
22 Grand Prix Disco
23 New King Lim Restaurant
24 Kusina Dabaw
25 Merco Restaurant
26 Hotel Maguindanao
27 Le Mirage Family Lodge
28 St Peter's Cathedral
29 Philippine National Bank
30 Men Seng Hotel & Restaurant
J R Disco
31 Sunburst Fried Chicken
32 Town Hall
33 Pension Felisa
34 Post Office
35 Bankerohan Market
36 El Gusto Family Lodge
37 Tourist Lodge

Places to Eat

Good cheap Chinese meals are to be had in *Dencia's Kitchenette* in Pelayo St, in the *Shanghai Restaurant* in Magsaysay Ave, which closes at 8 pm, and in the *Men Seng Restaurant*, in the hotel of the same name in San Pedro St, which is open round the clock.

Other good restaurants in San Pedro St are the *Kusina Dabaw* with Chinese and Filipino dishes and the *Merco Restaurant*, which also has good ice creams. The best fried chicken is probably at the *Sunburst Fried Chicken* in Anda St.

The *Harana II Restaurant* and the *Sarung Banggi II Restaurant* both in Torres St are known for good barbecues of anything from native steaks to spare ribs and chicken drum-sticks.

The *Eateries* in the Muslim Fishing Village near Magsaysay Park are strong on grills of almost anything that swims, mainly tuna and squid. A good spot for those who enjoy the rustic life.

Entertainment

For a reasonable nightclub with live music and a floor show that is not too expensive, try *Jimm's*, a bit outside the city centre on the MacArthur Highway. Also out of town, in the direction of the airport, in a side street to the right, 300 metres before the Taoist temple, is the *Square Circle Disco*, which has go-go dancers. It's on every night in the *Casino* in Laurel St in the north-west out-skirts of the city.

Bronco in Rizal St has live and disco music, and there's a good lively atmosphere at the *One Down Disco* downstairs in the Apo View Hotel (the entrance is at the back). By contrast, the *J R Disco* in San Pedro St is quite simple, as are the little bars off Claro M Recto St, between Palma Gil and A Bonifacio St. Night owls gather cosily from 2 am in the *Kamayan Restaurant* in Bangoy St.

If you prefer something different, you can

have a keep-fit massage in the nearby Plaza Romana.

Getting There & Away

Air PAL has flights from Cagayan de Oro to Davao and back on Monday, Wednesday, Friday and Sunday, taking 35 minutes.

PAL has flights from Zamboanga to Davao and back on Tuesday, Thursday, Saturday and Sunday, taking 55 minutes.

Bus From Butuan several Bachelor Express and Ceres Liner buses go to Davao daily, taking six hours or more. The last bus leaves around noon.

From Cagayan de Oro several Bachelor Express, Ceres Liner and Fortune Liner buses run to Davao daily, taking 10 hours. The last one may leave quite early in the morning.

From Cotabato numerous Mintranco buses run daily to Davao, taking six hours.

From General Santos City numerous Yellow Bus Company buses run daily to Davao, taking four hours. The last bus leaves at about 3 pm.

From Surigao four Bachelor Express buses run to Davao daily between 4 and 9 am, taking over eight hours.

Boat The Sweet Lines' MV *Sweet Glory*

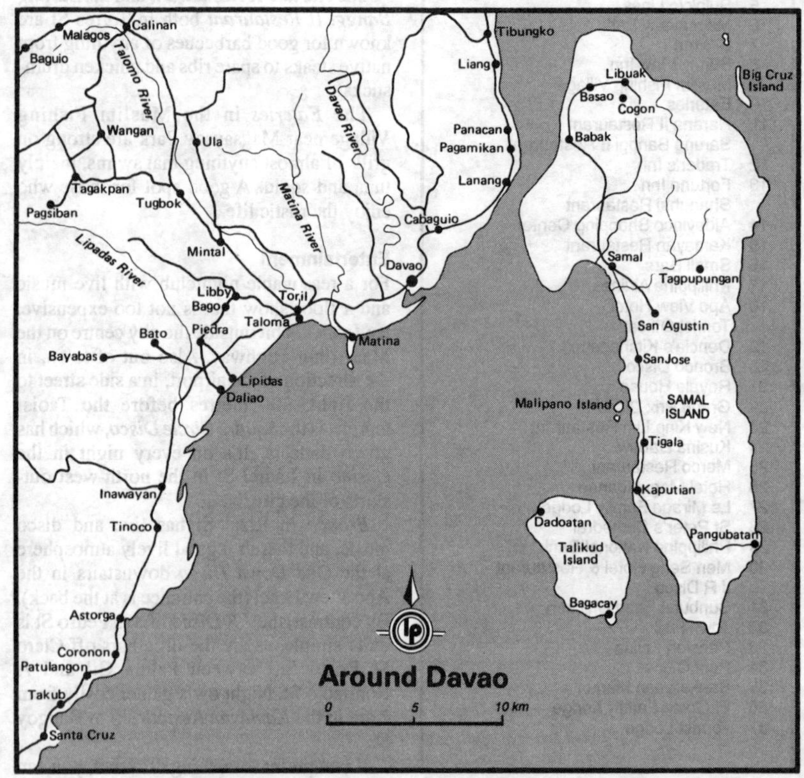

sails from Zamboanga on Thursday at 9 am for Davao, taking 23 hours.

The William Lines' MV *Manila City* sails from Zamboanga on Saturday at noon for Davao, taking 20 hours.

Getting Around

Airport Transport The airport is 12 km north-east of Davao, between the districts of Lanang and Panacan. A taxi shouldn't cost more that P50. It's cheaper to go by tricycle to the main road for P1 and then get a jeepney to Davao for P2. You might have to wait a few minutes though.

AROUND DAVAO

Samal Island

A romantic pearl diving atmosphere is missing on Samal, as the prosperous times of the Aguinaldo Pearl Farm seem to be over. You can, however, enjoy great diving in the water around the Aguinaldo Pearl Farm on Malipano Island, where the wrecks of two WW II ships lie 30 metres below water. Big and Little Cruz Islands, north-east of Samal, are good for diving. They used to be called the Liquid Islands. The white Paradise Island Beach on the north-west coast is the best beach on Samal; north of it are the cottages of the Coral Reef Beach Resort. Further to the north, at San Jose, is a Muslim fishing village built on piles over the water. There is said to be a good beach resort south of Kaputian.

To get there, go by jeepney from Davao towards the airport and Sasa. Get out before the bridge, just before Lanang, and follow the river to the right, towards the Caltex oil tanks. From there you can get a boat to take you over to Paradise Island Beach. The entrance fee is P10. Tours to Samal Island are sometimes arranged at the Davao Insular Inter-Continental Inn.

Talikud Island

This little island south-west of Samal has a cave with reputedly well-fed pythons and a couple of nice beaches with very hungry sharks. At least that's the story told by the

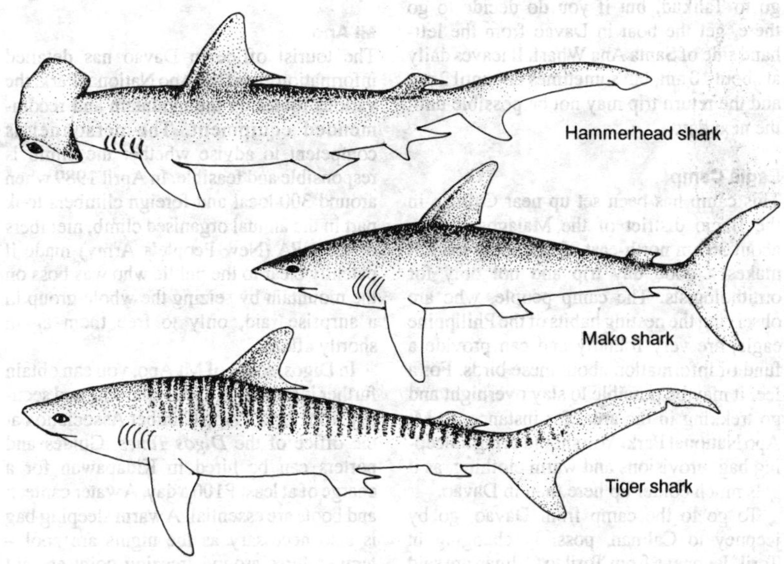

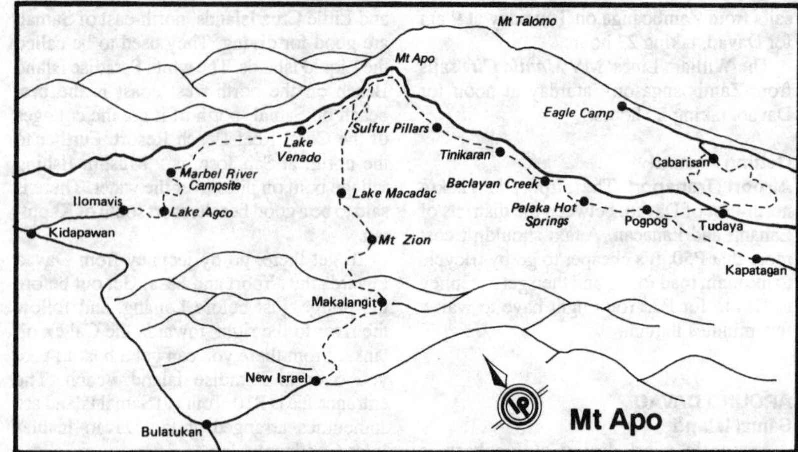

friendly islanders. You can stay overnight with the mayor. It should be possible to go across from here to the beach resort near Kaputian on Samal.

You can expect problems if you want to go to Talikud, but if you do decide to go there, get the boat in Davao from the left-hand side of Santa Ana Wharf. It leaves daily at about 10 am, but sometimes not until 2 pm and the return trip may not be possible until the next day.

Eagle Camp
This camp has been set up near Calinan in the Bagio district of the Malagos region, about 36 km north-east of Davao by road. It makes a good day trip and not only for ornithologists. The camp people, who are observing the nesting habits of the Philippine eagle, are very friendly and can provide a fund of information about these birds. For a fee, it may be possible to stay overnight and go trekking in the area, for instance, to Mt Apo National Park. You should bring a sleeping bag, provisions and warm clothing, as it gets much colder up here than in Davao.

To go to the camp from Davao, go by jeepney to Calinan, possibly changing in Toril. Jeepneys from Toril to Calinan are said to go only at 6.30 am and noon. You have to do the remaining five km from Calinan to Eagle Camp either by Special Ride in jeepneys or on foot. The last jeepney from Calinan to Toril leaves at about 3 pm.

Mt Apo
The tourist office in Davao has detailed information about Mt Apo National Park, the various routes up the mountain and recommended equipment. The personnel is competent to advise whether the climb is responsible and feasible. In April 1989 when around 300 local and foreign climbers took part in the annual organised climb, members of the NPA (New People's Army) made it patently clear to the public who was boss on the mountain by seizing the whole group in a surprise raid, only to free them again shortly after.

In Digos, south of Mt Apo, you can obtain further information about climbing and security from the Mt Apo Climber Association at the office of the *Digos Times*. Guides and porters can be hired in Kidapawan for a charge of at least P100 a day. A water canteen and boots are essential. A warm sleeping bag is also necessary as the nights are cool – temperatures around freezing point are not uncommon. Take your own provisions, not forgetting salt, to prevent dehydration.

The climb is not easy. Even though sprinters have completed it in one day, five or six days is a more realistic schedule, and certainly make the climb more pleasant.

Kidapawan Route This recommended four-day schedule includes travel to and from Davao:

Day 1 – Go from Davao to Kidapawan by Mintranco bus headed either for Kidapawan itself or Cotabato. This takes over two hours. Leave early as the last jeepney from Kidapawan to Lake Agco, via Ilomavis, usually leaves at about 3 pm. From Lake Agco it's a good three hours uphill on foot to the Marbel River Campsite, where you can stay overnight in the shelter.

Day 2 – This is six to eight hours' hard climbing; it's about five hours to Lake Venado. You will have to sleep outside, so take a plastic sheet, or better still a small tent, as it's uncomfortable if it rains.

Day 3 – Allow for two hours to reach the summit, then return to Lake Venado or the Marbel River Campsite.

Day 4 – Return to Kidapawan or Davao.

New Israel Route As well as the popular Kidapawan, or North Cotabato, route, there is the alternative New Israel route. The mountain village of New Israel is the home of the Alpha & Omega Sect, widely known in the region for its faith healer.

From Kidapawan, take a jeepney to Bulatucan; from the village it's about two hours on foot. Occasionally a jeepney goes all the way, but in bad weather this would be almost impossible. For a small donation, you can stay overnight in the sect's guesthouse and you can hire guides and porters there.

The climb from New Israel up Mt Apo takes about 13 hours altogether. The members of the sect make the climb once a year and have built overnight shelters on the way up. In Makalangit a capacious store camp has even been provided; a small donation is expected for its use. From there it takes five hours.

An alternative descent would be down the North Cotabato route, via Lake Venado and Ilomavis to Kidapawan, which would take about 12 hours.

GENERAL SANTOS CITY (DADIANGAS)

Maguindanao Muslims and B'laans were the sole inhabitants of this city up to the beginning of the 20th century. The first influx of immigrants arrived in 1914 to 1915 and more followed in the 1930s. In 1939 pioneers from Luzon and the Visayas led by General Paulino Santos made a settlement on the Silway River in Sarangani Bay. In 1965 Dadiangas was renamed General Santos City in his honour. The old name is also used today.

The city's economy depends mainly on pineapple, bananas (Dole Pineapple Plantation and Stanfilco Banana Plantation) and cattle (Sarangani Cattle Co).

Places to Stay – bottom end

Concrete Lodge (tel 4876) on Pioneer Ave has rooms with fan and bath for P75/110 and with air-con and bath for P170. It is unpretentious but good. *South Sea Lodge I* (tel 5146, 2086) on Pioneer Ave has rooms with fan for P78/112, with fan and bath for P112/157 and with air-con and bath for P224/420. It is clean and relatively good and has a restaurant. The *South Sea Lodge II* is in Salazar St, on the corner of Magsaysay Ave.

Pioneer Hotel (tel 2422, 2812) on Pioneer Ave has singles with fan and bath for P105, singles/doubles with air-con and bath for P150/210 and suites for P255. It is homely and has a restaurant and coffee shop.

Matutum Hotel (tel 4901, 2711) on P Acharon Blvd has rooms with fan and bath for P145/230 and with air-con and bath for P200/270. Suites are from P350. It is clean and good and has a restaurant and disco.

Places to Stay – top end

Phela Grande Hotel (tel 2950, 4925) on Magsaysay Ave has rooms with air-con and bath for P314/440, and suites for P660. It is clean and good and has a restaurant and coffee shop.

Pietro's Hotel (tel 4333, 4831) on the

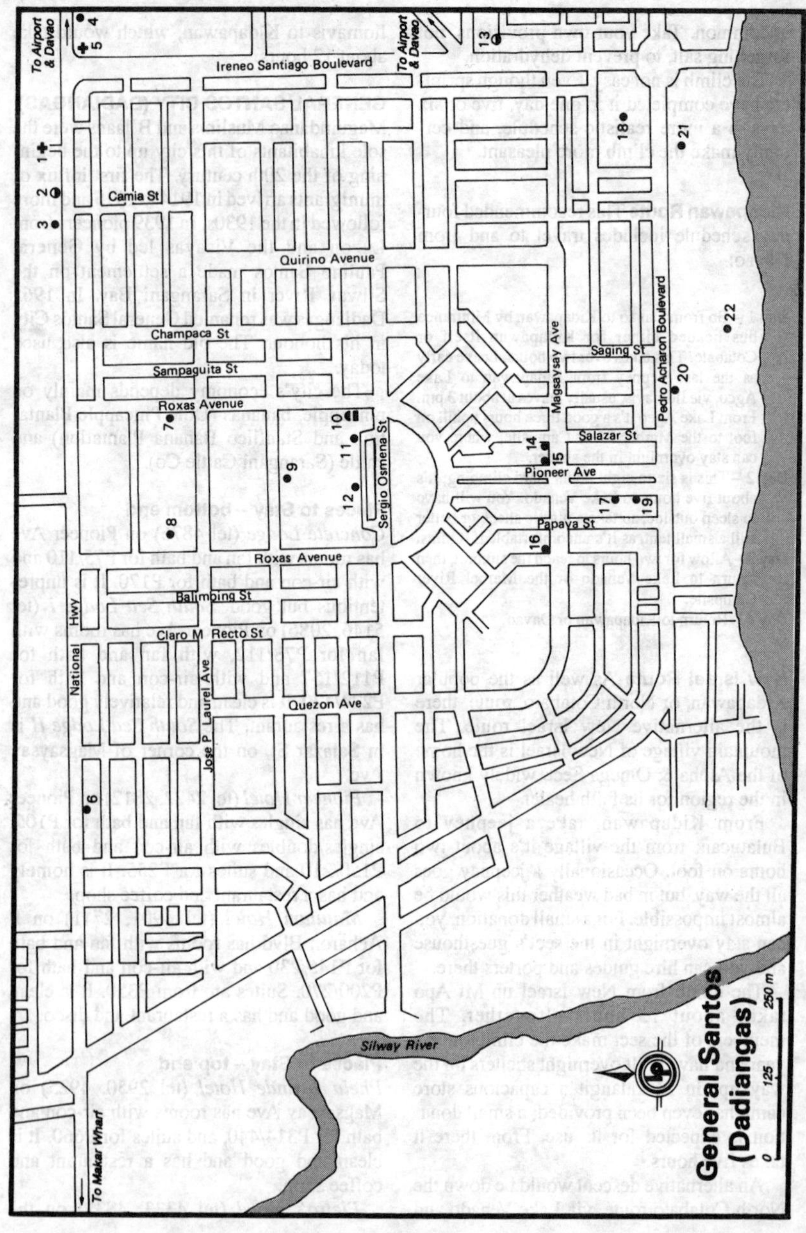
General Santos
(Dadiangas)
To Airport & Davao
To Airport & Davao
To Makar Wharf
Ireneo Santiago Boulevard
Camia St
Quirino Avenue
Champaca St
Sampaguita St
Roxas Avenue
Roxas Avenue
Balimbing St
Claro M Recto St
Quezon Ave
National Hwy
Jose P Laurel Ave
Sergio Osmena St
Magsaysay Ave
Pedro Acharon Boulevard
Saging St
Salazar St
Pioneer Ave
Papaya St
Silway River
0
125
250 m

1 Doctor's Hospital
2 Yellow Bus Company Bus Terminal
3 Oscar's Country Inn
4 Philippine Airlines
5 St Elizabeth Hospital
6 Pietro's Hotel
7 Immigration Office
8 Mindanao State University
9 Police Station
10 Post Office
11 Philippine National Bank
12 Town Hall
13 Bus Terminal
14 South Sea Lodge II
15 Concrete Lodge
16 Phela Grande Hotel
17 South Sea Lodge I
18 Market
19 Pioneer Hotel
20 Matutum Hotel
21 Fish Market
22 Magsaysay Park

National Highway, on the edge of town, has rooms with air-con and bath for P210/271-296 and suites for P486. It is clean and good and has a restaurant and disco.

Oscar's Country Inn (tel 2313) on the National Highway has rooms with air-con and bath for P395/470, suites for P640. It is pleasant and attractive and has a restaurant.

Getting There & Away

Bus From Davao numerous Yellow Bus Company buses run daily to General Santos City, taking four hours. The last one is likely to leave at about 3 pm.

From Koronadel (Marbel) numerous Yellow Bus Company buses run daily to General Santos City, some going on to Davao. It takes one hour. There are also minibuses.

Boat The William Lines' MV *Manila City* leaves Davao for General Santos City on Sunday at 10 pm, taking nine hours.

The Sulpicio Lines' MV *Philippine Princess* leaves Zamboanga for General Santos City on Thursday at 6 pm. It takes 11 hours.

KORONADEL

Koronadel, also known as Marbel, is the capital of South Cotabato Province. Mainly Maguindanao and B'laan, members of the original native ethnological groups, live here, but there are also immigrants from other parts of the Philippines. The Maguindanao call the town Koronadel, while the B'laan call it Marbel. It is a good starting point for a trip to Lake Sebu.

Places to Stay

Samahang Nayon Home (tel 272), on the corner of Osmena and Roxas streets, has singles/doubles with fan and bath for P72/135, and doubles with air-con and bath for P195. It is unadorned but relatively comfortable and has a restaurant.

Alabado's Home, on the corner of Alunan and Rizal streets, is a reasonable place; it has rooms with fan and bath for P70/135 and with air-con and bath for P200/240.

Places to Eat

The Chinese meals at the *Capitol Restaurant* in Roxas St, just around the corner from the Samahang Nayon Home, are good value. The *D'Breeze Restaurant* a little further on has good Chinese and Filipino dishes.

Getting There & Away

From Davao several Yellow Bus Company buses run daily to Koronadel via General Santos City, some going on to Tacurong. It takes four hours from Davao and one hour from General Santos City. From General Santos City there are also minibuses to Koronadel.

To go from Lake Sebu to Koronadel via Surallah, you go first by jeepney to Surallah, then to Koronadel in a Yellow Bus Company bus bound for General Santos City. It takes two hours or more.

SURALLAH & LAKE SEBU

Surallah is a small town in the south of the Alah Valley. It provides access to Lake Sebu, deep in the Tiruray Highlands, perhaps the loveliest inland sea in the Philippines. Around Lake Sebu live the tribespeople called the T'boli. They live in almost total seclusion and produce rice, maize and sugar cane. They are well known for the quality of their brass ware and weaving. (For more details, see the section on Cultural Minorities in the Facts about the Country chapter.) Try to arrange your schedule so as to include the colourful Saturday market, or, even better, the annual tribal festival on the second Friday in September, which lasts several days and includes struggles with wild horses as a high point.

You will only enjoy visiting the Lake Sebu area if you are interested in the traditional life and culture of the T'boli. Those after more modern attractions, such as discos, will soon be bored and will not be welcomed by the locals.

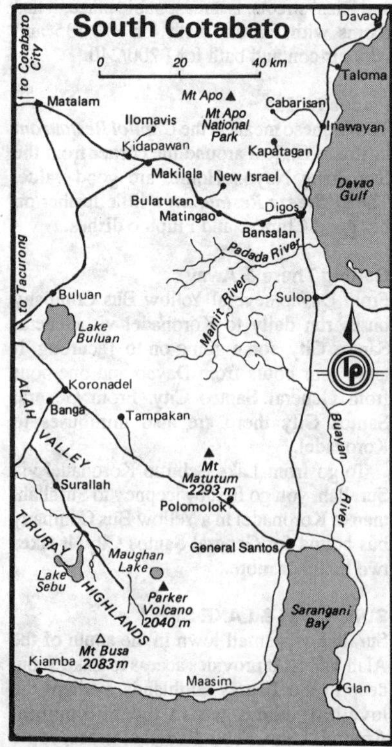

Places to Stay & Eat

Bonns Haus in Surallah has basic rooms for P40/80. *Santa Cruz Mission* on Lake Sebu has rooms for P25/50. Board can be arranged for an agreed price. The guesthouse is equipped with a small kitchen and you can bring provisions from Surallah, though there is a small store with not much choice in the town. Otherwise, try the small eating places that are 30 minutes' walk away.

If the few beds in the guesthouse are taken, you can use your own tent or arrange private board through the Santa Cruz Mission.

The *Ba-ay Village Inn* by the lake has rooms for P40/80. The owner, Bao Ba-ay, is a pure T'boli and can tell you a great deal about the T'boli culture. His wife, Alma, is an Ilokana and is a good cook. They also have their own fish farm.

Getting There & Away

Jeepney Several jeepneys go from the market at Surallah to Lake Sebu daily, taking an hour or more. You can ask to be set down at the Santa Cruz Mission. The last jeepney from Surallah usually leaves at about 3 pm.

COTABATO

Cotabato is on the Rio Grande de Mindanao, one of the country's longest rivers. The town appears to be predominantly Muslim, but statistics show that the population is 60% Christian and only 40% Muslim. The people here are known as Maguindanao. Islam came to Cotabato in 1371, when the Arab Sharif Muhammad Kabungsuwan, who is said to be the founder of Cotabato, arrived. The Jesuits only came in 1872 and settled in Tamontaka, seven km south-west, to build a church and establish Christianity in the area.

Places to Stay

Padama Pension House in Quezon Ave, near the bus terminal, has simple rooms with fan for P50/60 and with fan and bath for P70/80, but the rooms facing the street are noisy.

Hotel Filipino in the city plaza on Sinsuat Ave has reasonable rooms for P55/80, with fan and bath for P65/90 and with air-con and

Top: Sea gypsies in the Sulu Sea (JP)
Bottom: Sitangkai, the 'Venice of the Far East', Sulu Islands (JP)

Top: Badjao woman (JP)
Bottom: T'boli woman (JP)

bath for P130/190. It also has a restaurant. Some rooms have a good view over the city.

Castro's Pension House (tel 2709) at 99 Sinsuat Ave has good rooms with fan for P75/105, with fan and bath for P95/180 and with air-con and bath for P170/250.

El Corazon Inn in Makakua St has homely rooms with fan and bath for P104/141 and with air-con and bath for P172/227. Suites cost P300.

New Imperial Hotel (tel 2075, 2077) at 51 Don Rufino Alonzo St has rooms with air-con and bath for P300/380. It is comfortable and has a restaurant and disco.

Places to Eat

The restaurant in the *Hotel Filipino* has a reputation for good, reasonably priced food. Equally good and generous is *Jay Pee's Dan Restaurant & Snack House* in Don Rufino Alonzo St.

Entertainment

The disco upstairs in the *New Imperial Hotel* is expensive and has rather austere décor. The disco on the first floor of the *Sampaguita Hall* is better and you can listen to folk music on the second floor.

Getting There & Away

Air PAL has daily flights from Iligan to Cotabato and back, taking 40 minutes. It also has daily flights from Zamboanga to Cotabato and back. The trip takes one hour.

Bus From Davao numerous Mintranco buses run daily to Cotabato, taking over five hours.

From Koronadel many Maguindanao Express and J D Express buses run daily to Cotabato, taking three hours. Yellow Bus Company buses go at least as far as Tacurong; from there jeepneys run to Cotabato.

The bus trip from Pagadian to Cotabato by land is not advisable even if one is available. (See the Getting There & Away section under Pagadian.)

Boat A boat leaves Pagadian for Cotabato daily at 5 pm, taking eight hours.

The Sulpicio Lines' MV *Cotabato Princess* leaves Zamboanga for Cotabato on Monday at 8 pm, taking 11 hours.

TO/FROM MINDANAO

You can get to Mindanao from Bohol, Camiguin, Cebu, Leyte, Luzon, Negros, Panay and Siquijor (see the Transport from Luzon section of the Manila chapter and the relevant To/From sections of this and the Visayas chapter).

To Basilan

Boat From Zamboanga to Isabela, the Basilan Shipping Lines' MV *Estrella del Mar* leaves daily at 7 am and 1 pm, taking over an hour, and their MV *Dona Ramona* leaves daily at 10 am and 5 pm, taking over one hour.

From Zamboanga to Lamitan, there is a ship leaving daily in the afternoon. The wharf at Lamitan is outside the town.

To Bohol

Boat From Butuan to Jagna, the Carlos Gothong Lines' MV *Don Calvino* leaves on Sunday at noon, taking six hours.

From Cagayan de Oro to Jagna, the Carlos Gothong Lines' MV *Dona Lili* leaves on Sunday at noon, taking seven hours.

From Cagayan de Oro to Tagbilaran, the Trans-Asia Shipping Lines' MV *Asia Thailand* leaves on Tuesday at noon, taking seven hours.

From Ozamiz to Tagbilaran, the William Lines' MV *Misamis Occidental* leaves on Tuesday at 3 pm, taking seven hours.

To Camiguin

Boat From Balingoan to Binone, the Tamula Shipping Lines' MV *Ruperto Jr*, MV *Hijos* and MV *Anita* leave at 6.30, 7.30, 9 and 10.30 am and 1.45 and 4 pm, taking over an hour. The ship leaving at 6.30 and 10.30 am may go to Guinsiliban, south of Binone.

From Cagayan de Oro to Mambajao, the Georgia Shipping Lines' MV *Luzille* leaves twice a week, taking four hours.

To Cebu

Air PAL has daily flights to Cebu City from Butuan, Cagayan de Oro, Cotabato, Davao, Dipolog, General Santos City, Ozamiz, Pagadian and Surigao.

PAL also has flights to Cebu City from Bislig on Monday and Friday; to Iligan on Wednesday and Thursday; to Tandag on Tuesday, Thursday and Saturday; and to Zamboanga daily except Friday.

Boat Several ships go to Cebu City from various towns on Mindanao.

From Butuan the Carlos Gothong Lines' MV *Don Calvino* leaves on Monday, Wednesday and Friday at 6 pm, taking 12 hours, and their MV *Our Lady of Lourdes* leaves on Thursday at 6 pm, taking 11 hours.

From Cagayan de Oro, the Carlos Gothong Lines' MV *Dona Lili* leaves on Monday, Wednesday and Friday at 7 pm, taking 10 hours. Trans-Asia Shipping Lines' ships leave daily.

From Iligan the Carlos Gothong Lines' MV *Don Benjamin* leaves on Tuesday, Friday and Sunday at 7 pm, taking 11 hours.

From Ozamiz the Carlos Gothong Lines' MV *Dona Cristina* leaves on Monday, Wednesday, Friday and Sunday at 7 pm, taking 12 hours. The William Lines' MV *Misamis Occidental* leaves on Sunday at 9 pm, taking 10 hours.

From Surigao the Sweet Lines' MV *Sweet Home* and MV *Sweet Heart* leave on Monday, Tuesday and Thursday at 5 pm, taking 12 hours.

To Leyte

Bus From Davao and Cagayan de Oro, Philtranco air-con buses leave twice daily for Manila via Surigao, passing through Liloan and Tacloban on Leyte.

Boat From Surigao to San Juan, Kasamahan Shipping Lines has one ship weekly, leaving on Wednesday at midnight and taking five hours.

From Surigao to Liloan, MV *Maharlika II* leaves at 5 pm from Lipata, 15 km north of Surigao, and takes three hours.

From Surigao to Maasin, the Sulpicio Lines' MV *Surigao Princess* leaves on Tuesday at midnight and takes four to five hours.

To Luzon

Air All planes go to Manila. PAL has daily flights to Manila from Cagayan de Oro, Cotabato, Davao and Zamboanga. From Butuan, PAL has flights on Monday, Wednesday, Thursday and Saturday.

Aerolift has a daily flight from Dipolog, and a flight on Monday, Wednesday, Friday and Sunday from Surigao. It also has flights on Tuesday, Thursday and Saturday from Iligan.

Bus From Davao, Philtranco air-con buses leave twice daily for Manila. The 45 hours' travelling time includes the ferries from Surigao to Liloan and from San Isidro to Matnog.

Boat There are several ships that go to Manila from Mindanao. From Butuan the Carlos Gothong Lines' MV *Our Lady of Lourdes* leaves on Saturday at 6 pm taking 35 hours.

From Davao, the Sweet Lines' MV *Sweet Glory* leaves on Saturday at 8 am. It goes via Zamboanga and takes 57 hours. The William Lines' MV *Manila City* leaves on Sunday at 10 pm. It goes via General Santos City, Zamboanga and Odiongan on Romblon and takes 78 hours.

From General Santos City, the William Lines' MV *Manila City* leaves on Monday at 3 pm, going via Zamboanga and Odiongan on Romblon and taking 61 hours.

From Surigao, the Sulpicio Lines' MV *Surigao Princess* leaves on Tuesday at midnight and takes 35 hours, possibly going via Maasin on Leyte.

From Zamboanga, the William Lines' MV *Manila City* leaves on Tuesday at 4 pm, going via Odiongan on Romblon, and takes 36 hours. The Sweet Lines' MV *Sweet Glory* leaves on Sunday at 7 am and takes 36 hours.

Birds of the Philippines

Philippine eagle
(Pithecophaga jefferyi)

Palawan hornbill
(Anthracoceros marchei)

Seloputo owl
(Strix seloputo wiepkeni)

Philippine trogon
(Harpactes ardens)

Philippine kingfisher
(Halcyon chloris qullaris)

Palawan peacock pheasant
(Polyplectron emphanum)

To Negros

Air PAL has flights from Dipolog to Dumaguete on Tuesday and Thursday.

Boat From Dipolog to Dumaguete, the MV *Jhufel*, MV *Don Joaquin* or MV *Don Victoriano* of George & Peter Lines leaves daily, taking five hours. The harbour at Dipolog lies between Dipolog and Dapitan and is called Dapitan Port. A tricycle from Dipolog costs about P10.

To Panay

Boat From Cagayan de Oro to Iloilo, Negros Navigation Lines' MV *Santa Ana* leaves on Sunday at 4 pm, taking 15 hours.

To Romblon

Boat From Zamboanga to Odiongan, the William Lines' MV *Manila City* leaves on Tuesday at 4 pm and takes 22 hours. The boat comes from General Santos City and Davao.

To Siquijor

Boat From Plaridel to Larena, Sweet Lines' MV *Sweet Time* leaves on Sunday at noon and takes over three hours.

To Sulu Islands

Air PAL has daily flights from Zamboanga to Jolo and Tawi-Tawi. Tawi-Tawi Airport is on Sanga Sanga Island, near Bongao.

Boat SKT Shipping Lines has three ships going from Zamboanga to Sitangkai. The MV *Lady Ruth* leaves on Tuesday at 7 pm and takes 44 hours, going via Jolo (12 hours), Siasi (20 hours) and Bongao (31 hours).

The MV *Lady Helen* leaves on Wednesday at 7 pm and takes 44 hours, going via Jolo, Siasi and Bongao.

The MV *Dona Isabel II* leaves on Saturday at 7 pm, taking 44 hours and going via Jolo, Siasi and Bongao.

The Zamboanga-based Sampaguita Shipping Lines and Magnolia Shipping Lines have numerous ships on this route or parts of this route, including the good, big MV *Sampaguita Lei*.

Basilan

The southern end of Basilan meets the northern end of the Sulu Islands, and its northern end is just across the Basilan Strait from Mindanao. Since 1973, Basilan has been a province, comprising a main island and numerous smaller ones. About 200,000 people live here, roughly one third of whom are Yakan, an ethnic minority found only on Basilan, except for some families living near Zamboanga on Mindanao. They are peace-loving Muslim farmers and cattle raisers, who are well known for their hospitality towards visitors and for their colourful and elaborate ceremonies, festivals and weddings. As well as the Yakan, Basilan is inhabited by the Chavacano, Visayan, Samal, Tausug and a few Badjao tribespeople.

Basilan is hilly and rugged and its centre is virtually unexplored. In the north of the island, the climate is fairly stable and there is no obvious dry or wet season, but rain may fall at any time of the year. The southern part, by contrast, has a fairly dry season from November to April.

The area's main industry is forestry and the processing of caoutchouc for rubber. Basilan rubber is considered among the best in the world and large international companies have invested in the plantations. Other crops are coffee, cocoa, pepper, African oil (a plant oil extracted from the dates of the African palm tree) and abaca; copper is also mined. Because the waters around Basilan abound with fish, mussels and seaweed, the province is one of the most important suppliers of seafood in the southern Philippines.

ISABELA

The capital of Basilan Province, Isabela, is a small town with not much to see. You can go across the harbour in a few minutes in an outrigger boat to see Malamaui Island, where a few Badjao live in pile houses. The beautiful White Beach is the best known beach on

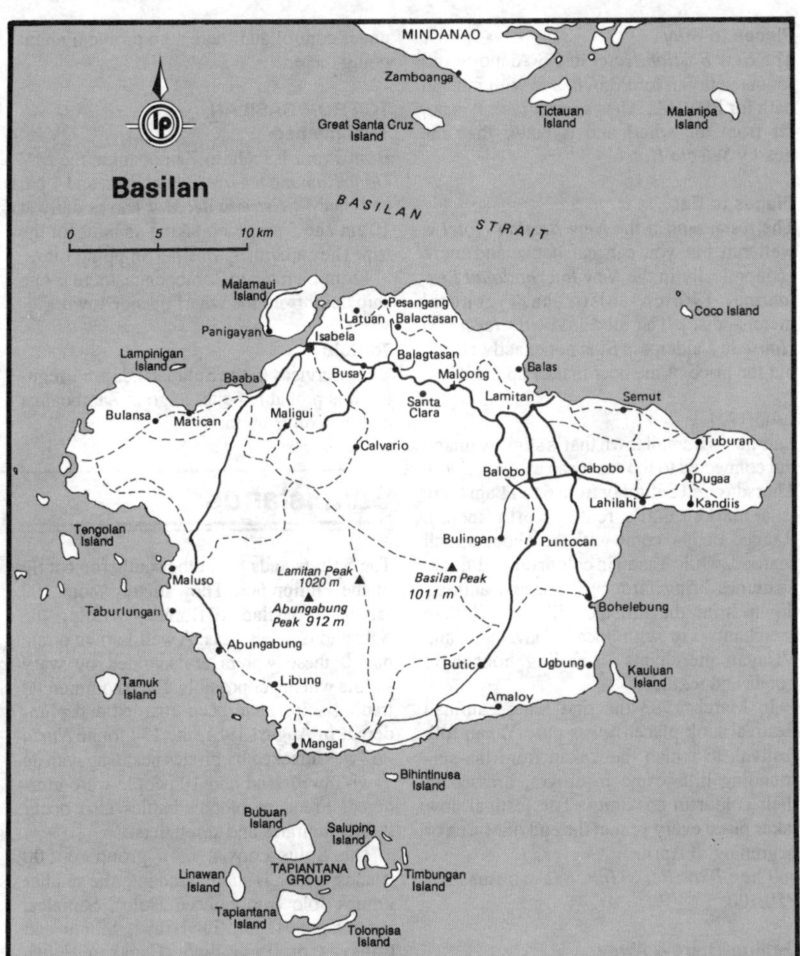

the island, but, in spite of this, is practically deserted. It's about an hour on foot from the landing place. You can get there by tricycle but there is no regular return service, so you either have to ask the driver to wait, order the tricycle for a fixed time or walk. The charge for waiting should be about P20 per hour. The last boat back to Isabela leaves around 4 pm.

A few km from Isabela are coffee, pepper and date plantations belonging to the Menzi family. On the way there you pass the Menzi manufacturing plant, where you can see exactly how rubber is produced from caoutchouc. Coffee beans are roasted there in the open air. It is closed on weekends. Before you reach the factory, you pass a mansion belonging to the wealthy Alleno family, who own the electricity plant and a shipping company, among other enterprises.

Places to Stay

The *New Basilan Hotel* in J S Alano St has rooms with fan for P35/70, and with fan and bath for P50/100; it has a restaurant. It is not far from the wharf and is better than the nearby *Selecta Hotel.*

Places to Eat

The restaurant in the *New Basilan Hotel* is well run but you can eat better and more economically in the *New International Restaurant* (which also has general merchandise). The food in *Awin's Icecream House* in Valderossa St is not exactly cheap, but the price of the beer makes up for it.

LAMITAN

Lamitan is a small town that is slightly inland but connected to the sea by an estuary. Every Thursday and Saturday from 6 to 11 am there is a market that's really worth seeing. Ragged Badjao come with their boats to sell seafood, while Yakan in colourful traditional costumes bring farm produce and animals down from the hillside villages. Chinese merchants vie with local Chavacano and Visayan merchants in selling household goods and textiles.

In March 1983 the first Lami-Lamihan Festival took place. It was pure Yakan folk festival, to which the Yakan from the surrounding hills came in droves, dressed in their colourful costumes. The festival now takes place every year at the end of March or beginning of April.

The *Traveller's Inn* has rooms for P50/100.

Getting There & Away

Several buses leave the market in Isabela for Lamitan from 5 am, taking 45 minutes. There is also a white nonstop bus which does the 27 km stretch in 20 minutes.

MALUSO

Until recently travellers were warned against going to Maluso, a fishing village which is the third largest settlement on Basilan, because of the very high risk of ambush or kidnapping. Nowadays, things are said to be under control and there's no problem about going there.

TO/FROM BASILAN

To Mindanao

Boat From Isabela to Zamboanga, the MV *Dona Ramona* leaves daily at 7 am and 1 pm and the MV *Estrella del Mar* leaves daily at 10 am and 5 pm, each taking an hour for the trip. They are run by Basilan Shipping Lines.

From Lamitan to Zamboanga, there is one ship daily from the wharf outside town.

To Sulu

Boat Services to the Sulu Islands are irregular. It is probably better to go to Zamboanga and then on from there.

Sulu Islands

The Sulu Islands are at the southernmost tip of the Philippines. They stretch about 300 km from Basilan to Borneo, dividing the Sulu and Celebes Seas. A well-known pirate haunt, these waters are avoided by wary sailors whenever possible. Even commercial trading ships have been boarded and plundered. In August 1981, the 134 tonne *Nuria 767* was attacked by pirates near Cagayan de Tawi-Tawi Island and 10 people were murdered. Frequent bloody battles also occur between pirates and smugglers.

The Sulus consist of a group of 500 islands, which is subdivided into the smaller groups Jolo (pronounced Holo), Samales, Pangutaran, Tapul, Tawi-Tawi, Sibutu and Cagayan de Tawi-Tawi (Cagayan Sulu). There are two provinces: Sulu, whose capital is Jolo, and Tawi-Tawi, whose capital is Bongao.

Attempts by the Spaniards to gain a foothold on these islands failed and the Americans were no more successful. At present government troops are trying to prevent the MNLF (Moro National Liberation Front) from realising its aim of political autonomy.

Among the most significant cultural

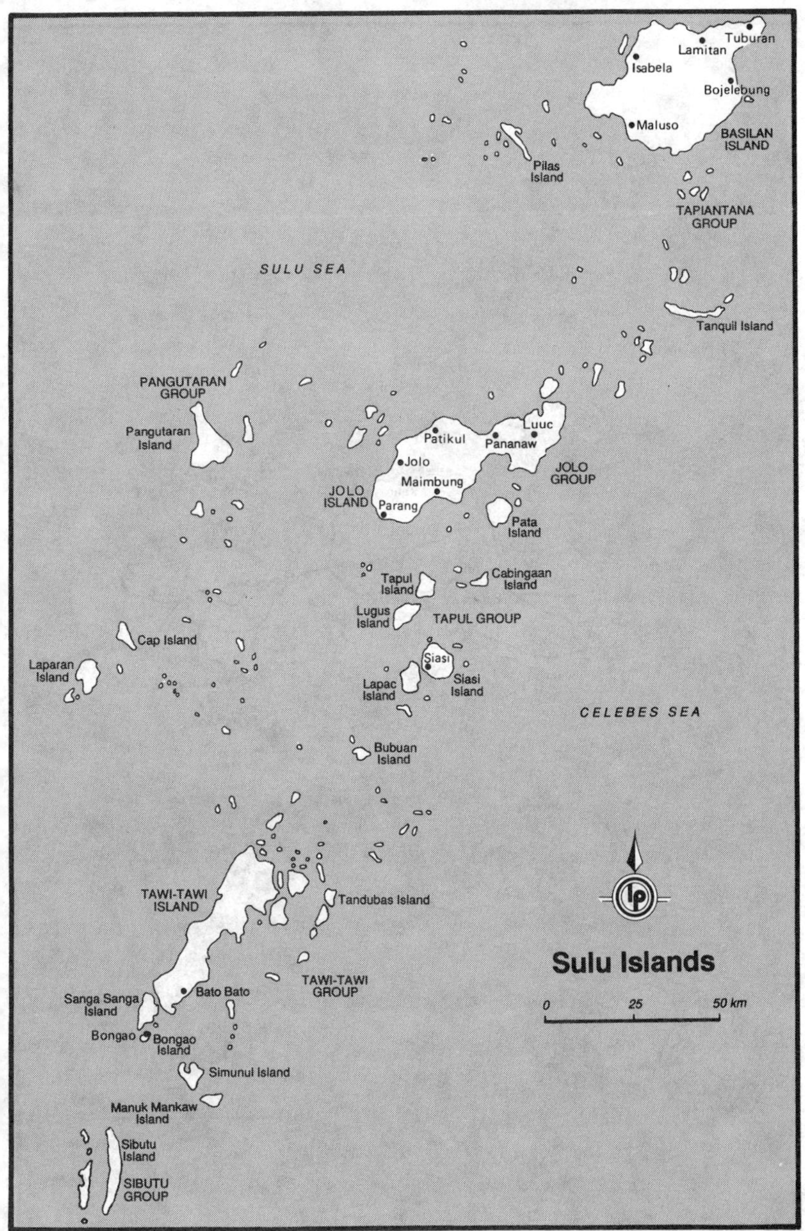
Tuburan
Lamitan
Isabela
Bojelebung
Maluso
BASILAN ISLAND
Pilas Island
TAPIANTANA GROUP
SULU SEA
Tanquil Island
PANGUTARAN GROUP
Pangutaran Island
Luuc
Patikul
Pananaw
Jolo
JOLO GROUP
Maimbung
JOLO ISLAND
Parang
Pata Island
Cabingaan Island
Tapul Island
Lugus Island
TAPUL GROUP
Cap Island
Laparan Island
Siasi
Siasi Island
Lapac Island
CELEBES SEA
Bubuan Island
TAWI-TAWI ISLAND
Tandubas Island
Sulu Islands
TAWI-TAWI GROUP
Bato Bato
Sanga Sanga Island
0
25
50 km
Bongao
Bongao Island
Simunul Island
Manuk Mankaw Island
Sibutu Island
SIBUTU GROUP

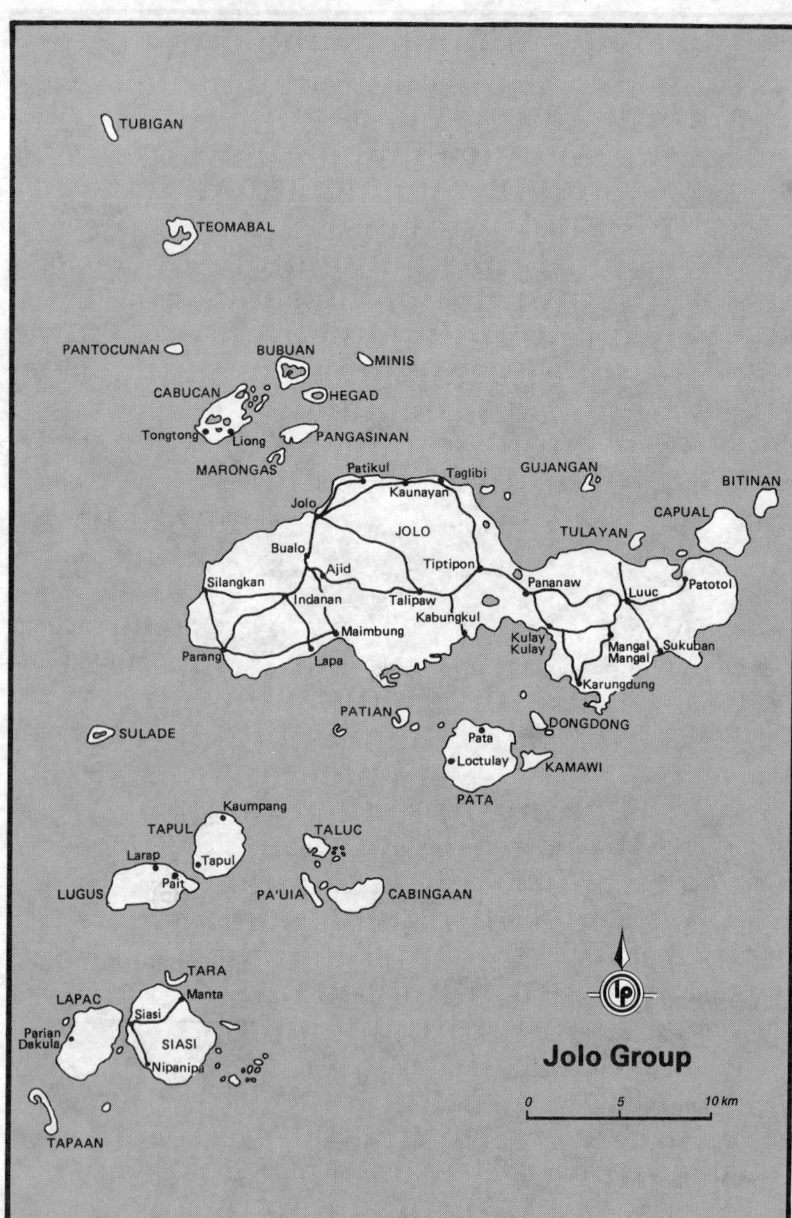
TUBIGAN
TEOMABAL
PANTOCUNAN
BUBUAN
MINIS
CABUCAN
HEGAD
Tongtong
Liong
PANGASINAN
MARONGAS
Patikul
Taglibi
GUJANGAN
BITINAN
Kaunayan
Jolo
JOLO
CAPUAL
TULAYAN
Bualo
Ajid
Tiptipon
Silangkan
Pananaw
Luuc
Patotol
Indanan
Talipaw
Kabungkul
Maimbung
Kulay Kulay
Mangal Mangal
Sukuban
Parang
Lapa
Karungdung
PATIAN
DONGDONG
SULADE
Pata
Loctulay
KAMAWI
PATA
Kaumpang
TAPUL
TALUC
Larap
Tapul
Pait
LUGUS
PA'UIA
CABINGAAN
TARA
LAPAC
Manta
Siasi
Parian Dakula
SIASI
Nipanipa
TAPAAN
Jolo Group
0
5
10 km

minority groups are the Samal and the Badjao. Both seem very gentle and peaceful. The main islands inhabited by the Samal are Siasi, Tawi-Tawi and Sibutu islands. These people are Muslim and make their living predominantly from fishing, agriculture and small-scale trading. Their houses are always close to the water, often standing in the water on piles.

The Badjao live on boats throughout the entire archipelago, but are concentrated around Tawi-Tawi and Sibutu. They are sea gypsies and their religion is generally thought to be animism. A lot of them, especially those who have ceased to be nomads and live in houses on piles like the Samal, have accepted the new way of life and converted to Islam. Of all the inhabitants of the Sulu Islands, the Badjao are on the lowest rung of the social ladder. Like the Samal, they feel oppressed by the Tausug, the largest and most politically and economically advanced tribe.

The Tausug are Muslim and are considered powerful, aggressive and independent. Quite a few generations have lived by piracy, smuggling and slave-trading. The original inhabitants of the Sulu Islands, the Buranun, are said to have been the forefathers of the Tausug. They too were converted to Islam and their descendants have remained so, except for small communities of Catholics and Buddhists.

From 1974 until the end of 1981, the Sulu Islands were totally out of bounds to tourists. You could sail there from Zamboanga but were not permitted to disembark without a permit. This permit was issued by the military authorities in Manila (Ministry of Defence, Camp Aguinaldo). If you did not have an acceptable reason, such as an officially recognised study proposal on the Badjao or Tausug, you could give up hope of ever getting a permit.

Now, however, foreigners are allowed into the area without permits or restrictions on where they go or how long they stay. This sounds good, but in fact many islands or parts of the islands are still inaccessible because of constant tension, such as that between Tawi-Tawi and Jolo. There are other islands like Laa, near Simunul, or Sipangkot, near Tumindao, which no boat operators will visit because they fear or dislike the inhabitants.

It is essential to take warnings seriously. When I wanted to cross from Bongao to Bilatan, the boatman only gave a discouraging 'Maybe tomorrow'. That evening there was a real shoot up on Bilatan. A few days earlier I had been refused a ride from Bongao to Laa through fear of an ambush. That night you could clearly hear a long fusillade of shots from across the water. There was probably a good reason, too, for the marine escort given to our boat from Sitangkai to Bongao.

Added to this are accommodation and water shortages. Only in Jolo, Bongao and Sitangkai is any commercial accommodation available. Elsewhere you have to find private lodgings and you should pay a reasonable price for them. On the southern islands, like Bongao, Sibutu, Tumindao and Sitangkai, there is a severe water shortage. You get a guilty conscience even brushing your teeth! Any washing is done in sea-water polluted with sewage and refuse. You can almost feel the hepatitis threatening your liver.

Nevertheless, a trip to the Sulu Islands is a unique experience. The impressions gained are many and varied and well worth the effort.

JOLO

Jolo is the capital of the island of the same name and also of Sulu Province. It is the only place in the entire archipelago where the Spaniards, after a relatively short period of 20 years, finally gained a foothold and built a fortress. This was at the end of the 19th century, about 300 years after they first reached the Philippines.

In February 1974, Jolo was partly destroyed in fighting between Muslims and government troops. Even today the military is still present in the city. Although no permit is required for the city itself, foreigners need a military permit to travel around this volcanic island. It is remarkable to see the many

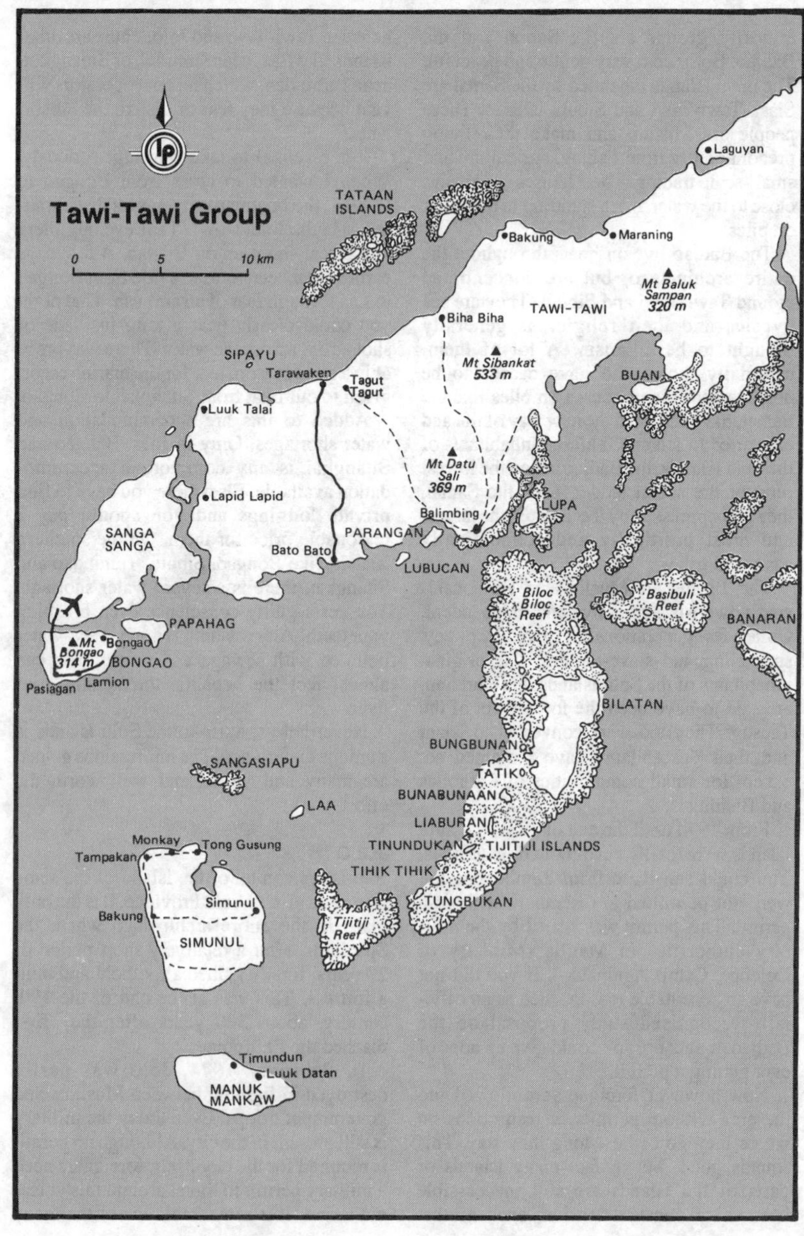
Tawi-Tawi Group
0 5 10 km
TATAAN ISLANDS
Laguyan
Bakung
Maraning
Mt Baluk Sampan 320 m
TAWI-TAWI
Biha Biha
Mt Sibankat 533 m
SIPAYU
Tarawaken
Tagut Tagut
BUAN
Luuk Talai
Mt Datu Sali 369 m
Lapid Lapid
Balimbing
LUPA
SANGA SANGA
PARANGAN
Bato Bato
LUBUCAN
Biloc Biloc Reef
Basibuli Reef
BANARAN
PAPAHAG
Mt Bongao 314 m
Bongao
BONGAO
Pasiagan
Lamion
BILATAN
BUNGBUNAN
SANGASIAPU
TATIK
BUNABUNAAN
LAA
LIABURAN
Monkay
Tong Gusung
Tampakan
TINUNDUKAN
TIJITIJI ISLANDS
TIHIK TIHIK
TUNGBUKAN
Simunul
Bakung
Tijitiji Reef
SIMUNUL
Timundun
Luuk Datan
MANUK MANKAW

trishaws standing around the great mosque. Don't miss the colourful fish market and the Barter Trade Market in the halls next to the harbour, where goods that come mainly from Borneo are sold. The lovely, sandy Quezon Beach is about three km north-east of Jolo. You can get there by jeepney, getting out before Patikul. A little further east in Taglibi is another wide, sandy beach with crystal clear water.

Places to Stay

Ricni Hotel in Astorias St has rooms with fan and bath for P50/80 and is simple and relatively clean. *Helen's Lodge* (tel 104) in Buyon St has rooms with fan for P40/70, and with fan and bath for P70/90. It is simple and relatively clean and has a restaurant. Travellers passing through can use the sanitary facilities for a small charge.

Places to Eat

If you have just arrived from Zamboanga, you will have your first experience of the island's coffee shops in Jolo. Whether you order coffee or a Sprite (the popular soft drink in Sulu), you will be offered a large tray of all sorts of cakes.

Good restaurants are the *Bee Gees* in Sanchez St, the *Plaza Panciteria* in Sevantes St and the *L C Snack House*.

SIASI

This island is a crisis area according to locals. Certainly the little port of Siasi is not very inviting: it has lots of damaged or totally burnt-out houses, a boarded-up Sultan Hotel, and few restaurants with little food. People are rather unforthcoming and it is difficult to make yourself understood in English.

BONGAO

Bongao, on Bongao Island, is the most important town in the Tawi-Tawi Island group. It's bigger than Siasi but smaller than Jolo, and has two harbours, a market, two cinemas and a main street with several side streets. The Provincial Capitol Building stands out like a mosque on the hillside. The Badjao village of Tungkalang, on the south-west tip of Sanga Sanga, which has been described in some old travel books, no longer exists. Sea gypsies have settled near Bongao, in the bay by the hospital, and Notre Dame College. Americans here aren't called 'Joe' (a holdover from 'GI Joe', popular after American troops helped liberate the islands from Japanese invaders in 1944 to 1945) but 'Milikan'.

The military camp, Philippine National Bank and PAL are all on the outskirts of town. Beyond them, you come to quite a nice swimming place, where the road meets the shore. At low tide you can walk across to a sandbank that is good for snorkelling.

The little village of Pasiagan is 5 km from Bongao. This is the start of the trail leading up Mt Bongao, a 314 metre mountain worshipped by both Christians and Muslims. Anjaotals, a member of an old royal family, is buried on the summit. Prayers said in the four-sq-metre enclosure with its wall draped in white cloth are said to be more powerful than any medicine. (If you visit the enclosure, you must take off your shoes.) Paths right and left of the grave lead to good lookout points that are clear of trees. The climb takes about an hour and is hot and tiring.

As this is a holy mountain, you should not defile it in any way and offensive behaviour like swearing should be avoided. It is believed that people who touch a monkey here will soon die or lose their wits. It's as well to take some bananas for these inquisitive animals. There are numerous snakes, though they're not easy to see, so don't grab blindly at trees or vines. In early October, Bongao has a fiesta and the hill is alive with people.

From Bongao you can catch small boats to the islands of Bilatan, Simunul and Manuk Mankaw. Bunabunaan is the burial island of the Badjao and can only be reached by a Special Ride. When in Bongao, I was constantly advised not to visit Tawi-Tawi.

Places to Stay

The *Southern Hotel*, opposite the mosque, has basic rooms for P60/80 and doubles with

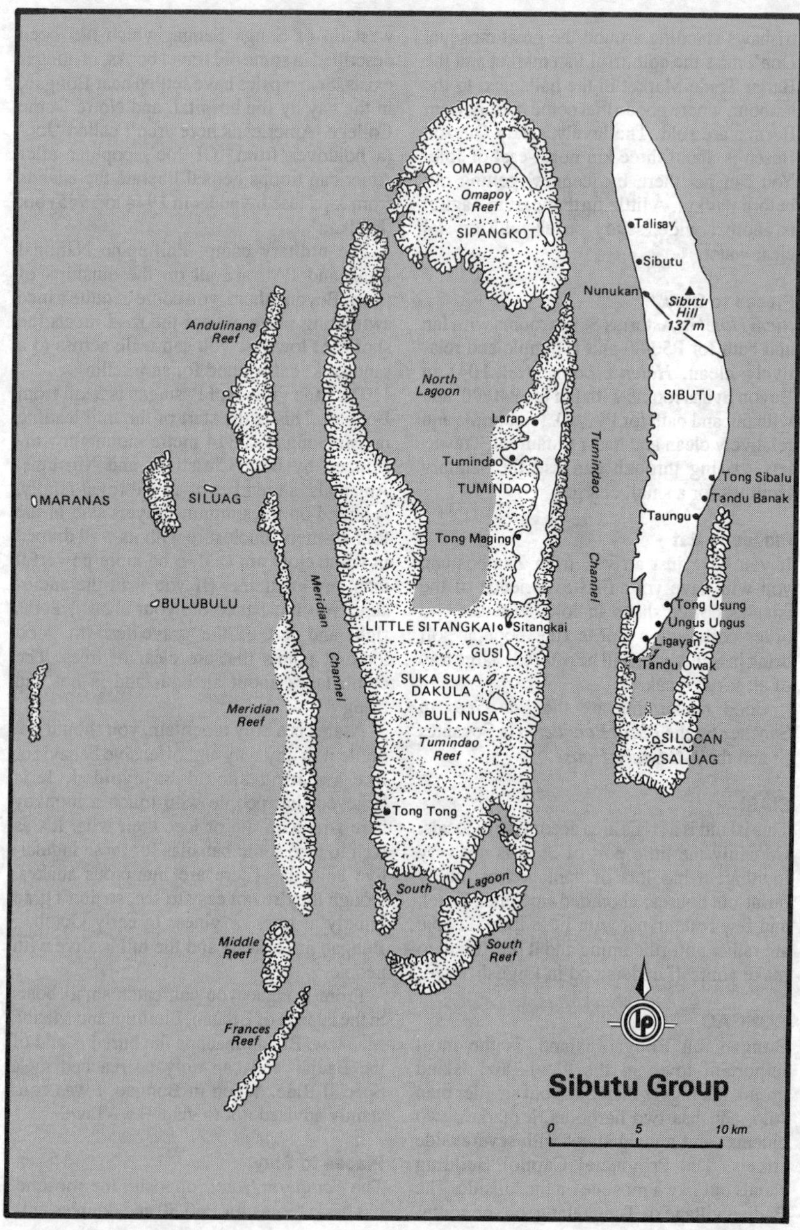

OMAPOY
Omapoy Reef
SIPANGKOT
Talisay
Sibutu
Nunukan
Sibutu Hill 137 m
Andulinang Reef
North Lagoon
SIBUTU
Larap
Tumindao
Tumindao Channel
TUMINDAO
Tong Sibalu
Tandu Banak
MARANAS
SILUAG
Taungu
Tong Maging
Meridian Channel
BULUBULU
Tong Usung
Ungus Ungus
LITTLE SITANGKAI
Sitangkai
Ligayan
GUSI
Tandu Owak
SUKA SUKA DAKULA
Meridian Reef
BULI NUSA
Tumindao Reef
SILOCAN
SALUAG
Tong Tong
South Lagoon
Middle Reef
South Reef
Frances Reef
Sibutu Group
0
5
10 km

fan and bath for P100. It has a restaurant and two pleasant balconies.

Getting Around

Airport Transport The airport is on Sanga Sanga Island, north of Bongao. The jeepney trip to the town costs P5, or P40 by tricycle.

SITANGKAI

It is said that more than 6000 people live in this 'Venice of the Far East' in houses built on piles on the giant reef. The water is so shallow that big ships have to anchor three km away in the Tumindao Channel and ferry their freight and passengers across in small boats.

There are more Badjao villages built on piles scattered over a large area west of Sitangkai. The largest, and furthest away, is called Tong Tong and is made up of 50 houses. It's not far from the Meridian Channel, which is 50 to 100 metres deep. Here as elsewhere the Badjao have laid out underwater seaweed fields; sea cucumbers are another main source of income.

From Sitangkai small boats run to the two bigger islands of Tumindao and Sibutu.

Warning Because of the many people who travel illegally on the smugglers' boats from Sitangkai to Sempora on Borneo (in the state of Sabah, East Malaysia), you may only be allowed to leave the ship at Sitangkai after showing a passport and a valid visa, as well as a permit from the Tawi-Tawi Task Force. You can obtain this permit at the appropriate office in Bongao. If you can show a return ticket (eg from Zamboanga to Cebu), it will help to cut down the question time.

Places to Stay

The *Plaza Hotel* is the only guesthouse in Sitangkai and has rooms for P30/60. If you have the chance to stay with the Badjao for a few days, do so but be generous with food and supplies, as these friendly people don't have much. Hadji Musa Malabong, the teacher at Sitangkai, and his brother, Hadji Yusof Abdulganih, can arrange private accommodation.

TO/FROM THE SULU ISLANDS

You can get to the Sulu Islands from Mindanao and probably also from Basilan. (See the To/From Mindanao section of this chapter.)

To Basilan

Boat Connections to Basilan from the Sulu Islands are irregular. However, merchant ships, which will also take passengers, are said to leave Jolo quite often for Isabela.

To Mindanao

Air PAL has daily flights to Zamboanga from Tawi-Tawi (the airport is on Sanga Sanga Island, near Bongao) and Jolo.

Boat See the timetable for SKT ships in the Getting Around section at the end of this chapter.

To Palawan

Boat If you have time, you could try the following route: go from Jolo to Pangutaran Island, then on to Cagayan de Tawi-Tawi, where you can occasionally get a freighter to Rio Tuba or Brooke's Point in south Palawan.

GETTING AROUND

Ships of various companies ply more or less regularly between the islands. Ships of the Magnolia Shipping Lines, the Sampaguita Shipping Lines and the SKT Shipping Corporation cover the route from Zamboanga to Sitangkai via Jolo, Siasi and Bongao and back. The timetable of the SKT ships is as follows:

MV *Lady Ruth*	Arrives	Departs
Zamboanga	Sat 5 pm	Tue 7 pm
Jolo	Wed 7 am	Wed 11 am
Siasi	Wed 3 pm	Wed 6 pm
Bongao	Thu 2 am	Thu 11 am
Sitangkai	Thu 3 pm	Thu 11 pm
Bongao	Fri 2 am	Fri 6 pm
Jolo	Sat 5 am	Sat 7 am

Swords

Single and double-edged swords of various designs are an integral part of the arts and crafts of the Muslims in the south of the Philippines. In Mindanao and the Sulu Islands in particular, the art of forging blades and shaping handles remains important. In Sulu, the classical type is the *kris*, called *kalis seko*, and the *kampilan*. Although they are rarely used in battle these days, swords are still of social and symbolic significance to the wearer.

1 Barong: a leaf-shaped, single-edged blade
2 Kampilan: the handle is supposed to represent the open mouth of a crocodile
3 Kris: a wavy-shaped blade
4 T'boli-bolo: the handle is decorated with brass curls
5 Dagger-kris: a weapon preferred by women
6 Talibong: a sabre with a single-edged, curved blade

MV *Lady Helen*	Arrives	Departs
Zamboanga	Mon 6 am	Wed 7 pm
Jolo	Thu 7 am	Thu 11 am
Siasi	Thu 3 pm	Thu 6 pm
Bongao	Fri 2 am	Fri 11 am
Sitangkai	Fri 3 pm	Fri 11 pm
Bongao	Sat 2 am	Sat 6 pm
Siasi	Sun 2 am	Sun 11 am
Jolo	Sun 3 pm	Sun 6 pm

MV *Dona Isabel II*	Arrives	Departs
Zamboanga	Thu 6 am	Sat 7 pm
Jolo	Sun 6 am	Sun 11 am
Siasi	Sun 3 pm	Sun 6 pm
Bongao	Mon 2 am	Mon 11 am
Sitangkai	Mon 3 pm	Mon 11 pm
Bongao	Tue 2 am	Tue 6 pm
Siasi	Wed 2 am	Wed 11 am
Jolo	Wed 3 pm	Wed 7 pm

Palawan

Palawan, in the south-west of the Philippines, is 400 km long but only 40 km wide and separates the Sulu Sea from the South China Sea. Beautiful empty beaches, untouched natural scenery and friendly inhabitants make this a very attractive island. A further 1768 islands make up Palawan Province, the most important being Busuanga, Culion, Coron, Cuyo, Dumaran, Bugsuk and Balabac. Most of Palawan consists of mountainous jungle. At 2073 metres, Mt Mantalingajan is the highest mountain.

Only a few coastal regions can be used for agriculture. The main crops are rice, coconuts, bananas, groundnuts and cashew nuts. The richest fishing grounds in the Philippines are off the Palawan's northern coast. About 60% of Manila's staple food is caught between Coron, Cuyo and Dumaran islands and especially in Taytay Bay. If you like fish, you will think this is paradise, as the fruits of the sea are really plentiful here. You could try a different fish dinner every day, choosing from crayfish, mussels, sea urchin, lobster and many others. Even jellyfish are eaten here.

The El Nido cliffs and the limestone caves of Coron and Pabellones islands, off Taytay, are home to countless swallows' nests. Hotels and Chinese restaurants all over the country get their supplies from these places to make that oriental delicacy, birds' nest soup. The jungles also harbour plants and animals which are found nowhere else in the Philippines. These include the iron tree, the mouse deer (chevrotain), the king cobra and many rare parrots and butterflies. In fact, more and more Japanese come to the island each April and May to catch butterflies because of the rarity and beauty of some of the specimens.

Economy

Since the discovery of oil off Palawan's north-west coast, the development of that industry looks promising. Another important industry is forestry, which is dominated almost without exception by Pagdanan Timber Products (PTP) and Nationwide Princesa Timber (NPT). Both companies are controlled by one person. Up to 1989, when the Aquino government imposed a logging ban, Palawan had lost 20,000 hectares of forests every year since 1979. That is about 2½% of the total forest reserves of this island, which has such a rich flora and fauna. It is becoming increasingly obvious, however, that the law is not being observed. As so often in the Philippines, the letter of the law and practical reality are two different things. This stripping of Palawan is likely to frustrate the promising plans of the Department of Tourism. In a few years there will be dead coral reefs caused by fishing with explosives and barren hillsides because of uncontrolled deforestation. These will so alter the face of the island that nature lovers will no longer have any reason for visiting.

People

Palawan is thinly populated, with most inhabitants coming from several islands in the Visayas. The Batak and Pala'wan are among the aboriginal inhabitants of Palawan. The Batak are very shy. If you want to find them and visit their villages, you need plenty of time and a competent guide.

The Negrito, nomads who live by hunting, are found in the north. Attempts to convince

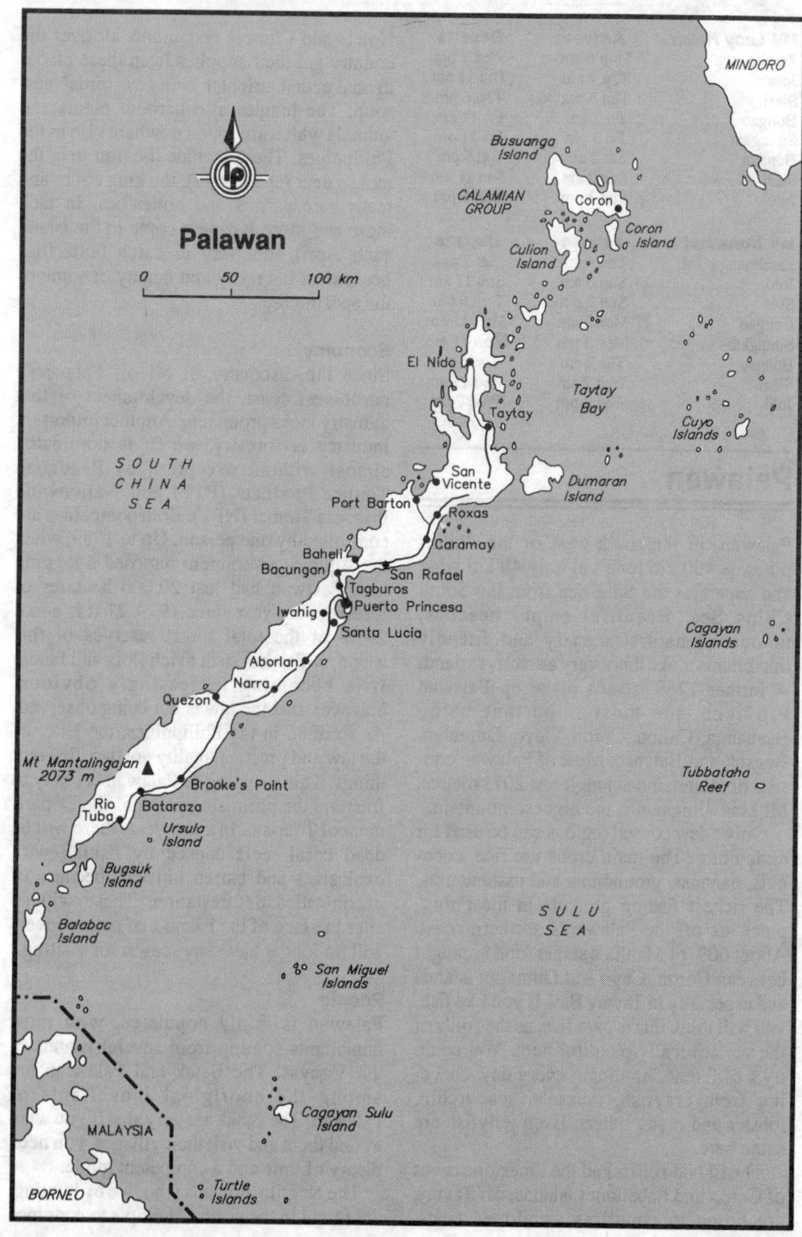
MINDORO
Busuanga Island
CALAMIAN GROUP
Coron
Coron Island
Culion Island
Palawan
0
50
100 km
El Nido
Taytay
Taytay Bay
Cuyo Islands
SOUTH CHINA SEA
San Vicente
Dumaran Island
Port Barton
Roxas
Caramay
Baheli
Bacungan
San Rafael
Tagburos
Puerto Princesa
Iwahig
Santa Lucia
Cagayan Islands
Aborlan
Narra
Quezon
Mt Mantalingajan 2073 m
Tubbataha Reef
Brooke's Point
Rio Tuba
Bataraza
Ursula Island
Bugsuk Island
Balabac Island
SULU SEA
San Miguel Islands
Cagayan Sulu Island
MALAYSIA
BORNEO
Turtle Islands

them of the benefits of agriculture and of settling the land have nearly always failed. Some of them go to school but then disappear into the jungle again.

In the extreme north of Palawan are the Tagbanua, a seafaring people who rarely settle in one place. On the other hand, the Tagbanua who live near the coast and along the rivers of central Palawan live in settled village communities. Like the Hanunoo on Mindoro, they use a syllabic writing system.

The Tau't Batu in the south of Palawan were only discovered in 1978. They live in caves in the Singnapan Basin, a few km east of Ransang, as they have done for about 20,000 years. Their habitat has been declared a protected area and is absolutely off limits. This prohibition must obviously be respected.

Information

Health Warning Outside of the capital, medical services are inadequate. Even if you can find a doctor, there won't be a pharmacy which stocks the necessary medication. In case of illness, head straight for Puerto Princesa.

Malaria is widespread on Palawan, so it's important to take antimalarial tablets, always sleep under mosquito netting, and wear insect repellent. (See the section on Health in the Facts for the Visitor chapter.) If you get a fever, remember that it could be malaria and head straight for Puerto Princesa. The doctors there know more about malaria and how to treat it than do doctors in Manila. On a more positive note, you won't see a mosquito during the dry season in large parts of Palawan. This is also when most people visit. Mosquitoes are usually only a problem in the wet season, and then especially in the south.

During the summer months, deadly jellyfish called *salabay* may be found in the coastal waters.

Things to Do

Palawan has a great potential for adventure. You can try jungle expeditions, gold seeking, deep-sea fishing, cave exploring, diving, trekking, searching for shipwrecks or living like Robinson Crusoe, among other things.

Places to Stay

Finding accommodation is not easy on Palawan, apart from in the main and most frequently visited centres. You are often dependent on the locals' goodwill, but the mayor will usually find you somewhere to stay.

PUERTO PRINCESA

Puerto Princesa is a relatively new city with about 60,000 inhabitants. Although more and more houses are being built, you can still find beautiful buildings in the traditional style. The town is dominated by the cathedral. At the waterfront there are fishermen's huts built right over the water.

The scene on the wharf at sunset is good fun. Puerto Princesa Bay also has some interesting places for diving. For about P200 you can hire an outrigger boat for a few hours and sail, swim, dive and fish in the bay.

White Beach on the eastern edge of town is good for sunbathing but swimming is only possible at high tide. Keep a good look out for pickpockets, who have been encouraged by unwary tourists. You can get to White Beach by tricycle by going in the direction of the airport and getting off at the Ice Plant. Just before the Ice Plant is an old gate; this is where the track to the beach starts. It's about 10 minutes' walk down to the beach. In the dry season you can go right to the beach by tricycle.

Each year there is a week-long festival which starts on 7 December. It includes concerts in Mendoza Park, Caracol boat processions, a beauty contest, quizzes, competitions, and so on.

Information

The Tourist Office has a counter at the airport but there is hardly ever anyone there. An office for Palawan Province is in the Provincial Capitol Building. For the most reliable and up-to-date information about Palawan, try the hostels, such as the Duchess Pension House and Abelardo's Pension.

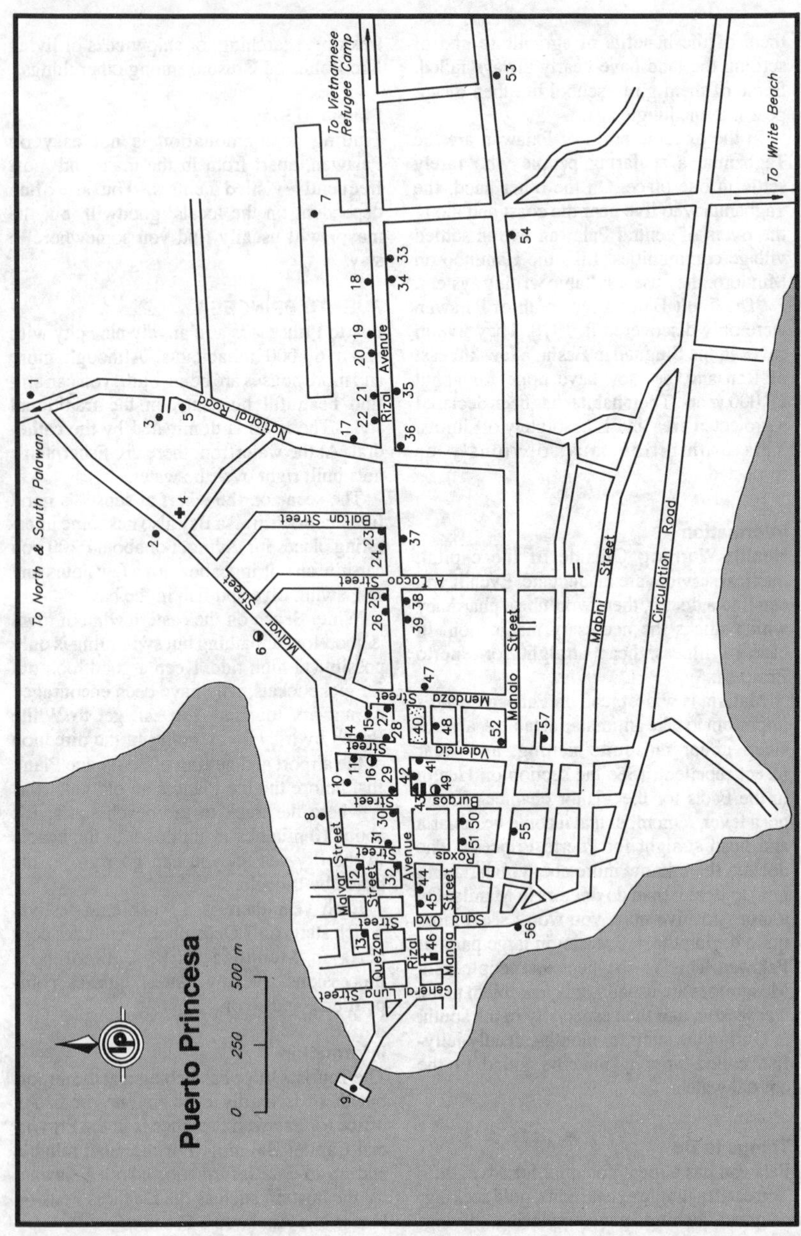
Puerto Princesa
0
250
500 m
To North & South Palawan
To Vietnamese Refugee Camp
To White Beach
National Road
Rizal Avenue
Malvar Street
Baltan Street
Lacao Street
Manalo Street
Mabini Street
Circulation Road
Mendoza Street
Valencia Street
Burgos Street
Roxas Street
Sandoval Street
Manga Street
General Luna Street
Quezon Street

1	Nightclubs	29	Roadside Pizza Inn
2	Emerald Hotel	30	Dynasty Hotel
3	Rafol's Hotel Palawan	31	Puerto Pension Inn
4	Provincial Hospital	32	Pink Lace Restaurant
5	Philippine National Bank	33	Double J Coffee Hauz
6	Charing Bus Lines	34	Palawan Hotel
	Jeepney Terminal	35	Badjao Inn
7	Airport		Bottle Ground Disco
8	Puerto Royale Bus Lines		Ihaw Ihaw Restaurant
9	Wharf	36	Provincial Capitol Building
10	Market	37	Kamayan Folkhouse & Restaurant
11	Bowling Lanes	38	Ellen Jenn Disco
	Cinema		Bottle Ground Disco
12	Holy Trinity College	39	Karla's Antiques
13	Ignacio Restaurant	40	Mendoza Park
14	Rengel's Store	41	Circon Lodge
15	Civens Lodge		El Tabon Disco
16	Jeepneys to Iwahig	42	Café Nostalgia
17	Bavaria Beer Garden	43	Post Office
18	Crystal Forest Grill Park	44	El Burrito Restaurant
19	Paradise Nightclub	45	Tipanan Restaurant
20	Island Divers Shop	46	Cathedral
21	Bistro JWS	47	Swimming Pool
	Rover's Inn	48	Police Station
22	Sheena's Little Garden Restaurant	49	Jeepneys to Santa Lourdes
23	William Lines	50	Palawan Shipping Corporation
24	Café Puerto	51	Abelardo's Pension
25	Garcellano Tourist Inn	52	College
	PCI Bank	53	Sonne Gasthaus
	Zum Kleinen Anker	54	Yayen's Pension
26	Golden Horse Restaurant	55	Fishery Bureau
27	PT&T Office	56	Mrs Abordo
28	Edwin's Food Palace & Disco	57	Duchess Pension House
	Metro Bank		

Diving Palawan is becoming more and more popular for underwater enthusiasts. For information about good diving places, ask Norman Songco of Island Divers in Rizal Ave. This diving shop runs organised trips. Hiring a complete outfit costs US$30 a day and you can get goggles and a snorkel for P80 a day. Diving tours for two or more divers cost US$40 per person a day. This includes transport, two tanks, a belt, a backpack, two dives a day and a meal. You can do a one-week diving course for US$300. Mr Gus in Sand Oval St, diagonally opposite the Ignacio Restaurant, also has tanks, backpacks, snorkels and goggles.

Plane Charter Pacific Airways has a six-seater Cessna for charter at P4000 an hour. Contact the pilot Captain Ely Bungabong at the airport.

Places to Stay – bottom end

Mrs Abordo (tel 2206), private lodgings in Sand Oval St, has basic but habitable rooms with fan for P35/70. *Duchess Pension House* (tel 2873) in Valencia St has singles/doubles with fan for P40/80 and doubles with fan and bath for P150. It is unpretentious but good. The managers, Joe and Cecille, are friendly and can give reliable travel information. They prepare meals to order. Girls from the Puerta 'scene' are not encouraged here.

Abelardo's Pension (tel 2068) at 62 Manga St has fairly good rooms with fan for P50/100 and with fan and bath for P75/150.

Garcellano Tourist Inn (tel 2314) at 257

Rizal Ave has singles with fan for P60 and singles/doubles with fan and bath for P80/120. It is unadorned and fairly good and has a large courtyard.

Civens Lodge is in a quiet location in Mendoza St and has basic rooms with fan for P65/75.

Yayen's Pension (tel 2261) in Manalo St Extension has rooms with fan for P40/80, with fan and bath for P100/130 and with air-con and bath for P270. It is homely and has a coffee shop and a garden. The owners have their own little island with a cottage in Honda Bay (see Honda Bay).

Sonne Gasthaus is a quiet place at 366 Manalo St Extension; it has rooms with fan for P80/120 and cottages with fan and bath for P200, as well as a restaurant.

Places to Stay – middle

Plaza Pension House at 353 Rizal Ave has rooms with fan for P150/180 and with air-con and bath for P350/450. It is clean and good and has a restaurant.

Circon Lodge (tel 2738) in Valencia St has rooms with fan and bath for P150 and with air-con and bath for P270. It is clean and fairly good and has a restaurant. It also has a nice balcony and offers transport to the airport.

Badjao Inn (tel 2761) in Rizal Ave has rooms with fan and bath for P200 and with air-con and bath for P350/385. The air-con rooms at least are clean and good, and there is a nice garden.

Palawan Hotel (tel 2326) is a comfortable place with a restaurant near the airport in Rizal Ave. It has rooms with fan for P260/320 and with air-con and bath for P370/435.

Places to Stay – top end

Emerald Hotel (tel 2611, 2263) in Malvar St has rooms with air-con and bath for P450/540. It is pleasant and attractive and has a restaurant and swimming pool, as well as transport to the airport.

Rafol's Hotel Palawan (tel 2022, 2111, 2212) in National Rd has rooms with air-con and bath for P795/925. It is beautifully kept and has a restaurant, swimming pool and disco.

Places to Eat

There are lots of restaurants in the side streets, but Rizal Ave alone offers a bewildering range of places to eat, reflecting the cosmopolitan range of tourists in Puerto Princesa and Palawan generally.

You can enjoy a good meal in an attractive setting at the *Café Puerto*, where the English chef Andrew prepares excellent French dishes. It is open from 11.30 am to 2 pm and from 5.30 pm to midnight. If you like Italian cuisine try the spaghetti and pizzas at the *Roadside Pizza Inn*.

The cuisine at the friendly *Pink Lace* includes Filipino, Chinese, Indian, Mexican and Vietnamese dishes and cakes. The Filipino dishes at the *Kamayan Folkhouse & Restaurant* are good and you can eat on the terrace or in the tree house.

At the cellar bar *Zum Kleinen Anker*, Achim and Honey serve Filipino and German meals and cold beer from 8 am to 10 pm. *Sheena's Little Garden Restaurant* also has good Filipino and German meals as well as good breakfasts. The *Tipanan Restaurant* and *El Burrito* serve good seafood as well as Mexican dishes.

At the entrance to the Vietnamese refugee camp, about two km out of town behind the airport, you will find the *Pho Dac Biet Restaurant*, which is open to the public. You can eat good cheap Vietnamese meals there as well as French-style bread from the camp bakery.

Entertainment

Films are shown on a big screen at *Edwin's Food Palace & Disco* at noon and 5.30 pm. From 8 pm this large Chinese restaurant becomes a disco. The *Café Nostalgia* entertains its guests with golden oldies, while the *Kamayan Folkhouse & Restaurant* has male and female folk singers.

Among the most popular discos are the *Rig Disco* in Rafol's *Hotel Palawan*, *El Tabon Disco*, behind the Circon Lodge, and the *Bottle Ground Disco*, which also features go-go girls.

Several nightclubs, such as *Eduardo's*, *Today's*, *Mina-Vic* and *Mahaligaya Mena Rosa*, are on the northern edge of town.

Getting Around

Airport Transport A trip in town by tricycle costs P1 per person and from the airport to town is about P2. Chartering a tricycle should not cost more than P30 an hour.

AROUND PUERTO PRINCESA

Balsahan

There is a resort by the river in Balsahan where the locals like to go on short holidays to relax and celebrate family occasions.

No direct connection exists between Puerto Princesa and Balsahan. At about 9.30 am a jeepney leaves Valencia St, near the market, for Iwahig. For a couple of extra pesos the driver may make the detour from the highway to Balsahan and pick you up again at about 1.30 pm.

Iwahig

The Iwahig Penal Colony is 23 km south of Puerto Princesa. Prisoners live here as in a normal village. They fish, cultivate rice and so on. There are no walls as the jungle and the sea make escape impossible. The warders and administrators have a good time here and are never short of workmen. Tourists are welcome as the souvenir shop sells handicrafts made by the prisoners. The prison colony also works as an advertisement for the government's modern and liberal penal policy. At the moment, about 4000 prisoners, called colonists, live there. About 65 of them have their families with them. This penal colony is self-supporting and needs no financial assistance from the State. The rate of recidivism of former prisoners is said to be markedly lower than in traditional prisons.

On the road to Iwahig is a crocodile farm kept by Japanese which is open to the public in the afternoon.

Getting There & Away A jeepney leaves Puerto Princesa for the Iwahig Penal Colony at 9.30 am from Valencia St, near the market, and returns at 1.30 pm. If you want to return later, you can walk to the highway and wait for a bus or jeepney coming from the south.

You can get a tricycle for the half-day trip to the Balsahan Resort, the crocodile farm and the prison colony, costing about P150 for the round trip.

Santa Lucia

Santa Lucia is a subcolony of Iwahig. There is a hot spring but you'll have to walk the seven km there and back. It's a favourite for weekend outings, after which the pool is cleaned out on Monday.

Several boats a day leave Puerto Princesa harbour daily for Santa Lucia as required.

Honda Bay

The islands in Honda Bay make a good day trip from Puerto Princesa. You can also stay there overnight. An almost intact coral reef exists between Canon and Pandan islands. The latter is among the best known islands in Honda Bay, but hardly anyone ever visits it. It should not be confused with the Pandan Island north of Roxas, which is the site of the Coco-Loco Resort. Snake Island is sandy and has a shallow coral reef on the landward side which is ideal for snorkelling. If you want to camp there for a few days, you have to take drinking water and provisions.

Near Snake Island is beautiful little Yayen's (Polding) Island, which belongs to the owner of Yayen's Pension in Puerto Princesa. In the late afternoon swarms of bats fly from Bat Island to the mainland.

On one small island, you will find the Starfish Sandbar Resort. Admission is P20 per head and you will get a sun shelter and two hammock-chairs. You can hire snorkel equipment and a small sailing boat there.

Places to Stay *Yayen's Cottage* on Yayen's Island has rooms for P35/70. There are plans to rebuild the decrepit cottage. You can get the latest news on this at Yayen's Pension in Puerto Princesa.

Meara Marina Island Resort on Meara Island is under Austrian management and

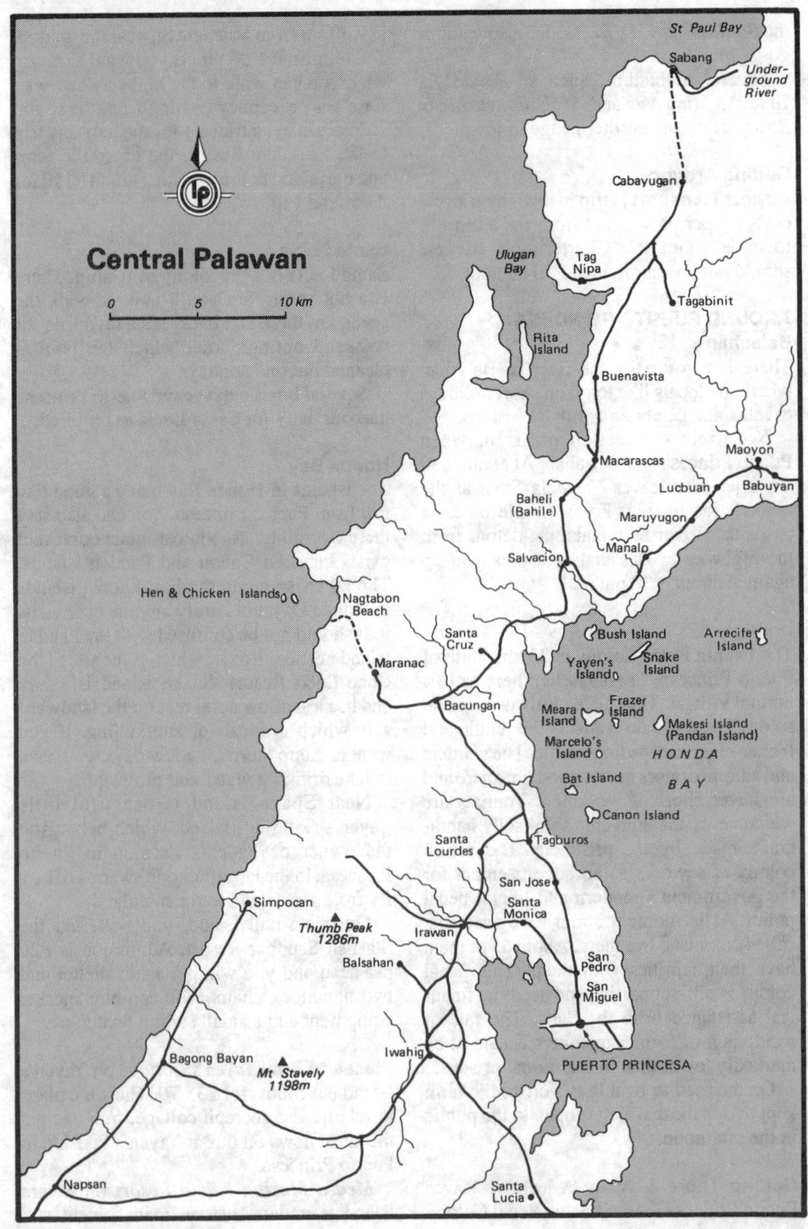
Central Palawan
0
5
10 km
St Paul Bay
Sabang
Underground River
Cabayugan
Ulugan Bay
Tag Nipa
Tagabinit
Rita Island
Buenavista
Macarascas
Maoyon
Babuyan
Lucbuan
Baheli (Bahile)
Maruyugon
Manalo
Salvacion
Hen & Chicken Islands
Nagtabon Beach
Santa Cruz
Bush Island
Arrecife Island
Yayen's Island
Snake Island
Maranac
Bacungan
Meara Island
Frazer Island
Makesi Island (Pandan Island)
Marcelo's Island
HONDA BAY
Bat Island
Canon Island
Santa Lourdes
Tagburos
San Jose
Santa Monica
Simpocan
Thumb Peak 1286m
Irawan
Balsahan
San Pedro
San Miguel
PUERTO PRINCESA
Iwahig
Bagong Bayan
Mt Stavely 1198m
Napsan
Santa Lucia

has doubles for P300 and cottages with double rooms and bath for P500. It is pleasant and attractive. The price includes breakfast and there is a restaurant and diving, including courses for beginners. Diving equipment is available. You can write to Franz and Marianne Urbanek at PO Box 4, 5300 Puerto Princesa.

Getting There & Away You can go from Puerto Princesa to Santa Lourdes Harbour (on the highway, north of Tagburos) by jeepney or bus going north. They leave from the jeepney terminal or from the market. Get off at the big Caltex tank and walk towards the waterfront, where you can hire a boat. Bong, the owner of *Norma*, has a good name for reasonable hire prices. The price for a round trip should be about P350 to P400.

A tricycle from Puerto Princesa to Santa Lourdes harbour costs P20.

NAGTABON BEACH

White Nagtabon Beach lies on a beautiful calm bay looking out on Hen & Chicken Islands. Unfortunately, as on many Palawan beaches, the tiny 'nik-niks' are always around ready to attack unprotected sun worshippers. An effective protection against these troublesome sandflies is coconut oil mixed with a few drops of insect repellent such as Autan or Off.

Places to Stay

Georg's Place has cottages for P75 and with bath for P100/200-250. There is a restaurant with Filipino and European cuisine. Georg and Lozy Bauer are a German-Filipino couple. Their postal address is PO Box 067, 5300 Puerto Princesa.

Zeny's Place has cottages for P80 and also has a restaurant.

Getting There & Away

There is a daily jeepney from Puerto Princesa to Nagtabon Beach at 7.30 or 10 am. If there are not enough passengers, the trip may finish at Maranac. From Maranac it's about an hour's walk down to the beach. A Special Ride from Puerto Princesa to Nagtabon Beach costs P500.

UNDERGROUND RIVER

Baheli and Macarascas are two starting points for trips by outrigger boat to the Underground River. Most tourists leave from Baheli, where the round trip by boat costs P600; from Macarascas it only costs P300. It takes about three hours to reach the small bay with an entrance to the Underground River. From there small paddle bancas go into the cave, officially known as St Paul's Cave, whose system has an overall length of seven km. In the light of the kerosene lamp you can see countless bats which come to life at night. Night trips are possible; if you want to take photos, you will need a powerful flash both during the day and at night.

The trip to the Underground River from Baheli or Macarascas is not possible during the south-west monsoon season from June to November, when the waves in the South China Sea are simply too big for outrigger boats. You can, however, go overland at this and other times.

From Baheli an outrigger boat normally leaves daily at 1 pm for Tag Nipa, taking an hour or more. The hike from Tag Nipa to Sabang via Cabayugan takes about three hours. From Sabang you walk along the beach and over a hill to the ranger's house in St Paul's National Park. The guides there will take you to the Underground River and provide information about it for P50. It is worth spending a few days in Sabang to enjoy the fine beaches, the nearby jungle and primitive landscape.

If you want to get from Sabang to Puerto Princesa in one day you will have to start at about 4 am, as the boat from Tag Nipa leaves for Baheli between 7 and 8 am.

You can also go to the Underground River from Tanabag near San Rafael by a three-day walk right across Palawan, and from Port Barton in one day by boat.

Places to Stay

Between Baheli and the Underground River,

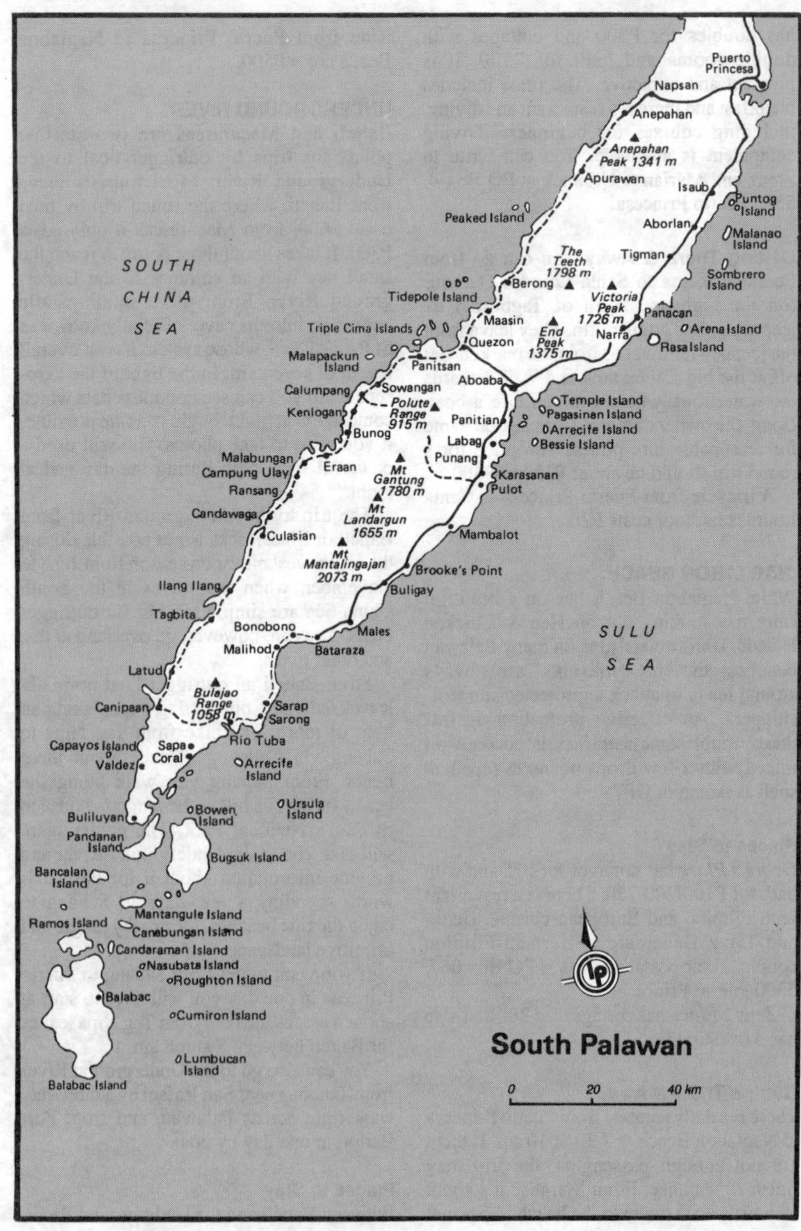

SOUTH CHINA SEA
SULU SEA
Puerto Princesa
Napsan
Anepahan
Anepahan Peak 1341 m
Apurawan
Isaub
Puntog Island
Peaked Island
Aborlan
Malanao Island
The Teeth 1798 m
Tigman
Sombrero Island
Berong
Victoria Peak 1726 m
Tidepole Island
Panacan
Maasin
End Peak 1375 m
Arena Island
Triple Cima Islands
Quezon
Narra
Rasa Island
Malapackun Island
Panitsan
Aboaba
Calumpang
Sowangan
Temple Island
Polute Range 915 m
Pagasinan Island
Kenlogan
Panitian
Arrecife Island
Bunog
Labag
Bessie Island
Punang
Malabungan
Eraan
Campung Ulay
Mt Gantung 1780 m
Karasanan
Ransang
Pulot
Mt Landargun 1655 m
Candawaga
Culasian
Mambalot
Mt Mantalingajan 2073 m
Brooke's Point
Ilang Ilang
Buligay
Tagbita
Bonobono
Males
Malihod
Bataraza
Latud
Bulajao Range 1058 m
Canipaan
Sarap
Sarong
Rio Tuba
Capayos Island
Sapa
Coral
Valdez
Arrecife Island
Ursula Island
Bowen Island
Buliluyan
Pandanan Island
Bugsuk Island
Bancalan Island
Mantangule Island
Ramos Island
Canebungan Island
Candaraman Island
Nasubata Island
Roughton Island
Balabac
Cumiron Island
Lumbucan Island
Balabac Island
South Palawan
0
20
40 km

you can stay the night at Jonis Oli's in Macarascas, Nelson Relovao's and Tatang Gonzales's in Tag Nipa, Joe and Helena's in Cabayagan and at the park ranger's in Sabang, for about P25 per person. It is basic accommodation and the meals are mostly simple.

Getting There & Away

There is a jeepney from Puerto Princesa to Baheli at 8 am, taking two hours or more. This jeepney may go on via Macarascas to Cabayugan; it is planned to build the road as far as Sabang.

You can also hire a boat from Port Barton to Baheli for P1500 for the round trip.

From Baheli to Puerto Princesa, a jeepney leaves at 8 am.

QUEZON

Quezon is a small fishing village on Malanut Bay. It is the departure point for the Tabon Caves, whose main entrance is on the north-west side of Lipuun Point. By boat the trip to the caves takes only 30 minutes and should not cost more than P150.

This giant system consists of 200 caves. Only 29 have been explored and are open to the public. Tabon Cave is the biggest and Diwata Cave, 30 metres above sea level, the highest and most beautiful. Because of prehistoric finds, they are of great importance. Human bones going back to the Stone Age have been found here and are thought to be the remains of the original inhabitants, the Pala'wan.

Ask at the National Museum in Quezon for an experienced guide to the Tabon Caves. Don't expect too much from the caves, however, as all you can see are some large holes in the mountainside.

After you've gone cave exploring, you might be tempted to go island hopping on the nearby islands with their white beaches, for example on Sidanao or Tataran islands. Far offshore on Tamlugan Island is a German called Frederick living a Robinson Crusoe existence together with a collection of animals, including sea eagles, chickens and goannas. If you want to visit him, you will need to take your own supplies. Two basic huts are available for visitors, and, although Frederick does not have a fixed charge for their use, he does expect a moderate contribution towards the completion of his tropical Garden of Eden.

A Belgian named Theo wants to set up cottages on nearby Palm (Mansaruyan) Island. He also runs the Tabon Village Resort on Tabon Beach, four km north-east of Quezon, which is where you'll probably find him. From here it's about an hour's walk to the Tumarbon Waterfall, or you can go by boat on the Tumarbon River through dense jungle. It takes 45 minutes to reach the mouth of the river and another 30 minutes to reach the waterfall.

Places to Stay

Dias Boarding House is right by the wharf and has rooms for P25/50. It is comfortable and has a restaurant. You can also obtain information about boats to offshore islands. *Paganiban Lodge* has simple rooms for P35/70, as well as a restaurant and disco.

Tabon Village Resort on Tabon Beach, about four km north-east of Quezon, has rooms for P50/70 and cottages with bath for P90/120. It is simple and fairly good and has a restaurant.

Places to Eat

Dias Restaurant and *Paganiban Restaurant* are both basic but serve good and reasonable meals. A bit dearer but very good are the meals in the tastefully designed and decorated *Mutya ng Dagak* (Pearl of the Sea). It is part of the Tabon Village Resort and is on an artificial island that is connected to the beach by a bridge.

Getting There & Away

Charing Bus Lines buses run daily from the Puerto Princesa jeepney terminal to Quezon at 7 and 9 am and 1 pm. The trip takes over three hours.

From Quezon to Puerto Princesa, the buses leave at 6 and 11.30 am.

Several jeepneys leave early in the

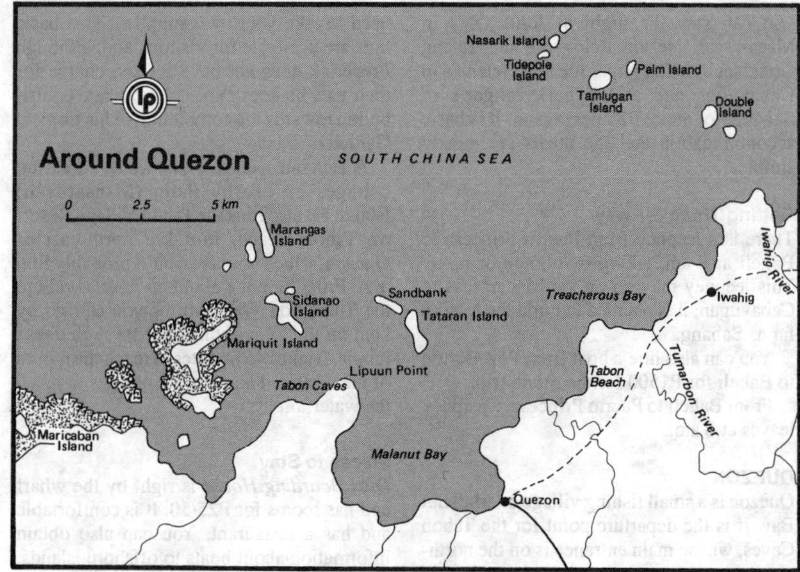

morning from both Quezon and Puerto Princesa.

NARRA

Narra makes a good stop on the way to South Palawan and nearby are the Estrella Waterfalls.

Places to Stay

The *Tiosin Boarding House* in Panacan Rd has rooms with fan for P35/70. It is a simple place and has good, well-priced meals.

Gardenia Boarding House has fairly clean rooms with fan for P40/70 and with fan and bath for P100/150.

Mount Victoria Lodge has rooms with fan for P40/80. It is simple, clean and quiet.

Getting There & Away

Many jeepneys run daily from Puerto Princesa to Narra as do several buses, some going on to Quezon and Brooke's Point. The trip takes two hours.

BROOKE'S POINT & URSULA ISLAND

Thousands of birds used to nest on Ursula Island, where they would return in swarms in the evening after foraging on other islands. However, a plague of rats has caused most birds to shift their nests, mainly to the faraway Tubbataha Reef. Ursula Island is uninhabited and there is no drinking water.

About 10 km north of Brooke's Point, near Mainit, are a small waterfall and hot sulphur springs.

The area to the west and south-west of Brooke's Point may be a crisis area and dangerous for travellers.

Places to Stay

Villa Senor Boarding House has rooms for P80/90 and with fan for P85/95. It is unadorned, clean and good and staff will prepare meals if you order them in advance.

Silayan Lodge has dorm beds for P40; rooms with fan for P50-80/100; with fan and bath for P120/140; and with air-con and bath for P230/250. It is unpretentious but good.

Sunset Travel Lodge & Garden has basic

rooms with fan and bath for P40-50/80-110-180, and with air-con and bath for P275.

Getting There & Away

A few Puerto Royale buses run from the market at Puerto Princesa to Brooke's Point in the morning, taking five hours.

You can get special outrigger boat rides to Ursula Island from Brooke's Point, Bataraza and Rio Tuba for about P500.

RIO TUBA

Occasionally freighters are supposed to sail from Rio Tuba to Cagayan de Tawi-Tawi Island (Cagayan de Sulu Island), where there are sometimes opportunities for onward travel to Jolo or Zamboanga via Pangutaran Island.

You can stay overnight at Rio Tuba in basic hostels at the wharf. The price is a matter for negotiation.

Getting There & Away

From Brooke's Point a large outrigger boat sails daily at 8 am for Rio Tuba. At midday a jeepney runs from Brooke's Point to Rio Tuba via Bataraza. Outrigger boats also travel between Bataraza and Rio Tuba.

SAN RAFAEL & TANABAG

San Rafael has only a few huts, which are strung out along the highway, a school and two small shops, where you can't buy much anyway. From San Rafael you can go and visit the Batak with a guide. Two excellent and sensitive guides to this ethnic minority are Nelson Pagayona and Gabriel. They are also good at helping with treks through the central jungles of Palawan, both in planning and in undertaking them. Whether you want to visit the Batak is something you will have to decide for yourself. The few remaining tribes of these nomadic people certainly do not need any contact with travellers.

Two km east of San Rafael is the little village of Tanabag. From the unique prison on the highway, a road leads to the beach with the Duchess Beachside Cottages. You will like this place if you want peace and quiet. It is also a good departure point for longer treks, such as St Paul's National Park with its Underground River, on the other side of Palawan.

Places to Stay

Duchess Beachside Cottages has singles for P30 and cottages with singles/doubles for P70. It is basic but habitable and there is a restaurant.

Getting There & Away

Between 5 and 7 am, three Puerto Royale buses a day run from the market in Puerto Princesa to San Rafael, going on to Roxas. The trip takes two hours. In the morning there are also several jeepneys from the market or the jeepney terminal.

ROXAS & PANDAN ISLAND

Roxas is a pleasant little place right by the sea. Fish and fruit are on sale in the relatively large market at reasonable prices. If you want to stay on a desert island in the north of Palawan, Roxas is the last place for buying equipment. You can get things like canisters and buckets in out-of-the-way places such as El Nido, but not less common items like cookers. The extensive bay beyond Roxas has several small islands, including beautiful Pandan Island with the Coco-Loco Resort. Every day at about 2 pm the resort's outrigger boat returns to the island after buying supplies in Roxas. You can get a ride for P45 per person.

Places to Stay

Gordon's is a simple place in Roxas with rooms for P25/50. *Gamalain Inn*, another basic place in Roxas, by the market, has rooms for P30/60. There is a restaurant which doubles as a disco at night.

Tito's Canteen in Roxas has rooms for P30/60. It has a restaurant and the friendly landlady has a lot of information about the Coco-Loco Resort and Port Barton.

Coco-Loco Resort on Pandan Island has cottages with singles/doubles for P120/150. It is homely and has a restaurant. It also has windsurfing, outrigger boats, paddle bancas, billiards and table tennis.

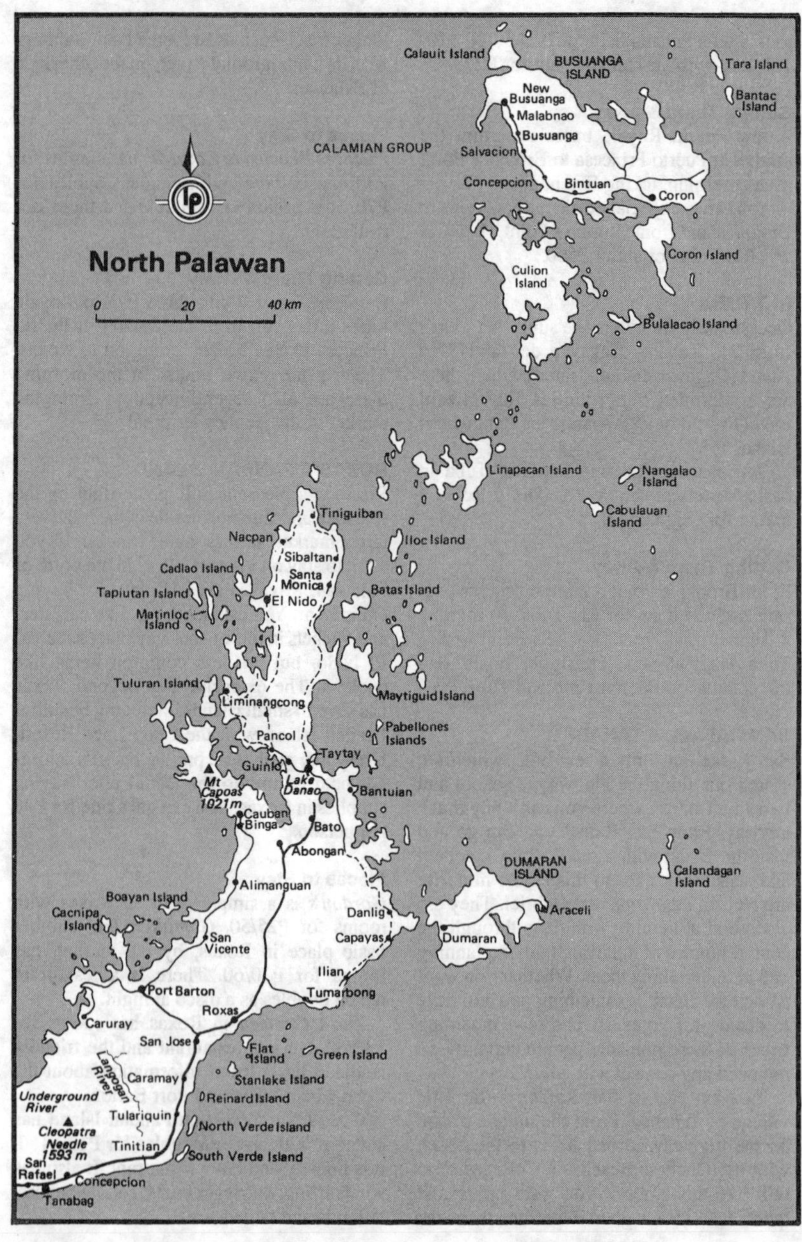
North Palawan
0
20
40 km
CALAMIAN GROUP
Calauit Island
BUSUANGA ISLAND
Tara Island
Bantac Island
New Busuanga
Malabnao
Busuanga
Salvacion
Concepcion
Bintuan
Coron
Coron Island
Culion Island
Bulalacao Island
Linapacan Island
Nangalao Island
Cabulauan Island
Tiniguiban
Nacpan
Iloc Island
Sibaltan
Cadlao Island
Santa Monica
Batas Island
Tapiutan Island
El Nido
Matinloc Island
Tuluran Island
Liminangcong
Maytiguid Island
Pabellones Islands
Pancol
Taytay
Guinlo
Lake Danao
Mt Capoas 1021m
Bantuian
Cauban
Binga
Bato
Abongan
DUMARAN ISLAND
Calandagan Island
Alimanguan
Boayan Island
Danlig
Araceli
Cacnipa Island
Capayas
Dumaran
San Vicente
Ilian
Port Barton
Tumarbong
Roxas
Caruray
San Jose
Flat Island
Green Island
Langogan River
Caramay
Stanlake Island
Underground River
Reinard Island
Tulariquin
Cleopatra Needle 1593 m
North Verde Island
Tinitian
South Verde Island
San Rafael
Concepcion
Tanabag

Getting There & Away

Three Puerto Royale buses leave the Puerto Princesa market for Roxas daily between 5 and 7 am. In case of demand there may be another one at about 9 am. In the morning several dusty jeepneys also make the run. The trip takes five hours.

PORT BARTON

Port Barton has only a few houses. It is on Pagdanan Bay and has an extensive, reasonably good beach. You can hire outrigger boats for P300 a day and visit the nearby islands, some of which have really beautiful white beaches. You can enjoy good snorkelling off Inadawan (formerly Tomas Tan) Island and in the so-called aquarium. The colourful coral reefs off Exotica and Albaguin islands have unfortunately been largely destroyed by dynamite fishing. In the country around Port Barton there are several waterfalls. Honeybee Valley is on the way to Caruray.

Port Barton has become a popular rendezvous in northern Palawan. For many travellers it is the last stopover in this direction. That will change once El Nido and the north-west coast, with its innumerable offshore islands, have better transport connections. If you want to economise, you won't like Port Barton, as everything has a fixed price. Boat outings in particular are strictly regulated. No boat can take more than six passengers or take on passengers from another boat, nor can anything but the fixed price be charged. If boat operators do not stick to these regulations, which were made in 1989, they will soon get into trouble with KAMADA. This is a kind of trade union which has outlawed free competition in Port Barton 'for the protection and safety' of tourists.

The following round-trip fares were binding in 1990: Island hopping P300, San Vicente, Boayan and Albaguin P400, Baheli P1800, El Nido P2000, Underground River P1000. The charge for waiting time is P400 per person a day.

The boat trip from Port Barton to the Underground River takes at least four hours. It is important to leave early or you'll have no time to see the river.

Places to Stay

Elsa's Beach House has rooms for P40/80 and cottages with singles/doubles and bath for P150/200, as well as a restaurant.

Swissipini Lodge has rooms for P40/80 and singles/doubles/cottages with bath for P120/150/160; there is a restaurant. Be warned: Martin, who is Swiss, and his wife, Flora, assume that guests will eat there. If you want to find another restaurant, you had better let them know or they will charge you for meals.

El Busero Inn has rooms for P80/100 and cottages with singles/doubles and bath for P120/150. It has a restaurant. The owner Urs, also Swiss, does diving trips, too.

The *Paradiso Beach Resort* has dorms for P30, singles for P50, doubles with bath for P100 and cottages with bath for P70/100.

At the eastern edge of Port Barton, the *Shangri La Beach Resort* has cottages with bath for P100 to P350, depending on the size of the cottage. There is a restaurant, and you can hire snorkel and windsurfing equipment and paddle boats.

Manta Ray Island Resort on Capsalay Island has cottages with singles/doubles for P750/1500 including meals. It is a beautiful place with a restaurant and is managed by Paola, an Italian.

Places to Eat

The places just mentioned serve good and plentiful meals but the owners appreciate prior notice. The village itself has a small, cheap restaurant called *Evergreen* on the main road. The restaurant-bar *Ginger's Cave* serves drinks until quite late. They also show video clips and movies.

Getting There & Away

Several jeepneys run daily to Port Barton from the jeepney terminal in Puerto Princesa, taking six hours. Occasionally there are faster jeepneys with relatively few passengers and ample space for luggage, but they cost double the normal fare. You can also go

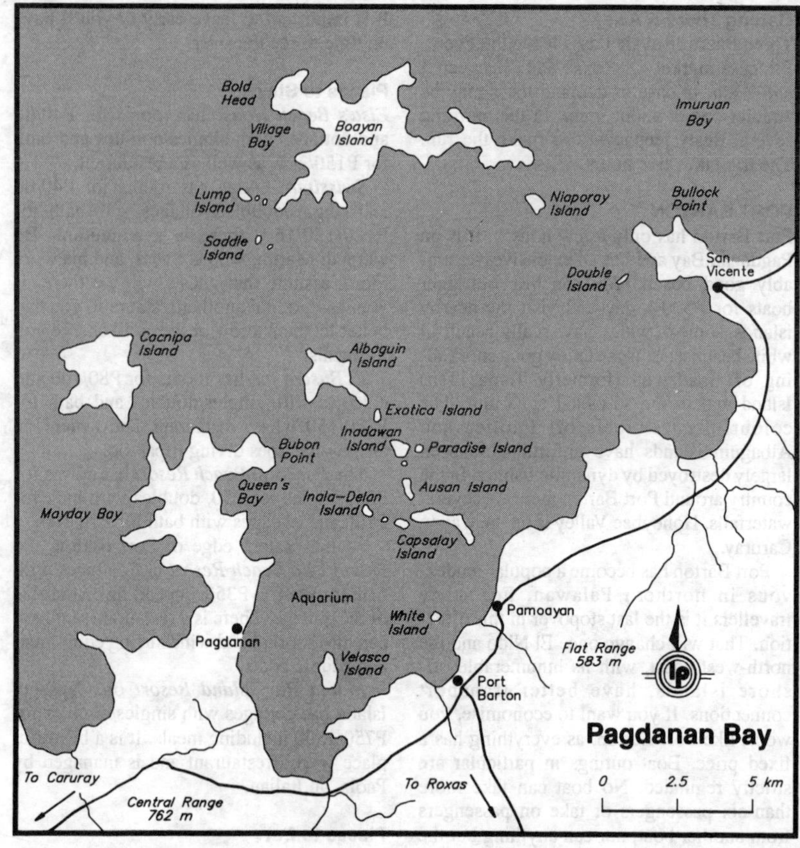

first to Roxas by bus or jeepney and then catch a jeepney going to Port Barton.

Several jeepneys a day leave Roxas market for Port Barton, taking one hour.

A jeepney runs daily to Puerto Princesa from Port Barton market at 6 am; a Special Ride costs about P1500. Two jeepneys go to Roxas daily from Port Barton at 6 am.

SAN VICENTE

San Vicente lies on a peninsula, about 18 km north-east of Port Barton. On the other side is a long beach that you will like if you want to be alone. You have to find private accommodation to stay overnight in San Vicente.

Getting There & Away

Since the road from Port Barton to San Vicente was finished it has deteriorated so much that you can't travel between the two by jeepney. The trip by outrigger boat takes one hour.

There is a jeepney connection between San Vicente and Roxas.

ABONGAN & TABUAN

Abongan is a tiny place on the Abongan

River. The trip from Roxas leads through a beautiful landscape, some of it dense jungle. The track to Taytay turns off just before Abongan. It takes about 30 minutes to walk from Abongan to Tabuan, a small river port which is also on the Abongan River.

From Tabuan you can get a boat to Liminangcong and Embarcadero or Taytay. A boat leaves for Liminangcong on Friday, Saturday and Sunday at about 11 am, costing P50 per person. The departure times are not completely reliable and you may have to charter a boat; a Special Ride to Liminangcong costs P500. The trip takes four hours.

You can also go to El Nido by boat, which costs P100 per person and P800 for a Special Ride. The trip down the Abongan River is beautiful and animated – the river still has crocodiles! Further on you go through Malampaya Sound, which is a giant fish trap.

Places to Stay

In Tabuan there is only private accommodation. Baby and Manuel Padernilla, who live by the footbridge over the river, charge P25 per person.

Getting There & Away

A few jeepneys leave Roxas market daily for Abongan, taking three hours or more.

TAYTAY & EMBARCADERO

Taytay is the old capital of Palawan. You can still visit the fort which was built by the Spaniards in 1622 and of which only ruins remain. The church is about 300 years old. There is a hospital and numerous shops which have an astonishing range of goods.

From Taytay you can go to the Pabellones Islands by outrigger boat, which takes about one hour. These are three small islands with sheer limestone cliffs. The many caves and cracks yield birds' nests for bird's nest soup. Elefante Island has a lagoon which is good for snorkelling.

Only a few km south of Taytay is Lake Danao, which is 62 ha in size. It has small islands and is surrounded by primaeval forest. It takes about 30 minutes to get there by jeepney.

Embarcadero is about six km west of Taytay. Almost daily, but at least twice a week, outrigger boats leave Tabuan, near Abongan, and go down the mangrove river to Malampaya Sound and then on to Liminangcong. You can also get a Special Ride further north to El Nido. A Special Ride costs P350 to Liminangcong and P700 to El Nido. Tricycles run between Embarcadero and Taytay, and you can sometimes also get a jeepney.

Places to Stay

Publico's International Guest House in Taytay has rooms for P40/80. It is simple, clean and good and has a restaurant. *Pem's Cottage Inn* in Taytay on Taytay Bay, near the fort, also has a restaurant. It has quite good rooms for P30/50, with fan for P40/70 and with fan and bath for P70/120.

Embarcadero Riverview Guesthouse in Embarcadero has rooms for P10/20. It is unadorned but good and has good cuisine, especially seafood.

Getting There & Away

A jeepney leaves Roxas for Taytay daily at noon after the the bus from Puerto Princesa arrives. The trip takes over four hours. From Taytay the jeepney to Roxas leaves between 7 and 8 am.

LIMINANGCONG

During the north-east monsoons, Liminangcong becomes a fishing centre. People there are friendly and helpful and the place itself is surprisingly peaceful as there are no cars. There is a cinema, for a change, and a small restaurant.

From Liminangcong you can go to the small offshore Saddle and Camago islands. You can also get boats to islands further north. Apart from that, there are always irregular shipping connections to Manila. The shopkeepers often know more about departure times than the coastguard.

Butterflies of the Philippines

Demoleus demoleus

Graphium anthipathes itamputi

Troides magellanus

Papilio idaeoides

Papilion doson gyndes

Zeuxidia semperi

Graphium agamemnon agamemnon

Papilio trojana

Pantoporia maenas semperi

Salatura genutia

Places to Stay

There is only private accommodation, for instance with Mr Abrina opposite the school for P30.

Getting There & Away

From Tabuan several outrigger boats a week leave for Liminangcong, almost certainly on Friday, Saturday and Sunday at 11 am, taking four hours. The fare is P50 per person and a Special Ride costs P500.

From Embarcadero several outrigger boats a week leave for Liminangcong. A Special Ride costs P350.

To travel to El Nido costs P25 per person, but you usually have to charter a boat. This is worthwhile if you want to get to know some of the islands in the Bacuit archipelago. A Special Ride to El Nido should cost about P300.

EL NIDO & BACUIT ARCHIPELAGO

El Nido is probably the most beautiful place in Palawan. Surrounded by steep, sheer limestone cliffs, it has attractive and well-maintained streets and houses. What's more, there are no cars.

You can go on some fascinating trips from El Nido to the offshore islands of the Bacuit archipelago, which have been almost ignored by tourists. The only development has been on Miniloc Island, half an hour by boat from El Nido, where the Japanese company Ten Knots has built the El Nido Resort. The deeply indented coast, a little to the north of this establishment, leads to a beautiful lagoon in the island's interior which is only accessible by boat.

Jock Gordon, a Scotsman, and his Filipina wife, Beccy, keep a small resort on Pangalusian Island. Unlike most of the other islands in the archipelago, which are steep and rocky with small sandy bays, Pangalusian is flat, covered in dense growth and has a long palm-fringed white beach. If you are travelling by boat from Manila to Liminangcong and want to get off at Pangalusian Island, ask the operators to blow the horn twice. A boat will then come from the island to meet you.

Inabuyatan Island is another South Seas dream island with a white beach covered in palms.

Pinsail Island looks like an insignificant rock but it has a cathedral-like cave which you can enter and is especially impressive when the sunlight streams in from above.

The archipelago abounds in reefs of living coral and colourful fish. The passage between Tapiutan and Matinloc islands is very attractive, as is Binangculan Bay in the north-west of Tapiutan Island, which has small white beaches. You will also find beaches and interesting coral in Calmung Bay on Matinloc Island and on the southern tip and west coast of North Guntao Island, where you can climb and get a wonderful view. Ubugun Bay, on Cadlao Island, is great for snorkelling but only from a boat.

Ellis Lim charges P300 a day for boat hire, including fuel. If that's too much, and you still want to go snorkelling and visit beaches other than El Nido, try Karong Karong Bay, three km south. From there for you can get the fishermen to drop you off at the small sand beaches of the peninsula's south-west coast for P20.

Snorkel and diving equipment can be hired from Willy, a German diving instructor, who runs diving courses and trips for a reasonable price.

Places to Stay

There are several places in El Nido. *Mr Austria Lodge* has dorm beds for P20, rooms for P30/60 and a restaurant. Both *Gloria Fernandez Cottage* and *Ellis Lim's Pension House* have rooms for P40/80 and meals can be arranged.

The *Bay View Inn* has rooms for P70/100, is comfortable and has a nice balcony. You can get good meals next door or in the place opposite the hotel.

Lally & Abet Beach Cottage & Lodging House has rooms with fan and bath for P50/100. There is a small restaurant.

Pangalusian Island Resort on a beautiful, long beach on Pangalusian Island has cottages with bath for US$42 per person, including two excellent meals.

El Nido Resort on Miniloc Island has very

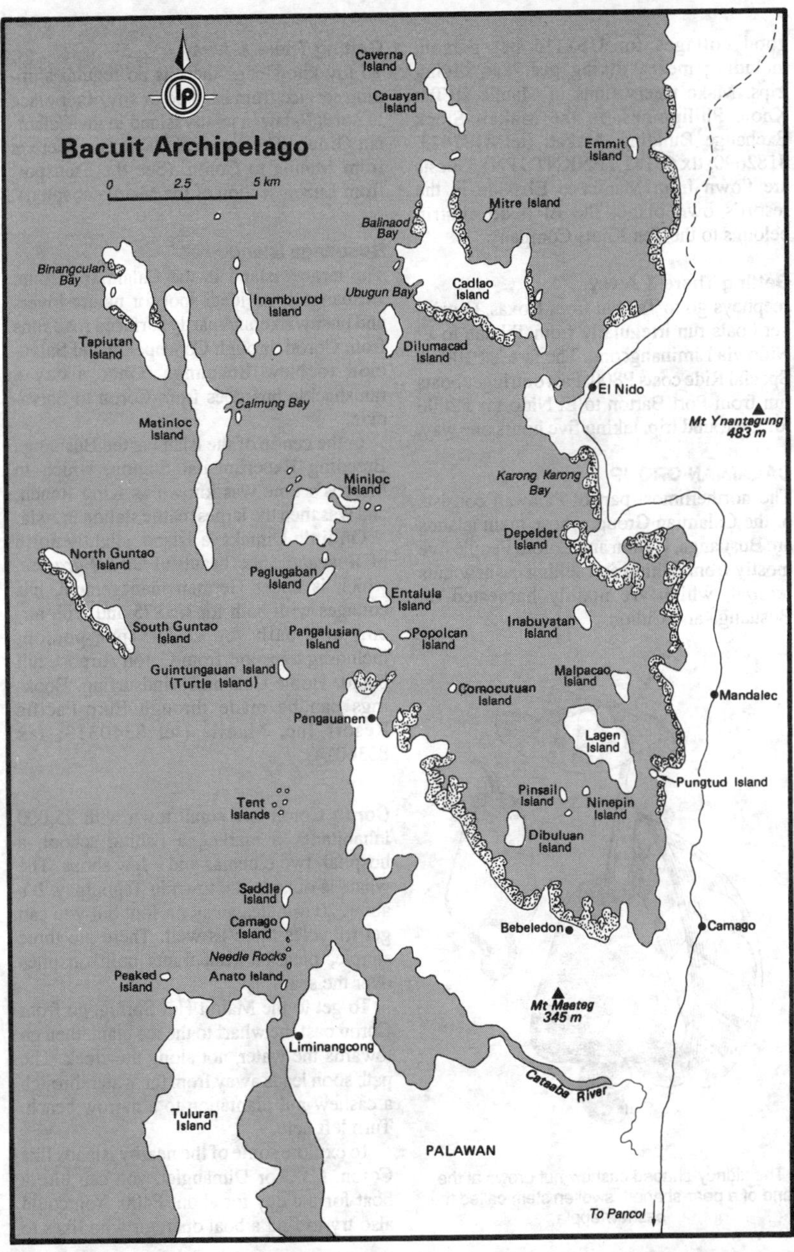

Bacuit Archipelago
0 2.5 5 km
Caverna Island
Cauayan Island
Emmit Island
Mitre Island
Balinaod Bay
Binangculan Bay
Cadlao Island
Ubugun Bay
Inambuyod Island
Tapiutan Island
Dilumacad Island
El Nido
Calmung Bay
Matinloc Island
Mt Ynantagung 483 m
Karong Karong Bay
Miniloc Island
Depeldet Island
North Guntao Island
Paglugaban Island
Entalula Island
South Guntao Island
Pangalusian Island
Popolcan Island
Inabuyatan Island
Guintungauan Island (Turtle Island)
Malpacao Island
Comocutuan Island
Mandalec
Pangauanen
Lagen Island
Pungtud Island
Tent Islands
Pinsail Island
Ninepin Island
Dibuluan Island
Saddle Island
Camago Island
Camago
Bebeledon
Needle Rocks
Peaked Island
Anato Island
Mt Maateg 345 m
Liminangcong
Cataaba River
Tuluran Island
PALAWAN
To Pancol

good cottages for US$115 per person, including meals, diving gear and diving trips. Make reservations in Manila at Ten Knots Philippines, in the Makati Stock Exchange Building, Makati (tel 8182623, 8182690; tlx 63141 TENKNTS PN). Guests are flown from Manila to El Nido in the resort's own plane; the El Nido airstrip belongs to the Ten Knots Company.

Getting There & Away

Jeepneys go to Tabuan from Roxas. Outrigger boats run irregularly from Tabuan to El Nido via Liminangcong. The fare is P100. A Special Ride costs P800. Fast outrigger boats run from Port Barton to El Nido for P2000 for the round trip, taking five hours one way.

CALAMIAN GROUP

The northernmost part of Palawan consists of the Calamian Group, whose main islands are Busuanga, Culion and Coron. People live mostly from fishing and selling cashew nuts *(kasoy)*, which are mainly harvested on Busuanga and Culion.

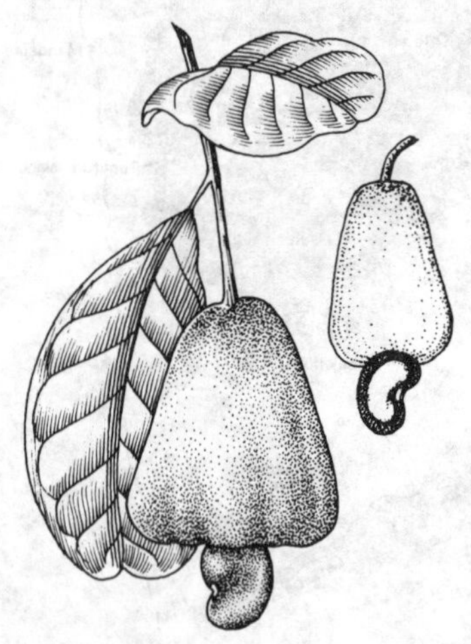

The kidney-shaped cashew nut grows at the end of a pear-shaped, swollen stem called the cashew apple

Getting There & Away

To my knowledge there is no regular shipping service from El Nido or any other place in north Palawan to any island in the Calamian Group. The simplest way to get there is from Manila to Coron. (See the Transport from Luzon section of the Manila chapter.)

Busuanga Island

The largest island in the Calamian Group, Busuanga is an ideal spot for nature lovers and bushwalkers. A partly surfaced road runs from Coron through Concepcion and Salvacion to New Busuanga. Once a day a ramshackle bus goes from Coron to Salvacion.

In the centre of the island is the Busuanga Breeding Experimental Station, which in Marcos's time was known as King Ranch, and was then the largest cattle station in Asia.

On little Dimakaya Island, slightly north of Busuanga, the beautiful *Club Paradise*, which is under German management, has cottages with bath for US$75 and with aircon and bath for US$95 per person, including transport from Coron Airport, full board, Hobie Cats and windsurfing. Bookings can be made through Euro-Pacific Resort Inc, Manila (tel 8340313; fax 8336014).

Coron Coron is a small town with 25,000 inhabitants, a market, a fishing school, a hospital, two cinemas and a few shops. The wharf is outside the town in Tagumpay. It's about 20 minutes away on foot but you can get tricycles there as well. There are three simple, pleasant restaurants built on piles over the sea.

To get to the Mainit Hot Spring, go from Coron past the wharf to the ice plant, then go towards the water, not along the creek. The path soon leads away from the water through a cashew-nut plantation to a narrow beach. Turn left here.

To explore some of the nearby islands like Coron, CYC or Dimanglet, you can hire a boat for the day for about P400. You could also try to find a boat operator who likes to

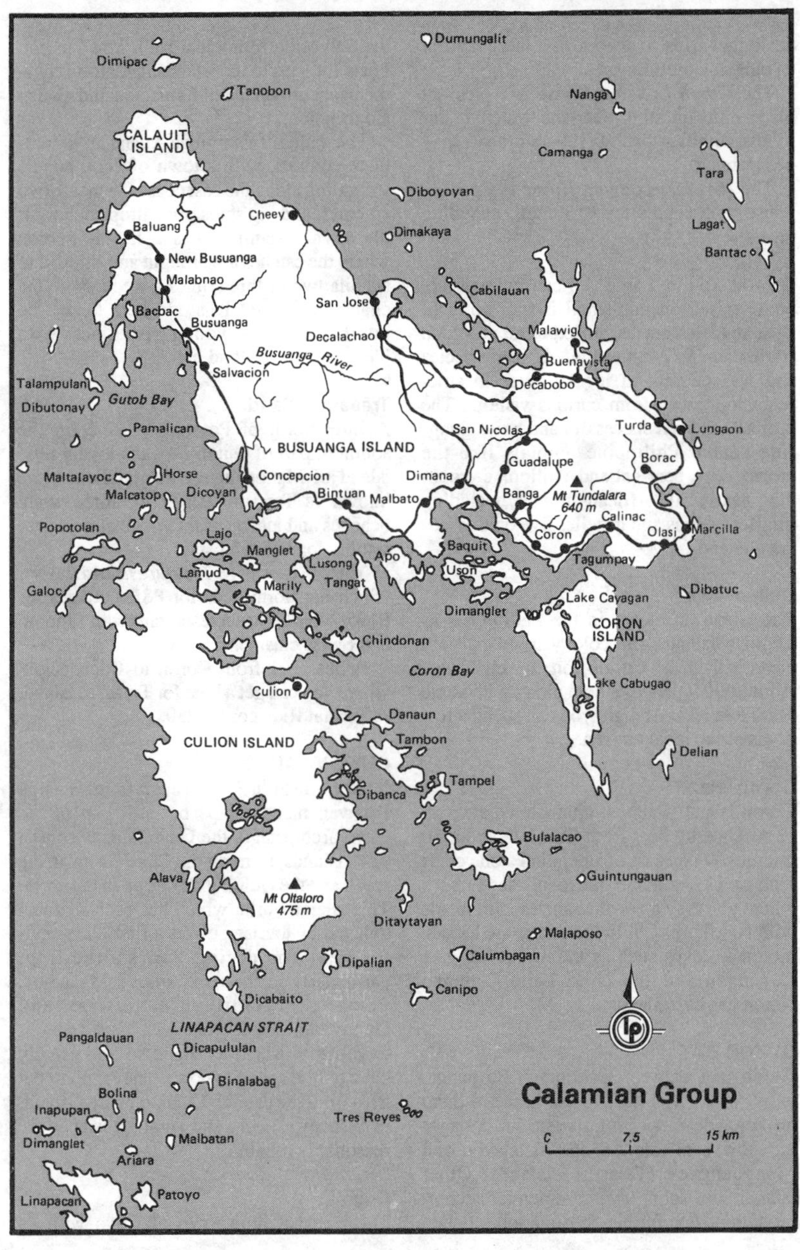
Dumungalit
Dimipac
Tanobon
Nanga
CALAUIT ISLAND
Camanga
Tara
Diboyoyan
Cheey
Baluang
Dimakaya
Lagat
Bantac
New Busuanga
Malabnao
San Jose
Cabilauan
Bacbac
Busuanga
Decalachao
Malawig
Busuanga River
Buenavista
Salvacion
Decabobo
Talampulan
Gutob Bay
Dibutonay
Turda
Lungaon
Pamalican
San Nicolas
BUSUANGA ISLAND
Guadalupe
Borac
Maltalayoc
Horse
Concepcion
Dimana
Mt Tundalara 640 m
Malcatop
Dicoyan
Bintuan
Malbato
Banga
Calinac
Popotolan
Marcilla
Lajo
Coron
Olasi
Manglet
Baquit
Tagumpay
Lusong
Apo
Lamud
Uson
Galoc
Marily
Tangat
Dibatuc
Lake Cayagan
Dimanglet
CORON ISLAND
Chindonan
Coron Bay
Culion
Lake Cabugao
Danaun
Tambon
CULION ISLAND
Delian
Tampel
Dibanca
Bulalacao
Guintungauan
Alava
Mt Oltaloro 475 m
Ditaytayan
Malaposo
Calumbagan
Dipalian
Canipo
Dicabaito
LINAPACAN STRAIT
Pangaldauan
Dicapululan
Binalabag
Calamian Group
Bolina
Inapupan
Tres Reyes
Malbatan
Dimanglet
Ariara
Linapacan
Patoyo
0
7.5
15 km

do longer trips to places like the beautiful islands in Gutob Bay.

The *Coron Lodging House* is a pleasant place built on stilts over the water. It has rooms with fan for P60/120 and meals may be arranged.

The *Bert Lim Lodging House* is a private house with rooms for P130/260, including meals.

Calauit Island Large African animals are being raised on this small island, north of Busuanga Island, as an experiment which started in 1977 with eight African species and was carried on for 10 years in strict seclusion, away from curious visitors. The project has been successful and now, alongside scarce Philippine animals like the mouse deer, bear cat and Philippine crocodile, nearly 500 African animals, including giraffes, zebras and gazelles live on this isolated island.

Culion Island

The island is known in the Philippines as Leprosy Island. The colony is in the very clean village of Culion, on the cliff face. About 600 lepers live here along with some 4000 relatives. At night you can spend a few hours at the local cinema.

Coron Island

Coron Island is almost uninhabited and can be reached by boat from Coron in about 30 minutes. It consists of steep limestone cliffs with caves and numerous lonely sandy bays where you may meet Tagbanua seminomads with Negrito blood. In the centre are hidden mountain lakes such as the turquoise Lake Cayangan and the large Lake Cabugao which has two islands.

GUTOB BAY

Gutob Bay, between Culion and Busuanga, is full of lovely little islands. Some of them are being developed for tourism and cottages are now available, as on Maltatayoc and Manguenguey (Treasure) islands. Other islands will soon have commercial accommodation. For further information, contact the Salvacion Municipal Hall. You can hire boats for trips to the islands in Gutob Bay in the peaceful village of Salvacion and also in Concepcion.

The larger Talampulan Island is a complete contrast, with a town of 2000 people straggling along the east coast. There are two cinemas, and big ships often drop anchor off the town. Talampulan is a fishing centre, where the catches are brought and shipped to Manila two or three times a week. Note the chance of a ride! It is odd here to see the number of very young fishermen with bleached straw-blond hair.

Treasure Island

A little north of Pototótan Island, in the southern part of Gutob Bay, the lovely little island of Manguenguey has lately become known as Treasure Island. Its three white beaches and intact coral reef are almost irresistible for an island stay.

You can stay at the *Treasure Island Resort*, which has dorm beds for P85, cottages for P195/275; there is a restaurant with Filipino and Swiss cuisine.

A bus goes from Coron to Concepcion, where you can get a boat for Treasure Island. A Special Ride costs P250.

CUYO ISLANDS

In the north Sulu Sea, set apart from the large Palawan main islands but still part of the Cuyo archipelago, the Cuyo Islands consist of 40 islands, forming the Cuyo Group in the south and the Quiniluban Group in the north. This island world, which has been scarcely touched by tourism, offers a first-class environment for diving and snorkelling, particularly in the reefs around Manamoc, Pamalican, Tinituan, Alcisiras and Quiniluban islands. However, it's not easy to travel from island to island so you usually have to hire a boat to do so. The regular boat trips from the capital, Cuyo, on Cuyo Island, to Bisucay, Cocoro and Agutaya islands are reasonably reliable.

Cuyo

The pleasant little town of Cuyo with its

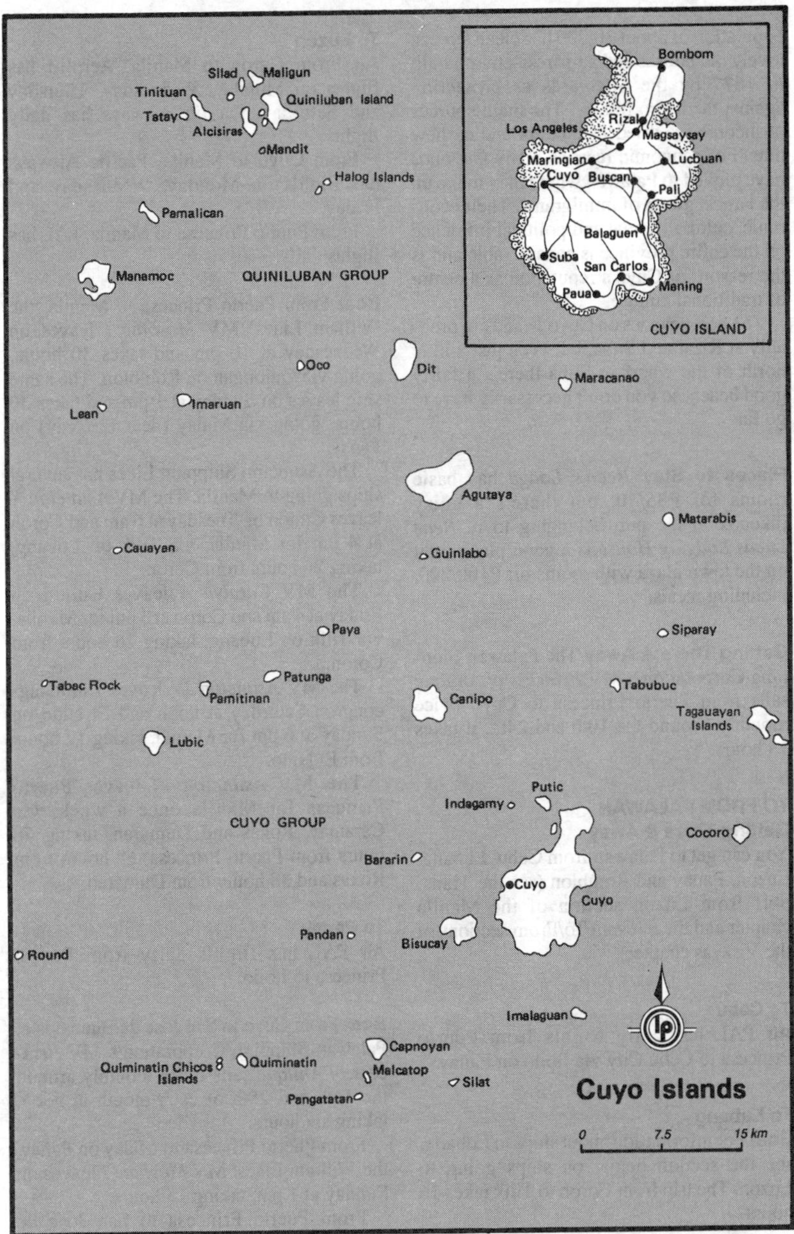
Bombom
Rizal
Los Angeles
Magsaysay
Maringian
Lucbuan
Cuyo
Buscan
Pali
Balaguen
Suba
San Carlos
Maning
Paua
CUYO ISLAND
Silad
Maligun
Tinituan
Quiniluban Island
Tatay
Alcisiras
Mandit
Halog Islands
Pamalican
Manamoc
QUINILUBAN GROUP
Oco
Dit
Maracanao
Imaruan
Lean
Agutaya
Matarabis
Cauayan
Guinlabo
Paya
Siparay
Patunga
Tabac Rock
Pamitinan
Canipo
Tabubuc
Tagauayan Islands
Lubic
Putic
Indagamy
CUYO GROUP
Cocoro
Bararin
Cuyo
Cuyo
Pandan
Round
Bisucay
Imalaguan
Capnoyan
Quiminatin Chicos Islands
Quiminatin
Malcatop
Silat
Pangatatan
Cuyo Islands
0
7.5
15 km

population of about 30,000 has clean streets, lovely old houses and a fortress-church built in 1677 by the Spaniards as protection against the Moro pirates. The main sources of income are dried fish, copra and cashew nuts. For economic reasons many Cuyonos have moved to Palawan where they make up the largest group of immigrants. Their economic, cultural, social and political influence on the entire province is considerable and is the reason for Cuyo's reputation as a centre of traditional culture.

The best beaches on Cuyo Island are probably at Rizal and Suba, but even just a little north of the wharf in Suba there's a fairly good beach, so you don't necessarily have to go far.

Places to Stay *Ireen's Lodge* has basic rooms for P35/70, but there's a noisy jukebox in the pub belonging to it. *Rene Lucas Lodging House* is a good place right on the town plaza with rooms for P100/200, including meals.

Getting There & Away The Palawan Shipping Corporation's MV *Princess of Antique* sails from Puerto Princesa to Cuyo twice monthly, around the 10th and 24th. It takes 14 hours.

TO/FROM PALAWAN

Getting There & Away

You can get to Palawan from Cebu, Lubang, Luzon, Panay and Romblon (see the Transport from Luzon section of the Manila chapter and the relevant To/From sections of the Visayas chapter).

To Cebu

Air PAL has daily flights from Puerto Princesa to Cebu City via Iloilo on Panay.

To Lubang

Boat For information about ships to Lubang, see the section below on ships going to Luzon. The trip from Coron to Tilik takes 16 hours.

To Luzon

Air From Coron to Manila, Aerolift has flights on Monday, Wednesday, Thursday and Saturday. Pacific Airways has daily flights.

From Cuyo to Manila, Pacific Airways has flights on Monday, Wednesday and Friday.

From Puerto Princesa to Manila, PAL has flights daily.

Boat From Puerto Princesa to Manila, the William Lines' MV *Masbate I* leaves on Wednesday at 10 pm and takes 30 hours, going via Odiongan on Romblon. The same ship leaves on Sunday at 1 pm and takes 30 hours, going via Malay (near Boracay) on Panay.

The Asuncion Shipping Lines has several ships going to Manila. The MV *Asuncion X* leaves Culion on Tuesday at 6 am and Coron at 4 pm for Manila, via Tilik on Lubang, taking 26 hours from Coron.

The MV *Catalyn A* leaves Culion on Friday at 4 am and Coron at 3 pm for Manila, via Tilik on Lubang, taking 26 hours from Coron.

The MV *Asuncion IV* leaves Liminangcong on Saturday at noon and El Nido on Sunday at 6 pm for Manila, taking 17 hours from El Nido.

The MV *Asuncion VI* leaves Puerto Princesa for Manila once a week, via Caramay, Roxas and Dumaran, taking 78 hours from Puerto Princesa, 68 hours from Roxas and 38 hours from Dumaran.

To Panay

Air PAL has flights daily from Puerto Princesa to Iloilo.

Boat From Cuyo to San Jose de Buenavista, Palawan Shipping Corporation's MV *Princess of Antique* sails twice monthly around the 11th and 25th of each month at noon, taking six hours.

From Puerto Princesa to Malay on Panay, the William Lines' MV *Masbate I* leaves on Sunday at 1 pm, taking 15 hours.

From Puerto Princesa to San Jose de

Buenavista, the Palawan Shipping Corporation's MV *Princess of Antique* sails twice monthly around the 10th and 24th of each month at 4 pm and takes 26 hours, going via Cuyo.

To Romblon

Boat From Puerto Princesa to Odiongan on Tablas, the William Lines *MV Masbate I* leaves on Wednesday at 10 pm, taking 17 hours.

GETTING AROUND

Touring is difficult in Palawan. The roads between the villages are only good in parts but road works are progressing. There is only one 'highway', which is partly sealed, leading from Brooke's Point via Puerto Princesa and Roxas to Taytay. If you want to travel on side roads, you either need lots of time or lots of money. Jeepney drivers and boat operators always try to make you pay for a Special Ride. If you agree because you can't wait, you will certainly be paying for all the other passengers, too, so everybody will get in and enjoy the free ride.

It's difficult and sometimes impossible to travel by road in the rainy season as some of the routes become impassable after a few days' rain. If, as a result, you can only travel by boat, you will have to pay through the nose to get anywhere.

Index

ABBREVIATIONS

MAPS

TEXT

Guides to South-East Asia

South-East Asia on a shoestring
The well-known 'yellow bible' for travellers in South-East Asia covers Brunei, Burma, Hong Kong, Indonesia, Macau, Malaysia, Papua New Guinea, the Philippines, Singapore, and Thailand.

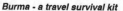

Bali & Lombok - a travel survival kit
This guide will help travellers to experience the real magic of Bali's tropical paradise. Neighbouring Lombok is largely untouched by outside influences and has a special atmosphere of its own.

Burma - a travel survival kit
Burma is one of Asia's most interesting countries. This book shows how to make the most of a trip around the main triangle route of Rangoon–Mandalay–Pagan, and explores many lesser-known places such as Pegu and Inle Lake.

Malaysia, Singapore & Brunei - a travel survival kit
Three independent nations of amazing geographic and cultural variety — from the national parks, beaches, jungles and rivers of Malaysia, tiny oil-rich Brunei and the urban prosperity and diversity of Singapore.

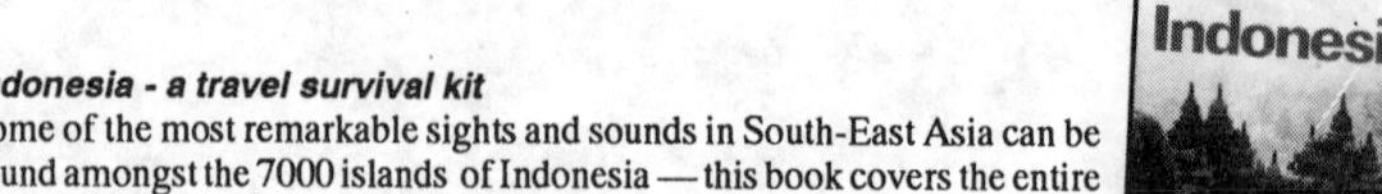

Indonesia - a travel survival kit
Some of the most remarkable sights and sounds in South-East Asia can be found amongst the 7000 islands of Indonesia — this book covers the entire archipelago in detail.

Hong Kong, Macau & Canton - a travel survival kit
A comprehensive guide to three fascinating cities linked by history, culture and geography.

Thailand - a travel survival kit
This authoritative guide includes Thai script for all place names and the latest travel details for all regions, including tips in trekking in the remote hills of the Golden Triangle.

Vietnam, Laos & Cambodia - a travel survival kit
This comprehensive guidebook has all the information you'll need on this most beautiful region of Asia – finally opening its doors to the world.

Also available:
Thai phrasebook, ***Burmese*** phrasebook, ***Pilipino*** phrasebook, and ***Indonesia*** phrasebook.

Lonely Planet Guidebooks

Lonely Planet guidebooks cover every accessible part of Asia as well as Australia, the Pacific, South America, Africa, the Middle East and parts of North America and Europe. There are four series: *travel survival kits*, covering a single country for a range of budgets; *shoestring guides* with compact information for low-budget travel in a major region; *walking guides*; and *phrasebooks*.

Australia & the Pacific
Australia
Bushwalking in Australia
Islands of Australia's Great Barrier Reef
Fiji
Micronesia
New Caledonia
New Zealand
Tramping in New Zealand
Papua New Guinea
Papua New Guinea phrasebook
Rarotonga & the Cook Islands
Samoa
Solomon Islands
Tahiti & French Polynesia
Tonga

South-East Asia
Bali & Lombok
Burma
Burmese phrasebook
Indonesia
Indonesia phrasebook
Malaysia, Singapore & Brunei
Philippines
Pilipino phrasebook
South-East Asia on a shoestring
Thailand
Thai phrasebook
Vietnam, Laos & Cambodia

North-East Asia
China
Chinese phrasebook
Hong Kong, Macau & Canton
Japan
Japanese phrasebook
Korea
Korean phrasebook
North-East Asia on a shoestring
Taiwan
Tibet
Tibet phrasebook

West Asia
Trekking in Turkey
Turkey
Turkish phrasebook
West Asia on a shoestring

Indian Ocean
Madagascar & Comoros
Maldives & Islands of the East Indian Ocean
Mauritius, Réunion & Seychelles

The Lonely Planet Story

Lonely Planet published its first book in 1973 in response to the numerous 'How did you do it?' questions Maureen and Tony Wheeler were asked after driving, bussing, hitching, sailing and railing their way from England to Australia.

Written at a kitchen table and hand collated, trimmed and stapled, *Across Asia on the Cheap* became an instant local bestseller, inspiring thoughts of another book.

Eighteen months in South-East Asia resulted in their second guide, *South-East Asia on a shoestring*, which they put together in a backstreet Chinese hotel in Singapore in 1975. The 'yellow bible' as it quickly became known to backpackers around the world, soon became *the* guide to the region. It has sold well over ½ million copies and is now in its 6th edition, still retaining its familiar yellow cover.

Today there are over 80 Lonely Planet titles – books that have that same adventurous approach to travel as those early guides; books that 'assume you know how to get your luggage off the carousel' as one reviewer put it.

Although Lonely Planet initially specialised in guides to Asia, they now cover most regions of the world, including the Pacific, South America, Africa, the Middle East and Eastern Europe. The list of *walking guides* and *phrasebooks* (for 'unusual' languages such as Quechua, Swahili, Nepalese and Egyptian Arabic) is also growing rapidly.

The emphasis continues to be on travel for independent travellers. Tony and Maureen still travel for several months of each year and play an active part in the writing, updating and quality control of Lonely Planet's guides.

They have been joined by over 50 authors, 40 staff – mainly editors, cartographers, & designers – at our office in Melbourne, Australia, and another 10 at our US office in Oakland, California. Travellers themselves also make a valuable contribution to the guides through the feedback we receive in thousands of letters each year.

The people at Lonely Planet strongly believe that travellers can make a positive contribution to the countries they visit, both through their appreciation of the countries' culture, wildlife and natural features, and through the money they spend. In addition, the company makes a direct contribution to the countries and regions it covers. Since 1986 a percentage of the income from each book has been donated to ventures such as famine relief in Africa; aid projects in India; agricultural projects in Central America; Greenpeace's efforts to halt French nuclear testing in the Pacific and Amnesty International. In 1990 $60,000 was donated to these causes.

Lonely Planet's basic travel philosophy is summed up in Tony Wheeler's comment, 'Don't worry about whether your trip will work out. Just go!'

Mail Order

Lonely Planet guidebooks are distributed worldwide and are sold by good bookshops everywhere. They are also available by mail order from Lonely Planet, so if you have difficulty finding a title please write to us. US and Canadian residents should write to Embarcadero West, 112 Linden St, Oakland CA 94607, USA and residents of other countries to PO Box 617, Hawthorn, Victoria 3122, Australia.

Europe

Eastern Europe on a shoestring
Iceland, Greenland & the Faroe Islands
Trekking in Spain

Indian Subcontinent

Bangladesh
India
Hindi/Urdu phrasebook
Trekking in the Indian Himalaya
Karakoram Highway
Kashmir, Ladakh & Zanskar
Nepal
Trekking in the Nepal Himalaya
Nepal phrasebook
Pakistan
Sri Lanka
Sri Lanka phrasebook

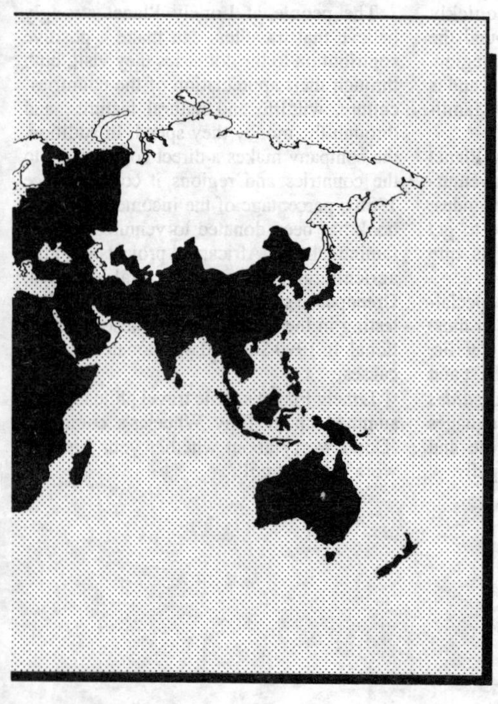

Africa

Africa on a shoestring
Central Africa
East Africa
Kenya
Swahili phrasebook
Morocco, Algeria & Tunisia
Moroccan Arabic phrasebook
West Africa

North America

Alaska
Canada
Hawaii

Mexico

Baja California
Mexico

South America

Argentina
Bolivia
Brazil
Brazilian phrasebook
Chile & Easter Island
Colombia
Ecuador & the Galápagos Islands
Latin American Spanish phrasebook
Peru
Quechua phrasebook
South America on a shoestring

Middle East

Egypt & the Sudan
Egyptian Arabic phrasebook
Israel
Jordan & Syria
Yemen